T0381553

The "OD" Years: WWII Americana

Randolph C. Pierson

Order this book online at www.trafford.com/08-0729
or email orders@trafford.com

Most Trafford titles are also available at major online book retailers.

Printed in Victoria, BC, Canada.

ISBN: 978-1-4251-8021-8 (sc)

ISBN: 978-1-4251-8022-5 (e)

*Our mission is to efficiently provide the world's finest, most comprehensive book publishing
service, enabling every author to experience success. To find out how to publish your book, your
way, and have it available worldwide, visit us online at www.trafford.com/10510*

 www.trafford.com

North America & international
toll-free: 1 888 232 4444 (USA & Canada)
phone: 250 383 6864 ♦ fax: 812 355 4082

INTRODUCTION

Recording these memories has not been a labor of love: it has become a responsibility! What started out as an account of my experiences in the U S Army Field Artillery during WWII has evolved into a series of episodes which took place during the early 1940's, a time now referred to as the 'World War II Years.'

Since retiring, I have written, rewritten, and reorganized this material to fulfill a dream, and what I feel is my responsibility to future generations. This period of American history must be recorded and not become buried by the shifting sands of time, nor changed by individuals who choose to rewrite history to meet their own goals.

Why now? Because the grim reaper is rapidly taking his toll on us old WWII veterans. Unrecorded memories suffer the same fate as an old soldiers, "They don't die; they just fade away."

The events of December 7, 1941 changed the lives of millions of living, and yet to be born Americans. On that day, I was 17 years old and a Freshman at the University of Florida. What I experienced, and learned, during the 1940s was not typical. After much research and reflection, I found my experiences were extremely unique. Sometimes sad, sometimes humorous, and sometimes almost unbelievable. How many young men survived spinal meningitis during basic training; endured the cold, snow, sleet, and mud of the miserable 1943–44

Tennessee winter maneuvers; and 'lived-it-up' at the Port of Embarkation, near Boston, for one month before departing for combat, and possible death on a battle field in Europe? The answer of course is, " Probably None."

To the generation which became of age during the 1950's, the term 'O D' related to a feature newly introduced in automobile transmissions, the 'Over Drive.' The generation of the 1960's gave the term 'O D' a new meaning – the drug related 'Over Dose.' But to us born before the Great Depression, 'O D' stands for only one thing – 'Olive Drab.' Olive Drab was the color of the 1940's. During WWII, Olive Drab was the color America painted trucks, artillery pieces, and planes. 'O D' was the color of our cots, blankets, towels, and tents. It was also the color of our pants, jackets, and overcoats. 'O D' was even the color of our underwear, hand kerchiefs, and socks. If you were a soldier during WWII, khaki and Olive Drab were your colors.

DEDICATION

This book is dedicated, first and foremost, to my wonderful wife, Marion. She too 'grew up' during the 'O D' years. Without her help, support, encouragement, and understanding, these memories would never have been recorded.

This book is also dedicated to the young men with whom I served in the 1940s, and to those with whom I fought in four European WWII Battles. These are memories of special friends, some who paid the ultimate price, others who were severely wounded, and those men of the 589th FA Bn, who were captured and were tough enough, mentally and physically, to survive the Hell of their inhumane treatment received in German POW Camps.

These comrade-in-arms include:

† Calvin Abbott   † John Gatens,   † Charles Jacelon
† Eldon Miedema   † John Rain   † Bernard Strohmier
† Frank Tacker   † and possibly others.

These men continued to fight 'another type war' with honor and distinction. These comrades, and their families, paid a heavy price while serving this country. They have earned my gratitude and eternal respect.

It is my intent to memorialize the "Olive Drab Years," the many total strangers who were exceptionally kind to this young GI, the brave young men with whom I served in the 589th Field Artillery Battalion of the 106th Infantry Division. Also the men of the 82nd and 101st Airborne Divisions with whom I served as a Forward Observer while in the XVIII Airborne Corps Artillery.

Randolph C. Pierson,
Former Captain, Field Artillery, USAR

FORWARD

My future sister-in-law, eleven year old Dorothy Drexel, remembers her Valdosta Elementary School teacher telling her class the Japs had bombed Pearl Harbor, but not to worry, Pearl Harbor was very far away from Valdosta, Georgia. With two older sisters, an older brother, her mother and father, a secure home, and a young child's attitude, Dorothy Drexel was not overly concerned. She mostly remembers seeing stars her neighbors proudly displayed in windows indicating some member of that family was serving their country in the military.

My future wife, Marion Drexel, only two years older than her sister Dorothy, with a slightly more mature point of view, remembers hearing the news of the Japanese attack on Pearl Harbor. Marion knew Pearl Harbor was in Hawaii, and was concerned about the safety of her Uncle Fred, an Air Corps Officer stationed at Hickam Field near Pearl Harbor and a cousin, a seaman, stationed aboard a battle ship, the USS Arizona.

Although the memoirs in this book are mine, I should mention a few of my wife Marion's WWII memories as a youngster, while living in Valdosta, Georgia. This brief recording of her experiences offers a vivid contrast to lifestyles experienced to those in the military during the 'Olive Drab' years. Her recollection of the war years include:

† Changes to the city of Valdosta caused by activation of nearby Moody Field, an Air Corps pilot training facility. The opening of a USO Club to entertain the ever expanding number of Air Corps personnel visiting Valdosta on leave. Her older sister Bertha becoming a USO Hostess. Marion, too young to be a Hostess, attended USO functions as an observer. She discovered that many of the lonely servicemen would sit, talk, and treat her like a younger sister. Marion loved to watch the older couples dance. She became 'friends' with the pianist of the Air Corps Dance Band from Moody Field. She was amazed that he could talk and play the piano at the same time. When asked about this ability, he told her he learned to do this when he formerly played with the famous Paul Whitman orchestra.

† As a result of the influx of military personnel, the City of Valdosta liberalized it's 'Blue Laws' and allowed bars to stay open longer and also allowed the moving picture theaters to open on Sundays. These were drastic changes in the 'bible belt' of south Georgia. One grand matron, of social and political influence, stated, "Valdosta will change it's blue laws over my dead body!" My wife notes this fine lady died years later of natural causes.

† The bowling alley was a favorite place for the aviation cadets from Moody Field to gather. Marion's mother and father occasionally took their three daughters to the bowling alley. They sat in the spectators gallery, equipped with theater type seats for the convenience of spectators and for those who were waiting for an open lane. During these trips, several aviation cadets became friendly with the elder Drexel's. As a result, an ever increasing number of cadets came calling to date Marion's older sister, Bertha The Air Corps cadets were always welcomed by Mrs. Drexel, who maintained an open house almost every weekend. To Marion's amazement, 'Bert' averaged at least one marriage proposal per month. 'Bert' was a popular and attractive young lady! It was very thrilling to be invited to a Moody Graduation Ceremony when Silver Wings and Second Lieutenants bars were awarded to the young graduating cadets. Marion still has a pair of silver wings given her by a graduating 'friend' which she cherishes to this day. Cadet visits to the Drexel home changed when Royal Air Force Cadets arrived from England to be trained at Moody Field. Marion remembers the English cadets vividly.

The RAF cadets seemed more mature, and almost to a man, sported a bushy mustache. An older friend of the Drexel family met, dated, fell in love with, and became engaged to one of these British RAF pilots. They planned to be married in England after the war. Both Marion and her family were saddened when this brave young Englishman was killed, his Spitfire shot down over the English Channel. o War-time shortages ranks high on my wife's memory list. People saving cooking fat, when turned in to a collection center, was made into explosives. Metal was collected: worn-out pots, pans, farming tools, even fencing. The City of Valdosta crews ripping up trolley tracks to be made into vital war materials. Clothing containing rubber, nylon, and/or leather were in short supply and rationed. Sugar, coffee, and meats were also rationed. Competition for sugar in the Drexel household was so fierce Mrs. Drexel provided a jar to each member of the family to hold their portion of the sugar ration. Dad Drexel was the biggest sugar filcher of them all.

† The local Ration Board controlled gasoline and tire consumption. This board determined a families need for automobile use. Once necessary usage was determined, a classification sticker was placed on the automobile windshield. Families without a special need were assigned an "A" classification and issued a ration book containing detachable 'A' coupons. These coupons, plus cash, were necessary to purchase gasoline and tires. This system of rationing worked fairly well, but it did spawn a fairly large black market for those willing to pay more than the controlled price of gasoline and tires.

† Wrapping bandages for the American Red Cross and selling War Bonds occupied much of Marion's time. War Bond rallies were extremely popular. These rallies provided the opportunity to feel patriotic in addition to investing money wisely. War Bonds and stamps were sold from a small booth in the center of town, manned by volunteers. At Moody Field, on open house days, a Bond purchase got you a ride in a military jeep driven by a young non-commissioned officer. To Marion, this was a special event to remember

† R. J. Drexel, Marion's father, was a veteran of World War I. At 44 years of age, with a family of five, he joined the Georgia State Defense Corps. Too old to fight overseas, he was a patriot and volunteered to defend his homeland.

He entered the Guard on May 1, 1942 and served until the fall of Japan in 1945. Marion still tells stories of how her father placed targets in their back yard for rifle practice. He also taught my wife how to shoot an army rifle. Marion maintains to this day, her father was a good shot, but she was better. History records Georgia was not invaded during WWII. I believe Georgia was not invaded because of my father-in-law, and patriots like him.

† During WWII allied forces took their first prisoners-of-war in the North Africa Campaign. These soldiers were 'the cream of the crop' in the German army, serving in the Africa Corps, commanded by the 'Desert Fox,' Field Marshal Rommel. After processing, many of these prisoners were, transported to, and imprisoned in the United States. Some of these German prisoners were housed in the stockade at Moody Field. Once there, these prisoners enjoyed better living conditions in Georgia than they had experienced back home in Germany. Many of these Germans learned to speak English. To keep these young men occupied, and in good health, they were allowed to volunteer for work details outside the prison. Farmers in the Valdosta area soon negotiated an arrangement for the government to transport able-bodied-men to farms in the area. These prisoners performed manual labor which produced food for the war effort. In exchange for their labor German prisoners were paid and allowed to purchase personal items from the Base Post Exchange. Marion was favorably impressed with the handsome young men from the elite *German Afrika Korps'* who worked on a friends farm.

† Three family happenings are indelibly imprinted on my wife's mind: One, when she received the good news that her uncle Fred was not wounded during the attack on Pearl Harbor. Two, the bad news when she learned her cousin serving on the USS Arizona was missing in action and presumed to be dead. And three, when her older brother said "Good Bye," and left home to join the U S Air Corps.

† †

Although I was never in the regular army I served, nine years, eight months, and two days of active duty in the Field Artillery during WWII and in an

Armored Field Artillery unit during the Korean conflict. Serving in two combat branches of the Army, and fighting in two different wars, gives me a unique and sympathetic point-of-view toward veterans, and their families, who made personal sacrifices to defend our country in times of crisis.

Combat has changed since my unpleasant experiences in Europe and while fighting in Korea There I served with the South Korean Army at war with the Russian backed Chinese hordes and the North Korean Army. A political war constrained by an imaginary line across Korea, called the 38th parallel. A war America and South Korean forces could have won, but for political reasons, were not allowed to win. In 1953 I returned home to my wife, Marion. No one, other than my immediate family, knew where I had been for two years. No one cared! At least I was not spat upon, and called a 'baby killer,' by anti-war activists, like the returning Vet Nam War Veterans.

Over the years, I have collected many items concerning veterans. Two such items have stayed with me and express my gratitude and respect for the men and women in the Armed Services. These are not my words. I cannot locate the authors to obtain permission to use their work in this Forward. These words express my feelings so strongly, I sincerely wish I could claim these words as my own. Please let me share these thoughts with you.

I want you to close your eyes and picture in your mind the soldier at Valley Forge, as he holds his musket in his cold and bloody hands.

He stands barefoot in the snow, starved from lack of food, wounded from months of battle, and emotionally scarred from the eternity away from his family.

Surrounded by nothing but death and carnage of war, he stands tough. With fire in his eyes and victory on his breath he looks at us now, in anger and disgust, and tells us this…

THE SOLDIER'S LEGACY
I gave you a birthright of freedom born in the Constitution
and now your children graduate too illiterate to read it.
I fought in the snow barefoot to give you the freedom to vote
and you stay home and do not vote because of rain.

I left my family destitute to give you the freedom of speech
and you remain silent on critical issues because it might be bad for business.
I orphaned my children to give you a government to serve you
and it has stolen democracy from the people.
It is the soldier, not the reporter who gives you the freedom of the press.
It is the soldier, not the poet who gives you the freedom of speech.
It is the soldier, not the campus organizer who allows you to demonstrate.
It is the soldier who salutes the flag, and serves the flag,
whose coffin is draped with the flag that allows the protester to burn the flag.
"Lord, hold our troops in your loving hands.
Protect them as they protect us.
Bless them and their families for selfless acts they perform for us
in out time of stress.

Amen

AN AMERICAN SOLDIER DIES
When the Soldier gets to heaven,
to Saint Peter he will tell,
"Just another Soldier reporting in, Sir.
I've served my time in Hell."

Cartoon courtesy of Mr. Donald Taylor, Monticello, Florida
A WWII Veteran and My Friend

Join me now on a trip down memory lane, A time when our nation was solidly united behind the war effort and everyone was eager to serve their country. These were the 'Olive Drab Years,' the time in our nation's history when 'The Greatest Generation' came of age.

CONTENTS

Fall 1941—Bob Hope playing in My Favorite Blond (top)

U of F Freshman—Robert (Red) Kaiser and Author, (bottom); 'Red' on Athletic Scholarship from Rochester, N.Y., Randy on working Scholarship from Cocoa, Florida

University of Florida ROTC Cadets (top)—1941
Infantry (long pants), Artillery (boots)
Author 2nd from left, 'Red' Kaiser 2nd from right

17 year old Author, Randy Pierson, perched upon a
1918 model horse-drawn French Caisson, (bottom)
University of Florida parade grounds—1941

I

America Enters The War

University of Florida — Freshman Class of 1941
Gainesville, Florida — September 1941

My introduction to the "Olive Drab" years and my love/hate relationship with the military started in September 1941, when I enrolled at the University of Florida. As a freshman, it was mandatory that each young man enroll in either Physical Education or Reserve Officers Training. I chose the Reserve Officers Training Corps. By the luck of the draw, I was assigned to Field Artillery, rather than Infantry ROTC training.

By 1941, the army had phased out horses and was using trucks as prime movers for artillery pieces. However, due to economic considerations, the University of Florida ROTC program was still training with World War I vintage, horse-drawn, "French 75" artillery pieces. Ammunition for these weapons was carried in a horse-drawn "Caisson." In fact, the lyrics to the Army Song contains reference to "Caissons rolling along." This became one of my favorite songs. I remember the words well, "Over hill, over dale, we have hit the dusty trail, and those Caissons go rolling along."

The words and music written and composed in 1908 by a young Artillery Lieutenant named, E. L. "Snitz" Gruber, bring forth vivid memories to me. Beautiful horses on the ROTC parade ground, rearing and snorting nervously. The excitement of horse-drawn French 75's and Caissons, bouncing across the uneven parade ground, the Caissons trying desperately to unseat the riding Field Artillery Cadets, and the drifting, swirling dust, which rose to cover both spectators and the marching foot soldiers of the Infantry units. These are fond memories indeed!

The author of those lyrics, Lieutenant Gruber, had certainly captured the true spirit of the horse-drawn Field Artillery. I was proud to be a Field Artillery Cadet!

Sunday, December 7, 1941, changed my life and the lives of millions of US citizens, and marked the beginning of the Olive Drab years in America. My college roommate, Robert "Red" Kaiser, from Buffalo, New York, and I had spent Saturday, December 6th, in Daytona Beach and were returning to Gainesville on our motorcycles that ill-fated Sunday. We were very cold and stopped in a little crossroads store in Interlochen, Florida to get warm. As we entered the country story, the proprietor blurted out, "What do you fellows think about Pearl Harbor?"

Blank-faced, we looked at each other, shrugged, and wondered what was on his mind.. Red's casual response was, "What is Pearl Harbor?"

The proprietor's irritated answer was, "It's a large American Navy Base, and the Japs just bombed it!"

This information piqued our interest, and Red asked, "The Japs bombed Pearl Harbor? What state is it in?"

By now the storekeeper realized we knew nothing about the circumstances and turned-up his radio so we could listen. That Sunday, cold and hungry, in an isolated country store, we learned of the sneak attack by the Imperial Japanese Navy upon the American Pacific Fleet, at Pearl Harbor in Hawaii.

After two doughnuts, and a hot cup of coffee, we cranked-up our motorcycles and headed west toward Gainesville and the University campus. By the time we arrived, I was cold, and shivering so hard, I decided to go directly to the infirmary. Red came with me and we parked our motorcycles in the lot north of the infirmary building. It was Sunday and the medical staff was at a minimum. When we arrived, the staff was clustered together and talking animatedly. One nurse finally broke away from the group and told us they were discussing the bombing of the US Fleet at Pearl Harbor and some staff members were already talking about leaving the University to accept commissions in the Medical Corps. However, when she haw I was not well, she stopped the conversation and led me to an examination room.

In a short period of time a University doctor entered the room, checked my vital signs, looked at my personnel records, and admitted me for treatment and observation. By this time I was no longer cold, I was burning with fever. His diagnosis was simple, I had the flu. When the doctor found out Red was my roommate, he let Red accompany me to my room.

In the room, Red told me he would place a cover over my motorcycle on the way to the dorm, get something to eat, and bring my toilet articles to the infirmary later.

By the time Red returned, I had received fruit juice and medication and was already feeling better. The nurse told Red she thought I would be out of the infirmary in a couple of days, barring unexpected complications. That was good news, and Red agreed to come and visit every day to see if I needed anything. The nurse then wanted to know if my parents should be notified of my illness. We both said no, because I already felt better and I did not want to worry my mother.

A good nights rest did wonders for me. However, the atmosphere of the Infirmary had changed by breakfast time Monday morning. People were everywhere and they were all excited. The whole campus, both students and faculty, were excited. After breakfast a nurse took me to a window at the north end of the hall which overlooked the campus. From there I could see cars doubled-parked and students carrying belongings from their dormitory rooms to the waiting cars. This scene reminded me of a colony of worker-ants. The nurse made the observation that at least one half of the student body was getting ready to leave school and go home.

About noon that day, Monday, December 8th, the infirmary received word the University President, Dr. John J. Tigert, was suspending classes that afternoon and asked all university students, faculty, and employees to assemble at Florida Field for an important message. On his way to the stadium, Red stopped at my infirmary room and said when the assembly was over, he would return and tell me what Dr. Tigert had to say. In the meantime the doctors and nurses, who were required to remain on duty, vacated a room on the second floor which overlooked the stadium. They invited me to listen to Dr. Tigert's speech from there.

The gathering at Florida Field was impressive. Dr. Tigert spoke from the center of the football field and used a public address system which could be plainly heard at the infirmary. He stressed the gravity of the situation and acknowledged everyone's concerns about how best they could serve their country. He stated the best course of action was to remain in school, and added, if and when our country needed us, it would call. His message was logical, and easily understood.

When Red returned to the infirmary, he flopped onto the bed next to me. We talked at length about the speech and our options and finally agreed we should both remain in college.

He was nineteen and draft age, I was not quite eighteen.

† †

My Hometown
Cocoa, Florida — June 1942

By the time the second semester ended, in June 1942, it was obvious I would not be returning to the University of Florida in the fall. Due to low grades as a freshman, I did not qualify for an extension to my scholarship, and mothers income was not sufficient to pay my college expenses for anther year.

The changes which had occurred in Cocoa during my nine months absence surprised me. When I left for college the previous September, Cocoa had been a small agricultural town, sitting squarely in the middle of Brevard County, and the Indian River citrus growing section, on the central east coast of Florida. Now, nine months later, the quickly expanding Banana River Naval Air Station south of Cocoa Beach was changing Cocoa into a thriving boom-town. I found the town struggling to accommodate the needs for the ever increasing numbers of Navy personnel and civilian construction workers. The town had not been able to gear-up quickly enough to meet the new demands for housing and recreation.

Competition for female companionship caused friction between young Navy enlisted men and local males. This fact caused jurisdictional problems between the tiny Cocoa police force and the ever-present Navy Shore Patrol.

Competition for the favors of females often erupted into fights in the two local "juke joints," and added to the "bad blood" between civilians and military personnel. The civilian construction workers played hard, worked hard, had money to spend, and overtaxed the limited local bar and pool hall facilities. While public institutions struggled, local merchants prospered as never before. The economy was a mixed blessing. The side effects of the war, both good and bad, had descended upon my small home town with a vengeance.

The realities of war came to Cocoa during 1942 also. German "U Boats" operated in the Gulf Stream east of Cape Canaveral with immunity. Merchant ship after merchant ship fell victim to German torpedoes almost under the nose of the Navy at the Banana River Naval Air Station. Survivors from merchant ships sunk of Cape Canaveral, who were brought into Cocoa, testified to the close proximity of the war. German saboteurs from an off-shore German submarine who landed at Ponte Vedra Beach, reinforced the realities of war when they were captured enroute to Jacksonville, Florida. Their mission was to damage vital shipyard operations in the Jacksonville area.

Since I was now eighteen, and marking time until my nineteenth birthday, and the receipt of my "Greetings from the President of the United States," I decided to apply for a job at the Banana River Naval Air Station. The process was simple, and the results were favorable. The Civil Service interviewer arranged for me to talk with the Director of Public Works. You can imagine my surprise when the Director turned out to be the father of an attractive high school senior I had just started dating. He and I discussed my experience and academic qualifications. When he discovered I had taken three years of mechanical drawing in high school, and made an "A" in solid geometry in college, he checked his list of job vacancies and asked how much time I had available for additional interviews. Sensing we were making good progress, I told him that my time was his time. We drove around the busy Naval Air Station (NAS) and the Director pointed out the work he had underway – both Navy and civilian contractors – that was under his direct jurisdiction. For an eighteen year old, this was a heady experience, riding with the head man, in his plainly marked Navy provided pickup truck, and having civilian job superintendents and Naval officers falling all over themselves, trying to impress him. The tour of the NAS ended at the Administration Building where we went to see the Resident Naval Officer in Charge of Construction (RNOICOC), whom the Public Works Director explained was his boss.

The Resident Naval Officer's secretary was seated behind her desk and smiled sweetly as we entered. The Director returned her smile as he asked if the Resident Officer was available for a couple of minutes. Without even checking, she ushered us into the spacious office of a Naval Lieutenant Commander, and announced our arrival.

The Lieutenant Commander looked up from his desk-work and casually commented, "Well Joe, what brings you to the temple from which all knowledge flows?

Good news, or bad?"

"Commander, I've been showing this young man around the station and I thought you might like to meet him."

"Fine, what do you have in mind for him?"

"He is local, his mother is a school teacher who has a fine reputation, he has completed one year of college, and has been trained as a draftsman – both high school and college."

"Joe, do you want to start him in the Navy drafting room, or with the civilian architects?"

"He does not plan to return to the university in the fall. This will make him subject to the draft in about one year. The Public Works Department is in the process of acquiring a new type blueprint machine, it is called an OZALID. It uses a dry – rather than wet – paper process, and is very quick. The OZALID field representative could start training him on our new machine next week, if we decide to put him on the payroll."

"Sounds like your timing is perfect Joe. Why not introduce him to the Chief Draftsman while you are in the building?"

"That is a good idea Commander, glad you mentioned it."

This type of friendly banter between such important men was new to me, consequently I asked the Director what would happen if the Chief Draftsman did not want me?

The Commander laughed as the Director glanced at me with a fatherly look and said, "The Commander likes you, I like you, my wife likes you, and my daughter likes you. Why would the Chief Draftsman not like you?"

† †

Banana River Naval Air Station
South of Cocoa Beach, Florida—June 18, 1942

Inside the air conditioned drafting room of the Administration Building, the wail of the air-raid sirens were clearly audible. This was the first time I had heard this warning signal and did not know what to do. I assumed it was some type of drill for the Navy personnel. The Second Class Yeoman who worked for me corrected me immediately and indicated something was really wrong. He got on the phone and called a buddy stationed on the flight line and found out a German "U-Boat" had been sighted on the surface, east of Cape Canaveral, and the Navy was dispatching six huge PBM (Patrol Bomber Martin) "flying boats" to engage and sink it. The Yeoman told me if I wanted to see a great sight, I should follow him and we could watch the six, large, lumbering bombers take off.

From a vantage point overlooking the Banana River, we watched six, large, dark blue, twin engine amphibians, start their motors and begin to taxi out into the channel of the river for take-off. Many other civilians and Navy people were watching nearby, and talked nervously, as we watched this process. This was exciting! The enemy was only ten or twelve miles east of us.

We watched intently as the huge "flying boats" took-off, one by one, and started forming a single attack-line in the sky. The take-offs were routine, until the sixth, the last plane to become airborne, headed directly toward the tall NAS water tower. Even on the ground, you could almost feel the straining arms of the pilot and co-pilot, as they pulled at the controls of the lumbering patrol bomber, trying desperately to gain enough altitude to clear the menacing water tower. With agonizing slowness, the giant aircraft struggled and its engines tried heroically to climb, but it could not. The Navy pilots around us were yelling, "PULL UP! PULL UP! For Christ's sake, PULL UP! Give it more power, PULL UP!"

At the last possible moment, the skilled pilot dropped his left wing to almost vertical and executed a dangerous racing turn around the NAS water tower. In the same motion, he dropped within a few feet of the roof of the Batchelor Officers Quarters (BOQ) to gain air speed. You could hear the roar of the radial engines as the pilot gave them full throttle. He pulled the yoke back, and the big bird began a graceful climb, much to the relief of the crowd below, and of course, to the relief of the plane-crew itself. The PBM then took its place at the rear of the line of flying boats which rapidly moved out of sight in search of their prey.

Back in the Administration Building there was much talk about the take-offs, the close call with the water tower, and the closeness of the enemy. Te chief draftsman even posed the question, "If German 'U-Boats' can get this close, why don't they just come within gun-range, surface, and shell the Naval Air Station?"

The prevalent answer to his question was, "The giant PBMs carry many depth charges and machine guns as ordnance, and no 'U-Boat' on the surface would stand a chance against even a single PBM." The US Navy felt it was prepared for any eventuality, and was confident it could handle any situation.

The events of this day shook the confidence of the US Navy, and cast doubts upon the Navies ability to adequately defend the Banana River Naval Air Station. Of the six PBM bombers that left to dispatch the enemy submarine, only five returned. The after-action debriefing of the pilots, and crew members involved in the attack on the submarine, reveled the lost PBM was the lead bomber of the flight.

With depth-charges set to explode at a shallow depth, and its 50-caliber nose guns blazing, the lead PBM made a straight, low-level, head-on, bombing and strafing run. Instead of making the anticipated, sudden crash dive, the submarine commander unexpectedly ordered his crew to man the forward, three-inch, deck gun. The second round from the deck-gun struck the slow, lumbering PBM. The aircraft then virtually disappeared from the sky in a gigantic ball of flame.

Fortunately the remaining five PBMs aborted their low-level attack, withdrew, reformed, and pressed the next attack from a high altitude after the submarine had submerged. Although all depth-charges were dropped, no oil slick, nor wreckage, was detected by the PBM crews. Consequently, no conclusions were reached concerning the fate of the German war-ship.

In a series of meetings, with both Navy personnel and civilian employees, the Navy Department stressed the seriousness of the situation, and the need to withhold this information from the press and the general public.

Speaking only for myself, I have only discussed this incident recently, and have found no one who can confirm it.

✝ ✝

Banana River Naval Air Station
South of Cocoa Beach, Florida—July 6, 1942

The weather was hot! I mean scorching hot! It was a typical central Florida summer day. The ocean tide was at dead low and there was not a breath of air moving. I was glad to get out of the drafting room, but I missed the comfort of the air conditioned office. The Public Works truck I was driving was equipped with what we laughingly called a "2–50" air conditioning system. Two windows open, at fifty miles per hour.

The Public Works Director was short of construction inspectors. I had been detailed to inspect the construction of six observation towers the Navy Department was building along the east side of US A1A, south of Cocoa Beach. This was neither a technical nor a quality inspection, merely a look-see, and report back to the Director on the completion status of the six towers. The Navy and the Civil Defense people were beginning to get testy about these towers. The towers were to be manned twenty-four hours a day by civilian volunteers as quickly as possible, and were being established as lookout positions to detect enemy submarine and/or aircraft activities.

I had not expected to see a large earth-mover working on the ocean side of A1A , inside the NAS, during this trip. Curiosity, and ample time, prompted me to stop and investigate this activity. The construction foreman, noting the Inspector markings on my truck, assumed I was a civil service inspector, came quickly to the truck as I pulled to a stop. To my surprise, he told me his crew was digging artillery gun-pits for the new artillery weapons the Navy Department had obtained for the defense of the NAS against attack from the sea. He also added this was the third of six such locations selected by the Navy.

During the conversation, he said a Navy gun crew was emplacing one of the new weapons an a completed gun-pit south of this location. Since I was headed in that direction, I thanked the foreman for the information and decided to take a look at the new weaponry the Navy Department had obtained for the defense of the Naval Air Station.

The scene I discovered at the newly finished gun position was chaotic. I found a group of Navy enlisted men, under the command of an ole "salt water" Chief Gunners Mate, milling around an artillery weapon I had seen many times before. I could not believe what I saw. The artillery weapon was a World War I vintage "French 75," the artillery weapon I had trained on during my one year of Reserve Officers Training at the University of Florida.

Sitting in the Public Works truck, I sensed the frustration of the Chief Gunners Mate. The gun-pit was not constructed to properly accommodate the "French 75" and the Chief obviously knew nothing about the artillery weapon itself. I wanted to be of assistance, but I knew it would be difficult because I was a teenaged civilian. But what the hell, I decided to try!

My first attempt to be friendly with the Chief was met with indifference and sarcasm. His attitude was, "Who in the hell is this civilian, this teenaged kid, and what does he want from me when I am busy?" When I asked him what was his problem, he pointed to the ancient artillery piece and said, "There were no instructions in the Cracker Jack box this damned thing came it." When I told him I was familiar with this weapon and might be able to help him, he looked at me like I was an alien from outer space. I could almost read his mind, "How could a young kid know anything about a WWI artillery weapon?"

By this time, some of the other enlisted men were joining the conversation. Finally a First Class Petty Officer spoke-up and told the Chief, "Let the kid put his money where his mouth is." Most of the other enlisted men chimed in, "Yea Chief, what we got to loose?"

That is when I began to shine. I organized the group into two gun sections, taught them how to use the sighting system, the somewhat complicated drum and plateau system, the dangers of the eccentric breach block mechanism, and several techniques of conducting direct fire. By this time, the sailors, and the Chief, were all ears. They knew I had been schooled on this particular weapon, and was not just some bragging, snotty-nosed kid.

The time spent with these sailors was interesting, but I realized I had a job to perform for the Director. I was getting into a time-bind and told the Chief I had to move on. He thanked me for the help, bemoaned the fact that he still had other problems to solve, and asked for my name, supervisor, and my on-base telephone number in case he had to get in touch with me.

As I continued my trip southward on A1A, toward the site of the last observation tower to be inspected, I felt sorry for the Chief Gunners Mate and his crew. Only I realized how much they did not know about actually firing a "French 75," however I dismissed their situation from my mind because I knew I would not be involved with the Chief and his men again.

Banana River Naval Air Station
Administration Building—The Drafting Room—July 8, 1942

My telephone rang with authority, as most Navy telephones had been adjusted to do. I answered in the prescribed Navy manner, "Drafting Room, Pierson speaking, Sir!"

The female voice on the other end of the connection was the sweet, but somewhat officious, voice of the secretary of the Resident Naval Officer in Charge of Construction. She advised me the Commander wanted to see me in his office. When I asked for fifteen minutes to complete what I was doing, she ordered me to her office immediately, "The Commander is waiting." It seemed peculiar to me how secretaries, with a lower civil service rating than mine, always assumed the superior rank of their bosses. This was a principle I questioned, but was wise enough not to challenge. I immediately dropped what I was doing and walked swiftly down the long corridor to the Commander's office.

There was an unfamiliar Navy Lieutenant seated in the Commander's office when I arrived. They were engaged in pleasant conversation while they waited for someone to join them. To my surprise, the person they were waiting to see was me. The Commander introduced the Lieutenant as the Naval Air Station Gunnery Officer.

There was an awkward silence until the Commander told the Gunnery Officer I was the person he wanted to interview. It was apparent the Gunnery Officer expected to meet someone more mature than the eighteen year old he had just met.

As the Commander leaned back in his leather executive chair, the Lieutenant began his interview. "Are you the gentleman who gave instructions on the 'French 75' to one of my Chief Petty Officers?"

"Yes sir, I'll have to plead guilty as charged."

"Where did you get such detailed information on this particular weapon? And, I don't know how to address you, should I call you Mr. Pierson, or do you hold a military rank?"

I looked at the Commander. He nodded, and I began. "I have completed one years training on the 'French 75' in the ROTC program at the University of Florida. I have never actually fired one, but I was taught the nomenclature, idiosyncrasies, and history, of this weapon. I have also been trained on the functions performed by each member of a 'French 75' gun crew, including the section chief. I do not hold a military rank, I am a civil service employee who works in the Navy Drafting Room, and everyone, including the Commander, calls me Randy."

"May I call you Randy also?"

"Yes sir, you certainly may."

"Well Randy, do you feel qualified to instruct some of my enlisted men on these aspects of this weapon?"

"Lieutenant, I have been taught the '75' is a very fine weapon, especially for direct fire. The weapon itself has some peculiarities. Some of these tricky features can be dangerous to members of the gun crew. I'm sure the Chief Gunners Mate

I talked to knows more about ordnance in general than I do. But it is obvious he does not know the finer points of this particular artillery weapon. If I can be spared from my civil service duties, I will be glad to pass on to your people the information I have learned."

With this pronouncement, the Gunnery Officer glanced at the Commander. The Commander asked the Lieutenant, "How many weapons have you received?"

The Lieutenant replied, "We have received only one weapon, no instruction manuals what-so-ever, and a strange looking trailer called a Limber." He then added, "I don't have the slightest idea what a Limber is."

The Commander nodded his head in silent agreement and then looked at me.

This conversation was becoming a little embarrassing to me. Neither officer had the slightest idea of the problems involved. They needed help, but I did not want to come across as a know-it-all. As diplomatically as I knew how, I explained the strange looking trailer was a specialized wagon designed to transport 75mm ammunition and was designed to be pulled by horses. I explained, "The British call these wagons Limbers, but the French and the Americans call them Caissons."

Both officers remained silent after this explanation.

Being a diplomat himself, the Commander finally spoke, "Lieutenant, I guess the Public Works Department can loan Randy to the Gunnery Department for a few days. It looks like the Navy might learn something from a first year Artillery ROTC Cadet."

Banana River Naval Air Station
Gunnery Depart Training Facility – July 14, 1942

Training manuals, personal notes taken while attending lecture sessions, and completed test materials I had acquired from the Military Department at the University of Florida made my class preparation fairly simple. In fact, the gunnery rated sailors attending my class had been instructed in other types of ordnance and took to the "French 75" training like a group of ducklings take to water. They were in their element, consequently they tested me frequently. In most cases I passed the tests, but in the few cases where I fell on my face, my sense of humor, sprinkled with self ridicule, seemed to enhance my standing with the students.

News of the class spread spontaneously throughout the NAS, and it was not uncommon for senior Naval officers to monitor the proceedings. Many of these officers were qualified aviators and wore their Navy "Wings of Gold" proudly. They seemed to enjoy the light, but productive, atmosphere in the classroom. They seemed impressed with the two artillery type gun sites we had prepared for training purposes.

During gun drill, as the Navy called it – I called it the "Cannoneers Hop" – the enlisted men competed, crew against crew, and each crew was timed with a stop-watch to determine which crew could identify, sight on, fire upon, and destroy a target the quickest. This type exercise was accomplished by "dry-runs" at first when only dummy ammunition was used.

As the gun crews became more proficient, the dry-runs gave way to actual firing exercises. The crews then fired live ammunition at a stationary target mounted on a large barge anchored several hundred yards off shore in the Atlantic Ocean. The gun crews became extremely proficient, very quickly, in firing at stationary targets.

Next came the tough question, "Could they hit a moving target?"

Both the Gunnery Officer and I were concerned with the safety of the small Navy tugboat, and its crew, which had been assigned the job of towing the target while it was under live fire from the shore guns. The tugboat captain, a salty, deep water, veteran Chief Petty Officer, actually made the final decision. He had towed targets for live firing practice many times and had brought standard Navy target towing cables – about the length of four football fields – to be used during our training exercise. He promptly dismissed our concerns for the safety of his tug and crew, and seemed anxious to get on with his assignment. The Gunnery Officer was not totally convinced the live firing drill would be safe, but he was not about to override the judgment of the experienced skipper of the tugboat.

Never having been in the vicinity of exploding artillery shells, I was thankful I was not a member of the tugboat crew.

The sun rose early the morning of the "final exam." We assembled the equivalent of twelve trained gun crews, each with a crew chief. The firing position was east of highway US A1A and well south of the main base. The Navy established three-way radio communications between the tugboat, the gun site, and a PBY Catalina Flying Boat, which carried the Gunnery Officer who was acting as the range safety officer. The vantage point of the airborne Flying Boat, above and beyond the towed target, offered the safety officer an unobstructed view of the entire operation.

As much as I would have like to say the second set of tests, firing at moving targets, were a howling success, they were not! The gun crews mastered the technique of hitting the target as long as it was moving parallel to the shore line. Under these circumstances, once the range was established, all the gunner had to do was lead the moving target. However, in reality, most targets would also move toward, or away from the gun, while moving to the right or left.

Some gunners were able to master changes in direction and range quickly, wheras others could not. It became obvious that gunners who had become proficient in firing at moving aircraft, and those "country boys" who had shot quail, ducks, and dove on the wing, were the gunners who were hitting the moving target. The others were not. I was glad the weeding-out process was the responsibility of the Navy and not mine.

The live firing exercise proved the Navy gun crews knew how to use the "French 75" sighting system, they knew how to transport the weapons from position to position, they were familiar with "shifting trails" within the position to track fast moving targets, and they also knew how to properly handle the 75mm ammunition. And best of all, I knew none of the Cannoneers would have a hand severed at the wrist by improper use of the infamous "French 75" eccentric breach block.

I knew my job was finished and I could contribute no more. This knowledge made me feel good as I drove back to my office in the Administration Building.

† †

Banana River Naval Air Station
Office of the Public Works Director—July 21, 1942

The Public Works Director was very specific when he advised me, over the phone, to be in his office at 4 o'clock sharp this afternoon. He offered no explanation. I asked no questions!

Later during the day, the chief draftsman advised me that he and I were to ride to the Public Works Building with the Commander at 1545 hours. It was confusing to me when people at the NAS mixed civilian time and military time in their conversations. I had to stop and think, 1545 hours military time meant 3:45 o'clock civilian time. I appreciated the offer of a ride, it was a convenient way for me to get from the Administration Building to Public Works, but I did not connect the Commanders invitation with the Directors instructions to be at his office at 4 o'clock sharp.

Many unfamiliar vehicles were in the parking lot adjacent to the Public Works Building when we arrived. More than I could remember seeing gathered there in the past. Of course, the lack of vacant parking spaces did not concern the Commander, he merely pulled into his reserved parking space near the front entrance of the building. In true military fashion, I departed the vehicle first, opened the two front doors, and hurried down the walkway to open the front door of the Public Works Building for my two superiors. The Commander entered the open door first and strode briskly down the corridor to the Directors office, followed closely by the chief draftsman, with me at a respectful distance in the rear.

There was an almost overflow crowd already assembled in the Directors anteroom when we entered. The crowd was made up mainly of Naval Officers, many of whom I had never met. Although I had never met him personally, I recognized the senior officer present, he was the Commanding Officer of the Naval Air Station. This distinguished gentleman was a four stripe Captain, resplendent in his immaculately tailored uniform, proudly displaying his "Navy Wings of Gold", and a triple row of multicolored ribbons on his manly chest. He and the

Resident Naval Officer in Charge of Construction, the Lieutenant Commander, exchanged pleasantries and then the Captain took charge of the meeting.

The Station Commander surprised me when he made a short speech to the assembled group about my contribution to the war effort as a civilian employee of the Banana River Naval Air Station, and presented me with a Certificate of Commendation for the training I had conducted in the Gunnery Department.

I was nervous and my unplanned acceptance speech was extremely brief. In fact, it was almost nil. I was overwhelmed by the unexpected presentation and did not know what to say.

The resulting applause from the standing Naval Officers was loud and sustained. They were either appreciative of the fact that I was genuinely sincere in my acceptance, and/or were extremely receptive to my brevity, which allowed them to leave and retire to the Naval Air Station Officers Club for an early start on their "Happy Hour."

I suspect it was the latter!

† †

Banana River Naval Air Station
Office of the Resident Naval Officer in Charge of Construction—
November 30, 1942

The Commander was conducting a meeting in this private office. Attending the meeting was the Public Works Director, the Chief Draftsman, and me. The subject of the meeting was my future. My "Greetings from the President of the United States of America" had finally arrived. I was to report for my initial physical the first week in January, and there was no reason to suspect I would be given a deferment from the draft.

All three of my superiors were pleased with me as an individual, and also well satisfied with my job performance. The Commander made a suggestion, he said he was in a position to offer me a permanent civil service rating which would entitle me to a deferment from the draft because of the essential nature of the work involved.

While flattered by this offer, I did not wish to remain a civilian in Cocoa, now dominated by the Navy, for the duration of the war. I was aware of the personal safety and good pay involved in this offer, and was grateful for the effort the Commander had exerted in my behalf, but I did not wish to be thought of as a draft dodger by my contemporaries.

This position was easily understood by my superiors. After all, one was a Naval Officer, and the two civilians were well beyond the maximum age of the draft.

The commander then offered me a second, and more appealing, alternative. This offer involved being sworn into the Navy as a Chief Petty Officer and being assigned to the Public Works Department at the Banana River Naval Air Station.

For a young man who would probably never earn more than three or four stripes in the Army, the prospect of starting a military career with six stripes in the Navy certainly had appeal. Chief Petty Officers commanded respect from both enlisted men and officers, and made lots of money with their base pay and other allowances. This offer was very tempting on the surface.

The main drawbacks, from my point of view, were the facts that I would never leave Cocoa, and would probably live out the war in my mother's home. All my close friends were leaving home, learning new skills, making new friends, and gaining new experiences by traveling to distant parts of the world. These were the things I really wanted. As much as I enjoyed my job, and the people I worked with, I knew if I stayed, I would be trapped in my small hometown environment, and be thought as a "mama's boy" for the rest of my life.

I quickly declined this offer also. This refusal prompted my superiors to ask if my choice was to enter the military as a recruit. They advised me to seriously consider the implications of the three alternatives and to inform them of my decision.

With a large amount of uncertainty, I told my superiors I felt I should not avoid the draft, and naively told them it was time for this little bird to test his wings and leave the nest. It was now time for me to become a man and take my changes.

This announcement terminated the meeting. The Chief Draftsman and I were dismissed, and the Director was asked to stay.

As the Chief Draftsman and I passed the Commander's secretary, the Chief Draftsman and I stopped to pass the time of day. What happened in the Commanders office was not meant for my ears, but I plainly heard the Commander say to the Director,

"Joe, Randy will be hard to replace, so get right on it. By the way, I don't want to be loosing people to the draft every six or eight months. Replace him with a female."

2

The Induction Process

U S Army Induction Center
Camp Blanding, Florida — January 1943

"Skunk Hollow" was the popular name for that portion of Camp Blanding dedicated to receiving civilian inductees from Florida and processing them into the military. Transportation from Cocoa to Camp Blanding was by a chartered Greyhound bus. This bus, leased by the army, accommodated about sixty people. It had started picking up inductees at Ft. Pierce and was about one-half full by the time the Cocoa group boarded. It continued to pick up additional inductees as we motored toward Camp Blanding and by the time we reached our destination, the bus was full.

Every Florida inductee remembers the total chaos of inductee processing, and the hell-hole called Skunk Hollow. Even time can not soften these harsh memories. To me, with one year of college ROTC training, I could not believe this was the army, it was a nightmare come true. We were herded, shoved, debased, cursed, and were required to say "Sir" to, and to salute corporals. We stood in long lines, unclothed, ashamed and vulnerable, and were constantly reminded by corporals that we were the lowest form of homo sapiens. Corporals relegated us to latrine duty, trash detail, and rudely awakened us at ungodly hours to serve on Kitchen Police (KP) detail. Corporals were forever marching us somewhere; to the mess hall, to the supply depot, and to the hospital to be examined, scrutinized, poked, and punctured by excruciatingly painful, dull hypodermic needles. For days on end, we saw nothing but corporals. I began to believe the entire army was populated with nothing but recruits and corporals. My main line of thought made me believe I had been damned stupid to give up the life of a Navy Chief Petty Officer for this.

Several days into processing, after we had passed all mental and physical tests, we were marched to an extremely large warehouse. There we were formed into a line to be issued our army clothing, boots, and field equipment. As the inductees completed this process, they signed a receipt for what they had been issued, and exited the building carrying two barracks bags stuffed with olive drab colored gear. They looked much like pack animals as they staggered back to their barracks carrying this heavy load.

I believe this agonizing trip back to the barracks marked the first time in our short military careers that we were not formed into a line and marched by officious corporals.

As I entered the warehouse, it was interesting to observe this process in action. Inside was a table, about one half the length of a football field, with inductees on one side of the table and supply clerks on the other. Behind the supply clerks was the largest assortment of clothing and gear I had ever seen. Army clothes and equipment were stored on shelves as far as the eye could see. As an inductee reached a spot on the table, or station as they were called, the supply clerk at that station would ask, "What size do you wear?"

When the inductee answered, "Size 34," the supply clerk would go to the shelf, remove six size 34 garments from the shelf, and place the garments on the table in front of the inductee. The inductee would then place the six garments into his barracks bag and move to the next station. This process was repeated numerous times until the inductee had been issued what the army wanted him to have. The inductee was then required to sign a receipt for all the clothing and equipment he had been issued. From that day forward, the inductee was responsible to the US Government for all the clothing and equipment he had been issued.

In the event the inductee subsequently lost any of this equipment, he was required to prepare a Statement-of-Charges form describing the loss. Upon receipt of the executed Statement-of-Charges form, the benevolent army then took the value of the lost equipment out of the inductees monthly pay.

Toward the end of the day, some sizes would become depleted. When an inductee would ask for a size 38, the clerk might issue him a size 36. If the inductee noticed the discrepancy and complained the size was too small, the supply clerk would curtly reply, "Don't worry about it! The army will work that excess gut off of you."

As I approached the table, I noticed a distinguished looking Master Sergeant coming toward us. After being castigated by corporals for several days, we all froze, afraid to move, like we were being approached by God! The Master Sergeant stopped and spoke to one of my friends from Cocoa, who was very nervous when he pointed his finger toward me. The Master Sergeant then approached me and asked, "Are you the son of Mrs. May C. Pierson?"

In a squeaky voice I answered, "Yes Sergeant."

He smiled and said, "That is nice son. Now get out of line and follow me."

This seemed strange, but I did as I was told and immediately stepped out of line, fell in behind him, and obediently followed him around the end of the supply table and into the bowels of the warehouse.

We passed mountains of army supplies as we walked farther into the cavernous building, finally reaching a closed-in office area. The Master Sergeant opened the door and motioned for me to enter. The office area contained many non-commissioned officers who were pouring over records and inventories. They hardly looked up as we walked by. At the rear of this large office area was a private office with a sign on the door that identified it as the office of the – Induction Center Supply Sergeant – Master Sergeant M. A. Hall.

Once in his office, Master Sergeant Hall sat behind a massive desk and motioned for me to sit facing him. As he introduced himself, I read his name-tag, M/Sgt M. A. (Mike) Hall. Then Mike said, "I didn't think you would remember me. I left Cocoa several years ago to join the army. You were just a small child. I'll never forget your mother, she taught me in high school. As a youngster I was always in trouble and she helped straighten me out. She taught me responsibility and discipline. Randolph, she was the best teacher I ever had!

I thought to myself, "He actually knows my name is Randolph."

Master Sergeant Hall continued, "Randolph, how does your mother feel about you being in the army?"

"Sergeant Hall, my induction was no surprise. When the letter finally arrived, she seemed to accept reality the way most mothers do when they are prepared for the inevitable."

The Sergeant seemed relieved and said, "I owe your mother, and I will try to repay her through you. The least I can do is make certain the boots and clothing we issue fit properly."

He then admitted his men tried to fit all inductees properly, but due to the sheer volume of bodies being processed each day, it was almost impossible. He then called a "Buck" Sergeant (three stripes) into his office and instructed him, in no uncertain terms, to issue me boots and clothing that fit. When the task was complete, the Sergeant was told to bring me back to his office so he could check the fit.

From that moment on, the process for me was much like selecting items of clothing in a huge, well stocked, department store. I was allowed to try-on everything; pants, shirts, jacket, boots, overcoat, everything!

After being issued my GI (Government Issue) clothing, I remained dressed in a "Class A; uniform and we returned to Master Sergeant Hall's office. He was extremely busy, but told us to enter, As he glanced at me, standing at attention before him, he commented, "Randolph, you look pretty sharp in your uniform. Where did you learn how to wear a uniform?"

I told him, "I took one year of Artillery ROTC training at the University of Florida. They made us Cadets stand personal inspection."

"It shows! Be sure and tell the records clerk to enter the Artillery ROTC training in your personnel records. It is very important!"

The Buck Sergeant excused himself when he saw Mike was pleased with the cut of my uniform. After the sergeant left, I asked Mike a few questions about the reception center and how it operated. He easily answered my questions, and then volunteered some additional information. He said the Staff Sergeant in charge of the Reception Center barracks was a friend of his. As I prepared to leave, and was thanking Master Sergeant Hall for his help, Mike told me he would call his buddy in charge of the barracks and let him know I was his friend also.

At the Retreat Formation that afternoon, the barracks corporal called me front-and-center, slipped a red arm-band around my left arm, and told me to wear the arm-band at all times until I reached my permanent duty station. He then turned and addressed the assembled recruits and announced I was now Acting-Corporal Pierson.

From that day forth, I pulled no extra duty such as KP or Latrine Duty, until I reached my permanent duty station, Fort Jackson, South Carolina. My chance meeting with Master Sergeant Hall had taught me a valuable lesson which later served me well. What you know is always important in the military, but sometimes who you know is just as important. No wonder I still remember Master Sergeant Hall.

Several days later, when processing was complete, and orders were issued assigning us to our permanent units, most of the fellows from Cocoa, including me, were assigned to the 106th Infantry Division, a brand new infantry division being formed at Fort Jackson, South Carolina.

When the happy day arrived, to leave Skunk Hollow, we were marched to a group of waiting Greyhound busses. Each bus was loaded from rear to front, leaving a front seat vacant for personnel records and the acting-corporal in charge of the detail.

At my bus, I was handed a box of personnel records and told to deliver both men and records to the Fort Jackson Reception Center.

The civilian bus driver laughed as I received my instructions, but I readily accepted the responsibility. The army had issued me a red arm-band and put me in charge.

I was proud to be an acting-corporal!

3
Army Basic Training

106th Infantry Division
Fort Jackson, South Carolina—February, 1943

The bus trip from Camp Blanding to Fort Jackson took almost all day. Enroute we stopped two times for rest stops and once for the mid-day meal, otherwise the trip was uneventful. After several hours into the trip, all the inductees seemed withdrawn and deep in thought, or sound asleep. No telling what went on in each man's mind. For me, I was wide-awake and looking forward to a new way of life.

A very bored bus driver finally delivered us to the Fort Jackson Reception Center. We were met by non-commissioned officers and drivers from the various units to which we had been assigned. In my bus load, all the inductees but me were assigned to one of the three infantry regiments, the 422nd, the 423rd, or the 424th. After sorting out who went where, the men and their records were loaded into waiting GMC trucks to be transported to their respective units. Finally only I remained.

I waited at the entrance of the Reception Center for quite some time. I was alone, tired, confused, and both my body and paper work were still unclaimed. Finally a jeep arrived. The Staff Sergeant driving the jeep eventually spotted me and my gear, drove to where I was standing, and asked, "Is your name Pierson?" When I nodded yes, he said gruffly, "Get in."

Unassisted, I stowed my barracks bag into the rear of the jeep and took the seat up front next to the Staff Sergeant. He immediately asked, "What in the hell does that red band on your left arm mean?"

"It means I'm an acting-corporal."

"Who made you an acting-corporal?"

"The Barracks Sergeant at Camp Blanding promoted me."

The Staff Sergeant looked me straight in the eye, and with a tone of authority told me, "Pierson, you ain't no acting-corporal no more! Take off that damned rag and remember this, and remember it good. You are a private, a lousy recruit, the lowest damn thing in this man's army. You got any questions Pierson?"

Without so much as one simple question, I removed the red are band, crammed it into my pocket, and replied, "No Sir!"

Unfortunately for me, this triggered another tirade, "Do you see these four stripes on my sleeve, Pierson?" Without waiting for an answer, he continued, "I'm a Staff Sergeant, not an officer, and you don't ever call a non-com Sir."

The rear wheels of the jeep skidded as he quickly released the clutch and revved up the engine. We were quickly on our way, but I had no idea where we were going. After riding past rows and rows of buildings in silence, I finally spoke, "Sergeant, can I ask you a question?"

"Permission granted," was his reply.

"Sergeant, where are we going in such a hurry?"

His answer was simple and to the point, "You are assigned to Headquarters Battery of the 589th Field Artillery Battalion. That is where we are going, and with my luck, you will probably be assigned to my section."

We completed the remainder of the trip in complete silence.

Fort Jackson was a permanent army post designed to accommodate three infantry divisions, plus several special units. It was a spacious, well laid-out, military reservation, and was excellently maintained. Camp Blanding, on the other hand, was hastily built, and reflected it's temporary nature in every respect. My new home with the 589th Field Artillery Battalion was a vast improvement over the past accommodations at Skunk Hollow.

When I arrived, the 106th Division consisted of about ten thousand men, and the remaining five thousand were arriving daily. My Battalion, the 589th, was at full strength, with Field Artillery orientation and basic training already in progress.

Basic training was scheduled to last thirteen weeks and is designed to transition a civilian body and attitude into a healthy, fine-tuned body, with a military mind-set. This change greatly enhances an individuals ability to function as part of a team, and to survive the rigors of war-fare. Army basic training is time tested, and extremely effective in accomplishing these necessary changes. Basic training is also HELL!

During basic training the artillery units are subjected to the same physical training as the infantry. Long endurance marches, calisthenics, and short speed marches, with heavy back-packs and lots of double time. However, the artillery specialty training is quite different from the infantry. With one year of artillery ROTC training behind me, I was assigned to the Battalion Fire Direction Center, immediately placed in s sergeant's slot, and started my technical training as a fire control operator.

This type of training was interesting and "duck soup" for me. I was a fast learner, and in time, I became friendly with my S-3, Major Arthur C. Parker, III and the Battalion Commander, Lieutenant Colonel Thomas P. Kelly, Jr. as I worked with them daily. My popularity with these senior officers did not please my Battery Commander, Captain Black. Captain Black thought I should be under his direct control because he was actually my commanding officer. However, at the request of Major Parker, I began spending more and more time at Battalion Headquarters and less and less time under Captain Black's control, performing menial battery duties.

For me, things were going great until the fifth week of basic training, when I started getting splitting headaches. Each morning I would complain and the Major would send me on sick-call. The Battalion Surgeon, a First Lieutenant medical officer, fresh out of medical school, strongly suspected that all GIs were goof-offs and/or "Gold Bricks." Each time I went on sick-call, he asked me questions, gave me the usual APC pills for pain, and returned me to duty. This predictable process lasted four days. In the meantime my headaches were becoming progressively worse, and I finally developed a high fever. The day of the high fever, the doctor finally excused me from duty and confined me to the barracks, where I finally passed-out in my bunk.

† †

Fort Jackson – Columbia, South Carolina
Station Hospital – Spinal Meningitis Ward – March 1943

Three days later I woke up foggy, and in strange surroundings. I was in a private room, and certainly not in the barracks. In the process of getting out of bed to determine where I was, and what was going on, I fainted, collapsed, and fell to the floor. The noise created by the fall brought people running to the room. It took two male orderlies, under the supervision of a nurse, to lift my unconscious body from the floor back onto the bed.

The process of getting me back onto the bed, plus a lively discussion concerning the use of restraints to keep me there, spawned my question, "Where am I?"

The nurse terminated her conversation with the male orderlies and replied, "You are in the Station Hospital at Fort Jackson. You have been in a coma for three days with spinal meningitis, which can be fatal, and you are very sick, Private Pierson."

At the time, this information did not register with me because I felt lousy, and frankly, I didn't know what spinal meningitis was and didn't care if it could be fatal.

After twelve days of individualized care and medication in the private room, I was moved into a large ward that held two dozen beds. There had been an epidemic of spinal meningitis at Fort Jackson, and several hundred soldiers were hospitalized. All the guys in my ward were privates, recently inducted into the army. This fact resulted in a lack of discipline as we began to recuperate and feel better.

Our head nurse – we rarely saw a doctor – was an older regular army nurse. She was very strict, but very caring. We became "her boys," and to us she became "The Major." Even though she valiantly tried to maintain discipline in the numerous wards under her jurisdiction, it was obvious she did not understand how to control, or motivate, a group of young men who were not yet soldiers, but still civilians at heart.

The winter meningitis epidemic, of 1942-43, was the first time sulfa drugs were utilized to combat this dreaded disease. We became medical guinea pigs. In fact, very lucky guinea pigs, because the sulfa treatment proved to be quite effective. During the winter of 1941-42, another army post experienced a meningitis epidemic which was treated with different medication. The 1941-42 treatment resulted in about ten percent fatalities and a huge percentage of crippled survivors. The results of the sulfa treated epidemic of 1942-43 was much better, with some three percent fatalities and almost no crippled survivors. If you were lucky and received the entire sulfa treatment, you were moved from your private room into the ward. After rehabilitation, and recovering your strength, the chances are that you would be returned to duty. If not, you left the private room feet first, covered with a white GI sheet.

To be effective, the sulfa drug had to be administered for fourteen consecutive days. If a patient survived this period of time, and his blood count remained satisfactory, the chances of complete recovery were good.

In my case, the white cell count increased to the point that administration of the sulfa drug had to be suspended on the twelfth day, three days short of the treatment objective. Much to my chagrin, I heard a private conversation between "The Major" and a doctor that hinged on my chances of survival if the treatment was ceased, versus the chance of killing me if they continued to administer the drug. Finally a joint decision was made to cease the sulfa treatment and closely monitor my white blood cell count.

During sulfa treatment, and into the recuperative period, each patient was required to consume large quantities of liquid. All liquid intake was carefully measured and recorded. By the same token, we were not allowed to urinate in the latrine. We were required to urinate into graduated glass urinals, called "ducks." These urinals were provided at the bedside of each patient. Periodically an orderly would enter the ward to record, and loudly announce, the amount of urine which had accumulated in each "duck.' Once this ceremony was performed, the ducks were taken to the latrine, empted, washed, dried, and returned to the bedside of each patient.

By measuring and recording the fluid intake and outflow of each patent, "The Major" could determine if our kidneys and bladders were functioning properly. She constantly reminded the patients and orderlies the importance this process.

For some reason, boredom probably, the ritual of recording and announcing the accumulated contents of each individual "duck" stimulated the spirit of competition in some of my ward-mates. Within a few days, friendly wagers were being placed between patients to see who could accumulate the most urine in their bladder for the first reading each morning. It didn't take long for almost every patient in the ward, including yours truly, to begin participating in the "Pee-in-the-Bottle-Contest" each morning. As the money-pot grew in value, even some of the hospital orderlies joined the wagering, betting on patients with the best win/loss record. With the ever increasing amounts of money to be won, the competition became more and more serious. It was not uncommon for the last two or three hold-outs to lie in bed each morning in pain, strained looks on their faces, groans escaping from their tortured bodies, and waiting until the last moment to void their bladders. This had indeed become very serious competition!

When "The Major" found out about our "Pee-in-the-Bottle-Contest," she was furious! We received the lecture of our lives about the damage we were doing to our young bodies, how hard she and the army were trying to cure us, and worst of all, how we had violated her trust and let her down. We were properly advised this type activity would not be tolerated in the future, and she gave us her word, if we pulled another such trick on her, we would be disciplined. Later, when we heard the orderlies who had aided and abetted our illegal competition had been transferred to front line units as combat medics, I decided it was not wise to make "The Major" mad again.

The families I had known in Cocoa had names like Williams, Green, Smith, and Jones. My developing circle of army friends included names such as Petrocelli, Feinberg, Silvertooth, and Andrasophski. To me, these names were strange, and these people were different. I didn't mind the different accents or the different religious and family traditions, I actually found the differences to be interesting. One of the more interesting guys I became friendly with was Vito Petrocelli. Vito had also contracted meningitis and occupied the bed to my left in the meningitis ward.

During our first get-acquainted session, Vito and I compared notes. His accent was Italian, mine Southern. He was Catholic, I was Protestant. I was nineteen and naive, Vito was twenty-three, sophisticated, street-wise, and played saxophone in a dance band. He was handsome, well built, an "Italian Stallion." I was a tall, skinny, country boy. We talked about our differences, got to know each other in the process, and became fast friends. A true case of opposites attract!

Every night after the evening meal, and before lights-out, male orderlies would enter the ward with large bottles of rubbing alcohol and offer to give us a body rub. I thought this was a great idea. This feeling was shared by most of the other patients. These rub-downs were refreshing. They provided a break from the tedium of being bed ridden. Vito, street-smart and forward looking, refused his rub-down the first night.

When the night nurse came on duty, a "pitiful Vito" complained the orderly gave everyone in the ward a rub-down but him. To placate "poor Vito" the attractive night nurse gave him a rub-down herself.

It didn't take Anne, the night nurse, long to realize that Vito wanted more than a mere rub-down. I'm certain many young men had made passes at Anne. She was a pert looking Second Lieutenant with a body that would stimulate any man, young or old. No doubt about it, she stimulated Vito, but she knew how to handle horny men. The third night Vito pulled his act on Anne, she told Vito to take off his pajama top and lie on the bed face down. She then started to rub his neck slowly, with her head close to his, whispering into his ear. Then she rubbed his shoulders and upper back. By this time, Vito was smiling and whispering back to Anne, who was now smiling at him. As she started to rub his lower back, Anne casually reached under Vito's stomach, untied his pajama bottoms, pulled them down to his thighs, and exposed his muscular buttocks. This maneuver surprised Vito, but he took it in his stride, still smiling broadly. Without comment, Anne shifted her attention to his waist, then moved her hands under his stomach and rubbed the front of his thighs. She then brought her hands together, beneath him, and began to massage the valley between his thighs slowly, methodically, and erotically.

This was more than Vito had bargained for. He ceased whispering to Anne, buried his face in the pillow, started to groan, and make funny sounds. When she knew she was in complete control, she said in a gentle voice, "Vito, roll over onto your back."

Vito refused!

In a more stern voice, Anne repeated, "Vito, roll over onto your back." Again, Vito refused to move.

With the authority of an officer addressing an enlisted man, this time Anne commanded, "Private Petrocelli, if you don't roll over onto your back, I will have two orderlies roll you over. Do you understand me?"

In desperation, Vito grabbed the sheet, and pulled it up to his chest as he rolled over. The result was no surprise to Anne, nor to any of the GIs who had been witnessing this performance. The sheet over Vito's lower abdomen looked as if it was supported by a sturdy tent pole.

In a mock, sweet, and tender gesture, Anne gathered the sheet around Vito's erection, displaying it even more prominently, and squeezed it gently. Vito lay there not knowing what to do, or what would happen next. Obviously savoring the moment, and pleased with her handy-work, Anne stood there, fondly gazing at the strained look on Vito's face, as she held his healthy erection in her left hand. Only Anne, and the orderlies, knew what would come next.

Without warning, and with professional precision, Anne sharply thumped the head of Vito's erection with the trained middle finger of her right hand. The blow was unexpected, sharp, and expertly placed. Even though I was not involved in this charade, I could almost feel the painful sting of that blow. The effect on Vito was almost instantaneous, his "tent pole" collapsed suddenly, much like a burst balloon.

Anne bent over the bed, looked into Vito's dark eyes, patted him lovingly on each cheek, and asked, "Is that what you had in mind lover boy?"

During our entire friendship, that was the only time I remember Vito being speechless.

The next day all Vito could talk about was getting even with Anne. The only thing that bothered him about last nights episode was the fact that a female had rejected him, and he was obsessed with getting even. Something to do with his Italian blood, I guess. Even though other friends tried to talk him out of getting even, Vito was determined.

As time passed, Vito and Anne remained outwardly cordial, but Anne kept her distance. I'm certain Anne liked Vito because he was a very likeable person, but she was an officer, he was an enlisted man, and in the army, the two were not allowed to mix.

Several nights after the massage incident, Vito looked, and acted, as though he was not feeling well. He asked Anne if she would please check his temperature because he thought he was running a fever. During the process of checking on Vito, Anne leaned over the bed and Vito suddenly grabbed her around the waist pulling her onto the bed beside him. Anne was obviously surprised and struggled to get back on her feet. Vito was too strong for her and rolled her over on top of his body. As she lay there struggling, he firmly kissed her on the mouth. In the process of releasing her, Vito slowly ran his hands over her shapely back and firm breasts, while announcing, so all could hear, "Now we are even!"

We were all as surprised as Anne and could tell she was quite upset. I wondered what would happen to a buck private who forcibly kissed, and fondled, an officer in front of more than twenty witnesses. Anne removed herself from the bed, stood there momentarily straightening her uniform, and as she walked away, Anne turned and calmly said, "Vito, you should not have done that."

Anne never returned to our ward. We wondered why, and we wondered what would happen to Vito. Two weeks later we received terrible news from an orderly, Anne was a patient in the hospital. She had contracted spinal meningitis. This news troubled us all, especially Vito. He had no idea he was infectious when he kissed Anne.

A few weeks later, after we had completed our rehabilitation program and passed our physicals, "The Major" advised us we would be returned to our units, and would be assigned light-duty for two weeks before returning to a full-duty status. I had no idea what comprised light-duty, but it sounded good to me. I still did not feel strong enough to complete a long hike carrying the expected full load of equipment, but I was glad to get out of the hospital, nine weeks was a long time.

The next morning while waiting for transportation to the 589th, Vito surprised me. He said the orders placing us on light-duty were not worth the paper they were written on. He strongly suspected "the Bastards" in our Battalion would put us back on full-duty the minute we arrived. I did not understand why he felt so strongly that this would happen, but I did know one thing, Vito had pretty good instincts.

† †

106th Infantry Division – 589th Field Artillery Battalion
Headquarters Battery – Return to Duty

I told Vito "so long" when the driver dropped me off at the 589th Headquarters Battery Orderly Room. As the jeep pulled away to take Vito to "A" Battery, I knocked on the Orderly Room door. When a deep voice said, "Come In," I recognized the voice of my First Sergeant.

The First Sergeant seemed glad to have me back and asked for my hospital discharge papers. While he was reading them he shook his head and said, "Pierson, you and I better go see the old man." He called Captain Black on the intercom. After a short conversation got up from behind his desk and motioned for me to follow him.

When we entered his office, Captain Black returned our salute, looked me over, and motioned for us to sit. He cleared his throat and asked me about being ordered to light-duty. I told him we had just completed a short period of physical therapy and the doctors thought we should be slowly eased back into full-duty. The Captain shook his head in a negative gesture and said, "Pierson, there is no such thing as light-duty in this unit now. While you were in the hospital, we completed basic training and will start unit training in a few days. This means we will be living in the field most of the time and subjected to all kinds of inclement weather. Now is the time we must separate the men from the boys. I can give you two choices: you can remain in this Battery on full-duty, or, I will have you transferred to another unit where you can start basic training again."

His position caught me totally off guard. I looked at the First Sergeant, then back at the Captain, and said, "With your permission Sir, I would like to think about my options and talk them over with Major Parker." My request went over like a lead balloon! Captain Black got red in the face, and told me in no uncertain terms, that Major Parker had nothing to do with my decision. The decision was mine to make, and I should make it now. He said, I should be grateful that he had given me the opportunity to make the choice.

Perspiration started to trickle from my arm pits. I had not expected to be placed under this type of pressure, it was not necessary. I did not want to leave my friends in the Fire Direction Center, and I respected Major Parker and Lieutenant Colonel Kelly. It was too bad I did not feel the same way about Captain Black. After vacillating back and forth in my mind, Captain Black became irritated again and demanded, "Alright Pierson, we don't have all day. Which is it? Do you want to leave or do you want to stay?"

I thought to myself, you son-of-a-bitch, it will take a better man than you to run me off, and calmly replied, "I'll stay."

The First Sergeant stood and signaled to me the meeting was over. We saluted and left the Captain's office. The bastard never even looked up or returned our salute.

Back in the Orderly Room the First Sergeant explained what had happened while I was gone. Part of the original Cadre had left and many of the new recruits had been promoted and were filling the vacancies created by the departing Cadre. He told me my old sergeant's slot had been filed and I would have to wait a long time before I would get a promotion. He advised me to check with Sergeant Tacker, who was now the Operations Sergeant, and tell him that Captain Black wanted me in his platoon. He also advised me to hotfoot it to Battalion and let Major Parker know I was present for duty. While there, ask the Major if he could slot me back into the Fire Direction Center.

I thanked the First Sergeant for the advice and as I was leaving he said, "I forgot the Captain has a thing about you and how much the senior officers like you. Don't think the old man is all bad, he is really trying to turn you civilians into an effective combat unit. In the end, we will all depend on each other. We can't afford to have a weak link in the chain."

Sergeant Tacker was an inductee from Nashville, Tennessee who entered the service at Fort Jackson slightly before I arrived from Florida. Prior to being drafted, he had attended a military prep school. During the first few weeks of basic training, he rose head and shoulders above the rest of us recruits. I was not surprised to learn he had already been promoted to Sergeant. When I entered the barracks, "Tack" was just leaving the Operations Sergeant's private room. He recognized me immediately and invited me into his room so we talk in private. Sergeant Tacker had class, he had a military bearing, he was a religious young men, and was a perfect gentleman. This combination of personal characteristics tended to set him apart from a majority of us recruits. Before I got sick, we were training for the same fire direction assignment. After getting caught-up on our personal lives, I finally told him the First Sergeant had advised me to talk to him and then hotfoot it to Battalion to let Major Parker know I had returned to duty.

Tack smiled and told me, "Randy, it is a good idea to show Major Parker this courtesy, but the Major already knows you have been returned to duty."

I did not realize the Major knew I was back, but Tack assured me he did. Tack also anticipated my big question and said, "The Major kept track of you while you were in the hospital, and has held a job open for you at Battalion Headquarters. The Major wants you back in Fire Direction when the opportunity presents itself." I felt as though I had hit the jackpot!

Sergeant Tacker finished his work while I was getting settled at my bunk, and decided to go to Battalion Headquarters with me. We entered the headquarters building and went directly to the Sergeant Major's office to determine if Major Parker would see us. Sergeant Major Moody was probably the sharpest looking soldier on the Post. He was Regular Army, with more than twenty years service, and had turned down the opportunity to go to Officers Candidate School (OCS) many times. His main reason for refusing this opportunity was that officers don't shoot craps. In the army, enlisted men shoot craps, whereas officers play poker. The Sergeant Major was my kind of guy.

Sergeant Major Moody greeted us with a friendly gesture and said, "Sergeant Tacker I presume, who is the 'goldbrick' you have with you?" Sergeant Tacker retorted, "I don't know him, he just showed up at the barracks, tired, hungry and begging for shelter." Then Tack became serious and asked, "Sergeant Major, would it be possible for us to see Major Parker for a few minutes?"

The Sergeant Major shrugged his shoulders, as if to say, I don't know, but responded, "He is in with the Colonel." Without thinking I pushed the issue, "Sergeant Moody, I'd like to see them both."

The Sergeant Major pressed a button on his intercom, without comment. When Lieutenant Colonel Thomas P. Kelly, Jr. answered, the Sergeant Major advised our commanding officer that Sergeant Tacker and Private Pierson would like to see the Colonel and Major Parker. After a pause, the Sergeant Major was told, "Send them in."

The Colonel, and the Major, had paper spread on a work table, and appeared to be extremely busy, but motioned for us to enter anyway. We entered the room, saluted, and moved quickly to the work table. I could see from the expressions on the faces of the two senior officers that we were welcome. Sergeant Tacker then informed them that Private Pierson had just been returned to duty. Tack volunteered he would like to have private Pierson assigned to the Operations Platoon. Major Parker nodded in agreement, but explained that my old job had been filled, and I might have to remain a private for a long time before a non-commissioned officer's job became vacant again.

I told both senior officers the options Captain Black had outlined to me. I also made it clear I would like to remain in the 589th, return to the Operations Platoon, and somehow, get back into the Fire Direction Center. Both officers understood my position and a brief discussion occurred between them. Finally Major Parker asked, "Pierson, can you drive?"

"Yes sir."

"Do you have an army drivers license?"

"No sir, I do not."

Major Parker thought for a moment and replied, "If you can get an army drivers license issued, I'll ask Captain Black to assign you as my driver." My outburst was spontaneous, "Sir, you just got yourself a driver!"

Sergeant Tacker and I talked all the way back to the barracks. I was happy to be back where I felt comfortable. Tack was glad to have me because we were accustomed to working together. He also knew I could handle almost any job in his platoon.

To me, the most important things I could do were to stay away from Captain Black, study hard, and play catch-up on the different fire direction functions, because I had no idea which job would become available, or when.

In garrison, driving for Major Parker was a snap. He did not require transportation very often. Waiting for him gave me more time to study, and study I did. When I was driving the Major, he was either teaching me new techniques, or he was verbally testing me to determine what I had already learned.

† †

Fort Jackson South Carolina
Training Range—The Last 30 Mile Hike

About one week after I returned to the unit, I walked over to "A" Battery to see Vito one evening. We propped up under a pine tree in front of his barracks and compared notes. During our conversation Vito asked, "Randy, did you get assigned to light-duty when you returned to Headquarters Battery?"

"No Vito, Captain Black told me there is no such thing as light-duty in Headquarters Battery. But it doesn't matter to me, driving a jeep is not hard work."

With this answer, Vito became agitated and informed me, "Battalion has scheduled a thirty mile hike, with full field pack and gear. I was told I will have to participate in this damned hike, and I don't think this is fair."

"Vito, the hike is scheduled for what day?"

"My First Sergeant says it is set for day after tomorrow. Have you been told you have to go on this stupid hike?"

"No one has said anything to me about a hike, Vito."

Vito became livid, "It is damned unfair for the army to pick on me. I am going to call my mother, she has political connections, and she is going to get somebody in deep shit for picking on me."

I hated to find Vito in this frame of mind because he seemed mad at me, even though I had no control over this hike situation. I was only a private and had no input into this decision. Vito should know that no one ever asks privates for an opinion.

The sun was sinking in the west when I returned to my barracks. As I flopped onto my bunk, my buddy, T/5 (Corporal) Delbert Miller, from Des Moines, Iowa told me Sergeant Tacker was looking for me. Since I had no idea what Tack wanted, I strolled to the other end of the barracks, knocked on his door, and announced, "Sergeant, its Pierson, do you want to see me?"

"Come on in Randy."

I found him seated at his small work table with a picture of his Tennessee sweetheart, Betty Jean, facing him. He was writing her a letter. Tack turned, and motioned for me to sit on his bed.

Sergeant Tacker began, "Randy, I have some bad news for you. Day after tomorrow we have a thirty mile hike scheduled that starts at 0400. It is a test to see what physical condition the Battalion is in. We will make this hike with full field equipment, all sixty pounds of it. I asked Captain Black to excuse you. He refused! I went to Major Parker and told him I didn't think you could finish the hike. Major Parker said this was a decision made at Division Artillery Headquarters and he could not change their orders."

"Tack, I just heard about the hike over at "A" Battery. One of the guys over there who had spinal meningitis is pretty shook-up."

"Randy do you think you are strong enough to walk thirty miles carrying a full load?"

My talk with Vito had started me thinking about this hike, but I really didn't know whether I could hack-it or not. "Tack, thirty miles in this summer heat, and carrying sixty pounds! Man, I really don't know. I think I can walk the thirty miles OK, but carrying full field equipment, I just don't know. What choice do I have? What are my alternatives?"

My answers and questions relieved Sergeant Tacker somewhat. "Randy, get a good nights rest, and leave the details with me. I'll try and work out something.

We really want this to be a team effort, and I want everyone in my platoon to complete this march."

The next night the barracks were in an uproar. All the guys were packing gear and getting ready for the hike which started the next morning at 0400. Tack and Dell Miller came by my bunk and helped me prepare for the hike. Instead of packing the required gear, we padded my pack and bed roll with crumpled-up paper. We agreed that once the Battalion departed camp and was on the road, I would give my steel helmet to Dell and pass my carbine to Sergeant Andrasophski, a friend from Cleveland. With no steel helmet, no carbine, a lightened bed roll, and a paper-filled back pack, I would be carrying about twenty pounds instead of the normal sixty. These changes relieved my anxieties about my ability to complete the hike. I knew it was important for everyone to finish the hike and I did not want to let anyone down. The thought of my lightened load also made my short nights sleep much more pleasant.

At 0400, the Battalion was formed and our march column started leaving the battery street. It was still dark and the night air was cool. As we picked up the normal marching cadence, I actually felt exhilarated. The plan was to walk three miles in fifty minutes, and rest for ten. This was the normal pace for an endurance march, and we had done this before.

As we marched briskly in the total darkness, I could not see much detail, only the men in front and on each side of me, but I could sense I was part of a huge movement of men. This feeling was reinforced by hearing the various platoon leaders chanting the cadence, "You Left, You Left, You had a good home but you Left." It was similar to marching on the ROTC parade ground at college. At three miles per hour, plus one hour to eat the mid-day meal, the march should last approximately eleven hours. If all went well, we would be back on the battery street by 1500 hours.

As the miles melted away, the sky became lighter and the South Carolina sun became hotter and hotter. Sergeant "Andy" Andrasophski asked me at every break if I wanted him to carry my carbine. Pride entered the picture each time Captain Black walked by and gave me a contemptuous look. Consequently I kept telling Andy I was OK and refused to surrender my carbine.

At the noon break all the fire direction team huddled around my prone body as I lay on the ground exhausted. They made certain I was drinking plenty of water, taking my salt tablets, and sweating freely. They removed my back pack before I lay down, and replaced it after I was standing. This way, I did not have to struggle to lie down or to rise and stand. Everyone in the Operations Platoon was helping me, any way they could, to complete this hellishly hot endurance test. The main thing that kept me going was the knowledge that Captain Black wanted to see me face down, and passed-out, in the damned dust. I refused to give him that satisfaction..

The last six miles were tough on the healthy men, but for me it was hell-on-earth! I was super heated, weak, my fatigues covered with salt rings from dried salty sweat, and, like the rest, had walked twenty four horrible miles. By now, at every ten minute rest break, some of the men tried to continue, but could not. They were exhausted and totally spent. Neither body or spirit would answer their feeble call. When a man stayed down, a non-com, or an officer, would check him and call for a medic. Soon the "meat wagon" would arrive. The medics would load the spent GI into the ambulance, throw his gear in beside him, and the ambulance would whisk him back to camp.

Heat exhaustion and fatigue were taking their toll on all members of this march. My body was getting weaker, but my desire to finish this march grew stronger as we neared the end of this test. I was fighting two personal demons, my pride, and Captain Black. I was determined to prove the damned Captain was wrong, or I would die trying. I promised myself I would show that bastard I was as good a man as he was!

At the last rest stop, three miles from camp, I was so weak I finally gave my steel helmet to Dell and my carbine to Andy. On the last leg of the hike, when the barracks were less than one mile away, my Heavenly Father gave me one more shot of adrenaline. I asked for my helmet and carbine. Both Dell and Andy looked at me in disbelief, but returned my gear.

On what had to be my last gasp, I picked up the step. Tack fell in beside me asked, "Randy, are you going to finish the hike?"

My belligerent answer was, "You can bet your ass on it!" In response Sergeant

Tacker commanded, "Pierson, fall out and move to the head of the column."

With no idea of what he had in mind, I complied, because it was an order. Dell Miller was in the lead position and carrying the Battalion Guidon. Tack told Dell to drop back one rank and took the Guidon from him. As I took Dell's place in the front rank, Tack handed me the Guidon. The next thing I knew, I was the Battalion Guidon Bearer with Andy to my left and Dell behind me, ready to catch the Guidon and me, if I faltered.

As Sergeant Tacker moved to the side of the column, into the platoon leaders position, I could hear him say to Dell, "Isn't that a sight to behold? Randy is six foot two, weighs 120 pounds soaking wet, his fatigues are so big they are falling off, his pack is hanging crooked on his back, and he is making three tracks, because his ass is dragging on the ground. But look how proud he is, carrying that Guidon!" Dell just laughed, "What more can I say?"

We entered the Battery Street, chanting as one man, "You had a good home but you LEFT. You had a good home but you LEFT. Jodie was RIGHT, you ain't very BRIGHT. You had a good home but you LEFT!"

In front of our barracks, Sergeant Tacker yelled, "BATTERY –––HALT! RIGHT –––FACE! PARADE –––REST!" I dropped the Guidon one arms length, to the parade rest position. The First Sergeant came over, took the Guidon, and handed it to the Supply Sergeant for storage. He looked at me with new respect, and said, "Nice show kid!"

The First Sergeant called us to attention and dismissed us quickly. He knew we were dead tired. Relieved from duty, we struggled into the barracks, dropping gear helter-skelter on the floor, and threw our exhausted bodies onto the waiting bunks. With mixed emotions caused by fatigue, and pride in completing the march, pride swiftly gave way to fatigue, as bodies replaced harsh reality with deep sleep. Fatigue melted quickly, as it normally does in healthy, strong, young bodies. Guys began to come by my bunk to tell me how proud they were the entire Operation Platoon completed the hike. I told them I was proud of the platoon also. However, I never mentioned to anyone that I had cheated slightly. What the Hell, I only cheated by forty pounds!

Dell Miller aroused me at 1630 and told me to get cleaned up for the Retreat

Formation. I felt better after my short nap, and even more refreshed after a quick shower, shave, and clean clothes. After Retreat we headed for the mess hall where the Mess Sergeant had gone all-out for the evening meal. Even the officers table was full because some of the battalion officers choose to eat with the enlisted men. They considered our food better at Headquarters Battery than the food they were served at the Officers Mess.

After supper, Dell and Tack decided to go to the movie at Post Theatre 2 and asked if I wanted to join them. As much as I wanted to go, I told them I had to go over to "A" Battery and find out how my buddy, Vito, did on the hike. At "A" Battery I was surprised to find Vito packing a civilian bag with class "A" uniforms. When I asked him how the hike went, he winked and said, "I passed-out at the six mile marker, and couldn't get up. Sergeant Alford, that friend of yours form Pensacola, called the medics and had me loaded into the meat wagon. When I told the medics I had just been discharged from the Station Hospital after having spinal meningitis, they took me directly to the hospital.

"What happened there?"

"I was examined by a couple of our former doctors and 'The Major,' our former head nurse. They were very upset when they found out all the 106th Division patients had been placed on full, rather than light-duty, as the hospital had ordered. The Chief Medical Officer spoke with the Inspector General and the 106th Division Commander about this situation. In the meantime, my mother called her US Senator, who contacted the Department of Army, and 'the shit hit the fan' after that. The Senator called my mother back and advised her she could tell me, and all my sick friends, the army would issue rehabilitation furloughs for all of us. My good buddy, that's why I am packing. Tomorrow, you and I will get orders to go home and relax for two weeks!"

This information was difficult for me to digest. I was not accustomed to political influence and manipulating people, but Vito's prediction was accurate. My furlough papers arrived in the orderly room shortly after breakfast the next morning. Private Pierson, Randolph C. was immediately placed on a rehabilitation furlough for fourteen days, with two days travel time authorized in each direction. Any way you cut it, that meant I would be gone for eighteen days. Of course, I was elated over the thought of going home, but then it hit me, this time-off might place my job in jeopardy again.

I decided to discuss this situation with Sergeant Tacker. He took the news calmly, "Randy you are included in the long range plans for fire direction. Don't worry about your job. Just go home, relax, and enjoy the time off."

† †

Cocoa, Florida—My Home Town
A Rehabilitation Furlough

Unfortunately, the furlough did not live up to my expectations, it was an example of anticipation being better than realization. Mother, while delighted to have me home, was furious because the army did not allow her to come to Fort Jackson to take care of her sick son. I understood her feelings about her only teenaged son, but it was not difficult for me to understand the army point of view. How could the army possibly accommodate several hundred anxious, and overly concerned mothers?

Rationing had started for civilians about the time I was drafted. Fortunately I remembered to purloin five pounds of sugar, and some coffee, from the mess hall and brought it home with me. When mother found the sugar and coffee on the kitchen table, she was so excited she almost dropped the sugar. But when the excitement waned, she started accusing me of committing a crime. After assuring her that five pounds of missing sugar and a small amount of coffee would neither make of break the US Army, she settled down, determined to enjoy her newly acquired luxuries.

Mother was a small town school teacher, a Methodist minister's daughter, highly respected, straight-laced, and honest to a fault. All these sterling qualities resulted in her being issued an "A" gasoline rationing sticker, while others who embellished the truth, and deserved no more special treatment than my mother, received "B" stickers. For some reason, the "A" sticker on the old Chevy windshield made me think mother was not treated fairly. With the mileage that "Ole Chev" got on a gallon of gas, mother was in dire danger of walking if she tried to drive more than thirty-five miles each week.

Not knowing in advance that I would be coming home, mother had not accumulated extra gasoline stamps in anticipation of my furlough. Only seventy miles of driving during the two weeks I would be home did not satisfy me. Rather than stay home and rot, I decided to wheel-and-deal a little on the, small but thriving, local gasoline black market. Once driven to this decision, I found out it was relatively easy to acquire small quantities of illegal gasoline. The owner of the local taxi and bus company, who was not rationed, felt sorry for me and helped with my problem. Several local filling station owners were also sympathetic, but my largest benefactor was the Banana River Naval Air Station. I was able to acquire fairly large quantities of high-octane Naval aviation gasoline from both civilian and military sources at the NAS.

This aviation gasoline had one disadvantage, it had to be mixed with lower-octane civilian gasoline, or it would do irreparable damage to older automobile engines. I received expert instructions from my suppliers concerning the proper mix-rate for "Ole Chev." Having wheels and a good supply of gasoline made my furlough much nicer.

Food and commodity rationing was another inconvenience for which I was not prepared. Mother had almost none of the food I was accustomed to eating, nor in the quantities provided by the army. Although perplexing, this problem was also solved. I went to the local rationing board, where I was welcomed home like a conquering hero. After the amenities, I asked about extra ration stamps while I was home. My request was honored and the board promptly issued me Red Stamps for items such as meat, butter, and fats; and Blue Stamps for canned goods. Mrs. Ponder, a friend of the family, told me it might be difficult to find some of these items in the local stores, and suggested I wear my uniform and go to the Naval Air Station Commissary to purchase the more scarce items. She certainly knew the situation and her advice was right on the money. I returned from the Navy Commissary loaded with food mother had not seen in months. Of the items purchased, I personally valued coffee the most. The army had already taught me to drink coffee by the gallons.

The days slipped by pleasantly, but Cocoa had changed. I was not able to see people I wanted to see, and those I did see, were too engrossed in the war effort to spend much time with a lonely soldier. After only one week at home, I caught myself thinking of my friends in the army, and thinking about my return to Fort Jackson. The next to last day of my furlough, I returned to the Navy Commissary and stocked up on grocery items my mother wanted. With her pantry shelves partially filled, and a full tank of gasoline in "Ole Chev," I felt I had done my duty and felt better about leaving mother when the time came.

At the bus station, our parting was painful, mother cried, and tears came to my eyes. I had to keep reminding myself, I am a man, a nineteen year old soldier, and soldiers do not cry!

4
Army Unit Training

589th Field Artillery Battalion
Fort Jackson, S.C. – Summer of 1943

The 589th FA Bn had completed Basic Training and had begun what the army termed Unit Training by the time I returned from rehabilitation furlough. Basic Training had been personal, mostly physical and psychological in nature, aimed at each individual recruit, to turn him into a disciplined and physically hardened young man. On the other hand, while still physical in nature, Unit Training was more task oriented, and taught each soldier his designated job skills. Unit Training was designed to implant these skills so firmly in the individuals mind that functions would be performed under all types of mental and/or physical duress.

Much to my delight, in Unit Training, I became immediately immersed in text book training, which was augmented with actual fire direction experiences gained on the artillery range at Fort Jackson. Of course, personnel from the three firing batteries were being trained on their 105mm howitzers at the same time. The experience was great and I thrived in this environment.

During the early phases of Unit Training it became evident that Major Parker was giving me cross-training in all phases of fire direction functions. It was never formally discussed, but we all knew I would ultimately be qualified to fill any position in the event anyone was transferred, or fell along the way.

Captain Black even assigned another driver to Major Parker when I got more involved in formal fire direction training. I was glad to be relieved as a driver, even though I enjoyed my brief personal encounters with the Major, I found being a driver was very monotonous and not very challenging.

My first formal training involved learning to read military maps and the symbols used by the army to designate military units, both friend and foe. How to read map coordinated and prepare firing charts using the proper symbols for firing batteries, target locations, and observation posts came next. This phase of training included instructions and practice in communicating with firing batteries and forward observers by radio and telephone. Although not hard to learn, it required untold hours of practice to accurately record target information from forward observers, plot this information onto firing charts, convert this information into commands to be used by the gunners at each 105mm howitzer, and pass these commands to the firing batteries, via radio or telephone, utilizing the required, concise, terminology.

Under the tutelage of Major Parker, we practiced and practiced, in the classroom and in the field. We conducted "dry run" after "dry run" until all procedures became routine. After several weeks of this simulated training, Major Parker finally announced we were ready for our first "live firing" exercise. Live firing involved the use of newly trained gun crews, live 105mm ammunition, and actual targets, with battery officers acting as forward observers. All of us in fire direction were confident we could handle the real thing with "no sweat," and even bragged about it. But deep down inside, without the bravado, we were a little nervous. In fact, the fire direction team, the howitzer crews, and even the forward observers, were all a little nervous.

When the day arrived for our first live firing exercise, the survey crew established coordinates for the observation post, the base piece of each firing battery, and three targets. I carefully prepared the firing charts, plotted the coordinates provided by the survey crew, and designated them on the firing chart with the proper symbols. The communications crew established land-line (telephone) connections between the observation post, fire direction center, and the three firing batteries. The liaison crew established a radio-net which also connected all artillery positions to a simulated infantry regimental command post. Everything went well in fire direction that special morning on the artillery range at Fort Jackson. Under a hot summer sun, and a cloudless, clear blue, South Carolina sky everything in Headquarters Battery went well!.

Major Parker, and Lieutenant Colonel Kelly checked and rechecked all details and seemed satisfied. Lieutenant Colonel Kelly then left the command post and rode to the "A" Battery howitzer positions. Everything at "A" Battery must have checked out to his satisfaction, but for some reason he elected to stay with the howitzer crews during the exercise and did not return to the battalion command post. While we waited, the Colonel and Major Parker had several private telephone conversations. The first thing we knew was when the command post radio blared the first message of the exercise, "Fire Direction, this is Able Observation Post (OP)–FIRE MISSION!"

My heart missed a couple of beats when Sergeant Tacker grabbed our radio microphone and responded with his best military protocol, "Able OP, this is Fire Direction–PROCEED WITH YOUR MISSION!" The remainder of the first live fire mission reminded me of our numerous classroom exercises. Major Parker double checked everything as the information flowed from the forward observer, through fire direction, and out again to each firing battery. The main difference between the classroom and this field exercise was the feel of the ground trembling and the sound as the howitzers fired, and the sound of faint explosions in the distance when the105mm projectiles exploded in the target area.

When the first forward observer, Lieutenant Clausen, the Battalion Survey Officer, finished adjusting the base piece of "A" Battery he barked into the radio the command we were waiting to hear, "FIRE FOR EFFECT!" We could feel the ground shake as all four howitzers of "A" Battery fired in unison at the target. Moments later, we heard the four explosions in the target area, and were hoping to receive the command from Lieutenant Clausen to, "CEASE FIRE–MISSION ACCOMPLISHED–END OF MISSION." Instead of the prescribed ending to the fire mission, Lieutenant Clausen got slightly over enthusiastic and sent the following message, "CEASE FIRING–END OF MISSION–WE CLOBBERED THE SON-OF-A-BITCH!"

Major Parker grimaced when he heard this transmission, but the enlisted men laughed, we thought the transmission was funny and quite descriptive!

The remainder of the fire missions were carried off with clock work precision until the last mission of the day, then we experienced an unwelcome surprise.

In the field artillery, the message, "ON THE WAY" is relayed to the forward observer when a battery fires. This message serves notice to the forward observer that the battery has fired, and gives him several seconds to focus his field glasses on the target area so he can observe where the projectiles burst in relation to the target. The observer then "senses" where the projectile explodes in terms of yards from the target. Sensings such as: "100 LEFT, 200 SHORT" or "200 RIGHT, "400 OVER" are typical.

Trained fire direction technicians then translate these Sensings into firing commands which enable the howitzer crews to make changes in range and direction that will hopefully move the next round they fire closer to the target. When the next round is fired, using the adjusted data, the howitzer crew reports, "ON THE WAY" to fire direction, who immediately passes this message to the forward observer. This process is repeated until the target is hit and the mission is accomplished.

In this case, however, the forward observer received the message, "ON THE WAY," was ready to observe, but saw no round burst in the target area. Consequently the forward observer sensed the round, "LOST." This message brought the firing exercise to a screeching halt! Major Parker checked the accuracy of my firing chart and the written records of the data which was verbally given to the firing battery. To my relief he found everything to be correct. On the observation post, the gunnery instructor asked other student officers what, if anything, did they see or hear in the target area. At the firing battery, Lieutenant Colonel Kelly was checking the sight settings on the howitzer for accuracy. This was serious business, and it was a very busy time. But at the end of the verification process everyone was puzzled, because everything checked out OK.

A telephone conversation with the gunnery instructor revealed that one of the student observers thought he heard a round explode far out into the firing range—far beyond the target. However, none of the student observers saw a shell burst in our target area, they thought the faint explosion, that one of them heard, was a round fired by another artillery unit firing on this huge range.

At the firing battery, Lieutenant Colonel Kelly knew we were firing at a relatively short range, he also knew we were using only three of the seven powder bags which come in every 105mm brass shell casing. Very few fire missions require the use of all seven powder bags to reach the target. Lieutenant Colonel Kelly decided to check the unused powder bags. Under the direction of the Battery Commander, the Battery Executive Officer ordered the howitzer section chiefs to gather all spent brass casings and lay them in a row behind each howitzer. This represented the total rounds fired by each individual howitzer. Lieutenant Colonel Kelly then asked his Battery Commander to have the each section chief to associate four powder bags with each spent brass shell casing. The results spoke for themselves, behind one howitzer there was one brass shell casing with no matching powder bags – conclusion, this howitzer fired one round at charge seven. The "LOST" round fired at charge sever, instead of charge three, landed several miles beyond the intended target.

Back in garrison, after the exercise, we felt sorry for the Cannoneers who goofed, and for their section chief. We knew they would be disciplined in some way, this was a serious mistake and someone could have been hurt or killed. However, the feeling of pity did not last long. It was quickly washed away at the Post Exchange (PX) with pitchers of 3.2 GI beer during our "after the first live firing exercise" party.

We were in a good mood because the fire direction center passed the live firing test with flying colors! Major Parker was proud of us.

Fort Jackson and Columbia, S.C.
Army Life – The Summer of 1943

I have no idea how many soldiers were stationed at Fort Jackson while the 106th Infantry Division was stationed there. I personally found it to be a very accommodating post. Unfortunately, I did not feel the same about *circa 1943*

Columbia, S. C. To me, the town, and its citizens, were the pits! Prominently displayed on some lawns were neatly lettered signs that carried a pointed message, "SOLDIERS AND DOGS STAY OFF THE GRASS." Merchants were eager to take our money, but reluctant to provide service or even a friendly greeting. The citizens of Columbia wanted high paying government jobs and generous government benefits at Fort Jackson, but wanted the soldiers to go away.

In reality, there were just too many soldiers stationed at Fort Jackson for a community the size of Columbia to absorb graciously.

When soldiers went on pass to Columbia they usually had the "Three Bs" in mind: Broads, Booze, and Brawling. No wonder we were so hard for the locals to like. I quickly discovered broads were expensive and scarce, whereas beer and brawls were inexpensive and plentiful. With my hard-shell Methodist upbringing and a private's pay, broads were out of the question. For me, this left beer, and on occasion, a brawl in some downtown bar on a Saturday night.

Since we normally got into trouble with the Bar owner, the Columbia City Police, or other military men, we went on pass in groups. There was safety in numbers. The guys I normally bar-hopped with were: Private David Dunham, Corporal Jerry Costello, and Sergeant Wilhelm Unger. I called them Dunham, Jerry, and Sergeant Ugh, respectively. They were all extremely likeable, but all were characters. We were quite different in stature and personality, but we bonded, and bonded firmly. We felt like the four musketeers, one for all, and all for one, and all that psychological stuff.

Dunham was from the hills of Tennessee and about as countrified as they come. Dunham loved to fight! I never knew if this was the heritage of a mountain-man from Tennessee or not, I was not wise in such matters. All I know is, Dunham loved to fight! He endured each day in the army merely to exist until Saturday night so he could go to town and pick fights. He was a modestly built young man, about five-foot-nine, weighed 165 pounds, was not excessively muscular, but had reflexes like a panther. He was quick, super quick! Dunham could hit you several times while you were trying to hit him once. His blows were sharp and accurate. Many times I saw him whip larger men who out-weighed him by fifty pounds. In the process, Dunham would hardly break a sweat.

On the bus going from Columbia to Fort Jackson one Saturday night, actually it was early Sunday morning, Dunham and I shared the back seat of a bus which was so crowded soldiers were standing in the isle. Dunham was unhappy, he had provoked only two fights. For him, this was a most unsuccessful Saturday night. In desperation, and to salvage the remains of Saturday night, Dunham suddenly stood up on the back seat of the bus and yelled at the top of his voice, "My name is Dunham, I'm from Tennessee, my blood is red, I think yours is yellow!"

This pronouncement had an immediate effect on our fellow travelers. I wondered, "What in the blue-blazes is going to happen to my buddy Dunham?"

I moved to the side of the bus, to get out of the way, and to give him swinging room. GIs were lining up in the center isle to defend their honor. As I prepared myself for the worst, I suddenly realized I had underestimated my friend. He was smart enough to realize that on this crowded bus only one man at the time could face him in the center isle. When the first adversary reached him, Dunham decked his with three sharp blows to the chin. This worthy adversary never knew what hit him. Then a strange thing happened. The remainder of Dunham's potential adversaries had to drag the unconscious soldier to the front of the bus to clear the isle so the next adversary could get to Dunham.

This predictable process continued until Dunham had decked six soldiers. By this time the remaining GIs on the bus had come to the conclusion their honor had been sufficiently defended and lost their savage desire to see some of Dunham's red Tennessee blood. During this entire melee, the indifferent bus driver kept his eyes on the road, his foot on the accelerator, and as if this were a routine trip, kept the bus moving steadily toward the main gate of Fort Jackson.

The only noticeable damage Dunham sustained during this action was a bloody uniform and bruised knuckles. Incidentally, the blood, even though red, did not belong to Dunham.

Another pass partner of mine was Sergeant Unger who was affectionately known as Sergeant Ugh. Sergeant Ugh was part of the cadre from the 80th Infantry Division that initially staffed the 106th Infantry Division. He was a Regular Army non-com, German to the core, sturdy as an ox, loved beer to a fault, and had developed a protective attitude toward me when we were off-Post. Sergeant Ugh was not belligerent or pugnacious by nature, but he valued his privacy, and did not want to be disturbed by strangers while drinking his beer. Depending upon the length of the evening, his beer consumption would vary between eight and twelve bottles per sitting. He paid absolutely no attention to the bar women who tried to hustle us for drinks, and usually dismissed them with a wave of his muscular arm and a very stern look. Every now and then an aggressive drunk would approach our table and attempt a conversation. The drunk would be greeted with a grunt, a flex of the biceps, a penetrating stare, and a slow drag of beer straight from a cold, brown, long-necked bottle. No one in his right mind could misread these signs. If the inept drunk was so desensitized by alcohol he could not understand this strong body language, he lived to regret his transgression. Sergeant Unger's retribution was quick and to the point.

Don't get me wrong, Sergeant Ugh was not immune to the female body beautiful, he was just choosy. He preferred the occasional company of Marcia, the attractive young blond wife of Corporal Jennings. Corporal Jennings was also a Regular Army non-com, who at the rank of Corporal had reached the apex of his military career. Jennings was so untrustworthy he owed his army longevity to his boss, Sergeant Unger. Corporal Jennings and Sergeant Unger were exact opposites. Sergeant Unger was a man of few words, whereas Corporal Jennings rattled-on incessantly—his favorite subject being his numerous sexual conquests. Unger was a large and powerful man! Jennings was a small man and well proportioned, except in one respect.

In the course of barracks living, I showered with Jennings on several occasions and could not help but notice the great contrast between his small body and his huge male genitals. Without a doubt, he had the largest set of balls and the most magnificent penis in the entire battery. Well almost!

Staff Sergeant Stovall, the Mess Sergeant, who was a much larger man than Jennings, could actually make Corporal Jennings hang his head in shame. Only the genitals of a prize Brahman bull could humiliate Staff Sergeant Stovall.

It was common knowledge in the battery that Sergeant Ugh covered-up for Jennings' screw-ups just to keep him around. Maybe I should say, to keep

Marcia around. When Sergeant Ugh got horny and felt the urge for female companionship, he would call Marcia. They would agree on the day and time of their meeting, and Sergeant Ugh would conveniently have Jennings assigned as Corporal of the Guard that night. We all saw this happen time and time again.

When Sergeant Ugh returned to camp, after a night with Marcia, he seemed contented, more relaxed, and actually smiled for a couple of days. Poor Jennings, I almost felt sorry for him. He either did not know what was going on, or simply did not care. I could never figure out which.

Corporal Jennings' most frequently told story describes, in excruciating detail, his experience on a three day pass in New Orleans, where he unwittingly participated in a "Blue Ribbon Special." For the uninitiated, the "Blue Ribbon Special" reported by Jennings was a rather spectacular sex act performed by professional "ladies of the night," and derives it's name from the fact the female participant ties a tight blue ribbon around her male partner's rigid penis during foreplay. He relates, "She picked me up in a bar on Bourbon Street, and offered to show me a good time, and man, she certainly kept her word. In the hotel room I remember lying there looking at myself and thinking about the bow she tied on my dong. The blue bow was pretty, all blue and fluffy, it looked kind of like an ornamental flag flying at half-mast. In all my experiences with women, this was the first time any gal had tied a bow on my dong. She said the ribbon kept men hard longer and gave women more satisfaction. I don't know about that, but I do know what it did for me. She climbed on top, and after a good work-out, I started to groan. That was her signal to reach between her thighs and untie the knot. Then she waived the blue ribbon in the air, and started riding me like a jockey riding a horse in the Kentucky Derby. Then it happened! Man, that was something!"

Jennings would normally pause at this stage of the story, either for dramatic effect, or to savor the thrill of the moment, I never knew which. Then, with a faraway look in his eyes, he would continue, "At the end, what I remember best is, lights flashing, bells ringing, shuddering, and thinking this is the way I want to die. The strangest part of this evening was the fact she didn't even ask me to pay for her services."

Corporal Jennings, with the rapt attention of his audience would say, "The next night I found out why she wouldn't take my money. Some buddies and I decided to take in a peep-show. We were ushered into a semicircle viewing room by a gorgeous little chick dressed in a long hostess gown. The room, in a hotel, was well decorated, strictly first class, up-town in all respects. The hostess seated us in the audience facing several large one-way mirrors. When the lights came on, and the show began, I was surprised."

By this time, someone in the audience, who had not heard this story before, would ask, "Jennings, what would surprise you in a peep-show? You say you have been everywhere, and done everything."

Jennings would respond to this question by saying, "The female star of the show was the same chick who picked me up and took me to bed the night before. I wondered if anyone watching the show last night is watching again tonight and recognizes me."

† †

Corporal Jerry Costello was cast from another mold. He was like Vito, a first generation American of Italian descent. Jerry was my age, only nineteen, but he was so serious minded, he could have been thirty-five. Large, handsome, and extremely powerful, Jerry was family oriented and totally Catholic. Every week his mother sent him a large box of Italian food, as though the army would not properly feed her "little boy." She sent Mozzarella, Parmesan, Pepperoni, Salami, and Pastrami. Food I had never heard of and had never tasted. The only Italian food I had ever eaten was spaghetti with meatballs in tomato sauce from a can. Jerry was constantly teaching me the intricacies of Italian cuisine, customs, and family traditions. All this was new and extremely interesting to a "Son of the Old South."

As our friendship grew, Jerry and I accidentally stumbled onto a risky money making routine. He had been a member of his high school wrestling team, and liked to wrestle. I could walk and run with the best of my peers but, even before I had spinal meningitis, I did not have much upper body strength. After the evening meal, when we were confined to camp, Jerry would move onto the lawn in front of our barracks and challenge anyone to wrestle with him. At first he had many takers, but slowly his opponents dwindled as they learned what a good wrestler he was. In desperation one night he challenged me to wrestle with him. With much bravado I accepted his challenge and loudly proclaimed, "I, 'The Great Southern Flash,' am going to teach this 'Italian Greaser' a thing of two about wrestling!" As we squared-off on the grass, I warned him, "Jerry be careful, don't you hurt me." He replied, "Don't worry 'Southern Flash,' I'm going to teach you some of the tricks-of-the-trade in professional wrestling."

The match started slowly and gained momentum. I grabbed one of his out stretched arms, spun, and pulled down. To my great surprise, he went flying over my shoulder and landed on his back with a thud. As he lay there, obviously in great pain, and gasping for breath, I thought he was hurt. I fell beside him, my arm across his chest, as though I was going for the pin, and asked him, "Jerry are you hurt?" With obvious pain written on this face, he whispered, "Randy, roll me over in an arm lock."

I was now more puzzled than ever. I knew I wasn't strong enough to throw Jerry over my shoulder in the first place. Then it dawned on me, he was just play-acting. He was "on stage." He was play-acting, and having fun.

We practiced our act several times. He taught me throws, rolls, locks, holds, and most important of all, how to grimace with pain. I became an expert and learned to throw him, hold him in "painful" arm and head locks, and then pin him as he pounded the ground in pain and anger. Jerry taught me everything about wrestling, including acting, and our show always drew a crowd, many people from near-by units. Even if I do say so, Jerry was a natural ham and we did put on an good show.

When strangers appeared, GIs from Headquarters Battery bet money on me. All the strangers had to do was look at me, then look at Jerry, and common sense told them that Jerry could wipe me out in a matter of minutes. The outsiders naturally covered all the local money which was bet on me. I would win, the GIs from my battery would collect, and the outside GIs knew they had been had.

In some instances, a macho GI from another battery would try to get his money back by challenging Jerry. You could almost read his mind, "If that tall, skinny, GI can beat that dago, I know I can whip him good." Jerry would then proceed to lower the boom on this GI, and we would win some more outsider money. We had a good thing going for several weeks, until the First Sergeant made us quit. He said we were going to start an inter-barracks war if we kept on with our scam.

In town on pass, Jerry and I did run into some sore losers who wanted their money back, but when Sergeant Ugh and David Dunham joined with Jerry and me, the argument ended quickly. I'll admit it was a scam, one which happened by chance and just grew. We didn't scheme to take this GI money, they were stupid, they gave their money away. This entire experience was unique, but I had no regrets, the army was full of scams!

While we were on pass in Columbia, Jerry would drink a small amount of wine while the rest of us swilled beer. He was somewhat like Sergeant Ugh in that he would shrug off the local bar women, but unlike Sergeant Ugh, he tried to avoid hurting their feelings. During these social drinking sessions, he and Sergeant Ugh pulled my chestnuts out of the fire on many occasions when I "Stood Up" when I should have "Shut Up." Without a doubt they saved my butt several times. They were good friends indeed.

† †

Several weeks into Unit Training, the non-commissioned officers, who were the original Cadre for the 589th, started leaving. Destined to become Cadre again for another unit being formed by the army. For me, this was both good news and bad news. I hated to see Sergeant Unger leave because I valued his friendship and appreciated what he had done for me. True to form, Ugh arranged for Corporal Jennings transfer to the same new unit. This meant Sergeant Unger could continue to visit Marcia the nights that Jennings was on Guard Duty.

In a way, I would miss Jennings and the wild tales of his sex exploits, also Jennings had one characteristic I would always remember. When he got excited he stuttered, and every time he mentioned his trip to New Orleans and his "Blue Ribbon Special," he always stuttered.

Fort Jackson, S.C.
589th Field Artillery Battalion—My first promotion

The exit of the original Cadre was expected. It was obvious that many of these older and experienced Regular Army non-coms were good at turning raw recruits into soldiers, but they were loners and did not fit well into a new organization. The good part about the Cadre leaving was that as they left, their assignments and ranks became available for people like me. I had been waiting patiently for months for the opportunity to be promoted, now it appeared my days as a buck private were numbered.

Due to the bout with spinal meningitis and my decision to remain in the 589th FA Bn, I had almost become the ranking Private in the United States Army. At least it felt that way to me. At an afternoon Retreat Formation, shortly after the first group of Cadre non-coms left, I noticed Major Parker standing near the orderly room, apparently waiting for the Retreat ceremony to begin. After lowering the flag, the First Sergeant called the battery to attention and proceeded to read from the Order of the Day, "Effective today Private Pierson, Randolph C., Army Serial Number 34547144, is hereby promoted to the permanent rank of Private First Class. By order of Lieutenant Colonel Thomas P. Kelly, Jr., 589th Field Artillery Battalion, Commanding."

Even though the battery was at attention, the roar of laughter and various cat calls came from the ranks so the First Sergeant sternly ordered the formation back to attention. I was slightly stunned because orders of this nature were routinely issued and posted on the bulletin board to disseminate this type information, not formally announced at Retreat formations. The First Sergeant called me front-and-center and with great pomp and ceremony pinned one stripe on each sleeve. Again, a great cheer, followed by good natured laughter, came from my friends in the ranks. Above this din, the First Sergeant asked, "Pierson, is there anything you would like to say?"

In my best military manner, I called the battery to attention, and announced in a voice with great authority, "Now hear this! In the near future I am going to make some serious changes around here!"

Without pomp or ceremony the First Sergeant growled, "Pierson, get your miserable ass back in the ranks."

After the First Sergeant dismissed the battery most of the men in the operations platoon surrounded me, yelling and slapping me on the back, many asking if I was now ready to sign-up and go Regular Army. This was a happy occasion for me, I had waited a long time to be recognized. Suddenly things became quiet, the crowd parted, and Major Parker walked toward me and simply said, "Congratulations Pierson," as he shook my hand. We were all so surprised to see him, we forgot to salute this senior officer. The Major obviously enjoyed the humorous ceremony and did not seem to mind the lack of military courtesy. We could hear him laughing and see the smile on his face, as he strode briskly up the Battery Street toward his office at Battalion Headquarters.

106th Infantry Division
Pay Day in the Army

Depending upon each soldiers situation, pay-day was a day of joy, or a day of sorrow. Joy, when you were present and god paid. Sorrow, if you were not present to be paid, or if you had been 'Red Lined' by the Finance Corps who prepared the payroll records. The pay-day process was very straight forward. If you reported for pay-call and the paymaster had your money, you were promptly paid after you signed the payroll If you were absent from pay-call for some reason, the paymaster drew a red line through your name on the payroll, and your money was returned to the Finance Corps to be disbursed to you one month later.

The worst case scenario happened when some desk-jockey in Finance got your pay records screwed-up and you were 'Red Lined' before the paymaster even received the payroll and money. When the screw-up was complicated, or the error hard to locate, some soldiers did not get paid for months and months.

This situation, no pay for months, or, just running short on money, temporarily, created another army phenomena. This phenomena could be accurately called an in house loan-shark industry. Only a lucky few, mostly first three grade sergeants, had enough money to lent to the unlucky majority who required immediate cash. Those of us who had to borrow money from Regular Army non-commissioned officers had no choice but to pay the standard going rate of interest, which went something like this, "I'll loan you ten bucks today, but you have to pay me back twenty bucks on pay-day."

If you were desperate enough to borrow money one week before pay-day, the interest you paid on your loan amounted to a staggering annual rate of more than Five Thousand percent. No wonder many of the Regular Army non-coms chose to remain in the service. They were getting rich lending money!

Just as certain as death and taxes, pay-day was always the beginning of a mammoth floating crap game. For some reason, unknown to me, an unwritten army law mandated that officers should play poker and enlisted men should shoot craps. The enlisted men's crap games followed an orderly pattern. They started in the barracks and in the recreation rooms. This starting pattern resulted in many games with relatively small stakes. As the marathon continued, the grand winner of these small games then moved to larger stakes games which lasted until they too had one winner. This process normally continued until each barracks produced one grand winner. Later, at a designated time and place, the barracks winners appeared with large amounts of money, body guards, and selected outsiders who acted as bankers. The purpose of these extra people was to keep the ultimate game honest and legitimate.

These "Super Crap Games" were grueling marathon affairs that lasted hours and hours. But ultimately there emerged one "Super Winner" who walked away from the game with thousands of dollars and his very nervous body guards. I never participated in these floating crap games at any level, but I watched in amazement as I saw the "old pros" do things with dice that were unbelievable. To me it was not a game of chance, it was more like charity because only a select few became consistent "Super Winners." I thoroughly enjoyed watching these games which provided drama and suspense, they provided great entertainment. With such huge amounts of money changing hands, they were also very exciting.

Fort Jackson Firing Range
Country Boy, City Boy—Pay Back Time

Headquarters Battery, 589th Field Artillery Battalion, contained approximately one hundred and thirty enlisted men, the vast majority being from the northeast, and the large cities of the central states. I was one of the minority from the rural south, and was constantly reminded how backward and ignorant southerners are. One of my most antagonistic detractors was a young man of Irish decent, from the upper east side of Manhattan by the name of O'Hare. O'Hare, like many men of Irish decent, had a big mouth, drank hard Irish liquor to excess, and had an inflated sense of self worth. His mistaken philosophy of life dictated that the more he put other people down, the higher he became by comparison. He rode me unmercifully. On several occasions I declined his drunken proposal to settle our differences man to man. I knew he was drunk, I knew I could handle him physically, but I wanted to humiliate him. This opportunity presented itself on an over-night bivouac. Late in the afternoon, after the evening meal, and before the beginning of the night exercise, we started to look for locations to pitch our pup tents and lay out our bed rolls. O'Hare, with his big mouth and normal Irish bluster, started bragging about the location he chose and how superior it was to mine. As a friendly gesture, I agreed to inspect his location.

When I saw the location he had selected, I noticed his tent was surrounded with fresh green leaves growing on crawling vines. I had seen these vines many times and recognized them instantly. I asked O'Hare if I could pull some of these vines and take the foliage back to my tent to place under my bed roll because it would make the ground softer and my bed more comfortable. O'Hare took the bait and swallowed the hook, "This is my location and these are my vines. Go find your own vines you damned Reb!"

I replied, "Go to hell you stingy Mick, I'll find my own vines." As I walked away, O'Hare had removed his shirt, and was busy gathering arm loads of tender leaves to place under his bed roll. Dell Miller had watched the discussion between us and asked, "Randy, what were you doing with your good friend O'Hare?"

"Not too much Dell. The dumb Mick has pitched his tent right in the middle of a patch of poison ivy."

"Did you tell him?"

"Hell no! He started out on me again and called me a "Reb" and I got mad, so I encouraged him to gather poison ivy and make a soft layer of leaves under his bed roll."

Miller asked, "You did what?"

"Wait until you see him tomorrow, then you will know for sure what I did."

As I predicted, the next morning at sunrise, the medics arrived in our bivouac area with an ambulance. As the medics were loading O'Hare, and his gear, into the ambulance, Sergeant Tacker walked over and asked, "Who are they taking to camp?"

"Private O'Hare."

"What is wrong with him?"

"Tack, he has the damnedest poison ivy infection I have ever seen. I hope he doesn't die. There isn't one square inch on his body that isn't red and all puffed up."

Upon his return from the hospital, Private O'Hare avoided me like the plague, and never referred to me as a 'Reb' again.

† †

589th Field Artillery Battalion—Fort Jackson, S.C. The End of Unit Training

As the summer season of '43 began to give way to fall, we spent more and more time in bivouac on the Fort Jackson firing range. We learned to shoot, we learned to move, and we learned how to communicate. These are the three most essential skills a highly effective field artillery unit must master.

We participated in field exercises with the 422nd Infantry Regiment, the regiment which we would support with artillery fire in combat. We learned how the infantry units were organized to fight. In army terms, we were learning how to operate as a Regimental Combat Team.

As early winter approached, we were advised we would participate, as a Division, in the Second Army Winter Maneuvers in Tennessee. This gigantic exercise later became known as the "Tennessee 43-44 Winter Maneuvers."

By this time, everyone in the battalion had accumulated furlough time. A decision was made to allow as many men as possible to take furloughs during the upcoming Christmas holidays. The unlucky remainder would be allowed to take their furloughs earlier, during the Thanksgiving holidays. In my unit, Headquarters Battery, each man was assigned furlough time by a random drawing. I drew Thanksgiving.

After my earlier recuperation furlough, mother decided to retire from the Brevard County school system. She gave up our rented Florida home, stored most of her meager belongings, and moved to Jesup, Georgia to live with her sister and brother-in-law for the duration of the war. As a youngster, I had spent several summers in Jesup with my Uncle Ed and Aunt "Frank" while mother continued her college education in summer school. I knew Jesup well, and had many friends there. I looked forward to the visit.

Shortly before Thanksgiving, I arrived in Jesup and found much the same situation which existed when I furloughed in Cocoa. Most of my Jesup friends were gone. To make things worse, mother had sold "Old Chev" and I had no wheels. I became more dejected when I learned the girl in Jesup I was most sweet on was dating a Naval officer from Brunswick and would not be seen with a lowly Army Sergeant. Jesup became a drag. Over mother's protest, I took a bus to Cocoa and completed my furlough there.

† †

Last Furlough Before Going Overseas
Cocoa, Florida — A Pleasant Surprise

One unexpected and exceptionally rewarding thing happened while I was in Cocoa. I ran into an old friend, George McGhee. I had not seen George since 1939.

During the depression years of the 30s, even though we were poor, mother always managed to have female domestic help. The lady who worked for mother was named Viola McGhee. Viola was black, proud, intelligent, a single parent, and had several children. George was her only son. George was two years older than I. He was also larger, stronger, and quicker than I was. We loved to tussle with one another, and were fast friends. Ours was an uncommon relationship in the deep south, during the depression years of the 1930s.

When Viola's older daughters grew up and left home to go to college, Viola would baby-sit George in our home while she worked for mother. George graduated from the 'Colored Cocoa High School' in 1939, two years before I graduated from Cocoa High School. After graduating from high school, George left home and I lost track of him.

You can imagine my surprise when I ran into George on Brevard Avenue in Cocoa one day. He was on furlough also. He was visiting his mother prior to going to North Africa. When we met, George looked great! His athletic build complemented his tailored Air Corps uniform. George was a Second Lieutenant, and wore the wings of a pilot. This fact surprised me, I did not know Negroes could be pilots.

George's initial reaction was the same as mine, surprise. Suddenly something happened, George froze in his tracks, and that competitive look I had seen many times came over his face. For a long moment he looked at me and finally asked, "Sergeant Pierson, isn't it customary for an enlisted man to salute a commissioned officer?"

This question absolutely floored me! He knew the answer to his question as well as I did. Yes, a salute was customary, but normally not on social occasions. I considered this a social meeting and assumed he would consider it the same. This was one thing I disliked about officers, especially Second Lieutenants. Next to Privates, they were the least respected rank in the Army. But George was obviously in the Air Corps, maybe he did not know much about military courtesy, and more probably, he just wanted to pull rank on me.

Still jarred by his question, I gave him the best ROTC / US Army "High Ball" I could deliver. Second Lieutenant George McGhee, a newly commissioned fighter pilot in the United States Air Corps, did not return my salute, instead he "broke-up" and started to laugh uncontrollably. The act that brought us both back to reality was when George picked me up in his strong, muscular arms and almost bear-hugged the wind out of me. When I started struggling to get loose, he put my feet back down on the ground, and with a big grin on his face said, "Buddy, lets go have a cherry coke at the drug store. This one is on the US Air Corps."

George had completed three years of college when he volunteered, and was accepted as a student pilot by the US Air Corps. He had learned of an experiment the armed forces were conducting with black men. It was known as the Tuskegee Experiment, and was designed to determine if black men were capable of being trained to fly aircraft. George became a part of this experiment.

History has recorded the fact that qualified black men were as easily trained as whites, and vindicated the people who had faith in the black mans ability, including that of the wife of the President of the United States, Mrs. Eleanor Roosevelt. These Negro fighters pilots established a WWII combat record second to no other bomber escort group in Europe. George's P-51 fighter unit never lost a single bomber to enemy aircraft during the escort missions they flew. They were known as the "Tuskegee Airmen."

After our chance 1943 meeting in Cocoa, Florida, I never saw or heard from George McGhee again.

† †

Fort Jackson, S.C.
December 1943 – My First Christmas Away From Home

In December, a mass exodus of people from my battalion was caused by the Christmas furloughs. I had been awarded a third stripe just before my Thanksgiving furlough and was not required to pull extra duties, with one exception, that being Sergeant of the Guard. Post Exchanges and Post Theaters began to close, and many mess halls consolidated their operations. The Post was almost deserted and it was lonely in the almost empty barracks. At the last minute, I decided to spend Christmas Eve and Christmas Day off-post and made a hotel reservation in Columbia. At least that way I would be around people and enjoy their Christmas cheer.

I checked into the hotel just after noon, on December 24th. The lobby was beautifully decorated with Christmas trees and ornaments. This was a sharp contrast to my Spartan barracks. Outside, people were scurrying up and down the main streets, ducking in and out of stores, frantically completing their last minute shopping. That evening, back at the hotel, several Christmas parties were underway. Judging from the age and dress of the revelers, these parties appeared to be the extension of office parties which spilled over into the hotel. The party-goers were mainly well dressed, older civilian men and younger, sharp looking, professional women. Fortunately I was invited to attend one party and gladly accepted. The party was lively. I had a wonderful time dancing with the attractive females, eating from the seemingly endless supply of finger-food, drinking at the free bar, and explaining to the older men why I was still in Columbia and not at home on furlough. That night when I went to bed, I was in much better spirits and glad I had come to town.

Christmas morning was much different. When I got out of bed and looked out of the window, the sky was gray and a slow, cold rain was bouncing off the window pane. Hoping to find a companion for breakfast, I showered, shaved, and dressed. Down stairs the lobby was empty, nothing was stirring. In the restaurant the one waiter was brusque, as though it was my fault he had to work on Christmas day. This was not what I had expected, and certainly not what I needed.

The lonely breakfast did nothing to lift my spirits even though the food was excellent. After breakfast the lobby was still deserted, the sky was still gray, and the cold rain was still falling. There was no one to talk to and no place to go other than to my room. Back in the room, I removed my shoes, hung my uniform, and reclined on the bed.

None of this helped me. I was not tired, nor was I sleepy, I was just lonesome. In desperation I moved an easy chair to the window and sat there looking out. All I could see was empty wet streets, dirty gray sidewalks, dark low hanging clouds, and the cold and still falling rain. I was alone, totally alone, there didn't seem to be another human being on the face of the earth. The more I looked at this dismal scene, the more lonely I became. This was the low-point of my young life.

Filled with self-pity, tears formed in each eye. I tried to reminded myself, twenty year old Army Sergeants are not supposed to cry.

Never-the-less, I wept!

5
1943–44 Tennessee Winter Maneuvers

Fort Jackson, S.C. – January 1944
Motor March to the Tennessee Maneuver Area

S hortly after New Years Day, 1944, all the officers and men of the 589th
FA Bn had returned from their Christmas furloughs and preparations
resumed to get personnel, equipment, and vehicles ready for the long
motor-march from Fort Jackson, South Carolina to the maneuver area near
Murfreesboro, Tennessee.

The 106th Infantry Division had done well in Basic and Unit Training and
had passed the Army Field Tests with flying colors. The army considered it a
superior Division at this phase of its training. The emphasis on youth had paid
off so far. More than three-fourths of the men in the Division were twenty-five
years of age or younger. The maneuvers in Tennessee would constitute the third
step in a four step training program for these young citizen soldiers.

The Second Army Maneuvers were scheduled to begin on 20 January and
end 27 March 1944. All equipment was to be carried into these war-games as
the Division would not be returning to Fort Jackson upon completion of the
maneuvers. Moving an entire Division, some fifteen thousand men and their
equipment, from South Carolina to Tennessee, by truck convoy, was no small
feat. The planning and logistics required to support such a move are staggering.

My Battalion, the 589th, along with the other Divisional units, was allocated travel-days, road-time, and road-space, to complete the five hundred mile trip. We were scheduled to make the trip in two long days, utilizing a truck convoy. The artillery battalions were lucky, they had numerous 2 1/2 ton GMC trucks to tow howitzers and haul ammunition, which provided ample capacity to move personnel and equipment. The Infantry Regiments, with many more men and fewer trucks, were not so lucky. The foot soldiers and their equipment were transported, jammed into trucks like cattle.

Our Battalion order-of-march consisted of five separate elements. The firing batteries A, B, and C, comprised the first three elements. Headquarters Battery the fourth, and Service Battery the fifth. The lead vehicle for the entire battalion was the jeep of Major Elliott Goldstein, the Battalion Executive Officer. Major Goldstein's vehicle set the predetermined pace for the road-march. Lieutenant Colonel Kelly, the Battalion Commander, flowed back and forth in his command-car, keeping tabs on everyone and everything. The rear, or clean-up vehicle, carried the Battalion Motor Officer, who, with his crew, was responsible for repairing or towing vehicles which broke-down on the march. During the road-march, strict march-discipline was maintained by the Battalion Commander via radio contact with the Battery Commander of each element.

The estimated time to cover approximately five hundred miles in two days was eighteen hours. This equated, each day, to two hundred fifty miles in nine hours. The road-march proved to be a test of endurance for both vehicles and personnel.

The fire direction team rode in a long-wheel-base 2 1/2 GMC truck which pulled a one ton covered trailer. When fully loaded with the fire direction gear, tents, etc., there was not much room left in the truck for people to sit. To get comfortable for the long trip, we carefully arranged back-packs, bed rolls, and tents so we could stretch-out prone on top of the packed gear. One of our serious problems was keeping warm, the weather during the move was colder than normal. The rear of the truck, although canvas covered, was not heated. While the vehicle was in motion, a brisk cold wind whistled around and through the trucks canvas covering. Even fully clothed in our winter underwear and outer garments, we were cold most of the time.

Private First Class Robert Hunt was the driver of our fire direction vehicle.

Robert was from Tennessee and had started driving trucks in his early teens. He was undoubtedly the most proficient driver in the battery, and he was happy to be going home. Even with an assistant driver, Robert drove the entire distance to the maneuver area himself. As we got closer to Murfreesboro, his grin got larger. By the time we arrived, Robert's face was all teeth!

For the rest of us, the trip was long, tedious, cold, and uneventful. The main problems centered on the cold, and corresponding, full bladders. In cold weather human kidneys seem to work overtime and keep constant pressure on the bladder. Even though we had planned rest-stops, these stops did not always coincide with our distended bladders. Early in the trip we learned that voiding ones bladder over the tailgate of a speeding 2 1/2 ton GMC truck was not desirable for two reasons. First, the liquid being released from the bladder tends to drift and cloud the windshield of the next closely following vehicle. Urinating on the windshield of the following vehicle did not cement relationships with existing friends, nor enhance the possibility of making new ones. Second, the turbulence caused by a speeding 2 1/2 ton GMC truck tended to pull the liquid released from the bladder back into the rear of the truck, drenching both the releaser and his nearby comrades. This uncivilized act of drenching ones closely packed friends with unsanitary liquid brought loud threats of slow and painful death to the perpetrator, in addition to the unsanitary conditions he imposed upon himself.

On the move, the soldier with a full bladder had only three viable options: First, to groan and bear the pain until the next rest stop. The Second, which occurred on several occasions, was to relieve yourself within the confines of your pant-leg, which had its obvious drawback of soaking wet clothing in freezing weather. Or Third, to remove the steel shell from your helmet-liner and use the steel helmet to hold the sloshing yellow liquid until the truck came to a halt. This third option had several drawbacks also. This technique required arms of steel and a steady hand to confine the liquid inside the steel helmet as the truck moved. It also cast doubt upon the cleanliness of your helmet the next time you were required to use it as a cooking utensil.

A major problem with the planned rest stops was the length of the march-column. Several times, Major Goldstein's vehicle pulled to the side of the road and stopped the convoy in a designated rural area for a rest stop, when another portion of the march-column was still in a populated urban area. This situation happened to our vehicle once during the two day trip. Our driver, Robert Hunt, tried valiantly to move our vehicle through the populated areas before we dismounted from the truck to relieve ourselves. But try as he always did, this time he did not succeed.

On this occasion, my bladder was so full I thought it would burst, consequently I moved to the rear of the truck, anticipating the stop. When the truck started to slow and pull to the side of the road, I opened the rear canvas flap and looked out. To my surprise, the truck had come to rest in a residential section of a small town.

Out of curiosity, many of the town folks had come to their porches and front yards to view the parked military vehicles which had disgorged numerous men dressed in fatigue uniforms. This attentive audience created a serious dilemma for the GIs who had stopped to stretch, get warm, and urinate. I was in such pain I could not wait until the next rest stop to urinate. I made up my mind to relieve myself and suffer the social consequences rather than do permanent damage to my urinary system. As I zipped down my fly and started to relieve myself, I could not take my eyes off of a dignified looking, elderly lady who was seated in a chair facing me, and rocking back and forth slowly on her front porch. She seemed to be extremely alert and intently observing all the strange sights now offered by the United States Army. Eventually our eyes met and locked. She smiled at me graciously and I bashfully returned her smile, but continued to relieve myself.

Of course I was not the only citizen soldier in this situation and gradually yellow liquid began to run in the gutter.

The thought of what we were doing embarrassed me. As we prepared to leave, I leaned over the tail-gate of the fire direction truck and looked in the direction of the elderly lady. She was still rocking slowly back and forth with a motherly looking smile on her face. When she saw me looking in her direction, she waved, the type of wave a mother would give to her son as he left home for the first time. The warm wave and tender smile of affection erased my feeling of guilt and made me feel much better.

Physically relieved and comfortably stretched-out inside the truck my mind started to wander. I thought of my mother and my aunts who cared for me while my mother was away at college attending summer school. Then my mind returned to the little lady who had just waived good-bye so tenderly and wondered how many ladies in this great country of ours would have been so gracious to us under these same circumstances.

This gracious little lady must have had sons or grandsons in the armed forces.

106th Infantry Division – Tennessee Winter Maneuvers
Outdoor Living Conditions Near Murfreesboro, Tennessee

The farther north we traveled the colder the weather became. By the time we reached the bivouac area between Murfreesboro and Lebanon, Tennessee, the weather was a miserable combination of sleet and rain. The army furnished us no barracks, no mess halls, no buildings of any kind to shelter us from the terrible weather. We were told we must live under simulated combat conditions for the next six weeks, whether we liked it or not! For the entire time we were in Tennessee, I never met anyone who liked the outdoor living conditions, and that included those of my friends, like Robert Hunt, who were 'native sons.'

Truthfully, the individual days spent during maneuvers had no significant impact upon me. The days seemed to connect endlessly and each day had no beginning nor end. Only instances, or situations, seemed to break the monotony of constantly living with rain, sleet, snow, mud, cold, and personal filth.

The Second Army maneuvers in Tennessee were designed to train both infantry and artillery units to endure, and to function effectively, in harsh winter combat conditions. The only ingredient purposely omitted was live ammunition. The troops involved in these war-games were divided into two opposing 'Armies,' the Red and the Blue. These opposing armies were placed in various geographical locations and assigned opposing objectives, such as, one army to defend and the other to attack. Impartial umpires, designated with white helmets and white arm-bands, roamed freely among both armies, and depending upon the information they received from the pseudo-combatants, the umpires designated specific people as being killed, wounded, or captured.

It was my good luck to get 'killed' early in one mock engagement. This fact caused me to spend the rest of the battle in the umpires 'graveyard.' This graveyard consisted of sleeping in a warm tent, on a soft cot, and eating three hot meals each day while 'dead.' However, of all the benefits of being declared 'dead,' the greatest luxury of all was the ability to take a long, hot shower each day while in the 'graveyard.'

The only thing better than getting 'killed' was getting 'seriously wounded.' Those lucky enough to be so designated became liter patients and were evacuated to a training medical facility and treated as though they were actually wounded. This training field hospital environment offered all the amenities of the 'graveyard' plus the extra ingredient of live, luscious, Army Nurses. Unfortunately I was not lucky enough to get 'seriously wounded' during the winter maneuvers and had to rely on the stories told by my friends who were.

During one mock engagement, our Battalion Commander, Lieutenant Colonel Thomas P. Kelly, Jr., ventured too far forward of the friendly lines. He, and his driver, were ambushed and captured, by the enemy. Although the Colonel argued hard and heavy with the umpires, the two of them were declared prisoners and spent the rest of the engagement in a Prisoner of War Enclosure. The one time I tried to query my CO about his experience as a prisoner, my embarrassed Battalion Commander refused to discuss the mater, but vowed to me solemnly he would never be captured again.

The living conditions we endured during the maneuvers for two months is difficult to describe. In fact, if I could describe these conditions properly, you could not comprehend them, because you were not there. This gigantic military experience involved many thousands of military personnel, whose movements flowed back and forth through a large area of Tennessee, between the towns of Murfreesboro and Lebanon, severely impacting the lives of the local citizens and land owners. During the process of the war games fences were broken and destroyed, farms and pasture land became rutted by heavy military equipment, farm animals escaped through open gates or ruptured fencing, private and public roads were severely damaged, and probably the greatest indignity of all, latrines were dug and human waste deposited in large quantities on private property. In my opinion, the army did not embrace the qualities I would be looking for in a good neighbor.

Natives of the great state of Tennessee are much like all other Southerners, some are friendly and gracious, even in adversity, while others became belligerent and hostile. A small minority of the local citizens in the maneuver area were neither, they became successful overnight entrepreneurs! I can remember examples of all types. Fortunately, I remember best the friendly and gracious folks of rural Tennessee.

But first, the entrepreneurs. Tennessee and Kentucky are noted for smooth 'sipping whiskey,' a sour mash bourbon. Of the thousands of military troops involved in the 1943-1944 winter maneuvers in Tennessee, I have no idea how many were accustomed to drinking 'moonshine whiskey.' The men in the 589th FA Bn were young and from diverse sections of the country, therefore, I would assume most of these men were not familiar with 'moonshine,' because it was consumed mainly in the south.

Two of my good buddies, David Dunham and Robert Hunt, although not yet twenty-one years of age, had been sipping Tennessee moonshine for years. They not only sipped it, they were connoisseurs of moonshine quality. They also understood how to obtain superior quality moonshine at a reasonable price, and in large quantities. They provided a valuable service for members of our battalion by keeping us well supplied with moonshine during the entire time we spent in the maneuver area. The men of the 589th owed these two native sons a debt of gratitude for this endless supply of reasonably priced 'morale booster.'

The men of the 589th paid their debt of gratitude to these two entrepreneurs by allowing them to 'tack-on' reasonable service and delivery charges. We also granted these two enlisted men the honorary rank of 'Morale Officers.'

Other groups of maneuver entrepreneurs came from the local Tennessee residents themselves. One of our great problems was personal hygiene. We, and our clothes, were constantly wet and covered with tight clinging Tennessee mud. The military offered no centralized bathing facilities and it did not take long for a group of locals to discover this fact. We ultimately found one group of locals who had converted an old milking barn into a large and drafty shower facility. This building provided a cramped, unsecured, space in which we could undress and redress; and a large, partially open, concrete floored area which had formerly been used for hosing-down milk cows prior the milking process. This concrete floored area was converted into the shower room itself.

These enterprising farmers obtained an old, inefficient, wood burning boiler to heat water. They then connected the water output from the boiler to several rows of overhead galvanized pipe which had been pierced with small holes to allow a mixture of scalding hot and freezing cold water to spray on the concrete floor below. They charged one dollar for a so-called shower, and the number of takers was enormous.

The shower process went something like this. Lines of GIs would start to form in the rain, sleet, and snow, early each morning in front of the make-shift shower building. The first forty GIs in line would be allowed to enter the undressing area after paying the one dollar shower charge. About two or three minutes were allowed for the undressing process and to get situated, soap in hand, under the perforated overhead water pipes. The boiler whistle would blow and the water would flow, the water both scalding and freezing each man simultaneously. In exactly one minute, the boiler whistle would blow again, and in fifteen seconds the water was turned off. It made no difference whether you were clean, still dirty, or covered with soap-suds, the water was shut off fifteen seconds after the whistle.

Following the water shut-off, all GIs, dripping wet and shivering from the cold, were herded into the dressing room, whether they had completed their shower or not. Those people who felt clean enough, or had no more money, dried themselves, changed into clean underwear and socks, donned their filthy outer garments, and exited the building. Those people who remained undressed, paid another dollar, re-entered the shower room, stood there shivering from the wet and cold, waited until the shower room was filled with new patrons, and resumed their shower when the boiler whistle would blow and the water would flow.

Each day this process repeated itself again and again, for seven days each week during the entire time we were in the maneuver area. Of the numerous showers I took at this facility, I was never able to complete a shower without paying at least two dollars. I really resented the treatment we received from these hard-hearted, money-grabbing locals, but in retrospect, I have to admit, these scalding/freezing showers were better than no showers at all.

Of course I do not know the education level of these local entrepreneurs, but I doubt they studied economics in college, however one thing is perfectly clear, these locals certainly understood the laws of supply and demand. They immediately recognized a demand, and for two short months, they provided a popular service for which they were handsomely rewarded. Using simple mathematics, these local farmers collected forty dollars from military personnel every ten minutes they were in operation. Their gross income from each ten-hour day was approximately $2,400 and they operated the shower facility for about sixty days. This resulted in a gross income of some $144,000 in unreported cash sales. Not bad income for the two months work in the year of our Lord, nineteen hundred and forty four.

Of course, not all Tennessee families fared this well. Take the case of the Tennessee farmer who, during one exercise, was unfortunate enough to have his home located only a few hundred yards in front of a 589th FA Bn firing battery. As I have previously explained, sipping whiskey was easy to obtain, relatively inexpensive, and when sipped in sufficient quantities seemed to diminish the hardships encountered while living in the great out-of-doors in this horrible Tennessee winter weather.

During a lull in our exercise, the Executive Officer, whom we will call Lieutenant "X," apparently had been sipping moonshine to excess, and to relieve his boredom decided to create a little action. He walked to a howitzer position and ordered the unsuspecting gun crew to, "Fall-in Behind The Piece" (Assemble behind the Howitzer). His alcohol befuddled brain had concocted a brilliant idea in which he would fire fence-posts in-lieu-of the normal projectiles the army refused to issue his battery during the war games. He ordered one half of his men to obtain a supply of new, rounded, wooden fence-posts he observed stacked neatly behind the Tennessee farmers barn. The other one+ half of his obedient gun crew was dispatched to acquire as much 105mm blank ammunition as they could find. It did not take the obliging gun crew long to return with both the fence-posts and the blank 105mm ammunition.

Members of the gun crew wondered what their Executive Officer had in mind, but only Lieutenant "X" understood he now had the propellants and projectiles necessary to perform a most unusual experiment using a US Army 105mm howitzer and a highly trained howitzer crew.

Lieutenant "X," now ready for his noble experiment, gave his crew the standard order, "Fire Mission!" The highly trained gun crew obediently "Fell-in" and assumed their normal firing positions around the howitzer. Upon the command of Lieutenant "X," the howitzer crew, without hesitation, loaded a blank round into the breech of the howitzer and rammed a new cylinder-shaped wooden fence-post down the howitzer tube (barrel). When the elevation and direction, ordered by Lieutenant "X," was set, the crew chief reported the weapon ready to fire. Lieutenant "X" then gave the command to "FIRE," and a cannoneer pulled the lanyard.

The following sequence of events created a spectacular first in the annals of modern warfare. A muffled roar, as the powder in the blank round exploded, followed by acrid white smoke belching from the muzzle of the howitzer, the somewhat zigzag flight of the four foot wooden fence-post as it passed through the misty white smoke, the Executive Officer standing behind the howitzer, binoculars at the ready to observe the erratic flight of the fence-post, the excitement of the gun crew, who could sense they were a part of an important and noble experiment, and last, but certainly not least, the high arching flight of the fence-post as it soared majestically through the frosty-cold winter air.

The first portion of this exciting experiment concluded with the distinctive sound of splintering wood, and the unexpected sight of the first fence-post ever fired by the United States Artillery embedded firmly in the highly pitched shingled roof of the unfortunate Tennessee farm house.

Undaunted, Lieutenant "X" sensed the round as "Short," lowered his binoculars, and gave instructions to his howitzer crew to raise the elevation, reload the howitzer, and report when ready to fire.

By now, members of his somewhat sobered crew were beginning to question the merits of this experiment. Behind them, Lieutenant "X." whom they all liked and respected, stood tall and positive, issuing legitimate orders in a military fashion. But in front of them, approaching across the open field separating the howitzer position and the farm house, was an obviously disturbed Tennessee farmer who was armed with a double barreled, twelve-gauge shotgun.

Most of the Cannoneers felt like warriors, armed with the latest US Army weapons, but unfortunately they had been issued only blank ammunition. They reasoned the approaching "Mountain Man" was carrying a shotgun probably loaded with "oo" Buckshot. Consequently all but the Executive Officer and his loyal section chief made a strategic withdrawal and took cover behind a stand of trees which was located just beyond Buckshot range.

For some unknown reason, fate stepped into this tense situation and instead of harsh words and gun-play, cool and polite dialogue prevailed. The mountain man had three sons in the service: two in the Army and one in the Navy. He was sympathetic to the army training needs and anxious to do his part, but he could not fathom the need for shooting one of his own fence-posts through the new roof of his home. The now-sober and smooth-talking Lieutenant "X," aided by his loyal section chief, convinced the patriotic farmer the howitzer crew was actually engaged in a highly secret mission which was of great importance to the nation's war effort.

An agreement was finally negotiated, on the spot, between the government of the United States and this native son of the great state of Tennessee. As the duly authorized representative of the US Government, Lieutenant "X" agreed to cease fire, return the farmers unused fence-posts to the pile behind the barn, and to make restitution the next morning, in cash, for damages caused to the farmers new roof. These actions and full restitution was guaranteed by the full weight of the United States Government, provided the Tennessee mountain man gave his solemn word that he would never reveal to anyone, under any circumstances, the vital military secrets he had learned that day.

Those of us who could not hear this privileged conversation were surprised to see Lieutenant "X" and his section chief snap to attention and salute the farmer. We were also surprised to witness the civilian as he shouldered his shotgun, do a snappy about-face, and begin the march toward home across the plowed field. We could actually see a touch of pride on the farmer's face as he envisioned how much he had helped the war effort, and contemplated the confidence the government had placed in him by sharing with him this highly valuable and secret military information.

This event grew in stature until it became a legend among the enlisted men of the battalion. Lieutenant "X" was a well-liked officer who had the best interests of his men at heart. He was also an intelligent man who became bored too easily with the tedium of army life which caused him to drink too much. Although it was rumored that Lieutenant "X" was the son of a wealthy man, the section chief made the rounds that night and collected funds from many of the enlisted men in the battalion. By the next morning, the 'Official US Government Restitution Fund' had grown to a substantial amount of money.

All the cash gathered was formally presented to the farmer the next morning, as promised, by the section chief, who, on this occasion, acted as the official representative of the United States Government.

I do not believe the senior officers in the battalion were ever aware of this incident, although several junior officers actually contributed to the 'Official Fund.'

† †

Even though I encountered numerous residents of the area during maneuvers, there are two ladies I recall vividly because of their unusual acts of kindness toward us soldiers. One, a diminutive, silver-haired widow, a resident of Nashville, five feet two inches tall, about sixty-five years of age, and weighed no more than one hundred pounds. The other lady, by contrast, was a farmer's wife. She was a large framed, pleasant looking middle aged mother, with 'men-folks' in the service, who desperately wanted to do everything she could for young men in the service.

First let me recall a weekend pass and my experience with the gracious little silver-haired widow in Nashville.

Four of us were lucky enough to get a weekend pass to visit Nashville and were ordered to wear Class A winter uniforms. Our personal belongings had been stored in duffel bags for weeks, with literally tons of other gear stowed on top of them. When I finally found my bag and retrieved a complete dress uniform, the uniform suffered from what is known as a 'duffel bag press.' My clothing was not an awe inspiring sight. I donned the uniform, surveyed the results, and came to the conclusion I would not be accepted in civilized society looking like this. My only consolation was the fact that other three looked just as terrible as I did.

Our army transportation deposited us directly in front of the main Nashville USO Club. As the driver departed to return to the maneuver area, he advised us he would pick us up at this same location the following afternoon at 1700 hours and return us to our unit. He emphasized that failure to meet the truck at the appointed location and time would result in harsh and vengeful treatment by the proper authorities.

During the trip to town, the four of us agreed on a sequence of events. First, we would get our uniforms pressed and our shoes shined. Second, we would obtain overnight accommodations from the USO so we would not be forced to spend a portion of Saturday night sleeping on a park bench. And third, we would do as many night spots in Nashville as we could, money permitting.

A female volunteer, resplendent in her freshly pressed USO uniform, viewed us with distaste as we walked toward the reception desk. Being the senior non-commissioned officer present, I introduced myself and explained our desire to get our uniforms pressed and our shoes shined. She looked relieved when she found our we were from the maneuver area, and quickly made a call in our behalf. She then directed us to a combination dry-cleaning/tailor-shop that also boasted a shoe shine parlor. We were surprised to learn that all of these services were conveniently located in one nearby business establishment.

We quickly discovered we were not the only soldiers in town with uniform problems when we entered the dry-cleaning establishment. We found it jammed with soldiers in need of sprucing-up in varying degrees. When I approached the counter, I was greeted by a grinning, slightly plump, Chinese man, who looked me over, nodded, and before I could say a word told me,. "Take tickey and get in line."

The process was relatively fast, much like an assembly line in an automated factory, only here, you paid first. When your number was called, you moved behind a small "modesty curtain," removed your jacket, shirt, trousers, and your "Go to Hell" cap, paid the cashier, received a receipt, and then moved into the line leading to the shoe shine chairs. We stood behind a waist high railing which supported a dangling curtain the proprietor had provided to shield our olive drab under shorts and white bare legs from the darting eyes of delicate southern females who seemed to pass the large plate-glass window in front of the shoe shine chairs in an unending procession.

Much to their delight, our bare legs and olive drab under wear were fully exposed to these innocent daughters of the South when we were seated in the high shoe shine chairs. To maintain some type of modest dignity, while seated in these highly visible chairs, most soldiers engaged in what is described as the "fig leaf stance." This stance entails nothing more than cupping both hands loosely and placing them in a strategic location slightly beneath the belly, and squarely between both legs. While thus waiting, my freshly pressed uniform appeared as if by magic, to coincide with the completion of the shoe shine. This was truly Chinese/American ingenuity at its best!

All four of us looked much better in our pressed uniforms and shined shoes. I might even say we looked sharp when we returned to the reception desk at the USO Club. There we explained our need for overnight accommodations and asked the receptionist for suggestions. After determining the four of us were together, she checked her records and made a call. Her first call resulted in accommodations, for the four of us, in a private residence situated in a suburban section of Nashville. The receptionist advised us we must return to the USO Club no later than 2230 hours for USO provided transportation to our accommodation. Although 2230 hours sounded early to us, we decided these terms were better than staying up all night, so we agreed to be on time.

For the remainder of the day, we visited with cute USO hostesses, ate free USO food, and took in a free movie. When darkness fell and the city lights began to shine, we started to bar-hop. Although the bright lights and night life of Nashville held our attention, I remained acutely aware that the USO frowned upon drunken GIs so I drank in moderation. My three companions were not so cautious however, and let it all hang-out. When time came to head back to the USO, they were full of fun, still ready to party, and hard to convince we had to call it a night. I made them wait outside the USO Club while I checked in at the reception desk. The hostess there gave me an approved transportation voucher and told me to present it to any cab driver stationed at the curb outside the building. We piled into the nearest vehicle for hire and enjoyed a nice trip to the outskirts of Nashville. At the address on the transportation voucher, I asked the driver to wait at the curb while I verified that we were expected.

At the door, a darling little lady looked up at me, with tenderness written all over her face, and told me sweetly that she was glad to have us spend the night in her home. She said she lived alone, had plenty of spare rooms, and liked to visit with nice young gentlemen. By this time I was beginning to compare her with my doting grandmother. She continued by asking me to bring my friends in, and added she was so glad we were such nice young men, because a couple of times the US had sent soldiers to stay with her who had been drinking, and who were rowdy.

All I could think of was my three tipsy friends, who were well into their cups, sitting in the parked cab, singing "Ninety-Nine Bottles of Beer on the Wall" loudly, in unison with our jovial driver. I knew if I could hear them, she could hear them also. Determined that they would not frighten this genteel lady, I returned to the parked cab, gave the driver the signed voucher, so the USO would pay him, and in no uncertain terms impressed upon my traveling companions that if they did anything, and I meant anything, to frighten our elderly hostess, they would spend the rest of the maneuvers digging latrines and/or scrubbing pots and pans for the mess sergeant.

Sufficiently forewarned, the four of us entered this prim ladies home and were treated like royalty. All of us were visibly touched by this gracious little lady who willingly shared her home with strangers, and was also delighted to share some of her most personal and prized possessions with us. She served us hot tea and petit fours while talking with us until almost 0100 hours.

The next morning we were awakened by the smell of food being prepared and a beautiful female voice downstairs happily singing hymns. When our hostess heard us moving around in our rooms, she invited us to dress casually and come down stairs for breakfast. She said we could shower and shave after we ate and then she would arrange for transportation to take us back to town. She strongly suggested we attend church services of our choice before returning to the maneuver area later that day.

The four of us were served breakfast in the kitchen by a much younger woman, who was obviously an employee of our elder hostess. The breakfast was literally fit for a king! We ate like starving Armenians and when we had finished it suddenly dawned on me, we had probably consumed all the rationed food that she could accumulate in a month of doing without. When I asked her about the food, she explained she was able to obtain additional food stamps from the Ration Board, to feed visiting service personnel.

This sweet, charming, and generous lady made an incredible impression on this young soldier. She was so giving of herself and her home to total strangers I have often wondered if she actually told me the truth about the availability of extra food stamps to feed 'her boys' in the service.

† †

I met the farm-wife under entirely different circumstances. We were in the middle of a military exercise when I met this fine country lady. The Battalion Survey Officer had dispatched his crew to survey additional artillery positions because the battalion was planning to move. The survey crew was gone for much longer than expected, and could not be reached on their vehicle radio. The Survey Officer became concerned and anticipated some type of trouble. He showed me, on a map, where he thought his crew might be and asked me to take his jeep and driver to see if we could locate them.

Outside the Command Post tent, the weather was a combination of sleet and rain, the temperature hovering around thirty-two degrees. I was not too happy about having to leave the comfort of the Command Post tent, but in this case, the Survey Officer's request was really an order, so I had no choice.

During this war-game, concessions had been made to actual combat conditions. Canvas vehicle tops could remain in place, and windshields could be left in the upright position to facilitate leaving the canvas top in place. In addition, the survey jeep was equipped with a heater. With these advantages, I decided the trip would not be too bad in spite of the harsh, cold weather, but I dressed in my warm foul-weather gear anyway.

We looked for the survey truck in several obvious locations, to no avail. Finally in desperation, we started looking in more unlikely places. Along a main road, I spotted a group of army vehicles partially hidden behind a large wooden farm house. The driver and I decided to take a closer look so we could check the vehicle unit designations. There we spotted the 3/4 ton Dodge survey truck, and parked our jeep close to the rear of the farm house. I dismounted from the jeep, climbed the stairs to the back porch, approached the rear door, and knocked.

The back door opened, revealing a large-framed, pleasant-looking, middle-aged, motherly type, lady who insisted the driver and I should get out of the bitter cold, come into the house, and get warm. This was an invitation I could not refuse, so I motioned to the driver to leave the vehicle and come up onto the back porch. The door on the back porch opened into a long center hall that ran from the rear to the front of the generously sized home. This entrance hall was typical of farm house construction and is often referred to as the "dog-trot." The term "dog-trot" is self explanatory if you are familiar with the life style of farmers who possess both house dogs and yard dogs.

To say I was surprised to discover what I found in her home would be an understatement. I was actually overwhelmed! The first door to my left, as we entered the dog-trot, opened into a large and well equipped country kitchen. This room was filled to capacity with soldiers who were gorging themselves on some of the best country cooking imaginable. This generous farm wife had two domestic helpers who were taking orders, cooking, and cleaning dishes simultaneously. It was as though I had entered a well organized and busy commercial restaurant. As I took in this scene, I spotted T/4 Ruona, the survey crew chief, and his entire crew, enjoying a generous, cooked to order, served at the table, hot farm breakfast.

Duty obligated me to tell Sergeant Ruona that he and his crew were delaying plans for the battalion to move. He grinned sheepishly and said, "Don't get your bowels in an uproar Sergeant Pierson. Why don't you and your driver sit down and join us for breakfast?" His suggestion was enthusiastically endorsed by the gracious housewife.

After being served, restaurant style, one of the best meals I had ever eaten, the housewife came to the table and recorded our names, rank, home address, and next of kin. As we departed, I tried to pay our hostess for the meals. When she refused to accept money, I realized these meals were a labor of love. We thanked her the best way we knew how, because her hospitality meant so much to us. The answer we received was a motherly smile, a tender hug for each individual, and the explanation that she had 'men-folks' in the service. She added, this was the only way she knew how to serve her country, when so many young men, away from home, needed a mother's care.

During the ride back to the Command Post I felt touched by the generosity and sincerity of this caring Tennessee lady, and prayed that her 'men-folks' would return home safely from this terrible war.

Once back at battalion and caught-up in the every-day problems of the maneuvers, this gracious incident finally slipped from my mind. However, weeks later, a letter from my mother caught up with me. In her letter, mother told me she had received a letter from a total stranger, a lady in Tennessee, who said I had visited her home, with friends, and told my mother what a nice young man I was. The Tennessee lady also told mother she should be proud to have a son like me.

To think this farm wife, who had "men-folks" in the service and was so kind to me, would write my mother such nice things about me was very touching. No wonder I still remember this dear farm lady some sixty years later.

† †

One fortunate thing about these winter war-games was the fact that I almost never came in contact with Captain Black. His main responsibilities, other than being Headquarters Battery Commander, was functioning as the Battalion Communications Officer. The adverse weather conditions, plus the fact the battalion moved frequently during these games, was challenging to the communications section. Telephone lines were constantly in need of repair, new lines being laid while old ones were being recovered, radio communications were intermittent, requiring constant maintenance, repair, and/or the replacement of parts.

Giving the Captain his due, he kept his communications section busy, and most of the time left the fire direction personnel alone. He was a persistent man however, and would not let go completely. To maintain his authority over "his troops," he had an infuriating habit of making nocturnal rounds of the Command Post area to inspect the quality of the fox holes we had dug. Of course in his opinion our fox holes were never deep enough, nor large enough, nor numerous enough, to protect all the personnel on duty at the Command Post. To make his point and to assert his authority, he would make a grand entrance into the Command Post tent and loudly proclaim his findings, and ask the Colonel or the Major if he could "borrow" some of the men on duty to go out into the cold, wet, black of night, to correct these horrible deficiencies.

When things were slack, and his timing was impeccable, we were temporarily released to our taskmaster and had to do back breaking work improving our fox holes with our entrenching tools. In semi-frozen, or sloppy wet ground, this was a thankless and inhumane task, and we hated his guts for subjecting us to this unnecessary, grueling work. While improving our holes one night, we devised a plan, but had to wait several days to implement it.

At our next new position, someone was smart enough to obtain several full sized long handled shovels. These shovels were ten times more efficient for digging deep holes than the small, short handled, entrenching tools. We chose our hole locations carefully, placing them in the middle of natural breaks in the forest which we hoped Captain Black would use as a path during his next nocturnal visit. We dug them deep, we dug them large, and we dug them in numerous locations. Although it was extremely hard work, we hauled water and dumped it into each hole. We then covered each hole with frail branches.

Our task complete, we cleaned ourselves and reported for duty in the Command Post as usual. I can't speak for the rest of my partners in crime, but I prayed that tonight we would catch a big, fat, Captain in one of our traps.

As the night wore on, I became more and more disappointed because Captain Black had not paid us his normal nocturnal visit, and I was afraid all of our hard labor would be in vain. I really wanted to get back at the Captain, but it appeared that Captain Black would win again.

With no prior warning, but clearly audible in the confines of the CP tent, we heard the sounds of tree limbs cracking, water splashing, and cursing. The oaths of anger contained words I had never heard before. These were the expressions an ex-prison guard might utter, but now they came from the mouth of an army Captain, an officer and gentleman by an act of congress. The voice was unmistakably that of Captain Black.

I looked at Staff Sergeant Tacker and my mouth formed the silent words, "We finally got the son-of-a-bitch!" Tacker's only response was a slight affirmative shake of the head.

Moments later Captain Black, drenched with mud and cold water, threw open the entrance flap to the Command Post tent and stepped inside. His body-language was aggressive, and his facial expression fierce, as he looked at the GIs in the tent. His fixed stare finally centered upon Major Parker, who had no idea what was happening, and the enraged Captain finally spoke, "That's the way I want those God Damned fox holes dug!"

Without uttering another word, the "Captain who had been had" exited the tent. This episode occurred near the end of the maneuvers, and the Captain made no more nocturnal inspections of our fox holes after the "Captain Trap" incident.

† †

By the latter part of maneuvers, strong relationships had been formed between men. Some relationships were good, some not so good. I had made many friends in the enlisted ranks, but I had learned to avoid officers. In retrospect I believe this was normal at this point in my military development. There were three officers I could not avoid however: my Battery Commander, Captain A. R. Black; my Battalion Operations Officer, Major Arthur C. Parker, III; and my Battalion Commander, Lieutenant Colonel Thomas P. Kelly, Jr.

To say a Technician 4th Grade had a close personal relationship with a Major and a Lieutenant Colonel may seem strange, but from my point of view, I worked closely with these two senior officers every day, and I idolized both men, but for different reasons. My relationship with my Battery Commander, Captain Black, was, putting it mildly, strained. Even though I was under the Captains direct command, I did not work for him. I worked for Major Parker in the Battalion Fire Direction Center, and was not normally available for battery duties as Captain Black expected. This fact irritated Captain Black, who often called me names such as; smart-ass, college-boy, and gold-brick. In return I referred to him as an ignorant back-water-hick and a pain-in-the-ass, but not to his face of course. To be truthful, the Captain was not ignorant, but he was a "Red-Neck," and in civilian life, he was a prison guard in the Texas penal system. Captain Black and I were opposites, and this was one case where opposites did not attract. He was a big man, tall, over weight, had as large gut, was socially course, and was physically strong; whereas I was tall, slender, scholarly, and not physically inclined at all. Even though I had passed all the Army Ground Forces physical tests, after my bout with spinal meningitis, Captain Black still considered me a sissy.

My personal traits, which irritated Captain Black, pleased Major Parker and Lieutenant Colonel Kelly. These senior officers recognized the value of brain power over brawn for persons assigned to read maps, to plot firing data, and to calculate firing commands for the three firing batteries in the battalion. By selecting me to become a fire direction technician, they successfully placed a round peg in a round hole. A perfect fit! My niche in fire direction work was quickly established by Major Parker, and I was grateful to be away from the heavy manual labor required by other assignments. This scholarly Major became my mentor, my educator, my role model, and fortunately for me, my protector from the ire of my Battery Commander, Captain Black.

The Major, as all members of the fire direction team called him, took personal interest in each and every member of his team. He taught us, cross trained us, tested us, and then he taught us more. He was a demanding taskmaster who believed that repetition was emphasis, and was a splendid educator. To give credit where credit is due, the Major became one of the dominant role models for this young and impressionable soldier.

The Colonel, as we called Lieutenant Colonel Kelly, was not as old as the Major. In fact, he was quite young to have attained the rank of Lieutenant Colonel. In civilian life he was a successful attorney from Tampa, Florida, but in the military, he was a natural leader with an uncanny ability to motivate and inspire men. The Colonel was a handsome man with an athletic build, which, combined with his tailored uniform, gave him an impressive military bearing. He was energetic, enthusiastic, and his mind never seemed to rest. Like the Major, he took personal interest in the officers and enlisted men who worked with him on a daily basis. He demanded excellence and gave excellence in return. Over time, during my close contact with the Colonel, he became my father figure, or my authority figure, which I did not have as a youngster, being raised solely by my mother. There was great respect given in both directions.

During maneuvers, one test, or exercise, the army imposed upon the 589th FA Bn was a personal endurance test. Both officers and men were subjected to severe combat conditions, with no rest periods given for an extended period of time. This "stress test," if you will, applied to both officers and enlisted men alike.

After about thirty hours of constant and frantic activity, the less determined personnel started to fold. Evidence was clear that personnel were becoming fatigued, errors were being made, tempers flared, and weaker men were going to sleep in the middle of their duties. Not so for the Colonel! Lieutenant Colonel Kelly remained physically active and mentally alert for about forty hours.

At the end of the exercise, the umpires, who had been allowed to work in shifts, started to prepare their critique and rate the battalion performance. Major Parker, who noted the Colonel was starting to fade, suggested the Colonel retire to his tent and get some rest while the umpires were preparing their critiques. Begrudgingly the Colonel accepted this suggestion and I was summoned to accompany the Colonel to his tent and make certain he got bedded down properly. The Colonels main concern was to be present when the chief umpire presented his critique of the battalion performance.

Lieutenant Colonel Kelly did not want assistance when we reached his personal tent, however, I remembered the Majors instructions and stayed with the Colonel as he partially undressed. As he wearily slipped into his sleeping bag, he said, "Pierson, I will rack your butt if I miss the umpires critique. I will be hard to wake up when the time comes. I will probably lie to you just to get fifteen more minutes of sleep. I might even try to intimidate you and pull rank on you. But no matter what I say or do, it is your responsibility to stay with me until I am fully awake and fully clothed before you leave me. Do you understand the situation, and are my instructions clear Sergeant?"

"Yes sir, very clear. Don't worry Colonel, I'll get you up in time for the critique. You have my word sir." "You are a good man, Pierson." Before I could respond to his statement of confidence, he was dead to the world. Sound asleep!

Major Parker half laughed and half snorted when I told him of my conversation with the Colonel. The Major said, "It will be almost impossible to get him up in just a few hours. He is obviously totally exhausted. That is what this exercise is all about, to determine how people operate under fatiguing conditions. But Sergeant Pierson, he meant exactly what he said, he will fight you with everything he can think of just to get a few more minutes of sleep. It is important for you to know this, and it is also important for you to realize this task is your responsibility. You gave the Colonel your word you would get him to the umpires critique, and you had better not fail. He is depending on you. I will give you as much advance notice of the critique time as I can, but getting the Colonel there is your responsibility!"

We received word from one of the umpires a few hours later who advised us the chief umpire would cover the 589th critique in about one hour. He emphasized that all senior battalion officers should be present during the presentation. The Major acknowledged the news and promptly dispatched me to awaken the Colonel.

Lieutenant Colonel Kelly was sleeping so soundly when I reached his tent I felt sorry for him. However, I had my instructions and I knew I had better carry them out. In an effort to awaken my Battalion Commander as discretely as possible, I politely cleared my throat. This mild action produced no results at all. My next effort was to lightly touch the prone body surrounded by the heavy sleeping bag. Again, nothing! Beginning to wonder if the Colonel had died since I saw him last, I grabbed the top of the sleeping bag and struggled to get his inert body in a semi-sitting position. This course of a action produced a groan and a slight body movement.

Thinking I was making progress, I released my grip on the sleeping bag, only to see the semi-sitting body, slowly but surely, wilt into a prone position. This was bad news—the Colonel had fallen asleep again. The realization that I might have to "lay hands" on a field grade officer did not appeal to me, but I had this awesome responsibility to fulfill, no matter what. This time, I rudely jerked Lieutenant Colonel Kelly to a full sitting position and stuffed his duffel bag behind him in an effort to keep him from going prone again. This time, the Colonels eyes opened slightly and with a wispy voice of recognition he muttered, "Thanks, I'm OK sergeant, you can leave now."

Both he and Major Parker had warned me about how hard it would be to awaken him, so I tried to keep him awake with conversation. Into my second sentence, I noticed his head had fallen to his chest, his eyes were tightly closed, and I could detect steady and rhythmical breathing—all symptoms of deep sleep. I was really worried, and wondered if I was ever going to be able to awaken this man.

Desperation engulfed me. This time I took a firm hold of the Colonel's shoulders and shook him vigorously. Slowly color began to rise in his face, his head lifted from his chest, his eyes opened, and he stared at me with unseeing eyes. Suddenly he became belligerent and growled, "That's enough Sergeant! Now get the hell out of my tent!" I was glad he was awake, but I certainly did not like the way he told me to leave. The situation was complicated, he being a field grade officer and me being an enlisted man, so I moved slightly toward the tent flap.

Simultaneous with my move from the tent, the Colonel shut his eyes and his head started to droop in the direction of his chest. I thought, "SHIT! This is not working! I am damned if I do and I'm damned if I don't." I knew I would be in deep trouble if the Colonel missed the critique. The situation called for more drastic action, even if I did end up losing my stripes and maybe going to prison. With many reservations, I cupped my left hand under his chin, held his head erect, and slapped him sharply around the face with the palm of my right hand.

This drastic action worked! Something in his subconscious reared its ugly head and he took the offensive. "Damn you Pierson, you just struck a superior officer." His blood now boiling, he continued, "I'm going to have your ass for this. Do you know anything about the Uniform Code of Military Justice? Well I do! You have just committed a military crime. I'm a damned good lawyer and I'm going to nail your ass to the guard house wall for this." "But Sir, you …"

"Don't but sir me. I didn't authorize you to cuff me around. Now get the hell out of my face, and get out of my tent – that's an order Sergeant!"

When I left his tent I knew he was mad – furious. I also remembered he said he might try to intimidate me, and I knew I could get into serious trouble by striking a commissioned officer, but only his ego had been damaged. His adrenaline was obviously flowing by now and I reasoned it would keep him awake. What I did not know was, what he would do when he got dressed and we returned to the Command Post.

I decided to wait outside his tent and see what developed. I was certain he was aware I had not left for the Command Post because he kept assuring me from inside the tent that he was OK, but I chose to wait and listened intently for continued sounds of movement inside his tent. I was not disappointed, my hunch was correct, he remained awake and continued getting dressed.

The tent flap finally parted, the Colonel stuck his head outside and looked pleased. During the short walk back to the Command Post he was wide awake and very alert. As we walked, he looked at me, chuckled, and asked two questions. "Will we get to the critique session on time?" And, "Did I give you a hard time while you were getting me up?" The pleasant expression on his face assured me I was in no danger of being reduced in rank or being sent to prison, so I confidently answered his questions, "Affirmative to both questions, Sir!"

† †

Tennessee maneuvers ended in late March 1944 with much jubilation and anticipation of moving from the harsh Tennessee field conditions to the relative comfort of living in barracks and garrison life.

These winter maneuvers were tough! They served as the burning embers and smoking oil, while the rugged terrain and inclement weather of the Tennessee winter served as the cold anvil and heavy hammer, which tempered the 589th Field Artillery Battalion and forged it into a strong, hard, and efficient fighting unit.

My Buddies in the 589th FA Bn Survey team, (above)
We all went to Europe together—some made it home, others did not.
Pictured here on the Artillery Range at Camp Atterbury, Summer 1944—
Sergeant Pierson, center, Survey Crew, L–R, Sergeant Ruona Crew Chief,
Private Slack, Private 'Fish' Feinberg and Private Kaughman.
I was a privileged friend and honored to have served with them.

Sergeant Pierson receiving training as a Forward Observer, (opposite top)
Captain George Huxel, left, training Sergeant Pierson, center,
in Map Reading and Forward Observation techniques
on the firing range, Camp Atterbury, Indiana—Summer of 1944.
The Lieutenant on right is unidentified.

My good friend Staff Sergeant Francis P. Aspinwall, (opposite bottom),
on the Artillery Firing Range at Camp Atterbury.
Francis survived combat in Europe and later became the 589th FA Bn historian.

6
Advanced Army Unit Training

Camp Atterbury, Indiana
Near Indianapolis—April through September 1944

The 589th FA Bn arrived at Camp Atterbury on 30 March 1944 and moved into a newly refurbished Battalion Area. Lieutenant Colonel Thomas P. Kelly, Jr., the Battalion Commander, quickly made plans to allow members of his command, with accumulated leave time, to visit their families, while the remaining personnel started developing a rigorous training schedule to accommodate the Advanced Unit Training program which the battalion must successfully complete before departing for overseas.

Garrison life for members of the 589th like me, who did not go on furlough, gradually developed a dichotomy of hard work and equally hard play. Although Camp Atterbury was not a Fort, which boasted permanent barracks, our barracks at Atterbury were well maintained and quite comfortable. Spring, in the agricultural Indiana country side, was a beautiful contrast to the mud and slop he had experienced during the Tennessee winter maneuvers. And Indianapolis, WOW, what a service man's town! I honestly do not remember the recreational facilities provided at Camp Atterbury because I spent as much time in Indianapolis as possible. The city was literally crawling with beautiful, single, and some not so single but available, females. All of whom seemed to be looking for male companionship.

Two main sources of female companionship that appealed to me most were quite different in nature. The state of Indiana had a large medical facility in Indianapolis which provided both nurses and student nurses. I found both categories to be friendly to service men, however I identified with the student nurses the most. Primarily because of age and education. The second source of female companionship I quickly discovered was a huge commercial establishment which catered to singles, both male and female, provided alcoholic beverages, had great dance bands, numerous tables, and the largest dance floor I had ever seen. This "dance-land" was called the Indiana Roof.

† †

In Indianapolis I first started dating student nurses, and quickly became entangled with a fresh looking, all American, sweet and delightful, daughter of a Hoosier farmer. Our relationship was great and under different circumstances would probably have developed into a permanent arrangement called marriage. However, there were two factors which impeded our friendship. First, neither of us had much spending money. She was in college and each month I was sending the lions share of my military pay home to help support my dependent mother. Our time together was usually spent "necking" in a darkened movie theatre, or just talking in the student lounge on campus.

The second problem stemmed from the fact that she wanted to get married before I went overseas and was opposed to premarital sex. Yes, she wanted to have sex with me, as I did with her, but she was determined to give herself only after marriage. On the other hand I wished to have a good time and avoid entangling situations. For some unknown reason, I had a strong feeling I would go into battle and be killed. I did not want to leave a widow, and possibly a child, and not be there to provide them with love and support. Our differences placed a tremendous burden upon our otherwise wonderful relationship.

A weekend trip to her farm home in rural Indiana administered the *"Coup de Grace"* to our relationship. While visiting with her parents, they made it extremely clear that they expected us to marry soon, and were already making plans for a large wedding. That Sunday night at the Greyhound Terminal in Indianapolis we hugged and kissed good-bye. She heading back to school, and I catching the bus to Camp Atterbury. This was a bitter-sweet parting for me because in my heart I knew I loved her, but I also knew I would never see her again.

Of course I do not know when she realized our Sunday night parting was final. What I do know is she was a wonderful person and I hope she found someone else with which to share her life. "Pete" deserved someone very special.

The Indiana Roof was the largest dance hall in Indianapolis. It was huge! The Roof, as it was called, was quite unique in the way it was operated. Alcoholic beverages were for sale, management provided first class, live dance bands, encouraged singles, and undoubtedly was the best place in Indianapolis to find a date. It was easy to form the wrong impression on your first visit to The Roof. I certainly did! I found out the management of The Roof had "zero tolerance" for drunks and rowdies. They employed large, stern, and muscular bouncers, who constantly patrolled the tables and dance floor. Any man accused of, or suspected of, misconduct toward a female patron received a swift and assisted one-way trip to the front door. The proprietors of The Roof operated a legal business, accommodated sell-out crowds, enjoyed numerous repeat customers, and were making money hand-over-fist. Why should they let some drunk troublemaker ruin a good thing? Simple, they did not!

My first visit to The Roof was with my good friend, T/4 Delbert Miller, also from Headquarters Battery of the 589th FA Bn. Dell was in his late thirties and much older than I. In civilian life he worked as a traveling salesman for the Rath Meat Packing Company in Des Moines, Iowa. Dell was as experienced and street-wise as I was naive. We were close friends and a case of opposites attract. I could not believe the way Dell acted when we first started strolling among the tables which ringed the enormous dance floor of The Roof. He acted like a Sultan surveying his Harem while selecting his mate for the evening. After a somewhat prolonged inspection tour, he stopped at a table occupied by four attractive females who were slowly sipping their drinks and intently watching couples perform on the dance floor.

Dell leaned over, whispered something to one of the girls, received a tremendous smile, and an affirmative nod. She then excused herself to her companions, and she and Dell melted smoothly into the flow of dancing couples.

This sequence of events presented me with a perplexing problem. Dell was a smooth talker and also an accomplished dance partner. Both he and his partner were enjoying themselves, but this fact did not help me. I simply did not know what to do. I just stood there with both arms dangling at my sides and did nothing. Finally one of the females at the table stood up and asked if I would care to dance. When I sheepishly said yes, she took my hand and slowly led me into the crowd on the dance floor. We remained on the dance floor for several numbers and seemed to "click." I was actually a better than average dancer, but she was great. She was so fluid she could have been a professional. This young stranger danced so close our bodies remained in constant contact, yet we never once bobbled a step. Her body was gorgeous, I could see it, but even better, I could feel it as she gracefully moved to the rhythm of the music. Her face was beautiful as she smiled the entire time we were dancing, constantly looking up into my eyes, her eyes seemed full of untold promises.

She removed her hand from my shoulder, when the dance band stopped playing, to take a break, and led me toward her table. On the way, she told me her name was Patricia, but everyone called her Pat. I reciprocated by telling her my name was Randolph, but everyone called me Randy. At the table, we found Dell and his partner deep in conversation, and Pat explained her name was Rosemary, but everyone called her Rosie. When I asked about the other two girls who had formerly been at the table, Rosie looked up and quickly told me they had left and I should not worry about them.

Even though we were almost total strangers, Dell had already made arrangements for us to meet Pat and Rosie again. Knowing that Dell had taken the initiative for himself, and also me, made me feel more at ease, because I liked Pat and really did want to see her again. The weekend after our next pay-day, we met the girls as planned at The Roof. Rosie was more gregarious than I had remembered, and was a really attractive gal, but to me she could not hold a candle to Patricia. Pat bordered on beautiful, she had sinuous movements on the dance floor, and no one had more expressive eyes than Pat. As our second evening progressed we danced, socialized, and learned more about each other. The girls were open in their plans for the future. They both desired no entangling relationships with men, but did wish to have a continuous relationship with the proper men. They found it time consuming to sit at tables, waiting to be picked-up, only to find they did not care for one or both of the swains trying to be their date for the evening. They wanted a relationship they could plan and count on, and Dell and I seemed to fit their needs.

Although Dell and Rosie were quite vocal about our forthcoming relationships, I was reluctant to participate in these extremely personal negotiations, I nodded my head in the affirmative many times, much to the delight of Patricia. By the time our second dates ended, we had a firm understanding. For the remainder of our relationships, Dell belonged to Rosie, and I belonged to Pat.

It came as no surprise that Pat and Rosie were roommates. Pat was the younger of the two, single, and about 21 years of age. Rosie was married and about 30. Her husband was a Marine Corporal serving in the Pacific. Both girls worked at the enormous Allison Aircraft plant, near Indianapolis, which made twelve cylinder engines that powered Army Air Force P-51 fighter aircraft and a marine version which powered Navy PT boats. Both girls were fully qualified mechanics even though we referred to Rosie as "The Riveter." They were lonely females living in a town with virtually no men of their age except men already in the military. Both girls were well paid by Allison, and both girls wanted access to semi-permanent escorts and were willing to pay for this service.

Dell and I seemed to fit their wants and needs. We readily agreed to their terms and our friendships thrived. The relationships went something like this. The first night in town after our pay-day, Dell and I took Rosie and Pat out for the evening. We wined and dined them. We then took cabs all over Indianapolis to night clubs and bars until our money was entirely exhausted. When we were undisputedly broke, Rosie and Pat bought us a round trip bus ticket between Indianapolis and Camp Atterbury and gave us each two one dollar bills. This two dollars represented the total amount of spending money we had until we returned to see the girls again. The girls were relatively certain we could not get into much trouble with only two dollars to spend. On each subsequent date until our next payday, the girls would foot the bill for all entertainment. Rosie and Pat were very generous with their money, but try as we did, Dell and I never persuaded the girls to give us more than two dollars when we returned to camp. We maintained this relationship until the 589th FA Bn left Camp Atterbury in late October for the Port of Embarkation in Boston.

Not once did this unique relationship become strained. We simply enjoyed being with each other. Pat was intelligent, well organized, interesting, and a take-charge type young lady who happened to think I was "cute." At six foot two inches tall compared to her five foot six, I wasn't certain what being "cute" meant, but if that was the way she wanted to think of me, I certainly did not mind.

During the summer and early fall months we saw each other frequently, not doing much in particular, but doing everything in general. We loafed in their apartment in the morning, took bus tours, walked in the parks or went to the movies in the afternoons. At night we almost always ended up at "The Roof," or in some bar, where we could dance. Pat was such a smooth dancer she made me look good. We put on quite a show as we danced, the sexy young lady with the terrific figure and a beautiful smile, who seemed to devour her tall, slender Sergeant with her expressive bedroom eyes. We enjoyed each other totally—intellectually, socially, and physically, but we both played by the agreed upon rules, no long term commitments!

The 589th FA Bn lost its first group of trained personnel during May 1944. The Department of Army (DOA) assessed the 106th Infantry Division some 2,000 men to be sent to the European Theatre of operations as replacements. The assessment was mainly for privates and corporals, however our battalion lost a sprinkle of sergeants and officers also. This action by the Department of Army literally cut the heart out of our unit because the back-fill for these fully trained artillerymen came from untrained new recruits and "wash-outs" from various Army Air Force training schools.

The second DOA assessment came in June to replace soldiers who were casualties of the Normandy invasion and the subsequent attack into France. The June assessment rendered the 106th Infantry Division even more impotent due to the intake of additional untrained men. This fact accelerated our Unit Training program.

One such filler was Private Brown, who immediately became "Brownie" to all the members of headquarters battery. No one knew Brownie's age, but he must have been over forty. He was an architect in civilian life whose strong sense of duty caused him to lie about his age when he volunteered for army duty. Brownie was neither mentally, nor physically, suited for military service in a combat unit. He was intellectual by nature, well educated, grossly overweight, and had no sense of urgency. He was also a loner who had been patronizing bars by himself for many years. This habit is dangerous in an environment which contains many military predators. I had learned, at a tender age, there is safety in numbers. Brownie was assigned to Headquarters Battery as a radio/telephone operator. An assignment for which he was eminently over-qualified.

The only life-threatening thing that happened to a headquarters battery man while we were stationed at Camp Atterbury happened to Private Brown during one of his solo passes to Indianapolis. No one really knew what Brownie did while he was off-post because he never went to town with a friend. When you got right down to the facts, because of his advanced age, he didn't have a close friend. Scuttle-butt had it that he just went to town, sat of a bar-stool, minded his own business, got drunk, paid his tab, and managed, unaided, to get back to his bunk in the barracks.

One Saturday night Brownie did not return from his pass to Indianapolis. Captain Black, our Battery Commander, was furious. The First Sergeant came to our barracks Sunday morning, asking questions about Brownie's whereabouts. No one knew anything about him and we all started wondering. I personally thought something must have happened to him because I didn't think Brownie would "go over the hill," but no one really knew what made Brownie tick.

Monday morning the First Sergeant received a call from the Base Hospital, Wakeman General, to advise the Commanding Officer of Headquarters Battery of the 589th Field Artillery Battalion that a Private Brown had been admitted for multiple bruises, lacerations, exposure, and possible internal injuries. The word of Brownie's hospitalization spread through the battery like wildfire.

Immediately after the evening meal, several of the headquarters battery non-coms took a ride over to Wakeman General to visit with Brownie. I was one of the few allowed to enter the ward. Brownie was a mess! His facial features were distorted by swelling, cuts, and abrasions. He was heavily sedated against his obvious pain and had a plastic breathing tube inserted into his nose. Although sedated, he was able to tell us what had happened.

He had gone to a bar Saturday night, one he had frequented before, to have a few drinks before returning to camp. Apparently the bartender, or another bar patron, slipped him a "Mickey," took him into an alley, beat the hell out of him, robbed him, and of all things, stole his uniform and shoes. They, he seemed to remember more than one, left him in the alley all night, semi-nude, where he was found Sunday afternoon by an Indianapolis police officer. Since he was not coherent and had no identification, he ended up in the city jail. It was not until Monday morning the Indianapolis police suspected he might be a serviceman and notified the Camp Atterbury Military Police. The base MP's quickly provided an ambulance which transported Brownie to Wakeman General. There he identified himself and the medics notified our First Sergeant of his where-a-bouts.

Our emotions were mixed when we learned the truth. We were sorry for Brownie and mad as hell at the bartender and the bar owner. How could anyone do something like this to a nice guy like Brownie? A group of us non-coms talked about this incident for the rest of the week. As our anger grew, we decided to teach the bar owner and bartender a lesson. By Friday night, several of us in headquarters battery had formulated a plan to prevent something like this from happening again. The plan was not without personal risk, but by Friday night we didn't give a damn about the personal risk involved, we had decided to take action. We planned retribution that would be severe enough to attract attention and send a message to all the bar establishments in Indianapolis.

Eight of us left camp for Indianapolis late Saturday night, each armed with a piece of iron pipe about the length of a police baton. We drove directly to the address of the bar where Brownie was assaulted, and arrived at approximately midnight. In mass, we entered the small neighborhood bar. I moved to the telephone sitting on the end of the bar and immediately demolished it with one blow of my piece of pipe. After ripping the demolished telephone instrument from the connecting block I glanced at the bartender who looked as though he might go for a gun hidden under the bar. Quickly I moved behind the bar and thrust my iron pipe under his chin, grabbed the other end of the pipe and tightened it against the shorter man's Adam's Apple in a painful chocking hold. After that, we stood behind the bar, perfectly still, and silently watched the show.

We saw another headquarters man expertly demolish a pay telephone mounted on the wall by the Men's Room while the other six men physically encouraged the few remaining bar patrons to leave.

The bartender watched in terror as I held him in a choke hold and the other seven men started to systematically destroy his place of business. The soldiers did not miss destroying one glass, one bottle of spirits, one chair, one table, one toilet fixture, his neon sign, or a light fixtures. The only item in the bar which was spared destruction was the mirror behind the bar. We had saved this for a special purpose. We left a prominent message on the mirror for the proprietor of this bar and every other bar owner in Indianapolis. The message was: "THE 106TH INFANTRY DIVISION WAS HERE – DO NOT FUCK WITH US!"

Time was running out, we felt one of the bar patrons may have notified the police by now, but we had a more personal message to leave with the bartender. As I released my choke hold, another member of the wrecking crew made him place both hands palms down on the bar. As quick as a heart beat, one of the non-coms delivered a crushing blow, with his metal baton, to the right hand of the bartender. The effect of the blow was devastating. We then quickly left the bartender, crumpled on the floor, writhing in pain behind the bar, amid the shattered whiskey bottles and drinking glasses..

Due to my assignment, to hold and subdue the bartender, I had not yet had the opportunity to vent my anger and relieve my deep desire to destroy something. Without thinking I turned as I passed through the front door and whacked the large plate glass window of the bar with my iron pipe. I was totally unprepared for the aftermath caused by the blow. The large sheet of plate glass broke at about chest high, a majority of the sharp shards spraying into the damaged bar room from the force of the blow. However, the remaining pieces of plate glass dropped straight down from the top of the window frame, much like four or five giant guillotines, and in the process, lacerating the back of my striking hand and narrowly missing my right foot on their short, but violent, journey to self destruction on the concrete sidewalk below.

The sound of breaking glass hastened our journey to the nearby parked cars. To avoid detection as much as possible the drivers of the two vehicles took different routes back to Camp Atterbury and arrived at the main gate at different times. Neither group encountered anything unusual during their trip from town back to the base.

Circumstances surrounding this event thwarted all efforts of the Indianapolis Police Department and the Camp Atterbury Provost Marshall to determine who wrecked the bar and assaulted the bartender. The civilian police did not know where Brownie was stationed when they released him to the Military Police, and the MPs did not know where the assault upon Brownie took place. Both police agencies treated the incident with Brownie as a stupid soldier getting drunk and getting rolled. No big deal, just an everyday occurrence.

The sign we left on the mirror behind the bar did make reference to the 106th Infantry Division, but we were not dumb enough to point a finger at our battalion. After all, there are 15,000 men in a division and that is a lot of people for the police to interrogate. The wrecking crew's late departure for Indianapolis was not witnessed, and our return, well after midnight, was routine.

The retaliation was the talk of Camp Atterbury for several weeks, even Pat and Rosie knew about it, but neither police organizations ever came close to identifying the perpetrators. The damage to the bar and to the bartenders hand sent a clear message to certain portions of the Indianapolis business community. After the retaliation, soldiers wearing the shoulder insignia of the "Golden Lion" division were treated with respect in Indianapolis.

All-in-all, we accomplished our mission and in the process apparently committed the perfect crime!

† †

My eyes started giving me trouble in mid-May. By the middle of June I was suffering almost constantly from severe headaches. During one of my weekends with Pat, she told me to quit fooling around with sick call and the Battalion Medical Officer and go to the Post Hospital and get examined by an Ophthalmologist. I explained this was easier said than done. To get to the Eye, Ear, Nose, and Throat (EENT) Clinic, I had to be referred by the Battalion Medical Officer, and he thought there was nothing wrong with my eyes because I could read the chart used to check visual acuity.

Patricia was adamant. She insisted I go on sick call Monday morning and exert myself, or what ever it took, to get the Battalion Medical Officer to refer me to the Wakeman General Hospital EENT Clinic. Thank goodness, common sense prevailed when I explained I had been born cross-eyed (Strabismus) and had worn corrective glasses since I was five years old. The Medical Officer seemed amazed to hear this and asked me why the Army had not issued me corrective glasses. He seemed ever more amazed when I responded, "The Army will not issue me corrective glasses for the very same reason you are reluctant to refer me to the EENT Clinic. I can read the eye chart without glasses."

This statement on my part prompted a general discussion about my visual problems and the fact that I had been wearing my civilian glasses until I recently broke them, and had no money to buy replacement glasses. He displayed no reluctance as he prepared the inevitable Army Form necessary to get me admitted to the EENT Clinic. I never knew why he had been reluctant to refer me in the first place, but that was now immaterial. With Form-in-hand, and in Major Parker's jeep, I proceeded directly to Wakeman General Hospital. I had a splitting headache, but felt something good would happen when I got to see a real, honest-to-goodness eye doctor instead of a brand new Medical School graduate.

Wakeman General was the official name of the Base Hospital. Even though Atterbury was a Camp, not a permanent Fort, Wakeman General was a large, well equipped, permanent medical facility. At the EENT Clinic receiving desk I was logged in: Name, Rank, Army Serial Number, and Unit. The receptionist, a medical corpsman, verified I was having eye problems. He then gave me a folder containing hospital forms and directed me to the Eye Center, within the EENT Clinic.

At the Eye Center I was directed to a typical eye examination room. After a short wait, I was relieved when a mature man, probably in his middle forties, entered the room and introduced himself as Doctor Hurley. On his collar points, underneath his white medical jacket, I noticed a medical insignia and the golden oak leaf of a Major. Doctor Hurley asked me some routine questions concerning my general health and then questioned me about my specific eye problems. During this question and answer session he made notes on various forms and never looked at me. There was something detached about his approach that made me think I had been moved back to square one again.

Suddenly he pushed his rolling stool directly in front of me and said, "Sergeant, look directly at my nose with both eyes." This was impossible for me because I was cross-eyed. Some how mother nature intervenes with cross-eyed people and causes them to have what is known as single vision. In other words, I could look at the doctor's nose with either my right or left eye, but not with both eyes at the same time. This condition, single vision, caused me to change eyes back-and-forth rapidly in an effort to focus both eyes on his nose.

Doctor Hurley watched the process intently and the look on his face became almost fatherly as he watched me struggling to obey his order. He cleared his throat and finally spoke, "You can't do it can you Sergeant? You have strabismus and single vision. No wonder you are having headaches, your eyes are constantly fighting a duel with each other for control. Your right eye must be your dominant eye because it seems to be winning the struggle."

"Major Hurley, may I ask you a question?"

"Yes Sergeant you may. But up-front, they call me Doctor Hurley here. I've been a doctor much longer than I have been in the military. I would prefer you call me doctor."

"Yes sir, doctor suits me fine. Doctor Hurley, you seem to know what is wrong with my eyes, can you help me?"

"Sergeant Pierson, correcting your eye problem is a fairly straight forward procedure, You need an operation, and I have performed this procedure many times. The problem lies in Army Regulations, the army does not authorize this type operation. Theoretically, the army would not allow a person with strabismus to enter the service. You should have been classified 4-F. How did you get into the army in the first place? How did you pass the eye exam?"

"Sir, I just took off my glasses and read the eye chart hanging on the wall. Then a corporal indicated on my physical exam form that my eye sight was normal."

"That figures!"

"Doctor, if I need an operation but the army won't authorize it, where do I go from here? What do you suggest I do? My headaches are killing me! They get so bad I get dizzy and almost pass out. I don't have enough money to buy a new set of glasses, let-alone to pay for an operation in a civilian hospital. I really need help!"

"Sergeant, your condition is not rare and is relatively simple to correct. Maybe if we work together we can solve your problem. First, I will perform the operation to straighten your left eye on my own authority, but I will have to do it off the record. Second, you will have to remain in the hospital for seven days after the operation. And third, since there will be no official record of the operation, or your stay in the hospital, you will have to arrange for your Commanding Officer to carry you present for duty on his Morning Report for these seven days. Do you think you can arrange that with your Commanding Officer?"

"Doctor Hurley, I really don't know, in fact, I doubt it. Captain Black, my CO, and I don't get along very well."

"That is unfortunate Sergeant. Would it help if I called Captain Black and explained the situation to him?"

"I don't know how the Captain will react. I get along real well with the First Sergeant. Let me get some advice from him and we will go from there. If this arrangement is OK with you, I'll talk to the First Sergeant. How can I get in touch with you after we talk? Do I need to go through the Battalion Medical Officer again?"

"Sergeant Pierson, as of today you are my patient, and under my care. You don't have to come through the Battalion Medical Officer, or the EENT Clinic, to see me. Either you or Captain, what's his name, should call me direct."

"My Commanding Officer's name is Black, sir."

"Oh yes, Captain Black. I think I can convince Captain Black you have a serious eye problem and it needs correcting."

As I left the Eye Center, I was given a stronger pain killer. I took a dose immediately and later found out it was much more effective than the APC pills the Battalion Medical Officer had been giving me. By the time I parked Major Parker's jeep in front of the Headquarters Battery Orderly Room I was feeling much better. Maybe from the more potent pain killer, or maybe from feeling a real, honest-to-goodness Ophthalmologist who understood my problem could fix it. Which ever, I was grateful.

The next task was convincing the Captain to agree to Doctor Hurley's plan. While sitting in the jeep I decided to tackle the lion in his den, right away, not later. I dismounted from the jeep and a short walk brought me to the Orderly Room door. Outside, I paused momentarily, looked toward the heavens, muttered a short prayer, took a deep breath, knocked on the door, and then waited.

The Battery Clerk finally responded, "Enter!"

Upon entering the outer office of the Orderly Room, the battery clerk looked up, smiled in recognition, and asked, "What can I do for you Sergeant Pierson?"

"I'd like to talk to the First Sergeant in private."

Before the Battery Clerk could reply, the First Sergeant called from within his office and said, "Come in Pierson," and asked gruffly, "what do you want?"

I wanted to explain my situation properly and took too much time answering his question. This delay agitated the old soldier and prompted a curt statement, "Shut the damned door and make it quick. I ain't got all day!"

This display of insensitivity caused me to blurt out the entire story concerning my crossed eyes, my debilitating headaches, my troubles with the Battalion Medical Officer, my talk with Doctor Hurley, the proposed unauthorized operation, and my request to be carried "present for duty" on the daily Morning Report, when I would technically be Absent Without Leave (AWOL).

This scenario obviously intrigued the old soldier who thought he had been everywhere and seen everything. As my tale of woe started to unfold, I could see his tough demeanor soften, his body language relax, and half smiles flickering across his craggy, sun tanned face. It was almost as if the old soldier was preparing himself to become a major player in a conspiracy to right a grievous wrong.

The First Sergeant caught me unprepared. I thought I had the First Sergeant eating out of my hand. I had not anticipated check questions. This expression of doubt shook my confidence. Everything I had explained to my top non-com had been straight forward and truthful. In desperation, I finally exclaimed, "First Sergeant, I know better than to try and bull shit you. You can spot bull shit a mile away, in the dark."

"So what you are asking me to do is stick my ass in a crack and cover for you for about eight days while you plan to go AWOL. Is that a fair statement?"

"No First Sergeant, I don't want you to get in trouble trying to help me. I am asking you to help me convince Captain Black that this operation is necessary and this is the only way I can get my eye sight corrected."

"Pierson, do you really think the Captain gives a damn whether you have head aches or not?"

"There is one thing I am certain of First Sergeant! I'm certain the Captain will be pleased to know I live in constant pain. That knowledge should make him a happy man."

"Who is this doctor you talked to Pierson? Can I call him and verify what you told me is true?"

I handed the First Sergeant the note Doctor Hurley had given me and told him, "The doctor is Major Hurley. He specializes in eye surgery in civilian life. His private telephone number is on the note. You have his permission to call him any time you wish. I told Major Hurley I was going to ask you for help. The Major said if anyone doubted my story, he would talk to Captain Black personally."

The First Sergeant thought carefully as he digested the doctor's note. After a few moments he spoke into his intercom and I heard him say, "Captain, Sergeant Pierson and I would like five minutes of your time. Are you free now?"

I could not hear the Captain's answer, but the First Sergeant immediately stood up behind his desk and said, "OK Pierson, lets go. The Ole Man will see us now. Just keep your trap shut and let me do the talking."

We walked over and knocked on the Captain's door. When the First Sergeant heard the command, "Enter," he opened the door and ushered me into our Commanding Officer's office. We both approached the Captain's desk, stopped, stood at attention, and saluted.

Captain Black reared back in his high backed executives chair, looked at us sternly, returned our salute, and ordered us to "Stand at Ease!" He then addressed the First Sergeant, "What does Pierson want this time, First Sergeant?"

The First Sergeant briefly related my eye problems and Major Hurley's solution. Captain Black shook his head in disbelief and finally asked, "Do you believe this cock-and-bull story First Sergeant?"

"Yes Sir!"

"Have you personally checked it out?"

"Yes sir," the First Sergeant lied.

"Does Battalion Headquarters know Pierson will be gone for more than a week?"

The First Sergeant looked at me intently, read the look on my face, and replied, "No Sir."

"Not without check questions himself, Captain Black then addressed me, Pierson, isn't that Major Parker's jeep I saw you parking outside the Orderly Room?"

"Yes Sir."

"You sure you haven't discussed these arrangements with Major Parker or anyone else at Battalion Headquarters?"

Trying to anticipate his reaction, I replied, "Captain Black, the only persons I have confided in are my doctor, Major Hurley, and the First Sergeant. You are my Commanding Officer. You are the proper person to help me with this problem. The decision is yours. I do not plan to burden anyone else with my problems."

The Captain paused in thought, seemed to like my answer, and dismissed us by saying, "First Sergeant, handle the details, but don't let Pierson get the bit in his teeth. He has a tendency to be a little free spirited. It will be your ass if he decides to go over the hill."

The First Sergeant acknowledged his responsibility with, "Yes Sir," and I acknowledged my appreciation with, "Thank you Sir." We both saluted, did an about face, and left the lion's den.

Back in the anteroom outside the First Sergeant's office, the First Sergeant instructed me to make the necessary arrangements with Major Hurley and then advise him of the specific details. He also told me something else, "Pierson, I hope you learned something about the Ole Man today. Captain Black really is a good Commanding Officer. He proved it today! You should stop bullshitting him about how important you are to Major Parker and Colonel Kelly at Battalion Headquarters. It would make life a lot more pleasant for all of us if you Battalion Headquarters guys would stop irritating the Captain."

The operation on my eyes was something else! For reasons I could not understand, the thought of getting my eye muscles cut terrified me. Doctor Hurley told me the operation would not be particularly painful. He said he was going to use a local anesthesia because he needed to talk to me during the procedure. I knew I could handle the pain, the pain did not concern me. I was concerned that something would go wrong during the procedure that would cause me to loose the sight in my left eye.

Lying on the operating table, covered only by a sheet, a surgical nurse had placed my head on a small firm pillow and propped either side of my head with what appeared to be large and immobile sand bags. She told me, through her face mask, the restraints were to hold my head still during the procedure and warned me of the serious consequences which could occur in the event I moved my head, even slightly, during the procedure. In this rigid position, the bright lights above the operating table were shinning directly into my eyes. I complained of the intense heat and that I was going blind looking directly into the bright lights. Perspiration caused by the heat and my own anxiety was making the immaculate white sheet stick to my body. In desperation I moved one hand upward to wipe the sweat from my eyes and forehead.

The surgical nurse grabbed my forearm before it was shoulder high and forced my arm back onto the operating table. The same nurse who had sandbagged my head warned me again about the consequences of moving.

Before I knew what was happening, restraints were placed around each wrist and both hands were secured firmly against the stainless steel side of the operating table. The only concession the surgical nurse made to my obvious discomfort was to instruct another nurse to get a towel and keep the sweat from my forehead, face, and shoulders, and to "do something" to take my mind off of the operation.

When Doctor Hurley finally appeared on the scene, he did turn off the overhead lights which were shining in my eyes. He then bent over the operating table and asked how I felt. I told him quite truthfully I was ready to call the whole thing off and leave. He chuckled and said, "Sergeant you can stand the discomfort for an hour. After that you will be all fixed up and back in the ward with nothing to do for one solid week except let these lovely ladies wait on you hand and foot." Then, to no one in particular he asked, "Why don't we get started?"

The procedure started with eye drops in the left eye to block pain. Then the surgeon explained the purpose of the two devices he was beginning to attach to my head. One was to measure angles and to determine the number of degrees the left eye had to be moved to the left to make it parallel to the right eye. The second was a special clamp-like device which would hold my left eyelid away from the left eyeball while he partially lifted the left eyeball from its socket. This, he warned, would be the most unpleasant, although not painful, part of the procedure.

As doctor Hurley was explaining the necessity of removing the eyeball from the socket so he could manipulate the muscles which moved the eyeball and attached the eyeball to the socket, my imagination took over. Immediately my body stiffened and again sweat began to flow freely. This reaction was not lost on doctor Hurley who asked me what was wrong. In a gush of words, straight from the heart, I told him I was afraid I would move, or something else might happen during the operation, that would leave me blind in my left eye.

Again, the doctor assured me nothing bad would happen if I would just follow his instructions during the procedure, and resist the urge to move for just a short period of time. This assurance had no calming effect on me at all. My anxieties were in full control and the doctor finally realized it. He ordered a syringe and a mild tranquilizer. Fortunately, the medication worked quickly, and the doctor was satisfied with my reactions to his verbal instructions, but the heat of the operating room lights, combined with my somewhat suppressed anxiety, maintained a steady flow of perspiration from every pore in my body.

The procedure went smoothly until doctor Hurley reached the point where the muscles behind the left eye ball were exposed for his examination. Then he exploded, "Damn it, I see scar tissue. Sergeant, have you had this operation previously?"

"Yes sir, when I was five years old, but it was not successful."

"This is quite a surprise. Why didn't you tell me about the previous operation, Sergeant?"

It must have been the effect of the tranquilizer that made me feel comfortable with my answer, "Because you never asked me, doctor Hurley."

"Damn it Sergeant, you know what this means don't you?"

Again, feeling rather pleased with myself, I replied, "No sir, I don't have the slightest idea what this means, but I'm ready to call the whole thing off if you are."

"Sergeant, don't get smart with me! It means I will now have to operate on your right eye. I can't take a chance on a second operation on your left eye. You haven't had this operation on your right eye too, have you?"

"But Sir! My right eye is straight, it is the left eye that is crooked!"

"Does that answer mean your right eye has never been operated on?"

"Yes sir, but …"

"Don't sweat the details Sergeant, I'll just make your right eye pop-eyed."

That was not the news I wanted to hear. Anxiety suddenly overcame the medication, my body became rigid again, and I replied, "That is just great doctor Hurley! Now you're telling me I'll have two messed-up eyes instead of one. That's just what I need, two screwed-up eyes!"

At this point the surgical nurse, who was removing the clamp from my left eye lid and moving it to my right eye, sensed my anxiety was turning into anger, and immediately interjected herself between doctor and patient. "Sergeant Pierson, you are getting way out of line. Doctor Hurley is eminently qualified to perform this procedure. I can assure you, his decision to operate on your right eye is correct. I have assisted in this procedure a number of times. I have seen surgeons operate on both the straight eye and the crooked eye. Circumstances influence which eye the surgeon chooses for the procedure. If we had known your left eye had been operated on previously, we would have setup the procedure to be performed on your right eye to begin with. Just try and relax, act like a soldier, and lets get this small unpleasant experience behind us."

"But I don't understand why he wants to screw around with my straight eye."

"Sergeant, doctor Hurley is not going to screw around with your straight eye. He is going to make the right eye parallel with your left eye. It is really very simple."

"It may be simple for you because you will not be walking around with your head turned crooked for the rest of your life."

Obviously getting exasperated herself, the surgical nurse demanded, "What in the world do you mean, with my head turned crooked?"

"If doctor Hurley makes both of my eyes look to the right, I'll have to turn my head to the left to see straight ahead. That's what I mean."

This pronouncement created the first laugh of the day among the operating room personnel. The sound of their laughter made me feel better. At least I had made them aware of my specific concerns, and they thought them funny. Doctor Hurley told the surgical nurse to explain what would happen after my eyes were made parallel, and added, "He seems to understand you better than he understands me."

The surgical nurse again explained the left eyes would be made parallel to the right, but in a short period of time, mother nature would pull them back to the straight ahead position. Actually this process of nature would happen within hours after my bandages were removed.

With a blink of my eyes, indicating I understood, the procedure started again. This time on the right eye. Maybe I relaxed because my serious concerns had been addressed, maybe because the medication took effect, or maybe because a cute young nurse started gently stroking my bare stomach and thighs under the starched white surgical sheet.

During the process, I was neither fully awake or asleep, just somewhere in the fuzzy middle. My first return to reality was when a nurse began applying a lubricant to both eye lids. This was preparatory to covering each eye with a gauze-like material and the application of a holding bandage around my head to keep the gauze in place. This was to be my dark and sightless environment for the next seven days.

The trip from the operating room to the eye ward was by wheel chair. The surgical nurse was in charge of my trip to the ward, and as I sightlessly whizzed along the hallways I could not see, she told me it was OK to slowly move my head, but I must not move my eyes in any direction until the bandages were removed. Actually, in my totally blacked-out world it proved easy to avoid moving my eyes.

In the ward, I had a change of command when the surgical nurse turned me and my records over to the nurse in charge of the eye ward. My new boss, the ward nurse, was of a much different temperament than the surgical nurse. I suspected the surgical nurse had been a First Sergeant in a former life and was accustomed to ordering people around. The ward nurse was totally dedicated to her charges and gushed the milk and honey of tender compassion. Frankly, I liked the ward nurse, she obviously cared for her patients.

The temporary sightless environment proved to be both pleasant and frustrating. Pleasant because being waited upon was a nice change, and the total privacy of being sightless provided me the opportunity to "live by myself," instead of sharing my life for twenty-four hours each day with more than one hundred sweating, cursing, and sometimes obnoxious GIs. Frustrating, because I could not maintain visual contact with what was going on around me.

This sightless environment helped to hone my senses of hearing and touch. It also taught me how to navigate around fixed obstacles by retaining a picture of the ward, its beds, and the latrine in my mind. This is a valuable experience even for a sighted person. In my darkened world, I realized how much I missed my sight and decided to become more observant once my sight returned.

The first time Pat and Rosie came to visit me, I wanted to see Pat in the worst sort of way. I wanted to see her lips, her eyes, her face, in fact I wanted to see her whole trim, beautiful body. I even wanted to see the more bawdy Rosie, my "Rosie the Riveter," but of course I could not. It took time for Pat to realize I could "see" through touch. Once she realized this, she placed my hand on her shoulder so I could run my fingers through her hair, and brush her cheek and neck gently with my finger tips. This affection was not new to us, we had done much more touching than this in private, but I had a feeling the whole ward was watching. This show of affection in public made me feel a little uncomfortable.

On this first visit, Rosie totally surprising me, she decided to take the matter into her own hands. Being quite a sport, and not the least bit inhibited, Rosie moved to the side of the bed. I could more or less feel her sweep Pat aside as she took my hand in hers, and promptly placed the palm of my hand firmly upon one of her ample breasts. She held my hand there, resisting my natural impulse to remove it, and finally challenged me, "Is there any doubt in your mind who this is KIDO?"

The laughter of the nurses and the groans of jealousy from the sighted GI patients removed all doubt whether or not we were being watched. Trying to set the proper tone, and rise to the occasion, I answered Rosie's question by saying in a loud voice, "I'd know that boob anywhere. You have to be Rosie!"

Either Pat or Rosie visited me every day I was in the hospital, depending on their work schedule at the Allison plant. They also brought friends with them to visit the ward, many of which I had not met. These young females wished to do their part in the war effort, and their presence in the ward pleased both the patients and the nurses. Many friendships blossomed between the GI patients and the other "Rosie the Riveter" type girls from Allison. Some of these friendships continued until we left for overseas. I was pleased when other GIs in the ward discussed the nice girls they had met through their ole buddy, Sergeant "Killer" Pierson.

Guys from the units also came to see me. Staff Sergeant Frank Tacker, Sergeant Barney Alford, T/4 Delbert Miller, and others. Our conversations ran towards what was going on in the Battalion and what to expect when I returned. The First Sergeant, remembering Captain Black's admonition, came to see me twice. He was surprised to see both eyes bandaged and nurses waiting on me. He kept telling me I could fall into a barrel of raw manure and come out smelling like a rose. In retrospect, I think he was jealous.

In seven days, God created the earth and every creature on it! For me, on the seventh day, doctor Hurley was to create sight for me. I was led into a private examining room which was darkened. There, a nurse carefully removed my retaining head bandage. Doctor Hurley told me to keep my eyelids closed until the nurse removed the two gauze eye pads and cleaned away the seven day collection of "gook." He was right, judging from the feel of the cleaning activity, there was plenty of "gook" to remove. During this cleaning process doctor Hurley reminded me that both pupils would be fully dilated, having been exposed to no light for seven days. He instructed me to open both eyes slowly, admitting as little light as possible, and above all, if things did not appear normal at first, to please control my anxiety.

This process went smoothly in the subdued light of the darkened room. When I finally had both eyes fully open, the attending nurse stood me erect and gently guided me to the examination room door, opened it, told me to look down the corridor, and then asked me what I saw.

The brighter light of the corridor bothered me and brought tears to my eyes. As I fought away the tears, and my pupils began to return to normal, I could determine the form of a woman in civilian clothing approaching rapidly. Her pace was brisk and bouncy. With prompting from the attending nurse, she asked me to describe what I saw.

Somewhat confused and bewildered, I stammered, "I see a lady dressed in civilian clothes. She has a great shape and beautiful red, shoulder length hair. She is getting closer and is coming into focus. I can see her more clearly now, but…"

"But what, Sergeant?" the nurse demanded.

"But…she has four big, and beautiful, bouncing boobs!"

At this point doctor Hurley and the nurse broke up and howled.

✝ ✝

Summer passed quickly. The autumn cool was refreshing. My eye problems and headaches were now gone. I was grateful to Major Hurley for his help and had more respect for Captain Black because of what he had done for me. Life, without headaches, was pleasant again. My feelings for Patricia had deepened, as had her feelings for me. By mid-September we were spending more time by ourselves and less time double dating with Dell and Rosie. Our conversations and actions indicated we knew the end of our relationship was drawing near. In spite of our deep feelings for each other, we maintained there could be no commitments when I left

† †

The 589th was now spending much time on the firing range. Last minute stuff, not really unit training, but personal training a soldier should carry into combat. I easily qualified as "Expert" with the 30 caliber M-1 Carbine, my prime personal weapon. I was not surprised, but some members of the unit were. I had hunted with a rifle and shotgun for many years before I was drafted. Most of my "city slicker" friends had never fired a rifle previously and were terrified by the noise and recoil of the weapon. I prayed my life would never depend upon their pitiful marksmanship.

While the other guys were struggling to qualify with the carbine, I had an opportunity to qualify with the Model 1911, 45 caliber, semiautomatic pistol. To everyone's surprise, including my own, I qualified as "Marksman" with this weapon. Little did I know it at the time, that this was to become my primary weapon during the war. This side-arm was not an easy weapon to master and not everyone did, however, my long-gun experience provided me an advantage when firing the Model 1911 pistol.

Strange as it seems, for sheer pleasure, I enjoyed firing the 50 caliber, air cooled, machine gun. It was a Brute! I found it easy to fire in all three modes: single rounds, short bursts, and extended bursts. Our table of equipment authorized quite a few 50 caliber machine guns in Headquarters Battery, primarily for anti-aircraft defense. These weapons were normally mounted on ring-mounts installed on our 2 1/2 ton GMC trucks for anti-aircraft protection. But when mounted on tripods and fired at ground targets, they were devastating at great distances. It was fun to zero the 50 caliber at four or five hundred yards and shoot at individually deployed targets. I quickly discovered I could "snipe" with this gun, although it was not intended as a sniper's weapon. You know, one shot–one kill!

The most fun however, was firing the 50 caliber as an anti-aircraft weapon. In this mode, extended bursts were necessary in order to get enough tracers into the air to provide a visual trail to the moving target. Our targets were ground controlled drone air planes which were highly maneuverable, and piloted from the ground by expert technicians. This type practice was as close to combat as you could get. The technicians used every maneuver in the book to keep his drone intact against the skills of the gunner trying to shoot it down. In most contests, the technician and the drone won, but occasionally a gunner would get a hit and the technician would electronically pop a chute which enabled the damaged drone to float to the ground. The technician would then retrieve his drone from the firing range, assess the damage, and if necessary, trailer the drone back to camp to be repaired to fly another day. This was great sport, and as in most sporting events, wages were occasionally placed. This time by technicians, gunners, and spectators who wagered upon the outcome of these mock battles. This was the type of gunnery skill where country boys had a marked advantage over their city slicker comrades. Most country boys had hunted dove, quail, and ducks since they were old enough to shoulder a shot gun. Shooting aircraft was much like shooting wild fowl on the wing.

Experience gained while hunting fowl gave us good eye-hand coordination and the ability to estimate the angle necessary for the projectile to intersect with the intended target. The guys who wagered on me, against the drone, made more money than they lost.

Of all the firing I did at Camp Atterbury, the most intimidating I experienced involved firing direct fire, with a 105mm howitzer, at a moving target. As a member of the Fire Direction Team, I was not directly involved with the firing of howitzers. My function involved the preparation of firing data to be used by gun crews in firing indirect fire where the target was not visible from the firing battery position. However, my friend, Sergeant Barney Alford, a 105mm howitzer section chief in Battery A, arranged for me to become a member of his section for a day. The day was spent on the firing range during a familiarization exercise in direct fire techniques. This was an experience I will never forget.

The concussion from a 105mm howitzer firing a maximum powder charge,

charge 7, is a powerful force. This force can actually pull the steel helmet from the heads of the Gunner and Cannoneers. For this reason, many members of gun crews remove their helmets while engaged in this type of firing, although regulations require wearing steel helmets at all times. While acting as a Cannoneer I lost my helmet on the first round fired, much to the delight of the seasoned members of Barney's gun crew.

The noise level around a 105mm howitzer while firing is intense and while firing direct fire at relatively short ranges of five to seven hundred yards, you get a double dose of explosions. First, when the howitzer fires, and second, when the round explodes a split second later. After continuous firing for a short period of time, the Cannoneers hearing becomes so impaired that commands must be shouted at the top of your voice to make them heard and understood.

The target at the Camp Atterbury firing range consisted of an old tank hull securely mounted on a flat railroad car. This car was pulled by a specially designed low profile engine. The railroad track was laid out in a meandering route between high earthen revetments. These revetments served two purposes: first, to protect the engine and railroad car carrying the target from direct hits, and second, the revetment obscured the route of the railroad tracks, thus making it more difficult for the gunners to anticipate the future direction of the moving target. This range was well laid out and presented a challenge to the gunners.

Near the conclusion of the hot and noisy day, the Battery Executive Officer allowed me to act as gunner, not on a moving target, but using a stationary tank hull located deeper in the firing range. I removed my steel helmet, took the gunners seat, and Sergeant Alford asked me to estimate the range to the tank hull. I estimated the range to be 800 yards. Barney put his field glasses to his eyes and said my estimate was too short, and advised me to set my range to 900 yards. I increased the elevation slightly, checked the level on the gun sight, set the cross hairs of the sight directly on the tank hull, and gave the command to fire. The effect was clearly visible in the gun sight.. The tank hull actually twitched from the physical impact of the high velocity 105mm projectile. Next we saw the orange-red glare and dark black smoke of the exploding shell. This explosion was instantaneously followed by a rising cloud of light gray dust pierced by flying tank parts. We then witnessed the violent rocking motion of the tank itself, quivering like some gigantic, prehistoric animal writhing in its death throes.

As the Cannoneers were gathering spent brass and ammunition crates after the exercise, the Executive Officer strolled over and congratulated me on my good shooting. He added jokingly, "Sergeant Pierson, if you would like to change jobs, I can work out something for you in our firing battery."

Without even having to think I replied, "Thanks, but no thanks Lieutenant. It was lots of fun, but Major Parker needs me in the Fire Direction Center."

7
Last Furlough Home

In late September 1944 rumors started circulating that the 106th Infantry Division was going overseas. Some of the rumors were unnerving. Here we sat, almost dead center in the middle of the United States, we could be shipped West just as easily as we could be shipped East. No one wanted to go into combat, but for me, if I had to go somewhere, I wanted to go to Europe. Nothing about the Pacific Theatre appealed to me at all.

These rumors started me thinking about getting home once more before departing for overseas. By this time I had learned enough about warfare to realize there was a possibility I would never see my friends or home again. Strangely enough, the thought of death did not upset me as much as the possibility of becoming severely wounded, to the point of being totally disabled for life. The first step in getting home, of course, was to find out how much furlough time I had accumulated.

The Battalion personnel section advised me I had accumulated only five furlough days. There was no way I could get from Indianapolis to Cocoa, Florida to visit friends, travel to Jesup, Georgia, where mother now lived with her sister, and get back to Camp Atterbury in five days.

Disappointed, and about to forget the whole thing, I decided to talk to the

First Sergeant. He agreed I should try to go home before we went overseas, because in his opinion, we would be gone a long time. He explained it was possible to tack a three day pass on the end of my five furlough days, but he said the Captain was against authorizing three day passes this way. Since I had nothing to loose, I continued my tale of woe, hoping the First Sergeant would give me the three day pass anyway. The First Sergeant, for all his rough ways, was a good man and finally called the Battery Clerk into the conversation. This was a good move for me. The Battery Clerk had a buddy in the Air Corps stationed near the huge Allison plant who was a dispatcher for incoming and outgoing cargo planes. The Battery Clerk called his Air Corps buddy to find out if it was possible for me to hitch a ride in a military plane going to Florida. After his conversation with the Air Corps dispatcher, the Battery Clerk called Battalion Personnel and asked them to cut orders for a five day furlough, destination Cocoa, Florida, and authorize military air transportation if available. He gave them the beginning date of the furlough, which coincided with a Military Air Transport plane's departure date from the Allison plant. The Clerk advised the First Sergeant he would get Sergeant Pierson's furlough papers and combine them with a "tacked on" three day pass the First Sergeant would have to sign, thus giving Sergeant Pierson eight days to get to Florida and return.

The First Sergeant smiled, nodded, and then asked smugly, "Well Pierson, is there anything else I can do for you while you are here?"

As I left the Orderly Room, I realized I had just learned an important lesson. Almost anything is possible in the armed forces if you know the right people and the right procedures. These arrangements also set up a journey I will never forget.

Bright and early on departure day, I checked into the flight shack at Allison and located the Airman who was the Battery Clerk's buddy. He was a pleasant young man who said he was expecting me. After our initial amenities, he told me I would be flying in a Military Air Transport Service twin-engine C-47. Flight time was approaching swiftly, and I had to sign a receipt for the parachute he was required to issue me. This news caught me by surprise because I had never flown military before, but I gladly signed the receipt and the Airman passed a large parachute pack across the counter. He then reminded me I would have to turn in the parachute pack to him when I returned.

A waiting jeep carried me, my duffel bag, and the newly issued parachute to the waiting C-47. When the jeep arrived, I met the pilot, a young Second Lieutenant, who was on the tarmac making an exterior inspection of the beat-up looking cargo aircraft. When I saluted and introduced myself, the Lieutenant did not return my salute and told me to get my gear aboard because we were about to depart. As I was throwing my two pieces of gear on board, the co-pilot stuck his head out of an open cockpit window and asked of it was time to wind-up the 'wind mills.' When the pilot nodded yes, I heard him mutter to himself, "I hope this crate can make the trip all the way to Miami." That was my first inkling of our destination, and the possibility that we might not get there.

The interior of the cargo plane was much different than I had visualized. Instead of empty space, equipped with cargo tie-downs imbedded in the floor, the aircraft contained litters, two high, installed along each side of the fuselage. My surprise must have been evident to the Staff Sergeant, a medical technician, who approached on the steeply slanted floor. He grinned with a friendly expression and introduced himself as Gene Evans, as we shook hands. Staff Sergeant Evans explained this particular C-47 cargo carrier had been refitted as a medical evacuation plane. He said we would have to sit, or lie down, on a litter during the flight as no seats were available. He indicated he was occupying the lower litter next to the cockpit door, on the port side of the aircraft. With a wave of his arm, Staff Sergeant Evans indicated I should take the corresponding litter across the isle on the starboard side.

He continues, "Sergeant Pierson, we are the only passengers on the plane. The trip is scheduled to be non-stop, but who knows what will happen. This is my third trip with these two Lieutenants. They are good pilots, but they are young and not experienced in cross-country navigation. They like to fly at low altitudes so they can read city names on water towers, and follow main highways when they get lost."

"When they get lost?"

"Oh yea, they get lost very often. When they find out they are lost, they make up excuses to land to get something repaired on the aircraft. While they are on the ground, this gives them a chance to get more flight instructions. This makes a trip with them quite interesting. The reason I suggest you use a lower litter is because flying so low, these flights get pretty rough. If you get thrown out of the litter while you are asleep, you don't have as far to fall."

Following his instructions I stowed my luggage under the litter and Staff Sergeant Evans laughed when he realized one piece of my luggage was a parachute. When I asked what was so funny, he told me, "The parachute. The Air Corps makes you sign for a parachute that probably wouldn't work if you had to use it, but the Air Corps does not issue a chute to anyone else on the plane, and that includes the two pilots, medical technicians, nurses, and the plane load of patients being evacuated."

"That is a strange regulation. What are you folks supposed to do if an engine quits, or a wing falls off?"

"I guess the Air Corps wants us to go down with the plane. You know, 'live in fame, or go down in flames,' or something like that."

This policy struck me as being odd, but not necessarily funny. As I was about to say something, the aircraft shuddered, the two engines sputtered, blue-gray smoke boiled from the oil stained exhaust pipes, the radial engines caught and revved up, and the C-47 began to move. Gene Evans yelled at me to sit on the edge of my litter and explained we had a long taxi ride across the airport before we reached the end of the runway for takeoff. The C-47 seemed to be equipped with square wheels. We bounced slowly along the taxi strip to a rhythmical Ka-thump, Ka-thump, Ka-thump. We hadn't even left the ground yet, and the ride was already getting rough.

At the end of the taxi-way the aircraft did a quick pirouette, a 90 degree turn to the right, and abruptly stopped with tortured brake-drums squealing like demons. I found myself clawing at litter handles and suspension chains in an effort to avoid being thrown from the canvas litter onto the hard aluminum cabin floor.

Staff Sergeant Evans, who was watching my frantic efforts to remain on the litter, yelled above the screeching of the tormented brakes and deafening roar of the aircraft engines, "Hang on Sergeant, you ain't seen nothing yet!"

The pilot held the aircraft at the end of the runway, the two radial engines pulsing and throbbing, the wheel brakes groaning against the pull of the two large propellers, and the body of the plane shivering in anticipation of becoming airborne. Finally, the control tower gave permission for take off, much to the relief of the groaning brakes, when the pilot ceased the tug-of-war between the brakes and propellers. The C-47 started to roll again, Ka-thump, Ka-thump, Ka-thump. As the plane gained momentum, the tail gradually lifted from the ground until the floor of the cabin was more-or-less level with the ground. Lying on my side, I could look out the port side windows and see runway markers flashing past. As airspeed increased, the plane became lighter on the runway and the Ka-thump, Ka-thump of the tires became less prominent. However, the plane seemed to be still on the ground, in effect, taxing at a very high rate of speed. I sensed the end of the runway must be near, but we were not airborne yet!

Questions, unpleasant questions, came to mind. Did the young pilot know how to fly? Had he and the co-pilot gone to sleep? How much airspeed do we need to get a C-47 off the ground? As these unanswered questions raced through my mind, I saw the end of the runway pass beneath the port wing and simultaneously felt two sharp impacts jar the C-47. Had we had hit something at the end of the runway? I visualized my grizzly death – burned to death in a firry crash, incinerated inside the plane with three total strangers. This is not the way I had planned to die, but at least I would go quickly, and in a blaze of glory. My mind was wandering as my body tensed for the crash. I actually started humming the Air Corps Song and remembered the words, 'We will fight in fame, or go down in flame, for nothing can stop the Army Air Corps.'

Lying there on the litter and waiting for my last moment on earth, I glanced out the port windows again and observed the ground slowly dropping away as the plane gradually gained altitude. Then it dawned on me, the jolts I had felt a few moments ago were actually caused by the heavy retractable landing gear as it seated itself into the bowels of the aircraft.

Only then did I appreciate he faultless takeoff and the gentle assent of the aircraft. Although the two pilots looked like they should still be in high school, the pilot had a beautiful feel with the controls. Now, more relaxed, I glanced at Staff Sergeant Evans. He was stretched full length on his litter and already sound asleep. Since there was nothing for me to do except listen to the steady drone of the aircraft engines, I decided to take a nap myself.

The heavy hand on my shoulder, combined with the lurching of the aircraft woke me with a start. Gene Evans was holding onto the litter above me with one hand while he shook my shoulder with the other. He was not smiling as he told me we would encounter some pretty rough turbulence shortly, and I had better sit up and stay awake so I could hang onto something stable. My mind, still muddled with sleep, could not seem to grasp the severity of the situation. I finally got my mind functioning and asked, "What's up?"

"Sergeant Pierson, what's up is this—you are going to experience a real rough ride in this old bucket of bolts. When the Air Corps converted this C-47 from a cargo carrier to a medical evacuation configuration, they removed some of the fuselage reinforcements to make space to hang litters. The fuselage is now much more flexible than it was originally. If you look closely, you can see light shining through empty rivet holes. These holes in the outer skin of the aircraft were not filled during the conversion process.

Sergeant Evans was correct. A close visual inspection from where I sat revealed glimpses of sunlight mixed with blue sky were plainly visible through the many open rivet holes. Gene Evans continued, "When we fly through 'the weather' ahead, pray that we do not fly through rain. This aircraft leaks like a sieve in the rain."

These dramatic statements took me by surprise. I had no experience with aircraft and had a naive conception that for man to fly an airplane, the airplane would be in perfect condition before it left the ground. To make his point about the weather ahead, Staff Sergeant Evans motioned for me to follow him as he made his way forward in the cabin, moving toward the small door located at the rear of the cockpit.

There was not enough room in the cockpit area for four people. Gene Evans squeezed into the small space between the pilot and co-pilot, while I got my head and shoulders into a position to see and hear what was going on. I also had an excellent view through the windshield and could look through both side windows of the cockpit. The weather I saw in front of us was rather grim. Nothing in sight but huge gray-black thunderheads billowing high into a partially overcast sky. Both radial engines were clearly visible and uncomfortably close to the cockpit. They were mounted on the forward portion of the aircraft's single wing and slightly behind the two pilots. Of course the propeller shafts protruded in front of the engine nacelles, placing the whirling propellers in a position to decapitate occupants of the cockpit in the event a propeller came loose from it's shaft. Not a pleasant thought, although it did not seem to concern anyone but me.

The almost childlike pilot turned his head, and with a grin that spread from ear to ear, advised us, "I can't fly over that front and I can't fly around it, so I guess we will just have to fly through it." As an afterthought he said, "We'll hit it at about six thousand feet, I hope the ole crate makes it through. This should be fun." Without paying anymore attention to his two passengers the pilot started talking to his co-pilot and asked him to radio for the current weather advisory and to determine how deep the squall-line was in the direction we were now flying.

Both Gene Evans and I stayed in the cockpit area to receive the news. The news was, we had almost two hundred miles of bad weather in front of us and the prevailing winds associated with this front quartered against our line of flight. The co-pilot estimated we would be lucks to average 120 miles per hour in ground speed against this wind. This information translated to about one and one-half hours of tough flying. Both pilots seemed to be unconcerned, but the pilot instructed Staff Sergeant Evans to break out the 'barf-bags' in case someone got air sick.

Two things bothered me initially as we approached the clearly defined front. First, I could see vivid flashes of "zigzag" lightening in the distance, and second, the wings of the flexible C-47 were beginning to flap up and down, much like a huge bird in flight. I first asked about the anticipated violence in the forth coming turbulence. The co-pilot turned in his seat and told me, "Vertical assents and descents of several hundred feet are very common in this type of weather. This aircraft is designed to take that kind of beating, but sometimes it is tough on occupants. Particularly to occupants who are not strapped down, because a violent decent can slam them against the cabin roof."

A second question addressed my concern about lightening strikes on the all metal plane. The pilot fielded this question rather clinically, "Since the aircraft is not grounded, it does not attract lightening strikes like trees or buildings on the ground. Occasionally however, an aircraft in flight is struck by lightening. These mid-air strikes can produce problems of varying degrees, or in many instances, produce no problems at all."

"Please be a little more specific about the problems a lightening strike can cause, Lieutenant."

"Sergeant, I don't want to alarm you, but a strike can over-heat and knock-out electrical circuits, it can blow fuzzes, and in some instances, a strike can start a fire, either electrical or fuel. I would be less than honest if I tried to tell you a lightening strike would not be serious. That is why I will try to fly around lightening centers when I can."

By now movement of the wings had become very pronounced because we were entering the western edge of the squall line. The pilot told the co-pilot to help him with the manual controls which were now fighting the pilot's hands and arms. He simply dismissed us by telling Gene Evans to take me to the cabin and strap me to the litter because he was going to be busy for a while and did not want to be concerned with his passengers. One thing that still bothered me was the fact the two young Lieutenants seemed to be enjoying the challenge ahead, whereas I thought the adventure could end in tragedy at any moment.

Strange as it seems, lying in the now darkened interior of the aircraft and strapped to the litter, I became more calm and adjusted to the sudden movements of the C-47. Since my fate was in the hands of the 'two young warriors' in the cockpit there was nothing left for me to do but sleep. This I did – the mark of a well trained soldier.

When Staff Sergeant Evans awakened me, the aircraft was relatively stable and he was laughing. "Sergeant Pierson, this is funny, but our officer corps wants to see you in the cockpit. They have problems."

"Sergeant Evans, I don't know anything about flying a C-47, how can I help them with their problems."

"Just un-strap yourself and go to the cockpit, you'll find out."

The cockpit was a mess. It looked like someone had squirted a garden hose into the cockpit and let it run for several minutes. The pilots were soaking wet. The seats, the floor, and the instrument panels were all wet, and the co-pilot was trying to unfold soggy maps that were tearing freely each time he handled them. I could not believe my eyes, they looked like kids playing in a mud puddle. To attract their attention, I asked, "Do you gentlemen wish to see me?"

The pilot glanced over his shoulder with a sheepish look on his face and answered my question. "Yes Sergeant, we do wish to talk with you. You are from Florida are you not?"

"Yes sir, my home town is Cocoa, Florida."

"Sergeant, where in Florida is Cocoa located?"

This line of questioning did not seem relevant to our current situation, but never-the-less, I responded, "Cocoa is located on the east coast of Florida, almost midway between Jacksonville and Miami."

"Thank you Sergeant. You possibly do not realize it, but the front, the one we just passed through, caused us some minor problems. We experienced heavy rain squalls, and some precipitation made its way into the cockpit. This precipitation has ruined our navigation maps. In the process, the water seems to have shorted-out our radio. The prevailing winds accompanying the front have forced us from our intended flight path and we are having some difficulty in determining our present location."

Confronting me with these problems, I thought, *Why Me Oh Lord?*" but I bit my tongue and said, "I understand Lieutenant. What would you like to discuss with me?"

"Hypothetically Sergeant, if you were the aircraft commander, how would you get to Miami from here?"

The answer was so simple, I just blurted out, "I would just fly on an easterly heading until I reached the coast. Then I would do a right face and follow the coastline south until I reached Miami."

Back in the cabin, Gene Evans was actually laughing as I returned from the cockpit. He asked me if I had passed the quiz on how to reach Miami? I told him it seemed pretty simple to me if you knew anything about the geography of the United States. He agreed, but said it made them feel better hearing this from me, since I was a resident of Florida.

The whole incident puzzled me. Why couldn't two pilots, trained in navigation, solve a simple dead-reckoning navigation problem without consulting with an artillery trained non-commissioned officer? I decided to forget the whole matter and try to get a little more sack-time, not realizing there was more excitement yet to come.

† †

My next nap was peaceful, but brief. Gene Evans was almost apologetic when he awakened me. "Sorry Sergeant Pierson, they want to see you in the cockpit again."

Still groggy, I nodded my head and asked, "What do they want now?"

Evans shook his head and muttered, "They can't figure out where they are supposed to land when we get to Miami."

The co-pilot was gingerly trying to unfold an extremely wet map when I stuck my head into the cockpit area. He immediately asked me, "Sergeant, do you know anything about Miami?"

"A little bit Lieutenant. What do you need to know?"

"Our orders are to land at the airstrip near Coral Gables, but I can't seem to find the right map. It looks like there are about three airports in the Miami area, but I can't determine which one is in Coral Gables."

"Lieutenant, I don't know whether I can help you or not. All I know about Coral Gables is that it is located west of Miami."

"OK Sergeant, thanks, that will help a little."

While in the cockpit I was surprised to see the weather had turned clear, the air over the ocean was smooth, and I was delighted to see the wings of the C-47 were no longer flapping up and down. We were cruising about 160 miles per hour, and rapidly closing on the city of Miami. My thoughts were cheerful as I anticipated a good time on my furlough in Cocoa. My only real concern was how I could get from Miami back up the east coast to Cocoa. In Miami, I would be about three hundred miles from home.

Back in the cabin, Evans and I discussed my transportation problem. He was very helpful. He suggested I grab my luggage and beat it over to the Operations Office as soon as we landed. He thought I might be able to hitch a ride on some type military plane headed north. Evans also said he thought he could get the pilot to put in a good word for me in the Operations Shack, but I quickly said, "Thanks, but no thanks! I think I can do better without the Lieutenant's help."

Gene Evans broke off the conversation as the C-47 slowly dropped its starboard wing in a graceful right-hand turn and started the gentle decent toward Miami. Gene made a quick trip to the cockpit, returned, started strapping himself to his litter, and suggested I do the same. It was obvious, even to me, we would be landing soon. Evans stated the pilot had spotted a long landing strip west of Miami, and was going to set the aircraft down there.

This matter-of-fact statement prompted me to ask a fairly simple question, "Have they checked with the tower to get their landing instructions?"

Staff Sergeant Evans reminded me, "They can't call the tower, the radio is still on the blink. Guess it hasn't dried out yet. Don't worry, they will make it. I've flown with this pair before, they always come out of a situation smelling like a rose. The good Lord takes care of drunks, pilots, and Second Johns."

The view of Miami was beautiful as we passed over the bay and city. The large airstrip was clearly visible as the C-47 banked into a northeast heading preparatory to landing. Below, huge military aircraft covered the tarmac and parking areas. The runway was not in use, and the airspace over the runway was clear of aircraft.

Deftly the pilot made contact with the runway and smoothly brought the C-47 to a halt, using no more than one half the length of the runway. I had to admit, the 'young warrior' was a good pilot. He revved the radical engines, moved the C-47 onto an adjacent taxi strip and started his ground trip toward a group of buildings at the end of the taxi strip. As we gained speed on the taxi strip, strange things began to happen.

Racing toward us on the taxi strip was a column of several speeding jeeps. Each jeep contained four men, the driver, two Military Policemen armed with sub-machine guns held at 'the ready,' and most sinister of all, the fourth occupant was manning an air-cooled 30 caliber machine gun, with cartridge case attached, mounted on a pedestal attached to the rear of the jeep. A Military Police officer riding in the lead jeep was frantically waving his arms in a highly agitated manner, while an enlisted man in the rear of the jeep kept us covered with his machine gun. The scene became a little unnerving when the lead jeep skidded to a stop and blocked the taxi strip. This action caused our pilot to cut power to both engines and slam on brakes to avoid a collision with the jeep. When the C-47 finally came to a stop, it was dangerously close to the muzzle of the lead jeep's 30 caliber machine gun which was trained directly at the 'fifty mission crush hat' perched jauntily on the pilot's head.

The non-pulsed pilot opened his side window as Evans and I reached the cockpit. Before the pilot could speak we heard the outraged Military Police officer screaming over the noise of the still running aircraft engines, "You can't land that pile of Crap on this runway. Who in the Hell do you think you are?"

The pilot yelled back, "This is a Medical Evacuation flight. We have orders to land here."

"Like Hell you do! This is a Strategic Air Command Base and you can't land that lousy C-47 here!"

"But our orders are to pick up hospitalized military personnel at Coral Gables. This is Coral Gables isn't it?"

"Well, technically you could call this Coral Gables, but it certainly is not a medical evacuation facility. This is a SAC facility, and you can't land here."

The 'young warrior' pilot was also beginning to get testy himself and his changing attitude showed clearly in his response, "Damn it, don't tell me I can't land here, I already have! Stop telling me I can't do something I have already done!"

From the jeep came a slightly moderated answer, "I mean you can't land here legally. Why didn't you call the tower and get instructions?"

"That's simple, we didn't call the tower because our radio doesn't work."

By now the MP officer was beginning to settle down and saw some humor in the situation. He sat down in the jeep, took the jeep radio mike in his hand and started talking to an unknown person. When he replaced the mike to its holder, he yelled up to the pilot again, "I just talked to operations and informed them I had a lost medical evacuation plane out here on the taxi strip. They advised me what we should do. I am to escort you to the end of the runway and head you northeast for take off. There, the operations tower will give you a visible green light when you are cleared for take off. You are to level off at two thousand feet and turn due west. About ten miles in front of the aircraft you will see a much shorter runway. Circle that runway, make a northeasterly approach and land there. They are expecting you. If you understand your instructions nod your head in the affirmative."

The pilot nodded his head in the affirmative and closed his side window. The lead jeep turned around sharply, displaying a large "FOLLOW ME" sign mounted on its rear bumper, and headed briskly down the taxi strip with the large twin props of the C-47 nipping angrily at the "FOLLOW ME" sign.

Both the pilot and the co-pilot seemed pleased with the military escort which led us majestically down the taxi strip toward the take off area. When we received the green light from the operations tower, the pilot saluted 'Thanks' to the MP officer, set his brakes, and revved up his engines. As the pilot released the brakes, the C-47 shuddered slightly, and as it started to roll the MP officer returned the salute, and the machine gunner in the rear of the jeep waved goodbye.

The remaining ten miles of our long journey proved uneventful.

The Medical Evacuation facility was more civilian oriented than military. The four of us checked in with the operations office. The two pilots started reporting deficiencies in the aircraft to be corrected, arranging to get the aircraft serviced, and developing plans for their return flight. Staff Sergeant Evans was busy checking with the medical facility to find out when the patients were to be delivered to the airport to be loaded aboard the aircraft. I decided to take Evans' advice and introduced myself to a very polite civilian who didn't seem to be too busy. We discussed my problem about getting transportation to Cocoa. He pondered a moment and then got on the telephone. After talking for a few minutes, he excused himself from his phone conversation and asked me if a flight to the Banana River Naval Air Station would be OK. I advised him such a flight would be perfect and he returned to his telephone call.

Two hours later, I had loaded my gear and was seated in the co-pilots seat of a small twin-engine Navy Beachcraft. The pilot, a Navy Lieutenant Junior Grade, told me to relax, he had two scheduled stops to make before reaching the Banana River NAS. He was flying a courier route and had pick-ups and deliveries to make en-route. He admitted Banana River was not a scheduled stop on this particular trip, but, "What the Hello," I had orders authorizing military air travel and that was good enough for him. During the flight the JG confided he had the 'hots' for a cute Navy nurse stationed at the Banana River NAS. With a knowing wink, he explained how often his aircraft developed trouble in the vicinity of the Banana River NAS, forcing him to land there to get the trouble corrected.

† †

Maybe I expected too much, but my furlough in Cocoa was a dud! The young lady I wanted to see was away at college and could not get home while I was there. I did enjoy visiting with the friends I formerly worked with at the NAS before I was drafted. Not much had changed in the Public Works Department since my departure. The only change in the Drafting room was the lady who took my job when I left. She was the only person who was not happy to see me.

My main problem in Cocoa was caused by the lack of an automobile. The first two days, I borrowed a taxicab from the father of a friend of mine who owned the local cab company. This was a nice arrangement, however, on the second day he apologized and asked me to return his vehicle. Then the mother of my girl friend felt sorry for me and loaned me her new Lincoln Zephyr for the remainder of my furlough. The Lincoln, I called it "Old Abe," was a large automobile, powered by a V-12 engine, and was a gas-guzzler. When the gas gage dropped to one-fourth full, I would drive to the NAS and park in the Public Works parking lot. While having coffee with the guys I would comment on my lack of fuel. Invariably, one of the gang would ask for my car keys. He would then leave the group and return a few minutes later and throw the key ring back to me. No words were ever spoken, only a wink or a nod, but when I left the base, "Ole Abe" would be full of gasoline. One time I tried to thank my benefactor for his help. The response I received was a shrug of the shoulders and the response, "What the Hell."

For a guy just bumming around, the time passed quickly, however the uncertainty of how I would get back to Camp Atterbury was always on my mind. As it turned out, the return trip was very interesting. The first leg was easy to arrange, it was another Navy courier aircraft which took me from the Banana River NAS to the NAS in Brunswick, Georgia. During the short hop to Brunswick, the pilot, this time a Navy Lieutenant, proved very friendly and was interested in my experiences as a civilian employee at Banana River. I told him friends at Banana River had arranged for me to fly from Brunswick to the Great Lakes NAS, outside of Chicago. He said I must have good friends at Banana River, and of course, I told him they were the greatest. He was very sincere when he looked me in the eyes and said, "What the Hell," and then added, "That's what good friends are for."

The leg of my journey to the Great Lakes NAS was not very comfortable. This long flight was in a single-engine, two-place, Navy Torpedo Bomber. The pilot was a rather 'up-tight' Navy Lieutenant JG, who was on a cross-country training flight, and was not sure it was proper to have an Army Sergeant as a passenger. Thank goodness the Operations Officer at Brunswick outranked him by one-half stripe and finally convinced the pilot that my Army orders authorizing military air transportation were just as binding on the Navy as they were on the Army Air Corps. Reluctantly, the pilot said, "What the Hell," and took me to his Torpedo Bomber on the tarmac. There he instructed me how to wear my parachute and how to communicate with him on the intercom system. By now, I had learned to appreciate the Navy phrase, "What the Hell," it seemed appropriate for all occasions.

The ride in the Torpedo Bomber was an entirely new experience for me. The aircraft was deceptively large for a single-engine, two-place plane, but after all, the aircraft had to accommodate a very large torpedo. It was heavily armored, and designed for low-level flying, as torpedoes are normally released close to the surface of the water during an attack upon a target ship. While durable, the aircraft seemed to be unstable because it was constantly moving up and down, and/or side to side. Perhaps this movement was due to over-correction by an inexperienced pilot, or caused by a flaw in the design of the aircraft. Whatever the cause, I was eternally grateful that I was a non-commissioned officer in the Field Artillery, and not the pilot of a Navy Torpedo Bomber.

It was a relief to remove myself from the rear seat of the bomber and to separate myself from the noise of the powerful engine when we reached our destination. The Navy JG was still 'up-tight' and paid me no attention as he reported in to the Operations office. This suited me fine because I had made up my mind I would never fly in a Torpedo Bomber again, even if it meant I would be AWOL. I would rather take my chances with a courts martial than to ride in one of those things again. I hate to admit it, but I felt a little sorry for the 'up-tight' Naval officer.

My good luck held at the Great Lakes NAS! I was able to arrange a flight on Military Air Transport Service (MATS) to Indianapolis. This C-47 was arranged to transport both cargo and passengers, thus had a few seats to accommodate passengers. With my orders I was lucks enough to rate a seat. In the Operations shack, an Army Air Corps First Lieutenant, told me he was not scheduled to stop in Indianapolis, but "What the Hell," I had orders, so he would modify his flight plan. There was that phrase again. I had come to love those words!

The entire trip from Cocoa to Indianapolis went so smoothly I actually arrived in Indianapolis one day early. I immediately turned in the parachute which had been my constant traveling companion and placed the receipt safely in my wallet. Relieved of this burden I left the Operations Shack and rode public transportation directly from the airfield to Pat's apartment in Indianapolis. Fortunately Patricia was at home when I arrived. She was so glad to see me she called her shift supervisor at Allison and reported out sick. It only took one night and one day with Pat to remind me how much I had missed her. We were good for each other and seemed to provide each other the normal day-to-day relationship the war had taken from our lives. It was a wonderful feeling, too bad the feeling could not be permanent.

The night my three day pass ended, Pat went with me to the bus stop where I normally caught the bus back to camp. We both knew I would be going overseas soon and I did not want to leave her that night. However, at her urging, and the urging of the impatient bus driver, I finally boarded the waiting bus. Feeling sorry for myself, I rode to camp all alone with my thoughts, even though the bus was jammed full with drunk and boisterous soldiers.

The walk from the bus stop in camp to the Headquarters Battery Orderly Room was short. I entered the orderly room without knocking. The Charge of Quarters (CQ), a surprised Corporal, looked up from his comic book and exclaimed, "Hi Sergeant Pierson! How was the furlough? Gee, it's 2355 hours, you still have five minutes of furlough time left."

"Yea, I timed it pretty good. Anything happen while I was gone?"

"Not much Sarge. Just the same old stuff. Oh, I almost forgot, the Battalion is starting to turn-in all the heavy equipment. You know, trucks, howitzers, and that kind of stuff."

"Why?"

"Smart money says we will ship out in about a week."

"Does smart money say where we are going?"

"I have a friend at Division Headquarters. He says we are headed for Europe."

"I hope your friend is right. I don't want to go to the Pacific. If I had my 'druthers,' I'd 'druther' stay right here. Sounds like tomorrow will be a busy day. Guess I'd better turn in."

"I think you are right Sarge, see you in the morning at chow."

"Yea, I'll see you at chow. Say, don't forget to change my duty status from 'Three Day Pass' to 'Present for Duty' on the morning report."

"Got you covered Sarge. Good night."

8

Port of Embarkation

On October 9-10, 1944, approximately 15,000 men of the 106th Infantry Division and their personal equipment, spent two days on troop trains being transported from Camp Atterbury, Indiana to Camp Miles Standish, Massachusetts. Along with other units in the 106th Infantry Division, the men of the 589th Field Artillery Battalion were ensconced within the cramped quarters of one of the troop trains. Our Battery Commander, Captain Black, told us as we boarded the train, "This two-day trip will be damned tough."

He was right! If you have never ridden in a troop train, you will not be able to comprehend the crowding, the discomfort, and the tedium involved. Let me try to explain.

The enlisted men of the 589th FA Bn were assigned seats in old fashioned day coaches, most of which were not equipped with toilet facilities. Of course the few passenger cars which were equipped with toilets could not accommodate the needs of all the troops. The army approach to this problem was to assign officers to the toilet equipped cars, and to restrict these few toilets for deification purposes only. The need to urinate was accomplished by the train pulling onto a spur track and halting momentarily, in what the army delicately referred to as a 'piss stop.'

This practice resulted in a mass exodus of men from the train each time it ground to a stop, and produced the impressive sight of hundreds of men, standing in a long line on the railroad ties, heads bowed as though in prayer, generating simultaneous arches of yellow liquid which sparkled magnificently in the bright autumn sunlight. This ritual, which occurred several times a day and into the night, reminds me of some pagan rite where all the young warriors of the village offered their holy water to the 'Bladder God.' It was a sight I had not seen since our truck convoy trip from Fort Jackson, South Carolina to the Tennessee maneuver area.

If an acute need to urinate developed while the train was in motion, the only way a GI could relieve himself was to make his way to the rear platform of his crowded coach and stand on the outdoor platform facing the rear of the train. Then with one hand, hold on for dear life against the erratic swaying of the coach, while unzipping his pants with the other. After stretching his penis to maximum length, and closing his mouth and eyes, he could let the liquid flow. Turbulence between the coaches turned the released liquid into a fine mist, thereby covering the uniform and face of the GI relieving himself with the released liquid.

This is fact, not fiction! I know, because I had to relieve myself on the moving train during the first night of this horrible journey.

The seating arrangement in the coaches was miserable! The coaches were obviously designed for commuters or for very short journeys. Two rows of seats lined each side of a narrow isle that ran the entire length of the coach. The seats were not generous and the fact that a man was assigned to each single seat, along with his duffel and musette bags compounded the problem. The only feature of the coaches which worked in our favor was the fact that the backs of the seats could be moved back and forth thereby creating a space for two or four men and their equipment. Of course the designer of the movable backs had in mind the accommodation of commuters, who frequently wished to sit face-to-face with other passengers to play cards, or engage in conversation during their commute to or from work.

After spending most of the first day sitting on and holding my personal baggage, I asked my seat mate Dell Miller to help find a more comfortable seating arrangement. During a trial and error period, we persuaded the two soldiers in front of us to reverse the backs of their seats. With the four seats facing each other we discovered we had created more usable space than we had with all seats facing in the same direction. This new arrangement allowed us to place the four duffle bags on the floor between the seats, thus creating a comfortable sleeping surface using the duffle bags and the four passenger seats of the coach. Musette bags were used as pillows and four of us were able to lie on this pallet, head to foot, in relative comfort.

To sit and read comic books, or play cards, we merely sat cross-legged on the pallet, resting our backs upon the cushioned seat backs. I am reminded of early advice given to me by my First Sergeant, "Don't never do nothing standing up that you can do sitting down. And, don't never do nothing sitting down you can do lying down." I took my First Sergeant's advice and spent most of the trip to Camp Miles Standish in the prone position.

Fortunately, this arrangement became standard in our car before nightfall on the first day. It accomplished two things. First, it cleared the center isle and made movement within the car easier, and second, it provided an environment which encouraged recreation. It was common to see Headquarters Battery soldiers sitting cross-legged on their pallets reading comic books, writing letters, or playing cards. The duffel bags made great card tables and helped relieve the boredom of the long trip.

I can't remember how many men occupied each day-coach, but the troop train was extremely long. The double steam engine train was transporting more than just our 500 man battalion, other troops were also included in this shipment. The sheer number of men on the train, coupled with limited food preparation facilities created severe problems in preparing and serving food, plus the subsequent cleaning of individual mess kits. However, as with every eventuality, the Army had a standard solution to this problem.

A five hundred man field artillery battalion consists of five batteries: three firing batteries, Able, Baker, and Charlie; headquarters battery; and a service battery. In garrison each battery has it's own mess hall and a permanent kitchen facility, staffed with a Mess Sergeant in charge and a trained cooking staff. Menial tasks, such as washing dishes, peeling potatoes, cleaning the kitchen and cleaning the eating tables and eating area, are performed by KPs (Kitchen Police). Only privates and privates first class are required to serve on KP duty, enlisted man wearing two or more stripes are exempt from this extra duty. Since KP duty is in the same category as latrine duty, trash detail, laundry detail, and guard duty, KP duty is not considered as punishment. However, it is one of the longest and toughest of the extra duty details, and some First Sergeants do use KP as an effective punishment for unruly privates. While in garrison, a field artillery battery mess normally prepares and serves about 350 hot, nutritious meals each day.

When a battery is in the field, such as training or combat, the kitchen facilities are highly efficient, but more restricted, and of course are mobile. Food preparation in the field separates the superior Mess Sergeants from the adequate Mess Sergeants. Good, hot, filling food is one of the best morale factors available for a soldier in combat.

For our two-day journey, the five battery field mess facilities were installed in closed baggage cars and interspersed among the cars containing the troops. Headquarters Battery, in my opinion, had the best Mess Sergeant and cooks in the Battalion. They labored for more than 48 hours straight, preparing and serving hot meals for us during the trip. The routine went something like this. The train would slow and come to a stop. The cooks and KPs would leap from the kitchen car and set-up their serving tables and food next to the railroad ties. Off to one side, they would set-up two powerful gasoline burners, place can holders around the burners, and place a large trash-can of boiling soapy water over one burner. Over the other burner they would place a trash-can of plain boiling water. The soapy water was for washing dirty mess kits, the plain water was for sterilizing the mess kit. Before a GI could eat, he had to sterilize his mess kit. After eating, the GI dumped any left-over food – if there was any – into a waste barrel, washed his dirty mess kit in the soapy water, then rinsed his cleaned mess kit in the clean boiling water. He then waived his mess kit in the air violently, hoping to dry it prior to folding it and placing the mess kit into it's OD canvas carrier.

This process was necessary, and saved many a GI from getting a severe case of dysentery while living in the field.

When the food was ready to be served, the Mess Sergeant would yell, "Chow Call" and the men would come running. One problem anticipated by the Mess Sergeant was the fact that 'Chow Stops' would also become 'Piss Stops,' and he was adamant the 'Pissers' and the 'Eaters' would be kept far apart. For two days, I was in charge of the 'Piss-Detail,' and if I do say so myself, I did an outstanding job of keeping the 'Pissers' and the 'Eaters' widely separated!

All troop trains were equipped with a Military Police detail. In our case, I did not feel the MP detail was necessary, but as I said before, the Army has set procedures. The MPs were not associated with the 106th Infantry Division in any way. They were a specialized unit assigned to do nothing but ride troop trains endlessly from 'Point A' to 'Point B.' They had their own rail-car, were an autonomous unit, and extremely self sufficient.

The MPs did not mingle with the troops being transported. Their single purpose was to make certain that every soldier who started the journey to the Port of Embarkation completed the journey. At each stop along the way, the MPs disembarked and were stationed along both sides of the train before any troops, officers or men, were allowed to leave their cars. Although I was not privileged to their orders, rumors reported they had orders to 'shoot to kill' in the event any passenger tried to 'go over the hill.'

Other than the tedium and discomfort, the trip from Indiana to Massachusetts, in the language of the military was , "Uneventful."

We were excited when the troop train pulled into the huge rail-head near Camp Miles Standish. Each unit disembarked when ordered, loaded themselves and their baggage into waiting trucks, enjoyed the ride into camp, and relished the thought of living in barracks again. What we did not realize was, our troop train trip was only a minor tune-up to the forthcoming, miserable, five day troop ship voyage we would have to endure on our way to England.

Troop accommodations at Camp Miles Standish were quite different from either Fort Jackson or Camp Atterbury. Miles Standish was a military post designated as a staging area for troops headed for the European Theater of Operations

(ETO). The turnover of troops there was constant. A unit deploying for the ETO stayed at Miles Standish an average of six or seven days. Miles Standish had good recreational facilities for enlisted men and the nearby city of Boston was a pleasant bus ride from camp. The bus schedule between the camp and Boston was geared to life of the troops at Miles Standish, and the round trip fare was moderate in price. A round trip ticket to Boston and back to Miles Standish was $1.80, and an enlisted man could not buy a one-way ticket. I never understood the logic in this policy, except perhaps the bus company wanted to make an additional 90 cents from each enlisted man who went AWOL and did not use the return portion of his ticket.

This brings up a point concerning the different rules at Miles Standish. This difference is covered in the Uniform Code of Military Justice. Military personnel who absented themselves without proper leave at the Port of Embarkation are not considered as Absent Without Leave (AWOL), they are considered as deserting in the face of the enemy. In plain language, being AWOL at the Port of Embarkation equates to being a Deserter. This is a major difference in Military Law that I became acquainted with later.

For the first time in my military career I sensed the Army was trying to make amends for the rough treatment I had received in training. I truly felt we were 'cannon fodder' about to be shipped to the slaughter fields of Europe and the Army was trying it's best to make us feel better just before the kill. Our food was delicious, prepared and served in a huge consolidated mess, and our Privates and Privates First Class pulled no KP duty. We pulled no guard or latrine duty, and no one was assigned to laundry or trash details. I could not believe the special treatment we were receiving at Camp Miles Standish.

In addition to relief from these everyday duties, we were required to undergo only light physical training. The only concrete requirements, or obligations, we had involved being present for two formations, or musters, each day. The first formation was at 0700, just before breakfast. The second formation was at 1900, just after the evening meal. The purpose of these formations was two-fold: First, to determine that all personnel were present for duty; and Second, to advise us the Unit had not received orders to move to the troop ship in Boston harbor. If the unit had received no orders to 'move out,' we were free to engage in recreational activities until the next formation. In other words, we were on a twelve hour alert.

It did not take long to learn to enjoy this carefree existence, even though the dark specter of death loomed in the immediate future. I had learned, as most service men do, to live in the present, not the future. I decided to leave camp as often as possible, and to engage in wine, women, and song. With the expert advice of my buddy, T/4 Delbert Miller, I got deeply involved with wine and women, although I do not remember singing very often.

Early on, as a Private, I made arrangements with the Army Finance Corps to send the major portion of my military pay home, as an allotment, to my mother. The purpose of this allotment was to help my mother in the event something happened to me. Also, if good fortune smiled upon me, and I returned from the war, I would have accumulated a small nest egg to help me resume my college education. By the time we reached Camp Miles Standish, several hundred dollars had accumulated in this nest egg. I mention this financial arrangement, because of the allotment the Army sent my mother, the money I received each month was small, even though I was a Sergeant.

On the other hand, Dell Miller was a mature, single man, who had received above average compensation in civilian life as a traveling salesmen for, the Rath Meat Packing Company, before entering the military. By my standards, Dell was a rich man! He always had enough money to satisfy his social needs.

After we bonded as friends, at Fort Jackson, Dell took my social education seriously. He was a street-wise and socially-active bachelor with untold experience to draw upon. I'll admit, he was an excellent teacher and I tried to be an apt pupil!

My social education started in earnest in Indianapolis at the Indiana Roof where Dell and I met Pat and Rosie. My several months association with Pat seemed perfectly natural because she was special to me. We liked each other, although we carefully avoided the word love. Knowing our time together would end, neither of us wished to develop a lingering relationship. But the fact remained, I already missed Pat, and suspected she missed me too. Here in Boston however, all I wanted was a good time. A 'Live for today, for tomorrow ye shall die,' sort of thing

As long as my money lasted, Boston offered good times aplenty. Dell and I liked to roam the bars and girly shows in the Scully Square area, such as the Old Howard and the Silver Dollar Bar. These places of business were operated to entertain transient service men who were on their way overseas and to make certain these men did not carry a surplus of cash with them when they departed from Boston harbor. Needless to say, my money disappeared swiftly and I needed an influx of cash so I decided to tap my savings.

Mother responded promptly to my first telegram requesting $200 for emergency purposes. This influx of cash lasted about as long as 'Pat stayed in the Army,' so I wired for a second $200. Mother took her time in responding to my second request. When the money finally arrived, it was only $100. Due to the delay in getting this $100, I immediately sent her a request for a third $200. I did not hear from my mother again! This inaction infuriated me, and had a tremendous impact upon the remainder of my stay at the Port of Embarkation.

Another act of fate extended our stay at Camp Miles Standish for an additional three weeks. The day the 589th FA Bn was scheduled to move to the Port of Boston, the movement orders were cancelled and we were ordered to sit tight. All HELL had broken loose at the Boston Navy Yard. Our transport ship, the USCCSS WAKEFIELD, was on fire at the dock, and sabotage was suspected.

I did not mind the delay because I was living life to the fullest, but this delay in going overseas exacerbated my financial problems.

The fourth night at Miles Standish, before my money problems became serious, Miller and I were having a short beer at the NCO Club on the base, when Miller asked if I would like to meet Sally Keith. I had heard of her, she was a popular headliner appearing in a girly-show, and famous for her unique 'Tassel Dance.' I had no idea what Dell had in mind so I replied, "Sure, why not?"

At the 1900 formation we were advised we were free until 0700 the next morning. Already dressed in Class A uniforms, we caught the next bus to Boston. Dell told me Sally did two shows nightly, one at 10 o'clock, and another at 1 AM. We decided to bar-hop in Scully Square before catching her 10 o'clock show.

About 9 o'clock we went to the combination bar, dance hall, and theater where Sally performed. Dell excused himself and left me in the lobby to watch the sights. When he returned, we were ushered to a table for four situated directly in front of the combination stage and dance floor. We were periodically hustled for drinks while waiting for the first show to begin. Dell took it all in stride and told me not to order the high priced drinks. When the show began, there were several attractive young females who came on stage and performed a variety of songs, strips, bumps, and grinds. Much to my delight, they performed only a few feet away and seemed to perform especially for me. Their sexually suggestive moves, sultry looks, and my vivid imagination, completely erased the horrors of war from my mind.

During a lull in the program, I glanced at Dell, he was obviously enjoying himself. I wondered if his big, happy grin came from his enjoyment of the warm-up acts, or from the pleased expression on my face. My glance at Dell was interrupted by a long drum-roll from the band and a man introducing the main act of the evening.

For me, it was love at first sight! Sally Keith was one of the most gorgeous woman I had ever seen! Her brief costume displayed her beautiful body to the fullest. She wore black high-heel shoes, two pasties that barely covered the brown nipple of each breast, and the smallest pair of panties the law allowed. From each pasty dangled a group of tassels, while another group of tassels dangled from the front of her panties covering the junction of her legs. The color of the tassels matched the bright auburn highlights in her hair.

As Sally walked to the front of the stage, her exaggerated body movements caused the breast tassels to swing from side to side and the lower tassel to move tantalizingly in and out between her legs. When Sally arrived at center stage, the undulating stopped and she stood there, feet spread, hands on her hips, talking and making eye contact with the patrons. Only then, when I was no longer fascinated by her tassels, did I look at her face. The crowd was obviously pleased with her entrance, and in turn, the flow of appreciation from the audience reflected in her face. Her wavy hair had an auburn cast which contrasted with her blue eyes and a peaches-and-cream complexion. She was truly a beautiful woman!

After speaking with the crowd, she suddenly bent over, her breast tassels almost touching my face, and whispered, "Randy, I will see you after the show."

I was speechless! Sally then stood erect, winked at Dell, and the band began to play a slow, bump-and-grind melody. As if by magic, the tassels started to move from side-to-side in time with the music. As the tempo of the music increased, the breast tassels began to whirl in circles. Sometimes the tassels circled in the same direction, but with a deft movement, Sally could change directions and the tassels would whirl in opposing circles. At the same time the breast tassels were doing their various movements, her lower tassel would swing back and forth between her shapely out-stretched legs. She was performing on the stage so close to me, I began to perspire.

After the floor show was over, Dell and I waited for Sally and a friend to join us at the table. Dell was very jovial and kidded me about my reaction to Sally's performance. I had to admit I was tremendously impressed, but I had no idea what other surprises Dell had in store for me that evening.

Meeting Sally and her friend Dolly produced mixed feelings. Sally, now completely clothed and without her stage makeup, was still a crowd pleaser. It made me feel special when I heard the groans of nearby patrons as she took the chair between Dell and me. Dolly, the other performer, was a contrast in looks and personality. Sally was sexy looking and pert, whereas Dolly was seductive looking and sultry. Sally lavished her attention on Dell and me, whereas Dolly had dark and roving eyes which were constantly scanned the audience as though looking for her next victim. Dolly's actions reminded me of a black widow spider, who carefully chooses her mate, seduces him, and then kills him.

After the first round of drinks, and the normal chit-chat involved in breaking the ice with strangers, Sally and Dell more-or-less began talking with each other. This left Dolly and me to our own devices. Dolly was easy to talk to, but she had these dark eyes which constantly wandered over the crowd and a face which displayed no emotion. When Sally talked with me, she looked me straight in the eyes, moved her hands, and had facial expressions which ran the gauntlet form fear, sorrow, and disbelief, to joy and laughter. In contrast, when Dolly talked with me, her hands were immobile, her face showed no emotion, and her eyes were always looking over my shoulder, not at me.

Even though Dolly was a gorgeous creature, and every other patron in the house wished she was gracing his table, I soon lost interest in her, and she in me. After about one half-hour of her inattention, I decided there was no way I was going to hang around until after their second show was over. When I announced to Sally and Dell I had better get back to camp, they looked surprised, but Dolly actually acted as if she was being relieved of a tremendous burden.

Sally was very receptive when I reached over, put my arm around her shoulder, gave her a peck on the cheek, and told her how much I enjoyed meeting her. I then reminded Dell of tomorrow's 0700 formation. He looked at Sally and when she smiled, he nodded to me and said, "Ole buddy, some things in life are more important than making an 0700 formation. If I'm not there, cover for me."

The next morning at 0700, Staff Sergeant Frank Tacker formed the operations section outside the barracks and started the roll-call. When he finally yelled "Miller," I answered "Here." Tacker knew that was not Miller's voice, looked up momentarily, but continued the roll-call. When Tacker finally completed the roll-call with "Zawolski," he executed a brisk about-face and waited for the First Sergeant to ask for the Operations Section report. Upon command, Tacker reported in his best military manner, "Operations Section all present or accounted for."

What the Hell, we were a team, we were trained to take care of each other, that's what buddies do. We covered for each other!

During what I consider to be phase II of my financial crisis at Camp Miles Standish, I had spending money, but not much. I concluded the only two chances of getting more money from my mother were slim, and none, so I decided to tone down my night life. During these two weeks I explored all the services offered by the USO and decided to take advantage of them. The USO in Boston did a fantastic job, it offered free food, movies, nightly on-premises dancing, and had attractive hostesses recruited from local families and nearby colleges. The senior USO hostesses arranged free historical and cultural tours for enlisted men who were so inclined. I took advantage of one such offer and visited a local family, played with their young children, and was served a marvelous home-cooked meal. This home-away-from-home visit was pleasant but I decided not to do it again. My personal problem stemmed from the fact that I sincerely believed I would not survive the war and did not wish to die a semi-virgin. I just wanted to spend my last days on earth, in private, with an attractive female who was sympathetic to my situation and who would accommodate my needs. There were many such young women at the USO, but they had taken an oath, on their mother's bible, they would not date enlisted men who frequented the club.

Earlier, at the USO Club, I had met a 19 year old sophomore from Boston College, named Dottie Wexler. She was attractive, a great dancer, and we became friends, but she would not break the USO rules and date me. Finally, one night I became more persistent than usual, and Dottie told me she and friends were going bowling after they left the USO Club and gave me the address of the bowling alley. However, she warned me this was not a date, but she could not stop me from coming to a public place of business. Needless to say, I went!

Dottie's group was not difficult to find in the enormous bowling alley. All I had to do was walk toward the mass of sailors who surrounded four teen-aged females trying to bowl on one lane. The strange thing to me was the way the Boston College Sorority girls dressed. They looked like clones, with their pullover cashmere sweaters, a single strand of pearls hanging from under the collar of a silk blouse, a wool skirt fitted at the waist, but pleated below, their saddle oxford shoes with short bobby-socks, and they all had shoulder length hair tied with a black ribbon. Their 'Sorority Dress Code' was as strict as the military's.

Getting through the sailors was not easy, however; I finally located Dottie, who offered me a seat beside her and introduced me to her friends. This was an interesting situation because I had no idea how the evening would progress. We bowled several lines before the girls decided to return to their Sorority House. Dottie paid for our bowling lines and told her friends she was not going to the Sorority House with them, but was going home to spend the night. This announcement definitely attracted my attention because I had absolutely no idea where she lived.

By the time we left the bowling alley, it was after midnight and Dottie convinced me she really was going home although her parents were not expecting her. She told me she lived in Brockton, and if I really wanted to, I could ride the bus home with her. I had no idea where Brockton was, but I could not refuse her offer.

On the bus, I learned Brockton was a bedroom community located south of Boston, and the bus ride would take quite some time. Dottie and I talked, held hands, and giggled on the almost empty bus. On one occasion, Dottie giggled and pointed at the driver. He had a huge grin on his face as he watched our shenanigans with his rear-view mirror. All too soon, we reached the end of the line. Dottie told me to wrap-up because it was cold outside and we had a six-block walk before we reached her home.

We walked with our arms around each other, as much to keep warm as anything else, and talked about nothing in particular. She fascinated me! Dottie was totally at ease with me, walking down a dark deserted sidewalk, after midnight, and all alone. It was as though we had known each other all of our lives. I was not paying attention to anything but Dottie when she suddenly said, "Well, we're here, we're home."

Immediately I looked around and saw an imposing ivy-covered stone wall divided by a large, ornate, wrought-iron gate. Dottie opened the gate, passed through, and motioned for me to follow. My impression of the house, as we walked up a curving slate walk, was that it was an ancient English castle. I fully expected someone to lower a draw-bridge so we could cross the moat. However, there was no moat, although a moat would have been appropriate in this grand setting.

We paused at the front door as Dottie searched for her door key. During the search, Dottie told me in subdued tones, her parents were not expecting her and we should be quiet when we entered the house so we would not disturb them. I did not question her instructions, but wondered if her parents worked here. Inside, the home was even furnished like an English castle. The rooms were enormous, the ceilings high, and even I knew the immense, expensive furnishings did not come from a local furniture store. In my mind, Dottie had to be the daughter of the caretaker or someone like that.

She led me down a generous entrance hall, through several large, exquisitely furnished rooms, and we finally ended up in a kitchen which most restaurateurs would be proud to own. There she announced she was hungry and asked if I wanted something to eat. Apparently we made too much noise as we raided the refrigerator and rattled pots and pans.

A worried female voice penetrated the closed kitchen door with a question, "Dottie, is that you?"

"Yes mom, it's me."

"What are you doing ?"

"Mom, it's OK. I'm hungry. I'm fixing something to eat."

The kitchen door opened slightly and I could see a distinguished looking lady, clutching he dressing robe. She looked at her daughter inquisitively, and said, "We weren't expecting you home tonight Dottie."

"I know mom. I just decided to come home and pick up some things I need. Come on in and meet Randy."

"Randy? I don't believe I know anyone named Randy. Is she a school mate?"

"No mom, she is not a school mate. HE is a Sergeant stationed at Camp Miles Standish."

As the door slammed shut, I heard the female voice say, "I will be right back. I must get your father!"

By this time I did not know what to expect, but Dottie came to my rescue and told me her mother did not handle surprises well, but nothing bothered her father. She assured me everything would be fine and continued to search the refrigerator for snacks while I nervously waited to see how I would be received by her father.

When the kitchen door opened this time, a medium sized man, also clothed in a dressing gown, entered the room and strode purposefully to his daughter. As they hugged and kissed, I could sense the love that passed between them. Finally Dottie grabbed her father's hand and brought him to the kitchen table where I was standing. She introduced me as Sergeant Randolph Pierson, who was on his way overseas, and introduced her father as Doctor Wexler, Chief-of-Surgery at Massachusetts General Hospital. He looked at me with great interest and finally said, "Sergeant, you must be quite some young man. You are the first service man Dottie has brought home for us to meet."

Not knowing whether to be flattered or not, I responded, "Sir, it wasn't planned, it just happened."

Dottie heard my remark and laughed just as her mother re-entered the kitchen, followed closely by two young boys, both desperately trying to rub the 'sleep' from their eyes. Dottie seized the initiative and introduced me to her mother, and then introduced her younger brothers, Timothy and William. Mrs. Wexler had obviously changed into an expensive lounging robe and had done something to her hair. My first impression of her was that she was distinguished-looking, but seeing her standing there, I changed my mind. Doctor Wexler was distinguished-looking, but Mrs. Wexler looked regal. She looked like a queen in her castle. It was certainly obvious that Dottie had inherited her beauty from her mother and her poise from her father.

I must have been staring, because Doctor Wexler broke the awkward silence when he said, "Sergeant, now you have met my family, how about telling us something about yourself."

Talking about myself had never been difficult for me, but the good doctor made it easier by asking me leading questions. Even the two young boys joined in. They seemed drawn to my uniform, my stripes, and of all things, my one chest-ribbon, the Good Conduct Medal. They thought it meant I was some kind of hero or something. Our 'man-to-man' conversation was periodically interrupted by questions from Mrs. Wexler and Dottie herself, Dottie trying to find out what everyone wanted to eat, and Mrs. Wexler trying to find out how long her daughter and I had known each other, and how and when we met.

The late night meal was delicious. Dottie and mom Wexler had prepared scrambled eggs, coffee for the adults, warm milk for the two boys, toast with butter and gobs of orange marmalade. We all ate hardily, except Mrs. Wexler, who obviously was concerned about her lovely figure. As usual, the conversation dwindled when we ate, but Mrs. Wexler would not give up on her questions concerning the relationship between me and her daughter. Finally Doctor Wexler looked at his wife and said gently, but firmly, "Mother, it doesn't matter. He is a lonely young man on his way to fight for our country. He is our guest, and he is our daughter's friend. Let's just leave it at that."

I was relieved to know that Doctor Wexler understood. He was a wise gentleman.

The last cup of coffee finished, and with Timmy and Will in bed, I told Doctor and Mrs. Wexler I must get back to camp because I had to be in a formation at 0700. The Doctor looked at his watch and remarked it was almost 3 AM and asked how I was going to get back to camp at this hour of the morning. With as much bravado as I could summon, I advised him I was accustomed to handling situations worse than this, and for him not to worry about me.

Mrs. Wexler excused herself and looked relieved when she learned I was not going to spend the remainder of the night in the Wexler home. As I prepared to depart, the doctor asked me for the name and address of my mother, told me I was always welcome to visit his family, and wished me good luck. Dottie put on her coat and walked me to the front gate. In the dark, we talked a little, kissed, and hugged each other. God, she smelled good and I could feel the pleasant contours of her body through her coat. I did not want to leave, but this was only prolonging my agony and delaying the inevitable. We kissed for the last time and I strode off into the darkness like I knew where I was going.

† †

Feeling very sorry for myself, I walked swiftly for about four blocks before I became aware of a vehicle driving slowly behind me. This was strange, because all the house lights were out and nothing on the street was moving but me. The vehicle followed me for another block, never catching me, but seemed to be keeping me under surveillance. I suddenly decided to confront my stalker! I stopped walking abruptly, turned, and faced the vehicle, which had pulled to the curb and also stopped. I prepared to defend myself the best I could. Then I read the sign on the side of the black and white vehicle. It read, BROCKTON POLICE DEPARTMENT.

The driver's side door of the police car opened and the dome-light illuminated the interior of the vehicle, revealing a large uniformed man behind the steering wheel, wearing the silver bars of a Lieutenant. In a loud voice that rippled with an Irish brogue, he addressed me, "Are you the Sergeant who was visiting the love of me life, Miss Dottie Wexler?"

I was so astonished I could only answer, "Yes Sir."

"Well Sergeant, get into the vehicle. Doctor Wexler has charged me with your safe-keeping, and I dare not let the good Doctor down."

"Lieutenant, am I under arrest? I didn't do anything wrong."

"I will not say you are under arrest me boy, but you did commit a grievous wrong. You have stolen the Wexler children hearts away. The good doctor is a pillar of our community, and strongly suggests that I, the Night-Watch Commander, take you into protective custody and personally deliver you, safe and sound, to your barracks at Camp Miles Standish no later than 0645 hours this morning."

"You mean to tell me that Doctor Wexler called and asked you to pick me up and take me to Camp Miles Standish so I will not miss my morning formation?"

"Yes, me boy, that's the way it is, and in Brockton, this public servant gives Doctor Wexler what he wants." With a wave of his massive arm, he ordered, "Get into the vehicle Sergeant!"

We stopped at the Brockton Police Station, where the Night-Watch Commander invited me in. I took a short nap in a cell and was awakened in time to get a fresh shave before the Lieutenant and I left for Miles Standish. The large Irish cop was easy to like. We talked constantly during the entire trip. He was from a large family and many of his relatives were cops. One thing I wanted him to know was how much I appreciated the wonderful things that good people had done for me in Tennessee, Indiana, and now in New England. I told him I expected to be treated well in the South, but I had been warned about the cold reception I would get in New England. I admitted I was surprised to find the people in and around Boston just as nice as Southerners. He beamed with a huge Irish laugh, and philosophized with me, "Sergeant, you will find that life is just one great mirror. You will receive back from the mirror only what you put in front of it."

I was not much of a philosopher, but I did realize this large, Irish Cop was right!

Brockton Police Department Night-Watch Commander, Lieutenant Michael Carney, had no problem getting past the MPs stationed at the main entrance to Camp Miles Standish. He had apparently developed a good working relationship with the Military Police, and they all recognized and respected him. I also realized he had made this trip many times before. He drove directly to my barracks and parked at the curb as the Operations Section was just starting to assemble for the 0700 formation. The conspicuous Black and White Brockton Police Car caused quite a stir in the crowd. Before I exited the vehicle, Staff Sergeant Frank Tacker walked to the side of the vehicle, clip-board in hand, recognized me, and asked if everything was OK. I nodded yes, and Tacker asked Lieutenant Carney, "Lieutenant, is he in trouble?" Then added, "He is my friend."

Lieutenant Carney read the name-tag on Tacker's breast pocket and replied, as if he had just kissed the Blarney Stone, "Sergeant Tacker, we are both extremely lucky men, for he is my friend also."

Lieutenant Carney slowly drove away and left us standing on the curbing. He momentarily flicked on his flashing lights, doffed his cap in a good-bye salute, and waved his huge Irish hand as a horde of Headquarters Battery men rushed to the curb to find out what had happened to 'Ole Randy' while he was on pass the previous night.

Try as I could, I was never able to convince my buddies I did not spend a miserable night in jail. The truth is, it was one of the most memorable nights of my young Army life. The icing on the cake came months later when my mother wrote me, while I was in England, that she had received a letter from some "nice doctor" at Mass General Hospital in Boston who thought I was a fine young man. In her letter she asked how I happened to meet him.

I did not think it was wise to explain to my sainted mother I met the 'nice doctor' the night I was trying, unsuccessfully, to seduce his beautiful young daughter.

† †

Phase III of my financial crisis was horrible. My money depleted, no more funds from home, and no one in the unit would loan me money. My credit was impeccable, no doubt about that, the problem was the situation in which we found ourselves. Friends who felt as I did, were 'living it up' before their expected demise. Other friends, with a more positive attitude toward survival, were not blowing their money on earthly pleasures, but were saving it for the future. Neither friendship not credit rating had ny bearing on the supply of money available to me.

The unit continued to receive rumors concerning repairs on the fire-damaged WAKEFIELD, nothing official however. We had already been at Miles Standish much longer than normal and common sense dictated we would be embarking soon. I decided to take one last fling at locating sympathetic female companionship in Boston. It would not be easy, I had exactly two dollars left, no more – no less. Two lousy one dollar bills! Round trip bus fare to Boston and back cost $1.80. That would leave me twenty cents for a night on the town. It would be tough, but I was willing to give it my best shot.

My first stop would be at the Silver Dollar Bar. The Silver Dollar was a magnificent watering hole which treated servicemen, and their money, with respect. After two short-beers – 10 cents each – and an apology to the bartender for not leaving a tip, I would wander over to the USO for a free meal, a movie, and later dancing. Maybe I would see Dottie, or one of her college friends. Who knows, maybe I would get lucky!

By the time I reached the Silver Dollar Bar, the early evening crowd was in full swing. I found an empty bar-stool and ordered my first ten-cent, short-beer. The draft beer was delicious and I nursed it as long as I could, intently watching the professional ladies of the evening working the crowd. They always worked the tables during the early evening hours when the floor was busy. It was only late at night they would work the bar itself.

A dedicated beer drinker can nurse a short-beer only so long. I shoved the empty glass to the bartender and motioned for a refill. Again my eyes drifted to the tables. It was interesting to see the various servicemen being hustled by the professional women. I was so interested in the crowd I was only slightly aware of the change on the bar-stool to my left. As I drained the last of the foaming yellow liquid from my glass, I heard a voice say, "Percy, what are you drinking?"

This question was both surprising and infuriating. Only a few close friends in high school had called me Percy. I did not like the nickname Percy because to me it meant being a 'sissy.' However my friends called me Percy because I was an 'egg-head' and made good grades without having to study, consequently I grudgingly tolerated the nickname. But this was a total stranger calling me Percy and I was ready to fight. I turned and faced the speaker. He was a large, red-headed, Navy Chief Electricians Mate, who looked vaguely familiar.

"You still don't like being called Percy do you? I asked you a simple question. What are you drinking? Is that question too tough for an Army Sergeant to answer?"

My anger died instantly, I could not believe my eyes. The Chief sitting next to me was my best high school friend, Howard Dixon. We had not seen each other for more than two years. Howard had enlisted in the Navy in January 1942 while I was still in college at the University of Florida. Pearl Harbor had been his incentive to join up and 'zap a Jap.' Now here we sat facing each other, in a bar, in the Scully Square section of Boston.

"Howard, what in the Hell are you doing here in Boston?"

"Well soldier-boy, I'm sitting here trying to get a drink. What are you doing here?"

"Damn it Howard, you know what I mean. I thought you went to the Pacific Theater. What brings you to Boston?"

"Well sport, I have one in every port. You know the old saying about a sailor. I just docked at the Boston Navy Yard. I've been at sea for a long time and I'm thirsty. I'll ask you just one more time, what are you drinking?"

"Oh brother, I hate to tell you this, but I'm flat broke. I don't even have the price of a beer on me. All I've got is a one-way ticket back to camp."

Howard reached into this pea-coat and pulled out a roll of bills that would choke a horse and said, "Don't sweat it Randy. I have almost three months pay here and I hate to drink alone."

With some of my initial embarrassment now gone, I asked Howard what he liked to drink. Without hesitation he answered, "Boiler-Makers!"

"Sounds good to me."

Howard immediately got the attention of the bartender, ordered two Boiler-

Makers, threw some bills on the highly polished bar, and told the bartender to keep them coming.

Seeing my best friend unexpectedly was such a pleasant surprise, I totally forgot why I had come to Boston. Howard told me he was stationed aboard a destroyer, The Macomb, which was pulling convoy escort duty between the United States and Europe. The Macomb had just returned from escorting a convoy of supply ships to the Russian seaport of Murmansk. On this particular trip, several freighters fell prey to a pack of German U-Boats. During the melee, his ship was slightly damaged and was now in the Boston Navy Yard receiving minor repairs, being fitted with advanced radar, and taking on fuel and supplies. He indicated he expected to be in port for several days.

He asked if I had heard about 'Scotsman.' Scotsman was the nickname for Billy Paterson, another good friend from the Cocoa High School Class of '41. Billy had joined the Navy about the same time as Howard and ended up a mechanic in a Naval Aviation Squadron. When I told Howard I had not heard anything about Scotsman lately, he ordered another round of Boiler-Makers and as we sipped our drinks, what he told me almost made me cry.

Scotsman had been a passenger on a Naval transport plane headed for Iceland when it developed engine trouble and went down into the stormy North Atlantic. The Macomb was the nearest Navy ship to the location where the troubled plane went down. The Macomb was dispatched to pickup survivors, but they found none. Howard was told later that William G. Paterson, from Cocoa, Florida, was a passenger in the ill-fated aircraft that crashed.

This was sad news for me. Billy was the first member of my High School Class to die in the war. We discussed his fate and Howard expressed his feelings when he said, "I hope Scotsman was dead when the plane hit the water. I hate to think of him freezing to death in the damned frigid water of the North Atlantic."

As we sat and drank, just two long-time friends talking, Howard finally remarked, in hushed tones, that the Coast Guard ship, The Wakefield, was tied up in the Navy Yard only a couple of piers from The Macomb. He knew The Wakefield was a former luxury liner, now converted to carry troops. He also knew it had suffered minor fire damage while in port, and was almost ready to depart for Europe. Since he also knew that troops staging at Camp Miles Standish were preparing to embark for Europe, it was simple for him to put two and two together.

Howard finally said, "Percy," – only this time it came out "Perthy," the powerful Boiler-Makers were beginning to take effect – "you unlucky bastard, you will be sailing in two or three days. We should get together again before you go to Germany and get your ass ventilated."

"Good thinking Chief! How do you think I can get to town with no money?"

As he dug into his pea-coat, he asked, "How much do you need? Is a couple of hundred enough?"

I quickly rose from my bar-stool to answer his question and suddenly realized the night was over for me. The room was spinning and tilting, I had to go to the latrine but could not remember where it was located, and most of all, I realized I had to get back to camp. I mean, I knew I was going to need help to catch a bus. Howard noticed me standing there rocking back and forth and asked, "Randy, are you OK?"

"I don't think so Chief. How many drinks have we had?"

Howard shook his head as he said, "I don't know. I haven't been keeping count."

As Howard was speaking, the bartender held up six fingers in answer to my question.

"Holly Shit, Howard, the bartenders says we have had six Boiler-Makers, and I had two short-beers before you came. If I don't get going, I'll probably pass-out and miss the last bus. I've got to find a sober buddy to help me get back to camp."

"Wait a minute Randy, I will call a cab and it can take you to your barracks."

"Don't sweat it Howard, I have had too much to drink before. The 'Ole Sarge' knows what he is doing. I'll catch the bus."

"Randy are we going to meet again tomorrow?"

"Chief, you can bet your ass on it. Same place, 2000 hours. The 'Ole Sarge' will be here."

The walk to the rest room was not too bad. I seemed able to accommodate my stride to the movement of the room without too much trouble. Thankfully, relieving myself in the urinal of what seemed to be quarts of liquid made me feel better. On the way out of the Silver Dollar, I reminded Howard I would see him again tomorrow. He nodded, indicating he understood, although he was still drinking and already in a serious conversation with another Chief Petty Officer.

Outside the comfortable warmth of the bar, the frigid night air made me shiver. I knew I would have to keep looking in bars until I found friends from the Battalion who would help me get back to camp. I remember going into several bars, but with no luck. Finally the body got weak and the brain gave out. I found an empty corner in a small bar, placed both arms and my head on the table and went to sleep. This must have been about midnight Friday night.

Slowly, oh so slowly, my brain started to function. I didn't remember too much, only that I would never drink Boiler-Makers again. My eyes were closed, but I could sense light through the eye-lids. Finally I got the courage to open my eyes. There was light out there, but my sight was blurred with a thick haze. As I rubbed my eyes, trying to rub away the fog, I accidentally touched my chin. The rough whiskers on my chin scratched the palm of my hand. What was going on? I badly needed a shave. As the fog started to lift, I realized I was on a bed, not a cot, and this bed was not in a barracks.

This realization fully awakened me. My pulse quickened and a shot of adrenaline bolted me to a full conscious state. Something was drastically wrong! The old fight or flight syndrome took over and I sat upright in bed. This bed was located in a bedroom, Army Barracks do not have fluffy white curtains covering the windows. My first conscious thought was, "My God, I have been rolled!"

I swung my feet to the floor, sat there momentarily, looked around, noticed I had been sleeping in my Olive Drab, army issue under-wear as usual, and realized I had a terrible hang-over. What puzzled me enormously were the strange surroundings and my lack of clothing. It finally dawned upon me I had not been rolled, because I had no money. I also reasoned if I had been rolled, I would be waking up in a filthy gutter and not in a nicely furnished bedroom. This was smart thinking for a brain which was not yet functioning at full speed.

This thinking process was interrupted when the bedroom door opened. In walked a smart-looking young female, probably in her early twenties, who was carrying my freshly pressed uniform on a coat hanger. She interrupted my stare with a witty comment, "My sister and I thought you had died. Welcome back to the world of the living."

The only witty response I could think of was, "Where am I?"

About the time I asked this question, a second female appeared. She was about two years older than the first intruder. She looked at me with an experienced eye and commented, "My, it is alive, isn't it!"

Again, the only repartee that would come out was, "Where am I?"

"Sergeant Pierson, to answer your question," the older female said, "you are in Brookline. In case you do not know, Brookline is a neighborhood in Boston. This room is our guest room. We are the Dempsey sisters. I am Bert and she is my younger sister Anne. You are a guest in our home, but from my point of view, an unwanted one."

"Wait a minute Bert, right now things are a little bit fuzzy. How did I get to be an unwanted guest in your home?"

"Anne felt sorry for you and made me help her bring you here. If it had been up to me, I would have let the Military Police have you."

"Just a minute Bert, how do you know my name?"

Anne answered this question. "It was simple, we just went through your wallet and read the information on your dog-tags."

"You went through my wallet? What did you find?"

Bert loosened-up a little and joked, "We certainly did not find money."

At this point Anne took charge. "Bert, he looks confused and he is probably cold, and sitting there in his under-wear can't be too warm. He is probably hungry too. Why don't I get him a robe and slippers and lets go downstairs to the kitchen?"

Good ole Bert couldn't miss this opportunity to make her point, "I told you she is a push-over. She not only takes in soldiers, she also takes in starving animals."

The Dempsey home was a small Cape Cod and the kitchen was typical New England. Everything spic-and-span, and everything in it's place. The Dempsey sisters were a study in contrasts. Anne, with her warm heart and gentle ways could have been straight from the deep south. Bert was distant, but I suspected she also had a warm heart. I felt Bert's brusque and wary ways were defense mechanisms. She probably let someone get too close in the past and got burned in the process. In times of war, these things happens!

Drinking sugarless tea and eating dry toast was not my idea of a hearty breakfast, however, beggars cannot be choosers. I was surprised when Bert told me she and Anne were cocktail waitresses in the small bar where, in my words, I went to sleep. In Bert's words, I passed out! The Military Police had checked the bar several times before it closed, and each time they started to remove me, Anne would intervene by saying I was her date and I was merely sleeping, waiting for her to get off work. The Dempsey sisters real problems came at closing time.

The bar owner, who shared Bert's opinion about letting the MPs have me, had to help them get me onto my feet. With one arm draped around each girl's shoulders, the three of us staggered into the cold outside air. Unfortunately, the cold air did not revive me as anticipated. The bar owner then had to use some of his precious gasoline to drive the three of us to the Dempsey residence in Brookline where he helped get me upstairs and into bed. There he refused to help undress me, and left that task to Bert and Anne.

It was hard for me to understand why two total strangers would sacrifice so much for me. When I asked this question, a tear ran down Anne's cheek as she explained, "The robe and slippers you are wearing belonged to our brother. He was killed in France, on Omaha Beach."

Anne had answered my question, but I was so stunned, I did not know how to respond.

Suddenly I remembered my 0700 formation and looked at my watch. It was already 0930 and here I was sitting in my under-wear, sipping tea like I had all the time in the world. The realization that I had missed a formation and was now AWOL caused me to exclaim, "What in the hell am I doing here? I have missed my 0700 formation and have to get back to camp. They will probably put me in the stockade when I get there."

Neither Bert nor Anne looked surprised, but Bert said it might be wise for me to get cleaned up and dressed while she arranged transportation to the bus terminal. Bert called for a cab while Anne escorted me upstairs and started running water in the tub. Anne handed me a razor, apologized for the dull blade, advised me to shave while I was in the tub, told me to go easy on the soap, and went back down stairs.

Let there be no mistake, I was very concerned. This was the first time I had ever been AWOL. My only salvation would be if Miller, or Tacker, or anyone, had covered for me at the 0700 formation. I had nothing on my mind but to get back to camp as quickly as possible. I realized I had really 'crapped in my mess-kit' this time!

Bathed, shaved, and dressed, I met my two benefactors in their living room. I could hear their heated discussion as I descended the stairs. "Bert, I know he hasn't got any money to pay his cab fare, but I don't see why we can't just give him some money and let him pay the cab driver."

"Anne, you will never learn, every soldier is not like our brother. There is no way I am going to give him money. He would probably go to the nearest bar and get drunk all over again."

"Well, how are you going to handle it? He has to get back to camp. You know he is stationed at Miles Standish and you know he is on his way over seas."

"Anne, I know all that, but I am not going to give him money. I'll just pay the driver before they leave."

I was embarrassed to overhear their conversation, but I had other important matters on my mind. I pressed the issue by asking, "When will the cab be here?"

Bert looked at me with a strange look and answered my question with a question, "Sergeant Pierson, what day do you think this is?"

A little irritated with her question, I asked, "What difference does it make?"

"It may make more difference than you realize! What day do you think it is?"

"It is Saturday, of course."

"Sergeant, for your information, today is not Saturday, today is Sunday."

This news hit me like a ton of bricks. I sat down and groaned, "Dear God! I have lost a day and have missed three formations, not just one!"

The cab finally arrived and as Bert negotiated the fare, Anne had me check my wallet to make certain I still had a bus ticket back to camp. Although I was extremely nervous and preoccupied, I did remember to thank the girls, and promised to write and repay the price of the cab fare. As the cab accelerated on the trip to town, I turned and looked out of the rear window. The Dempsey sisters were still standing at the curb, watching the cab disappear from view.

On the way to the bus terminal it dawned on me, I had failed to obtain their mailing address. Now I would not be able to return their money, or even worse, I could never thank the Dempsey sisters for their acts of kindness.

At Camp Miles Standish a group of friendly non-coms normally sat together in the huge consolidated mess during each meal. We had enjoyed our meal and were just sitting there 'bulling' with each other, when a red-faced Staff Sergeant Frank Tacker appeared at the table. He exploded, "Pierson, you dumb shit-head, where have you been?"

Tacker was really pissed! He did not normally use this type of language, but he continued his tirade, "I have been covering your ass for three formations now. I had decided to report you AWOL at 1700 hours this afternoon. I still might nail your ass for what you did. Don't just sit there with that stupid look on your face. Where were you?"

"Frank, don't get your bowls in an uproar, I'll tell you what happened. It really doesn't matter where I was since everything has turned out OK."

"Don't give me that crap about everything turning out OK. You smart-ass, this is not over until I say it is over!"

"OK Frank, if you want to show your ass, go on and show your ass, you have one more stripe than I do. But before you drop your pants in public, you had better listen to my side of this story!"

The details of what happened to me in Boston seemed to fascinate Frank and the other non-coms present. As the tale unfurled Frank settled down and I began to hear listening responses like, "She did?", "No kidding!", "Wow!", "I can't believe that", and "Holly Shit." By the time I finished my adventure story, Frank and I were friends again.

Later, in a less emotional environment, Staff Sergeant Frank Tacker, told me what pressure he had been under to cover for me because he believed that covering up was morally wrong. He explained I had placed him in the uncomfortable position of having to choose between friendship and duty. He also made it clear that regardless of what happened, the Army would have taken the position that I had 'deserted in the face of the enemy' if he had reported me as being AWOL. In wrestling with his conscience, he could not believe I would desert, but I had really pushed my luck, because 'desertion in the face of the enemy' is punishable by death.

At the afternoon formation we were advised of the news we all expected, but did not wish to hear. We were now confined to camp! This meant we would be making the brief train ride from Camp Miles Standish to the Port of Boston in a few short hours.

Lying on my bunk before I went to sleep that night, I realized how much Anne, Bert, and Frank had done for me. After I prayed for my mother, I told the Lord how much I appreciated the things these three people had done for me. As I lay there, thinking of the uncertain future, my anxieties seemed to disappear because I knew my Heavenly Father was at my side and watching over me.

The proof was too strong to ignore!

9

The Trip to England

Emotions were mixed on 10 November 1944 as we loaded into the special train cars which were to transport elements of the 106th Infantry Division from Camp Miles Standish to the Port of Embarkation in the Boston Navy yard. For the original members of the 589th Field Artillery battalion, such as myself, we had been training together for almost two years. We had come to know each other well, and had proved we could function as a unit. The Department of Army had made huge draws of personnel from the Division in May and June to be utilized as trained replacements in Europe after the D Day invasion. During August and September the 589th had received untrained men to replace those lost in the earlier draws. These replacement soldiers came from cancelled Air Corps Pilot Training Programs, cancelled Officer Candidate Schools, and young, recently inducted draftees. To say the least, the emotions of these new men could be described as apprehensive. They were not Artillery trained, had few or no friends, and as expected, did not feel comfortable going over seas with our Battalion.

Of course we were all apprehensive concerning the dangers posed by our long sea voyage through enemy submarine infested waters and the subsequent introduction into battle. Another emotional factor was the anticipation of action after more than one month of inactivity.

Although our spirits were high, and our physical conditioning at a peak, our emotions were mixed. This emotional mix happens when healthy young men go to war.

Each man, detraining onto the pier in the Boston Navy Yard was loaded with his personal gear, like a pack animal. I could not help but feel a twinge of pride as we struggled against our heavy loads while walking down the pier toward the waiting troop ship. Beautiful American flags waved, a crisply uniformed military band played, and American Red Cross ladies smiled and handed us coffee, doughnuts, and ditty bags. We were proud to be Americans! We would do our part! No matter what the cost, we would overcome the enemy!

The men of the 589th FA Bn were moved from the pier to levels D and E, centered in the bowels of the giant troop ship. We were assigned to rows and rows of canvas bunks which were stacked five high. There was a scramble to get the lower bunks due to the small storage space between the bunk and the gray steel deck. As it turned out, I ended up in the middle of the stacked bunks, the number three bunk. The men ending up in the first and the top bunks actually drew the worst bunk locations. The men on the top sweltered from the heat and constantly breathed air fowled with body odors, while the men on the bottom bunks were frequently vomited upon by their sea sick bunk mates above them.

During the time we were initially getting settled in the hold of the ship, we were briefed on the ship's history over the public address system. She, all ships are referred to as 'She' for some reason, was launched in 1931 as the USS (United States Ship) Manhattan, and served as a palatial pleasure ship. The USS Manhattan, 85 feet wide and 705 feet long, was one of America's largest ships. She cruised at 20 knots, powered by six powerful steam driven turbines.

During her peace-time service, she carried a crew of 478 and almost 1,250 passengers, a ratio of slightly more than one crew member for each three paying passengers. In June 1941 the United States government pressed her into military service, renamed her the USCCSS (United States Coast Guard Steam Ship) Wakefield, and manned her with a Coast Guard crew.

During her military service, I cannot recall the size of the Coast Guard crew, but I suspect it was less than the size of her peace-time crew. By comparison, the Wakefield carried 15,000 troops on each trip, which was about twelve times her peace-time capacity. As a carrier of military troops, the Wakefield was certainly no pleasure ship. To the 15,000 GIs who went to England with me, she was more like a ship from Hell.

Loaded to capacity, the Wakefield majestically pulled away from the pier and departed Boston Navy Yard about 1030 hours on 10 November 1944. The weather was squally and the slate-gray steel of the mammoth ship merged with the dense fog, misty rain, and the cold murky waters of the North Atlantic. Although no U-Boat activity had been detected in this area recently, the seasoned Coast Guard crew relished the rough weather because limited visibility rendered U-Boat activity ineffective.

Because of its great speed, the Wakefield was to make a solitary run for England, unescorted by Navy warships. At flank speed, no U-Boat could overtake the Wakefield from behind. To avoid U-Boats ahead, lying submerged and waiting, the Captain took evasive action by frequently changing course. The gamble was great, but the odds were probably better than sailing in a convoy, slowed to the speed of the slowest freighter. To me, the thought of being alone in the vast North Atlantic merely added excitement to this great adventure.

Of course this same blustery weather reeked havoc upon the GI passengers below deck. For two days this inclement weather held, and for two days the question was not, 'Will I be seasick?' The question was, 'How often and how bad will I get seasick?' My life spent boating on the East coast of Florida in the Indian River did nothing to prepare me for this experience. The first few hours at sea turned my compartment into an enclosure of fetid air, combining the smells of unwashed bodies, stale tobacco smoke, vomit, and expelled flatulence. The ventilating system was inadequate to remove the fouled air and replace it with air which was fresh. Soon body heat also became a comfort factor in the packed confines of the compartment. The heat, especially at the ceiling, became almost unbearable. My two-day trip on the troop train from Indianapolis to Boston was a relative snap compared to the first two days in the bowels of the Wakefield.

Other living conditions aboard the crowded troop ship were also terrible.

The weather was so disagreeable outside the ship that none but the hardiest GIs would dare to venture onto the open decks. Our toilet facilities consisted of a trough of sea water running beneath a seating area, equipped with seating holes. This arrangement was similar to the two-hole outhouse at my grandfather Pierson's farm. In rough seas, the great ship tended to roll. This rolling action caused the polluted water in the trough to move vigorously from side to side. The action of this moving water, at each end of the trough was predictable. Large volumes of water gushed violently from the seating holes on the low side of the trough, either pouring out onto the floor of the latrine (The Navy called it a Head), or producing seated GIs with an unexpected, and unsanitary, saturated bare rear-end and uniform.

I quickly learned, through the experience of others, the safest place to relieve myself on the long open latrine in turbulent weather was to sit in the middle of this ill designed contraption. Even this choice of a seating location was not one hundred percent immune from the sloshing latrine water in rough seas.

Eating also proved difficult, especially in rough seas. Two meals were served each day to those GIs hearty enough to eat. To reach the mess area from our compartment, it was necessary to get in a line, which slowly moved up several flights of steep stairs along companion ways for almost the entire length of the ship, then back down steep stairs into the huge mess area. This tortuous trip took about one hour, if nothing went wrong. Of course during the first three days of the trip, something usually managed to go wrong.

I'll give the Coast Guard cooks their due, once in the mess area, the food was excellently prepared, courteously served, and tasty to eat. When compared to Army chow in the field, I could not complain. We were served food, cafeteria style, in partitioned stainless steel trays, and not once did a Coast Guard cook slop ice cream into my mashed potatoes and gravy, a favorite trick of pissed-off Army cooks. We ate standing at tables designed for eating purposes. The tall stainless steel table tops had a fairly high ridge, or rim, around the top. This rim gave the person eating something to hold onto to brace against the motion of the ship. This rim also kept food trays and condiments from spilling onto the floor during rough seas. The drawback of these rims became obvious when a

GI became seasick in the mess area and unloaded the contents of his stomach onto the table. Of course, the vomit had no place to go and merely flowed back and forth on the table top, in concert with the movement of the ship, until mess personnel came out and cleaned up the filthy mess.

As we left the mess area, each man empted the contents of his tray into huge garbage cans, dropped his silverware into containers of soapy water, rinsed his tray in a large can of hot water, and stacked it on a table near the exit, to be washed by the mess personnel. This process was very efficient and orderly except for the one factor which was not predictable, sea sickness. In most cases, if 'mal de mer' struck near the exit, the sick GI successfully made it to a strategically placed garbage can to vomit.

On the third day of the trip, the weather took a turn for the better. The sea calmed and the weather became mild. If you were lucky, you could find an open space on deck and actually socialize with off duty Coast Guardsmen, who were also enjoying the mild, fresh, sea air. They told us the Wakefield was taking the longer, but more comfortable and safer southern route to England. This change in the weather brought wonderful changes into our living conditions. Mal de mer became a thing of the past, passengers enjoyed their food, and we were now able to take salt-water showers. The one thing the more pleasant weather could not change however was our cramped living and sleeping accommodations. Some of my buddies addressed these problems by actually sleeping on the open decks.

Try to conjure up the image of a full grown man, trying to read, write letters, store his duffel and musette bags, change clothes, and sleep in a three by six by two foot space. For men under six feet tall, it was bad enough, but for guys like me who were 6'-2", and taller than the bunk was long, it was hell. However, this was not the first touch of hell I had experienced, and it was not to be my last touch of hell on earth either.

During the afternoon of 16 November, land was sighted, and the Wakefield fell in behind another ship which was being guided by a British Destroyer Escort through anti-submarine mine fields off the coast of Wales.

I was lucky enough to get on deck the morning of 17 November and remember the sight of Wales and later a glimpse of Ireland in the distance. The

British Destroyer Escort later broke ranks and returned to the open sea as the Wakefield was now in the protected deep waters of the St. George's Channel. That afternoon, the Wakefield turned East and steamed unescorted to our final destination, the famous English seaport city of Liverpool. As we steamed slowly into the Port of Liverpool I witnessed the first defenses of England. We saw many anti-aircraft installations mounted upon tall steel platforms flanking all sides of the port As a trained artilleryman, I did not think I would care to be firing at attacking German aircraft from such an open and exposed location. The thought did not appeal to me at all.

The Wakefield docked at her assigned pier at 1600 hours. For the first time in a week her powerful turbines no longer turned and the ship stood still. We had crossed the Atlantic safely, without serious incident, and we all looked forward to being on firm, dry land again. Similar to the way we had embarked in Boston, we disembarked in Liverpool, England. The first troops disembarking were greeted by Red Cross ladies, flying flags, and spirited music of a British Military Band.

As I watched, chills ran up and down my spine. I was proud to be an American!

10
Life in England

Blackout conditions were strictly enforced in England when the Wakefield arrived. The 589th FA Bn disembarked at about 2000 hours, directly from the bowels of the Wakefield, onto a covered pier in the Liverpool Port. A thick fog surrounded the port area and infiltrated into the covered pier itself. By then, the Red Cross ladies had gone home, and the British military band did not greet the 589th. The sounds of muffled footsteps from shuffling artillerymen, quiet conversations, and nervous laughter of nearby friends combined with shouted orders from Non-Commissioned Officers echoed back and forth in the confines of the covered pier. These strange sounds plus the total darkness of the pier made me feel uneasy. I felt as though I would be attacked by 'The Hounds of the Baskervilles,' or confronted by 'Jack the Ripper.' Even though I was surrounded by more than five hundred able bodied men, I could feel fear in the air.

Once we boarded the troop train, which was to carry us to a staging area outside of Gloucester, this feeling of fear began to fade. The darkened coach lurched, and then slowly started to roll. Suddenly the lights in the coach came on, and we were confronted by a jolly English trainman, who looked much like Saint Nicholas. With a smile on his face, and a twinkle in each eye, he said his name was Tommy, and he wanted to welcome us to England. Tommy turned out to be our Ambassador, and during the ride to Gloucester, proceeded to explain the English people, their customs, their language, and their attitude toward Americans. Tommy advised us, we Brits have everything in common with the Yanks but a language." He explained, "When a British girl tells you she is 'knocked up,' don't get excited, she doesn't mean you got her pregnant, she means she is extremely tired." Among other things, Tommy warned us, "Never use the word 'Bloody,' it is the worst curse word you can use in England. A Brit is really angry when he uses the word Bloody."

Tommy continued, most Brits appreciate the sacrifice you Yanks are making, but you will frequently hear the phrase, "The trouble with you Yanks is: you are over-dressed, over-paid, over-sexed, and over here!" The Brits don't really mean it when they tell you this, but the phrase does carry a certain amount of truth in it.

Tommy was a big hit with the artillerymen in my coach. He kept us laughing and answered questions during the entire trip to Gloucester. Tommy was the personification of an Ambassador of Good Will!

† †

The staging area outside of Gloucester was nothing to brag about. The housing facilities were adequate, but primitive. Once we became settled, we were kept busy drawing the new equipment we would take to the continent, and in our spare time, we were briefed in what to expect once we were committed to battle. The briefing officers were combat veterans who had 'been there' and knew their subject matter from personal experience. Most of them had been too severely wounded in combat to be returned to battle.

The briefing on what to expect, if captured, made a lasting impression on me, particularly the portion dealing with escape techniques. At the time, I did not know I would use this vital information during my first days of combat in Germany, because at the time, the war still seemed very far away.

During the process of drawing equipment for the Battalion, I had opportunities to motor into the country side surrounding Gloucester. The sight of endless miles and miles of war materials stored in the open, along the English roads and covering the adjoining country side was almost beyond my comprehension. This overwhelming sight made me realize the Allied Air Forces totally controlled the skies and made me wonder why the entire island of Great Britain did not sink beneath the sea from the monstrous weight of these American produced war materials.

Back home I had heard of 'Fish and Chips' and had been told the English people drank their beer un-chilled. On my first pass to Gloucester, I made my way to a friendly pub and had a meal of fish and chips, washed down with room temperature, rich, dark beer. The experience was not unpleasant, however, I'll admit I would rather have had a hamburger all-the-way, with French fries, and a vanilla shake. The fish and chips were served in a cone, fashioned from a rolled-up newspaper. The newspaper served not only as the holder of the fish and fried potato slices, but also absorbed the excess fat left from the frying process, and the excess malt vinegar the proprietor liberally sprinkled over the contents of the newspaper cone.

Annie Dugan and I met outside a theater in Gloucester. She was a fair complected, red headed, teen-aged Irish lass who came to my rescue at the ticket sellers window of the theater. I was not accustomed to the English currency and could not understand the Cockney accent of the ticket seller. Annie, who was standing in the line behind me, came to my rescue by negotiating the ticket price, and retrieving my change. She was so pretty and helpful I decided to wait for her in the theater lobby. As she entered the lobby and approached me, she beat me to the punch and asked if I was alone. When I said yes, she took my arm and announced we would get the best seats in the balcony, and led me up the balcony stairs. I could not believe my good luck!

She was an attractive girl, with pretty red, shoulder length hair, and as I helped her remove her outer garments it was easy to see she had shapely legs and a very feminine body. She chose two seats on the front row of the balcony and as we waited for the show to begin we became acquainted.

Her family ran a hotel in a seaport town on the English Channel which was rented full-time by the United States Navy. She had a war-time job in Gloucester, and went home most weekends. She was perfectly at ease with Americans, in fact, she said she preferred the company of Americans because British men were too serious and did not know how to have fun. I thought I had stumbled onto a gold mine every time Annie told me more about herself.

During my three weeks stay near Gloucester, I saw Annie eight or ten times. We became good friends, enjoyed each other, did some serious necking in her apartment, but nothing more. Her attitude was much the same as Pat's back in Indianapolis, she wanted to enjoy male companionship, but she wanted no entanglements. I liked Annie, she was a likeable girl, but several months later I was exposed to another side of Miss Annie Dugan.

One of the first letters I received from my mother after the Battle of the Bulge in early February 1945, mother said she had received a letter from someone named Annie Dugan. The letter contained a return address of Gloucester, England. The letter stated I was the father of her unborn child. She had heard I was killed during the Battle of the Bulge and thought she was entitled to my $10,000 GI insurance benefits. Of course mother knew I was in England during November 1944 and was reported missing-in-action by the War Department in December 1944. From this knowledge mother thought I was not the child's father. Never-the-less, my straight laced mother took this news badly.

On several occasions I wondered how many other mothers, with sons in the service who passed through England, received a similar letter from Miss Annie Dugan.

† †

At 0545 hours, on 1 December 1944, the 589th FA Bn convoy started to roll as scheduled. As we left the staging area and reached the English highway system we started to gain momentum. Excitement was etched on every face. In the rear of the canvas covered Command Post 2 1/2 ton GMC truck we jabbered constantly above the road noise. With much bravado, we waved at the English civilians who gathered by the road side to watch the truck convoy pass. To each British girl along the way we blew a special kiss. Judging from our actions, we might have been college students on the way to a football game instead of soldiers going off to war.

Again, as the military would say, we reached our destination, Waymouth, England, 'without incident.' The Battalion was billeted in casual barracks and we spent the night on canvas cots after an evening meal of heated "C" rations.

At dawn on 2 December 1944, the Battalion moved by truck to nearby Portland Harbor and had a breakfast of coffee and doughnuts. Before we moved our vehicles, howitzers, and equipment on board the two waiting Landing Ship Tanks (LSTs), all men were issued life preservers and motion sickness pills. The rest of the day was spent at anchor in the harbor.

With time on our hands, many of the fellows speculated on what lay ahead. None of us were deep-water sailors. We had no idea how long it would take to cross the English Channel, and once across, we had no clue as to our final destination. This total lack of information led to numerous and heated debates concerning the future. I finally came to the conclusion that the guys who knew the least, argued the loudest.

After the evening chow, I smoked a Lucky Strike and hit the sack. As I drifted off to sleep, the last thing I remembered hearing was a heated argument on deck. Only this time the guys were arguing about who was cheating as they shot craps into the night.

Early on the morning of 3 December 1944, our two LSTs sailed from the calm waters of Portland Harbor and joined a sizeable convoy of ships heading for the port city of LeHarve, France, located at the mouth of the Seine River. The Coast Guard would classify the channel crossing as routine, but in December the Channel is not overly kind to landlubbers. We experienced rough seas and the flat bottomed LSTs had distinctive motions of their own in the turbulent waters of the English Channel.

The motion sickness pills probably helped, but at one time or another, most of the men of the 589th hung their heads over the rail of the LST and fed the fish. The effects of sea sickness are hard to describe to anyone who has not experienced the feeling. To those who have been sea sick, I need not explain. The memory is one you retain for a long time. To negate the motion of the LST, I tried to center myself on deck, breath deeply of the fresh sea air, and look at the distant horizon. These were techniques learned as a young Sea Scout in Cocoa, Florida. These actions tend to minimize the roll and pitch of the ship.

To get my sea legs, I decided to wander around the deck of the LST. I happened to spot my old Florida buddy, Sergeant Barney Alford, a 105mm howitzer section chief in Battery A. I sat beside him on the trails of his howitzer and we started to talk. "What are you doing Barney?"

"I'm just thinking Randy. What are you doing?"

"Oh, I'm trying not to get sea sick again."

"Christ, why did you bring up that subject? Don't you have something better to think about? Have they killed your brain in Fire Direction? You need to get a job and do something. I have a job open in my section that calls for a PFC. Think you could handle it?"

"Hell yes Barney! I'd give up two stripes any day to work for you. Every body says you're the worst Sergeant in the Army. Is that true Barney?"

"That may have been true until you came along, you Goldbrick."

"Now that we are sufficiently insulted, I have an artillery question for you."

"What is this now Randy? A quiz?"

"Yes, kind of."

"I don't know which is worse Randy, talking to you, or getting sea sick, but here goes. What is the question?"

"Barney, if a submarine surfaced to attack us with it's deck gun, could you hit it with your howitzer?"

He looked at me in surprise and asked, "What in the hell do you have on your mind?"

"Oh I was just wondering. Here we are, slowly cruising along on an unarmed vessel, and I just realized how easy it would be for a U-Boat to sink us."

"Well, for one thing Randy, we're in the middle of a convoy, with plenty of armed warships to protect us. The second thing, if a U-Boat wanted to sink a ship, it could do much more damage by sinking a major man-of-war than it could by sinking this dinky little LST."

"I know you are right Barney, but I was just thinking."

"To answer your question, ole buddy, look at the way this tub rides in the water, it bounces like a cork. From the deck of this LST, I don't think I could hit the continent of Europe with my 105, let-alone hit a half submerged sub."

"That's about the way I had it figured, but we have a lots of fire power here on deck. I like the idea of Sergeant Alford standing on the bow of the LST yelling to the Coast Guard skipper, Damn the torpedoes, full speed ahead."

As he shook his head and laughed Barney said, "Randy, your trouble is, you read too much."

We sat there lost in thought, as good friends do, and started to laugh at the ridiculous idea of trying to hit a moving target with a field artillery howitzer positioned on the deck of a pitching and rolling LST.

This unlikely hypothetical scenario produced the best laughs of the entire voyage.

The look-out on our LST sighted the coast of France in the late afternoon hours. Due to choppy seas and the numerous ships in the port of LeHarve the convoy commander decided to cruise in a circle about five miles off shore for the night rather than attempt to enter the crowded harbor under black-out conditions. We spent a miserable night pitching and tossing in the English Channel. The morning of 4 December 1944, we were extremely glad to see the sun rise and feel the increased forward motion of the LST as it moved into it's place in the convoy line headed for the sheltered waters of the seaport at LeHarve, France.

As we neared the port, we saw the first signs of war damage on the continent. The famous seaport had suffered heavy battle damage, probably from both sides in the war. However, the port was operational and overcrowded with Navy and merchant ships delivering war materials to the Allies on the continent. We were slightly puzzled when we steamed through the harbor and continued our journey up the beautiful Seine River, by-passing the port facilities completely. Whether this by-pass was planned initially, or dictated by the overcrowded port, was never explained to the troops. Never-the-less, we spent a peaceful night anchored in the calm waters of the Seine River a few miles inland from LeHarve.

Whatever dictated the decision did not concern me because I stayed on deck the entire trip from LeHarve to Rouen. The cruise up the river was incredibly beautiful, the river itself, the farmlands, and the villages. The French people along the way who stopped work to watch the ships cruise past were a sight that is hard to forget.

Our LST arrived on the outskirts of Rouen, France about noon 5 December 1944. We had been on the LST for almost four days and although the living conditions aboard the ship were not bad, the prospects of getting our feet on dry land again was pleasant.

The process of leaving the LST was relatively simple. The ship made a slow, wide turn in the river, and moved perpendicular to the shore. The forward momentum of the ship moved the bow onto the beach. The huge bow doors of the LST were swung wide open and a heavy-duty landing ramp was lowered to connect the ship to the firm bank of the Seine. We then started our engine motors and drove the vehicles, pulling their loads of trailers and howitzers, onto French soil. The process drew vast crowds of waiving and clapping French civilians and local military personnel, who welcomed us as conquering heroes. In appreciation, we showered the children with candy bars and chewing gum, an the adults with cigarettes. The landing produced a carnival like atmosphere.

During this unloading process I received my first real cultural shock. While sitting on the LST deck, awaiting our turn to leave the ship, I intently watched the crowd. One distinguished looking elderly gentlemen, probably a veteran of WWI, calmly walked to the edge of the river. There, in the midst of a crowd of women and children, he unzipped his pants, and proceeded to void his bladder into the pristine waters of the Seine River. No one paid the slightest attention to the old man. Both he and the others were perfectly comfortable with his actions. However, I could still remember how embarrassed I was when the sweet southern lady sat on her front porch and rocked, as she watched me urinate in her front yard while on the way to winter maneuvers in Tennessee.

The next day, 6 December 1944, we spent in a bivouac area outside of Rouen preparing our vehicles for the long motor march to our first combat position somewhere in Germany.

11

First Combat Position in Europe

The 589th FA Bn left the Rouen area early on the morning of 7 December 1944. The 422nd Regimental Combat Team, which included the 589th, then motored in convoy to a bivouac area near Roselle, Belgium. Enroute to Roselle, we witnessed the first evidence of war since leaving the port of LeHarve. During this portion of the trip we observed a landscape pitted with enormous bomb craters and substantial numbers of damaged motorized and horse-drawn German vehicles. The fact the invincible armies of the Third Reich were still using horse-drawn equipment was surprising to me.

The mood of the men in my unit became more somber as the cold and wet weather began to take its toll and the expectation of combat began to dominate our thinking. We rode steadily into the unknown, each man engrossed in his own thoughts, and enduring his own personal misery in silence.

The convoy reached the Belgian town of St. Vith the afternoon of 8 December 1944. This town was an important communications and transportation hub for both North-South and East-West traffic. Our Division, the 106th Infantry Division, ultimately chose this town as the location for its forward headquarters because it was located approximately in the center of the area the 106th Infantry Division was assigned to defend.

The men of the 589th FA Bn parked our vehicles on the side of a hill just north of town, ate a meal, then we waited for the return of our Commanding Officer, Lieutenant Colonel Thomas P. Kelly, Jr., who had gone to Division Artillery Headquarters to receive our latest orders. As ordered, we moved into a bivouac area near the village of Wallerode to service the vehicles and to spend the night. The weather was extremely cold and the snow quite deep. Sounds of distant artillery fire and the bright light of their muzzle flashes occasionally broke the stillness of the night.

The final leg of our journey to the front lines was completed on 9 December 1944. That day the 589th FA Bn relieved the 15th FA Bn of the veteran 2nd Infantry Division in defensive positions some two miles south of Auw, Germany.

† †

By 10 December 1944 the 422nd Infantry Regiment had established its defensive front, and was occupying pill boxes on the western side of the German Siegfried Line and all of the territory west of these fortifications. The Germans were securely dug-in and occupying fortifications about three miles east of the American forces. This created a type of no-man's land in the buffer area between the two forces.

The 422nd had several problems to cope with however. First, the front of their fortifications were facing in the wrong direction, with the rear, instead of the front, facing the enemy. Second, the Main Supply Route (MSR), over which the 422nd Infantry Regiment received supplies could not be considered an all-weather road, and Third, the Regimental front was so wide, and the infantry defenders spread so thin, this front could not be held against any type of determined attack.

As ordered, the 589th took over the positions of the 15th FA Bn, lock, stock, and barrel. We even left our new 105mm howitzers in the bivouac area for the withdrawing 15th FA Bn, and took over the worn 105s left by the 15th FA Bn. We were ordered to occupy their dugouts, howitzer positions, command posts, and observation posts, with no changes. The 2nd Infantry Division veterans advised us this was an inactive sector and we would gradually acquire our combat experience during the severe winter months. Being new to combat, we were grateful for this information, and immediately set about the business of establishing ourselves as an effective Field Artillery Battalion.

Even though we felt confident of our ability to provide effective support for the 422nd, and felt comfortable with the infantry between us and the enemy, the 589th had it's own problems. First, the 15th FA Bn had been in position long enough to improve the living accommodations for the howitzer crews, but the howitzer emplacements themselves were poorly designed, and did not contain the space necessary to shift the position of a howitzer so it could cover the entire width of the Regimental area of responsibility. This fact restricted the ability of our Artillery Battalion to mass all 12 howitzers on a single target in a reasonable period of time. Second, the firing batteries discovered, almost too late, their 2 1/2 ton prime movers could not reach the gun emplacements, making it almost impossible to withdraw the howitzers without a Herculean effort from the Cannoneers themselves. And Third, the left flank of the Battalion was not protected by the 422nd Infantry Regiment, but was inadequately defended, if defended at all, by a thinly spread Reconnaissance Squadron. This meant any enemy break-through to out north could quickly deny us the ability to withdraw the Battalion..

The 589th Battalion Command Post (CP) was located in a relatively large stone and timbered German farm house. The CP housed the senior battalion officers; Lieutenant Colonel Kelly, and Majors Goldstein and Parker, the Fire Direction Center and Message Center, plus the enlisted personnel necessary to man these centers 24 hours per day. Once ensconced in this building, I realized how lucky I was to be a fire control technician. The farm house was almost as sturdy as a pill box, and the ground floor was heated with a wood burning stove which also served as a cook stove. These were very comfortable quarters compared to being in a howitzer section, or in a communications crew, whose members were outside in the inclement weather a majority of the time.

Initially, as predicted, this sector turned out to be relatively inactive. Both American and German activity was mainly confined to infantry patrols, and small arms fire fights. The artillery action consisted of normal interdiction and harassing missions, with occasional missions fired by artillery forward observers upon targets of opportunity. By the time we had been in this position for three days, life had developed into a routine.

Several miles east of out Command Post, the Germans had installed 'Buzz Bomb' launching ramps. These German V2 rockets contained a ton of explosives, flew on short stubby wings, had a normal aircraft tail assembly, and were powered by a ram-jet engine. These flying bombs, which flew directly over our position at a very low altitude, were on their way to targets in Liege and/or Brussels, Belgium. The ram-jet engine made a sound similar to a four cylinder engine, running on two cylinders. The sound of these engines was very distinctive!

During the evening hours we could safely watch the light of the hot exhaust gasses from these engines as the bombs passed overhead. Off in the distance we often watched lines of lazy tracers trails from quad, 50-caliber machine guns valiantly trying to intercept the V2s as anti-aircraft batteries tried to explode the bombs before they reached their intended target. Occasionally we would witness a huge explosion when a bomb was hit. We would actually applaud when we viewed this spectacular sight.

After witnessing this sight for several nights some 589th machine gunners decided to join the war effort and planned to shot down a 'Buzz Bomb' as it passed over our position. Several 50-caliber machine guns were mounted at strategic locations in the area, and bets were placed on which machine gun crew would 'Pop' the first 'Buzz Bomb.' The gunners were right, the task turned out to be fairly simple. They 'Popped' the third 'Buzz Bomb' which flew above our position. However, no one had anticipated the disastrous effect caused by one ton of high-explosives being detonated about 600 or 700 yards above our heads.

The explosion caused several fatalities in a heard of milk cows grazing directly underneath the violent explosion. One heavily loaded supply truck was blown off of the road and onto it's side. The poor driver, badly dazed, was yelling he had his million dollar wound, and was going home. Several of the men from the 589th received headaches and experienced ringing in their ears from the explosion. Many guys thought we had been bombed, but those who knew the facts would not identify the perpetrator.

During the aftermath of this self-made disaster, no machine gun crew would take credit for the 'kill,' therefore all bets were cancelled.

On the afternoon of 15 December 1944, after I was relieved from my duties in the Fire Direction Center, I called Sergeant Alford at "A" Battery and invited myself over for a drink. When I arrived, Barney and his off-duty crew were sipping Cognac and had a low-stakes poker game under way. Their living bunker was warm from body heat and the heat from a small GI cooking stove. Everyone was in good spirits. Barney dropped out of the game and he and I lounged on a couple of built-in bunks, sipped Cognac straight from the bottle, and talked about the University of Florida and what we would do when the war was over.

While trudging through the knee-deep snow on the way back to the Command Post, I thanked the kind angel who guided me into the Field Artillery instead of the Infantry. Living outdoors in this weather would be impossible. When I reached the CP, I stuck my head into the Fire Direction Center and told Staff Sergeant Frank Tacker I was going to turn in for the night. Frank nodded and said he would have someone get me out of the sack in time for breakfast.

I partially undressed in the unheated attic of the farm house and slipped into my bed roll. In the silence of the attic, I could faintly hear the sounds of war in the far off distance. Not knowing what would happen tomorrow, I thanked my Heavenly Father for keeping me out of harm's way, and then fell fast asleep.

The German Winter Ardennes Offensive, later called "The Battle of the Bulge", (above), started early, the morning of 16 December, 1944, with a terrifying Artillery Barrage. Large German artillery shells exploding during the early morning darkness of 16 December, 1944

Fighting both the frigid weather and the advancing German forces during the daylight hours was fierce. A miserably cold and fatigued Sergeant Pierson, (right), rests on the bumper of a knocked-out Kraut half-track.

12

The German Ardennes Offensive Begins

Command Post
589th Field Artillery Battalion — 16 December 1944

At 0540 hours on 16 December 1944 dim flashes of lightening mixed with distant rolls of thunder awakened me from a shallow sleep. I had a strong urge to urinate but tried to fight it off. A trip to the latrine, outside the building, in the cold and deep snow did not appeal to me. The unheated attic where I slept was cold, but my bed roll was snug and warm. I looked at my watch, the GI luminous dial indicated 0540 hours. My shift in the Fire Direction Center did not start until 0700. Trusting my bladder would hold until then, I quickly went back to sleep.

Ten minutes later, Lieutenant Clausen, the Battalion Survey Officer, opened the attic door, looked in, and laughed. He witnessed eight enlisted men, dressed in long johns, long woolen socks, and woolen skull caps, sleeping on the attic floor in bed rolls. He then yelled, "Sergeant Pierson, drop your cock and grab your socks, we need you in Fire Direction." For emphasis, he added with authority, "RIGHT NOW" as he left the room.

Getting dressed in a hurry in the cold is easy. You learned quickly to keep your outer garments close at hand. In about three minutes , fully clothed, I made my way from the dark attic through the kitchen and down the cellar stairs. The double woolen blanked, used to black-out the cellar door, parted and

Lieutenant Clausen motioned me into the CP. Slightly peeved, I replied, "With your permission Sir, I have to take a leak."

The Lieutenant grinned, and with typical army humor, told me, "OK Sergeant, hurry up and take a leak, but only shake your pecker once. Shaking it more than one time is playing with it, and we don't have time for you to play with your pecker!"

Outside the building my eyes readjusted to the dark. At the enlisted men's latrine I started to void my bladder. The thunder and lightening flashes were north and east of our position. They seemed to be getting louder and brighter. Back home in Florida, flashes and thunder like this were common in the early morning hours.

Suddenly it dawned on me, this was not a Florida early morning thunder storm. This is Germany and this is combat. I was witnessing a heavy artillery barrage, several miles away, and thought, "Somebody north of us is catching Hell. I wish them no bad luck, but I'm damned glad it is them and not us."

Standing in the deep snow, astride the latrine slit trench, I obeyed the Lieutenant's order and proceeded to urinate and "Shake my pecker only once." Before I zipped the fly on my pants closed, I heard the unmistakable 'Woosh – Woosh – Woosh' of an incoming artillery shell. Promptly, I fell to the ground and heard the Command Post guard screaming at the top of his voice, "INCOMING MAIL!"

The loud noise and violent concussion of the nearby exploding shell froze me with terror in the total darkness. The 'Whir -r -r -r' of shell fragments flying through the air sounded like the flight of huge insects, while chucks of ice and frozen earth raining down upon my prone body intensified my fears. Stunned, shaking and with my heart racing, I lay there waiting for more shells to explode. I did not move until Lieutenant Clausen emerged from the farm house to check on the CP guard and yelled, "Sergeant Pierson, are you OK?"

"Yes Sir."

"Well get your ass back in this building – Pronto!"

We had occupied this position for six days with almost no action, and frankly, expected none. Our mission was simple, hold this ground until the

Allies mounted their spring offensive. Then we would head for Berlin!

As I entered the Command Post, the outside cold and darkness changed to warmth and light. This change was welcome! Still shaken, although not hurt, I noticed the CP was full. The Battalion Commander, Lieutenant Colonel Thomas P. Kelly, Jr. was talking to Division Artillery on the telephone and had a stern look on his face. Major Arthur C. Parker, III, the Battalion Plans and Operations Officer (S3), was plotting information on the situation map as Captain Joe Cox, the Battalion Intelligence Officer (S2), relayed information to the Major as he received it over the telephone from the Division Intelligence Officer. Only Lieutenant Clausen seemed calm and relaxed when he asked me, "Sergeant, did you shake your pecker more than once?"

Being the junior officer in battalion headquarters, he was much closer to the enlisted men than the older, more senior, officers. As a result, all of the non-commissioned officers, such as myself, liked him and confided in him. He was a good officer! I was in the process of telling him I was so scared, when I heard the incoming artillery shell, I forgot to shake my pecker at all, when Staff Sergeant Frank Tacker interrupted us. Tacker was in telephone contact with all three firing batteries and they were reporting many incoming rounds exploding in their battery positions. I immediately thought of "A" Battery and my buddy, Sergeant Barney Alford.

Lieutenant Clausen left us and informed both Captain Cox and Major Parker of the artillery attack on our positions. The Major immediately relayed this information to Division Artillery. Information was now beginning to flow!

Frank Tacker, the Intelligence Sergeant, motioned for me to move into the portion of the cellar designated as the Fire Direction Center. Once away from the intense senior officers I asked Tacker what was going on. He did not know many facts, only rumors. First rumor: Jerry had accumulated some excess ammunition and was just raising hell in our sector. Second rumor: A large scale German offensive was going to follow the heavy artillery barrage now underway in our sector. Conclusion—take your pick.

About 0630 hours we received our first fire mission of the day from 'Hotshot 1,' one of our forward observers up front with the 422nd Infantry Regiment.

'Hotshot 1' was excited! He reported no visibility due to fog, but infantry listening posts were reporting sounds of running motors and moving tracked vehicles at various locations along the entire Regimental front. He also reported a heavy, repeat heavy, artillery barrages impacting the entire 422nd Regimental front. Hotshot 1 requested unobserved fire immediately on eight pre-selected targets suspected of being German assembly and staging areas.

Before Hotshot 1 finished his requests for artillery support, Major Parker interrupted and told us in Fire Direction to, "Give him what he needs," and went back to confer with the Battalion Intelligence officer.

Lieutenant Clausen, now acting as the fire direction officer, took the phone from Staff Sergeant Tacker, told us to alert the firing batteries, and tried to get more information from the forward observer, Hotshot 1. Frank Tacker and I alerted the three firing batteries of multiple fire missions ahead and began to send fire commands: "Elevation 1390, Deflection 067, 1 Round, Charge 5, Shell High Explosive, Fuse Quick, Battery Right at Ten Second Intervals—Fire When Ready!"

Fifty one seconds later "A" Battery reported, "First Round on the Way," quickly followed by reports from "B" and "C" Batteries. Lieutenant Clausen reported "On the Way" to Hotshot 1 and continued to pump him for current information. Tacker and I were pleased with the firing batteries fast response-time to the first fire mission and Tacker commented, "A Battery got off the first round again," and half thinking out loud added, "Of course they usually do."

These first six fire missions, started the battle that Americans later called the 'Battle of the Bulge,' and the Germans referred to as their 'Ardennes Offensive.' The 589th delivered 72 rounds of 105mm high explosive shells with fuses set to detonate upon impact. Twelve rounds struck each of the six enemy target areas at 10 second intervals. This mission lasted about 10 minutes, from the beginning until the last firing battery reported, "Mission Complete." The Executive Officers of all three firing batteries reported sporadic incoming artillery rounds and asked Lieutenant Clausen if any of the battalion forward observers could spot the enemy artillery flashes and direct counter battery fire against the German artillery positions. All artillery forward observers reported negative. Vision was still impossible due to darkness and fog.

Hotshot 1 reported the sounds of moving tracked vehicles had diminished as the result of our first interdiction fire. With this information now available, Major Parker and Lieutenant Clausen studied battle maps and began preparing firing data for additional interdiction and harassing artillery fire in support of the infantry.

Tacker continued to talk with Hotshot 1 and the picture of the situation in front of the 422nd Infantry Regiment started to clear. The enemy artillery barrage had lifted in this sector and German infantry, heavily supported with armor, was probing outpost positions of the 422nd in earnest. German artillery fire, which had softened up the infantry, was now starting to concentrate upon the three firing batteries of the 589th Field Artillery Battalion. In fact, the firing batteries were now on the telephone reporting heavy enemy artillery fire landing in their positions.

Suddenly, about 0700, the conversation with Hotshot 1 was interrupted. The telephone line had been shot away, or cut by the advancing German infantry. We, of course, did not know which. The 589th switchboard operator reported the line completely dead. Frantically we changed to radio communications and finally made contact again with our forward observers. Hotshot 1 advised us the infantry outposts had been overrun and the main line of resistance (MLR) was beginning to crumble. He said he had been ordered back to Infantry Regiment Headquarters and would reestablish radio contact with us when he arrived there.

I never saw or heard from Hotshot 1 again!

By 0800 hours of the first day of the Battle of the Bulge, devastating German artillery fire had completely destroyed our forward telephone lines and the German signalmen were expertly jamming the radio frequencies we used to communicate with the infantry. We felt helpless and frustrated, we could no longer support our infantry! Lieutenant Colonel Kelly ordered Captain Beans, the Battalion Communications Officer, to take wire crews forward to locate and repair the damaged telephone wire net. Captain Beans, a huge man from Texas, did not blink an eye when he saluted the Battalion Commander and said,

"Yes Sir," and hurriedly left the Command Post. A few hours later I witnessed the body of Captain Beans sprawled across the hood of his shot-up jeep, the driver trying desperately to get the bloody and badly mangled body of this brave Captain to the Battalion Aid Station.

This was the last time I saw Captain Alva R. Beans. Almost fifty years later, I learned Captain Beans ultimately survived his heinous wounds but was never returned to battle.

† †

Communications were now limited to Division Artillery located in St. Vith, Belgium. Brigadier General McMahon, the Division Artillery Commander in St. Vith painted a dreary picture of the tactical situation to Lieutenant Colonel Kelly. A German panzer unit had breached the American lines to the north of the 589th FA Bn position. The breach was between the 14th Cavalry Group and the north flank of the 422nd Infantry Regiment. The 14th Cavalry Group was withdrawing under the weight of the enemy advance. The 422nd Infantry east of the 589th, was holding, but was defending itself on three sides, and could become completely surrounded within a matter of hours.

How did this affect the 589th Field Artillery Battalion? General McMahon advised Lieutenant Colonel Kelly that German armor, reinforced by armored infantry, would probably converge on the 589th howitzer positions from the north and east by 1400 hours. His specific orders were not firm at this time. For now, he suggested the 589th should prepare to defend itself in place. But, he added, also prepare to withdraw, under attack, utilizing elements of the 422nd Infantry that might fall back through the existing 589th artillery positions.

After talking with General McMahon, the Colonel immediately started to confer with his Executive Officer, Major Elliott Goldstein and his S-3, Major Parker.

The first decision was to close the Fire Direction Center as it could no longer be used in this situation. Major Parker ordered Staff Sergeant Tacker to, 'Close Station' for all but a skeleton Command Post crew and to prepare to withdraw to a farmhouse some 2,000 yards to the west of our current position. This location had been previously reconnoitered by our Executive Officer, Major

Goldstein and had been previously designated as 'CP Rear.' Within minutes, off duty personnel had been mobilized to pack and load communications and fire direction equipment, plus personal gear into the Command Post 2 1/2 ton GMC truck. The Command Post 3/4 ton Dodge truck was left empty to accommodate remaining equipment and the skeleton CP crew.

This task completed, Tacker and the majority of the CP crew departed to the CP Rear to establish a new Command Post and a communications network connecting to the new firing battery positions and Division Artillery in St. Vith.

The second decision was based upon the premise that the Battalion would be attacked from the north and/or the ease in a matter of hours. "B" Battery, being the center battery in the present location was not in a good position to defend itself from either direction. Consequently the Commanding Officer of "B" Battery was ordered to 'Close Station – March Order' and immediately began to withdraw to the alternate firing battery position designated 'Baker Rear.' Once emplaced, "B" Battery would be in a position to support the subsequent withdrawal of "A" and "C" Batteries, plus the remainder of Headquarters Battery. Major Goldstein was assigned the responsibility of commanding all personnel at the rear positions, plus relocating Service Battery, and designating a new supply route from Service Battery to the new Battalion CP.

The third decision was to turn the four howitzers of "C" Battery to face more northerly. "A" Battery required only minor adjustments to accomplish it's new mission at this time as it already covered the terrain to the east of our first position.

These decisions all proved to be rational based upon the information available to us. For instance, new reports received from Division Headquarters established the fact that both enemy armor and infantry had entered the town of Auw, Germany, which was located less than two miles north of us. There, the enemy was battering the exposed left flank of the vastly out-manned and out-gunned 422nd Infantry Regiment. To enable "C" Battery to provide effective fire in the direction of Auw, an observation post had to be established on the road which ran northward toward Auw. Major Parker called the "C" Battery Commander and advised him to position his four howitzers so they could provide indirect fire support to our infantry as they fought in, or were displaced from, Auw. It was also necessary for "C" Battery to be able to provide direct fire upon the Auw road in defense of his battery position against a direct infantry and/or an armored assault. The Major also advised him Lieutenant Clausen and a forward observation crew would contact him by radio once the "C" Battery forward observation post overlooking the Auw road was established.

As Lieutenant Clausen and his driver, a good friend of mine, Guy D. Smith, Jr. from Texas, prepared to leave on the trip to the new observation post I advised them both to take care, and waved good-bye as they left in their loaded-down jeep.

At the time, I did not know I would never see either of my friends again!

After addressing the reality of an attack from Auw, north of us, time was then spent debating the possibility of an attack from the direction of Prum, Germany which was located some twelve miles east of our current position and was a known marshaling yard for German soldiers and equipment. The potential threat from the east forced some minor changes in the mission initially assigned to "A" Battery. The new defensive plan for "A" Battery involved leaving the 3rd and 4th howitzer sections, on the right flank of the battery, in place to deliver indirect fire to the east toward Prum. The left platoon of the battery would be split and the howitzers re-emplaced. The 2nd howitzer section would be placed to cover the wooded area directly east of the battalion to protect against an infantry assault from that direction. The 1st howitzer section, commanded by my ole buddy from Florida, Sergeant Barney Alford, would be placed to cover the road leading eastward toward Prum. Any armored attack from the direction of Prum would be confined to the road itself because of serious icing and deep snow conditions. Also, the trees in this portion of the Ardennes Forest were so thick, Panzers could not leave the road.

Major Parker called Captain Menke, CO of "A" Battery and caught him in his command bunker. When Captain Menke was summoned to the phone he answered, "Good morning Major," and asked the question, "What in the hell is going on?"

"We don't know yet Captain, but Division Artillery thinks the 422nd Infantry will ultimately be surrounded. We are in a vulnerable position, sitting here behind them. Do you remember any of your old infantry training?"

"No I don't Major, I thought we were in the Field Artillery. You know, 'and those Caissons go rolling along,' and all that stuff."

The Major continued, "I have ordered "B" Battery to withdraw to 'Baker Rear' to cover the rest of the battalion if we have to withdraw also. The Colonel has also established a 'Command Post Rear' and placed Major Goldstein in command there. We've turned "C" Battery to face north to defend against an expected attack from Auw. I want you to leave your right platoon as is. Emplace one of your howitzers to cover our eastern side to defend against infantry infiltrating through the forest, and relocate your remaining howitzer section to cover the road from Prum with direct fire. If we encounter penetration through the 422nd Infantry, anti-tank fire will be required to defend against the approaching Panzers on that road. I'll be over in a few minutes and we will make a decision on the anti-tank position. Captain, do you have any questions?"

"Can't think of any right now Major. You have given me an idea of what we have to do. When you are ready, come to my command bunker, I'm certain I will have questions by then, we can discuss them over a cup of hot coffee."

Frank Tacker and I were busy closing down the Fire Direction Center when Lieutenant Colonel Kelly called for me. I walked over to the Command Post side of the cellar where Lieutenant Colonel Kelly and Major Parker were looking at the situation map which was still mounted on the wall. The Colonel asked me a very direct question, "Sergeant Pierson do you understand what we are trying to do?"

"Partially, sir."

Major Parker broke into the conversation and pointed to the newly updated situation map and then he said, "There is one missing piece," and inserted one more pin into the map. The location was east of the battalion and on the north side of the road leading to Prum. "We need an observation and listening post here." As I nodded my head in the affirmative, he asked, "Think you can handle it?"

This question caught me by surprise. I had assumed I would be going back to help establish the 'Command Post Rear.' I looked squarely at Major Parker, but got no response. After regaining my composure, I replied in a very unmilitary manner, "Sure, why not?"

"I know you can! We need eyes and ears on the east side of us. We expect infantry from the 422nd to be withdrawing toward us on the Prum road soon. We also think they may be followed closely by German Panzers and infantry. The idea is for us to let our folks through, but slow down, or stop, the following enemy. I want you to take a radio operator and a couple of men and establish an observation and listening post at the location indicated by this pin in the map. Think you can find it?"

It was clear to me the pin in the map was on the south side of a hill overlooking a deep and narrow cut where the Prum road ran through the hill. I looked at the Operations Officer and answered, "Yes Sir."

Lieutenant Colonel Kelly, an expert reader of maps, asked me a check question, "What terrain features do you see on the map that will indicate you are in the right location?"

The thought occurred to me, "Once a teacher, always a teacher." The Colonel was testing me now just as he had tested me during winter maneuvers in Tennessee and while we trained at Camp Atterbury, Indiana. In detail I explained to the Colonel how I would recognize the right location when my party reached it.

Apparently satisfied I knew how to find the proper location, the Colonel told me to get going as I had no time to waste. He added, "Sergeant, check in by radio when you get situated. Also, keep in mind, this is not a combat position, I need information. Stay under cover as much as possible, and remember, I need current information." His last statement to me was, "If, for some reason, you get separated from the unit, get your men back to Command Post Rear. If you find no one there, make your way south and west to Division Headquarters in St. Vith."

At the time I did not know it, but these were the last instructions I would ever receive from my respected Battalion Commander. After putting WWII experiences behind for many years, I joined the 106th Infantry Division

Association in the late 1980s. To my surprise, I learned that Colonel Kelly had survived WWII and had returned to his law practice in Tampa, Florida. Through telephone and mail contacts I was privileged to contribute to his published book, *THE FIGHTIN' 589th.*

† †

As I left the Command Post I told Private First Class "Brownie" Brown to dress warm, bring his carbine, a few extra clips of ammunition, a portable radio, and follow me. Outside I found Private First Class Jim Lemley and gave him the same instructions.

On foot, the three of us crossed the Prum road and entered the thick forest for cover. We turned east and walked parallel to the road. As we approached the rear of the "A" Battery position, an extremely nervous guard yelled, "HALT! Who Goes There?"

This challenge sounded so out of place I almost laughed, but when I heard a rifle bolt click and slam a round into the chamber, I yelled, "This is Sergeant Pierson and two guys from Headquarters Battery."

A cautions voice responded, "I don't know any Sergeant Pierson from Headquarters Battery."

Getting a little testy, I yelled back, "Well I don't know you either! Put the fucking gun down, we have to come through the "A" Battery position."

"Who told you to come through "A" Battery?"

"Colonel Kelly, you shit head."

"How do I know Colonel Kelly told you to come through "A" Battery? Do you know anybody in "A" Battery?"

"I'll answer both questions. You don't, and yes I do."

"Who do you know in "A" Battery?"

"That's enough of this bull shit! We are up to our ass in snow, we are cold, and we have to get through. Call Barney Alford and tell him Randy wants to talk with him."

"Do you know Sergeant Alford?"

"Yes he is from Pensacola, Florida, he chews tobacco, and he spits a lot."

"Yep, you know him. OK, come on through."

The walk out of the forest and through the "A" Battery position was much easier than breaking a new trail through the deep snow in the woods. On the way through "A" Battery we found Barney and Corporal Fairchild, the Battalion Artillery Mechanic, working on Barney's howitzer. Under the circumstances, the meeting was friendly, but brief.

"Well, as I live and breathe, this must be the lovable, tobacco chewing, and Cognac drinking, Sergeant Alford, the pride of "A" Battery. How are you doing Barney?"

"You lost? You Headquarters Battery, 24 carat, goldbrick. What in the hell are you doing in a firing battery? If you hang around here long enough, I'll get some work out of your skinny ass. We have to move this howitzer out to the road and set it up for direct fire, you know, like an anti-tank gun."

"I know, I heard Major Parker talking to Captain Menke about your assignment."

"Randy, what good will my 105 be out there on the road. In this fog, we can't see more than a couple of hundred yards."

"That's one thing we need to talk about Barney. I'm on my way to setup a listening post about a thousand yards down the road. We'll be located to the left of the road and about twenty yards up the hill that overlooks it. If you have to fire direct fire in that direction, for Christ's sake don't shoot to the left of the road. We won't be dug-in and we certainly don't want to get clobbered by fire from 'A' Battery."

"It's a good thing you told me where you are going. Damn, we could wipe you out by accident and you know we don't want to do that."

"Barney, you're one of the few firing battery idiots I trust. That's why we detoured by here to talk to you. I want a responsible person to know where we are."

"Who is with you, ole buddy?"

"Brown and Lemley."

"That's all?"

"Yea, they were the only guys I could find that were not nailed down."

"Randy, I think you could use some help. Could you use Corporal Fairchild?"

"I could use another man. I'd feel better with one more man in case something goes wrong. But Barney, Fairchild is from Service Battery, he would have to volunteer, I can't order him to come with us."

"Hold on a minute Randy." Sergeant Alford called Corporal Fairchild over and explained the situation. After several questions, Charlie Fairchild nodded his head and Barney introduced us. "Charlie, do you know Sergeant Pierson?"

"I don't really know him, but I know who he is. Is he a friend of yours Sergeant Alford?"

Without hesitation, Sergeant Alford emphasized, "Yes, he is a damned good friend. He has his tail in a crack and needs someone with common sense to help him."

The three of us, two Sergeants and one Corporal, the people who face the enemy and fight the skirmishes, decided the detail would take a bazooka, even though we were not expected to defend the listening post. As Barney and I talked about good times in sunny Florida, Charlie Fairchild went in search of a bazooka and ammunition.

Our observation and listening post was no more than a dot on a battle map. It was positioned to cover an east/west secondary road which connected Prum, Germany with a main north/south highway to our rear. This main highway connected St. Vith and Liege, Belgium. Our prime problem was visibility, we heard tank engines, but could not see them. We had almost zero visibility, a complete white-out. No earth, no sky, no trees, and no road. Nothing but pure white snow merging with dense white fog.

The four of us sat on our heels and waited on the south slope of a steep hill in the Ardennes Forest. The temperature hovered near twelve degrees and in a crouched position the snow was chest deep. The cold and the snow were both a curse and a blessing. Frigid cold numbed our senses, cracked our lips until they bled, pained our feet and fingers, and froze our carbines so they would not fire. The deep snow, however, hid us from the oncoming Germans, offered some protection from the merciless cold wind, and, being twenty degrees warmer than the air, tempered the penetrating cold somewhat.

Private First Class Brown whispered, "TANKS! I hear tanks moving Sergeant Pierson. The sounds are getting louder. They are coming our way! What should we do?"

My answer did not require much thought, "Brownie, fire up the radio and notify Colonel Kelly at Battalion Headquarters."

The creaking, clanking steel treads on frozen ground, combined with the undulating roar of the powerful and un-muffled engines indicated the oncoming vehicles were Panzers. American M4 Sherman tanks made a much different sound.

This fact posed more questions than answers. How many Panzers were there? How close were they? But more important to us, were they supported by infantry, or were they merely a motorized reconnaissance patrol assigned to make contact with the American main line of resistance? Despite the harsh weather and unanswered questions, the steadily advancing German Panzers were our immediate concern.

The temporary listening post was not defensible. I moved Private First Class Lemley one hundred yards east along the hill to warn us if infantry was advancing with the Panzers. I sent Private First Class Brown to the top of the hill behind us, to maintain radio contact with Battalion, and to alert us if enemy infantry approached from the rear. Corporal Fairchild and I remained in place. We assembled and loaded the 2.36 inch anti-tank bazooka, just in case.

The activity involved in getting ready for the frightening events to come calmed our frayed nerves. My natural instincts told me to get up and run, to bug-out, but my orders were to stay, listen, and report. Consequently, I stayed busy until the ground around me shook and the roar of powerful motors was deafening. Then I looked.

About thirty feet beneath us, and two hundred yards to the east, the white fog gave way to a mammoth, dirty gray monster festooned with contrasting black crosses highlighted with white backgrounds. The lead tank commander, in a Mk V Panther, was leaning out of the open hatch, eyes glued to the ground, issuing directions in German to the driver, desperately trying to keep his mechanical behemoth out of the ditch and on the ice-glazed road.

Suddenly I felt the bazooka resting on my shoulder and Corporal Fairchild tapping me on the helmet, the signal that the bazooka was ready to fire and he was out of the way of the back-blast from the weapon. Fairchild spoke, with his soft southern drawl, "She is loaded and locked. The sight is set for one hundred yards. Wait until the Panzer gets in range, Sarge. It will be like shooting a fish in a rain barrel."

Oblivious to the Colonel's instructions that this was not a combat mission, I aimed, and when the Panzer was what I judged to be one hundred yards away, I squeezed the trigger. The bazooka belched flames and gently kicked the side of my helmet. My eyes followed the flight of the projectile straight to the target. WHAM! A large explosion, a big flash, and the smell of acrid smoke. A direct hit!

Instantly the German tank commander dropped from sight and the hatch cover slammed shut. The Panther continued moving toward us, it's giant turret and 75mm cannon rotating to the right in our direction. The bazooka round was ineffective. It did not even scratch the hard metal armor plate of the oncoming Panther. Kneeling there bewildered, I silently watched the action below. Suddenly I felt a tugging on the bazooka and the now familiar tap on the helmet. An exceptionally calm Charlie Fairchild said, "Nice shot! One problem Sergeant Pierson, you aimed too high. This time aim lower, try to hit the tracks."

Taking his advice, I aimed lower. Again, the bazooka belched flames and gently kicked my helmet. Again, I watched the projectile fly straight and true. This time it hit the right front drive sprocket of the Panther with a loud explosion and flying chunks of jagged metal. The results were immediate. The Panther was still in motion when the projectile struck. The right side track dropped off the damaged drive sprocket and the Panther, still being driven by it's left track, spun broadside to the road. Wedged in the steep narrow draw, the disabled Panther completely blocked the road, rendering it impassable to the following Panzer column.

Suddenly Corporal Fairchild grabbed me and pulled me to my knees. At the same instant the Panther fired it's 75mm cannon in our direction. The powerful muzzle blast at close range, plus the savage concussion, caused by the passing high velocity projectile, tore away my helmet and knocked me flat. In the process, the chin strap of the helmet scratched my face and severely tore my nose, causing blood to flow freely. As I lay on the ground dazed, unable to move, my ears ringing, my sight blurred, and my life's blood staining the white snow red, I thought, "God, is this where I am going to die?"

On the verge of passing out, my mind recognized the sharp crack of small arms fire around me and the loud explosion of artillery shells. My reaction was to get up and run. When I tried to get up, I became dizzy and suddenly the lights went out.

† †

Brownie and Jim Lemley were talking a mile-a-minute as we back-tracked our way through the thick woods toward "A" Battery. They were fully charged with adrenaline. Charlie Fairchild and I were both half-sick, glad to be alive, and thankful to be helped along the trail by the two able PFCs. The forest was deathly silent. Charlie must have regained his senses more quickly than I, because he was the first to ask a question.

"Brownie, what happened back there?"

"Corporal, I can't believe that first shot. Sarge hit the damned Panther dead center and didn't even phase it. Just about the time you guys got the second bazooka round off, I got "A" Battery on the radio and told them where I thought the Panther was located. They alerted Sergeant Alford's howitzer crew. But before I could get any more information to them, the Krauts fired their damned 75 at you two, and I ducked. When I looked up I thought they got you two because I didn't see you in the deep snow, and then I heard small arms fire."

Jim Lemley jumped into the conversation explaining, "That was me! After the Krauts fired their 75, the hatch cover opened and the tank jockeys started to pile out of their damned Panther. I shot several of them, I don't know how many. I know I didn't get them all, because the hatch cover slammed shut again and some of them stayed inside. But I left a couple lying in the snow on the road."

The walk in the cold air and the animated conversation began to clear the fog from my brain. "Jim, I heard some loud explosions too. What were they?"

"I don't really know Sarge. I do know, what ever they were, they saved our butts!"

A still animated Brownie exclaimed, "It was Sergeant Alford! "A" Battery finally got a radio out to his howitzer position and I told Sergeant Alford we had got one tank, but I could hear some more coming up the road."

Lemley agreed, "I could hear them too."

Charlie Fairchild asked, "What did you tell Sergeant Alford, Brownie?"

"Well, not much, I was kind of shaking by this time. I didn't know what had happened to Jim and I couldn't tell whether that 75mm round got you two or not. Barney Alford couldn't see the Panther, and he didn't wand to fire blind because he didn't want to hit us. I told him I was high up on the hill, away from the road, but I didn't know where anyone else was. I told him the Panther was only disabled and should be destroyed so the others behind it couldn't use the road. About this time, the second Panther came into view and Barney told me to duck, then he fired. The damnedest thing happened. He fired just a little high and his 105mm HEAT (High Explosive Anti Tank) round passed right over the damaged tank and hit the second one. Boy, what a sight! That HEAT round penetrated the Panther armor like a hot knife cutting butter. The round exploded inside the Panther, set it on fire, and then all the Kraut ammunition inside the Panther started exploding. When I told Sergeant Alford what had happened, he said we might as well finish off the first Panther too. His second round of HEAT was a little lower and hit the first Panther. The same thing happened again; fire, exploding ammunition, the whole ball-of-wax. That is probably what you remember hearing Sarge."

Jim Lemley confirmed Brownies story and added, "I was closer to those tanks than Brownie was. What he probably doesn't know is, I heard a third tracked vehicle come to a stop, grind into reverse, and backed the Hell away from the fire and all the exploding ammunition. The way things were popping, I had to hit the ground. That's why Brownie couldn't see me"

"Jim, did you see, or hear, any Kraut infantry supporting the Panzers?"

"No Sarge, the three Kraut Panzers were probably just a patrol. No evidence of infantry—not ours, not theirs. I wonder what happened to our infantry? How did the Kraut armor get through them?"

"I don't know Jim. Brownie did you hear what Jim said? Two Kraut tanks destroyed, one got away, the road to Prum is blocked with two tank hulls, no infantry has been heard or seen—ours or theirs?"

"Yes Sarge, I heard him."

"Did you send that information to Battalion?"

"Damn Sarge, I've been too busy ducking shells and pulling you through this snow to fool with the radio!"

"Damn it Brownie, the Colonel sent us up here to obtain information. Now we have some. What good is it if we are the only ones who know it? Lets stop right hear and you call Battalion right now. Give them our information and ask them for permission to come in. If they say yes, call "A" Battery and tell them the four of us are on the way back. I don't want to argue with another fucking firing battery guard like we did last time. Think you can handle that Brownie?"

"Come on Sergeant, lighten-up a little, you know I can."

† †

About six hours after we had left to establish a listening and observation post on the road to Prum, Germany, we reached the howitzer position of Sergeant Barney Alford. During the time we were gone from Battalion, the situation for the 589th had changed drastically. Sergeant Alford and his crew still manned the 105mm howitzer which commanded the road to Prum. The rest of the firing battery seemed to be in constant motion. Vehicle wheels churning the mud and snow and personnel working frantically, preparing to withdraw. The confusion was not organized, it was more like every man for himself.

Barney had the familiar wad of tobacco bulging in his cheek. As we approached, he decided to spit, making a large brown stain in the snow. He grinned when he saw the four of us, shoved his helmet back on his head and asked, "Randy, what in the hell happened to you?"

My nose had started to swell and I had forgotten I had blood all over my face and overcoat. "I got the million dollar wound buddy. I'm headed back to the States!"

"Bull shit Randy, I've cut myself worse than that shaving. Have you heard the news?"

"No, my ears are ringing so loud I can hardly hear anything Barney. What's up?"

I heard "B" Battery was supposed to move back to 'Baker Rear' several hours ago, but it is still bogged down in their position. They can't even get one howitzer our to the road, let alone their ammunition. Division Artillery just ordered then to disable their weapons and abandon them. They are salvaging what equipment they can, but I don't think it will be much."

"What about "C" Battery?"

"They are reported to be under direct attack by armor and infantry coming from the north. The main German attacking force has broken through the town of Auw and is headed this way. "C" Battery can't withdraw under attack and they certainly can't defend themselves without infantry support."

"Have you heard anything about Lieutenant Clausen? He was supposed to establish an observation post somewhere on the road to Auw,"

"Yea, I know. Randy, nobody knows anything about the Lieutenant or his driver, your buddy Guy Smith. Dead or captured, I guess."

"Shit, I hate to hear stuff like that about Guy and the Lieutenant. What's going on in "A" Battery?"

"The Colonel gave us "Close Station – March Order and Withdraw" to 'Able Rear' about thirty minutes ago. We already got two pieces and their prime movers sitting on the road headed west. Of course my howitzer will be last, but I can get on the road in about five minutes. Somebody has to bring up the rear. We got problems with one section though. Both the howitzer and the prime mover are so deep in the mud you can't even see the axels. Captain Menke is about ready to leave both of them. Division Artillery wants some 105s back in the rear position and ready to shoot. Looks like all they will get is our three. Three howitzers our of twelve, that's pretty fucking sad, isn't it?"

"Barney, what about Headquarters Battery?"

"Oh, they are already gone. Only the Colonel is still here. He's with the Captain and talking about going forward to the Infantry to find out what is going on. I think you guys are supposed to hitch a ride with us when we withdraw to the rear position. Hang around and don't get lost."

"Barney, you couldn't lose me if you tried."

Corporal Fairchild walked up and announced he had found his 3/4 ton

Dodge truck and asked if Brown and Lemley could help him load it. He also offered the three of us a ride to the CP Rear. I accepted his offer and instructed Brown and Lemley to help Charlie load his truck and pick-up some extra cans of gasoline and a couple of cases of "C" or "K" rations because we might need them later. After the guys left, Barney and I propped up on the frozen parapet surrounding his howitzer and talked while I waited for the 3/4 ton Dodge to arrive, and Barney waited for permission to withdraw his howitzer and crew. Several vehicles and trailers passed, including the mess truck. The cooks hanging out the rear of the mess truck waved good-bye as they passed. It was now about 1400 hours. I had not eaten breakfast and was getting hungry. Oh well, we should be back at the rear Command Post by 1500 hours. Back there the mess truck would be set-up and the cooks could scrounge something for us to eat.

Barney and I noticed the fog was starting to burn away and we could see patches of clear blue sky. The air was cold and still. We were engaged in chit-chat when one of Barney's howitzer crew interrupted us. Pointing with his arm, he asked,, "Sergeant, what is that black thing on the hill across the field?"

Barney squinted and looked in the direction of the Cannoneers pointing arm as I uncovered my binoculars. Raising the binoculars to my eyes and adjusting them on the black object on the distant hill resulted in a spontaneous response, "OH SHIT! It's part of the damned Panzer patrol!"

Barney spit, threw his helmet into the gun pit, and jumped in after it. He beat the gunner to the gunner's seat on the howitzer and started traversing the 105 tube in the direction of the German tank. When the howitzer tube was pointed in the general direction of the Panzer, he yelled, "Give me a HEAT – Give me a HEAT!" Then over his shoulder he asked, "Randy, what is the range?"

It was easy to measure the height of the Panzer using the graduated cross hairs of my artillery binoculars. From this measurement I mentally estimated the range from the howitzer to the Panzer. "Six hundred yards, Barney."

With his eye glued to the sight, he adjusted the elevation of the tube and placed the cross hairs of the sight on the Panzer. As a cannoneer rammed a HEAT round into the breach, the 1 cannoneer slammed the breach-block closed and simultaneously yelled, "READY!"

The clear image in my binoculars told me we were faced with another Mk V Panther It was sitting broad-side to us on the crest of a slight hill, silhouetted against the now blue sky. The hatch was open and the German tank commander was studying the tree-line to our left. It was plain as day, we had spotted him, but he had not yet spotted us.

With the proper elevation set and the sight bubbles level, Barney gave the command, "FIRE!" Instinctively, the 1 cannoneer pulled the lanyard. Following a powerful muzzle blast and a sharp recoil of the tube, the HEAT round was on the way. As soon as the howitzer tube returned to battery from recoil, a cannoneer had another round of HEAT ready to load into the howitzer in case the first round missed the target.

The first round struck it's mark, slightly to the rear of the massive turret, almost in the engine compartment. A sure place for a kill. As seen through the binoculars, the explosion was clear, but seemed to be quite weak. Nothing like the terrible explosions I had seen on the firing range at Camp Atterbury when we were practicing direct fire. The explosion seemed to be against the exterior, not inside the Panther, and was almost puny. To my astonishment, and to the astonishment of the German tank commander, the clear air around the Panther was suddenly filled with flying paper. Almost like ticker-tape floating down on a Wall Street parade.

This weird display, clearly visible to the naked eye, surprised everyone in the howitzer crew. In fact, one cannoneer blurted out, "What in the Hell happened?"

Barney Alford's answer was extremely concise, "We hit the son-of-a-bitch with a shell PROPAGANDA! That's what happened. Each piece of paper you see fluttering around out there is a fucking Surrender Leaflet."

Being no mind reader myself, I had no idea what thoughts raced through the German tank commander's mind when I observed him grab a flying leaflet. All I know is that when he briefly read the large bold print that said in German, "ATTENTION–ATTENTION," "SURRENDER–SURRENDER," he quickly closed his hatch and the Panther disappeared into defilade behind the hill. The last thing I remember hearing was the sound of the powerful Panther engine getting softer and softer as it headed swiftly in the direction of Prum, Germany.

Second Day – Battle of the Bulge
589th FA Bn Command Post Rear—17 December 1944

Sitting on the floor of the unheated farm house, now designated as Command Post Rear, half asleep and still half into my bed roll, I thought, "Yesterday was just one big mess. Too many things had happened too damned fast!" Several things constantly reminded me how rough the day had been. My swollen, torn nose and my half scabbed-over face, smeared with Army Iodine, hurt like hell. These features, combined with two days growth of beard and filthy clothing made me look like something only a mother could love. My head ached and my ears still rang, in plain English, I was miserable!

Even in the ice and snow, the trip from the forward "A" Battery position would normally have taken fifteen or twenty minutes. However, yesterday we had been blocked by stalled vehicles and foot troops the entire journey. We encountered a few organized convoys of units trying to withdraw, but mainly the road was jammed with individual vehicles fighting for road space in an effort to leave the combat area. Many vehicles were marked with unit insignia I had did not recognize. It was the scene of a frantic rout, not one of an orderly withdrawal.

Charley Fairchild had driven the last mile using black-out lights called 'Cat Eyes.' The Command Post Rear was dark when Charlie pulled to a stop in front of the farm house. The four of us dismounted the 3/4 ton and I asked Charlie if he wanted to spend the night with us, but he declined, "Sergeant Pierson, I am supposed to be with "A" Battery so I guess I had better find where they are. I'll stay with Sergeant Alford's crew if I can find them." I hated for Charlie to be wandering around in the dark by himself, but what he had to do was his own decision, not mine.

Hot chow had already been served by the time we found the blacked-out mess truck and the only warm food still available was hot coffee. Staff Sergeant Webb, the mess sergeant, did heat a can of pork and beans for each of us by immersing the cans into the hot coffee for a few minutes. We then ate the semi-heated "C" rations and drank freely of the hot, black coffee. The total food for the day – one lousy "C" ration and a canteen cup of hot coffee.

Lieutenant Colonel Kelly had not arrived at Command Post Rear when Major

Parker finally let me sack down for the remainder of the night. No one seemed to know anything about the situation. Before I dropped off to sleep I hoped things would return to normal and would be more organized when I reported to the fire direction center in the morning. I thought, Fire Direction, that's a laugh, down to eight howitzers, no forward observers, and no communications with the infantry. Why set up a fire direction center anyway? With that question unanswered, I fell fast asleep.

† †

Someone shook my shoulder and aroused me from a troubled semi-sleeping condition, "Sergeant, Captain Huxel wants you in the CP."

Rolling up my sleeping bag and gathering my personal gear was a chore. I hated getting our of my warm 'fart sack' in a cold room. Brownie, Lemley and a couple of other guys were still asleep and I did not awaken them. I carried my gear to load into the Command Post truck, just in case we had to move-out in a hurry. The 2 1/2 ton GMC had not been unloaded, it was still full, but the 3/4 ton Dodge had been partially unloaded. Both drivers seemed worried as they briefly acknowledged me with a dull, "Morning Sarge."

The cooks at the mess truck had not unloaded, but were cooking, if you call it that, in the back of their 2 1/2 ton GMC. The Mess Sergeant loaned me a spare mess kit and served up scrambled dried eggs, soupy Cream-of-Wheat, soggy toast, and boiling hot coffee. As bad as it was, I almost enjoyed this hot breakfast. But things got worse! I scalded my lips on the burning hot metal rim of the canteen cup when I took the first sip of coffee. "How could the cup be so hot when the weather was so cold?" I then wondered, "Jesus, what can happen next?" Little did I know!

Major Parker and Captain Huxel were the only officers I found in the Command Post. Apprehension was obvious in the eyes of the enlisted men and each officer. We had lost communications with everyone except "A" Battery, which was just across the road. "A" Battery had established a listening post beside the main road, just east of our position, and observers were beginning to report sounds of movement in the darkness just before dawn. German or American?

No one knew!

At first light, Major Parker ordered "A" Battery to move to the road and start forming a convoy heading west. The Major left the remnants of "B" and "C" Batteries in place, facing east, to cover the convoy's withdrawal. Captain Huxel was ordered to start preparing Headquarters Battery to join "A" Battery in the now forming convoy.

About 0700 hours, the listening post reported hearing tank movement in the distance. This report confirmed the fact that the movement was German, there was no American armor in the vicinity. "A" Battery observer personnel were withdrawn to join the convoy.

By 0720 hours the head of the convoy was moving slowly westward on the ice-covered road leading toward Schoenberg. The column was to cross the Our River bridge, which was believed to be intact. Across the Our River, the column was to make it's way through the town of Schoenberg, which was weakly defended by the 81st Combat Engineers, but also believed to be partially occupied by enemy forces. Once successfully through Schoenberg, the convoy was to turn southwest and make it's way to the town of St. Vith, Belgium and the Headquarters of the 106th Infantry Division.

Major Parker remained behind to herd "B" Battery and the miscellaneous Headquarters personnel through Schoenberg. I, of course, was one of the remaining Headquarters Battery personnel. The Major asked me to make one last check of the Command Post while he went to "B" Battery.

As I hurried, making the rounds, burning secret documents and rousting guys out to the waiting vehicles, I heard the remaining Headquarters Battery vehicles beginning to leave the position. For some unknown reason I started wondering what happened to my friends in "C" Battery and hoped they had gotten out of their lousy position during the early hours of darkness last night. Finally all of my men were accounted for but Brownie. I then remembered the last time I had seen him he was asleep upstairs in the farmhouse. I bounded the stairs, and sure enough, Brownie was still asleep in his bed roll. A deep sleep, totally exhausted, almost like in a coma.

"Brownie, get up! The battery is leaving! Get the Hell up!"

Brownie seemed drugged. He sat up and stared at the wall. His eyes were open, but they didn't see. I shook him and slapped his face. "Brownie, it's Sergeant Pierson! Damn it, wake up!" He showed no signs of recognition, nothing happened. Brownie was covered with cold sweat. He was going into shock and I did not know why. I could not drag him our into the bitter cold, it would kill him. What could I do? I did the only thing I knew to do to save his life. I laid him back down in his warm bed roll, made him comfortable, and gave him a shot of morphine. With tears in my eyes and my heart aching with grief, I left my friend Brownie in the hands of our maker.

Outside, everyone and everything but one jeep was gone. I jumped into the driver's seat and turned the switch. The starter worked fine, but the engine would not start. I tried again and again, but the jeep refused to start. Frantically looking for what was wrong, I noticed the gas gage was on empty. Some lame-brained idiot had burned all the gas last night using the heater, trying to keep warm. I ran to the rear of the jeep and checked the spare five gallon gas can—it too was empty.

Standing alone in the quiet forest surrounding the farm house, I could now hear the sound of clanking tank treads on the ice-covered road plus the roar of tank engines in the distance and realized I had to get out of here! I half ran and half walked to the main road and looked east. Nothing was visible, but I could hear the oncoming tanks more clearly now. No one could outrun a tank on foot, but I started running west toward Schoenberg anyway. I needed to get some curves in the road between me and the oncoming Germans as quickly as possible so they could not spot me. My big problem, the road was very straight for about one mile. I had to run! I had to try! Adrenaline was now my best friend!

As I ran, a 3/4 ton Dodge weapons carrier pulled out of the woods and onto the road about four hundred yards in front of me and turned west toward Schoenberg. The weapons carrier was loaded with men, maybe eight or ten. I yelled and frantically waved my arms hoping to attract someone's attention. The truck slowed and I ran harder. When I got within one hundred yards of the vehicle, I heard some of the occupants yelling at the driver to speed up, while others were yelling for him to stop. At this point we were still on the straight part of the road and extremely vulnerable to tank fire.

The driver, in desperation, decided to accelerate the speed of the vehicle. The distance from me to the vehicle began to increase. Two hundred yards, three hundred yards – I was running and screaming. My heart was pounding. The cold air was freezing my lungs. My legs were turning to jelly. I suddenly thought I was not going to make it. Then a strange thing happened! In the cold crisp air, I could hear it as plain as day. A strong voice rose above the others, "It's Sergeant Pierson – STOP THIS DAMNED TRUCK!"

The Dodge brake lights came on, I will never forget the welcomed bright red glow as the vehicle came to a full stop. I continued to run as fast as I could. Three hundred yards – two hundred yards – one hundred yards – I thought maybe I'll make it. With the last bit of strength left in my spent body, I collapsed on the tailgate of the weapons carrier. Four strong arms grabbed my overcoat and roughly pulled me onto the back of the vehicle as an unknown voice commanded the driver to, "HIT IT!" The Dodge fish tailed severely and the four wheels spun as we gained speed on the icy road.

Reclining on top of the humanity packed in the bed of the weapons carrier I had an excellent view of the road behind us. As we entered our first long and sweeping curve in the road, the front end of a large gray panzer came into view. When we successfully negotiated the second curve in the road unseen, I prayed and thanked 'The Almighty' for his help.

The weapons carrier was now traveling too fast for the road conditions. Even though we wanted to put as much space between us and the advancing enemy as quickly as possible, this pace was dangerous. The up-front passenger finally spoke up, "Fairchild, slow this thing down. If we end up in the ditch, they will catch us for sure."

Charlie Fairchild slowed the pace of the weapons carrier gradually. When he had the vehicle under solid control he turned his head and said, "Welcome aboard Sarge. If I had known that was you back there in the road I wouldn't have made you run so hard." I was so thankful to be on board, so tired, and was thinking about Charlie bailing me out of trouble yesterday, all I could say was, "Thanks Charlie, now I owe you two big ones."

The 3/4 ton weapons carrier was an open truck. No top, no sides, only a windshield up front. It beat walking, but riding in the back of Fairchild's truck was cold! After riding a few miles, without observing either friend or foe, the fear of being killed or captured gave way to cold and the urge to urinate. By unanimous decision, Fairchild pulled to a stop on the side of the road. In unison, twelve men bailed out of the vehicle, unzipped their flies, pulled out their peckers, and started to piss. All you could hear was groans of relief and all you could see was twelve columns of steam slowly rising from twelve yellow holes in the cold white snow.

While we were trying to walk some warmth back into our cramped legs, I recognized only Corporal Fairchild and two others. I moved over to where Charlie Fairchild was inspecting his truck and asked him about the strangers. He said they were guys from the 422nd Infantry Regiment who had somehow made it back to "A" Battery during the night and he was supposed to get them to St. Vith.

As we started to get back on the weapons carrier an infantrymen swung himself into the front seat. Corporal Fairchild quickly admonished him, "Get in the back, Sergeant Pierson is the ranking non-com on board. He is in charge now, he sits up front."

As we resumed our travel toward the Our River, Charlie Fairchild and I discussed the situation. Not knowing whether the bridge was still intact, or whether or not the town of Schoenberg was under American control, we decided to park the weapons carrier in a wooded area just short of a hill which overlooked the Our River valley, and moved to the crest of the hill on foot. The ranking infantry non-com turned out to be a corporal, a rifle squad leader. Corporal Andy Donaldson was from Houston, Texas, and was all business. He was very cooperative when I asked him to establish a perimeter guard between the road and the hidden vehicle. After he had positioned his men, he returned to the hill to find out the next step.

"Charlie, Andy, I may be the ranking non-com here, but this is not my ball of wax. We have to evaluate the situation together and then figure out the best chance of getting to St. Vith. I think we should move to the crest of the hill, stay hidden for a while, and try to figure the situation. We must find the best odds to get down this hill, across the Our River, through Schoenberg, and over the hill west of Schoenberg.

Looking at the map, it looked like we will be in the open, and under observation, all the way. Do you guys agree?

17 December 1944
On a hill overlooking the village of Schoenberg and the Our River valley—
1030 Hours

From our vantage point on the forward slope of a hill on the east side of the Our River, the view was magnificent. The long graceful hill sloped to the river. A gently winding road meandered down the hill and connected with the still intact Our River bridge. The war damage to the buildings in Schoenberg was masked by heavy snow. The road running west, away from Schoenberg, snaked its way up the distant hill and disappeared over the crest of a ridge, on its way to St. Vith. This tranquil scene was very deceptive and gave us no clues to the dangers we faced.

Sketchy information led us to believe the Germans had pushed through the town of Auw, which was only five mile north and east of Schoenberg. We had been led to believe the Americans controlled the south western section of Schoenberg, and the Germans controlled the rest. Apparently the route we must take through Schoenberg traversed some type of no-mans-land, between the opposing forces.

Charlie, Andy, and I, took turns observing the beautiful panorama in front of us. through my field glasses. We could not detect movement of any kind, nor could we hear firing of any type, or sounds of vehicles moving. Slowly we put together our plan. With nothing else to guide us, the plan was based upon the assumption that once across the Our River bridge, the Germans would be on our right, and the Americans on our left. We hoped the Americans would not fire on us, and assumed the Germans would. Once fired upon, Charlie would drive like hell, get across the bridge fast, through Schoenberg as quickly as possible, and over the ridge west of Schoenberg as fast as the 3/4 ton vehicle would go. The plan was simple and primitive.

When we returned to the truck, we explained our withdrawal plan to the rest of the men. In return, we received blank stares and one questions. One of the infantry men asked Andy, "Corporal Donaldson, what if I don't want to go?"

Corporal Donaldson wasted no words, "Willie, you don't have to come if you don't want to. Nobody will make you come. However, if you stay here by yourself, you will probably be captured or killed. Willie, you better stay with the truck, I think it's your best chance to survive."

"OK Corporal Donaldson, I just wanted to know."

"Anybody else have a question? If not, lets get the show on the road Sergeant Pierson."

"Before we move out, Charlie how about checking the truck and make sure it is ready to roll. Andy, get your men to reload the truck. Have them place as much gear on the right hand side of the truck bed as they can. Try to make a barricade they can get behind and fire over. Charlie will drive, and I'll ride shotgun up front."

Corporal Donaldson spoke up, "Sarge, if you don't mind, I think Johnny, my BAR (Browning Automatic Rifle) man should ride up front. It will be cold, but if we put the windshield down, Johnny can lay down a lot of fire to the front of the vehicle while we are moving. The rest of us, in the back, can lay down fire on the right hand side. Since you seem to know where we are and where we have to go, I'd feel better if you would hunker down behind Corporal Fairchild and be ready to drive in case he gets hit."

"Andy, sounds good to me. Charlie, do you have any ideas?"

"Yea, a couple. Once we get going, I don't plan to stop for anything or anybody until we are west of the Our River valley and several miles down the road toward St Vith. Second, just keep your head down Sarge, I don't plan on getting hit."

"Charlie, Andy, I'm going out to the road and keep an eye open for vehicles. Get the gear rearranged in the weapons carrier, then load what weapons you have. When you are finished, move the truck out to the road and pick me up."

When I reached a vantage point where I could observe activity on the road, it was empty, nothing in sight. There were no sounds either. This situation gave me an eerie feeling, almost like being in the eye of a Florida hurricane, violent activity going on all around us, but perfectly quiet here. I finally heard Charlie start the truck motor, then heard the transmission growl as he shifted into low gear, and heard the crunch of freshly frozen snow as the truck began to move toward the road. Once on the road I climbed unto the bed of the truck and positioned myself directly behind Charlie, the driver. I told Charlie to take it easy until we got to the Our River bridge, or until we were taken under fire by the Germans, which ever came first, and then drive like hell. The trip up the hill gave me more confidence in Andy. He had barricaded the right side of the weapons carrier with gear and five of his men were ready to fire from that side of the truck. Up front, Johnny looked all business with his potent BAR. I thought, who knows, we might even make it to St Vith.

The road, winding down the reverse side of the hill was icy, but not what I would call treacherous. The ice and frozen snow were rough, not glazed, and provided half-way decent traction. Corporal Fairchild had the weapons carrier in second gear, and was able to keep it completely under control. During this decent, and about half way to the Our River bridge, we had neither seen nor heard anything. About three hundred yards from the bridge, the road started to level out and Charlie accelerated the movement of the weapons carrier slightly. Simultaneously a mortar round burst in the snow immediately to our rear. That round was the signal Charlie was waiting for! He shifted the transmission into high gear and the race began. The second mortar round exploded squarely behind us, leaving a dirty gray stain in the fresh snow. The enemy had obviously zeroed in on the bridge with their mortars. While we were crossing the bridge, the third mortar round exploded in the river nearby and drenched us with frigid water and flying chunks of ice.

After we safely crossed the Our River and entered Schoenberg, war damage to the town was now clearly visible. Buildings bore the marks of house to house fighting and many had no roofs. The cobble stone street was narrow, slippery, and winding. Fairchild had to reduce speed to negotiate sharp turns in the road. Our nerves were tense and our eyes moved constantly, always searching for signs of the enemy.

Fortunately Charlie Fairchild and Andy Donaldson were both blessed with common sense and I felt it was common sense, not army training, that would get us through Schoenberg and back to St Vith. Charlie raced the weapons carrier through the first two intersection. At the third intersection we drew fire, some 'Burp Guns,' but mostly rifle fire. Before we reached the fourth intersection, Charlie brought the truck to a halt beside a protective building. He revved up the engine, which sounded like a moving vehicle, and immediately all hell broke lose at the fourth intersection. The Germans had anticipated our crossing of that intersection and had laid down heavy small arms fire to nail us when we tried to go through. Eventually, when no vehicle crossed the intersection, the German firing stopped.

We sat there in the shelter of the building, the truck engine idling slowly, wondering what to do. How could we get through this intersection with the enemy sitting there, prepared and anxious to do us in. I'll admit, I was afraid and didn't know what to do. Slowly, but surely, Andy began to take charge.

"Johnny, take the BAR and three men to the intersection. Try to spot the source of the German fire. If we stay here very long, they will send a squad to find us. Charlie, move the truck to the shelter of the building just short of the intersection, and do it quietly. I will take three men through the intersection, on foot, while Johnny and his men cover us. When I give the signal, Johnny's squad and my squad will lay down covering fire so you can get the truck through the intersection. Charlie, don't go far, just far enough to get out of the cross fire. My men will give Johnny and his men covering fire so they can get to my side of the intersection. If anyone gets hit during the fire fight, we'll try to get him to the truck. When we are all in the truck Charlie, take off and keep going. We had better take a chance and run the rest of the intersections before the Krauts can get reorganized and come after us with a tank or something. Maybe the Krauts don't have enough people in town yet to cover all the intersections. Sergeant Pierson, you got any other ideas?"

"Andy, I'm not an infantry squad leader, I don't know anything about house-to-house fighting. Just do your best and try to get us through Schoenberg."

"OK Sarge, the plan stands. Johnny, you and your men, Move Out! I'll be right behind you. One last word Corporal Fairchild, once you get rolling, don't try to 'bug-out' you're our bus ticket out of this mess. I promise, if you do try to 'bug-out' I'll put an M-1 slug through your head!"

This warning was hard for me to take. "For Christ's sake Andy, don't talk to Charlie like that. We are not going to run off and leave you. That's my promise!"

Thankful to be relieved of the current responsibilities and to have the infantry making the decisions, I propped up on the barricade in the back of the weapons carrier, checked my carbine and extra ammunition clips, and waited.

We heard scattered bursts of small arms fire when Andy and his three men scurried, one by one, across the intersection. Johnny's squad returned the enemy fire and seemed to squelch the Kraut attack somewhat.

At the intersection, everyone now in place,, Andy gave a motion to move the truck forward slowly. Charlie inched the vehicle forward and stopped in the shelter of the designated building. For a brief moment there was a dead silence. By voice command, Andy yelled at the two squads to "Commence Firing," and by hand, gave us the 'Double Time' signal to quickly move the weapons carrier across the intersection.

We caught the Germans by surprise. The whole action took less than thirty seconds. M-1s and Carbines firing, the BAR chattering, the vehicle vaulting, the Kraut's returning fire, and one of Johnny's men lying in the dirty intersection screaming, "I'm Hit! I'm Hit!"

Before anyone could react, heavy German fire was concentrated on the body of the wounded GI lying in the snow. The sight was awful, blood flying everywhere, the now dead body shivering and twisting from the force of enemy bullets. Even though I did not know the dead soldier, watching the GI's body being ripped to shreds by the barbaric volume of German fire made me sick. The poor guy did not have a chance. Fortunately, he did not suffer long.

Two infantrymen made a move in the direction of their dead friend, but they were immediately stopped by Andy. At his command, they all piled into the truck and Charlie started moving smartly down the slippery street. We crossed the remaining intersections without incident. Even though no one on board the weapons carrier was hurt, I noticed that one enemy round had struck the tail gate of the vehicle, leaving a jagged and ugly hole in the metal. As we crossed the last intersection in Schoenberg, and moved into open farm land we encountered a five man German patrol approaching from our right. Apparently they were not expecting trouble because they were walking with their arms slung instead of at the ready position, which would be normal for a combat patrol. Johnny spotted them first and fired a full clip from his BAR at them, the BAR set for automatic fire. The rest of us started firing from behind the barricade in the moving vehicle. Four of the German soldiers were dropped in the field immediately, either dead or wounded, the fifth fled behind a building, apparently unhurt.

Now, out of Schoenberg, Corporal Fairchild had the Dodge engine wound up tight, the engine growling as we raced over the rough iced surface of the road. About six hundred yards out of town, exploding mortar rounds started stalking the vehicle as it snaked westward across the Our River valley floor. We had survived about ten near misses when our luck ran out. One mortar round landed about ten yards to the right of the speeding Dodge. Shell fragments pierced the side of the truck in several places while other fragments passed over our heads, sounding like an attack of swarming insects. None of the fragments which struck the truck disabled it, but embedded themselves harmlessly in the thickly packed barricade.

I could feel the impact of the mortar fragments when they struck the vehicle and feared some of the men might have been wounded by this near miss. My fears prompted me to raise my head and check on Charlie and Johnny who were riding in the front seats relatively unprotected. I was relieved to find both men unhurt and hunched low to avoid the mortar fire and the searing cold wind. Feeling good about our continued good luck, I settled back down on the floor of the truck bed, only to have the infantryman next to me moan, "Sergeant, I think I'm hit."

Sure enough, one piece of shell fragment had penetrated both the metal of the truck body and the bulk of the barricade. It's force almost spent, the metal shard had embedded itself deeply into the soldier's left shoulder. The backs of his garments were torn and soaked with blood. The shiny metal shard was clearly visible in the mangled flesh of the open wound. His situation, as of now, was not fatal, but it certainly was not good. With the help of a buddy, we turned him face down and removed pieces of cloth from the wound. We sprinkled Sulfa powder from his first aid kit into the wound to prevent infection. We then tied a tight compression bandage over the wound to slow the bleeding. When that was completed, we rolled him over onto his right side and covered him with overcoats and canvas to help keep him warm and to prevent him from going into shock. During this process I was afraid to remove the metal shard. Removing it might aggravate the wound and cause added loss of blood. The constant jarring of the truck, as it bounced over the rough terrain, was not good for the wounded rifleman either, but this could not be helped.

Without looking, I could sense the weapons carrier was starting up an incline. We were leaving the valley floor and the exploding mortar rounds behind. Maybe we would be fortunate enough to pass over the western ridge of the Our River valley and reach the St Vith highway without suffering any additional casualties.

By this time, the initial numbness of the rifleman's wound was giving way to pain. The wounded man became restless and started to groan. Andy located a morphine Syrette and handed it to me. I injected the morphine into his torn shoulder and the rifleman gradually calmed down and fell into a blessed sleep. Blood was still oozing through the compress bandage. He wasn't losing blood fast, but the constant bumping of the truck seemed to keep his wound open. We had to get him to an aid station before it was too late!

Directly ahead the crest of the hill was a beautiful sight. We were out of mortar range, and so far, we had not attracted panzer or artillery fire. A few more minutes of good luck and the Krauts would no longer be able to observe our flight. As we briefly raced along the ridge, moving south parallel to the river, I raised my binoculars to get one last look at Schoenberg before we crested the hill. As far as I was concerned, nothing had changed, however for us, things were looking better.

Past the village of Schoenberg—On the road to St. Vith, Belgium
17 December 1944 – 1400 Hours

St Vith was about seven miles from Schoenberg, using the secondary roads through Heuen and Setz. Under normal circumstances it was a short and pleasant trip, but these were far from normal circumstances. We had been out of contact with everyone for more than twelve hours and lack of information complicated things. We knew the situation was SNAFU (Situation Normal, All Fucked Up) and felt we might run into Krauts at any moment. This was no pleasure trip and we were not on our way to a picnic in the country. Our survival was at stake!

The first mile and one half to Heuen was relatively uneventful, but we moved slowly and cautiously. We passed shot-up and abandoned vehicles and picked up four additional foot soldiers who were lost and not certain where to go. Other stragglers tried to bum a ride, but the vehicle was already overloaded and could not accommodate them. However, we did tell them how to get to St Vith, the only city in the immediate area we . knew was still under American control.

In the village of Heuen, things became more difficult. MPs were trying to stem the flow of stragglers and several infantry officers were trying to organize a defense of the village. One of these officers tried to stop us from passing through the village. I had to assert myself and told the officer we were under orders to report to the 106th Division Artillery in St Vith as quickly as possible, and I intended to carry out that order. I also pointed out I had to evacuate one of my wounded men and we had current knowledge that Schoenberg was now in enemy hands and that the Our River bridge was still intact, and our Division Commander needed this information. The obviously weary infantry officer finally 'got the picture,' and allowed us to depart the village.

From Heuen to Setz, another mile and one half, the trip was a different story. Our vehicle finally become entangled in what appeared to be a full scale retreat. We observed vehicles operated by frantic, wild-eyed drivers, competing for precious road space to the rear with lost, battle shocked, foot soldiers. Speed for all traffic was held to the pace of the slowest foot soldier. Occasionally a vehicle would run out of gas, or break down, and block the road, adding to the congestion. Things were out of control, no one was in charge. It took more than one hour to negotiate that mile and one half.

Things did not get much better between Setz and St Vith. By the time we reached the American main line of resistance, north and east of St Vith it was now past 1700 hours. The seven mile trip had taken more than three hours. Shortly after we crossed back into American held territory, Charlie Fairchild spotted a 589th Headquarters Battery jeep parked on the side of the road. Captain George Huxel was sitting on the hood and intently reading the unit designation on each bumper as the vehicles passed. A smile came on his face when he saw the 589th Service Battery marking on our weapons carrier, and waved us off of the road. Charlie parked next to the Captain's jeep and I crawled out of our cramped vehicle, reported to Captain Huxel, and began to engage him in conversation.

As Captain Huxel was asking about trailing vehicles and missing personnel, Andy Donaldson interrupted the conversation, "Captain, I'm Corporal Donaldson, Company B, 422nd Infantry Regiment. I have a wounded man to get to an aid station and I have to get my other men back to our unit. Will you help me Sir?"

A little surprised at Andy's urgency, Captain Huxel replied, "Of course I'll help you Corporal. Load your wounded man into my jeep, my driver will take you and him to an aid station. As for the rest of your men, I suggest they stay with Sergeant Pierson until we find out where you should report."

589th FA Bn—In bivouac west of St Vith, Belgium
17 December 1944 – 1830 Hours

Andy's men quickly loaded their wounded buddy into the Captain's jeep. Moments later the jeep and occupants were on the road to an aid station in St Vith. After his jeep had disappeared into the fading light, Captain Huxel climbed into the front seat of the weapons carrier, next to Corporal Fairchild, and started pumping me for information as we rode the short distance to the 589th Field Artillery Battalion bivouac area. During this interrogation I realized how physically and emotionally drained I was. It had been another long, tough, day! When we reached the 589th Command Post, Frank Tacker and Dell Miller started the interrogation all over again. Everyone was hungry for information. They were both surprised to learn the jeep they had left for me would not start, and how I had to leave Brownie. It really hurt me to leave Brownie, and I told them how bad I felt. They made me feel a little better when they assured me I had done everything anyone could have done except stay with him, and staying with him under the circumstances did not make good sense.

Miller finally asked me if I was hungry, and it dawned on me I had eaten only two meals in the past two days. I told Dell I felt lousy and maybe some food would help. Dell then walked me to the mess truck just in time to get fed with the infantry guys we had brought in. Thanks to our dedicated mess sergeant, we had a hot meat with lots of coffee. As Dell and I were finishing our second cup of coffee, Andy returned from the aid station. He wanted to talk about his men, but I told him to eat first, while the food was still hot. Between each mouth full, Andy told us his wounded man had lost lots of blood, the medics had removed the shell fragment, gave him plasma, and re-bandaged him for evacuation to the rear. The medics also told him they thought his man would be OK. Andy also told us he had located some rear echelon type from the 422nd Infantry Regiment in St Vith who told him where to find the remnants of the 422nd. Andy wanted to know if Fairchild would drive him and his men to the other side of town. Charlie was pooped also, but finally agreed to take the infantrymen wherever they needed to go. As the infantrymen loaded into the back of Charlie's weapons carrier, I thanked them all for getting us through Schoenberg and wished them good luck in the future.

On the way back to the CP, Dell showed me the location of the command post truck where my bedroll and personal gear was stowed. When Dell departed for the CP, I told him I was going to clean up a little and then get some sleep. I silently prayed I would be left alone and not have to pull duty in the Command Post until I felt better. Robert Hunt, the CP truck driver, wondered what had happened to me. He was glad to see me and helped me find my bedroll and musette bag, which contained my personal gear. While I was washing and shaving, we talked. He said no one knew where the Krauts were located, or what the situation was. He had heard German paratroopers had landed to our rear to cut off our supply and communication lines. He had heard about specially trained German soldiers, dressed in American uniforms who spoke good English, who were reversing road signs and acting like American MPs to give misleading information to American troops on the move. These specially trained German troops were also reportedly killing American stragglers. Robert had also heard of the massacre of a group of captured American Artillerymen at a town in Belgium named Malmedy. His assessment was, the situation is really SNAFU!

During our conversation I told Hunt I was dead tired and had to get some sleep, but I wanted to bed down where I would not be found, or get left in case the unit had to pull out in a hurry. My Tennessee buddy, Private First Class Bob Hunt told me, "Sarge, the truck is almost fully loaded, just put your 'fart sack' on top of the gear that is loaded up front near the cab. You should be safe and comfortable there. Get under the canvas top in case we get snow tonight." He also assured me, "I won't run off and leave you Sarge, you have my word on it!"

Another thing Bob, I don't particularly want anyone to find me if they come looking. "Don't worry Sarge, I ain't even seen you!"

Knowing that PFC Hunt would keep his word, I climbed into the truck, spread my bed roll on top of the gear near the cab, took off my combat boots, wiggled into my bed roll, and made myself comfortable. My anxieties slowly gave way to a full stomach, the warmth of the bed roll, and the realization that for moment I was safe. Quickly my conscious brain ceased to function, fatigue put out my lights, and I fell into a deep, but very troubled sleep.

Third Day—Battle of the Bulge
589th FA Bn
Orders are received to deploy to Recht
18 December 1944—0100 Hours

The stupor of deep sleep began to wear off. My troubled dreams had seemed real. I was relieved to hear friendly voices in the dark. Finally truck and jeep motors all around me coughed, sputtered, and finally came to life. Then people, real American GIs started climbing into the rear of the 2 1/2 ton GMC command post truck. One clown climbed right on top of me in the darkness, mistaking me for a duffle bag. I thrashed out with a free arm, trying to protect myself, and as I grunted a warning to my unknown tormenter, my friend Jim Lemley remarked in surprise, "Excuse me Sarge, I didn't see you. When did you catch up with us?"

"I don't really know Jim. What time is it anyway?"

"It's 0100 hours."

"0100 hours? 0100 hours of what day?"

"Come on Sarge, you must really be out of it. It's the 18th. What day do you think it is?"

"Hell Jim, when you jumped on top of me, I was sleeping so hard, I thought that damned Kraut Panther was still after us."

"Well Sarge, that Panther won't bother you again, we creamed it good almost two days ago."

"Lemley, it feels like the truck is rolling. What's going on?"

"We just received orders from Division to move to a little village named Recht and set up a road block there."

"I've never heard of Recht, is it in Belgium or Germany?"

"It's a little village in Belgium, six or seven miles north and west of St Vith."

"You mean there are Germans west of St Vith? I thought that area still belonged to the Allies."

"The Corps Commander thinks the Germans up north of us will penetrate to the west and then turn south. If they can do that, we will be cut off, then the Krauts would have us in some kind of pocket. The General doesn't want that to happen so he ordered us to Recht to set up a blocking action there. We are supposed to keep the northern portion of the German pincer movement from closing."

"Well that is interesting. How long do you think it will take us to get to Recht and set up this blocking action?"

"I don't know Sarge, but in this ice and snow, and driving at night under black-out conditions, I guess it will take three or four hours, even if we are lucky."

"Lemley, I'm going back to sleep. Be sure and wake me up when we get there."

"OK Sarge, get some shut-eye, I'll wake you up when we get there."

Headquarters Battery — 589th FA Bn
Recht, Belgium — 0450 Hours

The convoy arrived in Recht while it was still dark and what was left of the men in Headquarters Battery started establishing a Command Post. To my dismay, I found out "B" Battery had not been able to disengage from the enemy infantry and withdraw from the second position yesterday. Some of the men escaped, but the four howitzers and their prime movers had been destroyed during the encounter. The loss of four more howitzers and the "B" Battery men was a terrible disaster. To make things worse, Miller told me that "A" Battery had lost one howitzer and it's prime mover to panzer fire while they were trying to negotiate the streets of Schoenberg. We were now left with only three howitzers and were short on men.

By 0700 hours a formidable road block had been established on three sides of Recht, each howitzer commanding the north, east, and west approaches to the vacated village. Within the village itself, land mines had been strategically placed in the narrow streets. These mine fields were covered by .30 and .50 caliber machine gun positions to prevent enemy infantry from detecting and removing the mines. Bazooka team locations had been established to cover sharp turns in the narrow streets of the village. These sharp turns would stop a tank cold in its tracks and make it an easy target for a Bazooka as it tried to negotiate the tight turn.

Everything was in place, but no Krauts were in sight. By 0800 hours, warming fires began to appear all over the area. The serious business of making coffee, heating "C" rations, cleaning up, and keeping warm became the order of the day.

As if to mock, or frustrate us, the command radio crackled to life in the Command Post at 0830 hours. Some staff officer at Division Headquarters broke all security guidelines, and in the clear, ordered the Battalion to withdraw from Recht and to move promptly to Bovingy. The result of this order was a mad scramble to defuse and remove the land mines we had laid, reload the trucks, and study maps to determine where, in the name of goodness, the village of Bovigny was located. Bovigny proved to be located some fourteen miles south and west of our current location. Sitting on a major road intersection west of St Vith, Bovigny looked like a gate in the fence guarding the rear entrance to Division Headquarters. I began to think the people at Division were fighting invisible ghosts. I didn't see how in the world German forces could have advanced far enough to attack St Vith from the west.

In the Command Post, Major Parker was briefing Major Goldstein and Captain Huxel, plus a hand full of Non-Coms, on how to travel to a bivouac area east of Bovigny. He advised them to move out as quickly as possible, and move the Battalion in small elements. They were to go through the villages of Poteau, Petit Their, Vielsalm, cross the Salm River, turn south and proceed through Salmchateau, and on to Bovigny. Once there Major Goldstein, with the first element, should find a suitable bivouac area between Bovigny and the Salm River. They should post a road guard to direct other 589th vehicles into the bivouac area. Major Parker emphasized he would be riding in the last vehicle. If he did not make it to the bivouac area, of course Major Goldstein would be in charge.

Major Parker was our operations officer and I was accustomed to hearing his very specific and thorough briefings. In civilian life, Major Parker was an engineer, and his briefings were always structured like he was explaining how to construct a bridge, or something of that nature. But in this briefing, I was surprised that I had not seen our CO, Lieutenant Colonel Kelly, because the Colonel always participated in briefings of this nature and I wondered why he was not there. Frank Tacker answered my question. Lieutenant Colonel Kelly had left the first position two days ago to go forward and check on the infantry situation. He and his driver had not returned and no one had seen them since. This news came like a sledge hammer to my guts. It never occurred to me that anything bad could happen to the Colonel!

Headquarters Battery—589th FA Bn
In Bivouac—near Bovigny, Belgium, 1000 Hours

Compared to the move to Recht, the move to our new bivouac position was easy. Day light hours, better roads, and less traffic all helped. All vehicles, weapons and personnel reached the new bivouac area without incident. Major Parker ordered Captain Huxel to reconnoiter the road system west of Bovigny to select defensive positions while he contacted Division Headquarters to advise them where the Battalion was currently located. Before the Captain could leave the temporary Command Post, the Major said, "Hold it George, there has been another change in plans."

Additional conversation with Division resulted in a heated debate, but finally the weary Major terminated the conversation with a terse, "WILCO and OUT!" He turned to Captain Huxel and said, "Our new mission is to defend Joubieval and Baraque de Fraiture. We will have to split what is left of the men and equipment into two groups." This turn of events was too much for me to understand. I left the temporary Command Post, went to the Command Post GMC truck, sat in the cab, and talked to the driver, Bob Hunt. Neither of us could understand this order, or who would go where. As it turned out, Bob Hunt went to defend the village of Joubieval and I went to Baraque de Fraiture.

13
The Battle for Parker's Crossroads Begins

Baraque de Fraiture was not even a village, it was merely an intersection of two roads about one mile from the small village of Fraiture, Belgium. A good secondary road, running east from the Salm River at Salmchateau, crossed a main north-south highway, known as N-15, at Baraque de Fraiture. N-15 crossed the Ourthe River at Hoffalize and was the main highway running north to the city of Liege, Belgium. Hitler had designated Liege as a main military objective for his armies to capture on their march to Antwerp and to the sea. Hitler's time-table called for Liege to fall within forty-eight hours. Two reinforced German Divisions, the 2nd SS Panzer Division and the 9th SS Panzer Division, totaling approximately 30,000 highly trained and well equipped troops, had to pass through the Baraque de Fraiture area to accomplish this objective. Liege did not fall on 18 December 1944 as Hitler had scheduled. In fact, Liege was never entered by German armed forces during the Battle of the Bulge.

Major Arthur C. Parker, III, an engineer from Alabama in civilian life, established a road block at Baraque de Fraiture, Belgium, with the assistance of Major Elliott Goldstein, a distinguished corporate attorney from Atlanta, Georgia, with less than 100 men on 19 December 1944. The majority of the American troops that held the crossroads at Baraque de Fraiture were from the 589th Field Artillery Battalion, however, due to Major Parker's strong leadership and personal courage, he inspired stragglers from other units to stand and fight with the men of the 589th, and deny this crossroad to Hitler's finest troops for almost five days. Major Parker was severely wounded during this prolonged holding action and many US soldiers were wounded, captured, or killed. Subsequently Major Parker was decorated for valor by the Belgium and American governments and received a Purple Heart for his wounds. The 589th Field Artillery Battalion was awarded a Unit Citation by the French Government in honor of it's brilliant five day holding action at Baraque de Fraiture and the Belgian Government has erected a magnificent memorial to all of the brave men who fought there. The battle for the crossroads at Baraque de Fraiture is now referred to, in military and historical writings, as "The Battle for Parker's Cross Roads," a fitting tribute to a gallant citizen soldier.

Headquarters Battery—589th FA Bn—Day 4, Battle of the Bulge
Baraque de Fraiture, Belgium—19 December 1944, 1400 Hours

Once at Baraque de Fraiture, I could not think of the cross roads as a prime piece of real estate worth fighting for. We were told to expect overwhelming odds and were ordered to deny the crossroads to the enemy for, "As long as humanly possible." This seemingly insignificant "X" shaped crossroad, sitting in the middle of the XVIII Airborne Corps area was the responsibility of the 82nd Airborne Division to hold and defend. The problem, the entire 82nd Airborne Division had no reserves and was completely committed, already fighting valiantly trying to contain the advancing German 1st, 2nd, and 9th SS Panzer Divisions in other locations.

To make things worse, *Kampfgruppe Peiper,* was still a serious threat, having been identified as the German unit responsible for the horrendous Malmedy massacre. This German 'Battle Group' was rumored to contain American (not English) speaking German soldiers dressed in American uniforms, carrying American arms, and riding in American vehicles. These members of *Kampfgruppe Peiper* were specifically ordered and trained to disrupt Allied lines of supply and communications, to create havoc by changing road signs, to kill American stragglers, and to assassinate high ranking Allied officers, including the Allied Supreme Commander, General Dwight David Eisenhower.

Although we did not know it at the time, General Gavin, Commanding Officer of the 82nd Airborne Division had no troops available to block highway N-15 East of Manhay, Belgium. Simply put, that is why the battered remnants of the 589th Field Artillery Battalion were sent to Baraque de Fraiture—we could no longer function as a field artillery battalion, and we were expendable! We were expected to delay the Krauts until US Armored reinforcements could be brought in. Our mission was to buy time! Only the two Majors understood this, the rest of us expected to fire a few 105mm rounds at the advancing enemy and then withdraw. This was the only thing we had done so far in this lousy war.

Baraque de Fraiture was only a road intersection in the form of an "X" located in open farm land, a clearing in the dense Ardennes Forest about the size of ten or twelve football fields. Dotting these fields were about five structures—a Country Inn and two sturdy stone farm houses with out-buildings. The two roads actually crossed on the crest of a wind blown knoll at an elevation of 2,200 feet, the second highest point in the Ardennes Forest. The area offered almost no shelter from the frigid cold, fierce biting wind, and deep snow. It was obvious the occupants of these homes were long gone. The buildings contained minimal furniture but the out-buildings contained live and healthy milk cows, with well stocked hay lofts. So far everything about this war had seemed strange to me. We had been fighting like Infantry and Tank Destroyers. Except for a brief period of time the firing batteries had yet to function as we were trained, as a field artillery unit. The 589th Field artillery Battalion entered the 'Battle of the Bulge' with twelve 105mm howitzers three days ago—we now had three. During the first three days of the 'Battle of the Bulge' our five hundred troops had atrophied to about two hundred. Three hundred of our men had been either wounded, captured, or killed. Only one half of the remaining men in the battalion, four officers and less than one hundred men were here at Baraque de Fraiture, the others dispatched to Hell-and-Gone on another mission impossible. Our Commanding Officer, Lieutenant Colonel Thomas P. Kelly, Jr. was missing in action, as were many of the other battalion officers. We had yet to advance, only withdraw. Yes indeed, this was truly a strange war to me!

Only the two Majors seemed to understand the big picture. They were everywhere—checking weapons emplacements, giving instructions and advice, and making certain we were dedicated to holding this important ground. They kept us busy! We, the troops, did not have time to philosophize or complain. We were cold, wet, and tired, and we were apprehensive about the future, but they kept us too busy to realize it.

Major Parker established the Command Post in the largest stone building located near the intersection of the two roads. Telephone lines were laid to each of the three howitzer sections and outpost positions. Radio communications were established with the 106th Infantry Division Headquarters in St Vith, but our radio net was not very reliable for many reasons. Listening and observation posts were established to our east on the road to Vielsalm, and to the south on the road to Houffalize. Major Parker expected strong enemy pressure from each direction and wanted advance notice when it came. In the Command Post, Staff Sergeant Frank Tacker organized the message center, assigned radio and switchboard duties among the men, and asked me to organize the fire direction center and firing charts while he updated the situation maps.

Two officers and Sergeant Barney Alford commanded the three howitzers and received instructions from Major Parker on howitzer locations, fields of fire, the types of ammunition to prepare, the locations of the listening and observation posts, and where the local perimeter of defense was to be established. Sergeant Alford's crew, which already had tank kills to it's credit, was assigned to cover the road going toward Houffalize. Captain Arthur C. Brown, the former "B" battery Commander who escaped from the Germans at Schoenberg, was assigned to command the howitzer which covered the road going toward Vielsalm. The third howitzer was assigned to Lieutenant Thomas J. Wright from Service Battery, and was positioned to fire to the west, in order to cover what was expected to be our weakly defended rear.

Captain George Huxel was assigned the responsibility of establishing the listening posts and the perimeter defense against possible infantry penetration. Major Elliott Goldstein shared over-all command responsibility with Major Parker.

The perimeter defenses, located in the cleared fields around the road intersection, faced densely wooded areas of the surrounding Ardennes Forest. This defense was manned by cold, uncomfortable, and uneasy artillery men, equipped with small arms, machine guns, hand grenades, and bazookas, who were expected to perform like trained Infantry troops. Digging protective fox holes and slit trenches in the hard frozen ground was almost impossible. The only other alternative available consisted of wooden logs. Everyone not on duty at the Command Post spent much of the night felling trees, chopping away limbs, cutting logs, and reinforcing the defensive line and the howitzer positions. Once a position was deemed secure, the men assigned to the position rapidly spread shelter-half's and tarps over the logs to protect both men and equipment from the lightly falling snow. Within a short period of time these positions were perfectly camouflaged because they became totally covered with snow and blended perfectly into the heavy snow which covered the fields.

By midnight things had settled down to a routine in the Command Post. Frank Tacker had assigned me to the 2000 to 0200 hours shift. The men assigned to the 0200 to 0800 hours shift had crawled into their bed rolls several hours ago to get some well-earned sleep. We had assembled a folding cot in the CP for the Majors. Since no one knew what was going to happen, Major Parker, the senior officer now on duty, decided he would cat-nap on the cot in the CP when, and if, he got a chance.

Shortly after midnight I plugged into the "A" Battery jack on the field switchboard and gave the ringing crank a turn. Immediately a husky voice answered, "Sergeant Alford."

"Barney, this is Randy. What's going on over there?"

"Jesus Christ Randy, you scared the shit out of me. I thought this call would be something important."

"No, it's not important, I just wanted to know if you guys were dug-in and ready."

"Ready for what?"

"Hell, I don't know what's going on any more than you do Barney, Division can't tell us anything! Major Parker doesn't know too much himself. All the Major tells us is that holding this cross road is important to the Allies and we will deny the Germans access to this area as long as we can. What ever that means."

"Randy, if it was up to me to deny the Germans the use of this intersection, I'd take a few thousand pounds of explosives and blow the damned thing to kingdom come. Then I'd get the hell out of here. How about that approach?"

"Sounds good to me Barney, I think I'll put you in charge."

My conversation with Barney was cut short when Tacker asked, "Randy, who are you talking to?"

As I was knocking down the switchboard connection I told Barney, "I've got to cut out now, Tacker wants me for something. I'll try to get over to see you in the morning."

To answer Tacker's question, I explained, "I was just talking to Sergeant Alford in 'A' Battery."

Before Tacker could reply, Major Parker interrupted, "How are they getting along at the howitzer positions Sergeant Pierson?"

"Major Parker, they are doing OK, Sergeant Alford is griping about several things and you know what they say about griping GIs — they are OK. It's when they stop griping you have to worry."

"Yes Sergeant Pierson, I believe I have heard that saying before. Sergeant Tacker it might be wise for you to call the other two howitzer positions and the listening posts to see how they are getting along. In the meantime, I'm going to try and get a little rest. I really do not expect enemy activity before 0400 hours. If I am not awake by then, please awaken me. Do you understand Sergeant Tacker?"

"Yes Sir! If anything new comes in from Division do you wish to be disturbed?"

"By all means."

† †

Battle for Parker's Crossroads — Day 2
Baraque de Fraiture, Belgium — 589th FA Bn Command Post
0600 Hours, 20 December 1944

Private First Class Lemley threw his bedroll on the floor next to where I was sleeping and softly said, "Sarge, I'm sorry, but it's time to get up." After receiving no response, he added in a louder voice, "Sarge, if you want something hot to eat, you'd better get up and get going!"

To my sleep fogged brain, these were magic words, however it took a lot of willpower just to sit up in my bedroll. After debating with myself over whether to get up or not, I finally realized it was time for me to start my next six hour tour in the Command Post. I started wiggling my shoulders free from the sleeping bag which was wrapped inside my woolen GI blankets. The cold air of the unheated room made me shudder and prompted me to dig quickly into the sleeping bag and retrieve my already warm field jacket and slip it on—so much for my top half. Dressing the bottom half of my body was more complicated. Even though we all had well insulated sleeping bags, we slept almost fully clothed. We had learned to keep most of our cloths on for several reasons. First, the weather was hovering between 15 and 20 degrees below freezing at night. Second, none of the rooms where we had slept so far had been heated, and only a fool would want to put frozen clothing on over a warm body, fresh out of a sleeping bag. And third, but certainly not last, I did not want to take time to dress in case we had to leave the building quickly. I had already been left once, and the memory of having to leave Brownie was still fresh on my mind. One experience like that was enough for me!

My procedure, when getting ready to retire, was to place my legs partially into my sleeping bag, un-blouse my outer fatigue pants by pulling the legs from under the Government Issue (GI) condoms I had tied into a circle, like a rubber band, around the top of both boots. I would then roll the condom onto the toe of each boot, leaving them there so I would not lose them while sleeping. I then unlaced and removed my boots, removed my damp socks, massaged both feet to restore circulation, and put on the dried pair of socks I had previously left in the bed roll. Both the muddy boots and the damp socks were then moved to the foot of the sleeping bag to dry and to be kept warm. This foot care was important to prevent trench foot and/or frost bite, unfortunately, during combat all nights were not spent in buildings out of the weather, consequently many combat troops suffered from one or both of these conditions during the bitter European winter of 1944-45. Unfortunately this Sergeant was one of those GIs!

Of course the reverse was true when I extricated myself from a sleeping bag. While still sitting, I would reach into the sleeping bag, straighten my socks, tuck the ankles of my long johns into each sock, roll my olive drab woolen pants leg around each ankle and tuck then into the top of each sock With my underclothing firmly in place, I would don my boots, lace them, roll the condom up to ankle height and blouse my fatigue pants under the restraining condom. Most combat soldiers used some variation of these dressing and undressing procedures, if not they would ultimately get caught in some kind of an emergency with their 'pants down.'

As I was dressing, Lemley had already snuggled into his sleeping bag and I could hear him muttering something about early morning visitors, but he was almost asleep and I didn't really understand what he said.

For me, the short sleep had been deep, but quite restless. I thought I remembered hearing sounds of motors running and of tracked vehicles moving on brittle ice. I also seemed to remember hearing loud and excited conversations, but I assumed all these things happened in a dream. The reality of fragrant coffee aroma drifting into the room was the catalyst I needed to get me up and into the Command Post. There the thing that attracted my attention most were the changes which had occurred during my six hour absence. There was a cheery small fire burning in the fire place, a pot of coffee was heating over the fire, and Tacker had just started to fry some canned bacon in an old mess kit. As I looked around the CP, I noticed three non-coms I had never seen before – they were engaged in conversation with Major Parker. On the floor, beside the fire place, I noticed an open cardboard carton marked, US ARMY – 10 in 1 RATIONS. To attract attention as I entered the CP, I cleared my throat and slammed the door. Hearing the door open and shut, Major Parker turned and half said and half asked, "Sergeant Pierson, nice of to join us. Did you rest well last night?" Before I could comment he continued, "Freshen up and wash your mess kit. Sergeant Tacker has volunteered to fix breakfast." My glance at the 10 and 1 RATION carton on the floor prompted the Major to continue again, "The 10 in 1s are complements of Staff Sergeant William Jones of the 643rd Tank Destroyer Battalion. Sergeant Jones, meet Sergeant Pierson."

Staff Sergeant Jones extended a muscular hand and explained he had donated the rations to the cause, provided he and his men could chow-down with us. The Major seemed delighted to have added four, 3 inch, high velocity, antitank guns and their crews to his defense forces.

The other two non-coms had arrived in a light tank, in the dark of the early morning hours, low on gas, and with a screwed-up radio. They were members of the 87th Reconnaissance Squadron who had been sent toward Houffalize to make contact with the point elements of the advancing German Panzer Divisions. They had made contact, but could not report the point of contact to the Squadron Commander due to their dead radio. Not knowing what to do, they maintained contact with the advancing Germans almost all night, while trying to fix their radio. When they arrived at Baraque de Fraiture, which was occupied by friendly forces, they decided to stop, refuel, and see if they could find someone to repair their radio. The Major had convinced them that under the circumstances it was better for them to join us than to be running abound the Kraut infested countryside by themselves. After introducing myself and talking to the Recon men, I didn't think Major Parker had to give them a hard sell to remain with us, they appeared willing to become a part of our group.

One of the things I found interesting about the Recon men was the fact that their mission was to locate the enemy, report the position of the enemy, and to rapidly disengage from the enemy. They were not trained to stand and slug-it-out. Having faced superior German Armor only hours earlier on the road to Houffalize, they had parked their light tank behind the stone farm house so it could not be seen by anyone approaching from that direction.

The field telephone connecting the CP and one of the listening posts rang and interrupted our conversation at 0900 hours. I answered the phone and was surprised to be talking to my buddy, John Schaffner from "A" Battery. Schaffner had good news, he wanted to report to Major Parker that four half-tracks from the 203rd Anti-Aircraft Battalion were on the way to the Command Post. They had been kicked out of their position on a hill west of Houffalize by enemy infantry and armor. Their senior man, a Staff Sergeant, wished to speak to an officer. I thanked John, hung up, and passed this information to Majors Parker and Goldstein. Immediately the two Majors started discussing arguments on how to convince the 'Ack-Ack' men to join the holding action, and how best to utilize them and their tremendous firepower if they agreed to stay.

I was watching from a window in the farm house when the four half-tracks arrived. A Staff Sergeant exited the lead vehicle and reported to the waiting officers with a snappy hand salute. It was impossible for me to hear the heated conversation which followed. Gradually the conversation became more calm and as I left the window to answer the CP switchboard, all three heads had started nodding agreement. The call was from a Lieutenant Colonel at the 106th Infantry Division Headquarters who demanded to speak with the officer in charge. As Major Parker returned from the road to take the call, Major Goldstein left in the lead half-track with the 'Ack-Ack' Staff Sergeant, headed for the perimeter defense line, followed by the other three half-tracks.

Three of the half-tracks carried four .50 caliber machine guns mounted in a powered turret. The fourth was equipped with a rapid firing 37 millimeter anti-aircraft gun. Although designed to repel low flying aircraft, the quad .50 caliber machine guns, mounted in a motorized turret, was a devastating weapon for use against foot troops and even lightly armored vehicles. These four weapons systems would be a welcome addition to our defense capability. I was not as certain about the worth of the 37 millimeter gun. To me it had limited capability against anything but non-armed vehicles, never-the-less, these four vehicles and crews added substantial fire power to our cross roads defense. Major Goldstein and Captain Huxel were building quite an effective defensive perimeter.

At noon, the Command Post crew was treated to a 10 in 1 Dinner. Not only were the rations provided by the Recon crew, but the Recon men also prepared the hot portion of the meal on their portable gasoline burning, single burner stove. I considered this meal quite a treat when compared to the "C" type rations we had been eating for several days. The Recon Sergeant said this was his way of repaying the 589th Field Artillery men for fixing his radio and giving him enough gas to make it back to his unit. Once their radio became operational, the Recon Sergeant made contact with his Squadron Commander who gave him instructions to remain in place until the point of the advancing German forces reached Baraque de Fraiture, then report this fact to him and quickly withdraw to Samree, Belgium.

The remainder of my on-duty shift passed quickly, but I was glad to see the replacement shift start drifting in at 1400 hours. After briefing my relief, Dell Miller, I made my way across the icy Liege Highway, N-15, to visit with Sergeant Barney Alford and his 105mm howitzer crew. They were a sorry looking bunch of soldiers, dirty uniforms and dirty faces, but they were in good spirits and glad to see me.

Barney turned to his on-duty crew and half-heartedly commanded, "Ten Hut! We are about to be inspected by some gold-brick Sergeant from Headquarters Battery. You can tell he is from headquarters, note the clean uniform, the clean shaven face, and the lack of mud on his boots." This type of joking seemed to please his Cannoneers and tended to ease the obvious tension in each man's mind. Suddenly turning serious, Barney asked, "Randy, when will the main show begin?"

"Barney, I don't know, We have two guys from the 87th Reconnaissance Squadron at the Command Post now. They played tag almost all night with German infantry and panzers between here and Houffalize. They thought the Kraus would be here before now."

"I wish something would happen soon, me and the boys don't want to sit here like ducks on a small pond. That's what we are Randy, just sitting ducks, and ole buddy, you are sitting on the same pond."

"Yea, I know! No one wants to be a sitting duck, but right now, I'd rather be a sitting duck than a dead duck! Maybe the Krauts have run out of gasoline. The Recon tank was running on fumes when it pulled into the CP early this morning. Maybe the Krauts will change their minds and go home. Who knows what will happen? I wouldn't blame them if they go home. This frigging cold weather makes me want to go home!"

"Well, let me tell you something Randy, if I had my choice, I'd damned well rather be back in Florida. If I ever get back home, I swear to God, I'll never leave again. I didn't know how good I had it. This is a TARFU (Things Are Really Fucked Up) situation."

"Barney, changing the subject, is today the 19th or the 20th of December?"

"Why do you ask? What in the hell difference does it make?"

"December the 19 is my birthday."

One of Barney's crew chimed in, "Yesterday was the 19th. How old were you Sergeant Pierson?"

"Yesterday I became a man, I was 21 years old. Now I can vote, get drunk legally, and screw around with women of the night. Right now I vote to have a drink and celebrate becoming a man."

Barney agreed, "Under the circumstances, I think we should celebrate." Then disappeared into the log covered dug-out beside the howitzer. He reappeared, waving a bottle of Cognac in his glove covered hand. His white teeth contrasting sharply with his surrounding, three day growth of beard, as he smiled and invited us into the dug-out..

"Come on in Randy, the drinks are on me."

It didn't take long to finish the Cognac and declare the bottle to be a 'Dead Soldier.' The Cognac was surprisingly smooth and went down easily, straight from the bottle. Slowly the conversation turned to more pleasant things and our current concerns started to fade. Then the telephone rang.

Barney answered the phone and we all listened as he grunted, "Yep, yep, I understand, WILCO (Will Comply)." He handed the phone to a crew member and said, "Stay on the phone, we've got to prepare for a fire mission. I don't have the full details yet." He then instructed the rest of the crew to remove the protective tarp from the howitzer, un-case four rounds of High Explosive shells, open four time fuses, and prepare to shift trails. He then turned to me and said, "Randy, this is crazy! The 87th Recon Squadron Commander in Samree just called his tank, you know, the one parked by the CP, and said one of his Recon crews reported spotting enemy infantry approaching the village of Samree from the north. The Squadron Commander said he had an officer with the Recon crew who could adjust artillery fire. He asked if the 589th could provide him with some anti-personnel fire. The Recon Sergeant at the CP relayed this request to Major Parker and the Major has agreed to provide them artillery support."

"What is so strange about that? That is the business we are in. We provide anti-personnel fire all the time."

"Wake up Pierson, my howitzer is deployed to provide fire to the south and east, Samree is west of us. If the Recon people are right, we now have Krauts on three sides of us. We may damned well be surrounded."

"Holy Shit, you are right Barney, we probably are surrounded. That is just great! What in the hell comes next. How do we get out of Baraque de Fraiture? Things are getting complicated! It looks like the 'Fat Lady' is about to sing."

Charlie Fairchild stuck his head out of the dug-out and yelled, "Sergeant Alford, fire direction just told us to relax. They expect the first enemy contact to come from the direction of Houffalize, that is our area of responsibility. The Major has assigned another howitzer the mission to fire in Samree. We are to remain in place."

Barney nodded his head to acknowledge he understood and told the Cannoneers to replace the tarp over the howitzer and re-case the ammunition and fuses. Standing in the cold and snow, we discussed the implications of our situation, finally agreeing that neither of us knew what to expect. I thanked Barney for the Cognac and the party. Our future seemed very uncertain as we shook hands and I departed for the Command Post. On the way back to the CP I heard a howitzer fire the first round of the Samree mission. Many things were going through my mind. As Barney would say, at least we're doing something. The Cognac was good and made me feel better, but it didn't kill the cold. I started thinking, "Happy Birthday to Me. Yesterday I became a man. What is going to happen if we really are surrounded? How in the hell did we get into this mess anyway? How do we get out of it?" My mind would not stop asking questions, but it never received one single answer.

Finally I made up my mind – to Hell with it all, I'm going to take a nap when I get back to the CP, I don't give a damn about this war. I am not responsible for this war until I go back on duty at 2000 hours.

589th FA Bn – Command Post
Baraque de Fraiture, Belgium
20 December 1944 – 2000 Hours

My buddy, Sergeant Dell Miller, the non-com I was to relieve in fire direction was so keyed-up he did not want to be relieved. The news, or more accurately, the rumors from different sources concerning the overall situation contradicted each other. The situation map reflected these contradictions as I tried to sort through various military symbols placed on the map with different colored grease pencils. Black for us, and Red for the enemy, it had no Black line or Red line, representing opposing forces, with a no-man's land in between. The situation map was now covered with Black and Red circles, indicating who controlled the territory within each circle. I had never seen anything like this before—two forces opposing each other, but no front lines!

Dell said if I was trying to make sense out of the map, "Forget it!" His appraisal of the situation was the only road in the area still under American control was the road to Manhay. In his opinion, that road would not remain in our hands for long, and if we lost control of that road, he reminded me of something I already knew. We would get no more re-supply of food, gasoline, or ammunition. This was pretty scary stuff!

In the meantime the 106th Infantry Division Headquarters continued to notify us , by radio, how important it was to deny this main road to the enemy for as long as possible. Apparently Division expected us to conduct a John Wayne, Hollywood type shootout to the last man. This approach did not appeal to me at all! I asked Dell about the short Samree fire mission during the late afternoon hours. He said it was a strange mission. To begin with, we had no firing charts prepared to shoot behind us, so he and Frank Tacker made up a firing chart quickly, using information from the 1/50,000 scale situation map we had on the wall. Miraculously, the 87th Recon officer observed the first round as the shell burst in the target area. The forward observer then asked for a relatively small adjustment for the second round. When it exploded, he made no changes and asked us to "Fire For Effect" on the third round. After a four round volley from two howitzers, he reported scattered enemy infantry dead and the remainder in retreat. With the crisp orders: "Cease Fire"—"End Of Mission"—"Mission Accomplished." Miller said the entire mission had been fired as though a trained Artillery Officer had been the forward observer. The only deviation from SOP (Standard Operating Procedures) occurred when the Recon Officer added, "Thanks for your help, 589th!"

The 87th Reconnaissance Squadron evaluated this enemy action not as a combat patrol, but an intelligence gathering patrol to determine if Samree was occupied and defended by American troops. The Krauts obtained an answer, however, but how well defended, or for how long Samree was to be occupied by American troops remained to be seen,

Dell's adrenaline flow finally started to slow and fatigue began to set in. He made it perfectly clear where he would be bedded down and insisted I get him up in a hurry if things heated up during the night. I gave him my solemn word I would.

When I reported to Major Parker, I noticed he also looked tired and the worse for wear. He had been carrying a huge load since we lost Lieutenant Colonel Kelly, the Battalion Commander. After briefing me on the situation in general, the best he could, he suddenly changed the subject to Lieutenant Colonel Kelly. He was concerned that we had not seen nor heard of the Colonel in four days now. The Major had served with the Colonel for the entire time we had trained as a Battalion, they were good friends, and had tremendous respect for each other. The thought of the Colonel being killed, wounded, or captured distressed us both. Terminating our conversation with a desperate shake of his head, Major Parker walked to his cot, sat down as if in meditation, and then slowly lowered himself into the prone position. I could tell he was worn out by his awesome responsibility, the loss of many friends, and the terrible uncertainty of our mission. After lying there for only a few moments he finally slipped into a deep and merciful sleep.

With only two other enlisted men on duty with me in the Command Post, I suddenly realized I was the senior person awake, and the fact that I was 'in charge' finally sunk in. The three of us stayed busy for the next hour and a half, listening to radio traffic between units, performing the normal housekeeping chores, and answering the CP switchboard. At 2330 hours, the EE8A field telephone rang that connected the CP to the listening post in the woods adjacent to the Houffalize highway. The hushed voice of John Schaffner from "A" Battery whispered, "I've got to talk to the person in charge at the CP, right now!"

As I took the telephone handset from the operator, I answered, "Sergeant Pierson, what's up?"

"Randy, I don't know what's up, but we hear noises like people moving along the hard-road. Right now I can hear Krauts talking and laughing. I can't see them in detail, but they seem to be pushing bicycles."

"What else are they doing, John?"

"Nothing, just walking and talking. They are headed toward the CP. They act like they're going to a picnic or something."

"Is it only foot soldiers, or do they have some type of motor support?"

"I don't think they have any support at all, Randy. They're still headed toward you folks. Maybe they are lost."

"Schaffner, hold on a minute, I've got to wake up the Major and try to get things sorted our. You just hold on."

"Sarge, I'll hold on, but do not ring me back under any circumstances. The Krauts would hear the ring and know exactly where I am. They would be all over us like a coat of paint."

"Don't worry partner, I understand, just hang in there, I'm getting Major Parker."

The instant I touched his shoulder, Major Parker was wide awake. He asked me to assess the situation and I repeated what John Schaffner had told me. The Major thought briefly and said he did not wish to endanger the listening post personnel nor reveal the locations of his howitzers. He opted to utilize the quad .50 caliber machine guns mounted on the anti-aircraft half-track covering the Houffalize road. As the Major uttered this statement, the telephone operator on duty was calling to alert the Ack-Ack crew. The Anti-Aircraft Sergeant had two questions, how many enemy personnel were approaching, and at what range? Schaffner estimated about 20 enemy foot solders were some one hundred yards west of his listening post and still advancing toward the Command Post at a leisurely pace. These facts placed the enemy infantry about six hundred yards from the half-track. This information was passed to the 'Ack-Ack' crew.

In the still, cold night air, we at the CP could actually hear the distinctive, 'clack, clack – clack, clack' four times as .50 caliber cartridges were loaded into each of the air cooled anti-aircraft machine guns mounted in the half-track turret. The crew chief then reported back to the CP, "Turret ready to fire. We are aimed on target, waist high, awaiting your command to fire." At the Major's direction, I notified Schaffner we would be firing quad .50s, and other small arms down the Houffalize road. The fire would consist of four separate bursts. He and his men should stay in their holes and keep their heads down until two minutes after the fourth burst. At that time he should stick his head up and report the results of the machine gun fire.

An extremely nervous John Schaffner said, "Randy, make sure I got this straight.

Duck, four bursts, wait two minutes, then look up and report."

"You got it right partner – NOW DUCK!"

On command, the cold, black night exploded and burst into flickering orange-red light. The anti-aircraft gunner squeezed off twenty round bursts (actually eighty rounds for each burst as he was firing four machine guns) by counting the number of tracers fired. This was relatively easy for an experienced gunner because each fifth round in the ammunition belt was a tracer. He merely counted four tracers, released the firing mechanism for a count of ten, and then fired four more tracers. The gunner repeated this rhythmic sequence four times and in the process fired a total of 320 highly destructive rounds of .50 caliber slugs.

Once the firing started, Major Parker and I moved to the front of the stone building housing the CP to watch the fireworks. The muzzle flashes from the four .50 caliber machine guns silhouetted the olive drab half-track against the white snow surround it. Each muzzle burst cast eerie shadows behind tall mounds of snow and illuminated the dark tree line of the surrounding Ardennes Forrest. Cherry red tracers flew down the Houffalize road like four columns of giant lightening bugs and gracefully moved from side to side, like molten liquid from a garden hose, as the gunner gently traversed the turret to direct fire along both sides of the road. The accompanying noise level was awesome. This picture repeated itself three more times and the sight and sound was spell binding. I had difficulty in equating such a beautiful sight to the horrible death and destruction it was causing some six hundred yards from me.

As suddenly as this spectacle started, the night became black again, and the silence of death prevailed.

Two minutes later, Schaffner reported in over his field telephone, "Holy Shit

Randy, I didn't know those quad .50s could throw out so many rounds. I could see tracers going over and could actually feel the velocity of the rounds as they passed over our hole. I could hear the Krauts running around and screaming. Those Ack-Ack guys really caught the Krauts with their pants down."

"Schaffner, have you stuck your head up yet?"

"NO WAY!"

"Can you hear anything?"

"I haven't really tried yet. Hold on a minute. I think I hear some guy down the road moaning and groaning."

"Where is he from your location?"

"I can't tell, I'm pretty deep in my hole."

"Think you can stick your head up now?"

"Are those Ack-Ack guys through shooting?"

"For right now John, yes."

It seemed like I waited forever for Schaffner to get back on the phone. When he returned, there was excitement in his voice. He reported torn up bicycles and dead bodies all over the road. There was no one standing, walking, or running on the road, and he could hear nothing moving in the forest. The only sign of life he could detect was the moaning German soldier lying on the side of the road.

"Schaffner, can you detect any movement in the direction of Houffalize?"

"Sarge, it is spooky quiet out here. I mean real quiet. It is spooky, all I can hear is my heart beating."

"OK buddy, we won't do any more shooting, but stay put, and stay alert. I don't know whether the Major is going to send someone out to pick up the wounded Kraut or not,"

"Randy, unless my ears are playing tricks on me, I think I hear Captain Huxel out there now. Hold on and let me take another look. Sarge, I was right, warn everyone at the cross roads not to fire, the Captain and two other guys are dragging the wounded prisoner toward the CP right now."

"Thanks for the information John, I'll pass it along to Major Parker."

"Randy, before you hang up, I want to tell you I'm going to disconnect my phone."

"Schaffner, you can't do that, we might have to call you!"

"Just a damned minutes Sergeant, I'm not finished. I don't want this damned thing ringing. With that patrol wiped out, somebody will probably come looking for them later on. I don't want anyone to hear my telephone ringing. I'm going to disconnect the phone lines from my EE8A and hold them in my hand. If you need to call me, crank the magneto slowly, the shock will tell me to hook up the phone line. But remember, don't turn the crank hard, these magnetos can 'bite' you. I don't want to get 'bit' and drop the line and loose it."

"OK, I get the picture John. Stay down and hang loose. If you need me, call, I'll be right here."

Activity in the CP picked up. Major Parker was reporting to Division and all the local phones were busy, everyone wanted to know what the firing was all about and as Frank Tacker and Dell Miller entered the CP fully clothed, Captain Huxel and a medic dragged a half frozen, badly wounded, and extremely frightened German Corporal into the Command Post.

For some reason I thought of my conversation earlier in the day with Barney Alford. I was certain he felt as I did, that our position was untenable, that we had been declared expendable, and since the end was near, the 'Fat Lady' had already begun to sing!

Battle for Parker's Crossroads — Day 3
Baraque de Fraiture, Belgium — 589thFA Bn
Sergeant Alford's Howitzer Section
21 December 1944 — Early Morning, Before Day Break

Although Sergeant Alford's howitzer section had not been involved in the skirmish with the German bicycle patrol last night, Barney was fully aware of what had taken place. He had not slept well last night and down deep inside he knew he and his men would be severely tested today. He detested firing his howitzer using direct fire, like an anti-tank gun. His 105mm howitzer was designed for indirect fire, not direct fire, and although his howitzer was a powerful artillery weapon, it was slow to fire when compared with the gun on a panzer, and his crew members were not protected like the members of a panzer crew. Of course, the obvious advantage a panzer mounted gun had over his howitzer was the fact that the panzer could move about swiftly, whereas his howitzer could not. He knew these facts from training, and more recently from experience in combat. However he was determined his crew would be ready for the first wave of German armor which would obviously attack our positions today.

Corporal Fairchild, the Battalion Howitzer Mechanic, had the same basic feelings. When he sensed Sergeant Alford moving about in the dark of the cramped, log covered bunker, he decided to get out of his warm sleeping bag and get dressed for action also. Soon the light produced by a gasoline lantern and the heat produced by the tiny cooking stove, combined with the aroma of boiling coffee made the cramped bunker more bearable. Outside however, the ammunition crates were covered by several inches of new snow and the howitzer itself, under it's protective tarp, looked like a huge, harmless mound of snow, not like a sophisticated weapon of war.

Although the black coffee was steaming hot and the "C" Rations, marked on the can as 'Eggs and Bacon,' had been heated, this combination did not make the greatest breakfast Barney and Charlie had ever eaten. The best thing you could say about the "C" Rations was they were nutritious and filling and the caffeine in the coffee helped get the ole motor started. The worst thing about getting up under these conditions is going to the latrine. Urinating through four layers of tight clothing is difficult, no mater what the length of the penis. The usual outcome produced a slight leakage down one pant leg or the other. But having a bowel movement with your bared rear-end touching the snow is, putting it lightly, not a pleasant experience in below freezing weather. Most GIs waited as long as they possibly could to take a crap. This practice, along with the heavy spices and the high protein contained in Army field rations, caused each man to generate enormous amounts of intestinal gas. Since a large volume of this intestinal gas is passed during the sleeping hours, the sleeping bags, or bed rolls, were frequently referred to as 'fart sacks.' Not necessarily a polite name, but extremely descriptive! This morning, Sergeant Alford's closed-in bunker smelled pretty rotten, giving credence to the old GI adage, "It's better to fart and bear the shame, than not to fart and bear the pain."

In normal times Charlie Fairchild, as the Battalion Artillery Mechanic, was charged with the responsibility of maintaining twelve 105mm, truck drawn, howitzers. He was now serving as a member of Barney's howitzer crew, but continued to check the three remaining howitzers daily. In weather this cold, the main item he checked was the hydraulic fluid in the recoil mechanism. If this hydraulic fluid froze, or leaked out, the howitzer could sustain severe damage when fired, and most likely, one or more of the Cannoneers would be injured in the process. It was Fairchild's responsibility to make certain this type of accident would not happen.

Charlie Fairchild did not look forward to making his howitzer inspections this morning. The weather was particularly fowl, the three howitzer positions were widely disbursed and, it was difficult to get his 3/4 ton Dodge truck, which carried his heavy tools, close to any of these weapons. Since his truck was parked fairly close to Barney's howitzer position he decided to start his inspection tour here at first light.

Breakfast over, Barney reached into his musette bag and retrieved a partial box of hand rolled Cuban Panatela cigars. He carefully counted out four cigars, his quota for the day, looked at the almost empty box, and cursed to no one, in particular, "We'd better get out of this damned position before I run out!" Muttering to himself, he returned the almost empty box to his musette bag, carefully placed three cigars into a hard plastic cigar case, stuffed the case into an inner jacket pocket, and started to light his first cigar of the day. Once the cigar was properly lit, he headed through the deep snow toward the latrine to take a good, healthy crap.

Battle for Parker's Crossroads – Day 3
589th FA Bn – Command Post – 0540 Hours
Baraque de Fraiture, Belgium

The switchboard operator yelled, "Captain Huxel is reporting the outpost line between the Houffalize and Vielsalm roads is under heavy infantry attack." Major Parker looked at his wrist watch as he picked up the handset of his telephone and thought, "Jerry is right on time, exactly 0530 Hours." In his normal, unhurried, and gentle tone of voice, the Major asked Captain Huxel, "What is going on George?"

The Major had made many important decisions concerning the defense of the cross roads, but placing Captain Huxel in command of the outer perimeter defense was probably his most wise decision. Captain Huxel was by far the most physical and tough officer in the Battalion, and the men respected him for this personal toughness. His defense was well planned and potential enemy travel routes were covered by devastating and mobile firepower. The additional defensive force was not originally planned, but had been accumulated from other units passing through our road block who had been recruited by Major Parker to stand and fight with the 589th. To the less than one hundred 589th Field Artillery men and their remaining three 105mm howitzers, Captain Huxel now had four anti-aircraft half-tracks and crews from the 203rd AA Battalion, four 3 inch anti-tank guns and crews from the 643rd Tank Destroyer Battalion, and one light tank and crew from the 87th Reconnaissance Squadron. Our mission had not changed, we were to hold this open area, the size of a dozen football fields, which had been cleared from the dense Ardennes Forest years ago by Belgian farmers, for as long as possible.

While Captain Huxel was a smart man, he could not be accurately described as an intellectual. The word which described him best, was physical. At 5' 11", he weighed almost 200 pounds, all muscle, and no fat what-so-ever. An angular face topped with blond hair, a short cropped military style haircut, a crushing handshake, and penetrating sky-blue eyes, were his trade marks. The Captain had one peculiar theory which was unique for an officer, he felt the Army placed too much emphasis on personal hygiene and thought one bath each week was sufficient. This belief was hard for others to understand and placed him in a category by himself. Never-the-less, in combat he was truly respected by both officers and enlisted men. If you were engaged in a rough, tough street fight, you would want the Captain on your side. In my opinion we were about to be committed to the roughest and toughest pitched battle of our lives, and I was glad Captain Huxel was on my side!

Captain Huxel answered Major Parker's question in a brief and unemotional manner, "Major, the attack started with light fine from a single 60mm mortar. We have pretty well pinpointed the mortar location, but have no way to knock it out. We are receiving small arms and burp gun fire, not heavy, just enough to force us to keep our heads down. I'd estimate we are facing a reduced Company, maybe 60 or 70 people. Anything else you need to know?"

"George, is there any chance the Germans can break through our defense?"

"Major, I don't think so. They're still in the woods and don't have any punching power. To get to us they would have to advance about two hundred yards across open ground covered with deep snow. I don't think they could make it."

"What is your plan?"

"We're going to kick the shit out of them!"

"No George, I mean specifically. What about the mortar?"

"Sir, I would like for you to send me the Recon tank. The one behind the Command Post – Aw shit, excuse me Major."

After a long pause Captain Huxel returned to the telephone and continued, "We had to duck, that fucking mortar is bugging us. Major please let me use the tank, we definitely know the location of the mortar. The Kraut small arms fire can't hurt the tank. The tank crew should be able to take out the mortar easily with a couple of rounds."

"Consider it done George," the Major responded as he passed instructions to Staff Sergeant Frank Tacker, "Do you need anything else?"

"Yes Sir, we could use some 105mm rounds into the tree line directly in front of us. You know, like interdiction fire. Fuse Quick would be best. That would produce tree bursts and give the Kraut infantry something to worry about, in addition to killing some of the bastards."

"I'll give you the 105mm support very quickly. Need anything else?"

"No sir."

"Consider it done George, keep your head down and let me know if the 105mm support is effective."

Frank Tacker looked over my shoulder intently as I talked to Sergeant Alford on the telephone. "Barney, this is Randy – FIRE MISSION."

As Barney yelled "FIRE MISSION" to his howitzer crew, he said, "Go ahead

Randy, what's up?"

Captain Huxel needs interdicting fire into the woods about three hundred yards in front of him. The eastern side of the perimeter in taking small arms and mortar fire."

"We can hear the firing. My howitzer can lay down direct fire into that area. You gave the mission to the right crew. We have a good field of fire in that direction."

"Barney, here are the commands, Charge 3, Shell HE, Fuse Quick, Range 600 yards, Ten Rounds at ten second intervals, Fire when ready." As an after thought, I added, "Barney, rake the area and try to get tree bursts"

"WILCO, Randy. Tell the captain to keep his head down."

Major Parker reported to Captain Huxel, "Get down and stay down, the first round is on the way, nine more to follow at 10 second intervals. At end of mission, report results."

The situation at the east perimeter had escalated into a vicious fire fight. Mostly small arms fire, but periodically punctuated with the distinctive 'crump' of exploding German 60mm mortar shells. The Germans obviously did not know how to use their mortar effectively. The rounds were landing in the open area where the men of the perimeter defense were well dug-in. The Germans appeared to want to soften up the outpost positions and were paying almost no attention to the building which contained the American Command Post, nor the half-tracks or the howitzers themselves. During the night, German troops had moved toward the cross roads from Houffalize and Vielsalm and obviously expected to encounter light, or no resistance at all.

The first ten rounds from Barney's 105mm howitzer, bursting in the trees over the heads of the advancing enemy infantry had quite a dampening effect on their attack. The sounds of battle diminished perceptibly as the Kraut soldiers scurried in search of cover. Captain Huxel reported he was pleased with the suppressing effect of the howitzer fire, but wanted to know when to expect the Recon tank. While he was still complaining about the mortar fire that harassed his men, he reported he could hear and see the Recon tank making its way slowly in his general direction. The tank hatch cover was open and the tank commander was visible from the shoulders up. He was receiving sporadic, but ineffective, small arms fire during the short journey which made it necessary for him to duck inside the tank's protective armor frequently, thereby slowing his progress.

An infuriated Captain Huxel called for another ten rounds of howitzer fire. These tree bursts took the remaining fight out of the now retreating German infantry. Those soldiers not killed or wounded had started a frantic and disorganized withdrawal toward the town of Vielsalm.

With no small arms fire to contend with, the Recon tank commander reached Captain Huxel without additional trouble. As the tank slowed to a halt, the Captain climbed aboard and gave the signal to proceed. In short order, the tank moved eastward on the Vielsalm road unopposed. Once on the road, the Captain told the tank gunner to "load and lock with shell HE" and be prepared to fire when the tank turned left into a cleared fire break in the forest. He explained he expected to find the mortar and crew located there. When they reached the fire break, the tank driver was going to fast and as he made the left turn the tank slid sideways on the ice. In the moment it took to get the tank under control and stopped, the gunner saw the upright mortar and the crew men. In true artillery fashion, Captain Huxel bellowed above the rumble of the engine, "Range 300, Fire When Ready!"

The 57mm, high velocity, tank gun roared, the tank chassis shook, and the fire break in front of the tank was filled with black smoke, flying snow, a perforated mortar tube, and unrecognizable body parts.

The Captain then ordered, "Fire two when ready!"

For all practical purposes, the second round was not necessary, but it too produced spectacular results. This round triggered numerous secondary explosions of the remaining enemy mortar rounds.

Captain Huxel advised the Recon Sergeant he felt the mission was successful, but the Sergeant wanted to take a look around. He armed himself, and closely followed by Captain Huxel, climbed out of the protection of the light tank. They were covered by a nervous tank gunner, who manned a light .30 caliber machine gun from the safety of the turret. The Captain collected German 'Soldiers Books' from the mutilated dead bodies while the Recon Sergeant diligently searched for war trophies.

The tank encountered no enemy fire as it returned to the cross roads at 0745 hours. The occupants of the returning tank found 589th medics tending the German wounded, they saw enemy dead lying in the snow in a row at the edge of the clearing, and witnessed the new-to-combat 589th Artillery men, fighting as infantry, actively engaged in rounding up German prisoners of war.

Battle for Parker's Crossroads – Day 3
589th FA Bn Command Post – 2000 Hours
Baraque de Fraiture, Belgium

We had been in hard combat for six days now, however, the battle we had experienced this morning was the most intense combat we had experienced to date. The fire fight lasted about two hours, but to the artillery men involved, it seemed like a lifetime. In addition to taking care of ourselves, we had captured twelve German *Volksgrenadiers* we must guard, four of which were wounded. We had received no serious casualties, however, three of the 589th men had received lacerations from mortar fragments. The most prevalent damage to the American troops defending the cross road consisted of frayed nerves and an uncertain future. We had been severely tested and we had prevailed. Now the enemy knew we were here and we were determined to stay. For the enemy to continue their advance toward their immediate objective, the vast Allied supply dumps near Liege, Belgium, they must exercise one of two options: either bypass us, or overwhelm us.

There was no doubt in Major Parker's mind, we would stay, we would hold this ground as long as we could, and in the end, we would be overwhelmed because we were expendable. We were mere pawns in a gigantic, absurd, chess game, where winner takes all. He and Captain Huxel had spent all day rearranging the defense, re-establishing listening posts, and establishing a fall-back defense line to use when the enemy exerted even more pressure on the defenders later in the day. The Major felt pressure would be exerted with additional infantry, greater firepower, and armor support.

The fire direction crew on duty during the day had been busy after the morning attack. They were ready to go off duty when I reported to the Command Post. As I entered the room, Major Parker immediately cornered

Frank Tacker, Dell Miller and me. The Major looked exhausted, his shoulders drooped, his face was void of expression, and he looked at us with a vacant stare. In a monotone he began, "Gentlemen, I expect all hell to break loose just before dawn tomorrow morning." He paused, as though trying to organize his thoughts, and then he continued, "I believe the enemy will mass troops, armor, and artillery along the Houffalize and Vielsalm roads tonight." He paused again to let the message sink in. "We must be able to use our artillery to interdict and disrupt their assembly areas. To accomplish this, we must establish and man a forward observation post tonight." After pausing for the third time, to allow the full weight of his statement to sink in, he finally said, "I need a volunteer!"

No one spoke! The three of us looked at each other for what seemed an eternity. Still, no one spoke!

Without raising his voice, the Major repeated his request, "I need a volunteer who can adjust artillery fire."

The following silence was embarrassing, and to my utter surprise, I heard myself say in a high squeaky voice, "Major Parker, I will volunteer."

Major Parker bowed his head and said, "Sergeant Tacker, Sergeant Miller, thank you, that will be all. Sergeant Pierson, come with me, we need to talk."

Looking over an aerial photograph of the area, the Major pointed out a location, between the two roads involved, where a wire crew had run a telephone line to a fox hole hidden in thick trees. I was to take an EE8A (pronounced–Double E 8A) field telephone to that location, connect it to the line, secure myself in the fox hole, and report to fire direction when I was ready to listen and observe. I was to report enemy movement of any kind to the east or south of me, be it foot soldiers or vehicles. If my report resulted in a fire mission, I was to adjust artillery fire onto the target. Major Parker advised me I was to man this outpost until dawn, at which time I would be relieved.

This was a pretty tall order for an inexperienced Sergeant who would have limited visibility due to the dense trees and total darkness. On the other hand, with the supreme confidence inherent in a young, healthy, twenty-one year old male, I figured if anyone could do it, I could do it. Only this thought suppressed my fears and provided me the necessary courage to start the long, lonely walk to the observation post. All alone, just me, my EE8A, my trusty pistol, and my newly sharpened boot knife, I began walking east on the Vielsalm road. .

What lay ahead? I could only guess! The farther I walked, the more disturbed I became. All this darkness, the uncertainty, the obvious danger, and being alone, caused a nervous twitch in my left eye lid. My right hand dropped to my pistol holster and I unsnapped the protective flap. As I forced myself to keep walking, I kept asking, "Why did I volunteer?" The answer I received was always the same, "Because you are stupid! Stupid! STUPID!"

The luminous dial of my GI wrist watch indicated it was almost 2300 hours when I turned the crank on the EE8A and checked in with the fire direction center. When their telephone rang, Dell Miller answered and asked, "Randy – Are you OK?"

"So far, so good Dell. Tell the Major I'm all set, but I can't see anything. I can't hear anything either, and Dell, don't let anyone touch the crank on your phone. It's so quiet out here the Krauts could hear this damned thing ring a mile down the road."

"I'll tell the Major. Glad you made it buddy.!"

"Dell, I'm serious! You guard that damned telephone crank until I get back to the cross roads. I'm depending on you!"

"Don't sweat it Randy, I'll guard it. No one will call you."

"Dell, I'll check in with you guys every half hour, but I say it again Dell, DO NOT CALL ME!"

† †

Battle for Parker's Crossroads – Day 4
589th FA Bn – Forward Observation Post
In the Ardennes Forest east of Baraque de Fraiture, Belgium
22 December 1944 – 0130 Hours

"Dell, I can hear motors running every now and then. The darkness plays tricks on my eyes but I think I see a light over the tree tops every now and then. The light is hard to describe, it is very faint, just a glimmer."

"Where do you think the Krauts are?"

"About one mile east of me. Sounds like vehicles moving into a bivouac, or maybe a staging area."

"Which way do you think they are turning off of the Vielsalm road?"

"It's too dark to read a map, but I'd say they are turning south, maybe down a fire break, heading towards the Houffalize road. I can't pinpoint the sounds or the lights exactly."

"OK Randy, I'll talk to the Major. In the meantime, keep the line open, I'll need to talk to you in about one minute."

"I'll wait."

Dell was gone a long time and I hung on the line for what seemed like an hour. The EE8A telephone is equipped with a push-to-talk switch. Consequently when Dell put his receiver down, his switch was not depressed, and I could not hear what was going on in the Command Post. The line was totally dead, the air was getting colder, the night was moonless, I was alone, and the spooky forest was beginning to get to me. My nerves were as taut as stretched rubber bands and my straining eyes were seeing things which did not exist. Periodically I was brought back to the world of reality by the sound of a truck motor in the distance, the wind in the snow covered trees, or the occasional soft 'plop' when a clump of damp snow fell to earth from an overburdened limb.

The fox hole wasn't really large enough for me. I was starting to get leg cramps from the cold and lack of exercise and I already wished I was back with my friends at the Command Post. Why in the hell did I volunteer to come out here? I must be nuts, a candidate for a Section Eight (Mental Deficiency) Discharge.

"Randy, are you still there?"

"Of course I am! Where in the hell do you think I could go? What is going on at the CP? Did you guys take a nap?"

Ignoring all these snippy questions, Dell asked, "Can you hear increased activity east of you position?"

"No, I just hear a single motor every now and then. Sounds like a single truck, however, it may be the same truck over and over again. I don't know."

"OK, I'll tell Major Parker. He doesn't want to do anything yet. I'm going to sign off for now, be sure and check in at 0200 hours."

"Dell, I'll hang around a little bit longer, but I really want to come in. I feel like a red pimple in the middle of a big white rear-end sitting out here all by myself. And Dell, don't let anyone call me. You promised!"

"I promised, no calls you can trust me. You call us, we will not call you!"

There was nothing more to report during the calls at 0200 and 0230 hours. Time was dragging, I was very cold and uncomfortable, and it was getting difficult to stay awake. The only defense against the cold and going to sleep was body movement. I had to get out of the fox hole more frequently and exercise. For the 'umpteenth' time I looked at my GI wrist watch. The luminous dial told me it was 0250 hours. In ten minutes I had to check in with fire direction. When I did, I would tell them to notify our outposts not to shoot because I was coming in. I don't care if the Major does expect me to stay out here in this damned forest by myself until I am relieved at dawn. During my exercise session, of bends, stretches and knee lifts, I decided to make my way through the trees to the side of the road. The distance was not great. Once there I could definitely hear motorized traffic. The sounds were much louder, but not necessarily closer. As I listened more intently I could make out the distinctive sound of tracked vehicles. Apparently Jerry had been moving infantry into a staging area in trucks for two or three hours and now their supporting armor was beginning to arrive.

It was almost 0300 hours when Dell Miller answered the telephone, "Randy anything new?"

I was almost too excited to report, "I believe Jerry has dumped several truck loads of infantry into the woods about a mile east of here. Now I hear their armored support vehicles beginning to arrive. You'd better notify Major Parker."

"WILCO, hold on."

There was no mistaking the situation. Jerry was going to assault the cross roads at daybreak with a larger infantry force, this time supported by armor. The thought occurred to me, this really makes me a very small red pimple on a huge white rear-end. With Americans shooting at Germans over my head and the Germans fighting back, how was I supposed to get out of this fucking mess alive. One side or the other will surely kill me during the fire fight and I'll be just as dead no matter who pulls the trigger. I hope the Major will order me back to the Command Post before the shit hits the fan. If he does, with my luck, I'll probably get shot by one of the nervous 589th Cannoneers as I stumble down the road to the CP in the dark. CRAP!

My thoughts were shattered when Dell spoke into the telephone. "Randy, Major Parker wants you to adjust some artillery fire. We are preparing the gun data right now."

"Dell, I can't see anything because of the trees. How can I adjust fire when I can't see the target area or the shell burst?"

"We know you can't see the target area, just do the best you can. We are going to adjust with Shell WP (White Phosphorus) which will create a lots of light and maybe set something on fire, or maybe create a secondary explosion."

"Hey, pretty good thinking pal. Really sharp! Who thought of that?"

"I don't want to brag but it was your ole buddy Dell. Just taking care of a friend."

"That won't take care of me, but maybe the artillery fire will help."

When Dell reported, "First round on the way," I could actually hear a 105mm howitzer fire and realized it was not one of ours, but belonged to another Field Artillery Battalion located much to the west of the cross roads, and made a mental note to ask Dell what outfit was firing the mission for me. This question disappeared quickly when I left the protection of my fox hole to observe the burst of the white phosphorous round as it burst in the forest east of me. The flash was brilliant against the black sky and plainly visible to my naked eye.

"Did you see the first round Randy?"

"As plain as day."

"How do you sense the round?"

"Hang on Dell, I want to listen for a minute before I make up my mind. I want to know if the first round attracted the Krauts attention, or if it is so far away they aren't paying any attention to it."

Apparently the bursting White Phosphorous round attracted the enemies attention. From the sounds involved, both truck and tank motors were being started. In their haste to move out of the target area, some enemy drivers committed an unpardonable sin, they broke black-out discipline and turned on their head lights. From my vantage point, I came to the conclusion the first round of WP burst beyond the lights on the moving vehicles, which were moving slowly to my left.

I reached for the field telephone at the parapet of my fox hole and spoke into the transmitter in a low voice, "Miller?"

"Yep."

"The round is 400 over and 200 right."

"To enable me to follow what was going on in fire direction, Miller left the push-to-talk button of his EE8A in the ON position. I heard him as he made the corrections to the fire direction specialists, "Down 400, Left 200."

Things were starting to happen which made me forget the discomfort caused by the cold and eased the tensions caused by fear. Adrenaline began to flow and fight overcame the flight characteristics of the 'Fight or Flight Syndrome.' What I was doing now was one of the things I was taught to do in training. It was almost like being on the firing range back in Camp Atterbury. In short order, I received the report from Miller, "On the way." As I heard the swishing 105mm round go over my head, I thought, the howitzer crew firing this mission is pretty sharp, then my mind was brought back to focus by the brilliant flash of the second round bursting in the Kraut assembly area. My perception of where the second round burst seemed to be between me and the moving vehicle lights. We apparently had achieved what a good forward observer strives for—a bracket—one round short of the target, and one round beyond the target. Once the target is 'bracketed' you know it is located between the established firing data. The next sensing would ask the fire direction crew to split the bracket and "Fire for Effect." The only thing I now had to adjust for was for the slow movement of the vehicles to my left.

"Dell, try 200 Short, 200 Right, Change shell to HE (High Explosive), Fuse Quick."

Through his EE8A I heard Dell make the corresponding corrections, "Up 200, Left 200, Shell HE, Fuse Quick."

My request for a change in ammunition from White Phosphorous to High Explosive was more of an educated guess than a mere whim. After-the-fact, I thought it was going to be a foolish request. First, I thought I would not be able to observe the bursts of the HE shells through the trees, and second, the flight characteristics of the two shells were different. Logically I thought I had wasted a round, but more important, I felt I had given Jerry more time to flee and/or seek cover. With these thoughts running through my mind, I heard Miller report, "On the Way."

The third round of my adjustment burst in the target area, I heard it, but I could not see it. What I did see was a great ball of fire, surrounded by the low hanging clouds caused by the two previous bursts of white phosphorus shells. The target area now looked like heat lightening during a stormy night back home in Florida. Following this visual display came a second explosion which made the sound of the shell burst seem puny by comparison. The force of this explosion was so powerful I could actually feel the force of the explosion push upon my chest. Following this secondary explosion, two shafts of light rose above the crest of the tree line at a crazy angle. These two beams of light were stationary and clearly visible as they penetrated the haze and smoke caused by the previous WP shells. The secondary explosion had upended an enemy vehicle whose headlights had become the guiding beacons for the rain of 105mm shells which followed.

My sensing of this round was short and exhilarating, "Direct Hit – Fire for Effect!" As an after thought I added most unprofessionally, "Hit them with everything you've got, including the kitchen sink." Suddenly the still night was filled with explosions. Behind me the howitzers were firing rapidly and the target area in front of me had become an audible and visual mosaic of bursting artillery shells and multi-colored flashes. Entirely caught-up in the excitement of the moment, I finally heard Miller's voice on the telephone, which was still held to my ear, "Fire for Effect is Complete – Please Report the Results."

Still excited, I dropped the expected forward observer protocol and responded, "It looks like we did a lot of damage. Of course I don't know how much. We got at least one good secondary explosion and I know we got at least one vehicle. I cannot assess any other damage from actual observation because I can't see anything."

"Randy, do you require additional fire upon the target?"

"Dell, please do not give the firing battery an 'End of Mission' yet. I need more time to listen for movement. I'm going to move out onto the road and try to take a look at what the Krauts are doing. I'll be back in a couple of minutes."

"OK Randy, I won't release the firing battery until I hear from you again."

The view looking east on the Vielsalm road was not good because of the curves which followed the contours of the hilly terrain. Through the now quiet night I could see no lights, other than the flickering orange/red glow caused by something burning in the distance. The slanted beacons, which had marked the target area, were gone, either extinguished by the artillery barrage or by the hand of some brave and unknown enemy soldier. Not a trace of vehicular movement could be detected, but I had a feeling, a strong instinctive feeling, that there was silent foot movement, that I could neither hear nor see, along the road and in the forest. Instinct and common sense moved me back into the forest and to the cover of my fox hole where the feeling of movement to the east of me grew even stronger. My heart began to pound, my mouth went dry, and I breathed in short, quick intervals. The adrenaline was beginning to flow again. This time, would it be fight or flight?

After minutes of waiting and listening there was still nothing tangible to guide me, but I had a strange feeling that I was being hunted. Now I knew how a deer must feel as it waits in the thick brush for the arrival of an unseen hunter. I reported this feeling to Miller.

"Randy, do you think infantry is moving toward you as a result of our last fire mission?"

"All I know is this! We know the enemy is out there and they know we are here. Sooner or later we are going to lock horns, and I'm out here all by myself and caught in the middle."

"Suppose we drop some rounds into the forest between you and the target area and see if we can flush-out any of their infantry."

"That makes sense and makes me feel a little better."

"Randy, the Major has been listening. He thinks we should drop a few rounds of HE, with fuse quick, into the trees several hundred yards east of you and see what happens."

There was a painful delay as the fire direction specialists computed new data for the howitzers and relayed this information to the firing battery. Finally Dell reported, "First Round On The Way" and added a message for me, "Be sure and DUCK."

The first round of this second mission landed four or five hundred yards east of me with a spectacular tree burst, high above the ground. After the tree burst I could plainly hear under-brush moving, ice and snow crunching, and excited voices conversing loudly in German. It was instantly obvious to me, the enemy infantry was moving quickly in my direction. I sensed the round, "200 Over."

Dell took my sensing, but did not relay it to fire direction. He asked, "Did we stir up anybody?"

"You sure did, it is like a hornets nest out there. Get some more rounds on those bastards in a hurry if you want me home for breakfast." Over the telephone I could hear Dell order the fire direction technicians to reduce the range by 200 yards, and almost immediately reported back to me, "On The Way."

The second round burst in the tree tops much closer to my position, producing the sounds of shattered limbs falling and much louder and closer excited German voices. In desperation I sensed the round "200 Over – Fire For Effect!"

"Randy, according to the firing chart, if we drop the range another 200 yards, we will be bursting High Explosive shells in the trees right over your head."

"Damn it Dell, do it! Do it NOW! If you don't do it now you can kiss my southern ass good bye!"

"OK ole buddy. Duck and good luck!"

Deep in the fox hole I tried to cover my entire body with my steel helmet. I wanted anything I could get to protect me from the red hot steel fragments I knew would come. 'Friendly Fire,' as they call it, started bursting in the tree tops all around me. Tree tops were blown off, jagged tree pieces fell to the ground, and mind boggling explosions were everywhere. Vicious, hot steel shell fragments, flying through the cold air, seeking their final resting place, found the bodies of enemy soldiers, and caused the screams of wounded and dying men to mingle with the sounds of more exploding howitzer shells. As quickly as it started, this man-made hell-on-earth stopped. I was immediately conscious of three things: First, the moans of the wounded Germans around me; Second, the acrid smell of burned powder; and Three, there was even more movement of people in the forest, very near to my fox hole. I had survived the shelling unhurt, but I needed more covering fire. Knowing Dell and the Major wanted my report and the fact that I needed more fire, I reached up for the EE8A on the parapet of my fox hole, two feet above my head. It was gone! It had been shot away, not even the phone lines remained. The realization that I was totally alone, and with no support, drained the remaining strength from my body. I collapsed to the bottom of the fox hole, my heart pounding like a drum and almost afraid to breath. By accident, my right hand dropped to the top of my combat boot and felt the handle of the razor sharp, double edged, boot-knife sheathed there. An automatic reflex, born of my Ranger training at Camp Atterbury, caused me to withdraw the fighting blade from it's leather sheath. The Pawn Broker in Boston who sold me this knife while I was at the Port of Embarkation had assured me this knife was the finest 'fighting blade' money could buy and added, the purchase of this knife might someday save my life. Of course at the time I considered this a sales pitch, but I bought the blade anyway. For some reason I had worn the knife in my right hand boot ever since we had reached Europe.

I waited silently in the fox hole, knees slightly bent, with both legs positioned squarely beneath my torso. The leather wrapped handle of the fighting knife was firmly grasped in both hands, it's sharp steel tip pointed upward, toward the top of the fox hole. After several minutes of waiting in this position, almost paralyzed with fear, I could sense someone moving in my direction, thrashing wildly through the deep snow and fallen limbs. Suddenly a metal object dropped into the fox hole, striking my helmet, and finally coming to rest upon my shoulder. Was it a grenade? No, it was a German helmet! Before I could react, a bare headed body followed the helmet into the fox hole and landed head down on top of me with a guttural grunt. Strong body odor filled the air. I could smell his filthy uniform, his stinking wet leather boots, and worst of all, I could smell the foul breath which gushed from his mouth as a result of the unexpected fall.

My terrible fears suddenly turned into great strength and unleashed fury. The cold steel fighting blade was thrust upward with the power of both arms and legs. This thrust met the dead weight of the falling German body. The five inch blade entered the mans chest just below has Adams-apple, severing his sternum from top to bottom and in the process exposing steaming internal organs, and starting a fatal flow of his life's blood. Surprised, and in terrible pain, the German screamed, *"Gott In Himmel!"* The power of my upward thrust moved him completely out of the fox hole. With the German infantryman now lying on the parapet of the fox hole, I used the force of both arms to descend the fighting blade into the German's open chest and ripped toward his belly button. Only his metal belt buckle prevented the fighting blade from reaching it's intended destination.

Now standing fully erect in the fox hole, I withdrew the fighting blade from the man's body. His warm blood ran down both arms, staining the front of my overcoat in the process. Slimy entrails hung from his clothing with a smell of fresh feces. Mortally wounded, but not yet dead, he cursed his fate and frantically grabbed at my arms. I finally shook free from his grasp, and in desperation, slit his throat. His throat gurgled as if he had some last words to say, and then his body went limp. With a final shudder and gurgle, the enemy lay still, and groaned no more. Bloody, emotionally drained, and physically exhausted, I slumped to the bottom of the fox hole. Gradually my mind began to clear and the reality of my predicament set in. Suddenly I realized enemy troops were moving all around me. If I were to survive, I knew I had to escape discovery in some manner, but how? Gently I pulled the dead German into the fox hole and decided to stay hidden beneath the bloody carcass until I heard no more movement in the forest.

Time passed slowly with nothing to do but wait and think. Supporting the weight of the dead German soldier was physical torture and the smell of his ruptured intestines made me ill. Finally I could endure this experience no more! With no thought of personal danger, I heaved the bloody carcass out of my hole, stood up in the darkness, took a deep breath, and expected to die. I just didn't give a damn anymore! Fortunately, except for me, the forest was empty. With no communications with Battalion, I knew I was of no use to them here in the forest. I also knew I had no chance of survival if I remained with the slain German, so I thought, "If I stay I die. If I leave the forest I will die. What the Hell, what difference doe is make what I do?" With this thought in mind, I decided to leave the forest.

Battle for Parker's Crossroads – Day 4
Baraque de Fraiture, Belgium – A Walk in the Woods
22 December 1944 – 0400 Hours

Cautiously, and silently as possible, I slowly inched the short distance from the fox hole to the Vielsalm road. The only thing I knew for certain was, the Americans were to my left, but I had absolutely no idea where the enemy was located. Assuming the Germans were on my right, I turned left and started walking slowly toward Baraque de Fraiture and the 589th FA Bn Command Post. While training in England, combat veterans had told us that combat experience sharpens the senses. They claimed experience gained in combat enhances the basic instincts animals use for survival. I now believed this to be true. Instinct and training had kept me alive so far. Maybe these instincts, plus army training, would help me return safely through the American lines.

Progress in the ice and snow was slow at first. I caught myself moving from shadow to shadow, then remaining motionless in the shadows to look, listen, and feel. As I came closer to the cross roads, my concern over the Germans, whom I concluded were behind me, became less and less. My main concern now centered more upon the American troops in front of me. I knew they were on edge, easily spooked, and had heavy trigger fingers. This concern was very real. The pass-word and counter-sign are changed each night at mid-night. I had not been advised of the new words before I left the Command Post to man the observation post. Where did this leave me if I was challenged by an American sentry? I had no answer to my own question, but I wanted to get this ordeal over with as quickly as possible. Throwing caution to the wind, I picked up the pace and started walking down the icy road in the best military manner I could muster. Then what I feared happened!

A suspicious sounding voice in the distance rang out, "HALT – Who Goes There?"

Without thinking, or slowing my stride, I yelled back, "My name is Tommy Tit, and I don't give a shit!"

This response must have taken the unseen sentry by surprise because I heard a smothered chuckle, followed by, "Sergeant Pierson, what in the hell are you doing out here on the Vielsalm road with all this shooting going on?"

"Don't give me a hard time, I've had a bad night and I'm headed to the Command Post."

"Sarge. do you need anything from us?"

Wearily I replied, "Yes. Tell the other sentries I'll be passing through in a few minutes and I don't know the damned pass-word." As an after thought I added, "Also tell them to keep their fucking trigger fingers away from their triggers."

"Sarge, you got it! No problem. You take care now."

Battle for Parker's Crossroads – Day 4
Baraque de Fraiture, Belgium – Command Post – 589th FA Bn
22 December 1944 – 0430 Hours

Standing in the doorway of the CP I thought, "I'll be damned, I made it!" While I watched the frenzied action in the fire direction center, I realized I was a wretched looking sight, my sunken eyes staring from a blood covered face, and my woolen OD colored overcoat caked with dried mud and blood. Too tired to speak, I just stood and stared. I stayed there, motionless, for several minutes before someone finally noticed me. Major Parker exclaimed, "My God, Sergeant Pierson, we thought you had bought the farm. When the phone line went dead, we thought we had killed you." This apologetic remark mirrored the thoughts of everyone in the room. The Major broke the embarrassing silence when he asked, "Are you wounded? Should I call a medic?"

My monotone reply was, "I think I'm OK, but I could use a drink. Does anybody have a cigarette? I've had a rough time. I'm just cold and worn out."

Miller and Tacker both rushed to the door and took me into the fire direction center. As Tacker helped me remove my filthy webbing and overcoat, Miller lit a cigarette and stuck it in my mouth. As I took a couple of deep drags on the cigarette, Miller dug into the fire direction chest and removed a full bottle of French Cognac. Major Parker averted his eyes as Miller opened the bottle and motioned for me to take a drink.

In the meantime Tacker had dampened a cloth and was wiping away the dried blood and caked mud from my neck, face, and hands. As the mud and blood began to disappear, Tacker exclaimed, "Where did this blood come from? This is not your blood. You're not even wounded!"

Tacker's proclamation surprised most of the people in the room but it also relieved some of their pent up tension. The Major told Tacker to put me on his cot when he realized I was not seriously hurt, and added, "For now, Sergeant Pierson needs rest, let's leave him alone for a while, but the rest of us have plenty of work to do."

On the Major's cot, I finished my second cigarette and my third long drag from Miller's bottle of Cognac. Finally the warmth of the CP, combined with the effects of the undiluted Cognac started to relax me. For now, I was safe and with friends, I was warm and comfortable, and I was dog-tired and sleepy. Moments after I laid my head on the cot, I was fast asleep.

Battle for Parker's Crossroads – Day 4
589th FA Bn – Cross Roads Perimeter Defense Lines
Baraque de Fraiture, Belgium – 22 December 1944 – 0530 Hours

As expected, another determined enemy attack was mounted against the cross roads defense by ever increasing numbers of German infantry, now supported by heavy mortar fire. For some reason, the mortar fire was still directed at the artillery men in the perimeter defense lines who were deployed in fox holes located in the open fields surrounding the cross roads.

The ensuing fire fight was intense. Captain Huxel utilized the mobility and awesome fire power of his four anti-aircraft half tracks in conjunction with the fire power of the 57mm high velocity tank gun on the light Recon tank and his dug-in, stationary, automatic weapons. This attack lasted more than one hour before the badly mauled German infantry withdrew into the bowels of the protective Ardennes Forest. By 0730 Captain Huxel had men searching the edge of the forest looking for killed or wounded Germans, and those of the enemy wishing to surrender. By 0830 the Captain reported his after battle find to the Command Post: "22 enemy dead, 4 enemy wounded, 6 un-wounded enemy captured, and 4 slightly wounded American GIs." Major Parker thanked him for his report and advised Captain Huxel to prepare the defenses for an even more determined attack which would be launched shortly by the German troop commander.

The 106th Division Artillery headquarters called at 1155 hours to inform Major Parker that he should try to withdraw the remnants of the 589th FA Bn to Manhay, Belgium to get re-supplied by the 3rd Armored Division, who still occupied that town. The Major agreed that we desperately needed food, fuel, and ammunition, but he could not, in good faith, withdraw the 589th support from the troops of other units defending the cross roads who would be forced to remain. The Major stated that even though the town of Manhay might be secure, he doubted the road from Baraque de Fraiture to Manhay was still under American control. In the end, the decision to withdraw, or to stay, was left to the Major. Major Parker decided to stay.

By mid-day, most of the preparations to reinforce and prepare the perimeter defense had been completed. Feet were washed and dried, socks and underwear changed, hot "C" Rations consumed, ammunition redistributed, fortifications improved, and fire power planned for the anticipated afternoon attack. Earlier, the Major had arranged for temporary reinforcements from the 3rd Armored Division. The 3rd Armored, now hard pressed itself, dispatched a platoon to Baraque de Fraiture consisting of three medium tanks and one command type half-track. Upon arrival at 1425. the platoon leader reported he had received small arms fire on the road between Manhay and Baraque de Fraiture. He also reported advance elements of the *560th Volksgrenadier Division* were probing the southern flank of the Manhay defenses and he did not know how long he would be able to remain.

The third attack on the cross roads started at 1530 hours, with a vicious artillery and mortar barrage preceding the infantry attack. This advance barrage targeted all buildings, howitzer positions, and tracked vehicles, in addition to softening-up the men in the perimeter fox holes. The barrage lasted almost a life time, about twenty minutes. It was quickly followed by withering small arms fire, laid down by automatic weapons and designed to keep the American heads down during the relentless German infantry attack.

During the initial barrage, our positions received many direct hits, and near misses, resulting in our first serious casualties, one of which was Major Parker. He received a large, ugly body wound, in the left stomach and chest area. He was immediately treated by a medic who reported both bright and dark red blood coming from the chest cavity, indicating both ruptured veins and arteries. The prognosis for the Major was not good. The medic applied Sulfa Drugs directly into the chest cavity to fight infection, administered morphine shots to lessen the pain, and firmly packed sterile gauze into the open wound. He then applied a tight compress bandage to the entire wounded chest area to hopefully slow the flow of blood. Three of us then lifted the Major, carried him into the Command Post, and placed him on his cot in a sitting position.

This battle was vicious, both sides were determined to prevail, and it lasted until the Germans suddenly decided to withdraw into the shelter of the deep forest at 1800 hours. During this two and one half hours the battle raged, both sides suffered severe casualties to men and material. The cross roads defenders sustained numerous men killed and wounded, the light Recon tank destroyed, one of our 105mm howitzers damaged, two anti-aircraft half-tracks destroyed, and all of the Tank Destroyer guns captured. The American fire destroyed six German panzers and four armored assault guns. While withdrawing, the Germans left without removing their dead or wounded, which littered the open ground east of the perimeter defense line, on both the Houffalize and Vielsalm roads.

To accomplish this carnage, the American defenders expended more than 200 rounds of artillery shells, an estimated 3000 rounds of 50-caliber ammunition, more than 25 Bazooka shells, and untold 30-caliber ammunition. The outcome of this battle was in doubt many times as the fortunes of war ebbed and flowed. By 1800 hours, the American salient had barely won this fight, using superior leadership, grit, determination, and with excellent planning.

At 1845 the 3rd Armored Division contacted it's platoon leader by radio and ordered him to return to Manhay. The Armored Lieutenant offered to evacuate some of the more seriously wounded men in his half-track. Over Major Parker's strong objections, Major Goldstein insisted the Major accompany the Lieutenant back to Manhay. Upon consultation with the senior medic present, Major Goldstein decided to place Major Parker, three other seriously wounded GIs, and a medic in the half-track. Major Goldstein filled a 2 1/2 ton GMC truck with lesser wounded men and the German prisoners. He and his truck then joined the convoy of armored vehicles. The five vehicle convoy, headed by a lead tank, left for Manhay at 1915 hours maintaining strict black-out discipline, leaving Captain Huxel in command of the cross roads defenders.

Under the cover of darkness, Captain Huxel led an armed reconnaissance patrol into the forest east of the cross roads. Three hundred yards into the forest the patrol encountered German infantry digging in. The patrol broke off contact immediately and returned to American held territory. No shots were fired. The Captain returned to the Command Post to record and report what he had learned. Captain Huxel then began preparations to withstand another enemy attack at dawn.

Battle for Parker's Crossroads—Day 4
Baraque de Fraiture, Belgium—589th FA Bn—Command Post Guard Duty
22 December 1944—2000 Hours

My sentry partner for the night was John Schaffner from "A" Battery. John was normally an irreverent soul, always laughing and cracking jokes, but tonight, John was serious and all business. Our two man hole did not satisfy him. After the day's action, John wanted the hole larger and deeper. As he bluntly put it, he didn't want to be fighting with me for the bottom of the hole when things heated up. He was convinced we would be attacked and overrun this night. Word must have gotten around that I had killed a Kraut with a knife, because while we were in our hole eating dry cereal, John pulled out his sheath knife and stuck it in a fence railing we were using as a parapet in front of the hole. I felt more comfortable with mine sheathed in my boot, but prayed to the Almighty I would never have to use my fighting knife again. Finally the hole seemed to satisfy Schaffner because he sat in the bottom of the hole, wrapped himself in a blanket, and advised me it was my shift and he was going to sleep. This was news to me because we had not discussed who would stay awake for which shifts. Even though I had one more stripe than Schaffner and could have assigned him the first shift, I decided what-the-hell, I had taken a nap in the CP and besides, I wasn't sleepy anyway.

About 2000 hours we received several incoming mortar rounds, big stuff. These rounds were directed at a half-track a few hundred yards across a field from us. I was glad the Krauts were not shooting in our direction because the explosions were very powerful. However, the only effect these explosions had on Schaffner was to make him pull the blanket over his head more firmly, as though the blanket would protect him from flying shell fragments. As I watched, several more rounds exploded in the snow around the half-track and then the vehicle sustained a direct hit. The results of this hit were horrible to witness. The first thing we heard after the explosion was the wounded men in the half-track screaming for help. Next we heard the half-track ammunition starting to explode. By this time Schaffner was awake and standing beside me in the fox hole, but neither of us knew what to do. We were on guard duty and had a responsibility to the men working inside the Command Post, yet we felt one of us should leave our post and give aid to the wounded men regardless of the personal danger involved.

My quandary was short lived—the front door to the CP building burst open and Staff Sergeant Frank Tacker ran past us in the dark, shouting for someone to help him assist the wounded Ack—Ack men. My doubts now gone, I told Schaffner to stay put and I followed Tacker into the night running toward the burning half-track and it's exploding ammunition. Tacker reached the burning vehicle moments before I arrived. With one powerful vault, he cleared the side of the armored vehicle and landed feet first in the fighting compartment. In one fluid move he lifted one wounded GI over the side of the half-track and dropped him into my outstretched arms. I barely had time to lower the body to the ground when the second body came over the side of the half-track, quickly followed by Frank Tacker himself. At this point my heart was beating rapidly and my breathing was labored. We were horribly exposed to enemy fire standing in the white snow and highlighted by the brilliant light produced by the burning vehicle. Of course I could not speak for Frank, outwardly he was calm, but I was so nervous I was actually trembling. In plain view of the enemy, we stooped to check the conditions of the two wounded men. It did not take a medical doctor to determine that one man was dead, and the other badly wounded.

Tacker needed help to get the wounded man up and onto his shoulder. Once the man was in a typical fireman's carry position, Tacker started the long, slippery, and dangerous trek back to the Command Post and a waiting medic. I tried to drag the body of the dead GI away from the fury of the burning vehicle and the still exploding 50-caliber ammunition, but the badly burned flesh of the man's wrist and forearm came off onto my woolen gloves. I stopped trying to drag the body, moved away from the burning vehicle, leaned over in the darkness, and retched on the snow. The terrible sight and horrible smell caused by the burned human flesh was too much for my stomach.

How my friend Frank Tacker managed to carry the dead weight of the wounded man the distance to the Command Post through the ice and deep snow, in total darkness, is a mystery me. I do know Frank was a young man with considerable physical strength, a deep sense of responsibility, immense personal courage, and a man of high moral character.

I sincerely wish this experience had a more happy ending for the two Anti-aircraft men, but it did not. The second American GI died on the shoulder of Frank Tacker while being carried to the Command Post.

By the time I returned to the Command Post, Frank had already gone inside the building and I crawled back into the fox hole with Schaffner. John was excited and wanted to talk. "Randy what in the hell did you two guys do out there?" Why did you risk your ass for two guys you don't even know?"

"John, we just tried to help a couple of guys who were in big trouble. They would have done the same for us."

"Yea, but you could have gotten hurt out there."

"I didn't even think about it John. I just ran out there after Tacker when he yelled for help. It was just one of those knee-jerk reactions."

"You have to be nuts to do something like that. You could have gotten yourself killed."

"OK Schaffner, knock it off! I don't feel philosophical right now. I was so scared, I think I pissed in my pants. My pants are wet and cold, my nerves are shot, and my hands are shaking so hard I can't work my Zippo lighter."

"Yea Randy, I noticed. You want me to give you a light?"

With an affirmative nod, I sat down in the fox hole. With shaking hands I cupped the cigarette to kill the light as Schaffner applied the flame of the lighter to the end of my cigarette. When the cigarette was lit, John clicked the Zippo shut and commented, "Maybe tomorrow will be better Randy, Major Goldstein should be back with reinforcements."

After a few long drags on the Lucky Strike, I started to relax and finally told Schaffner to stay awake because it was now my turn to sleep.

AUTHOR'S NOTE:
As a result of these two incidents,
Major Goldstein later recommended me for a direct promotion
from Sergeant to 2nd Lieutenant.
In addition he recommended that I be awarded
a Silver Star for Valor.

Battle for Parker's Crossroads — Day 5
Baraque de Fraiture, Belgium — 589th FA Bn — Sergeant Alford's Bunker
23 December 1944 — 0330 Hours

Sitting in the dim light of the shell fragment damaged bunker, Sergeant Barney Alford exclaimed to Corporal Fairchild, "I don't like this shit Charlie. You know we are surrounded and don't have a chance, sitting here like two damned clipped-wing ducks. Look at the beating we took yesterday, Jerry is going to bury us! Then he will roll over the top of us, and there is not a damned thing we can do about it."

"I sure hope you are wrong, Barney. We've been sitting here for four days now. Maybe the higher-ups will get off of their gold braided butts and send us some help."

"Fat chance buddy! Nobody is thinking about saving us, they're too busy covering their own asses.. Forget it Charley, we won't get any help, we have been declared expendable, we're just part of the fortunes of war. No one gives a shit what happens to us but our mothers! Christ, we have shot up most of our ammunition and we are short on rations. What are we supposed to do, throw empty shell casings at the frigging German tanks when they come back later today?"

"Barney, let me ask you a question, now that Major Goldstein has gone to Manhay to try to get us some help, is Captain Huxel in charge?"

"Who else? He is the senior of the two Captains left!"

"If something happens to our last two officers, what happens then?"

"I guess we draw straws."

"Captain Huxel is a strange man. I don't know him very well, but he must be very brave. It seems like he exposed himself to enemy fire and awful lot. If he keeps doing that, we may be down to one officer pretty damned quick."

"Charlie, I don't know whether he is brave or stupid, but I do know this about Captain Huxel, he believes that Jerry has not made the bullet with his name on it yet."

"Do you believe that stuff about a bullet with your name on it? You know Barney, if it has your name on it, no matter where you hide it will find and kill you?"

"The way I look at it Charlie, they all have my name on them, but I'm going to keep ducking anyway."

"Do you really think we are going to die today Barney?"

"We all die when the time and place is right. Looks like this time and place may be right. Christ, I hope not! There are too many things I want to do and so many places I'd like to see. Oh Hell Charley, I don't know."

"Barney, did you ever read about the Alamo?"

"Yea, I think I did. Isn't the Alamo an old army fort somewhere in Texas?"

"That's right. A long time ago, a Mexican General, named Santa Anna or something, I don't remember his name, tried to capture the Alamo. A bunch of Americans, they were called patriots, decided they were going to stop this Mexican General. They were guys like Jim Bowie and Davey Crocket who decided to stop the Mexicans at the Alamo. All the American patriots at the

Alamo were killed in the battle, but they kept the Mexican army from capturing the Alamo. There were no American survivors!"

"Yea Charlie, I remember them, those guys made history. At the last minute Colonel Bill Travis and his Texans came rushing in and drove off the Mexicans while the Texans yelled and screamed, Remember the Alamo!"

"Barney, to me this battle at Baraque de Fraiture is something like the battle for the Alamo. I hope some historian in the future will remember this battle and call it *The Battle for Parker's Crossroads,* that would be a nice honor for Major Parker. We have an Alamo type defense going on here, the main difference is we are stopping Germans, in tanks, not Mexicans on foot."

"Lets not get too carried away Charlie. Dying is easy, staying alive gets hard sometimes. I've talked to guys who have been in combat before and they have a theory about being a good soldier and surviving. They say you can't change from a civilian to a soldier, I mean a good soldier, unless you accept the fact that if you stay in combat long enough you will be killed. Once you accept the inevitable, that you are going to die, you lose the fear of death and get on with the job of being a soldier. In the last few days, I guess I've made the evolution from civilian to soldier. I know I will die if I stay in combat long enough, so I quit worrying about dying and concentrate on getting my job done and surviving in the process. Why don't we stop talking about dying and start acting like good soldiers? We are in a combat unit and we are in combat. What more can I say. I promise you one thing though, when I go to the big PX (Post Exchange) in the sky, it will be one expensive trip for the Krauts. I'm going to take a bunch of those bastards with me, I'm not going to get captured and end up a POW (Prisoner of War)."

"Jesus Barney, cut the crap. I don't like to hear you talking like that. I don't want to hear any more."

"OK Charlie, I guess enough preaching is enough. Has that snow you are cooking melted yet? I need a cup of coffee – Bad!"

"I'm with you buddy, coffee will make us both feel better. I need a caffeine jolt to get started. It will be a busy day. If we are going to have some heavy action this morning, I need to check the howitzers." With an after thought Corporal Fairchild added, "It shouldn't take long, we have only two howitzers left."

Silence claimed the bunker. No conversation, just two grimy GI's deep in thought as they cradled their hot canteen cups of black coffee in their gloved hands, and tried to envision what was in store for them come the breaking dawn. Corporal Fairchild finally broke the silence, "I've got to check the weapons." As he left the shelter of the bunker and entered the frigid air of the pre-dawn darkness, he checked his GI wrist watch. It was 0410 hours.

Battle for Parker's Crossroads – Day 5
Baraque de Fraiture, Belgium – 589th FA Bn – Command Post
23 December 1944 – 0330 Hours

The fighting yesterday had taken its toll in men and equipment. Enemy fire had shot away all telephone lines and radio antennas. Enemy fire had severely damaged gun emplacements and protective personnel bunkers in addition to damaging the Command Post building. Throughout the night, Cannoneers, truck drivers, and fire direction personnel were pressed into service to restore the local communications network. The task was made difficult because of darkness, the treacherous frozen snow, and because of the sporadic interdiction fire being thrown at us by German mortars and artillery. By 0500 hours, local communications were considered adequate and most personnel had returned to their defensive locations and responsibilities. However, one fact remained, we could not communicate with anyone beyond our perimeter defense, and no one outside our perimeter defense could communicate with us. We were totally isolated. There was nothing we could do but await the fury of the eminent enemy attack at dawn.

The first shots of the pre-dawn enemy artillery preparation began at 0530 hours and were fired from 'German 88s.' The German 88mm all purpose field piece was one of the most versatile, mobile, and accurate artillery weapons used by any nation engaged in combat during WWII. It was not a howitzer, which is a moderately low velocity weapon with a short barrel. The 'German 88' was a long barreled gun which fired high velocity projectiles a great distance. The velocity of the '88' projectiles in flight gave the incoming round a distinctive sound. No soldier who was in the vicinity of an incoming '88' round can forget this unique sound.

In the CP we heard this sound, mixed with the crack of the exploding shell. The force of this explosion shook the sturdy stone Belgian farmhouse we were using as a Command Post. The first assault of the day on the cross roads had begun. The cross roads defenders hugged the ice covered bottoms of their protective holes, ready to pop out and challenge the infantry attack which always follows such an artillery preparation.

Captain Huxel had formed the cross roads defense perimeter in the shape of a new moon. The heavy portion of the defense faced east. At each end the defense line curved toward the west and covered our north and south flanks. This shape was designed to protect the main line of defense from an attack by enemy infantry who might infiltrate through the forest and attempt a flanking attack from the north or south. For four days this defensive formation had served us well. It effectively controlled the two main east/west roads the German armor must use to accommodate their heavy vehicles. The very light small arms fire from the northern and southern flanks had caused us no particular problems in the past. I sincerely hoped our good luck would hold today.

The pre-dawn artillery preparation was much lighter than expected. The initial pressure exerted by the combined armor and infantry attack came mainly from the two main roads and lacked the force we expected. As the fire fight progressed past daylight, a shift in enemy pressure was detected. More small arms and automatic weapon fire was originating from the forest directly north and south of the cross roads. It became evident Jerry planned to keep pressure on the defenders with armor and infantry from the east, while unsupported infantry was engaged in an encircling action on foot through the dense forest. This fire fight lasted until 0945 hours, more than four hours, with both sides suffering severe casualties.

By mid morning Captain Huxel faced the problem of trying to establish a complete circumference defense with ever dwindling numbers of people and weapons to accomplish the job. However, he had no alternative, other than surrender, and determined he must 'circle the wagon.' He knew the enemy would soon be attacking from all points on the compass. The current 'half moon' defense could no longer do the job. To 'circle the wagon,' Captain Huxel had to re-form his 'half moon' defense lines while establishing a tight defensive circle around the cross roads. With men and material bunched into this much smaller enclave, the targets for German mortar, artillery, and direct fire from tanks became more concentrated. This was not good, but the only other viable option was to try and disengage from the enemy and withdraw westward toward Manhay through ever increasing enemy held territory. The Captain's decision was the same as Major Parker's previous decisions, we would stand, and delay the enemy.

Reorganization of the defenses became frantic. New protective holes were dug, automatic weapons relocated, ammunition redistributed, and the smaller communications network revamped. All this was accomplished between 1000 and 1350 hours. This was a gigantic task to be accomplished by less than sixty cold, hungry, glassy-eyed and bone-weary men. No one could remember how it was done, but the fact is, it was done. By 1400 hours the defensive circle around Baraque de Fraiture was complete. We knew the German observers had watched the entire process and knew where every man and weapon was now located.

The second enemy preparation of the day started at 1430 hours and was concentrated in the now much smaller defensive area. This was the most concentrated and devastating artillery fire we had yet faced. It was totally terrifying and gut wrenching. Men broke and ran, even though there was no place to run, only to be cut down by shell fragments and small arms fire. Those who remained in their protective holes were shaken, deafened, and disoriented. Strange things happen to men's minds under this barbaric type of stress. Some men cringe and cry for their mothers through swollen faces and tear stained cheeks. Others squat, staring with non-seeing eyes, while rocking back and forth, and moaning through half opened mouths. Some become angry and extremely hostile, torn between the strong opposing instincts of fight or flight, and lash out at friends or foe, with little or no provocation.

While observing the action around our defensive perimeter, I stood precariously by a second story window of the CP building, my body partially shielded by the huge boulders which composed the outer wall of the building. Suddenly I heard the unmistakable sound of an incoming German 88mm artillery round. With no other place to go, I instinctively dropped onto the floor behind a large boulder. The '88' round, probably armor piercing, entered the first floor of the CP an exploded with an ear shattering burst that caused enormous amounts of chocking dust and acrid smoke inside the building. This violent explosion also caused the collapse of the portion of the second floor where I lay. The sudden collapse of this floor pitched me into the air and I landed violently in a heap on the first floor, the body of my friend Jim Lemley cushioning my fall. Miraculously Lemley was not seriously hurt by the explosion, the falling ceiling timbers, nor by me, but for some reason he became furious with me. He jumped up, shook himself off, and attacked me as though I had fallen on top of him on purpose. Quickly, I grappled with him, wrestled him to the floor, and tried to calm him down before either of us became a victim of our own confrontation..

Lying there on the debris covered floor, with mortal combat surrounding us, still grappling with each other, I felt Lemley's body go limp. Not knowing exactly what to do, I relaxed my death grip on his arms and turned his face toward mine. This large, strong, heroic young man had momentarily cracked. His body was shaking and tears were flowing from each eye, creating an uneven clean line down each dust covered cheek.

Cradling him in my arms, I kept reassuring him softly, almost tenderly, "It's alright buddy, it's alright." Between deep, body wracking sobs, this great hulk of a man moaned, "Sarge I didn't mean to hurt you. I'm sorry, I'm sorry, I'm sorry..."

By 1530 German infantry probes were occurring from all positions of the compass. The enemy probe from the east was by far the strongest. The newly arrived advance elements of the elite German 2nd SS Panzer Division started playing a prominent role in the attack, bravely exposing their panzers to our fire and then subjecting our defenders to exceptionally destructive fire from their high velocity tank weapons. Judging from the fire of the enemy gunners had decided to eliminate their main threat, our two remaining 105mm howitzers.

At about 1600 hours, Captain Huxel entered the Command Post cellar and made an announcement. Even though the situation was desperate, his voice was calm and he spoke deliberately. "The situation is hopeless. We can no longer resist these overwhelming odds. We have more than accomplishes our mission.

We have only two choices and must make a decision now. We can remain in place and be killed or captured, or we can try to escape. I will not make this decision for you. There is no correct choice, each man must make his own decision. Any questions?"

"Yes Sir, what are you going to do Captain?"

"I will try to escape. I plan to move northwest through the forest toward Manhay and try to reach the defensive line established by the 82nd Airborne Division in that area. Before I leave, let me offer to take anyone with me who wishes to escape. The German heavy preparation is complete. There is minimal small arms fire coming from the enemy positions. I'm certain the German commander feels he has an easy 'mop-up' operation ahead of him. I strongly suggest to each man who wishes to leave – do it promptly, and go in small groups. Regardless of your decision, I am honored to have served with you. Good Luck!"

His message complete, Captain Huxel gathered his gear and departed the cellar. No one followed him!

Much muttering and soul searching followed the Captain's farewell speech and lonely exit. Frank Tacker, Dell Miller and I quickly exchanged thoughts. I favored the Captain's approach. I wanted to escape from this Hell-Hole. I had made up my mind, I would rather be killed trying to escape than become a German POW. The thought of dying as a prisoner in a German POW camp did not appeal to me.

Dell's opinion was not as firm as mine. He could see advantages and disadvantages in each of the scenarios, but need time to think and to make up his mind.

Tacker was at the opposite end of the spectrum from me. As the senior non-commissioned officer present, he felt it was his obligation to stay with his troops as long as anyone else stayed. He viewed it as the responsibility of command. When Dell reminded Tacker that Captain Huxel had made the decision to allow each individual to decide his own destiny, Tacker argued he did not share the Captain's feelings and could not follow his example.

To me, precious time was being wasted in useless academic debate about command responsibility. Dell noticed I was getting fidgety as I gathered my personal belongings and asked if I had changed my mind.

With a negative nod of the head, and not looking at Tacker, I started up the cellar stairs. Above the murmur in the cellar I could hear Miller say, "Randy, wait for me, I'm coming with you."

We paused at the entrance of the building and closely observed the terrain. There was nothing that could prepare us for the ordeal we were about to experience. To survive, we needed mental discipline, physical strength, common sense, and above all, an enormous amount of good luck. A highly religious person might call survival under these circumstances, God's Will, God's Providence, or even Predestination.. All I knew was, we needed all the help we could get while crossing the five hundred yards across 'Dante's White Frozen Hell' and into the deep forest without getting killed..

First, we must cross the ice and snow covered road in front of the Command Post. This road was plainly visible to the surrounding enemy troops. Then cross a drainage ditch about two feet deep and six feet wide, which in fair weather would require one good leap. However in this weather crossing the ditch became a formidable obstacle. The next challenge about three feet beyond the ice covered ditch was a four foot high wire fence. Climbing this obstacle while encumbered by bulky winter clothing and equipment dangling loosely from our web belts would have been difficult under normal conditions, but these conditions were not normal, people would be shooting at us. The next portion of this obstacle course consisted of sprinting across frozen plowed ground about the length of two football fields. This ground was covered with slippery ice-covered foot high rows which ran perpendicular to our line of flight. Each row was barely distinguishable to the eye because the heavy snow cover made the ground appear flat. At the end of this field a second four foot wire fence reared it's ugly head and waited to be climbed.

Beyond the second wire fence was another plowed snow covered field. Some three hundred yards beyond this field a huge drainage ditch separated the open field from the dense Ardennes Forest. I thought if I could get to the deep drainage ditch and into the thick forest I might escape from the man-made Hell at the cross roads.

With the big picture in mind, I slowly moved across the icy road in a crouched position. Once I was safely across the road, across the ditch and over the first fence, Dell followed, maintaining an interval between us. Apparently we attracted no enemy attention until Dell started climbing the first fence. About half way across the first field, I heard small arms fire and looked back. I saw Dell struggling with his overcoat which was caught on a fence post, and observed tell-tale bits of ice flying near him as the enemy bullets hit the hard ice and ricocheted.

As much as I wanted to help my friend, there was nothing I could do. In a crouch, I turned and started to run with all my might toward the second fence, more than one hundred yards away. Even though the field was slippery and uneven, I was able to time my stride perfectly and cleared the second fence cleanly with a head first dive. I landed heavily on the frozen ground beyond the fence, face down, with the wind partially knocked out of me.

Luckily for me, I lay still, partially hidden by the snow, long enough to see small arms fire kicking up ice chips in front of me, where I would have been, had I not fallen on my face in the snow. The German gunners had anticipated the path of my flight, much like a hunter would 'lead' a bird in flight. It was clearly apparent the next three hundred yards would become a game of wits between the hunters and the hunted. Artillery fire did not concern me. No army operating short of supplies, as the German army was, would waste an artillery round on just one man. Rifle and machine gun fire were my prime concerns.

As I lay there, hidden and resting, the sounds of small arms fire increased. Although I could not see the action while lying down, I suspected Miller, and others, leaving the Command Post building were drawing fire. Consuming fear increased my impulse to get up and run. Fortunately for me, common sense told me to lay low, crawl, and seek cover between the rows in the plowed field where possible. The next portion of this perilous journey was very slow because the shelter provided by the rows in the field did not run directly toward the protection offered by the deep drainage ditch.

Ultimately, my slow progress was interrupted by the sound of an incoming mortar round. My instinct to freeze overcame my impulse to run. As expected, the shell hit the ground and exploded nearby. Suddenly the air around me was filled with white smoke and particles of white phosphorus. I could then smell the strong odor of burning cloth and realized this searing hot metal would soon reach my tender flesh. Quickly I sat up, disregarding cover completely, and started scooping handfuls of snow and forcing it into the burned holes in my outer garments. Then I remembered from my training that this would not stop the burning, white phosphorus will burn under water. Frantically I retrieved my boot knife and started flicking particles of hot white phosphorus from my clothing. The phosphorus burned more rapidly than I could flick. Quickly my attention moved from clothing to the burning areas of my legs. Probing my legs with the fighting blade hurt as much as the burn itself, however I knew it had to be done.

The smell of burning flesh was now mingled with the smell of burning wool. I probed deeper and worked faster with the sharp knife blade. As quickly as it started, the burning stopped. Only the pain remained. I was still alive and desperate. Throwing caution to the wind, I stood up and ran, my body fully extended, my pained legs pumping, my heart pounding, and my lungs screaming for oxygen.

Cherry red tracers joined the rifle fire. I was now the target of a Jerry machine gunner. Still I stayed erect and ran. The drainage ditch came closer. Should I drop to the ground or keep running? I was drawing intense small arms fire. I continued to run. The ditch was near. My heart was about to explode! From exertion, fear, or both? With one final burst of strength, I lunged into the air and over the edge of the drainage ditch.

The result of my desperate leap turned out to be the equivalent of jumping out of a second story window and landing on a concrete walk. The ditch was deeper than I had expected and the surface at the bottom of the ditch was rock hard ice. My landing was not graceful. I hurt my left shoulder, but no bones were broken. Thank goodness my entire body was well padded with heavy winter clothing.

The fall rendered me almost unconscious and I lay dazed on the ice in the bottom of the ditch. A mental fog kept appearing and disappearing. My left shoulder ached horribly, my legs burned constantly, and my eyes would not focus. My future did not seem bright!

A scuffling noise above me brought me out of my dazed state and quickly into the world of reality. A large body came sliding down the frozen side of the drainage ditch and came to rest behind me. I had a vivid flash-back to the night when a German soldier crawled into my fox hole. I panicked and screamed. A sturdy arm encircled me from the rear and a strong gloved hand covered my mouth. A hushed voice said, "Randy, stop screaming! Everything is OK. This is Dell."

I stopped screaming and my body went limp.

Escape from Parker's Crossroads
Lost in the Ardennes Forest
between Baraque de Fraiture and Odeigne, Belgium
23 December 1944 — 2000 Hours

Dell Miller and I agreed to take different escape routes when we reached the small creek bottom where the drainage ditch normally empted it's water. Neither Miller nor I had a map or a compass to guide us and had only a general idea of where we were. To make the situation worse, we had only a vague idea about the location of the area controlled by the American 82nd Airborne division. As I found out later, the hard way, the situation was still fluid, no front lines existed. In the area where we were, only small disorganized pockets of friends and foes existed.

We decided to take Captain Huxel's advice and try to work our way through the forest and reach Manhay. As the crow flied, the town of Manhay was about three miles northwest of our present location. By road, approximately five miles. Through the forest, we had no idea. Dell planned to walk about one mile due north toward the village of Fraiture, then turn west to reach Malempre and then on to Manhay.

My route would be south of Dell's and entailed walking west through the forest toward Odeinge and then North to Manhay. Of course neither of us knew what to expect during our journey. We decided to travel at night, for security reasons, and to hide and rest during the day.

When we shook hands and parted, I hated to see my buddy leave. Suddenly

I felt vulnerable, and miserably alone.

The weather was clear and cold, the temperature hovering around 15 degrees. Great weather for hypothermia and frozen feet. At night the plainly visible stars did give me a general sense of direction. After all, when I was a kid living in Cocoa, I did study elementary navigation while in the Sea Scouts.

There was no doubt in my mind about this trip, it was going to be tough. To stay alive and reach the American lines would be difficult. The deck seemed stacked against me. The enemy, inclement weather, no food, no heat, no shelter, the snow in the forest, and the dark increased the odds against me. I reasoned, what else can I do? I was not going to quit! I was going to give the chance of survival my best shot!

For more than eight hours I moved slowly, cautiously picking my way through deep snow and hanging limbs of the Ardennes forest. Occasionally, when I came to an opening in the forest created by a man made fire break, I glanced at the twinkling stars, trying to determine my location. I thought I had kept the Baraque de Fraiture to Manhay road on my right, but I had an odd feeling the road was farther to my right than I had intended. Had I stayed close, I would have been able to detect road noise, or see flashes of faint light. There was no man made noise audible in the forest, only the eerie sounds generated by mother nature.

At several locations during the journey I had smelled the smoke of burning wood. The smell apparently came from widely scattered dwellings located in clearings in the forest. Instinct made me avoid the warmth, and possible food, probably available in these homes. I had no idea who occupied these buildings. German troops, American troops, Belgian civilians? I simply could not take a chance trying to finding out.

Getting half the distance to Manhay, maybe two and one half miles through the forest, had been my first nights goal. Even though battling the elements, fatigue, and lack of specific direction, I should have been able to struggle this distance in eight hours, however I did not know where I was.

Suddenly I stumbled into a cleared firebreak which ran to my right. Even though I felt I should not expose myself, I turned into the cleared firebreak hoping it would assist me in locating the road I was trying to follow. Without giving my decision much thought, I quickened my pace, trying to reach the Manhay road before daylight. Once I became reoriented I would seek cover in the forest. There I could rest and resume my journey at nightfall. I glanced at my GI wrist watch, the time was about 0430 hours. While in the firebreak I noticed a shadow move. I froze motionless in place. The shadow materialized, it was a German sentry. I was looking down the muzzle of a German *Schmeisser 9mm Automatic Machine Pistol*, a weapon capable of cutting me in half in less than five seconds. A guttural German voice commanded, *"HALT!"*

With no chance to shoulder my weapon, I slowly raised my hands above my head and clasped them on top of my steel helmet. Before my hands stopped moving, I was completely surrounded by members of the elite German *2nd SS Panzer Division*. Whether I liked it or not, I was now a prisoner of the German army!

14
Captured by German SS Troops

Battle of The Bulge — Day 9
Temporary Forward Headquarters — German 11th SS-Panzerkorps
Ardennes Forest near Odeigne, Belgium
24 December 1944, 0700 Hours

S*S-Sturmbannfuher*, (Major) Frederick Rupp, a Waffen-SS intelligence officer, had been interrogating me for about an hour. He spoke fluent English, Oxford English, not American English. He had been alternating his interrogation approach between: good guy — bad guy — good guy — etc. He knew I was from the American 106th Infantry Division, he recognized my shoulder insignia. He had deduced I had been one of the defenders of the cross roads at Baraque de Fraiture, although I had not told his I was. He had asked me many questions I could not answer. Questions about supply depots, quartermaster units, troop dispositions. He was seeking strategic information to which no combat non-commissioned officer would have access. We both knew that under the rules of the Geneva Convention, the only information I was required to give him was my Name, Rank, and Army Serial Number. He had obtained this information more than an hour ago.

I could not make up my mind if this SS Major was really a bad guy, a good guy, or perhaps both. I knew one thing, his bad guy persona frightened me. I felt strongly that he could have me shot and have no regrets what-so-ever, if I pushed my luck and antagonized him. With this thought firmly in my mind, I continued to respectfully answer answer questions I thought would not furnish pertinent information to the enemy. What more information did he want? What information did I have that would be important to him? I didn't know! I concluded the more freely I talked without aggravating the Major, the longer I would live. He was now interrogating in his good guy mode and I had to guard against giving aid and comfort to the enemy. He was intelligent, well trained in his craft, and knew how to phrase his questions innocently.

"Sergeant, how old are you?"

"Sir, I became twenty-one years of age six days ago. December the 19th."

"How do you like being a professional soldier?"

"Major, I am not a professional soldier. I was drafted, I did not volunteer. I would much rather be a civilian."

"How much education do you have, Sergeant?"

"Do you mean formal education?"

"Yes Sergeant."

"Sir, I have completed one year of college."

"Do you plan to complete your undergraduate work after the war?"

"Major, if I survive the war and am financially able, I would like to return to college and get a degree."

"Speaking of surviving the war Sergeant, why did you fight so hard and bravely against a superior force at Baraque de Fraiture?"

I had to think about this question seriously. Even a naive artillery sergeant should know this question was 'loaded.' To stall for time to ponder this question, I said "That is a good question, Sir."

"Well Sergeant, if it is a good question, why do you hesitate to answer?"

"Sir, it is a good question, but there is no simple answer."

"Do you hate the German people and the Third Reich so much that you were prepared to sacrifice your life for such an unimportant cross road?"

Very carefully I began to answer his question, "First of all Major, I do not hate the German people. I confess I do not know much about the Third Reich. History and politics do not interest m The reason I fought hard and risked my life had nothing to do with history or ideology. My unit was surrounded and your people were trying to kill us. It was extremely personal. I fought very hard for only one reason. I wanted to survive, I did not want to die."

With a slight smile on his face the Major responded, "That is quite a scholarly answer from a first year college student. Which institution of higher learning did you attend?"

"The University of Florida. What university did you attend, Major?"

With a stern look on his face, and the tone of authority in his voice, the German Major replied, "Sergeant, I am the interrogator here, not you! You will refrain from asking me questions in the future! Do you understand?"

"I am sorry, Sir! I do not wish to offend you. I am just curious by nature."

"I happen to be an educated man. I received my undergraduate degree from Oxford University in England. My advanced degrees were awarded by the University of Berlin. Does that satisfy your curiosity, Sergeant?"

"To some degree Sir. You speak more perfect English than I do. I thought perhaps you might have been educated in England."

"You are very observant Sergeant. Under the circumstances, quite calm."

"Looks can be very deceiving Sir, I am quite concerned about several things."

"What things concern you Sergeant? Name them in order of importance."

"First Sir, are you going to have me killed?"

"Sergeant, I am an educated and sensitive man. I do not slaughter unarmed prisoners. However, your personal welfare depends upon how well you cooperate with your captors. What is your next concern?"

Major, I have not eaten in more than two days. I am hungry. Would it be possible for me to have some food?"

"You are in no position to bargain with me! For food or anything else. I advise you not to push me too hard. Do you understand me?"

"Yes Sir, completely. Possibly you did not understand my answer. I am very hungry and thirsty. You asked for my second concern. I am trying to cooperate with you by answering your question truthfully. I am not trying to bargain information for food. I doubt I possess information that would be of use to you. I am only a three stripe sergeant in the field artillery. My knowledge of important things is extremely limited."

"That is enough Sergeant. What is your next concern?"

Pulling up my left pant leg, I showed Major Rupp a portion of the ugly red and festering incendiary wounds I had received.

He looked surprised and asked, "Did you receive these wounds at the cross roads at Baraque de Fraiture? Have they been attended to?"

"Yes Sir, at the cross roads, and no Sir, they have not been attended to."

"Sergeant, I believe you have answered my questions truthfully. I have no more time. My interrogation is complete. I will now try to relieve some of your anxieties. I will not have you shot. My sergeant will see that you receive some food, although we do not have much to share. My sergeant will also obtain medical treatment for your wounds. After that you will be evacuated to the rear and be processed as a prisoner of war." Then surprisingly he let down his guard. Major Rupp answered my question about being basically a 'good guy' or a 'bad guy,' when he added, "Sergeant, good luck, I hope we both survive this war. If you are so fortunate, I advise you to resume your academic pursuits."

Immediately he was transformed into the role of captor again when he barked, at this sergeant, *"Oberscharfuhrer* Gruber, do you understand your orders? If so, remove the prisoner!" Sergeant Gruber saluted, motioned for me to precede him, and we left the warmth of Major Rupp's tent.

The German Sergeant Gruber carried out Major Rupp's orders very efficiently. After my wounds were cleansed, medicated and bandaged, and I had consumed a fairly large chunk of hard crusted dark bread and washed it down with a hot bowl of turnip soup I felt much better. Even though Gruber had treated me as Major Rupp had ordered he bothered me. He was a tough looking soldier, an SS Sergeant, the type of enemy who had a reputation for extreme cruelty. Even though Major Rupp seemed to be a decent man, I did not trust Sergeant Gruber! After my meal, Gruber motioned me into a holding area where other American prisoners were gathered. He motioned for me to squat in the snow, which I did immediately, my head bowed and looking at the snowy ground. I heard the crunch of crisp snow as Gruber walked toward me. I looked up and my heart literally stopped. The SS Sergeant was approaching with a professional fighting knife in his right hand and was looking directly at me with a determined look on his face. I bowed my head again, and awaited my fate.

You can appreciate how I felt when Sergeant Gruber placed his left hand on my right shoulder to steady me as I waited for my death blow. Also you can appreciate how relieved I was when the SS Sergeant started gently cutting the stitches which held the 106th Infantry Division insignia on the left shoulder of my outer garment, rather than cutting my throat. Thank goodness, Sergeant Gruber merely wanted a war trophy!

Walking Toward a German POW Collection Area
While Planning My Escape
24 December 1944 – 1500 Hours

There were thirteen American prisoners walking East with me, in single file, on an almost deserted road which led away from the sounds of battle. We were guarded by three wounded German soldiers armed with *Gewehr Model 24, 7.92mm, Czech made, Mauser bolt action rifles.* The guards had mounted their K98k bayonets, but carried their weapons on their right shoulder in the sling position. One guard was at point position and led the ragged column. The second guard walked in the road opposite the middle of the column, while the third guard brought up the rear.

All the German guards were 'walking wounded.' The had two immediate objectives: First, get us back to the rear echelon Prisoner of War Processing Center. The Second: Get themselves to the nearest field hospital for treatment of their wounds. However, the objectives varied between the Guards depending upon the severity of his own specific wounds. For no apparent reason, the rear guard seemed to be the most seriously wounded of the three. Judging from the manner in which the guards carried their weapons and the lethargic appearance of the American prisoners, the guards apparently did not anticipate any serious problems from the Americans. They seemed to be concerned only with their ability; to walk the distance to the collection area, to survive their own wounds, and to endure the terrible winter weather.

While walking toward the German POW collection area, my mind became very active. I still would rather die honorably, rather than slowly 'rot to death' in a POW Stalag. While staging in England, one combat instructor made several points about how to act if you were unlucky enough to be captured by German troops, especially SS troops. He advised: Do not be insolent, do not show fear, and, do not look your captors in the eye. I had used this advice successfully while being interrogated. This same instructor had explained what to expect of the German Army when they moved you from the battle field to the rear echelon as a prisoner. He said the Germans are very methodical and follow standing instructions religiously. My current situation was a classic case, straight out of their military procedures manual. For a prisoner to escape while enroute from the battle field, this instructor explained the principle of straggling. Separate the guards from one another, with as much distance as possible. Walk slowly to buy valuable time, and break and run for cover when an opportunity presents itself.

When we formed our march column, I tried to be the last American in line, but another GI fell in behind me. He, being the last, and me the next-to-last American in the column. Every now and then, I glanced at him. He wore jump boots and a unique type of outer jacket, which marked him as a paratrooper. As the column moved down the icy road, the prisoner in front of me started to struggle as we trudged along. The interval between him and the man in front of him was beginning to widen. It occurred to me he may be slowing his pace on purpose. Regardless of the reason, I decided to do the same. A quick look to the rear made me realize the intervals between me, the paratrooper, and our wounded guard, had increased also. The sluggish rear guard did not seem to detect the growing distance between him and the middle guard in front of us. Possibly he was so preoccupied with his own wounds he did not care. With the three rear prisoners now playing the straggling game combined with the physical problems of the rear guard, the distance between the rear and middle guards had become significant.

Within and hour, the column had become quite long. It had stretched to the length that the rear and lead guards could no longer see each other when we negotiated sharp turns in the road. The rear guard was walking slowly, head down, as if in pain. For me, the decision was not difficult. I made up my mind,

I would break from the column and run the next time we lost sight of the lead guard. If lucky, I would be able to reach dense tree cover before either the center or rear guard could react and fire their weapons. All my senses sharpened as I looked toward the head of the column. There appeared to be a sharp bend in the road ahead as it turned abruptly to the left. There was heavy snow covered foliage on both sides of the road at the turn. Thinking this would be the place, I decided to run left. If successful in not getting shot, I would then move deeper into the forest and hide until dark. I felt it was highly unlikely that any of the wounded guards would abandon their remaining prisoners and try to recapture me.

The curve in the road came closer and the lead guard disappeared from sight. The American in front of me almost stopped walking, intently watching the progress of the center guard. The split second the center guard vanished from sight around the bend in the road, the American in front of me bolted and ran swiftly into the forest on our right. This movement was all the catalyst I needed to jar me into action. For some reason before starting to run, I glanced at the rear guard. He was almost one hundred yards behind me and stooped over looking at the airborne trooper who was squatting in the center of the road, obviously in physical distress. From this distance I saw the trooper suddenly straighten his body and simultaneously strike the wounded German guard flush on the chin. The force of the blow was backed by all the leg and right arm power the rugged trooper could muster. This vicious martial arts blow dislodged the heavy German helmet and sent it and the guard's rifle crashing to the ground. The whip-lash effect on the guard's neck was similar to that caused by a severe rear end automobile collision. Immediately the guard fell to the ground badly hurt, or unconscious.

Like a tiger springing on a crippled prey, the trooper lunged at the dazed guard and lifted his rifle from the ground. With a classic infantry move the trooper smashed the unprotected head of the German guard with the steel butt-plate of the wooden rifle stock. The trooper never looked in my direction as he dropped the German rifle and fled into the forest. By the time I reached the prone German body the trooper had disappeared into the mist and snow of the Ardennes Forest. The whole incident happened so quickly I was not prepared for the final scene. The fatally wounded German soldier was lying in a puddle of blood with both arms extended and his hands faintly grasping the cold air. But worst of all, I saw the pleading look on the German's face, as if he was asking me for help. I did the only thing I knew to do. I picked up this rifle and plunged the bayonet through his heart, killing him instantly.

This whole experience disturbed me deeply! What else could I do? With a futile wave of my arms, I moved off of the road and into the cover of the forest, and did the only thing I knew to do. I ran, and ran, and ran...

† †

Battle of the Bulge – Day 11
Totally Lost in the Ardennes Forest
26 December 1944, 0500 Hours

For two nights I had wandered through the Ardennes Forest, hopelessly lost. While moving under the cover of darkness, I had lost all feel for direction and distance. In fact, once I caught myself traveling in a circle when I crossed my own foot prints in the snow. The past day had been spent hiding, burrowed into a snow bank which surrounded the base of a huge tree, trying to avoid the biting arctic air. I was out of food and afraid to eat more snow to ease my thirst and hunger pangs because my body temperature was already too low. Debilitating exhaustion had set in and I needed rest. I also needed to find another place to hide because it would soon be daylight. Fortunately, I wandered into a cleared field which contained large mounds of snow. An examination of the closest mound revealed it to be a stack of hay, covered with snow. Even though I knew a farm house must be near and I thought it best to avoid farm houses, I could go no farther.

Physically and mentally spent, it took a superhuman effort for me to claw my way into the middle of the enormous hay stack. When I formed a living cavity in the hay, I was able to make myself a soft bed and pillow of hay several inches above the frozen ground. I then covered the entrance hole I had made in the hay stack and lay resting in the total darkness. My ever present hunger pains forcefully told me I had not eaten during the two days since my German captors fed me turnip soup and black bread. Fatigue, hunger, and apprehension, coupled with the 15 degree temperature, were taking their toll.

In the darkness, the interior of the hay stack felt comparatively warm and secure. The air had the smell of musty hay. For no particular reason, I stuck a sprig of dry hay into my mouth and started to chew. The taste was not what I would call appetizing, but it wasn't too bad either. My mind started wandering as my body started to relax. I thought, "Where can I find some food? When? Where are the American lines? Am I safely hidden in the hay stack?" The last question I remember asking myself was, "How did I manage to get myself into this stinking rotten mess?" When sleep came, it came suddenly, like a drawn curtain. My body was weak and exhausted, however, my subconscious mind was still active. Instinctively I knew I was not safe, even while well hidden in the interior of this snow covered hay stack. There was always the danger that I might make a noise, a cough, a sneeze, or snore while asleep. I did not know where I was nor did I know who might lurk outside my frozen hideaway.

15

Prisoner of American 82nd Airborne Division

Battle of the Bulge—Day 11
Hidden in a Haystack
16 December 1944—0700 Hours

My short period of sleep ended abruptly. All of a sudden I was wide awake in the darkness of the hay stack. My heart beat rapidly. With every instinct focused on the world outside the hay stack, I lay silently trying to determine why my adrenaline was flowing so freely. Finally I sensed movement outside the hay stack and wondered, "Was it man or beast, or merely the wind?" "If it was man, was he friend or foe?" "Would the man move on and pass me by, or would he detect me?" "Would the man rescue or try to kill me?" The suspense was terrifying! I was unarmed, unable to fight, and I could not flee. All I could do was lie there, pray, and wait in silence. I could hardly force myself to take a breath! Suddenly the darkness of the hay stack was penetrated by a bright shaft of light which blinded me. An excited voice yelled into the breeched hay stack, "ROUSE, you KRAUT Son-of-a-Bitch! If you don't come out with your hands over your head, I'll blow your FUCKING brains out!"

With a voice squeaking under the stress, I yelled through dry, cracked lips, "Don't shoot, I'm unarmed! I'm an American! I'll come out head first on my hands and knees."

With equal emotion, the voice outside of the hay stack yelled, "You English speaking KRAUT BASTARD, if you come out head first, I'll blow your fucking brains out. You better get down on your hands and knees and back out slowly, Very Slowly, ass first. Do you understand me?"

"Of course I understand you. I told you I am an American. I'm going to start backing out right now, slowly. For Christ's sake don't get trigger happy. I don't want to get shot in the ass. As a matter of fact, I don't want to get shot any where."

The voice outside still sounded nervous as it responded, "OK, come on out slowly, ass first, and keep both hands on the ground. When I tell you to STOP, you damned well better STOP, and don't move. You got anybody else in there with you?"

"No, I don't have anyone else in here with me, I'm by myself. I'm coming out ass first, very slowly, with both hands on the ground. When you say stop, I'll stop. I don't want any trouble. I've got enough trouble already, I don't need any more."

"Don't try to soft soap me you Kraut Bastard." The voice then yelled in the opposite direction, "Sergeant, send a squad over here. I just found a fucking Kraut in this hay stack."

Off in the distance I could faintly hear an American voice responding, "OK Kennedy, I'll send over a squad. Keep him pinned down and don't kill him unless you have to. Remember we are supposed to bring in prisoners for interrogation."

"OK Sarge, but if the SOB even breaths hard, I'll blow him a new ass hole with my M-1."

"Kennedy, I said don't kill him unless you have to. We need prisoners. This is not a combat patrol, it is an intelligence patrol. We need prisoners to tell us who is in front of us and what their plans are."

All this chit-chat between an American Sergeant and his man Kennedy made me feel better. At least they were not Germans, they were friend lies on an intelligence mission, not a search-and-destroy mission. But as I started to back out of the hay stack on my hands and knees, I still did not trust this clown named Kennedy, who ever he was. I had a strong feeling he would like to kill this 'Fucking Kraus Bastard' even though I had insisted I was an American. Backing out of the hay stack was much harder than crawling in head first. My legs were numb, my stomach was cramping, either from fear or hunger, I didn't know which, and of course I could not see where I was going. That, of course, is what Kennedy wanted. Maybe he wasn't so dumb after all. As my legs started to break out of the hay stack, Kennedy yelled, "Slow down!" I yelled back, "I can't see what I am doing, damn it." Again, Kennedy instructed me to keep coming back slowly until he could see my ass.

His attitude was beginning to piss me off and I yelled back, "How in the Hell am I supposed to know when you can see my ass if I can't turn around to see where you are?"

For the first time I could sense the fact that Kennedy was now beginning to feel in control of the situation because he actually chuckled when he answered, "You'll know, you'll know!" To keep him happy, I continued to back out of the hay stack. Suddenly I felt the hard cold steel of a 30-caliber M-1 Rifle poking me in the rear end and I heard a rather jubilant Kennedy announcing, "Now you know I can see your ass Kraut Baby." He also announced to someone else, "Now his Kraut ass is mine!"

Another voice said rather firmly, "OK Kennedy we have him covered, let him out." As I emerged from the hay stack, the same voice said, "He looks American to me. He is wearing GI boots and fatigues."

"That doesn't mean a thing Sarge," Kennedy explained, "Lots of Krauts Bastards dressed in GI clothes have infiltrated our lines and are wandering around loose. I still think he is a German."

The other voice said, "I know that Kennedy. The way he is dressed doesn't make any difference, he is still our prisoner. We'll take him back to Regiment and let the S-2 (Intelligence Officer) figure out who and what he really is."

With much wiggling and straining I finally backed completely out of the hay stack. I remained on my hands and knees, facing the hay stack, afraid to turn and face my captors, or liberators, I knew not which. The bright sun light glancing off of the snow covered hay stack hurt my eyes. I had to blink constantly until my eyes adjusted to the light. Finally the Airborne Sergeant spoke, "Let him up

Kennedy, I want to see what he looks like from the front side."

Kennedy removed his rifle barrel from my rear end, and with authority, ordered me to get on my feet and turn around. Slowly, very slowly, I started to stretch and straighten my body. Again, slowly I raised my arms and interlocked my fingers on the top of my head. Only then did I turn to face the group. There were six of them, a typical infantry squad, standing separated by several feet as a well trained squad should be, all covering me with various types of weapons. They were dressed in airborne jump boots and airborne type fatigues. Only the Sergeant did not have his weapon trained on me. The Sergeant approached me and said briefly "You are a prisoner of the U. S. Army! Do you understand?"

Feeling a little more confident now that my captors would not shoot an unarmed man, I answered, "Of course I understand. I told you I am an American."

The Sergeant looked at me with no expression on his face and said to the squad in general, "We have done our job, lets move out and get this prisoner back to Regiment." He turned to Kennedy and said, "Good job Ken, put the prisoner in the middle of our column and move the squad out." With no reply, Kennedy motioned for me to fall-in behind the first three GI's and we started walking away from the hay stack in the bright sun lit snow of the Ardennes Forest..

505th Parachute Infantry Regiment—82nd AB Division
Command Post—South East of Manhay, Belgium
26 December 1944—1000 Hours

The trip, by foot, through the snow covered Ardennes Forest was slow, but relatively uneventful. We could hear small arms fire to our rear, possibly opposing combat patrols making contact with each other. We could also detect the distinctive 'crunch' of exploding mortar rounds in addition to the 'whoom' caused by larger artillery rounds exploding. During the march, I thanked my lucky stars that I had been captured by and American intelligence patrol. Had my captors been on a combat patrol with a 'search and destroy' mission, I would already be dead.

My first interrogation by an American officer was conducted by the Sergeant's platoon leader, a 2nd Lieutenant. The Lieutenant was so busy keeping track of his squads and staying in contact with headquarters he didn't take time to quiz me. He didn't have time to fool with me and told the Sergeant to take me back to Company Headquarters. At Company Headquarters, the commanding officer, a Captain, merely blinked when the Sergeant reported in and told his CO that he had a prisoner. Without even looking up from his battle map, the Captain instructed the Sergeant to deliver his prisoner to the Battalion S-2. The Battalion S-2 was another Captain. Harassed and strung out, he asked me a few questions. I could tell from his blood shot eyes and the wild look on his face he was exhausted and getting frustrated by the lack of information I was giving him. He dismissed me as a worthless piece of shit, and told the Sergeant to use his jeep and deliver the prisoner to Regiment because the Intelligence Officer there had more time to spend with the prisoner than he had.

The Sergeant moved me out of the Command Post. Outside he spotted the Battalion S-2 jeep and located the driver. The driver knew the Sergeant and offered to take us to Regiment without even checking with the Captain. An assigned guard and I got in the rear seat of the jeep while the Sergeant sat up front. The jeep ride over the logging trail through the Ardennes Forest, between Battalion and Regimental Headquarters, was rough. During the ride it occurred to me that I had done nothing but walk for more than a week. It was nice to let the jeep do the work because it was a long way from Battalion back to Regiment. At Regimental Headquarters the Sergeant took me into a farmhouse and reported to a Master Sergeant that he had a prisoner for the S-2. The M/Sgt called for a guard and relieved my captors of their responsibility and advised them to return to Battalion. At the time, the M/Sgt asked me if I understood English. I assured him I could understand English because I was an American Sergeant. The M/Sgt gave me a stern look and left the room.

Moments later a Major entered the room and introduced himself as Major Snowden, the Regimental Intelligence Officer. Fortunately for me, he was not as strung out as the Battalion S-2 had been. He asked me to be seated and motioned the guard to position himself behind me. We sat and silently looked at each other for a long time. It was difficult to evaluate my feelings. The room was warm and although I was seated in a straight back wooden chair, it was comfortable. There was no sound of war to be heard, and I was with Americans. Both my mind and body started to relax, I felt safe. Major Snowden finally broke the silence when he asked me for my name, rank and army serial number.

"Sir, my name is Randolph C. Pierson, may rank is Technician Fourth Grade (T/4), and my army serial number is 34547144."

"That is not a German name! The German army does not have a rank of T/4! Do you claim you are an American soldier?"

"Major, of course I am an American soldier, My unit is Headquarters Battery, 589th Field Artillery Battalion, 106th Infantry Division. I was born in Cocoa, Florida, December 19, 1923. I am just barely 21 years old and I am a draftee."

"I'm familiar with the 106th Division, if you are a member of that division, why are you not wearing a 'Golden Lion' insignia on your left shoulder?"

"Sir, it is a long story, but when I was captured, a German SS Sergeant cut the insignia off of my overcoat and took my 45-caliber pistol as war trophies."

"What do you mean you were captured? Where, and by whom?"

"Sir, I was lost in the woods and wandered into an outpost of the German *11th Panzerkorps*. The guards got the drop on me before I could use my weapon, or get away."

"What did they do with you?"

I then explained my interrogation by SS Major Rupp, my frightening experience with SS Sergeant Gruber, and the details of my escape while being marched to a German POW collection point."

"Your story doesn't hold water! If you were an American taken prisoner, you would be in a POW camp, not sitting here. You are obviously a German, dressed in the uniform of an American soldier you probably killed. I think you are a stinking, dirty, rotten German spy! You are probably a member of SS Colonel Skorzeny's well trained and infamous saboteur organization which is now operating behind American lines. You may think we are stupid, but you can't fool me! You are a German in an American uniform and I am going to have you executed as a spy."

This seemingly spontaneous outburst caught me by surprise. It was totally unexpected. I had really expected to be treated like a fatigued, malnourished, and wounded GI. In defense of myself, I blurted out, "Wait a minute Major, you are beginning to make me nervous as Hell! I will explain again, in plain English. I am an American non-commissioned officer in the U. S. Army, and I am wearing my identification dog tags. My identity is no secret, it can be traced through the 106th Division headquarters in St. Vith. I didn't come this far to get murdered by some paranoid, bird-brained officer, who happens to think he is God because he is wearing jump boots. You are not going to order me killed, you may have me thrown in prison, but not executed. I am exhausted, hungry, and have wounds that need attending. I demand to speak to the Regimental Commander, right now, not later!"

"That did it you insolent son-of-a-bitch. You know fucking good and well that St. Vith is in German hands and the 106th Division is all shot to hell, and what is left is spread to the winds. You know I can't trace your records, you slimy bastard!"

By this time, what little what little adrenaline I had left was beginning to flow. I was both terrified and furious. This damned paranoid airborne officer was casting himself as both judge and jury. I decided I was not going to let him have me executed without a fight. I did not get where I was by meekly caving in. Words started to flow and I YELLED at him, "You good-for-nothing, STUPID YANKEE, you'd like to kill another 'Southern Boy' wouldn't you? I can tell you don't like Southerners because you're a Damn Yankee and you think you are better than we are. Well let me tell you something, 'Mr. Jump Boots,' and I raised my voice even higher, "The South should have kicked your ass when we had a chance. I'm hungry and thirsty, I'm dead tired, and my legs hurt, but if you want a piece of me buddy, lets get at it, because I would like to kick your butt. I'm not going to take this shit from a Damned Yankee any more. I want to see your Commanding Officer and you'd better get him fast, because I want to see him now. Right Now!" I was livid! I was also on a roll.

Major Snowden was visibly shaken by my violent outburst. Both of his hands, which rested on the table between us, started to tremble. His face had taken on an ashen tone and his eyes were daring around searching the room behind me. He started to rise from his chair as if he wanted to stand. I thought, "Well here it comes. I'm dead meat!" The Major froze, half standing and half sitting as a well modulated voice behind me said, "Don't get up Major." and then spoke to the guard, "Corporal, why don't you get the prisoner a cup of coffee?" The same voice then said, "Son, stand up and turn around. I want to get a look at a guy who claims to be a good Southern soldier."

Getting out of the chair was difficult, I was getting stomach cramps again, but as I rose to my feet, I turned to face a distinguished looking 'full bird' Colonel. He was dressed in paratrooper fatigues and jump boots, an 82nd Airborne Division insignia on his left shoulder, and the name EKMAN stenciled over his right breast pocket.

Something happened in my head, reflex action, two years of military training, I don't know what happened, but my next action was involuntary. I snapped to attention and gave the Colonel a crisp military hand salute, and held it. Colonel Ekman returned the salute and spoke to me softly, "At Ease son. Did you say you are from Florida?"

"Yes Sir, Cocoa, Florida."

"I'm not familiar with Cocoa. Where is it located?"

"Sir, Cocoa is located on the east coast of Florida, almost midway between Jacksonville and Miami."

"Son, where were you inducted into the Army?"

"I was inducted into the Army at Camp Blanding, Florida, Sir."

"Where did you join the 106th Infantry Division?"

"Sir, at Fort Jackson, South Carolina, in February 1943."

Smiling slightly, the Colonel asked, "Do you remember what the recruits called the induction center at Camp Blanding?"

With this question, my tension started to fade and I smiled back, "Oh yes Sir. It was called Skunk Hollow." Even the guard standing behind me laughed when I answered this question. Everyone but Major Snowden seemed more relaxed.

"Why did they call it Skunk Hollow?"

When I answered this question, I forgot to use the term 'Sir' which protocol called for, and blurted out, "Because it Stunk!"

"Sergeant Pierson. You did say your name is Pierson, and you are a T/4 in the

U. S. Army Field Artillery, didn't you?"

"That is correct, Sir."

"Sergeant, if I may, I would like to make and observation."

"Please do, Sir."

"Sergeant, you are NOT a good judge of a person's heritage. Major Snowden is from Alabama. I happen to be a Damned Yankee. My home is in upper New York State." With a grin on his face, Colonel Ekman continued, "In view of this startling new information you have just received, are there any other thoughts you would care to share with us concerning Yankees?"

I thought, "This is too good to be true. I have just run into a senior officer with a sense of humor," and then replied sheepishly, "Not really Sir, except I have found some Yankee Officers are more tolerant than others."

"I'll accept that as a half-hearted apology Pierson." The Colonel suddenly turned to the soldier guarding me and asked, "Corporal, do you think this young man is a German?" The guard obviously caught off guard thought a moment and answered, "Colonel, I ain't never heard no Kraut talk with a southern accent like he does." The Colonel then turned to Major Snowden and said, "I think he is an American GI, but keep him under guard, get him fed, and let the medics take a look at him. Then, depending on what 'Doc' says, either evacuate him to Division Headquarters for more interrogation, or to the medical facility at the Corps POW Collection Center if he needs further treatment."

Without any emotion what-so-ever, Major Snowden responded to his order, "Yes, Sir." Then the Colonel turned to me, and the questioning began again, but this time along another vein.

"You are trained as an artilleryman are you not?"

"Yes Sir."

"Wasn't the 589th Field Artillery Battalion involved in the defense of the cross roads at Baraque de Fraiture, Belgium?"

"Yes Sir, we were heavily involved!"

"Were you personally involved in that action?"

"Yes Sir, I was at the cross roads from the very beginning until the bitter end."

"Is that where you were captured?"

"Well, no Sir, I escaped through the enemy encirclement at Baraque de Fraiture, but was captured by SS troops later."

"How did you manage to escape?"

"Another GI and I killed our German guard. Judging from the way the other GI was dressed, I believe he was one of yours. You know, a trooper."

"Who was the senior officer at Baraque de Fraiture?"

"We actually had co-commanders, Majors Elliott Goldstein and Arthur C. Parker shared the command."

"Did you know that members of the 82nd Airborne Division tried to reinforce you there?"

"Yes Sir, I was aware of that fact. Two different units tried, one Glider, and one Paratrooper unit, but they were unsuccessful and had to withdraw. The same thing happened with an armored combat command, but by then we were completely surrounded. I surely do wish you guys could have gotten us out."

"I do too Sergeant, we lost some good men trying! Do you know what Corps now calls the cross roads?"

"I have no idea, Sir."

"I thought you would like to know. We call it 'Parker's Cross Roads' in honor of your valiant holding action there. I understand Major Parker was badly wounded during that action."

"Major Parker got hit pretty bad, Colonel. The medics finally got him stabilized. Over Major Parker's objections, Major Goldstein had him loaded into a half-track, and evacuated with a medic and a couple of badly wounded GIs. That, of course, left Major Goldstein in sole command. I don't know what happened to Major Parker. I certainly hope he made it to a hospital and they can patch him up. He is one fine officer.

Turning to Major Snowden, the Regimental Commander reiterated, "I believe he is telling the truth, but follow my instructions to the 'T', and depending on whether 'Doc' recommends further treatment of his wounds, or not, evacuate the prisoner to a medical facility or to Division Headquarters. Regardless of where he ends up, the G-2 (Division Intelligence Officer) will want to talk to him."

As Colonel Ekman turned to return to the room he had set up as his Command Post, he asked another question, "Sergeant, are you qualified as a forward observer?"

At the time I thought that was an irrelevant question, but I replied, "Sir, I was formally trained as a Forward Observer at Camp Atterbury, Indiana, just before we were shipped overseas. I have already fired a few missions in combat."

"Thank you Sergeant. Good luck with the Division G-2. It is his responsibility to officially determine if you are a friend or foe. Just in case you turn out to be friendly, I will notify the Division Staff of your qualifications. We are extremely short of qualified Forward Observers."

Battle of the Bulge – Day 11
Regimental Aid Station – 505th Parachute Infantry Regiment
26 December 1944 – 1230 Hours

On the way to the aid station, we detoured by the mess tent. Because I was still officially a German POW, there were only two other persons present while I ate, the guard and a cook. I was obviously being isolated from most American troops regardless of the Regimental Commander's opinion. However, I did notice the Corporal guarding me was not quite as 'up-tight' as he was during my initial interrogation because now he referred to me as Sergeant. During the meal he told me, "Sergeant, you really 'pissed-off' the S-2. You know that don't you?" He acted pleased because an enlisted man 'pissed-off' a Major and got away with it.

"Well Corporal, he pissed me off too! Can you imagine an officer from Alabama thinking a GI from Florida is a Kraut? To me, that is pure stupidity!"

The Corporal thought for a while and then responded, "I don't know nothing about nothing. I just follow orders. But I'll tell you one thing, you don't look like no German to me."

"Thanks buddy, that is reassuring. Now what comes next?"

When you are through eating, I'm supposed to take you to the aid station and let "Doc" take a look at you. He'll decide whether you go to Division Headquarters or go to a medical facility."

"It will be good to see a doctor, I don't feel very good. I ate too fast, my stomach hurts, and I feel like I'm going to vomit. My leg hurts like Hell!"

"Well, 'Doc' ain't no real doctor, he is the non-com in charge of the aid station. Actually he is Staff Sergeant Dutch Schultz."

"With a name like Schultz he is an American. But with me, a name like Pierson makes me a German. That is just great. Sounds to me like you Airborne guys have everything ass backward."

"It wouldn't be the first time." Then the guard laughed at the thought.

"Tell me what you know about Sergeant Schultz."

"I don't guests it will hurt none to talk about Dutch. Him and me have served together since Jump School back at Fort Brag. I know him pretty good. He was born in Sycamore, Georgia. His momma and daddy moved from Germany to Georgia sometime after World War I. Dutch is from a farm family. A big family. His mamma and daddy still speak German, but all of their kids speak American. Dutch is the youngest boy. He was raised up on their farm. Grew tobacco for money and grew peanuts to feed their hogs. Then December 7th come along and Dutch decided to join-up so he could kill Japs. He loves America. He took his basic training, then volunteered for Airborne training."

"That is interesting. How did he end up a medic instead of killing Japs?"

"Dutch busted up a leg during one jump. He wanted to stay in the Airborne Infantry, but with a bad leg he couldn't qualify. One of his buddies in Personnel got him sent to a school for medics."

"How in the world did Personnel determine he was qualified to become a combat medic?"

"Because he had lots of experience at doctoring sick hogs. Ain't that funny? He is a damn good medic because he doctored sick hogs back home. That's Army Personnel thinking for you!"

"Did he ever get to the Pacific to kill Japs?"

"No, It's funny how things work out sometime. Somebody in Washington decided to let the Marines make all the initial landings in the Pacific instead of Airborne troops. Here in Europe Dutch is a good medic and also speaks good German. He also does a lots of interpreting work. Dutch carries a lots of weight with our senior officers even if he is only a Staff Sergeant. All the officers, including the Regimental Commander, listen to Dutch. They'll ask him what he thinks about you."

We entered the double flapped entrance to a large squad tent. The tent was well marked with a solid white circle surrounding the internationally recognized red cross. The well lighted interior of the tent contrasted with the overgrown wooded area we had been trudging through. Inside the warm medical tent I felt better, but not much. The heavy, rich food in my shrunken stomach couldn't make up it's mind whether it wanted to come back up, or stay down. Dutch 'Doc' Schultz turned out to be quite an imposing man. Tall, large framed, broad shoulders, heavily muscled, and a handsome, rugged face. His fatigues were freshly pressed, well tailored, and fit him like a glove. To me, he could have been a model dressed to make a picture for an Airborne recruiting poster.

Dutch looked me up and down, shook his head, and asked the guard, "What have you got here?"

"Doc, I don't know. He says he is a GI. Major Snowden thinks he's a Kraut, but the old man thinks he is American. The Colonel wants you to patch him up and either send him to the Division G-2 for more interrogation, or send him to the medical facility at the Corps POW Collection Center. It's your call."

Turning to face me, Sergeant Schultz asked, "What is wrong with you that a bath and a change of clothes can't cure?"

"Sergeant, my stomach hurts, I'm cold, I'm tired, my legs and feet are killing me, and I'm tired of being treated like a POW. I'm a T/4 from the American 106th Infantry Division."

"Anything else?"

"I'd appreciate it if you would take a look at my feet and legs first."

"What is wrong with them?"

"Frost bite and white phosphorous burns."

"Whose WP, ours or Kraut?"

"Kraut, they were trying to kill me."

"OK, strip down to your underwear and socks."

"Sergeant Schultz, I'm still cold and it is not very warm in here."

"How can I help you if you don't strip down? I've got to check you all over.

I can't do that with your clothes on. Go on and strip down."

I shrugged slightly, "I don't know, but please get me a blanket or something."

Sergeant Schultz nodded to the guard and said, "Go to the next tent and get me a couple of blankets and an aid man. I think they are over there shooting craps."

The guard protested, "Doc, I'm not supposed to leave the prisoner."

Dutch Schultz replied forcefully, "I don't need a lesson in military protocol from a damned Corporal. I didn't ask you, I told you to get me a couple of blankets and an aid man. Is that clear?"

'Doc' Schultz then directed his attention to me and asked me to get on the examination table. As an after thought he asked, "When was the last time you had your boots off?" When I told him they had not been off for about a week, he grimaced, shook this head and instructed me to start taking my boots off, but leave your socks on. Then take off all my outer garments. Even though I felt better having 'Doc' talking to me like I was a human being, I still complained about being cold.

As I was taking off my boots, he started looking me over, this time concentrating on minute details, looking into my eyes, evaluating my body language and coordination. Sensing my despair, he finally told me gently, "I know you will feel better in a little while, but right now I have to check you all over. This is very important!" This was not exactly what I wanted to hear, but the medic seemed sincere, so I climbed onto the cold metal examination table and continued removing my combat boots. The boots looked horrible, the buckles would not work and it was almost impossible to loosen the boot laces with my fingers. Once I got the boots open, my feet were so swollen I could not get my feet out of the open boots. This supposedly simple effort took so much concentration I was not aware the guard had returned with the blankets and an aid man. I finally looked at 'Doc', I was bewildered, and just sat there on the examination table immobile.

"Doc" Schultz motioned for the medic to come to the examination table and told him, "Ken, help him undress. We have a fatigue case on our hands." Then over his shoulder he asked me, "What size waist do you have?" This question puzzled me, but I replied, "Size 32." 'Doc' then told the guard to go to the supply truck and draw underwear, long johns, and heavy socks that will fit the prisoner. The guard reacted negatively, "I'll have to wake-up the Supply Sergeant and he will kill me. He will want someone to sign for the stuff. Whose name should I sign?"

"Adolph Hitler!"

"Oh come on 'Doc,' I'm serious."

"I'm serious too. Get your GI butt on the road, I don't want to tell you again. You don't have much choice, Who do you want to kill you, me or the Supply Sergeant. Either way you are going to be just as dead."

For some unknown reason I had followed the conversation and as the guard left the tent I muttered to no one in particular, "Some people never learn!"

Undressing turned out to be a more tedious process than I could have imagined. I was very little help because I was completely exhausted. The medic that 'Doc' called Ken, who was helping me, turned out to be Corporal Kenneth Yardley, a young trooper from some place I never heard of on Long Island, New York. He told me he was a conscious objector. He explained it was against his religious beliefs to take a life, but felt he had a duty to serve his country and also to help his fellow man. Apparently the Army understood his beliefs and trained him to be a medic. I had never heard of a conscious objector before.

Ken was very gentle and could not remove my feet from my open combat boots. He finally ended up cutting the boots from my swollen feet with surgical scissors. He also cut away the portions of my long johns that were stuck to the still open burns on my legs. With everything finally removed but my underwear and socks, 'Doc' told Ken to remove my underwear, wrap me in a blanket, make a pillow with the other blanket, and help me lie down on the examination table. 'Doc" told me they were going to leave my feet exposed because they were going to cut the socks from my swollen feet. He also warned me this process might be painful. As Ken trimmed away, 'Doc' kept reminding him to slow down and be careful. 'Doc' was right, the process was painful! Although I could not see my feet, I had the feeling Ken was pulling off flesh that had stuck to the filthy socks. When Ken thought he had finished his job and stood up straight, 'Doc' moved to the foot of the table and announced, "We have removed both socks." Then poked at my feet with an unknown object and asked me, "Can you feel that?"

After waiting for about one minute, I asked, "Feel what."

Ken and Dutch looked at each other and did not answer my question. Instead they discussed the possibility of frost bite or frozen feet. Dutch told Ken he really could not determine which it was until my feet thawed. He felt my feet should be thawed slowly, without administration of any kind of heat.

Right or wrong, 'Doc' was firmly in charge. He dismissed the guard and told him to return to the Regimental Command Post. I could hear the argumentative guard protest because he felt the prisoner was still his responsibility and said he had no intention of leaving without his prisoner. With a scowl, Dutch told the guard the prisoner was now the responsibility of the medics. Finally the guard got the message and as he left he advised Dutch that Major Snowden would want to know when to pick-up the prisoner and take him back to the Division Intelligence Officer. Dutch advised the guard forcefully, "You tell the Major, respectfully, the prisoner is no longer his responsibility. This afternoon the prisoner will be transported by ambulance to the appropriate medical facility. The Division G-2 will be notified by proper medical authority where and when the prisoner will be available for further interrogation. Do you think you can remember that?"

The still reluctant guard snapped back, "What if the prisoner escapes?"

By now it had become obvious the conversations between Dutch Schultz and the guard had deteriorated to something personal and someone needed to intervene. Corporal Yardley and I tried but failed. The two troopers just stood there toe to toe, glaring at each other. The time was ripe. Who was going to take the first swing? After what seemed an eternity, Dutch finally snarled, "You stupid headquarters bastard! How can the prisoner escape with two frozen feet, no boots, no warm clothing, and heavily sedated against pain? Now get out of my tent before I get mad!" Without another word, the guard slung his rifle and left the tent. Almost in silence I muttered again, "Some people never learn."

Corporal Yardley breathed a sigh of relief and bent over the examination table, lifted my head, handed me a canteen cup partially filled with cool water. He nodded at his other hand and told me to take an assortment of pills from his hand. When I asked what the pills were for, he told me, "The pills are to fight infection and to make you sleep." Since I was groggy anyway, I told Ken I didn't think I would need pills to make me sleep. Ken laughed and made me take all the pills he had in his hand and reminded me, "You just saw what happens to people when the piss Dutch off. You don't want to get him pissed at you, do you?"

The last thing I remember when a comforting fog descended and surrounded me with a feeling of pain free security and the fact that Dutch was not pissed at me, but was definitely on my side.

Battle of the Bulge—Day 11
Ambulance Ride to XVIII Airborne Corps Medical Facility
26 December 1944—1530 Hours

Slowly, very slowly, my eyes opened. I struggled to get them in focus. Driving away the translucent film that obscured my vision was difficult. My eyes partially focused on a frosty white ceiling above me. By rolling my; head from side to side, I could tell the walls of the container which held my body were also frosty white. My first semi-lucid thought was that I was inside a closed casket, but as my mind started to clear I sensed this container was too large to be a casket. Then another thought occurred. Maybe I was dead and somehow was on the way to heaven. If this is true, I came to the conclusion that dying wasn't too bad after all. I was comfortable and didn't hurt.

Semiconscious and still foggy, I lifted my head. Two vertical oblong shafts of bright light were penetrating the dim interior of my protective container. The next thing which attracted my attention was the olive drab blanket which covered my entire body. Almost simultaneously I sensed movement. A sudden and severe jolt jarred me into full consciousness and caused me to exclaim, "Where in the hell am I?'

A friendly sounding voice responded, "I do believe sleeping beauty is awake." The voice belonged to the medic, Corporal Ken Yardley. Even though I recognized Ken's voice, I did not comprehend what had happened. I asked the question again, in a more modulated voice, "Ken, where am I?"

"You are in an M-1, Government Issue, Dodge 3/4 Ton Ambulance on a bumpy road, headed toward a hospital. How do you feel?"

"I don't feel much of anything. Christ, I thought I was dead and going to heaven in some kind of white container traveling on two shafts of bright light."

"Man, that is wild! A 'Reb' going to heaven in a white container riding on two shafts of bright light. You must have been looking at the sun shining through the two windows in the rear of the vehicle."

"Ken, why is the tube in my arm?"

"We are feeding you pure Vodka, it seems to cure everything. Seriously, how do your feet feel?"

"Not too bad. They do burn a little. What is wrong with them?"

Ken chuckled and replied, "I don't doubt that they hurt, we had a hell of a time getting your socks off while you were asleep. You had on two pairs, the first pair came off real easy, but the second pair seemed glued to your skin. We pulled off lots of cold-damaged tissue to get the second pair off. Pal, you got one good case of frost bite. I believe you are lucky, Dutch doesn't think your feet were frozen. However, if you are unlucky, you might loose some toes."

"Holly Shit Ken! Do you have any other good news for me?"

"You might say so, you are alive! Your legs aren't the best looking things I have ever seen, but they do not show any signs of infection. Did someone treat your burns before we captured you?"

"Yea. When the SS guys first captured me, a Kraut medic made me drop my pants and long johns and rubbed some kind of axle grease on my legs. I don't know what it was, but it was really greasy."

"You should pray for that Kraut medic tonight, he might have saved your life. Now we will find out if an American doctor knows how to save your toes."

"Damn, you sound cheerful!"

Ken thought a while and said, "We have treated a lot of frost bite cases. Dutch has his own way of treating frost bite at the aid station. He thinks he can prevent some tissue damage if he thaws the feet slowly. He actually started the thawing process on your feet by putting them in cold water, then gradually warming the water. Since we pulled off quite a bit of cold-damaged tissue when we cut off your socks, we also used Sulfa Powder liberally to prevent infection. When you screamed too loudly, we used Morphine to kill the pain. Do you remember any of this? This process took quite some time."

Ken, I really don't remember anything about this afternoon."

"I'm glad you don't remember anything. This must have been a pretty painful process. We really had you knocked out. Probably used more drugs than we are authorized to use. What the hell, who counts pills and shots in combat? It is tough seeing someone suffer."

"Thanks a bunch Ken. I appreciate what you and 'Doc' did for me. I want to ask you another question, OK?"

"Sure, fire away."

"A few minutes ago you made a crack about a 'Reb' going to heaven. Do you think I am a Reb?"

Corporal Yardley looked down at me lying on the stretcher in the back of the bouncing ambulance. With an earnest look on his face, Ken said, "Sergeant Pierson, Dutch and I know you are a GI. You can't 'fake it' when you are sedated the way you were. Dutch will try to convince the Division G-2 that you are friendly, but the G-2 is a hard nosed Son-of-a-Bitch. There are other considerations too. You pissed the G-2s buddy, Major Snowden. That doesn't help your case at all."

"Thank God someone believes me. Ken, you don't know how upset I get when someone calls me a fucking Kraut. Those bastards tried their best to kill me!"

"Dutch and I know Sergeant, you fought Krauts in your sleep all afternoon, things must have been pretty tough on you and your buddies back at the cross roads."

Battle of the Bulge—Day 11
XVIII Airborne Corps POW Collection Center—Near the Ourthe River
26 December 1944—1730 Hours

The 'meat wagon' we were riding in bounced to a stop and a 'spit and polished' XVIII Airborne Corps Military Policeman stuck his head in the front window and asked the ambulance driver for his trip ticket. Checking the information on the trip ticket with the unit markings on the front bumper of the vehicle, he moved to the rear of the ambulance, opened the rear door and stepped back, while a second MP covered him. The first MP then stuck his head into the white interior of the ambulance and asked, "What has the mighty 505th Parachute Regiment brought us lowly earth bound soldiers today?"

Struggling to get past the stretcher where I lay, Ken Yardley made his way to the rear of the ambulance and answered, "Well hello Willie, I brought you a huge appetite and a wounded Nazi Field Marshall who has a personal message for General Eisenhower. Is the General around?"

"No shit Ken, did you guys capture a German General?"

"Willie, you know I am pulling your leg about everything but my appetite. We're hungry. The guy on the litter is an American Sergeant with a couple of bad legs and feet. Before we go to the Administration Office, I'd like to go to the mess hall and get three descent meals. Is that OK with you?"

"Why in the hell are you bringing a wounded GI here? You know as well as I do we don't treat GIs here. We only treat prisoners here."

"Come on Willie, it's a long and complicated story. I'll tell it to you later. Just let us in the compound, I know where the mess hall is and I also know where the Admissions Office is. I'll talk to you on the way back to Regiment and explain everything."

"As far as I am concerned, this is a routine trip. I'm checking three bodies into the compound with a destination of the Admission Office. I don't give a 'didley damn' if you detour by the mess hall to get some chow. But buddy, let me tell you one thing, I'm only going to let two bodies leave the compound. Remember that Ken and don't try to get tricky with me.

Willie kept the vehicle at the guard shack while he posted our destination onto the trip ticket and made a phone call to the admitting office. He then opened the double gates and gave a snappy hand signal to the driver to proceed unescorted into the bowls of the POW enclosure.

Visibility from the back of the 3/4 ton Dodge was very poor. There are no windows on the sides, only one narrow window on each of the two rear doors. Ken had obviously been here many times before, but the driver had not, consequently Ken moved to the cab of the vehicle to give directions to the driver. I had never seen a Prisoner of War compound so I propped up on the stretcher and tried to look out the rear windows. As we moved slowly down a narrow, bumpy, Belgian

Block road, I was able to see the guard house, the double security gates at the entrance to the compound, and the two tall barbed wire fences which connected to each security gate. Determined to see more, I sat erect on the stretcher with both hands braced against the ceiling of the ambulance to steady myself against the unpredictable movements of the moving vehicle. Apparently the XVIII Airborne Corps had taken over some type office or commercial complex, plus a large amount of vacant land from the Belgian government and turned it into a POW enclosure. From what little I could see, the enclosure was capable of accommodating hundreds, if not thousands of prisoners of war.

Once we were confined within the twin barbed wire fences and under observation by guards in towers evenly spaced above the tall fences, we were not challenged again by security forces. Once parked in front of a large stone building, Ken advised us this building housed the enlisted men's mess. Ken told the driver he was going talk to the Mess Sergeant, and for him to remain in the vehicle until he returned. Ken then turned to me and advised me to keep my fingers crossed because, by hook or crook, he was going to get me something to eat too. This thought appealed to me, so I immediately crossed my fingers

For the first time, the driver and I had a chance to talk. He was a nice young man, younger than I, and had just earned his first stripe. He was proud to be a Private First Class and thought his promotion was a good sign of better things to come. Time passed quickly and before we knew it Yardley appeared at the rear of the ambulance accompanied by two privates who were obviously assigned to Kitchen Police (KP) duty. The two KPs opened the ambulance doors, picked up the stretcher which held me, and the five of us marched, of course I was carried, into the mess hall. The mess hall was absolutely spotless. I had not seen a mess like this since we left England. The KPs placed each end of the stretcher on a table and positioned a third table so I could roll onto my left side and dine in comfort while reclining. I could not believe how nice they were treating me. Enlisted men seemed to understand my situation, but up until now only officers had given me a hard time. The Regimental Commander of the 505th seemed to be the only officer I could respect.

As the two KPs returned to their kitchen duties, a Staff Sergeant, dressed in a Class A, woolen OD winter uniform, walked across the room and approached where I lay on the stretcher. He looked down at me quizzically and said to Ken, "So this is the guy the brass thinks is a Kraut."

Corporal Yardley nodded, indicating affirmative.

The mess sergeant looked down again and asked me to say something.

This request, or command, caught me by surprise and all I could think of was, "You all have a nice mess hall Sarge. I hope the chow tastes as good as the mess hall looks."

What would you like us to fix for your meal?"

"Oh man, coffee, ham, eggs, biscuits, grits, and red-eye gravy would go pretty good right now. I haven't had any grits since we crossed the channel."

Without any more conversation, the mess sergeant yelled to his first cook in the kitchen, "Fix three good servings of what ever you have available for three hungry combat GIs," and told Ken rather matter-of-factly, "Yardley, you heard him ask for ham, grits, and red-eye gravy, and then refer to me as 'you all.' How in the hell could any body in their right mind, even an officer, think this guy is a Kraut?"

The meal, although not ham and grits, turned out to be a real treat. After thanking the mess sergeant and the first cook, we departed the mess hall in much the same manner in which we entered. The hospital for wounded and sick prisoners of war occupied the largest permanent building in the enclosure. Again, the driver and I waited in the ambulance while Corporal Yardley was in the admissions office completing the paper work necessary to transfer the responsibility of the 'prisoner' from the 505th Parachute Infantry Regiment to the XVIII Airborne Corps. This process took much longer than obtaining our three unauthorized meals. In fact, it took so long, coupled with the comfortable feeling generated by a large and delicious hot meal, that both the driver and I fell fast asleep in the ambulance while waiting for Ken to return.

When Ken finally returned, the relaxed atmosphere changed. The ambulance was surrounded by armed MPs who threw open the vehicle's rear doors and screamed, "Don't move, we have you covered!" Having no choice, I lay back on the stretcher, crossed my arms across my chest, interlocked my fingers, and yelled at the top of my voice, "Don't shoot! I surrender!"

Only one of the many gathered MPs thought my reply was funny and chuckled at the idiotic scene.

Immediately two white garbed medics bounded into the ambulance and with well rehearsed motions, immobilized me by securing me firmly to the stretcher with webbed restraints. Only then did the assembled MPs holster their side arms. The medical corpsmen removed me from the vehicle and started carrying me to the entrance of the medical building. In frustration, I called to Ken and asked him, "For Christ's sake Ken, what happens next?"

"I'm not sure, I had a hard time convincing the hospital administrator that you are a special case. He finally agreed to let me accompany you to the examination room, although you are no longer my responsibility. I'm going to talk to the doctor and the head nurse. You will like her, she is a regular army Major. She actually has more authority over how prisoners are handled than the doctors or the hospital administrator. She is tough, but she is a good judge of human nature, and old enough to be your mother. Try to get her on your side."

The examination room was not too different from the one at Regiment.. It was warmer, and the doctor was a Captain instead of a Staff Sergeant. The doctor entered the room and introduced himself as Captain Knox. Ken introduced himself, then introduced me as Technician Fourth Grade Randolph Pierson. This introduction caused the doctor to raise his eye-brows as if asking a question.. With an armed MP present, my restraints were removed and I was helped onto the examination table. After receiving instructions from the doctor, I completely undressed. For the first time, I saw my heavily bandaged feet.

Looking over my body, the doctor's attention finally moved to my legs. he asked Corporal Yardley a muffled question I could not understand. Ken answered, as they both looked at my feet. As the doctor started removing the bandage material I became aware that someone else had entered the room. Looking over my shoulder was awkward, but I tried. To my surprise, I saw two American nurses standing at the head of the examination table, intently watching the doctor working over my feet. One nurse, a motherly looking type, wore the golden oak leaf insignia of a Major on her collar. The second nurse was a First Lieutenant who was gorgeous. The unexpected sight of her made me gasp. Nothing in my recent experiences had prepared me for two American females, especially for a black haired and dark eyed, twenty-something year old beauty with a figure that just would not quit. This experience was quite a shock. When I finally realized I was lying there on my back, under a bright light, completely nude, and these females were looking at me with great interest, the shock became even greater. Highly embarrassed, I blurted out something which caught the head nurse by surprise.

The Major asked, "Does he speak and understand English?"

Corporal Yardley nodded in the affirmatively, and the head nurse asked me, "What is the matter soldier? Are you cold?"

Taught to answer questions directed to me by an officer, I automatically replied, "No Sir."

"Well soldier, speak up. What is wrong?"

This time I looked at Ken Yardley and asked meekly, "Ken will you please cover me up?"

He looked at the doctor, then the two nurses, shrugged his shoulders, said, "Oh!" and placed my long johns across my milky white crotch. Moving closer to the younger nurse Ken addressed her in subdued tones, "Lieutenant Davila, this is the sergeant from the 106th Infantry Division we were discussing."

The head nurse and the doctor heard the explanation and looked at each other. At once the Major asked Corporal Yardley why he had brought a wounded GI here when she had no facilities to house American soldiers. The doctor spoke up and expressed the same feelings. This opposition forced Ken to go on the defensive against much superior rank. He patiently explained that only the 82nd Airborne Division G-2 could officially declare me an American, and until that time came, I was to be considered a German prisoner of war. Ken pointed out that almost everyone who had dealt with me felt I was an American. Ken also explained the hospital administrator was responsible for reporting my whereabouts to the Division G-2 and advising him when I was physically able to be interrogated. This information caused the head nurse and the doctor to leave the room to engage in a private conversation. The young nurse, Lieutenant

Davila, approached the examination table, looked me in the eyes, smiled at me with moist red lips and beautiful white teeth, and moved to the foot of the table to examine my leg wounds and feet. When she moved back toward my head and bent over, I could read her name tag 'Davila, Anne Marie' which rode high upon her beautifully mounded right breast. For some unknown reason she decided to cover my bare body, and draped me from shoulder to feet with a fresh, clean smelling sheet. I liked the sensation of being covered, but it was nothing compared to the sensation caused by nurse Davila when she reached under the sheet with her soft hand searching along my thighs for the long johns Ken had used to partially cover me. I'm certain the expression on my face, and the visible on-coming erection under the sheet said more to the Lieutenant than words could possibly say. This chain of events caused Lieutenant Davila to laugh and smile at me again. Still smiling, she asked for my name and I told her, "Randolph Pierson."

"Where were you born, Randolph?"

"Lieutenant, I was born in Cocoa, Florida."

"What do your close friends call you? You know, your nick-name."

"Almost everyone calls me Randy."

"Did you participate in sports when you were in high school?"

"Not really Lieutenant, I worked most of the time to made spending money so I could date the cheer leaders.

"You don't know it, but I was a cheer leader in high school."

"I don't doubt that Lieutenant, you are a very pretty lady, and looking at your figure, I'd say you are still pretty athletic."

"Randy, may I call you Randy? You are already paying me complements. Are you trying to get something from me, or did the army teach you this technique?"

"Lieutenant, I'm not trying to give you a 'snow job.' Now to answer your second question, I was complementing pretty girls long before I got in the army. It just seems the natural thing to do. Do you mind if I think you are attractive? You know, you being an officer and me being an enlisted man?"

"Heavens no! I certainly don't mind receiving compliments. Most females love to receive genuine compliments from men. Changing the subject Randy, did you come through England on your way to Europe?"

"Yes. The 106th Infantry Division staged in England. While there, we were issued new trucks, howitzers and equipment before we crossed the channel. The US Army had so much stuff stored in England while we were there, I thought the whole island was going to sink into the North Sea."

"Did you have an opportunity to date any girls while you were there?"

I laughed and told the Lieutenant, "Oh yes! I dated one in particular, a red headed Irish lass named Annie Dugan. She was something else."

"What kind of reaction did you get when you told the English girls you were Randy?"

"That is a good question Lieutenant. I got some strange looks that I did not understand at first. Then, after Annie told me that 'randy' was an English slang work for being horny, I began saying, my name is Randolph and quit saying I'm Randy, although I guess I really was 'randy' while I was there. My first name, Randolph, was well received in England because it is a distinguished English name."

Then Lieutenant Davila asked if I had run into the term 'knocked-up' in England.

She gave me another gorgeous smile when I told her I almost fainted the first time Annie Dugan told me she was 'knocked-up' and told the Lieutenant I thought she meant she was pregnant. I knew I didn't put her in a family way. Lieutenant Davila broke in and explained something similar had happened to her when she was stationed in England. One night a British nurse she was rooming with came into the officer's quarters and announced she was 'knocked-up.' It took a little time for her to realize her British friend was merely announcing she was tired. We both laughed and Lieutenant Davila said she had heard the British and Americans had everything in common but a language.

The Lieutenant came closer to the table, placed her hand on my stomach, and stood there in silence, just looking at my face. After our conversation, this seemed strange to me, but I could tell she was deep in thought. I knew she didn't mean anything by placing her hand there, my stomach was merely a convenient place to put her hand, it was obviously just an idle gesture, but to me her touch was electric. I felt I was losing control of my emotions because my mind was wandering toward sexual fantasy and I was on the verge of having another erection. Her dark eyes started to come into focus as she completed her thought process. When her gaze fell to the bulge in the sheet between my legs, her eyes moved to my face and she softly said, "I believe you are excited and are blushing. Am I making you feel uncomfortable?"

"That is a hard question to answer. It is complicated by our difference in rank and the situation under which we have met. The truthful answer is, both 'yes' and 'no' because of the circumstances. I haven't been with a female in a long time, and you are so attractive, you are starting to get to me as a man, but I know you are 'off limits' because you are an officer. Damn it, I'm sorry, but I can't change how I feel about you."

"Randy, don't apologize to me, or say you are sorry about how you feel, you are having very normal and expected reactions. I am actually flattered you find me attractive. I am Hispanic! Hispanic women understand men. They also like men who appreciate them. I personally don't care about our difference in rank, but we are in the army, and we are required to play by the army rules. I am a Hispanic nurse by profession who just happens to be in the army and I will tell you something, you have many qualities which make you attractive to Hispanic females. Don't ever forget that! Stop worrying. Everything will work out for you in the end—but now I have to go and talk to the Doctor, the Provost Marshal, and the head nurse to find out what we are going to do with you."

Watching Anne Marie Davila walking across the examination room was a sight I had not experienced since leaving England. Her features fascinated me, her broad shoulders, trim waist and flat tummy, shapely legs, and her tantalizing fanny as it moved erotically underneath a tight fitting skirt As I lay there, thinking pleasant thoughts and starting to drift of into never-never land, I realized my fate was squarely in the hands of the authorities. All I could do now was—lie there, wait, and focus on the wondrous beauties of the form divine. However, my short reverie was shattered by a loud, spirited conversation taking place in the hall outside of the examination room. The Provost Marshal, a Military Police Captain, was the most vocal of the group, however, the two nurses seemed to be holding their own. The medical doctor remained strangely quiet. Again I found myself in a situation over which I had no control and this bothered me, but the pain in my legs and feet troubled me more. The pain killer 'Doc' and Ken had given me was obviously wearing off, and wearing off fast! As the conversation, which had by now turned into a full blown argument, continued, I gritted my teeth and endured the increasing pain as long as I could. In desperation, I finally called out, "Lieutenant Davila, I need help! Would you please come in here?"

Anne Marie immediately left the argument in the hall and entered the examination room, closely followed by Major Hartman, the head nurse. Genuinely concerned, Lieutenant Davila asked, "Randy what is wrong?" I pointed to my feet and said, "Anne Marie, they really hurt. They are killing me! Can you give me something to ease the pain?" As Major Hartman entered the room she heard me refer to Lieutenant Davila as Anne Marie. At the time, the Major said nothing but uncovered my feet and legs, and studied what she saw intently. When her examination was complete she ordered Lieutenant Davila to consult with the doctor, develop a schedule for treatment and obtain an order for medications, bandages, and pain killer.

In the hall, Lieutenant Davila interrupted the doctor and the Provost Marshall and obtained instructions on how my hospital treatments would begin. Anne Marie returned, conferred with Major Hartman, inserted an IV tube into my left arm and started the flow of clear liquid from a bottle suspended on a metal device above the examination table. She then rolled me over on my right side and gave me an injection in my buttocks. When I asked what the shot was for, she told me the shot would make me feel better and put me to sleep. Meanwhile, Major Hartman was preparing medications and bandage materials for my feet. When Anne Marie completely uncovered me this time, I didn't even care, the sedation was strong and working very quickly.

The last thing I remembered, before dropping off to sleep, was Major Hartman asking Anne Marie, "Lieutenant Davila, what is this 'Randy and Anne Marie' relationship between you and an enlisted patient? What ever happened to addressing people in the army by their rank and last name?"

To me, in my condition, this question was superfluous!

16

Allied Forces Medical Compound

Battle of the Bulge — Day 12
Medical Compound for Prisoners of War
American Army Nurses Quarters
27 December 1944 — 0530 Hours

The sound of movement near me aroused me from a deep drug induced dream. I could sense there was something moving, making a gentle noise in the darkness. I thought the Germans were infiltrating our defenses at the Cross Roads. I sat upright, wide awake, alert, and reached for my rifle, but it was not there! My mouth was dry and my heart was pounding, then I realized I was sitting on a bed and foolishly said out loud, "Where in the hell am I? Suddenly a dim light began to shine and the total blackness of the night turned to gray. I jumped as I felt a firm hand on my shoulder, but relaxed when I heard a soft female voice say, "Randy, it is me, Anne Marie. Are you OK?"

"Good God, Anne Marie, you scared the hell out of me. I was fighting Krauts back at the Cross Roads and couldn't find my rifle. Where am I?"

"Its a long story, Randy, but to keep it short, we decided to keep you here in the hospital. You have spent the night in the nurses quarters. More specifically, you are in my bedroom. My roommate, Second Lieutenant Susan Prell, temporarily moved out to make room for you."

"Slow down Anne Marie. Are you telling me I am still classified as a POW and I just spent the night with a female American officer in the nurses quarters? What kind of a war is this?"

"It is a crazy war and crazy wars are like politics, they both make strange bed fellows. Isn't this interesting, we all have to make sacrifices. You know what General Sherman said, 'War is Hell!' Susan now refers to our quarters as 'The Suite of Pleasure.' I like that, all the other nurses are jealous. You will like Susan when you meet her, she is a real sport, especially when it comes to men." Anne Mare quickly added, "Speaking of the real sport, I think I hear her coming down the hall."

Still confused about where I was and why I was there, I looked toward the door just in time to witness the grand entrance of Second Lieutenant Susan Prell. Susan was also a 'looker,' a twenty four carat knockout! Petite, shapely, effervescent, and blond. Almost a perfect contrast to Anne Marie, but still just as much a head-turner. She too was beautiful. Susan more-or-less burst into the room and with a bat of her mascara covered eye lashes cooed, "Hi Randy-baby, how do you feel this morning?"

This bubbly greeting surprised me and I did not know how to answer her question, consequently I introduced myself, "I am Sergeant Pierson. I don't believe we have met."

As Anne Marie laughed, Susan approached my bed with an exaggerated, hip-swinging walk and in a distinctly teasing tone replied, "Oh yes we have met Randy, you just don't remember the meeting. I helped Anne Marie bathe you last night."

Looking at Anne Marie, I asked, "Were there any other girls in on the fun?"

Susan giggled, she really was cute, and Anne Marie told me, "Only the two of us bathed you. It was a private party!"

I looked at Susan realizing she was enjoying my questions, and asked her, "Did you give me a 'spit bath,' or did you bathe me all over?"

"We bathed you all over, buddy! You were really cruddy! I'll bet you had not taken a bath in weeks. We used a GI brush and Octagon soap to clean your dirty hide." For some reason, unknown to me, Susan giggled again and looked at Anne Marie. It was as though they were sharing a deep dark secret.

Anne Marie looked at Susan, looked at me, then got serious. "Randy, while we were bathing you, you became sexually aroused. Susan felt we should relieve some of your sexual tensions, much like mother nature does with a 'wet dream.' I agreed, and Susan erotically massaged you. Judging from the results we witnessed, you were more than past due for some sexual activity. You should feel more relaxed this morning."

They both stood there waiting for my reaction. It took time for their message to sink in, but when it did, I admitted, "To be truthful, Anne Marie, I do fell more relaxed this morning than I did in the examination room yesterday. I'm sure you know what I mean."

By this time I was talking directly to Anne Marie, "But other things have happened to me that make me feel worse. These things happened to me too quickly and too violently. In the past twelve days, my Battalion Commander, Lt. Colonel Thomas P. Kelly, went forward to the infantry regiment we were supporting and never returned. He was my roll model, a perfect soldier. I don't know what happened to him and his driver, are they dead or alive? My Battalion S-3, Major Arthur Parker, was severely wounded and evacuated, I don't know whether he survived or not. The Major was my friend and mentor, who taught me all I know about artillery techniques. My Battery Commander, Alva Beans, was evacuated with terrible body wounds on the first day of the Battle of the Bulge. I remember his jeep driver returning to the Battalion area with Captain Beans draped over the hood of his jeep. Blood was running out of his body like water from a spring and he was just barely breathing. I don't know whether he survived or not. We had our differenced, but I will be the first to admit, Captain Beans was a brave warrior. I did not know our three firing battery commanders too well, but one was killed and another one wounded on 16 December 1944. They were two brave Captains trying to protect their men. The Battalion Survey Officer and his jeep driver, one of my best friends, Guy Smith, were ordered to establish an observation post overlooking Auw, Germany. Again, on the first day of the Battle of the Bulge, they and two other GI's left the Battalion Command Post, never to be seen again. What was the fate of these four friends? My buddies and I fought for and held the ground around Parker's Cross Roads at Baraque de Fraiture from 19 December, until 23 December 1944, in the most inclement winter weather in Europe in eighty years. We held our ground against overwhelming odds and pressure from Hitler's finest, the troops of the German 2nd SS Panzer Division. In the deep snow of the Ardennes Forest east of the cross roads, I was forced to kill my first human being, with my fighting knife, in hand-to-hand combat. Thankfully the Good Lord was on my side, and I killed the SS Trooper rather than him killing me. This was a horribly vivid experience and very traumatic for me. I will never forget that fight!"

By this time, all of my pent-up emotions had overwhelmed me. Tears came to my eyes and I began to cry for all of my courageous friends. "On 22 December, the Battalion Executive Officer, Major Elliott Goldstein, a prominent lawyer in civilian life who was from Atlanta, Georgia, realized we had fulfilled our orders: 'To hold this ground as long as humanly possible,' and tried to reach a higher command to obtain reinforcements, or to obtain permission to withdraw. Of course, with all communications to higher headquarters obliterated, he had no means of doing either. Consequently the Major decided he would personally try to obtain reinforcements, for what was left of the Battalion, from an Armored Division we thought was in control of Manhay, Belgium area. We all understood the dangers involved in getting from Baraque de Fraiture to Manhay and feared for his safety. He left and never returned! What happened to this fine officer? I don't know! By the morning of 23 December, all twelve of our howitzers had been lost to enemy action, this situation left us unable to defend ourselves against a German armored attack. Many of my enlisted friends were either killed, wounded, or captured. We fought, and held, Parker's Cross Roads at Baraque de Fraiture, Belgium for 5 endless days and 4 terror filled nights against impossible odds and weather and increasing pressure from Hitler's premier troops of the 2nd SS Panzer Division. A close friend of mine, Staff Sergeant Frank Tacker, and I risked out lives to save two unknown Anti-Aircraft gunners from a burning halftrack, but they died anyway. Later I was wounded in both legs with white phosphorous and my feet started hurting due to frostbite. I was captured by SS troops who robbed me of my personal possessions. The subsequent interrogation by an SS Intelligence Major, was extremely uncomfortable because I did not know what I should tell him. I wanted to be loyal to my country, but I knew the decision whether I lived or died lay in this German officer's hands. I am thankful for having survived this precarious situation. After the interrogation I escaped German imprisonment by killing a second human with a blade, this time with his own bayonet."

By this time, I was controlled by emotions which were totally foreign to me. All of my pent-up emotions were overflowing, tears came to my eyes again, as my story continued. "The morning of 26 December, two days after escaping from the SS troops who captured me, I was hiding in a snow covered hay stack, lost, cold, hungry, and in pain, when an 82nd Airborne Division patrol 'captured' me. They thought I was a German. Later I was ordered to be executed! The American High Command screwed up royally in our sector and it cost many American lives, and me, many friends. The only Americans who have treated me like a human being are the medics. But nothing has really changed, I am still a fucking POW! No one believes me or even gives a damn. I feel lousy! Get me a gun, leave me alone, and let me solve my problems permanently!"

The room became completely silent. Susan and Anne Marie were totally unprepared for this type of outburst, but they both recognized the symptoms of battle fatigue and suicidal tendency. Anne Marie asked Susan to hurry down to see the doctor to explain their situation and quickly moved to the bed to talk to me. By the time Susan returned with Major Hartman and antidepressant medication, Anne Marie was sitting on the bed and holding my head in her lap while telling me how lucky I was to be alive and getting good care. She insisted my feelings might be normal, but the solution I had suggested to solve my problems was totally inappropriate. She assured me they all believed me, and knew I was an American GI. Her touch and assurances lifted my spirits and I was feeling much more normal when Major Hartman addressed me, "Sergeant, what is all this nonsense about you wanting a gun?"

"Major Hartman, I couldn't hold my true feelings in any longer, they just all came out. Maybe I am not the man I thought I was, but I am OK. Lieutenant Davila has a calming effect on me. I must have been feeling sorry for myself."

"Sergeant Pierson, I hope you are not too depressed, I do not want to put you in restraints again, but if restraints are the only way to keep you from hurting yourself, I will! I want you to take the medicine Lieutenant Prell brought you, and Sergeant, that is an order! While we are addressing your many problems, I will remind you, Anne Marie is not your private nurse, she also has other duties to perform. Do you understand that?"

"Yes Major, I will take the medicine as ordered and hope I am not placing too much of a load on Lieutenant Davila." The Major continued to engage me in conversation until she was certain my depressing mood had passed. As the Major was leaving the room, Lieutenant Prell was in the process of bringing a glass of water to my bedside so I could take the anti-depressant. Major Hartman watched intently from the door way. When she was satisfied I had taken the medicine she closed the door and we could hear the military cadence of her footsteps as she 'marched' down the hall.

Once the three of us were alone, Susan dominated the conversation. It was obvious she wanted to change the direction of the conversation away from what was depressing me. "Randy, we told you that while we were bathing you we decided to help mother nature take its course. For some reason, Anne Marie did not want to massage you, but I didn't mind. It gave me an opportunity to practice a tension relieving technique I learned from our German nurse colleagues. From a nurse/patient point of view, it is a much different type relationship. From a medical viewpoint, it is super, it really works!"

Everyone seemed to like Susan! She was easy to look at, normally very animated, an interesting nurse, with a captivating personality. Susan not only knew medicine, but also understood applied psychology. She was determined to keep the conversation on the light side and avoid depressing topics, so she continued, "German doctors learned erotic type massage treatment made the wounded soldiers less aggressive, diverted them from feeling sorry for themselves, and also helped their healing process. When you massage a lightly sedated man properly the results are immediately visible, you can see the results right then and there. You see the patient's body become rigid, see him shudder, hear him groan in ecstasy, and watch a smile of satisfaction come to his face as his body completely relaxes. Germans medicine is way out in front of the Americans in this area of health care. Anne Marie has her reservations about this technique, but I think it is pretty neat! I am glad we could help, that is why we are here. It was obvious to both of us you were pretty darn tense."

"Thank you Susan, this information will remain with me forever. However you omitted information that is important to me and prompts two questions. "How often do you plan to relieve my tensions? and, May I remain awake during our next session?" Anne Marie had been patiently listening to our nonsense but tired of the endless banter between Susan and me. She finally pulled her rank on us, "All right you two. That's enough! Lets change the subject. Susan now that you have proved to Randy that you are a man-killer, aren't you supposed to be on duty in the ward with the German nurses? In response to Lieutenant Davila's strong hint for her to leave the room, Susan stopped at the head of my bed, ran her hand through my hair, gave me a long drawn-out, full-faced look, and told me seriously, "Randy, we know you are an American soldier and I believe everything that bothers you will work out alright. I'm with Anne Marie, I like you too." As she started to leave the room she glanced over her shoulder and added, "But I'll like you much more after you shave, soldier boy."

We could hear her laughing as she walked down the hall. With a smile on her face Anne Marie spoke up, "I told you she is a sport. She is truly a nice and caring person. You should have seen how gently she treated you last night. For some reason she just likes to appear sexy and worldly-wise around men."

Kidding around with Susan had answered some of my questions about what happened last night, but all of the details were not clear in my mind. To fill in some of the blanks I decided to ask Anne Marie, "What else happened in the hospital last night?" "For one thing Randy, you did an awful lot of talking while you were sedated. I am sure the Provost Marshal realizes you are an American soldier. It is very difficult, almost impossible, to lie while you are sedated." "What did I say Anne Marie?" "You talked about many things. The doctor kept you lightly sedated while the Provost Marshall asked you questions. The Provost Marshall is not supposed to interrogate prisoners, that is not his responsibility, but he interrogated you anyway. He has a problem on how to secure you. Mostly what you said is what you had already told us. You also added some nice things about me."

"For Pete's sake, I hope I didn't say anything that might get you in trouble!"

"Oh, the head nurse took it all in and later gave me the standard lecture about getting personally involved with a patient. Involvement with patients is a failing of mine and I get this lecture about every six weeks whether I need it or not."

"How did I end up in your room?"

"Under the circumstances, there was no other place to put you that would be secure. First of all, Major Hartman and the Provost Marshall agreed on one basic thing, they wanted to keep you away from the enemy prisoners for your own protection. Second, the Provost Marshall was required to keep you under the control of his security people until a higher authority decided you are, in fact, an American soldier. His position in this situation was to 'save-his-own-ass' in the event something went wrong. I finally understood where he was coming from. Other than the general POW compound, the hospital wards, and during the day, the Administration Office, the only other installation where MPs are on 24 hour duty is the American nurses quarters. This was the only guarded place in the entire compound that met his and Major Hartman's needs. Third, the Provost Marshall had one more 'ass-saving' need. He wanted an American officer, other than him, to be personally responsible for you. When I volunteered, I solved all his requirements."

"What about the doctor and the head nurse?"

"The doctor could care less. All he is responsible for is your medical treatment. Major Hartman agrees with this joint solution, she trusts me implicitly—she just reminded me that if you escape, I'll have to take your place in prison. Is that true?" "Anne Marie, I'm not sure, but I have heard the same thing. Regardless of what people say, you should not be concerned, you have my word, I am not going anywhere. Realistically, how could I? I have no clothes other than this 'split-back' hospital gown.

It is below freezing outside, and I don't even know if I can walk with my damaged feet or not. Believe me, you are not going to jail to serve my sentence, mainly because I don't plan to be placed in the stockade. Another thing to ease your mind Anne Marie, why would I want to leave and return to combat, only to be shot and killed, when I can get the kind of care that Lieutenant Prell gives me here?"

"Good God Randy, get serious, you are acting just like a horny GI." Looking at her watch, she exclaimed, I'm hungry and the mess is open, do you want to eat here in the room or try to hobble down to our little officer's mess?" "Anne Marie, if I have a choice, I would prefer to eat here in the room with you, if that is possible." "You should know by now Randy, anything is possible if you have the right connections, or enough rank." With that statement Lieutenant Davila called the officer's mess and ordered two substantial breakfasts to be delivered to her quarters as soon as possible. Within minutes a member of the kitchen detail delivered the piping hot meals and we starting to enjoy the excellent food and pleasant conversation.

As we sat eating and talking, Major Hartman unexpectedly returned to the room. "My, isn't this cozy," she exclaimed, directing this remark with a frown toward Anne Marie, then addressing me she added, "How do you like your accommodations here Sergeant?" The Major's comment and question seemed to be a little sarcastic and the relationship between the Major and her Lieutenant appeared antagonistic. This was my fault. I didn't know whether to try and explain my side of this triangle to the head nurse, accept the blame, or to try and smooth some ruffled feathers. I decided I would try humor, "Major, things must be looking up. You just called me Sergeant. I like that, it is a step in the right direction. If you keep up the good work, you just might become my all time favorite nurse."

"Don't you dare and try to soft soap me young man, I've been dealing with smooth talkers like you almost as long as you have been alive! How old are you?"

"Major I just turned 21, but I did not fall off of a turnip truck and land on my head. I'm not stupid enough to try and give a snow job to a head nurse, who is also a Major. Please cut me some slack, I am just trying to stay loose in a pretty tight situation. You still haven't told me what is going on, why don't you share the game plan with me?"

"Sergeant, I just dropped in to discuss these living arrangements with Lieutenant Davila. They are quite unorthodox, and I am the senior officer here. I do not want to make a mistake that will cause problems for any of us who are involved. Anne Marie, how do you feel about the Sergeant as a roommate?"

"Major Hartman, we get along fine. He is no trouble and needs someone to talk to. On the other side of the coin, I love Susan like a sister, but I need a break from her for a little while. I know Sergeant Pierson will be leaving the hospital shortly. His feet already look better, would you like to examine them while you are here?" The Major paused and looked at her watch, "Yes that is a good idea, and while I am thinking about it, get him a Class A woolen uniform. This type uniform, and the necessary accessories, can be obtained from the Provost Marshall's supply organization. Be certain the uniform fits and is pressed properly, I want this young man to look like a good soldier when Colonel Williams comes to debrief him this afternoon, and for goodness sake, get him something to shave with. Sergeant is there anything I can do for you before I leave?"

"Yes there is Major. First let me thank you for what you are doing for me. Then, who is Colonel Williams, and what is a debriefing?"

"I don't know Colonel Williams personally, but he is an intelligence officer in the headquarters of the American 1st Army. He has asked to talk with you when you are medically fit. He will debrief you – that means he wants you to tell him all of your experiences." This was interesting news to me, I thought no one was doing anything for me. Apparently more was going on than I realized. "Major Hartman, I was under the impression that someone was going to interrogate me to find out whether I am an American soldier or a German spy. Will he also do that? That is important to me!" "Sergeant Pierson, I can't answer that question, but I told him you would be available for debriefing at 1400 hours this afternoon. Why don't you ask him that question while you and he are talking? During the meeting, act in a military manner, be polite, tell the truth, and try to make a favorable impression on him. Anything else bothering you?"

"Major, I appreciate your advice, I'll be on my best behavior and I will do the very best I can. One thing before you leave. Would you please come closer to the bed so I can give you a hug." After saying that, my mind drifted back to the wonderful head nurse, a Major, we had at the Fort Jackson Station Hospital when I was hospitalized for Spinal Meningitis during basic training. There were similarities, but Major Hartman seemed to be more military than my head nurse at Fort Jackson, who 'mothered' me and hugged me when I left the hospital to return to duty. It occurred to me that maybe I had handled Major Hartman wrong, but I still wanted to penetrate her military veneer, so I decided to stretch the truth a little and added, "I have never been hugged by a Major."

"Sergeant, don't get fresh with me! If you try to hug me, I'll have you lying at attention every time I enter this room. Is that clear?" The Major then addressed Anne Marie, "Lieutenant Davila, I have to leave now. Your patient seems to be feeling frisky. Think you and handle him?"

"Major, he is a piece of cake!"

The rest of the morning was busy. The MP Anne Marie had requested arrived and stuck his head in the door and exclaimed, "I've never been in the nurses quarters before. Are you the prisoner I am supposed to get a Class A uniform for?" Without even thinking I responded, "I'm not a prisoner, I'm an American soldier, and looking at your sleeve, I outrank you by two stripes. Is that clear?" The MP reacted to this outburst with half a statement and half a question, "Suppose you are an American Sergeant, why are you here in the nurses quarters and why am I supposed to guard you?" "Answering your two questions would take two days. We don't have that long. I am supposed to be dressed in a Class A uniform by 1400 hours because a full Colonel from 1st Army Headquarters is going to be here and debrief me. How do you propose we proceed from here, you are the one with the gun."

This PFC was all business as he called his superiors and got instructions. He then arranged for a pair of long johns, heavy socks, overshoes, and some outer clothing to be delivered to the nurses quarters. He knew I would need them to keep warm during the trip to the supply building. That task complete, he relaxed and sat in a chair between me and the door as we waited for the clothing to arrive. There was still some hot coffee in the thermos container left over from breakfast. To break the ice with my guard, I asked him to wash Lieutenant Davila's cup and pour himself a fresh cup of coffee. When he returned from washing the cup in the bathroom, I asked him to pour coffee in mine. He thought this was a nice deal and as the coffee warmed our souls, he told me about his duties, and how boring they were, but he was quick to admit being bored was better than getting shot at. This brought him around to asking about my legs and feet. With my permission he came to the bed, and asked me how I got wounded. This question allowed me to tell him of my latest combat experiences at Parker's Cross Roads. He then advised me 'The Gods of War' now favored the Allies and plans to move this hospital to the rear had been cancelled. The Allied Air Force completely dominated the skies over Belgium, and more German POWs were arriving at the compound daily.

My temporary clothing finally arrived, delivered by an American medic who helped me out of bed and into the warm clothes. We had no trouble dressing the top part of my body, but getting the long johns over my sore legs and feet was difficult and painful. The process of placing my feet into the over sized socks was almost impossible. Finally the medic wrapped my legs and feet in a GI blanket and helped me into a wheel chair. I felt like royalty as the medic and MP gently pushed me down the corridor of the nurses quarters, through the administration office, and out to the awaiting jeep. Luckily the jeep was equipped with side panels for warmth. My guard climbed into the rear seat and the medic and driver gently lifted me into the front passenger seat. With the side panels closed and the heater going, the ride to the supply building was quite comfortable. At the supply building my legs and feet got their first real test because there was no wheel chair available there. With GIs supporting me under both arms, I walked to a nice heated room where I was properly fitted with not one but two Class A uniforms. Before I knew what was happening, a German POW took one of the Class A uniforms and left the room. By the time the rest of my gear was issued, folded, and placed into a duffle bag, the POW returned with a professionally pressed uniform replete with creases that would pass any white glove inspection.

When the supply people finished issuing my new clothing it was time for the noon meal. I accepted the Supply Sergeant's gracious offer to take me to their mess hall. The meal was nicely prepared, I enjoyed the comradery, and did not feel out of place because I was now dressed in an American uniform. After the noon meal, I returned to the supply building with the Supply Sergeant who called for a jeep to come pick me up and deliver me back to the administration building. Then we hit a snag that made me realize why I hated the army. The Supply Sergeant wanted me to sign a requisition form for the clothing I had just received. We argued about how I should sign the form for several minutes, then I gave in to army red tape and signed the name of a friend who had been killed in action and made up an army serial number to go with his name. When I left the supply building the triumphant Supply Sergeant looked at though he had just won the battle of the Alamo.

Battle of the Bulge—Day 12
Medical Compound for Prisoners of War
Administration Building—The Debriefing
27 December 1944—1400 Hours

During the debriefing session, Colonel Williams kept asking me the same questions over and over again. It was obvious he was trying to trip me up, much the same way the German SS Major Rupp had done. The main difference being that Colonel Williams did not pull the 'good guy, bad guy' routine on me like the German Major did. The Colonel was pretty straight down the middle all the time. I could tell he had conducted interviews of this nature many times before, and he was quite good at it.

At the end of the lengthy debriefing session, Colonel Williams let down his guard and the debriefing turned more-or-less into a conversation between two soldiers. He told me the holding action on highway N-15 at Baraque de Fraiture was now called the Battle for Parker's Crossroads in honor of Major Parker. He seemed surprised when I told him I was aware of that fact. The Colonel also told me of the German massacre of American troops at a village named Malmedy. This atrocity was committed by members of a panzer unit from the *11th German SS-Panzerkorps* about the time I was captured only a few miles away. This information explained why such a high ranking intelligence officer was interested in someone like me, as my experience was quite different from those GIs who were murdered at Malmedy.

This less formal atmosphere gave me the opportunity to ask about my future and tell the Colonel I was tired of being kept in the dark. Colonel Williams looked at the floor, shook his head, and admitted we were all in the dark right now. He then asked me what I wanted to know. This opened the door for me and I monopolized the conversation. I told him I was being well treated, but I wanted to get my feet fixed so I could wear combat boots again and rejoin my outfit. I wanted to find out what happened to our senior officers in the 589th Field Artillery Battalion, Lt. Colonel Kelly, Major Goldstein, Major Parker, my friends, and I was tired of being treated like a German spy. I would also like to know if he thought I was an American soldier born in Cocoa, Florida, or a *Swinehunt* born in Dusseldorf, Germany?

This mild outburst caught the Colonel off guard, but he handled it well. He told me he knew I was an American soldier, a soldier who had just been through a little personal hell, but I should thank God that I had survived, was here, and being well cared for. I was one of the fortunate ones! He told me the compound doctor had advised him I would be able to wear boots in a few days provided I did not develop an infection. A member of his staff had been able to locate the headquarters of the 589th Field Artillery Battalion. It is temporarily located in Chateau de XHOS-TAVIER, Belgium. The same officer talked with a Staff Sergeant Aspinwall and then a Captain Huxel, who both said they personally knew you and were glad you were alive As I paused to allow this information to sink in, Colonel Williams asked if his answers addressed my problems. It took a few moments for his information and question to sink in. When they finally did sink in, I told Colonel Williams I was happy to hear the Major and the Captain escaped from the cross roads safely, and was really glad to hear the good news about my friend Francis Aspinwall as I had not seen him since 19 December.

"In answer to your question Colonel, yes I have one more thing that bothers me. Most people here refer to me as 'the patient.' I would like to be addressed as Sergeant Pierson because that is who and what I am. If you can clarify this situation for me, I would appreciate it." Before giving me a direct answer the Colonel asked me a question, "I have heard several of the nurses and male medics refer to you as 'Randy,' does that bother you?" "No sir, because that is my nick-name and none of these people think I am a German spy." The Colonel admitted this situation gave him a problem also, however he would informally notify the Provost Marshal, the Doctor, and the Head Nurse that I would be declared an American Serviceman shortly. He added, however, due to army policy, I would be moved to another medical facility when he officially changed my status from foe to friendly. He asked if I wanted to be moved or stay here until my feet healed and I was able to return to my unit. He explained the timing of this official act would have to be made depending on my wishes. I reassured him I was being well treated here and would like to remain here until I could be released to my unit providing my current arrangements were approved by Major Hartman and did not inconvenience Lieutenants Davila and Prell. The Colonel reinforced the fact that Major Hartman would have the final 'say' in this decision. He smiled and admitted he did find my living arrangements to be most unique.

Battle of the Bulge — Day 12
Medical Compound for Prisoners of War
American Army Nurses Quarters
27 December 1944 — 1700 Hours

My feelings were mixed — part joy, sorrow, and relief. I didn't know which emotion dominated my feelings while I carefully hung my new uniform and changed back into the stupid hospital gown. But I definitely felt I had gained ground in my battle to become an American GI again. Lying there in Lieutenant Davila's bed, thinking about the meeting with Colonel Williams made me feel better, much better. Missing pieces were finally beginning to fall into place. I was so engrossed in thought I was surprised to see Lieutenant Prell as she walked through the door. She looked pooped and went directly to her locker, grabbed her bathrobe and a towel, pulled her shirt tail out of her uniform waist band, removed her bra from under her shirt, threw the bra on a chair, entered the latrine and shut the door. Almost immediately I heard the shower water running. A few minutes later Susan emerged from her bath in an oversized bathrobe, her wet hair wrapped in a towel, and clutching her outer garments, which she also threw on a chair. She carefully eased herself onto her bed, stretched like a cat, let out a sigh of relief, acknowledged me with a "Hi Randy" and fell fast asleep.

Activities involved in the daily processing of ever increasing numbers of enemy prisoners was definitely taking its toll on Susan.

When I was certain Susan was sleeping soundly, I hobbled the short distance to her side of the room. Although the room was not cold, it was not warm either. She looked like a dainty and exquisite Dresden Doll lying in her bed, but her hair was still wet and it wasn't difficult to see she had nothing on under her bathrobe. I knew she would get cold after the warmth of the hot shower diminished. As gently as I could, I rolled her to one side of the bed, freeing the blankets in the process. Then rolled her onto her back, straightened out her bathrobe, and then completely covered her with blankets. Standing there, looking at this strikingly beautiful young woman, moved my mind from the horrors I had recently experienced to the memories of more pleasant things I had enjoyed prior to combat. Looking at Susan was similar to viewing a gorgeous painting. While thinking about Susan and Anne Marie, I started wondering if the three of us would survive the war, and if so, what experiences lay ahead. I carried these thoughts with me as I returned to Anne Marie's bed. Once in bed, my thoughts turned to the good news Colonel Williams had given me, and I too fell into a deep and peaceful sleep.

Battle of the Bulge – Day 13
Medical Compound for Prisoners of War
American Army Nurses Quarters – Day of Departure
28 December 1944 – 1100 Hours

Lots of water had gone over the dam since the evening meal last night. This morning had been exciting and busy. Before breakfast Major Hartman had advised me the doctor had given his permission for me to return to the 589th Field Artillery Battalion, but with certain restrictions. Since the Battalion Commander, now Major Goldstein, knew where I was located and my status, the Battalion Daily Status Report had been changed to reflect I was now Wounded In Action (WIA) instead of Missing In Action (MIA), making the issue of whether I was German or American moot. My new commanding officer felt I should return to Headquarters Battery as soon as I was able to travel.

The compound doctor did not feel my bandaged feet was sufficient reason to keep me from making the trip, but insisted that I report-in to a medical officer immediately upon arriving at my unit. This decision, although sudden, seemed reasonable to all concerned. A driver and vehicle from the 589th FA was scheduled to pickup me and my belongings about noon today.

When I asked Major Hartman if she knew where the 589th FA was billeted, she told me she had checked a map and discovered the Chateau de XHOS-TAVIER was located near the small village of Hody, Belgium, some 30 miles from our present location and thought the trip would not be too straining. The Major also advised me to check with Lieutenant Davila just before I left because she would have several medications I would have to take with me, medication a normal Battalion Aid Station would not stock. Of course I had already planned to see Anne Marie before I left, and readily agreed to the Major's instructions. Finally Major Hartman reminded me I must be cleared by the Administrative Officer before I could leave the compound, and she assumed the 589th FA driver would meet me at the main gate. All this information was almost too good to be true.

In the room, busy packing, thinking about seeing my buddies again, and having mixed emotions about leaving my newly made friends, I was not aware when Anne Marie entered the room. I turned in surprise when she announced, "Well, this is the big day, the one you have been waiting for. My don't you look sharp in a uniform. Its funny, we've been roommates for a couple of days now and this is the first time I have seen you in a uniform." Even though I was feeling blue about leaving, I could not ignore this opportunity, "Anne Marie, I dressed for the occasion, I thought it was time for you and Susan to see me with clothes on."

A disgusted look came over her face as she spoke, "Randy – or should I address you as Sergeant Pierson? Major Hartman asked me to deliver this carton of medications to you – along with your medical records – and to instruct you to report to your Battalion Medical Officer immediately after you arrive at your destination." My blank stare caused her to continue, "Damn it Randy, I mean it! This is important! I want you to promise me you will follow my instructions." More than slightly shaken by her display of anger, I assured her, "Anne Marie, I promise I will check in with the medics the first opportunity I get and faithfully promise to take my medicine. However I doubt we have a Battalion Medical Officer any more. The senior medic will probably be a Staff Sergeant who will take good care of me."

"Another thing Randy, I have to say goodbye now, we are awfully busy. Damn it, I hate to have to say goodbye this way!" Anne Marie tilted her beautiful face upward with tears in her enchanting brown eyes. She was no longer mad, she was now silently sad, and it was breaking my heart. She moved forward and snuggled close with her arms around my waist. During a lingering embrace our thighs touched and her firm breasts pressed against my chest. My hands enjoyed the pleasant contours of her muscular back and wonderfully rounded hips. As I started to tell her my deep feelings toward her, she pulled away quickly and without a word, abruptly left the room.

My departure from the hospital was not developing the way I had anticipated, so I forced myself to put my thoughts of Anne Marie, Susan, and Major Hartman behind me and tried to concentrate on the future. The MP stationed as a guard in the nurses quarters was very helpful when it came time for me to leave for the Administration Office. He summoned a vehicle and a male medic loaded my duffel bag into the back of the closed jeep. The MP driving the jeep was friendly and extremely helpful too. He accompanied me into the Administrative Office and helped me complete the necessary paper work to clear the compound. This first task now complete, the MP driver suggested we go to the main gate of the compound to wait for my transportation, and make arrangements with the Sergeant-of-the-Guard to allow me to wait in the warmth of the guard shack until the 589th FA vehicle arrived to return me to my unit.

The guard shack was not a large building, but it was warm and comfortable against the inclement weather. While talking with the off-duty MPs, I found they were interested in my brief, but violent, combat experience. This gave me the opportunity to relax and tell some 'war stories'. The MPs told me the Americans were finally starting to push toward the east again, and in the process we were inflicting severe damage to the retreating German forces. All the off-duty guards were aware of the pounding the 106th Infantry Division took during the early days of the Battle of the Bulge. Time passed quickly and suddenly the problem of getting as midday meal became a reality. Since I had officially become just another Non-Com in the US Army, the Sergeant-of-the-Guard invited me to eat with him at the NCO Mess. The ease of solving this problem reminded me how great it was to be a Sergeant, and to be back in the American Army. The group in the guard house was deep in conversation discussing the benefits of having two female nurses as roommates when a jeep from the 589th FA stopped at the main gate. My heart skipped a beat when I saw the 589th FA Bn markings on the front bumper.

An American soldier, dressed in combat fatigues and a heavy woolen overcoat, got out to the driver's side of the jeep when he was challenged by the MPs on duty at the entrance to the compound. I don't know who I expected to come for me, but I could not believe my eyes. The tall slim soldier was Staff Sergeant Francis Aspinwall, from Headquarters Battery. We had not seen each other since the morning of 19 December when we had been sent to establish roadblocks at different locations. I had no reason to believe he had survived. With a thankful heart, I hobbled out into the cold and yelled a greeting to Francis. With a large grin on his face he walked to the guard shack, where we met and embraced, as only close friends do, both laughing with joy. In a joking manner, Francis told the smiling group of MPs, "I'm Staff Sergeant Francis Aspinwall, I have come to claim the prisoner."

The noon meal at the hospital NCO mess was a great reunion for us! We enjoyed the comradery and the well prepared meal, but as much as we wanted to linger and talk, Francis kept reminding me we had some pretty rough country to go through which was not completely cleared of enemy troops. He emphasized the importance of getting back to the 589th Battalion Headquarters before dark.

Outside the mess, with all four wheels spinning and a toot of the horn, we exited the main gate and headed south toward the Chateau. The weather was clear and cold, but the roads were rough and covered with rutted snow and patches of glazed ice. Fortunately for me, Francs had mounted the canvas side curtains on the jeep and the heater worked fine. In our heavy winter clothes we were comparatively comfortable. Still elated, we talked the entire trip. The only sobering part of the journey was the existence of two 45-caliber Thompson sub-machine guns Francis had placed in the jeep, just in case we encountered trouble along the way.

Battle of the Bulge — Day 13
The Chateau de XHOS-TAVIER, near Hody, Belgium
28 December 1944 — 1630 Hours

The trip from the hospital compound to the Chateau was rough and slow, but the time passed swiftly in conversation between friends trying to get 'caught up', consequently it was difficult to realize the thirty mile trip had taken three hours. During the trip, Francis tried to explain the layout of the Chateau and our living arrangements there. However, when we pulled into the private drive leading to the Chateau itself, I was not prepared for what I was about to see. The Chateau was huge and magnificent!. Francis said it had taken more than three hundred years to build. The only other building of this nature I had ever inspected up close was the Biltmore Estates near Ashville, North Carolina. I had visited the Biltmore Estates in the late 1930s as a tourist and remembered the main residence building as large and beautiful. However, the Biltmore Estates could not compare with the old European splendor of this enormous Chateau. The use of this imposing orange-gray stone structure to house our battalion had been volunteered by the Countess Jacqueline d'Oultremont and her husband, the Count Etienne d'Oultremont. Members of the d'Oultremont family were noble born Belgians and Count Etienne was an industrialist and a farmer with vast resources. The Battalion was extremely lucks to have such a persuasive commanding officer as Major Goldstein, who personally persuaded the d'Oultremont family to become our hosts for several weeks while we regrouped and nursed our wounds.

The Chateau was 'U' shaped, and the closed portion of the 'U' consisted of the stately 'Manor Building', the first portion of the Chateau to be constructed. This portion of the Chateau housed the d'Oultremont family, Major Goldstein, and his only remaining officer, Captain Huxel. The only enlisted man authorized to enter that portion of the Chateau on a daily basis was Staff Sergeant Francis Aspinwall, who had inherited the job of Battalion Adjutant, an assignment normally handled by a commissioned officer or a warrant officer. The sides of the 'U', which were added later, were designed to house the required domestic servants and field hands, along with assorted livestock and carriages.

The open end of the courtyard had been enclosed with an imposing stone wall, including a double gate constructed of elaborate wrought iron. When both gates were open, the entrance to the Belgian block paved courtyard was large enough accommodate any army vehicle, and the courtyard was large enough to park several GMC 2 1/2 ton trucks.

Less than 100 members of the 589th were billeted in and around the Chateau XHOS. These men were all that was left of a once proud, well trained, and well equipped field artillery battalion of some 500 men. At Francis Aspinwall's insistence, I decided to room with him. His living quarters, while Spartan, were located on the first floor and had interior access to office space setup for Major Goldstein and Captain Huxel in the 'Manor House' portion of the Chateau. Our living quarters were comfortable and far above average of those occupied by the other enlisted men. We had running water and heat from a military gasoline type heater, which also provided us a source of hot water for bathing, shaving, and making hot coffee. However living with Francis presented personal problems for me, because he was constantly on call and when the officers wanted him and could not locate him, they knew where to find me. My first night at the Chateau was filled with conversation with Francis and a couple of non-coms. Every one present wanted to hear my version of the Battle for Parker's Crossroads. I, in turn, was anxious to learn from them what had happened to my buddies and what was going to happen to the 589th. There were two scenarios concerning the battalion. One: It would be refilled with replacements, re-equipped , and returned to battle, and two: It would be disbanded and all men available for duty would be sent to other field artillery units.

The conversation was filled with 'scuttle butt' and personal reservations about the outcome of the war. As the second bottle of Cognac started to disappear Francis asked our visitors to leave so I could get some much needed rest after a very tiring day. Although I had enjoyed the general 'bull session' I was glad when only Francis and I were able to sit on our bunks and talk uninterrupted. Francis poured one more Cognac night cap and as we sipped the warming liquid he confided in me the real story of what was in store for our friends and the 589th. This was the first official, yet to be announced, news I had heard concerning the battalion and it's men. Francis told me that orders had been cut to send Barney Alford and John Schaffner to the 592nd Field Artillery Battalion. This unit had formerly been the medium (155mm howitzer) artillery battalion in the 106th Infantry Division Artillery. It was now short handed, needed trained filler personnel, and had become part of the XVIII Airborne Corps Artillery. He continued, Dell Miller was destined to be assigned to the XVIII Airborne Corps Artillery Fire Direction Center. And last but not least, Francis told me I had been temporarily assigned to the Headquarters of the skeletal 589th Field Artillery Battalion until the medics declared me fit for full duty. After being examined by the medics tomorrow morning, I was to report to Staff Sergeant Francis Aspinwall at Battalion Headquarters to be advised of my new duties.

Francis asked if I had any more questions. When I said no, he turned out the Coleman lantern and said, "Good night." As I lay there in my bed roll, stretched out on my single bunk, in a warm, dry room, my concerns seemed to gradually drift away as the Cognac took effect. I now felt secure among my old friends and after some tough and frustrating experiences, I had found my way home at last.

17
Return to Active Duty

Battle of the Bulge—Day 14
The Chateau de XHOS-TAVIER
589th FA Battalion—A Different Kind of Life
29 December 1944

S taff Sergeant Francis Aspinwall broke my sound sleep by raising and then dropping the foot of my bunk on the hard stone floor. As I fought away the webs of sleep from my foggy brain I exclaimed, "What in the hell is going on?"

"Sergeant Pierson, if you want some deliciously scrambled dried eggs, soggy toast, and boiling hot coffee, you had better shake a leg, breakfast will be served in the courtyard in about thirty minutes."

"Francis, in the hospital, they served me breakfast in bed."

"Forget it Randy, you are back in the army now. However, if you don't feel like going to the mess truck, I'll have someone bring your breakfast here. You have to get up and go to the medics anyway. Maybe it will do you good to get back in the swing of things. I've got to check in with Captain Huxel and get my day lined up before I go to breakfast. After you get your evaluation from the medics come to my office and we'll find out what the Captain has planned for you. OK?"

"Thanks for getting me up Francis. I haven't had much of a routine for a couple of weeks now. No time like the present to 'bite the bullet.' I think I can handle this morning OK. Don't worry about ole Randy, I'll make it."

Getting dressed was not too difficult. I added a second pair of heavy socks to the pair I had slept in, put on one of my new woolen OD uniforms and covered it with a set of fatigues and a field jacket, and then slowly placed my feet into a large pair of overshoes. My feet felt much better this morning, but I anticipated they would start hurting again the minute they got cold. The mess truck was parked very close to the location of our room. As I approached the mess truck, the mess sergeant came to greet me. After a pleasant exchange he led me back into the building to the room the men were using as a dining room, and told me one of the KPs would bring me my breakfast there. The description Francis gave me concerning the morning meal was a joke. The meal was expertly prepared and I was enjoying myself when Francis entered the dining room and sat down beside me. Most of the conversation changed when Francis sat at our table. Everyone was pumping him for information that he could not give them. It was only then that I realized I had been made privileged to information that no one else had. This made me realize what confidence Francis had in me. It was a good feeling!

The medics had established their Aid Station in a tent outside, but adjacent to, the Belgian block courtyard. I was correct when I had told Anne Mare Davila that we would probably not have a Battalion Medical Officer. I never learned what happened to the medical detachment, but a Staff Sergeant, not known by me, was the senior medic there. He accepted my medical records and then looked at the medication Major Hartman had given me, paused as if in thought, then asked me to get on the examination table while he and another medic removed my overshoes, socks, and bandages, so he could look at my feet. Other than a few small spots where the bandaging stuck to my skin, this process went smoothly and without pain. The Staff Sergeant told me he fully agreed with the medication Major Hartman had given me, and said he would try to get some more just in cans I needed it later. He stated my feet were healing nicely, but he estimated it would take several days for the swelling to get back to normal and I could not wear combat boots until that happened, and of course, as long as I could not wear boots, I could not be placed back on full duty. He said he would write a note to Captain Huxel to that effect. In the meantime, unless something drastic happened, he wanted to see me every other day, to wash, re-medicate, and re-bandage my feet. He suggested I raise my feet to chest level as much as possible, and of course stay out of the cold. I nodded my agreement and the Staff Sergeant began writing his evaluation for Captain Huxel.

The remainder of the day at the Chateau I hobbled around the estate looking at the outbuildings and made friends with two Belgian youngsters, Victor and Marie Collenge, children of the caretaker of the d'Oultremont estate. I did not know it at the time, but my friendship with the Collenge family would last for many years after the war. Louis Collenge was the general manager of the enormous estate surrounding the Chateau de XHOS-TAVIER. His employer, the Count d'Oultremont, spent most of his time in the other homes he owned in Brussels and Liege. Louis was a fiercely loyal Belgian who had fought honorably, as a rifleman against the 'Boche', during WWI. In addition to Victor and Marie, Louis and Madame Collenge had a beautiful fifteen year old daughter, Alice, who was enrolled in a private school in nearby Hody. Their fourth child was an older son named Eugene, who was old enough to serve in the military, however, his father had arranged for Eugene to attend school in England for the duration of the war. Thus he was exempt from conscription into the Belgian military, and out of the grasp of the German army. One of the great pleasures I experienced during this period of my life occurred the few days I spent with Louis, Madame Alice, and their mischievous children, Victor and Marie. Victor and his sister Marie were a contrast in both looks and personalities. Victor was bashful and large for his age, a pre-teenager who was already performing men's work with his father, while Marie was gregarious and small for her age, causing everyone to call her 'Petite Marie.'

My personal relationship started with Madame Collenge during my initial exploration of the d'Oultremont estate. At first she was concerned with the immediate attraction between Victor, Marie and me, and the rough and tumble play we engaged in. After she realized most of the 'rough housing' was caused by her children and not me, and I was obviously not going to hurt them, she too became more friendly. Once she invited me into their huge combination family kitchen, dinning room, and sitting room, we communicated very poorly as she spoke no English and I understood only a few phrases of French, but she offered me some warm fresh milk and a Belgian pastry, which I consumed with relish. On the walk back to the Chateau I decided to go by the mess hall and see what was available there. Perhaps I would be able to trade some of the canned army rations for fresh food which seemed to be available to the Collenge family. The mess sergeant thought this was a super idea, and he quickly assembled quite an assortment of canned rations such as: canned milk, powdered eggs, coffee, sugar, jellies and preserves, shortening, and even canned meat. The mess sergeant then loaded these 'goodies' into the back of a jeep and provided me with a driver who had studied French in high school. When the driver and I delivered this cache of canned goods to Madame

Collenge she could not believe her good luck. After accepting the army rations she made it clear to the French speaking driver that her husband Louis would respond by supplying the mess sergeant with fresh milk, eggs, poultry, fresh meat, and even though it was the dead of winter, they would share the contents of their well stocked root cellar with us. I quickly became the go-between and brokered scarce food items between the Collenge family and our Mess Sergeant. This was a 'win-win' situation. Madame Collenge obtained preserved food which could be stored almost indefinitely, and the men of the battalion received fresh food which was impossible to obtain through the normal supply channels. Madame Collenge followed us out to the empty jeep, and through the driver, made it perfectly clear that we were invited to have the evening meal with her and her family. I immediately accepted the invitation, but the French speaking driver declined, muttering that he was on guard duty that night and could not be relieved from that duty.

When I arrived for this first formal visit, Marie and Victor literally tackled me to the floor searching my many pockets to find the candy bars and chewing gum I had promised to bring. Chocolate had been in short supply for years in rural Belgium. To satisfy one of my passions, I brought Madame Collenge flour, shortening , sugar, and canned fruit. In return, she baked me the most delicious Belgian pastry I had ever eaten. After finishing this bountiful meal, I helped Madame Collenge tuck Victor and Petite Marie into their huge feather bed and faithfully promised to see them again tomorrow. When the Madam and I returned to the huge country kitchen I noticed Louis had arranged two comfortable chairs in front of the combination heating and cooking stove. As I started to help Madame Collenge remove food, silver, and soiled dishes from the dining table, both Louis and Madame Collenge protested loudly and Louis motioned for me to take a chair in front of the stove with him. Madame Collenge then produced a silver tray containing two crystal glasses and a bottle of Napoleon Cognac. As Louis was pouring the Cognac, I reached into my jacket pocket and withdrew two fresh cigars. For the remainder of the evening, Louis and I conversed in a mixture of English, German, and French, but the most effective means of communication was sign language and the comradery between two 'ole warriors' who had battled the 'Bosch' and survived.

When Louis began to yawn, either from the effect of the superb Cognac, or fatigue caused by a hard days work, I decided it was time to quit telling 'war stories from the two great wars' and leave. With a *'Merci'* and *'Bon Soire'* I left the caretaker's home and began walking the short distance to the Chateau in the dark. I don't know whether it was the wonderful food, the fine Cognac, the good cigars, the kindness of the Collenge family, the temporary respite from danger, or a combination of these factors which made me feel happy. Slipping on the icy, uneven road leading to the Chateau I realized my feet didn't hurt very much. As I approached the Chateau in the dark, the sentry on duty at the gates behind the Chateau challenged me, and asked, "Is everything OK Sergeant Pierson?" I thought about how lucky I was to be alive, among friends, and without pain, and reassured the sentry, "Ole buddy, things couldn't be better!"

In our quarters Francis was eager to talk and began telling me the story behind the death of an 8th Air Force Brigadier General named Frederick W. Castle, Commanding General of the 4th Combat Bombardment Wing. The name didn't mean anything to me but I was not sleepy, so I decided to humor Francis and listen to his story. It seems that

Brigadier General Castle was a well respected and rising star in the Air Force. When the weather cleared on 24 December, he led the largest single bombing raid ever mounted in any war. He commanded 2,034 bombers and

926 fighter escorts on this Christmas Eve raid designed to support the hard pressed ground forces involved in opposing the German Ardennes Offensive. While flying over the village of Fraiture, Belgium, his B-17G named the 'Treble Four' was attacked by several German Me-109 fighters and shot down. This fact attracted my attention, our battle for Parker's Crossroads at Baraque de Fraiture was only a couple of miles from the village of Fraiture, and although I had just escaped from the guards of the 2nd SS Panzer Division on Christmas Eve day, I vividly remembered the vast number of allied aircraft in the air that day. The multitude of white contrails left by the aircraft beautifully contrasted with the clear blue sky, creating an unforgettable picture in my mind.

Apparently Staff Sergeant Aspinwall realized he had caught my attention and continued his story by describing the appearance of two 8th Air Force Majors who appeared unexpected on 26 December with a written authorization signed by the Allied Supreme Commander, General Dwight D. Eisenhower to extend help, of any kind requested, by these officers in the performance of their duties. At the Air Force Officers initial meeting with Major Goldstein, they requested the exclusive use of one of the L-4 Liaison planes which belonged to the 589th FA Bn. This request was granted, and arrangements made for one of the Air Force officers to fly the aircraft from the Belgian airfield where it was now located. The second request was not so straightforward. They also wanted to make the Chateau their base of operations and install vital communications equipment here, and of course they would need to billet the ground crew personnel necessary to service the aircraft and operate the communications equipment. Major Goldstein stated we were 'merely guests here' and he would have to obtain permission from the owner before he could grant these requests. This answer surprised the Air Force officers because they had assumed the US Army had requisitioned the Chateau and controlled its use. However, within a few hours the Air Force officers were satisfied when the gracious Countess Jacqueline agreed to temporarily house the Air Force personnel. Almost simultaneously, the 589th L-4 aircraft, flown by the Air Force Major, landed in the pasture in front of the Chateau. According to Francis and Victor Collenge, who witnessed the landing, it was perfect. But upon examination of the landing area, the Air Force Major decided a fence across the pasture would have to be removed to provide enough runway space to insure a safe takeoff.

Young Victor was fascinated by the American airplane and displayed his maturity by explaining to Staff Sergeant Aspinwall in French that he and his father Louis could remove the fence. Francis gave this information to the pilot, who shook his head in amazement that a youngster would accommodate his request. Once the fence was removed and fuel made available, the two Air Force Pilots started making over-flights of the area, looking for downed B-17 parts. Once parts were located from the air, their locations were recorded and the Air Force officers required armed ground forces from Major Goldstein to search and identify bomber numbers and collect body parts for examination. Although he knew ground search activity was necessary, it gave Major Goldstein problems. He was trying to reorganize a Field Artillery Battalion, obtain trained filler personnel, form a cadre from his wounded and worn-out people, requisition new equipment, and could not spare any of his limited resources . When he resisted the request for people, it became necessary for the lead Air Force officer to explain the importance of his mission to our Commanding Officer.

The American high command had determined it was absolutely necessary to determine that General Castle was alive and captured by the enemy, or was as they suspected, killed in action. His vast personal knowledge of the operations of the 8th Air Force was too important to fall into the hands of the enemy. If they determined this had happened, most of the strategic objectives of the 8th Air Force would have to be changed. Of course, if General Castle had perished in the B-17 crash, this secret information would be safe. Under the circumstances, almost all of the 589th enlisted men had been engaged in this ground search. Pieces of the General's B-17 had been located and verified, and identifying body parts had been collected and flown to England, which later confirmed the fact that General Castle was one of the five airmen killed in this disaster.

Francis seemed to have lost some of his momentum at the end of his story, and I had definitely lost interest in the demise of General Castle. No disrespect was meant, but the death of the General was not as important to me as the recent loss of my close friends. The day had been quite fatiguing and both Francis and I were asleep within minutes after my close friend doused the light.

Battle of the Bulge—Day 15
The Chateau de XHOS-TAVIER
Life at the Chateau—30 December 1944

Everything considered, life at the Chateau was pleasant for me. With the help of friends I established a more-or-less daily routine. Pre-breakfast chats in our bedroom with Staff Sergeant Aspinwall—bull sessions at breakfast with my buddies—trips to the Medics to feet and legs tended to, and lively discussions over drinks of canned grapefruit laced with medicinal alcohol—followed by a not so easy walk to the Collenge cottage. The weather was still extremely cold and nasty, but I was not assigned any out-of-doors activities consequently the weather was a minor distraction to me. My feet and legs were healing nicely, but I could not wear combat boots yet, and the overly large goulashes made walking difficult. My attitude was returning to normal, even though it was difficulty to shake the grief I felt for my lost friends. However, the horrors experienced during past battles still remained and were reinforced by the fact that I would fairly soon be recommitted to combat.

Upon arising Staff Sergeant Aspinwall advised me the Count d'Oultremont and his lovely wife were hosting a small New Year's Eve party tomorrow night and we were both invited. He added that Sergeants Miller and Alford were also invited and Major Goldstein expected us to be 'spit and polished', dressed in Class A uniforms, on our best behavior, and to exercise restraints while consuming intoxicating beverages.

My reaction to this invitation, with all of its restraints, was mixed. "Francis I haven't seen my Class A uniform since we left England. I don't even know where to start looking."

"If I were you Randy, I would start with the supply Sergeant, he has all our duffel bags stashed somewhere. The supply room is located in one of the stable rooms on the ground floor of the north wing."

"Well, that is good news, I hope I can find my gear. If I do find it, my uniform will look like wipe-cloths it will be so wrinkled. Then I have the problem of boots. I can't get my feet into boots yet. You know I am still wearing hospital slippers inside my overshoes."

"Why don't you try to locate your uniform? Maybe Madam Collenge will steam out the wrinkles for you. Take her a couple of cans of peaches or something?"

"Francis, one more thing, why did we four Sergeants get invited to the shindig tomorrow night?"

"Randy, I really don't know. Just count your blessings and don't look a gift horse in the mouth. The four of us are invited, I don't really know why, but we will be entertained like Nobility, it will be an interesting evening, and we will have fun. Now you go and find your uniform while I try to locate a pair of low cut dress shoes for you. What size do you wear?"

With our tasks clearly defined we finished dressing and went to breakfast.

Battle of the Bulge – Day 16
The Chateau de XHOS-TAVIER
New Year's Eve – 31 December 1944

Yesterday had been a busy, hectic, and frustrating day. With the help of the Supply Sergeant and a helper, they finally located my duffle bag which had been in storage since we occupied our first combat position in Germany. After a diligent search or the crushed and out of shape bag, we finally assembled a full dress uniform, complete with jacket, pants, socks, shirt, belt, overseas hat, and a tie. The problem was, everything was wrinkled and moldy. Madam Collenge had taken everything from me, along with a large can of strawberry jam, an assured me the uniform would be good as new by the middle of the afternoon today.

About 1600 hours I entered the Collenge cottage and could not believe what Madame Collenge had done to my uniform. As I gazed at the uniform hanging neatly on a clothes hanger I knew the good Lord in Heaven was still taking care of me. I don't understand how she spruced up my clothes but everything looked brand new. Even my overseas hat with the red 'Artillery Piping' looked great. She had polished my brass and the few ribbons I had earned were pinned neatly above my left breast pocket. With the exception of shoes, I would look like a sharp garrison soldier.

On the way back to the Chateau I thought, "Maybe no one will notice my hospital slippers." When I arrived at our room in the Chateau, I found Staff Sergeant Aspinwall busy putting his uniform together. Still working on his uniform, Francis glanced over his shoulder, pointed toward the foot of my bed, and asked, "Think you can get your feet into those low cuts?" Fortunately he had borrowed a pair of shoes which were several sizes larger than I normally wore. I took off my hospital slippers and gingerly inserted my feet into the glossy shined shoes. "Francis, you are a genius! My feet will fit into the shoes and they don't hurt much if I lace them loosely. Thanks a million buddy!"

At the appointed hour, Francis and I knocked on the front door of the Chateau. We were immediately admitted by a beautiful, tall, coiffed, young woman, dressed in formal evening attire, who offered her hand to Francis. He lifted her hand lightly and brushed it with his lips. Still holding her hand lightly he asked in his most dignified manner, "Countess, may I introduce my good friend Randolph Pierson?"

This gorgeous creature removed her hand, gracefully turned to face me, extended her hand to me and replied, "Of course you may, Francis."

Frankly I did not know what to say or do. This was a new experience for me. I said something like, "Hi, thanks for the invitation," as I shook her hand. Staff Sergeant Aspinwall was surprised when the Countess asked him what my friends called me. "Countess, we all call him Randy." She smiled and asked Francis, "What type reaction did the English girls display when he said he is Randy?" Both the Countess and Francis laughed a knowing laugh although Francis did not answer her question. This moment was a little embarrassing to me, consequently I was surprised when the Countess offered her arm and said, "Randy, if you will give me your arm, I will escort you to the Count's chambers."

During the walk through the hallways which led deep into the center of the Chateau, I was acutely aware of the full, firm, breast which constantly pressed against my left arm.

When we arrived, Major Goldstein and Captain Huxel were already enjoying the Count's hospitality. Slightly later the two other Non-Commissioned officers invited, Sergeants Dell Miller and Barney Alford, arrived. Of the four enlisted men attending this social function, only Staff Sergeant Aspinwall appeared too be at ease.

Count Etienne d'Oultremont was an impressive gentleman. He spoke English fluently, was extremely poised, was gregarious by nature, and perfectly at ease with his American guests. He had obviously come to the conclusion the Allies would win the conflict in Europe. For a young, recently wounded Non-Commissioned officer like me who expected to return to deadly combat again, I did not know whether the Count's point-of-view was correct or not.

During the evening, most of the conversation centered upon the transition of Europe from a war-torn economy to free trade again and the numerous opportunities available to those business men involved in this transition. The Count left no room for doubt, he planned to avail himself of these opportunities. At my level, all I could think of was going back into combat and getting killed. To ease the pain of this thought, I helped myself to his fine Cognac, enjoyed the plush comfort of is quarters, listened to his vision of the future and tried to understand his point-of-view.

I considered myself fortunate. Not many American servicemen were privileged to this type of economic thinking. The Count, unknowingly, had contributed to my education and maturity.

At the stroke of mid-night, we all stood, raised our champagne glasses, and toasted the New Year, an Allied victory, and prayed for peace on earth for all mankind.

This evening was truly a great experience for a young man like me!

De-Bulging "The Bulge"–Late January 1945, (top)
155 mm howitzers of the 592nd FA Bn delivered effective
harassing and interdiction fire nightly on enemy roads and
troop positions

All fighting was not behind the lines in Artillery positions,
(bottom two)

Sergeant Pierson, Forward Observer,
(bottom left), up front with the Infantry

2nd Lt. Pierson, Forward Observer,
(bottom right), up front with the
Infantry, still carrying an M-1 Rifle

18

De-Bulging the Battle of the Bulge

Battle of the Bulge—Day 20
Reassigned to the 592nd FA Bn—Battery C
Back to Combat—0900 Hours—4 January 1945

Captain Huxel sent his jeep to the Collenge cottage to pick me up and deliver me to his office in the Chateau. There he advised me the Medics had just cleared me for combat duty and the Captain thought orders would be cut to transfer me to a combat unit any day now. My intuition told me he had already seen a copy of my orders.

I had enjoyed life at the Chateau but knew this life would end. My feet were healing, I was wearing combat boots now, and walked with only a slight limp.

Later that day, orders from 106th Infantry Division Headquarters arrived, and Captain Huxel summoned me to his office to discuss the orders. I had been ordered to report to the Battery Commander, Battery C, 592nd Field Artillery Battalion assigned to XVIII Airborne Corps. The 592nd Field Artillery Battalion consisted of twelve 155mm Howitzers, considered 'Medium' Artillery, and had previously been a part of the 106th Infantry Division Artillery. With the collapse of the 106th Infantry Division, the 592nd Field Artillery Battalion had been transferred to XVIII Airborne Corps Artillery and was now actively assisting in 'De-bulging the Bulge.'

I read the orders and realized I was being assigned to a Firing Battery instead of Headquarters Battery as I had expected. I looked at Captain Huxel and exclaimed, "SHIT

I don't know anything about a Firing Battery! The Captain shrugged his shoulders as if to say, "Just the luck of the draw." He then showed me a copy of his orders which assigned him to XVIII Airborne Corps Artillery as Assistant S-3 in the 211th Artillery Group. He commented he would be working with Sergeant Miller in the Artillery Group Fire Direction Section. He added I would be in the same Firing Battery with Sergeant Barney Alford and Corporal John Schaffner, and commented, "This isn't too bad, you three ex-589th Field Artillery guys can look out for each other.

This information made me feel a little better, but I clouded-up again when he reminded me that we still had to 'Strike the Colors, Turn out the Lights, and Lock the Door' when we left because we were the last remaining members of the now disbanded 589th Field Artillery Battalion. Captain Huxel told me to pack my gear in the quarter-ton trailer hooked to his jeep, and invited me to have lunch with him at noon in the Chateau as he planned for us to leave at 1330 hours. He planned to drop me off at Battery C of the 592nd on his way to report in at Corps Headquarters. He seemed pleased when I asked him if I cold take some rations to the Collenge family and have my noon meal with them. The Captain gave me permission and advised me he would pick me and my gear up at 1330 hours at the Collenge cottage and he expected me to be ready.

At precisely 1330 a jeep horn sounded in the courtyard of the Collenge home. I left the house with my personal gear and placed it in the trailer. When I turned around, the entire Collenge family stood in the bitter weather watching me. I ran to the group and my farewell to Louis, Madam Collenge, Victor and Marie was a sad occasion. As I hugged them good-bye, tears welled in the eyes of Madam Collenge and her two small, bewildered children cried openly when their mother explained to them their friend Randy was going back to war. Seeing my eyes start to water, Captain Huxel ordered, "Get in the jeep Sergeant, we have a long trip ahead of us."

As the jeep cleared the Collenge court yard, I glanced back and what I saw almost ruptured my heart, I saw the old Belgian Infantryman Louis Collenge standing at rigid attention and saluting while Madam Collenge was hugging her crying children trying to comfort them. I returned the salute that Louis was giving us and turned forward and thanked the good Lord that Captain Huxel and his driver could not see the grief in my face.

(Battle of the Bulge—Day 20
Northwest of Stavelot, Belgium
C Battery—592nd Field Artillery Battalion
January 4, 1945—1600 Hours

When Captain Huxel dropped me off at C Battery, wished me good luck, and told me good bye, Charlie Battery was engaged in a fire mission. The noise was deafening and the ground shook as each howitzer hurled it's screaming missile of death toward the enemy. At the Command Post, the Battery Commander was absent and the Executive Officer, a First Lieutenant, was actively engaged in coordinating the mission. I observed the management of the mission and thought, at least they seem to know what they are doing. At the completion of the mission, as the Executive Officer was not noticeably busy, I reported in for duty, The XO was a pleasant officer, but he lost his cool when he found out I was a Technician Fourth Grade, a Headquarters type T/4, with no firing battery experience. He told me I was the last thing on earth he needed right now, and immediately placed me in the same category as receiving a shipment of mosquito netting in a snow storm when he had requisitioned 155mm projectiles. He made me feel utterly worthless. I was advised to get in the corner of the CP and stay there out of his way, until the old man returned.

Of course I took his advice and found a folding chair, placed it in an out-of-the-way corner, and thought to myself, "So much for a warm and cordial welcome to the 592nd!"

Two more fire missions were received and completed while I waited for my new Battery Commander to return. I had to admit to myself the missions were expertly handled. Between the fire missions the XO left the Command Post and went out to the howitzer sections, checking with the howitzer crews. then back to the CP, talking with the Fire Direction Center. Charlie Battery seemed to be under the control of a centralized fire control system rather than firing missions using its own forward observer. This fact was interesting to me as I had never before operated in a Corps Artillery mode.

During a lull in the firing and when the XO was absent, an enlisted man came into the CP, looked around, spoke to everyone, and then noticed me sitting in the corner. He came over and spoke to me in a friendly manner, "You are a new guy aren't you? I am Corporal Wiener. What is your name?" Without getting up, I answered his questions, "Yes, I am a new guy, my name is Pierson, but you can call me Sergeant Pierson."

Still cheerful, even though my answer was a little frosty and I was not wearing my Sergeant's stripes on my sleeve, Corporal Wiener continued the one-sided conversation, "Where are you from and what is your assignment here in Charlie Battery?"

Thus began my friendship with Corporal Jerome T. Wiener. The over-weight Corporal Wiener looked and acted like anything but a soldier. He had shaggy black hair, darting dark eyes, and smiled almost constantly. I could not comprehend how a person could look that happy under such miserable circumstances. He was obviously intelligent, inquisitive, and had an out-going personality. Corporal Wiener was as Jewish as they come, and made it plainly clear from the beginning, he hated Nazis!

During our conversation I found out Corporal Wiener was a radio technician and wanted to become a member of a forward observation crew so he could actually see Nazis die. He liked the Executive Officer even though he found the him to be childish at times. When I asked Corporal Wiener what his friends called him, he told me the GIs called him various things: Wiener, Hot Dog, Jew Boy, Jerry, and sometimes Wienersnitzel. He seemed pleased when I told him I preferred Jerry.

Jerry found out more about me during our first meeting than I knew about myself. The two things that interested him most was the fact I had killed an German SS Trooper with my boot knife, and the fact that I had actually adjusted artillery fire in combat. Our conversation was finally interrupted by the Battery Commander when he returned from a briefing at Battalion Headquarters. He and his XO had a brief pow-wow about plans to move the Battery forward to enable it to provide better support for an up-coming counter attack planned by the XVIII Airborne Corps. The XO was dispatched to coordinate the details of the impending move with the other battery officers and the senior non-coms.

Seizing the opportunity when the XO left the Command Post, Corporal Wiener quickly brought it to the attention of the Battery Commander, Captain Baxter, that he had a new Technician Fourth Grade in his unit. Acting a little surprised, but more calmly than the XO, Captain Baxter talked to me and developed a picture of my background and skills. When the Captain looked somewhat disappointed, Corporal Wiener advised him that I was a trained forward observer and had functioned a one in combat. The Captain's expression changed immediately as he explained that most of the 592nd Battalion forward observers had been lost during the early days of the Battle of the Bulge and the Battalion Commander was having a hard time finding qualified replacements. After our brief discussion, the Captain advised Jerry to bunk me with the communications section until he could work out a permanent assignment for me.

The communications bunker was solidly built and was covered with a thick, sturdy roof. It was relatively warm and comfortable with individual bunks constructed from empty wooden ammunition crates. Since the day shift of the radio and wire sections were on duty throughout the battery, Jerry and I shared the bunker with the off-duty men who were fast asleep. Jerry pointed out a bunk which contained no bedroll and suggested I bunk there until the Captain made up his mind about my permanent assignment. Jerry volunteered to go back to the CP, get my personal gear, and bring it to the bunker. This was a good idea which gave me to get orientated. Later when Jerry returned with my gear and I began sorting and storing it, Jerry watched and we talked.

After I got things settled, Jerry suggested we take our mess kits and walk up to the mess truck. There Jerry introduced me as a transfer into the unit and his new friend. I took some good natured ribbing about being Jewish, although I did not explain I was a Methodist. I guessed being a friend of Jerry's automatically made me Jewish to them. We enjoyed a well prepared meal. Nothing like I had been eating with the Collenge family, but not at all bad for GI chow. As luck would have it, we ran into Sergeant Barney Alford and Corporal John Schaffner at the mess truck. The reunion was lively. They had left the 589th FA Battalion several days before I did and this was our first opportunity to talk since then. They were both surprised to find me in a firing battery and asked me about my assignment. I told them about meeting the XO and the Battery Commander and that both officers seemed disappointed at getting a useless 'Headquarters Battery Type Technician Fourth Grade.'

Barney laughed and said he could understand how they felt. I explained that the Battery Commander was going to talk to the Battalion Commander about my experience as a forward observer, but for now, I was unassigned. Barney really reacted when I told him the Captain was going to talk to the Battalion Commander and asked me, "How in the Hell did the Battery Commander find out about you being qualified as a forward observer?" Corporal Wiener jumped into the conversation and proudly said, "Sergeant Pierson didn't tell Captain Baxter, I did." Now it was Corporal Schaffner's turn. He tore into Jerry, "You stupid bastard, why did you tell the old man that? What are you trying to do, get Randy killed? Just because you want to be a forward observer so you can watch Nazis die doesn't mean everyone is as crazy as you are! Did you tell the old man that Randy had knocked out a panzer with a bazooka too? Maybe the Battalion Commander will assign Randy to an anti-tank team, as an additional duty, when he is not up with the infantry killing Nazis as a forward observer. Wiener, won't you ever learn to keep your big, fucking, mouth shut? You dumb shit-head!"

This outburst was fairly typical of the way Corporal Schaffner handled things, and he made some very valid points. I did not relish the thought of serving with the infantry as a forward observer because forward observers had a short life expectancy during this kind of combat. Dieing at the tender age of 21 was not part of my career plan. However, Jerry looked so crushed by this criticism I thought I should say something and asked my foxhole buddy, Corporal Schaffner, to ease-off a little bit because Corporal Wiener meant no harm.

That night, as I lay on my bunk, snuggly wrapped in my bed roll, I wondered what kind of an assignment I would draw and how life would be in a firing battery. Gradually my thoughts drifted back to the College family and I wondered if Louis was sitting in his easy chair in front of his huge kitchen stove, drinking Cognac, smoking one of the cigars I left for him, and blowing graceful smoke rings which gradually disappeared as they rose over the heat of the ornate stove. I suddenly realized how much I missed the precocious Collenge children, with their carefree, frolicking ways, and their loving mother, Madam Collenge.

Gradually my body became warm and relaxed, and I fell asleep to the steady rhythm of the 155mm howitzers as they methodically fired their nightly interdiction missions deep into the enemy held territory.

Battle of the Bulge – Day 22
American XVIII Airborne Corps
592nd FA Battalion – C Battery – Returned to Combat
6 January 1945, 0530 Hours

Life in a firing battery never ends, it is a 24 hour a day operation. Well before dawn, Corporal Wiener was bending over my bunk, with a cheerful look on his face, urging me to wake-up and get out of my bedroll. He was fully clothed and meaningfully waving a mess kit in my face. When I told him I would catch breakfast a little later and tried to turn my back on him, he physically restrained me. Jerry was excited, really worked-up, as he sat on the side of my bunk while I dressed. He explained he had arranged for a driver to take us to an XVIII Airborne Corps forward observation post. The purpose of the trip was for me to fire some missions while one of the Corps Artillery Officers checked me out. This wasn't the best news I had received lately, however I tried to accept it philosophically because most things which happened lately were all beyond my control.

The driver and Jerry talked constantly during the entire trip to the Observation Post. The jeep slipped and skidded on what seemed to be a logging trail which ran through thick snow covered evergreens. Only the expert skills of the jeep driver kept us on the road and out of the ice covered ditch running along each side of the poorly defined path through the forest. At the base of a hill the jeep slowed to a stop in the snow and the driver indicated this was the end of the line for his passengers. Jerry jumped from the rear of the jeep, handed me a 30-caliber carbine, to supplement my 45-caliber hand gun, and my binoculars. Jerry then slung the straps to a portable radio pack over his left shoulder and carried his 30-caliber carbine in his right hand. He and the driver agreed upon a pick-up time, then motioned for me to follow him up the hill.

The unmistakable sounds of combat erupted periodically while we trudged toward the crest of the hill. As we approached our destination I began to observe signs of human habitation along the way, such as, empty C Ration cans and telephone lines partially buried in the snow. Near the summit, a guarded voice, from an unseen source, told us to be quiet and to keep our heads down. Before we actually reached the top of the hill, Jerry waved, in recognition, to a snow frosted GI with a weeks growth of beard on his face and nicotine stained teeth showing between split and badly chapped lips. The sight of this face was not pretty, but the way my face burned in the icy cold wind, I began to wish I had not shaved this morning. The grungy looking GI turned out to be Sergeant Harvey Holt, a friend of Jerry's, and the Non-Commissioned Officer (NCO) in charge of the forward observation crew now on duty.

Sergeant Holt, or 'HH' as Jerry called him, briefed us on the current situation. 'HH' told us everything in this sector seemed to be, more-or-less, in a holding pattern and not much was going on but routine patrol activity. He said the Forward Observer, Lieutenant Green, was expecting us and proceeded to lead us to the observation site on the crest of the hill.

The site seemed inadequate to me. It consisted of a very shallow slit-trench which connected with three fox holes. This network had been laboriously dug into solidly frozen ground and in my opinion offered only the barest protection to the FO crew. The fox holes were located in the edge of the tree line on the crest of the hill. These open holes offered no protection from incoming mortar or artillery shells which would burst overhead, with devastating effect, when striking the overhanging tree limbs. The entire site made me very uncomfortable.

Lieutenant Green did not look much better than Sergeant Holt. The Lieutenant's appearance did not inspire me, but as it turned out, he was a West Point graduate and a very competent Artillery Officer. After our introduction, Lieutenant Green asked me questions about my training and operational background. He then gave me a quick check on my map reading ability. Apparently satisfied, he told me the next fire mission was assigned to me. During this initial probing, Corporal Wiener faced us, smiling and nodding his OK to every answer I gave the Lieutenant. Even with the bitter cold and biting wind out of the north, the morning passed quickly. During the morning trial as a forward observer, I handled four fire missions successfully, but I was glad to hear our jeep transportation crunching at the bottom of the hill as it returned to take us back to Charley Battery.

Also hearing the jeep motor approaching the bottom of the hill, Sergeant Holt relieved us as observers. Lieutenant Green decided to stretch his legs and walked down the hill toward the jeep with us. On the way, the Lieutenant told me I had done fine and he would pass this information along to his superiors. He did not know what the outcome would be. In his opinion, there were two possible scenarios: one, I could become the NCO in charge of a forward observation team like 'HH' Holt, or two, I might become a forward observer myself. He did not predict which scenario would prevail. His only comment was, "An enlisted man should not be asked to perform an officer's job without being given the rank assigned to the job."

The jeep ride back to Charlie Battery was much like the ride to the observation post, rough, extremely cold, thankfully without incident. Again, Jerry and the jeep driver talked non-stop as I thought about my future assignment. At the Battery, Jerry quickly spread the word concerning my ability to read maps and conduct successful fire missions. After a warm dinner at the mess truck, Jerry and I went to the communications bunker to get warm. After a short talk session with some of the off duty radio men, I decided to take a nap. Jerry awakened me rudely from a sound sleep and advised me the old man wanted to see me in the command post as soon as possible. Still clothed, I stumbled the short distance to the command post bunker and reported to the Battery Commander. Captain Baxter engaged me in a 'father to son' type conversation. He congratulated me on my performance this morning on the observation post and said the decision had been made at a higher command to assign me as an XVIII Airborne Corps Artillery Forward Observer. He continued, I would be attached to his battery for administration, logistic support, and assignments to support Corps Infantry Regiments as required. This news surprised me, made me a little nervous, and spawned several questions. "Captain Baxter, who will be my NCO in charge? Who will supply me with technicians? When will my vehicles be ready?" "All in good time Sergeant. The most pressing issue now is who will be your NCO, what is your opinion?" "Yes Sir! Jerry Wiener can handle the job."

Corporal Wiener was ecstatic when I returned to the communications bunker and told him I was now a Forward Observer, and Captain Baxter had assigned him to me on my Forward Observer Team as the NCO in charge. Jerry, still smiling, dropped his head and said a prayer in Yiddish that I did not understand, raised his head, and asked if either of us got promoted. When I said "No," we started discussing people, equipment, and vehicle requirements. I suggested he talk to other Forward Observer team members and come up with concrete suggestions for forming, equipping, and training our own team. Our objective was to become operational as quickly as possible. The next few days, Jerry and I worked our butts off to accomplish this next to impossible task.

Battle of the Bulge—Day 29
Charlie Battery, 592nd Field Artillery Battalion—My New Assignment
Early Morning—13 January 1945

On 13 January the XVIII Airborne Corps mounted a major counter attack on the north western portion of the German penetration into Belgium. The purpose of this attack was to push almost due south through the town of Houffalize and on to St. Vith, thereby returning control of St. Vith to American forces. Once St. Vith was secure, then connect with another large American force attacking from the south. The troops involved in the XVIII Airborne Corps counter attack were the 30th and 75th Infantry Divisions and the 424th Infantry Regiment of the badly mauled 106th Infantry Division. The now battle weary 82nd Airborne Division was placed in general reserve for the counter attack.

Charlie Battery of the 592nd started receiving additional ammunition at our new, more advanced, position on 11 January in anticipation of increased artillery support required by the planned counter attack. The next day, Captain Baxter advised all Charlie Battery Non-Commissioned Officers to advise their men that the entire Battery was on 24 hour duty, until advised otherwise.

Early the morning of 13 January the pre-counter attack artillery preparations were awesome. Brilliant flashes from literally hundreds of artillery weapons, supporting the counter attack in our sector, turned the cold, crisp, blackness of night into day. The loud sounds of powerful muzzle blasts and exploding artillery shells reverberated through the hilly terrain which threw echoes back in our faces, thereby doubling the ear splitting explosions.

About noon on 14 January, Captain Baxter sent a runner to the number four howitzer, where Jerry and I were helping the number four howitzer crew. The runner told us the Captain wanted to see us, "Right Now!" Jerry and I left the howitzer position 'on the double.' Upon reaching the command post we reported as ordered and Captain Baxter wasted no time in asking, "Sergeant Pierson, do you think you and your crew are ready to man an observation post the first thing in the morning?" Before I could answer, Corporal Weiner replied, "Yes Sir!" The Captain looked at me, then looked at Jerry, shrugged his shoulders, shook his head in disbelief, and handed me a battle map encased in a plastic holder with certain locations marked in black on the holder. Sergeant Pierson, you are to relieve the FO Crew at outpost 'Dog' at 0600 hours tomorrow morning. You are to report to a Captain from XVIII Airborne Corps Artillery who will coordinate the withdrawal of the existing crew and furnish you with mission orders. I need to know your call sign and furnish it to Corps Fire Direction before you leave. Have you chosen a name yet?" Again Corporal Weiner answered the Captain's question, "Yes sir! Sergeant Pierson is Hotshot 1 and I am Hotshot 2." I hoped we would live up to our names.

The people assigned to the 'Hotshot Crew' were on duty all over the battery area when I asked Jerry to locate each crew member, and advise his temporary section chief that Captain Baxter had activated his Forward Observation crew and the CO wanted this man released as he was now assigned to Sergeant Pierson. When everyone was located, I told Jerry I wanted to meet with the entire crew at the communications bunker. We would then discuss how and when we would move out. The unanimous decision of the crew was that we should leave Charlie Battery this afternoon and spend the night as close to the location of 'Observation Post Dog' as we could safely get. This would make it easier for us to report in at 0600 hours. With Captain Baxter's permission, the seven of us left Charlie Battery at 1600 hours. Our two vehicles, and one trailer, were loaded with radio equipment, personal gear, and enough supplies for the crew to be self sufficient for two weeks. In our search to find a comfortable place to spend the night we got lucky. We bedded down near a Medical Aid Station which was already receiving wounded GI's.

Battle of the Bulge—Day 31
XVIII Airborne Corps—Overlooking Houffalize, Belgium
15 January 1945—0600 Hours

Jerry and I arrived at 'Dog OP' on foot, via a little used trail, from a level spot on the reverse of the hill. When almost to the summit of the hill, we were challenged by a weary GI on guard duty, who said we were expected. He also said he was glad to see us because he wanted to get back to the rear, get cleaned up, get something decent to eat, and added, he was tired of getting shot at. He seemed to feel better when I told him we would relieve him as quickly as possible. On the summit of the hill we were greeted by an officer who asked if we were members of the relieving forward observation party.

I answered his question with a "Yes Sir. This is Corporal Wiener and I am Sergeant Pierson." In response, the Captain asked, "Where is the Forward Observer?" Jerry pointed to me and said, "Captain, you are looking at him." This brought a puzzled look to the Captain's face, who exclaimed, "I'm a little surprised, most of the FO teams are headed up by a Commissioned Officer." Again Jerry confidently told the Captain, "Don't give it a second thought Captain," and added, "We'll get the job done!" "Well Corporal," the Captain added, "I hope you are right, supporting this attack is very important."

Feeling a little irritated by Jerry and his attitude, and a little left out of the conversation, I suggested to the Captain that I get Corporal Wiener busy setting up our gear so the existing crew could withdraw before it got too light. I gave Jerry a nod toward the vehicles and the Captain and I cautiously approached the observation post. Upon arriving there, the Captain advised the officer in charge to report to Corps Fire Direction Center that his OP would be off the air for a few minutes.

The process of setting up our own equipment, and relieving the old observation post crew went smoothly. Corporal Wiener promptly reestablished communications, by radio and telephone, with the XVIII Airborne Corps Fire Direction Center, and the Infantry Regiment we were directly supporting. The relieved crew left and the last thing the XVIII Airborne Corps Artillery Captain did was to tell me our mission was twofold: First, to be assigned fire missions from the Corps Fire Direction Center, and Second, to seek targets of opportunity and direct fire upon them as requested by the infantry. He then wished us Good Luck, and departed.

When I made the first inspection of the observation post, the guys and Jerry assured me that everything was satisfactory and in order. We were now on our own, and determined to prove our worth. As the morning progressed, I handled several fire missions requested by the infantry. Each mission was handled efficiently with a final report of 'Mission Accomplished,' from the infantry. To me, these reports established the fact that we were doing our job effectively.

Life on an observation post, particularly in this kind of weather, is not pleasant. Constant exposure to the elements, limited opportunity to move around, and the danger of being detected by the enemy, complicates efficiency and attitude. From our vantage point, Jerry and I were able to observe the movement of both friendly troops and the enemy. The battle below us could be likened to an ebb tide of water flowing into and out of a tidal basin. The enemy defense seemed to withdraw and then counter attack against the American forces. During the afternoon it was obvious our attack had slowed down and was losing momentum. We spent our first miserable night under the worst of conditions, faced with freezing sleet and not knowing whether or not the American Infantry could hold it's hard gained ground.

Fortunately for us, with the help of massive artillery fire support, the early morning American infantry attack of 16 January was furious and the American forces regained momentum, gained control of the battered town of Houffalize, and moved on to continue it's attack toward our objective of St. Vith.

We had performed well in our first assignment as a team. During this period of violently contested combat, we had gained the respect of the Infantry Commanders we supported, and the respect of Corps Artillery Officers with whom we worked. I'll admit my feelings were personal, I was proud of our initial performance and I was very proud of my team.

Battle of the Bulge — Day 33
Corps Artillery Observation Post — South of Houffalize, Belgium
17 January 1945

Late in the afternoon of 17 January I was ordered to 'Close Station' at our existing location. We moved through Houffalize and established an observation post South and East of town. This OP was manned and remained active for several days. We were there long enough to build some overhead cover which gave us protection from enemy mortar shell bursts and gave members of my team a place to escape from the wet and cold weather. During this period of time, the attacking American Infantry rested, regrouped, received re-supplies and organized for the remainder of it's attack to liberate St. Vith.

During these days, I learned more and more about Jerry. Corporal Weiner was a unique person, his own man! He was truly dedicated to me, his team, and dedicated to killing Nazis. Jerry was fanatical about eliminating Nazis. I could not understand how he got so excited when he watched German soldiers die. While watching this gory scene through his binoculars we would actually clap his hands and scream with joy when he witnessed out artillery shells bursting in the middle of a German patrol, smashing and tearing at the enemy bodies.

My attitude toward killing Germans was basically self preservation. I tried to kill them before they killed me! Of course I was not Jewish and deep inside, I did not like the thought of killing anyone. But Jerry was Jewish and enjoyed eliminating Nazis.

Battle of the Bulge — Day 37
On the Counter Attack toward St. Vith, Belgium
21 January 1945

The 21 January American counter attack started just before day light and the weather was not favorable. We had to contend with more than thirty inches of dry snow on the ground and drifts of snow as high as my head. The wind velocity was high, blowing the newly fallen snow into great clouds of blinding white crystals. The temperature was extremely cold, the coldest recorded in Europe in forty years. This type of weather is as dangerous to combatants as the danger posed by enemy troops. If a soldier is unlucky enough to become wounded, and falls to the ground, he becomes almost invisible to his comrades in the deep snow. If he is not discovered in a very few minutes, he becomes completely covered by snow, quickly looses consciousness, and rapidly freezes to death. I was told by the Medics that this is a relatively painless process, and in many instances is the most humane solution for a seriously wounded soldier.

The predawn artillery preparation was ear shattering and powerful, however none of the forward observers could determine it's actual effect on the enemy. Visibility was limited to a few hundred yards and binoculars became snow coated and frozen within seconds after removing them from the protection of your great coat. This type of weather rendered artillery forward observers useless.

Fortunately for the attacking American troops, the weather limited the German defenses just as severely. The American infantry and armor advance toward St. Vith was agonizingly slow, but relatively steady. It wasn't until the next day that my team was able to contribute to the American advance. That morning a half frozen infantry platoon leader struggled through the deep snow to reach our observation post. Exhausted from breaking a trail through the deep snow, he asked if we were artillery observers. When I told him we were, he said his platoon needed help. His point squad was pinned down by a mammoth German panzer and wanted to know if we could take the panzer under fire. The infantry officer pulled a battle map from under his great coat and pointed to a small valley on his map. He then advised us the panzer was hidden there in the hilly terrain.

Unfortunately, neither the valley nor the panzer was visible from our observation post. I explained to the Lieutenant we would have to take a radio and an operator to some location where I could clearly see the panzer before trying to disable it. The platoon leader understood, and volunteered to guide us to such a location. Jerry and I got our gear together, left the rest of the team on the observation post, and left with our infantry guide in search of the "Mammoth German Panzer." The unbroken snow along our path was deep but the winds had abated, giving us fairly good visibility. As we neared a small incline, the leading infantry officer signaled us to keep low, and motioned to Corporal Wiener, who was carrying the radio, to stop. The Lieutenant then gingerly motioned to me to join him behind a thick stand of snow covered trees perched on the crest of the incline.

Immediately in front of us, the Lieutenant pointed out a low sweeping panorama of evergreen trees, This beautiful panorama was broken by a small meadow in a valley which contained a now frozen stream which ran perpendicular to our line of sight. On the gentle forward slope of the next hill I could identify the draw the infantry officer was indicating on his map. I uncased my binoculars and scanned the draw and the surrounding slope. Sure enough, I spotted the "Mammoth German Panzer," partially camouflaged with evergreen boughs, and located in an excellent position to command the valley.

The platoon leader gently backed into defilade when he was certain I had located the panzer's hiding place and Jerry brought the radio closer to my partially hidden location near the crest of the hill. There, we began a three way discussion of the situation and developed what we considered the best method of attack. Using the platoon leader's map, I established the coordinates of the target for destruction. I asked the platoon leader where his men were located and was assured that none of his platoon had crossed the frozen stream. Since I had never encountered this model panzer, I asked the infantry officer to describe it for me. With no hesitation he said it was a *Jagdtiger,* or as the Americans called it, a Royal Tiger. It was indeed a monster, 72 tons to be exact. It mounted a 128mm Pak 80 gun and had armor plate that no known anti-tank weapon could penetrate. The infantry officer complained that it was just his luck for the platoon to run into the world's largest main battle tank.

Cautiously, the three of us moved slowly back to the crest of the incline, trying our best to remain partially hidden from the tank by a snow covered tree. When Jerry had the radio in place and working, I instructed him to contact XVIII Corps Artillery fire direction center (FDC) and report a fire mission. When the FDC requested details of the mission, Jerry repeated slowly after me, "FIRE MISSION! Coordinates 176.832. 046.127, Request one 8 inch

Howitzer. Target is one stationary German Royal Tiger tank. Will fire target for destruction."

The answer came back from the Corps FDC, and Jerry repeated the answer to me, "Coordinates confirmed, largest ordnance available is 155 mm. Are you certain the target is a Royal Tiger?"

"Target is confirmed by the infantry platoon leader and the artillery forward observer. It is a Royal Tiger, 155mm ordnance is too small, find us an eight inch howitzer somewhere!"

"Message received. Standby!"

The three of us remained immobile and hidden while we waited, but kept the panzer under constant surveillance. I asked the platoon leader to keep his point squad in place for the time being because I did not want the panzer to get spooked and move. Even with an 8 inch howitzer, the most accurate weapon in the American artillery arsenal, I could not hope for a direct hit on a moving target while adjusting indirect fire.

After what seemed to be an excessive amount of time, Jerry reported FDC had finally acquired an 8 inch howitzer for our mission. He reported they were locked and loaded with shell high explosive (HE), fuse quick, and were awaiting our command to fire. I told the platoon leader to radio his people and advise them to keep their heads down as we were about to take the *Jagdtiger* under fire. When the platoon leader gave me the OK signal, I turned to Jerry and commanded, "FIRE!"

Jerry repeated the command into the radio transmitter, and almost immediately reported back to me, "ON THE WAY!"

The blast of the initial round was loud and clearly visible in the dense forest about two or three hundred yards beyond the *Jagdtiger*. Before the blackened snow and other debris from the explosion settled, two German soldiers exited the panzer and started removing the camouflage. To my surprise, some of the American infantry exposed themselves and opened fire with small arms to drive the enemy soldiers back into the safety of their panzer.

A light machine gun, mounted on the front main deck of the *Jagdtiger*, quickly joined the fray and returned withering fire in the direction of the exposed American infantrymen. I quickly decided to drop the second 8 inch round between the panzer and the exposed infantrymen. In doing this, I would establish a bracket (one round short of and another beyond) on the target, and force our infantry to keep their heads down and stay out of this one sided fight. I yelled to Jerry my first observation, "400 OVER – 100 RIGHT!" As Jerry relayed my observation to the Corps FDC, I noticed, to my dismay, a puff of blue-gray smoke erupt from the rear of the panzer. Someone was desperately trying to start the huge cold engine.

As the platoon leader was screaming instructions to his squad leader through his small radio, Jerry yelled at me, "ON THE WAY!" As expected, the second round exploded in the open meadow between the *Jagdtiger* and point squad of American infantrymen. I now had a good bracket on the panzer and had avoided dropping a powerful 8 inch round of High Explosives on our own infantrymen. Through the binoculars I thought I could detect two German bodies near the tracks of the panzer. The next adjustment in the mission was clear. I observed this round "200 SHORT!", and Jerry immediately transmitted this information to Corps FDC.

While waiting for the third round to explode, I viewed the battle ground and was concerned about the panzer moving. The panzer frame was starting to shudder slightly, as though the powerful engine was running. Then the *Jagdtiger* tried to move, the driver straining to rock the panzer back and forth, trying his best to break the ice covered steel tracks from the frozen ground. Suddenly the third 8 inch round exploded so close to the struggling panzer I could not tell if the burst was short of, or over the *Jagdtiger*. There was no time left to ponder, I had no choice, the panzer was about to move. I yelled to Jerry, "FOUR ROUNDS – FIRE FOR EFFECT!"

I was so intent in watching the ever changing situation below I did not remember hearing Jerry give the command to "Fire for Effect." My attention was riveted upon the dedicated American infantrymen, laying down small arms fire on the Royal Tiger in an effort to keep it buttoned-up and to restrict the vision of it's occupants. I was also witnessing the German machine gunner returning vicious, withering fire. From our vantage point, it looked as though our troops, lying semi-protected in the open snow, were getting slaughtered.

My concentration was broken when Jerry yelled, "ON THE WAY!"

My binoculars rose automatically from my chest to my eyes so I could closely observe the location and effects of the incoming rounds. It was amazing to me how quickly the four rounds landed. The gun crew manning that particular eight inch howitzer was "on the ball." It is unfortunate that such a crew was not privileged to witness the precision of their work.

From an artilleryman's point of view, the "Fire for Effect" was magnificent! The first three 8 inch HE rounds tore into the terrain adjacent to the *Jagdtiger,* moving all 72 tons violently from side to side. The fourth, and most devastating round, struck the *Jagdtiger* just aft of the turret. This created a brilliant flash, followed by huge chunks of flying metal and a ball of orange colored flames caused by the ignited panzer fuel. I felt as if I was watching a Dante created "Panzer Commander's Hell On Earth!" For the *Jagdtiger* and it's crew, the war was over!

Jerry totally lost control when the first round of the "fire for effect" struck. He dropped his radio transmitter and ran to the top of the incline to watch the rounds land and explode After the fourth round delivered a termination blow to the Royal Tiger, he jumped up and down in glee, screaming, "We got it, we got it, we got those Bastards!" I had to remind him we still had to report to the Corps FDC, "CEASE FIRE–END OF MISSION–MISSION ACCOMPLISHED!"

For a few moments I watched the carnage in an effort to determine if any of the panzer crew survived, or if there was any German infantry in the area. I detected no enemy activity of any kind. However I did see activity on the American side of the creek in the meadow and realized the platoon leader was talking to his squad leader by radio. The Lieutenant was nodding as he spoke, but had a concerned look on his face. When I asked what was wrong, he said two of his men were hurt, but the medic had patched them up, and the squad leader thought his non-wounded men could get the two wounded men back to the Battalion Aid Station.

Rather abruptly the Lieutenant said he had to check on his other squads and report back to his Company Commander. He wanted to know if Jerry and I could find the way back to our Observation Post without his help. I pointed to the ragged path we had made on the way to this location and assured him we could back-track to our OP without his help. The Lieutenant turned to leave, then slowly turned back and apologetically said, "Sir, I almost forgot. Thanks for your help. That was nice shooting. You probably saved the lives of that entire squad."

With a strange look on my face, I explained, "Lieutenant, you just called me Sir. I do not rate a 'Sir' I am an enlisted man. I am a T/4." He looked very surprised and asked, "You are a T/4, in what outfit?"

"Lieutenant, I am Sergeant Randy Pierson from Charley Battery, 592nd Field Artillery Battalion, XVIII Airborne Corps Artillery."

The platoon leader laughed, "Well I'll be damned. I thought you were a Liaison Officer, a Captain. I'll have to tell the Regimental Commander about the T/4 that saved our ass. Anyway Sergeant, "Thanks, it was good shooting!" As he walked away into the forest, he looked back and added, "I'm glad to have met you, and I am damned glad you are on our side!"

Common sense dictated that we should not loiter in this non secured territory. Jerry dismantled the radio and packed it into it's canvas carrying case as I picked up our side arms. The trek back to our OP was slow and arduous in the still deep snow. Of course Jerry maintained a one way dialogue for the entire distance, talking to himself about "killing those fuckers" and "blasting those Nazi bastards."

I was glad to get back to our Observation Post and among friends. My adrenalin burst had left me fatigued. What I needed now was a cigarette and a cup of hot coffee.

Battle of the Bulge—Day 38
592nd Field Artillery Battalion—Charlie Battery
22 January 1945

We were relieved from duty early on the morning of 22 January. Another forward observer team had established a new OP closer to St. Vith. The successful American advance had rendered our present location useless. Close-in artillery observation was needed to support the planned counter attack to recapture this town. St. Vith was a vital crossroad city which had formerly housed the 106th Infantry Division Headquarters at the beginning of the Ardennes offensive more than a month ago. For that reason, I felt disappointed that I was not going to participate in the recapture of St. Vith.

We had barely reached Charlie Battery when the battery clerk found us and told me to report to the Command Post on the double, and report in to the CO. Captain Baxter debriefed me on the actions at the old OP and then, in almost a casual manner, told me to get a woolen class A uniform cleaned up and pressed, if possible. When I asked why, he said he had received verbal orders to get Sergeant Pierson cleaned up and have him at the 106th Division Headquarters in Stavelot no later than 1600 hours today. When I asked the Captain the reason for the trip, he said he didn't know, but thought it was for some type of awards ceremony.

I left the CP shaking my head and wondering what would happen next. I knew I had several things to do, and I had to do them quickly. Instantly I thought of Jerry and immediately located him. As I hurriedly explained to him what I had to accomplish is a short period of time, an innocent smile appeared on his face and he started nodding his head as if he understood. Jerry said, "The battery clerk told me what was going on and I have already put things in motion. One of our crew has already located your tailored class A uniform and it is being steamed and pressed by one of the battery cooks. Transportation has been arranged. You are to use your own jeep" and Jerry informed me, "I will be your driver." At this point I stopped Corporal Wiener, "Hold it Jerry, I need your help to get to Stavelot by 1600 hours this afternoon, but you can't drive me, you will have to remain here and be in charge of the team while I am gone." Jerry was pleased with being "in charge" during my absence, but he really wanted to go to Stavelot with me. He said, "I was afraid you would tell me I could not go so I located an old friend of yours from the 589th, Private First Class Feinberg, has volunteered to drive you. I'll tell 'Fish' to get your jeep serviced and also get a proper trip ticket signed in case you need fuel, food, or anything else, while you are gone. By the way Randy, how long will you be gone?" "I don't know Jerry, but tell 'Fish' probably three days."

"Jerry, sometimes you frighten me with your efficiency. How do you do it?"

"Sergeant Pierson, it isn't that complicated. I just keep my mind on the problem in front of me, then I just do for you what I would like you to do for me if our roles were reversed." "Jerry, thanks again for the help. I am going to our bunker and pack some personal gear. I think I'll wear fresh fatigues on the trip. Please make sure my class A uniform gets to the bunker by 1200 hours. Also tell Fish to have the jeep at the bunker and ready to go by 1200 hours. I'd appreciate it if you would get the 1st cook to have our dinners ready by 1200 also. Fish and I should be on the road for Stavelot by 1230. That will give us three and one half hours to get to the 106th Division Headquarters. Do you have any questions?"

As I left to go to my bunker, Jerry replied, "No questions Sergeant. Don't sweat it, I've got you covered."

Packing my personal belongings didn't take long. I was accustomed to leaving the battery on short notice, my team and I were always going somewhere. Getting things together had become almost routine. I still could not believe how Jerry seemed to know more about what was going on than I did. About 1100 hours I debated whether to check on Jerry, or lie down on my bunk for a few minutes. About 1115 Jerry entered the bunker carrying my uniform on a coat hanger. The uniform was immaculate and professionally pressed with creases in the right places. Jerry was smiling as I asked him how the cook was able to do such a professional looking job. Jerry explained the uniform was steamed over a huge pot of boiling coffee to take out the wrinkles. After the clothing partially dried, the cook used a clean pot as an iron, constantly dipping it in boiling water to keep it hot. Jerry said it was no big deal, this particular cook performed this service for lots of guys going on pass. They usually paid for his services with war trophies.

The sound of a jeep motor just outside of the bunker disrupted my conversation with Jerry. PFC Feinberg walked into the bunker and announced, "Sergeant, your chariot is here." We laughed and I embraced Fish as I had not seen him in several weeks.

After exchanging pleasantries, I asked him, "Think you can drive that jeep Fish?" "I don't know Randy, you know I drove the Survey Crew 3/4 ton weapons carrier when we were in the 589th." "That's the reason I asked Fish. If I remember correctly the Survey Crew truck was the most beat-up vehicle in the battalion."

"Don't worry Sarge, ole Fish will get you there and back in one piece."

I glanced at my watch, and Jerry reminded me we were due at the mess truck at 1200 hours The 1st cook had promised to have something for the three us to eat at that time. We decided to walk to the mess truck. Upon arriving we found the 1st cook waiting for us. We were surprised to see the Mess Sergeant seated under the cover of a tarp hung from the side of the mess truck. He had placed four folding chairs around a small table he had set-up for the occasion. In surprise, I walked up to the Mess Sergeant shook his hand, and asked, "Why the special arrangements, what officers are you expecting?" His response was unexpected, "Randy, I understand you are going to be honored in some way tomorrow in Stavelot. This table is set up for the four of us. I decided I wanted to have a meal with a 'genuine hero,' that's what Wiener tells me you are." "I appreciate the honor and the effort Sergeant, but Wiener tends to stretch the truth some of the time."

Not only was the meal a wonderful send-off, the Mess Sergeant had prepared a cold meal for the road, just in case we were not at Division Headquarters while the enlisted men's mess was open. As we walked back to the bunker, the three of us talked about how lucky we were to be in a unit where everyone seemed to appreciate us.

Fish and I bid Jerry goodbye, left the bunker, and stopped at the Command Post. The Captain was not there so I left word with the senior noncom there that I was leaving the area to go to Stavelot as ordered by the Captain. When the noncom asked how long I planned to be gone, I told him I really didn't know but I thought about three days. One day going, one day there, and one day returning. This seemed to satisfy the battery clerk who decided to carry me on the Morning Report as: "temp duty -Div Hq."

Relieved that the war could successfully continue, now that it was officially recorded in the battery Morning Report that I was on temporary duty at Division Headquarters, I returned to the jeep and told Fish we were cleared to leave the area. In response, Fish put the jeep in four wheel drive, shifted into low gear, released the clutch, and with a flourish that would have made General Eisenhower proud, we were on our way to Stavelot.

We arrived at Division Headquarters later than I had planned. Along the way, Fish lost control of the jeep on an ice covered curve in the road and we ended up in a shallow ditch. We banged up the jeep a little bit but nothing serious. As for ourselves, only our egos were bruised. Even though our jeep was not damaged, it was wedged in the slippery incline in such a way that we could get no traction. After a short wait, a large 2 1/2 ton truck, with a strong winch mounted on it's front bumper, stopped and the driver offered his assistance. During the rather simple process of winching the jeep back onto the road, we discovered the truck was from the 106th Division Supply. The driver advised us he was on the way to Stavelot and suggested we follow him the rest of the way to Stavelot. Once there, he said he would show us where we should check in, get some food, and a place to bunk down for the night. We took his offer, it was too good to turn down.

We drove straight to the building the 106th Infantry Division was using for Division Headquarters. We parked the jeep where an MP indicated, and thanked the truck driver profusely for his help. Upon trying to enter the building, we were questioned by another MP. After answering what seemed to be more than enough questions, the MP finally told us where to go, who to report to, and let us enter the building..

Upon entering the building the first thing we noticed was two enlisted men standing in front of a desk with their backs to us To my surprise I recognized these men to be two old friends, Sergeant Barney Alford and T/4 Delbert Miller. The Staff Sergeant behind the desk was shaking his head from left to right, vigorously indicating 'NO' to their requests. I watched this scene for several minutes in silence, then motioned to Fish that we should join our friends. Fish and I marched, with authority, down the corridor toward the reception desk where I advised the Staff Sergeant that I was Sergeant Pierson who had an appointment with the Sergeant Major and asked him to advise the Sergeant Major that I was here. Something about my demeanor made the Administrative Sergeant reach for a clipboard holding a group of typewritten papers. He thumbed his way through the papers, apparently found what he was looking for, stood up and politely said, "Will you gentlemen please follow me, the Sergeant Major is expecting you."

This abrupt change in attitude came as a complete surprise to all four of us. In the Sergeant Major's office we got another surprise. The Sergeant Major came from behind his desk, shook our hands, gave each one of us a typewritten order pertaining to us, and asked, "Have you gentlemen been advised the reason you were ordered to attend this ceremony?"

Quick to answer for the three of us, Barney replied, "All we were told was to be here to attend an awards ceremony."

The Sergeant Major looked at the orders in his hand to confirm the fact that we were indeed, Sergeant Alford, T/4 Miller, and T/4 Pierson. He then asked about PFC Feinberg. I advised the Sergeant Major that Fish was my driver. Fish was then dismissed and told to wait at the reception desk for us. Then looking directly at the three of us the Sergeant Major spoke, "Gentlemen, let me be the first to congratulate you on your promotion to Second Lieutenant."

This totally unexpected statement caught us unawares and momentarily speechless. After a brief moment of silence, a barrage of questions was directed to the Sergeant Major. He was gracious and expertly fielded our naive questions. He explained we were among the first enlisted men in the 106th Infantry Division to be promoted directly to Officers. The awards ceremony would take place on the athletic field directly behind the division headquarters building. Before we received our gold bars, Sergeant Alford would receive a Silver Star for Heroism and T/4 Pierson would receive a Bronze Star for Valor, for actions during the Battle for Parker's Crossroads at Baraque de Fraiture, Belgium, between the dates of 19 December and 23 December 1944. We were advised that during this ceremony other enlisted men and officers would also receive similar awards.

The Sergeant Major continued and explained that our direct promotions to officer status is commonly referred to as a 'Battlefield Promotion,' which was news to us. He said the promotion ceremony would be presided over by the Acting Division Commander, Brigadier General Herbert T Perrin after the awards ceremony. He asked if we were aware of the Army custom of paying $1.00 to the first enlisted man who saluted us as officers. In unison we answered "No." The Sergeant Major smiled, reached into a desk drawer and withdrew three new, crisp $1.00 bills and handed one to each of us. As he handed the bills to us, he told us the money was courtesy of Brig. General Perrin.

This custom seemed strange to me, but the Sergeant Major pointed out this custom probably pre-dating the Civil War. He reminded us that one dollar represented a lot of money to an enlisted soldier in those days. The briefing by this senior Non-Com was cordial, interesting, and informative, but we knew he had much more important things to do than give three new officers a lesson in military customs. Barney, always ready to move on, broached the questions of changing uniforms, getting fed, and accommodations for the night. We were assured the Administrative Staff Sergeant would handle these details for us.

During our second meeting with the Administrative Staff Sergeant he was more helpful and persisted in calling us 'Sir.' His reason, the orders promoting us to Second Lieutenants was dated today, and as far as he was concerned, we were already officers even though we were still wearing three stripes on our sleeves. He offered us sage advice when he suggested we remove our stripes prior to the ceremony. This would avoid the confusion caused by simultaneously wearing Lieutenants bars on our collars and stripes on our sleeves. We all laughed at this thought and thanked him for the suggestion.

Arrangements for the four of us at the transient quarters were Spartan. However they were adequate and gave us a place to stow our gear, shave, remove our chevrons, and get ready for the ceremony tomorrow. Several officers who had also come to Stavelot to receive decorations, started kidded us Sergeants about 'ruining their neighborhood' until they asked us why we were removing our insignia of rank. When Miller explained we had just been promoted to Lieutenants, they started forming a 'promotion party' to be held immediately following the promotion ceremony to 'water down' our new bars. The enthusiasm generated by these unknown officers was genuine, and we gladly agreed to participate.

The following day my feelings about the two ceremonies were mixed. Unexpected things were happening so fast I could not understand the far-reaching implications. On the clear and bitterly cold day, while standing at attention on the snow covered parade ground, my mind wandered. Presenting the numerous awards, and reading each accompanying citation was painstakingly slow. It seemed it took hours to complete this part of the ceremony. When all medals had been awarded, every one was ordered back into ranks and the Assistant Division Commander, Brigadier General Perrin moved onto the field. The three of us were then ordered 'front and center.' General Perrin then read the orders promoting us to officers, and proceeded to pin crossed brass cannons on our collar points, designating 'Field Artillery' as our branch of service. Next he pinned gold bars on the opposite collar points, indicating our rank as 2nd Lieutenants. He then took three steps backwards and rendered us a snappy hand salute.

None of us anticipated the General's action, but we all three, proudly and promptly, returned his unexpected salute. The General then stepped forward, shook our hands, and individually wished us good luck. The formal ceremony ended when the color guard passed in review, dipping the Divisional Colors in a tribute to the honorees, and the Adjutant dismissed the troops. Everyone then broke ranks and ran for shelter to get warm. Before the three of us could run for shelter we were warmly congratulated by a group of Division Staff Officers on the spot. After thanking these officers, we too ran to the shelter of our transient quarters. My feet were still sensitive to the cold and the thought of a nice warm stove and a strong drink made me walk faster

I had not gone far when I felt a touch on my shoulder. Not knowing what to expect, I turned and was delighted to see the Division Sergeant Major. He stopped me, took three steps to the rear, saluted, and grinned. His actions caught me by surprise because I had been wearing my officers insignia for only a few minutes. I did manage to return his salute with a grin of my own. The look of pleasure on his face said it all. He had managed to give me my first salute.

Automatically I withdrew the crisp dollar bill, he had given me, from my pocket and handed it to him. He accepted it with both hands, looked at it as he turned it over and over, as if he wondered what to do with it. The Sergeant Major finally looked me in the eye and said, "In my fourteen year military career this is the first dollar bill I have ever 'earned' from a newly commissioned officer. It means a lot to me and I would like to keep it with my other memorabilia." The Sergeant Major paused, and then continued, "But as much as it means to me, I know it will mean more to you in the future." Then slowly, almost reluctantly, he returned to bill to me.

Later that night, after the 'watering down' activities were over, I obtained a V-Mail form and wrote my mother a short note advising her my rank and serial number had changed but the rest of my mailing address remained the same. I confided in her that as an officer I now had a job which involved no personal danger and could now censor my own mail. I omitted the fact that I had just received a medal for 'Valor' while engaged in combat.

19

The Battle for the Rhineland

The Battle for the Rhineland Begins
Charlie Battery – 592nd FA Bn – 25 January 1945

Thank goodness Fish and I left Stavelot shortly after breakfast because when we returned to the Charlie Battery position, they were not there. When Fish finally connected with Charlie Battery via our jeep mounted radio, he was advised the whole Battalion had moved forward during our absence. Fish had a difficult time obtaining instructions to get from where we were to the new battery location. The XO advised his operator not to give us the coordinates of the battery on the radio because he knew the Germans were monitoring his frequency. By using 'Pig Latin' and other slang expressions with the battery radioman, Fish finally advised me he thought he had enough information to find the new battery location.

It was almost dark when we finally found the Charlie Battery Command Post. When we checked in to let the First Sergeant know we were back. Captain Baxter heard us and immediately wanted to know where his 'errant hero' had been. The Captain listened intently as Fish and I told him about the awards ceremony, but he did a double take when I started explaining the promotion ceremony. His immediate reaction was, "They did what to you?" He obviously did not know I was going to get an award and also a 'Battlefield Promotion.' His reaction to this news was very mixed. He did not seem able to accept the fact that I was now a commissioned officer, yet he congratulated me on my promotion. He thought, and then said, "I send a T/4 to Division to receive a medal and they send back a decorated 2nd Lieutenant. How did this happen? I didn't recommend you for a medal or a promotion. I don't know you that well. Who in the hell recommended you?"

I could not answer his question, but I tried, "Maybe someone in the 589th FA Battalion recommended me, someone their had to had to write the commendation. It could have been Captain Huxel, or maybe Major Goldstein. They were the only two officers left in the battalion who knew what I did. What do you think Fish?"

PFC Feinberg agreed with me, "It must have Major Goldstein, he was running the battalion after the Battle for Parker's Crossroads." Captain Baxter nodded his head in agreement and said, "It must have been Major Goldstein," and asked no one in particular, Are you sure that Pierson was actually promoted or was he just made an acting officer?"

Fish quickly responded in my behalf, "Randy was definitely given a direct promotion. I heard General Perrin, himself, read the orders and saw him pin the crossed cannons and a gold bar on Randy's color points. I know all three of the Sergeants that got promoted. They all three deserved it.

Captain Baxley told Fish to 'cut the Bull Shit' and asked me, "Do you have a copy of the orders?"

Without comment I handed him a blurred typewritten copy of my orders and he read them. When he finished he asked, "Who is this guy named Miller? He is on this same order too. I see he is assigned to XVIII Airborne Corps Fire Direction Center. You are a fire direction technician Pierson, why didn't you get assigned to the Corps Fire Direction Center also?"

"I really don't know Captain Baxter, but I can give you an educated guess. Miller is much older than I am, he must be pushing 40, and Captain Huxel trained me to adjust fire from an observation post on the firing range at Camp Atterbury. Miller has never been trained to adjust fire and he wears thick glasses, I don't think he could see well enough through the binoculars that forward observers must use to adjust a round. The Corps probably needs Forward Observers and

Liaison Officers more than they need guys trained in fire control."

Captain Baxter finally admitted he did not know what to do with me. He said he wanted to discuss my situation with his Executive Officer and then sleep on it. He told me he had a Battery Commander's Call tomorrow morning at Battalion Headquarters and he would get the Battalion Commanders thoughts about me at that time. He promised to get in touch with me after he talked to his Commanding Officer. In the mean time I was to tell the First Sergeant and the battery clerk where I would be bedded down, and he told me to attend his officers call, tomorrow morning at 0700 hours, in his Command Post.

We located Fienberg's section, where I dropped him off with his gear, and left to find Jerry. Corporal Wiener and the other guys in my section had not yet completed our new bunker, however, what they had completed appeared safe, was comparatively warm, and reasonably comfortable. Jerry had constructed me a bunk, consequently I threw my sleeping bag and other personal gear on it, sat down, asked Jerry what was going on, and started taking off my heavy outer garments. Jerry rambled on about the rumors concerning an upcoming big push to de-bulge the 'Bulge.' How, this time, the Allies were going to 'kick ass' all the way to Berlin. He was about to tell me some recent 'war stories' when he noticed the crossed cannons and a gold bar on my shirt collar. In surprise, he asked, "Randy, what is that stuff on your collar, and where are your stripes?"

These questions aroused the interest of all the occupants of the bunker, so I said in a loud voice, "Listen up! Listen carefully! I am going to explain this only once! I'm no longer a T/4, I am now a 2nd Lieutenant. I have not changed, only my rank has changed. I don't know if I will remain in this battery or not. That decision is up to the Captain. Even he did not know we were going to receive a 'Battlefield Promotion.'"

Jerry broke in and asked, "We?"

"Yes, we. I was promoted with two other sergeants, friends, from the 589th FA Bn. They were Barney Alford and Delbert Miller. Lieutenant Alford was assigned as an officer in an artillery firing battery in the 82ns Airborne Division and Lieutenant Miller was assigned to the XVIII Airborne Corps Fire Direction Center as an Assistant S-3. Both men are well qualified for their assignments. I was assigned to this battery for administrative purposes, what ever that means. I do not know who recommended me for the promotion, or why. I'll probably find out more of the details at the Officers Call in the morning."

One of the radio men in the rear of the bunker asked, "Sarge, are we supposed to call you 'Sir' now?"

"Sparks, I'll put it this way. I am a newly commissioned officer. You should address me the same way you address all commissioned officers. I do demand one courtesy however. Don't ever, and I repeat, don't ever salute me in full view of the enemy, unless you are trying to get me killed."

This little attempt at humor seemed to be appropriate because in a few minutes we were all relaxed, joking, and well into a fresh bottle of Cognac. As we drank and talked, my mind started wandering and I wondered what I would find out at Officers Call in the morning. I also noted that Jerry was looking at me with an infectious grin on his face. He kept shaking his head back and forth, and mouthing in silence, "I can't believe they made you an officer."

I mouthed back to him in return, "You'd better believe it pal."

Battle for the Rhineland
Charlie Battery—592nd FA Bn
Officers Call—26 January 1945

At 0600, Corporal Wiener shook my shoulder and said, "Lieutenant Pierson, rise and shine, its chow time."

News had traveled fast. During the brief walk to the mess truck I was congratulated several times by various sergeants, but it was apparent the corporals and privates were giving the new officer a wide berth. I remembered when I was a private I did the same thing. That's the Army! When you are on the bottom of the totem pole, it's to your advantage to remain invisible.

At the mess truck, the Mess Sergeant and his on-duty cooks made me feel welcome. They seated me, with another officer, under a large canvas fly, which had been attached to the stake-body of the 2 1/2 ton GMC mess truck. This overhead canvas cover protected the officers from inclement weather as they ate. Under the protection of this overhead cover was a folding table which would accommodate six people. Metal cups, dishes, and cutlery were provided instead of the standard mess kit I had used for so long.

When I finished my breakfast, the first cook told me to leave the soiled utensils on the table, he would have a KP wash them. With just one day in grade, I was already beginning to appreciate the difference between being an enlisted man and an officer.

There were four people at the Battery Officers Call, Captain Baxter, the Executive Officer, the Motor Officer and yours truly. I recognized the Motor Officer as the silent 2nd Lt. with whom I had shared breakfast. He was unaware of my promotion. Captain Baxter had much information for us. A three Corps offensive was planned for the morning of 28 January. The 592nd FA Bn would remain in place and participate heavily in the opening artillery preparation supporting the attack.

Our Battalion would support General Ridgeway's XVIII Airborne Corps which consisted of four Divisions, the 1st, the 30th, and the 84th Infantry Divisions, plus the war weary 82nd Airborne Division, to serve as a reserve. The 592nd FA Bn would be in general support of this Corps. On our north flank would be General Huebner's V Corps and on our south flank would be General Middleton's VII Corps. If successful, this attack would signal the end of the 'Battle of the Bulge' and the beginning of the Allied drive to reach the Rhine River.

The Captain having completed his message, asked his XO and the Motor Officer if they had any questions. They nodded their heads 'NO.' As the Captain dismissed them he said, "You have a lots of work to do in the next 36 hours, now get with it!"

After dismissing his other two officers, Captain Baxley turned to me and said, "I learned a little more about you from the Colonel last night. He thinks you should be assigned to Battalion Headquarters, but he is going to leave you in Charlie Battery. He wants you to get some firing battery experience."

Captain Baxter continued, "I don't mind training you, that is part of my job, training people. You have a positive attitude and are above average when it comes too being intelligent. What bugs me about this situation is the Colonel. For some reason he wants you to get firing battery experience, yet he wants you to handle the liaison job between Corps Artillery and the 505th Parachute Infantry Regiment. You are to report to the Operations Officer of the 505th before noon tomorrow to coordinate their artillery requirements for the initial push. I understand the 5005th Regiment will be one of the point regiments during the initial push. Can you handle a Liaison Officers responsibilities?"

"Yes Sir, I can handle the job. Of course I have never been a Liaison Officer, but I am familiar with what they do."

"Pierson, don't let your ego over-load you ass. The Table of Organization (TO) calls for a Liaison Officer to be a Captain."

"Yes Sir, I know that. The difference in rank doesn't bother me. The TO calls for a Forward Observer to be a 1st Lieutenant. I handled that job as an enlisted man."

"Pierson. you give me a problem. For a brand new 2nd Lieutenant with no experience, I don't know whether you are full of crap and trying to Bull Shit me. or are just a cocky T/4 who happens to be wearing a gold bar."

"Captain, we don't really know or understand each other so I would like to try and explain how I feel. I'm going to do the best job I can do under the circumstances, but I will admit my knees knock when you explain what you expect of me. You do not have to remind me, I already know the importance of being the eyes and ears of the artillery when the infantry needs our support, I also know this job is dangerous. I only ask one consideration. To get this job done properly I need my forward observation crew intact."

"OK Lieutenant, you have your FO section intact. I'll even give you another Sergeant to take your place. Does that suit you?"

"No Sir. I need to have to have Corporal Wiener as my acting FO Sergeant, and I feel he should be permitted to pick his own Corporal."

"You mean you want 'Jew Boy' to be your Acting Sergeant?"

"Sir. people should not call Corporal Wiener 'Jew Boy.' He is intelligent, innovative, he gets things done, and we work well together."

"Pierson, I don't share your opinion of Corporal Wiener, but its your ass not mine. You can tell Wiener he is now an Acting Sergeant and has my permission to pick his own second in command. Is there anything else you want to discuss?"

"Yes Sir. As my first official act as an officer, I want to recommend that Acting Sergeant Wiener be promoted to Sergeant."

"Jesus Christ, I should have known better than to ask. You really are an arrogant son-of-a-bitch. Don't push your luck any farther. I might change my mind."

"Thanks for your help Captain. Now with your permission, I better get moving if we are going to get my team together and get to Regiment by noon tomorrow."

"Lieutenant Pierson, one last thing, this is going to a big show. Do your job well, many lives will depend on your performance. Be sure and fulfill your responsibilities. Give the infantry what they need, and rest assured we will deliver on this end."

The Battle for the Rhineland
Command Post—505 Parachute Infantry Regiment
27 January 1945

Our two jeep convoy slowed and parked under two snow covered evergreen trees. We were concealed in the forest about two hundred yards from the 505 Parachute Infantry Regiment's advanced Command Post. I told Jerry to wait with his crew while I checked in with the Regimental Operations Officer (S-3) to find out what he expected of us.

The Command Post and Operations Center were located in separate tents that provided protection from the snow and cold, but offered no protection from enemy activity. This fact concerned me. An armed guard intercepted me about half-way to the tents and satisfied himself that I was friendly. When I asked for the location of the Regimental S-3 he pointed to the Operations Center tent. He warned me the S-3 was busy as hell this morning, but fell silent when I told him I was invited to the party.

Battalion and Company Officers filled the tent as the S-3 briefed them on the attack plans, their areas of responsibility, specific objectives and time frames, and the time schedule for this entire attack. I began to appreciate the complexity and importance of this operation. The weather was terrible, the plan was extremely complicated, and required close contact and cooperation between the involved units.

Well into the briefing a Captain finally noticed me, disengaged himself from the crowd surrounding the battle maps, and approached me. He asked who I was and why I was at the briefing. He seemed relieved when I told him I was Lieutenant Pierson, the Liaison Officer from Corps Artillery. I informed him I had been assigned to the 505th Regiment to assist in the evaluation and the planning of their artillery requirements prior to and during the initial attack. The Captain informed me his name was George Smythe. Smiling when he explained, "That is 'Smith' spelled with a 'y' and an 'e.' Captain Smythe was a friendly officer, several years my senior, and under the circumstances, extremely relaxed. In contrast, I could feel tension beginning to take control of my body.

Abruptly, officers started gathering their map cases an personal belongings, then silently leaving the tent. The silence mirrored the fact they were already contemplating problems they and their units would experience tomorrow. The crowded tent emptied rapidly, leaving only a handful of Regimental officers still pouring over the battle charts.

Captain Smythe guided me too the map table, interrupted the intense conversation, and announced I was the Liaison Officer from Corps Artillery. The senior officer at the table, a Major, looked up, extended his hand, and said, "I'm Bill Blanton the Regimental S-3, we've been expecting you. Are you ready for the big show?"

There was something about the way the S-3 handled himself. He was direct, self-assured, friendly, but not chummy. He reminded me of Major Arthur Parker, my long time S-3 in the 589th FA Bn, and he immediately made me feel comfortable. I decided I would like doing business with Major Blanton. I answered his question by saying, "This is my first time out as a Liaison Officer and I'm a little nervous. Under these circumstances, I'm as ready as can be expected."

"A little nervous," he asked as he looked me over closely, then quickly added, "That is natural, that's a good sign." He then spoke with the remaining Regimental officers briefly, asked for questions, answered several, and then dismissed them. The Major then began his meeting with Captain Smythe and me. Captain Smythe explained the pre-attack artillery requirements to me. When the Captain completed the pre-attack artillery requirements, Major Blanton asked, "Does this plan present problems for you or the folks at Corps Artillery?"

I replied, "These are pretty much 'plain vanilla' requirements: road interdictions, destruction of fortifications, interdiction of enemy assembly and supply areas, and the destruction of enemy communications systems. The only things to be determined are relatively simple. All I need is the infantries target priorities and time tables for firing them. Acquiring the proper weapons and ammunition is my responsibility and I anticipate no problems in these areas. My main concern with your established plan is how to handle last minute changes in the plan. If such changes are required, it is my duty to clear these changes with Corps Artillery immediately." Neither officer thought there would be any changes in the pre-attack artillery requirements.

This brought up my next concern and I asked, "What do you expect from me after the pre-attack artillery requirements are fulfilled?" Major Blanton explained, "Once the situation becomes fluid, things become chaotic, and we need clearly defined channels of communication and responsibility. We expect moderate to heavy casualties in the initial phase of the attack. The enemy forces are well dug-in and the terrain in this sector forces our units to jump-off across a long, open, and sweeping valley. Once the dug-in defenders are dislocated, and starting to withdraw, the Colonel expects the casualties to become less severe.

The S-3 continued, "Once the attack begins, the Regimental Commander has a tactical concern about the forward movement of adjacent units. His main concern is his northern, or left flank. A regiment of the veteran 1st Infantry Division had the responsibility of guarding this flank, but traditionally regular army infantry units do not advance a fast as airborne infantry units. If history repeats itself, he fears the left flank of his regiment will be wide open to an enemy counter attack. He would like quick artillery response in this sector in the event a counter attack occurs."

During this discussion I indicated I had been given no operational instructions other than, be available to the Regimental Commander at all times, and to maintain back-up radio communications with Corps Artillery. These instructions gave me the flexibility to develop a plan that would meet the requirements of both the Regimental Commander and Corps Artillery. Then I asked if he would be receptive to my thoughts.

Major Blanton said, without hesitation, "Now is the time for opinions."

Since the Major obviously wanted my ideas, I began, "I have five men and two radio equipped jeeps with me. I believe my team should be split into two sections during the initial attack. One section should remain at Regiment to maintain direct liaison between Regiment and Corps Artillery. The second section should move to the 3rd Battalion, or possibly to the Command Post of the Company assigned to attack on the left flank of the Regiment. This plan would give Regiment a Corps Artillery presence in the sector of greatest concern during the initial attack. I stressed this arrangement would provide an overall point-of-view from where the two diverse units were trying to maintain contact on their respective flanks during the attack."

Major Blanton was deep in thought as I described how I felt my liaison group should be deployed. He asked how I proposed to divide my six man team, and who would remain at Regimental Headquarters. I suggested leaving Sergeant Weiner at Regiment with two men and a radio equipped jeep, and I would go forward with the attacking Battalion, or Company, with my jeep, driver, and a radio operator. I felt it would be to the advantage of the infantry if I was readily available to the attacking unit. If they needed additional artillery support I could act as a Corps Forward Observer.

The S-3 questioned my reasoning. He pointed out the Colonel normally dealt with a Liaison Officer who was a Captain and he had no idea how the Colonel would feel about dealing directly with an enlisted man.

I understood the Major's reluctance to recommend my approach, however I thought I was right, so I continued selling my idea. I explained when Sergeant Wiener contacted Corps Artillery, from Regiment, with a message or a request for a fire mission, he was relating the request of a full Colonel, a Regimental Commander, and it would be honored as such by the Corps Artillery S-3.

On the other hand, if an Infantry Platoon Leader, or a Company Commander, called Corps requesting additional artillery support, the Corps S-3 would more likely honor my request for a fire mission before one coming directly from a small infantry unit commander. As an added selling point, I advised the Major an assistant S-3 at Corps was a long time friend who would not leave me holding-the-bag if I called. He would help me, even if it was not authorized, because he owed me.

Major Blanton shook his head and said, "Pierson you still think like a sergeant. I have always suspected the Army is run by sergeants. Listening to you confirms my suspicions. I still have reservations concerning your approach, but I will discuss it with the Regimental Commander. But be prepared to get your ass chewed, he is a tough commander, and he likes to chew on the young, tender, asses of 2nd Lieutenants."

"I appreciate your offer to discuss my thoughts with the 'ole man' Major, but do not worry too much about my young and tender butt. When the Colonel gets through chewing on me, he will know he did not get a virgin."

"OK Lieutenant, so much for army humor. Captain Smythe, please get the artillery people settled-in near the Command Post, and let the Sergeant Major know where to find them. The Colonel will want to talk to Lieutenant Pierson and Sergeant Wiener after he and I have discussed the liaison situation,"

Captain Smythe took me to the Message Center, introduced me to Sergeant Major and the Regimental Clerk. He then asked for the best location where six artillerymen could bed down for the night. Before the Sergeant Major could make a suggestion, I asked where the Regimental Aid Station was located. When he said it was located nearby, I asked, "If it is convenient, I would like to take my team there for the night." This idea seemed to please the Sergeant Major because this arrangement relieved him of additional responsibility when he had more important things to do. The Captain viewed my request differently, and asked, "Why the Aid Station?"

To placate the Captain, I explained I had friends, regimental medics, at the Aid Station. They treated my leg wounds about a month ago, and I would like to thank them. I assured Captain Smythe they would be glad to see me, and would put-us-up for the night. This explanation satisfied the Captain and he instructed the Sergeant Major to have a 'runner' guide us to the Aid Station.

The Regimental Aid Station was located about four hundred yards to the rear of the Command Post, sitting in a small clearing in the dense forest. In defilade behind a small hill, it was well hidden from enemy view. This location offered access to an adequate, tree covered road which could accommodate the 'meat wagons' as they started arriving tomorrow morning, bringing dead and wounded men from the battle area. There were two 3/4 ton Dodge ambulances parked under thick foliage near the newly erected hospital type tents, all of which displayed the international red cross insignia, indicating they were tents and vehicles of mercy.

Our guide motioned for me to park the jeeps in the edge of the woods, maintaining proper distance between the jeeps, the ambulances, and the hospital tents. The guide accepted Jerry's offer of a ride back to the CP. As Jerry's jeep left, I told my driver to wait in the vehicle and asked the radio operator to contact both Corps Fire Direction Center an the Charlie Battery Command Post to let them know we had arrived at the 505th Regiment as ordered. I also instructed the radio operator to leave Captain Baxter a message that things at Regiment seemed normal.

Apparently the sound of running motors in front of the aid station aroused the non-com on duty. He opened the protective entrance flaps to the largest tent and stood there with his arms folded against the cold, watching intently as I fought my way through the quickly accumulating snow. As I approached the tent, he held back the protective flap and motioned for me to move inside. The interior of the tent was well lighted and surprisingly warm. A welcomed pleasure compared to the nasty weather developing outside. The medic asked me if I had any wounded with me. I answered, "No, I am looking for a place to feed and bed-down six relatively healthy artillerymen."

It was evident my answer was confusing him, so I tried another approach. I asked, "Is Dutch Schultz around?" He still looked puzzled, so I continued, "I am Lieutenant Pierson, Dutch and I know each other. I would like to talk with him. Will you get him for me?"

"Oh, yes sir, Did you say you and Dutch are friends?"

"No, I didn't say we are friends, I said we know each other. I am not certain he will remember me, but I would like to talk to him. Can you get him for me?"

"Yes Sir! He is in another tent playing poker, but he'll be pissed-off if I interrupt his game."

"Damn it, this is business, this is not a social call! Just go get him, piss him off, I could care less! I have seen him pissed-off before, and this probably won't be the last time I'll see him pissed-off. Just get his ass in here, RIGHT NOW!"

"YES SIR! I'll go get him Lieutenant, please wait right here."

As good as his word, the duty non-com returned with Staff Sergeant Dutch Schultz in tow. I could hear them approaching the tent, crunching through the newly ice encrusted snow. Dutch was muttering, "This better be good. I'm in the middle of winning or losing a big chunk of money. Who is this officer anyway?" I don't know any artillery officers. What does he want from me?"

In the middle of this one way conversation, Staff Sergeant Schultz burst through the tent flap and stated, "I'm Sergeant Schultz. What can I do for you Lieutenant?"

Dutch looked good, every inch the soldier I remembered. He was not an easy man to forget, not that I wanted to forget him. He had done a lot for me, I still owed him. But I could tell, he was pissed, really pissed-off. I thought I must have interrupted one hell of a poker game to get him this irritated. His belligerent mood showed in his face and he displayed hostile body langue. For the moment, I was glad I out-ranked him. Rather than let him simmer any longer, I offered my hand and said, "Hello Dutch, good to see you again. How are you doing?"

The large Dutchman's attitude slowly started to change. I could see the tension start to leave his body. The obvious irritation written on his face began to soften into a questioning look. I could almost read his mind. "Who is this guy anyway? Where did I meet him? He looks familiar, why can't I place him?" As hard as he searched his mind, he was not coming up with the answers.

I decided to help him with his problem, "Dutch, I came through your aid station about a month age. I was a T/4 from the 106th Infantry Division. One of your patrols had 'captured' me. I was wounded in both legs, white phosphorous burns. My feet were in bad shape too. The squad leader that captured me thought I was a German dressed in an American uniform."

Before I could continue, a grin of recognition spread over his huge face and he blurted out, "I remember you now, you and our Intelligence Officer, Major Snowden, had a go at each other. Ken Yardley ended up taking you to the hospital. We both wondered what happened to you."

"That's right Dutch, you and Ken did a great job on my legs and feet. The doctor at the hospital said if hadn't been for you two, I probably would have lost some toes.

"Well I'll be a son-of-a-bitch! It's good to see you again. I'm damned glad you came through your troubles OK. Everyone around here remembers you. You were a 'tough case' with Major Snowden. That took guts! We called you the Rebel."

"Dutch, I am from the south, but I am not a rebel. I had to do something drastic to defuse Major Snowden. He wanted to have me shot."

"Lieutenant, it feels strange calling you Lieutenant, I almost called you Randy. That is the way I remember you."

Interrupting him, I replied, "Randy is fine with me Dutch, as far as I am concerned there is no chain of command involved here. I am not accustomed to being called by my new rank yet. I've only been an officer about a week."

"How did you get promoted to Lieutenant Randy?"

"It's a long story Dutch. maybe later over a drink or something. Right now I have five GIs to look after. We have to coordinate the infantry/artillery action prior the infantry jump-off early tomorrow morning. In the meantime, I told the Sergeant Major I would like to bunk my men with the medics tonight. Can you accommodate six of us?"

"You know we will. We have plenty of room tonight Plenty! We have more than two dozen cots set up to handle the wounded we expect tomorrow. They are empty tonight, take your pick. But when the wounded start coming in tomorrow, I don't think we can accommodate you, we'll be real busy! We do have a new medical officer assigned to us for the attack. A nice guy, a 1st Lieutenant, but he does not know shit from shingles about handling trauma cases. His total trauma experience comes from about six weekends in the Emergency Room at Grady Hospital in Atlanta, Georgia."

"Thanks Dutch, I thought you could handle our problem for tonight. I don't know where we will be starting tomorrow morning. We will just have to play the cards as they are dealt. I will have Jerry, my section chief, get the guys out of the weather if someone will show them the tent and bunks to use. If it's OK with you,

I'll have Jerry throw my belongings on one of the cots, along with my men."

This time Staff Sergeant Schultz interrupted me, "Randy I can bunk you down with the medical officer, he is in a four man tent all by himself. Plenty of room. He probably would like another officer to talk to."

"Thanks, bit no thanks buddy. The six of us are a team. We work as a team. We depend upon each other. We live as a team. This team concept is important to our survival. I'm sure you understand."

"You don't have to explain it to me. I think being part of a team is very important."

"Good. By way, Major Blanton knows we are bunking-down with you. He wants me to talk with the Colonel later this afternoon. I would appreciate it if the medic on duty at the aid station is told to expect a call from the Major. You do have telephone connections with the CP don't you/"

"Yep, we're connected to the switch board, you can receive a direct call from anyone in this Corps. We have a good communications network, both radio and telephone."

"That is good to know. Dutch I hear a jeep motor, I think Sergeant Wiener is back. I'd like him to get our gear out of the weather and get the men bunks for the night.

I strongly suspect you want to get back to your poker game."

"Who told you I was in a poker game?"

"I don't want to get anyone in trouble buddy, but it was your duty non-com."

"That stupid bastard, I told him to never mention I am playing poker. The 'ole man' doesn't like me playing poker with the officers. It can get me in trouble. Today I'm on a roll, but you're right, I'd better get back to extracting their money. It's like taking candy from a bunch of babies."

"Don't worry about me Dutch, I won't tell the Colonel. You just finish your game and I'll try to find out what I have to do tonight. Then we can get together. I'd like to have a drink with you and try to relax. Tomorrow we will all be very busy."

On the way out of the tent, Staff Sergeant Schultz paused and said, "A drink sounds good to me, I like that. I'll furnish the booze to wet down your new bars. An Randy, you'd better relax tonight, tomorrow will be tough. Real tough!"

Battle for the Rhineland
505th Parachute Infantry Regiment—Start of the Attack
28 January 1945

At 0400 the Medical Officer came through the aid station tent, awakened us, and told us to vacate the cots we had used for the night. He again urged me to move my gear into his four man tent. He wanted to know how we were to operate, two twelve hour shifts, or what? I told him we had not been advised yet, but I thought three of us would be leaving and three would remain here. The Medical Officer told me, regardless of how we were divided, use the three empty cots and other space in his tent as I saw fit.

I dressed, rolled up my sleeping bag, shaved, and asked Jerry to move all of our personal gear into the Medical Officer's tent until Major Blanton gave me more details. We ate a quick, hot, and nourishing breakfast with the medics, then Jerry, a radio operator, and I, went outside to move his jeep closer to the regimental operations tent.

We could not believe how the weather had deteriorated during the night. It was horrible! I could not believe the Allies could mount, and sustain, a successful attack in this type weather. The tactical air force could not get into the air to support the ground troops and the visibility was so limiter, artillery observation was rendered useless.

Jerry had to move his jeep from the aid station to the regimental tent by walking in front of the vehicle, while shouting directions to his driver, to keep the jeep from wandering into a snow drift. If I had known this relatively short trip was going to be so treacherous, I would have left the vehicle near the operations tent yesterday afternoon.

Major Blanton, the Regimental S-3, bid us a weary good morning as the three of us reported for duty. He indicated he was anxious to establish our radio communications link with the Corps Fire Direction Center. Sergeant Wiener needed no instructions from me and advised he would report back when all channels were working properly.

The first information I needed from the S-3 concerned required changes in the pre-attack artillery preparations. When told there were none, I was not surprised. Plans for an operation of this magnitude have to be well thought out. I asked the Major for permission to leave and immediately found Jerry to give him our first official message to Corps Artillery, "No changes required in artillery preparation by 505th Regiment."

The subject of how the liaison team would operate was brought up next by Major Blanton. He had discussed my suggestion, to split the team, with the Colonel. The 'ole man' thought it was a novel idea, but felt more comfortable keeping the entire liaison team at regimental headquarters. Apparently I looked disappointed, because the S-3 told me the Colonel liked dealing with officers who expressed opinions. These stated differences gave the 'ole man' options, and he liked that. Major Blanton also explained that General Ridgeway, the Corps Commander, felt the attack would be best accomplished by the infantry, with as little tactical help from armor and the artillery as possible. The Corps Commander had advised that no, and I repeat no, buildings were to be destroyed by tank or artillery fire. All buildings which sheltered enemy strong points were to be taken by infantry action alone. These orders were issued because of the inclement weather. Once captured, the Allied troops needed the shelter of these structures for their own protection.

This news surprised me, but after the message was analyzed, it made sense. Now I understood at least two good reasons why the Colonel wanted the entire team to remain at regiment. First: It did not appear we would be firing many 'on demand' fire missions during the attack. Second: If we stayed at Regiment, no panicked Platoon Leader could pressure me into destroying a building which was an enemy strong point. Yes, the Colonel was a smart cookie!

Telephone and radio traffic was beginning to increase in the operations center. My conversation with the S-3 was being interrupted more frequently now, with front line unit commanders reporting in with current status reports. Finally I was able to ask the Major at what time should I make myself available in the operations center. He glanced at his watch and replied, "Be here no later then 0545 hours."

"Thanks Major, that gives me about thirty minutes. If you don't mind, Sergeant Wiener and I will get one last cup of coffee before we report back for duty."

The S-3 nodded his head in agreement and started walking toward one of his assistants who was waiving a telephone receiver, indicating the Major was needed to handle an incoming call.

Sergeant Wiener and I stopped at the tent's entrance before returning outside to the still dark and cold weather. I asked Jerry to get the rest of the team together and meet me back here no later than 0540 hours and told him I was going back to the aid station for one last cup of coffee before the big show started. I suggested he find the regimental mess facility and do the same for himself and his men,

Even though it was still dark, finding the way back to the aid station was fairly easy. The jeep had cleared a path in the snow that was easy to follow while using the subdued light from my 'cats-eye' flashlight. Two nervous sentries challenged me as I approached the aid station and asked for the pass word. I realized how out of touch with the infantry I was. No one had bothered to tell me tonight's pass word, and I had been to stupid to ask. I replied, "I am Lieutenant Pierson. I'm the artillery liaison officer. I'm sorry, I do not know the pass word."

"I don't care who you say you are. I asked you for the pass word."

Shining the dim black-out flashlight on my face and then directing the beam onto my holstered 45-caliber weapon, I told the sentry, "I said I am an artillery officer and I do not know the pass word. I just came from the operations tent where I was talking with Major Blanton. Now I want to get out of this damned ice and snow and talk with Staff Sergeant Schultz. Do I make myself clear?'

A second sentry entered the conversation, "We still don't know who you are. You better give us the pass word, or get on your knees and start praying, cause in about one minute we're going to start shooting."

I exploded, "Damn it, I'm not trying to attack the aid station all by myself. You stupid pricks, call the aid station and ask Dutch to come out here and vouch for me."

"What if Dutch ain't there?"

"Then get the fucking medical officer to come and identify me."

"All right, I'll try to get some body to identify you, but you had better stand still, cause if you move, you're dead meat! Do you understand me?"

"Yes, I understand you. But move your ass, I haven't got all night. I'm in a hurry."

In the darkness I could hear movement, someone was moving toward the aid station tent. Then I heard one of the sentries yell, "Sergeant Schultz, we have a guy out here who claims he is an artillery officer. He doesn't know the pass word and he wants you to come out and identify him."

I could hear the tent flap open and Staff Sergeant Schultz yelled into the darkness, "Randy, is that you?"

"Yes Dutch, it's Randy. Please tell these sentries to let me in."

In response to my request, Dutch yelled into the darkness again, "It's OK, I know the lieutenant. Let him get out of the cold."

When the tent flap closed, the nervous sentry ordered, "OK Sir. Advance and be recognized."

Inside the tent many changes had taken place. The tent now looked almost like a hospital. Medical equipment was every where. Obviously all available medics were present and ready to receive the wounded. To my surprise, Dutch and the Medical Officer were already busy tending to a wounded GI. When Dutch decided the Medical Officer could handle the wounds, he came over and asked if we were ready for the attack. I told him Major Blanton seemed satisfied. Dutch then asked if there was anything he could do for me. I nodded and said, "A cop of coffee would help right now and while I drink it we can talk for a few minutes."

Dutch grabbed a passing corpsman and asked for two coffees, one black and one with light sugar and light cream. He explained the lieutenant likes cream and sugar. As the corpsman left, Dutch pointed to two closed medical supply chests sitting in a corner of the tent. He said, "Lets sit over there, out of the line of traffic. All I get before a big action is a lots of questions. Everybody gets keyed-up and jumpy."

Getting out of the line of traffic seemed a good idea. While sitting on the medical chest waiting for our coffee, the traffic in the tent kept getting worse. I even noticed a Chaplin and his aide had appeared on the scene. I thought, before I forget, I'd better ask Dutch for the pass words. He told me, "The pass words for tonight are 'Betty Boop' 'Betty' is the sign and 'Boop' is the counter sign. Think you can remember that until midnight? At midnight the pass words changes to 'Orange Crush.' 'Orange' is the sign and 'Crush' is the counter sign."

"I think I can handle that. Who in the hell thinks up these words anyway?"

"Some lame brain back at Corps Headquarters. If the war lasts long enough, they will run out of words. I thought of a couple of words the Krauts wouldn't understand. You play poker, how about 'Full House' or 'Royal Flush.'

Dutch continued to talk, "Randy, as of 0600 hours this morning you officially become a combat qualified airborne officer. Have you thought of that?"

"No Dutch, I really haven't thought about it, I've got too many other things on my mind right now. Why do you ask?"

"Well first, look at your lousy combat boots."

"What's wrong with my combat boots?"

"Airborne officers don't wear combat boots, they wear jump boots. That's their badge of distinction. What size boots do you wear Lieutenant?"

"I wear size eleven, what difference does it make?"

"The difference is, you are my buddy, my friend. Buddies look out for each other."

"What are you going to do Dutch, get the Supply Sergeant to requisition a pair of jump boots for me?"

"Don't you worry about ole Dutch, he has ways. Just leave the details to me."

"OK ole buddy, I know you move in mysterious ways, so I'll leave the details to you." Looking at my watch, I exclaimed, "Oh shit, I've got to get back to Major Blanton. Thanks for the coffee, it hit the spot. Please tell the Medical Officer my entire crew of six will be remaining with Regiment for a short time, and we accept his offer to let us use part of his tent while we are here. Oh yes, before I go, how did the GI on the examination table get shot before the attack began? Did he have an accident?"

:No, the poor bastard didn't have an accident, he has an 'SIW."

"Dutch, what the hell is an SIW?"

"SIW stands for a self inflicted wound. The dumb bastard shot himself in the foot."

"On purpose?"

"It happens every now and then when a man cracks and can't tolerate combat any longer. What they don't know is that a 30-caliber slug through the instep breaks about a zillion small bones in his foot and no military doctor can put the foot back together again. It's kind of like Humpty Dumtpy. That kid will get a Bad Conduct Discharge (BCD) and will limp the rest of his life,

"Dutch, thanks again for the coffee, and don't forget to tell the Medical Officer he will have guests for a couple of days. You know Dutch, maybe having a gimpy foot and a BCD is better than getting killed."

"Maybe for you buddy, but not for me!"

The Attack Starts to Fail
505th Parachute Infantry Regiment—Medical Aid Station
29 January 1945

Staff Sergeant Dutch Schultz, the Medical Officer, and I, were drinking coffee, and discussing the beginning of the attack. yesterday. The operation was planned as a *'Blitzkrieg'* type attack. A hard initial blow, quick penetration of the enemy front lines, a sudden burst into the enemy communications zone, followed by a swift advance deep into enemy held territory, then an eighty mile advance in five or six days. A grand master plan, but it was not going to happen. What did happen on the first day of the attack was a well executed artillery barrage. This had been the Medical Officer's first experience watching a massive pre-dawn artillery barrage. He had gone outside to watch the spectacle, and described it in terms of a sunrise with thunder and lightening. He said the barrage lasted more than thirty minutes, starting slowly and gaining momentum until it reached its maximum furry. During this time, the doctor described the first feeble flashes from intermittent artillery fire as a soft, flickering, pre-dawn light. But as the firing tempo increased, he said the whole horizon became alive with a bright, continuous light, much like that of the rising sun.

The sounds of the barrage reminded him of rumbling thunder as sound waves rolled through the air. He experienced loud thunder from nearby artillery pieces hurling missiles of death at the enemy. This sound was mixed with the softer, more distant thunder, from missiles exploding in enemy territory. The bitter cold air, and the surrounding hilly terrain, turned these mixed sounds into eerie reverberating echoes.

I found his description of this intense terror, raining down from the skies, to be rather poetic and almost childlike.

Another topic of conversation concerned the casualties which passed through the aid station yesterday. Fortunately, the Regimental Commander's forecast for heavy casualties during the first day of the attack was not accurate. The casualty rate had been light. The beefed-up group of medics had been able to handle the flow of wounded with no major problems. Why were the casualties so light? Would you believe it, it was the stinking, lousy, bitter cold, weather. The first day plan was to move North and East for about ten miles. The first day our infantry advanced about one half of one mile. The reason for the short advance was, of course, the inclement weather.

The experience I gained as a Liaison Officer on my first day at Regiment was zilch, zero, nothing! My two main duties consisted of receiving situation reports from various attacking unit commanders, and explaining to Corps Artillery why no one was requesting supporting artillery fire. I became so frustrated by the questions from Corps Artillery I almost gave them some useless fire missions to shut them up. Their not so subtle insinuations that I was not handling my responsibilities properly prompted me to advise them I was giving Regiment all the help it needed, and asked a Corps Artillery Assistant S-3 if he would like to verify this fact with the Colonel. Everyone, including the XVIII Airborne Corps Commander himself, was frustrated because the attack had stalled. The Corps Commander made hurried visits to all the Regimental Command Posts to personally express his disappointment.

Dutch said he had a tent full of foot soldiers who were suffering from nothing more than hypothermia and physical exhaustion. He explained the guys would probably thaw-out and get their strength back in 48 hours, but they were completely exhausted from breaking trails through chest deep snow like human bulldozers. This was a non-ending task, and ground was gained yard by yard from a determined and well entrenched enemy. The weather did not permit the normal leapfrogging of platoons, and limited the attack to just one tediously slow effort to gain enemy held ground.

During this grim conversation, Dutch suddenly changed the subject, "Randy, I have something I want to give you."

"Something for me? What is it?"

While the Medical Officer watched with a 'I know something you don't know' grin on his face, the Dutchman reached behind a medical chest and withdrew a pair of gleaming, highly polished, jump boots. With a flourish of obvious satisfaction he exclaimed, "They are size elevens Lieutenant. Why don't you try them on?"

"Dutch, where in the hell did you get these boots?"

"As I said before Lieutenant, don't sweat the details. Just leave the details to ole Dutch."

The Medical Officer and Dutch watched as I removed my rough, dirty combat boots and tried on the smooth leather jump boots. First the left, and then the right. Next, stomping on the hard packed dirt floor of the tent. Then walking, striding, the entire length of the tent, back and forth, testing the fit of the new boots. My combat boots were comfortable but so were the jump boots. My combat boots looked like hell whereas the jump boots looked great. The Medical Officer nodded his head in approval as I eyed and tested the jump boots.

"Dutch, these jump boots fit like they were made for me. I'd like to keep them. How much 'bread' do I owe you?"

"You don't owe me nothing. Just wear them with pride. They are a gift from a Trooper you don't even know. He got his 'million dollar wound' yesterday. He will be in a hospital in the states for a long time. Uncle Sam will issue him a new pair of boots to fit his new leg when he gets it. In the meantime he wants you to have his boots. It is an Airborne tradition. The wounded Trooper wants his boots to be with his buddies even if he can't be there. Lieutenant, wear these boots with pride. These boots belong to you now."

Again, the Medical Officer nodded his head to indicate he was in total agreement with the unknown Trooper's gift.

Today's north easterly advance through the Loshiem Gap was progressing better than expected. In Herresbach, elements of our regiment captured the

German unit assigned to defend this village. During the day, the 505th Regiment also secured the villages of Holzheim and Emmerscheid for the Allies. Today the aid station received a steady stream of dead and broken bodies.

When Sergeant Wiener assumed my duties at the Operations Center, I went straight to the aid station in search of 'medicinal alcohol' and to get away from the responsibilities of war. When I entered the tent, the aid station was a beehive of activity. It was apparent I was not the only person who was sleep deprived and dead tired. One particular examination table caught my eye. It was surrounded by several medics, who were themselves surrounded by angry armed Troopers. On the table, half lying and half sitting, was a German soldier, a hated German SS Officer. He was severely wounded in his left leg and was arguing loudly, in German, with Staff Sergeant Schultz. This scene interested me, so I joined the group just in time to see Dutch pull sharply on the SS Officer's wounded leg. The German Officer screamed in pain, rose to one elbow, and slapped Dutch smartly across the mouth. Blood sprang from the Dutchman's cut lip, and complete silence reigned in the tent.

Wording my way through the silent GIs to the edge of the examination table, I saw the bleeding lip and the slap mark on my friend's face. What concerned me most was the look of extreme hatred on the medic's face, and the fear on the face of the SS Officer. I stood there wondering what had happened between these two, then I looked at the German's feet. He was wearing regulation U S Army jump boots! I looked at Dutch again. He was furious! Dutch was so mad he was loosing control. The eyes of the surrounding combat troops contained the same look of intense hatred. They all knew how the SS Officer had obtained the jump boots. Every one of them wanted to kill this German. Here, and now!

I realized it was time for cooler heads to prevail and defuse this dangerous situation. I asked the combat troops to leave the tent. When no one stirred, I ordered them to evacuate the tent. Grudgingly they left, one by one, muttering as they passed by the wounded SS Officer. The only incident occurred when one trooper paused, looked the German in the eyes, and spat directly into his face. This airborne non-com then glanced knowingly at Dutch as he left the tent.

The Medical Officer, sensing something was wrong, came to the examination table and looked at the wounded prisoner. He and Ditch had a brief conversation after which the Medical Officer motioned for Dutch to resume tending to the wounded man. Apparently finished here, he quickly left to continue his work in another part of the tent. Dutch had a dual responsibility while dealing with a prisoner. First, to treat the prisoners wounds, and Second, to interrogate him prior to turning him over to the Intelligence Officer for a more detailed interrogation.

The still angry Dutchman resumed cutting away the outer pants and the underwear from the wounded leg. The SS Officer started to relax. His period of relaxation was brief however. When Dutch started to remove the jump boot from the shattered leg, he unlaced the boot and used a mighty tug on the boot to remove it. The prisoner screamed, a scream of the damned, and immediately passed out from the pain.

I could not believe an American medic would do such a barbaric thing. For the first time in our friendship, I questioned the actions of Staff Sergeant Schultz. "Dutch, did you administer morphine to the prisoner before you tried to remove his boot?"

The angry medic snapped back, "They weren't his boots!"

"Answer my question Sergeant!"

"Is that an order?" He almost snarled, and then added, "Sir!"

"Yes Sergeant Schultz, that is an order."

"No, I did not administer morphine to the prisoner, Sir."

"Then you just wanted to hurt this wounded human being?"

"No Sir, I am saving the morphine to ease the pain of our own wounded men."

"Sergeant Schultz, I do not believe you. I know you have plenty of morphine. You just wanted to torture this prisoner because he was wearing American jump boots."

Staff Sergeant Schultz was getting boiling mad again, but this time he was mad at me. He realized I had brushed friendship aside and now this was strictly an enlisted man/officer situation. His thought process began to change as he carefully phrased his response, "Lieutenant, First, he slapped me hard enough to draw blood. He slapped me in front of my superiors and subordinates. Second, he took those boots from a dead or wounded Trooper. I will not let him get away with that."

"Sergeant Schultz, I am not going to argue with you. I know what you say is true. But it is common practice in the German Army for officers to slap enlisted men. That slap was just an automatic reaction. It is also common in both armies to remove clothing from the dead. Dead bodies don't need clothing, but living bodied do."

"Yes Sir."

"If it is medically correct, I want you to give the prisoner some pain killer, remove the boot, treat his wounds, wake him up, and interrogate him. This is a request. If necessary, I'll make it an order.'

"Yes Sir."

This whole process was painful for me. Dutch was my friend, but his actions were wrong. I did not like having to talk to him in this manner, with other medics watching and listening. As I left the scene, I cornered the Medical Officer and told him I had disciplined Dutch in front of his peers and didn't know what effect my actions would have on his people. He told me not to worry about my actions, they were normal, and advised me to go to his tent and forget what had happened. "While you are there, you may want a drink. I think you know where I keep the alcohol and grapefruit juice."

I thanked him as I left. I was emotionally drained and suddenly felt tired. Once alone and in his tent, I mixed a stiff drink and rapidly empted the entire cup. The second cup of 'medicine' was consumed much more slowly. Thankfully, the two drinks started to salve my frayed emotions. The drinks did not solve my problems, but they made me feel better. Finally, my strong desire to talk to Dutch caused me to return to the examination tent. I felt better when I saw the German Officer sitting on the side of the examination table. His shattered leg and bare foot neatly bandaged. The agony was gone from the prisoner's fact, the pain now blocked by morphine injections. Dutch gave me a stern look as I approached his treatment table and gruffly asked, "Does that job suit you Lieutenant? Did I fix the son-of-a-bitch to your satisfaction?" Before I could respond, he continued, "Now the SOB wants to go to the latrine, He wants to take a crap. I've got a good mind to make him sit here and crap in his fucking pants."

"Come on Dutch, ask one of your medics to escort him outside to the latrine."

"No Lieutenant, I'll escort the bastard myself. I can talk with him, the other medics don't speak German. He would try to escape from one of the younger guys."

"It is your call Dutch. Handle it your own way. It is none of my business how you run things here. I feel rotten because I've stuck my nose in your business too much already."

Apparently the huge medic accepted my indirect apology because he replied, "Don't sweat it Lieutenant, you are a good young officer. And Randy we all know you mean well."

With that said, Dutch went to a tent pole, removed a hanging web belt and suspenders, and donned them. Hanging on the web belt was a 45-caliber pistol in a leather holster. Strapped to the suspenders with medical tape were two fragmentation grenades. Dutch said something to the prisoner in German and motioned toward the rear tent flap. As they exited the tent I thought, "All is well that ends well," and returned to the Medical Officers tent.

While sipping straight grapefruit this time, I began to unwind, a comfortable cot, a warm tent, and no frenzied activity. It really felt good.

Suddenly my reverie was broken by a loud, but muffled explosion. Was it caused by an incoming mortar round, a bursting artillery shell, what had exploded? I hit the dirt and waited for the second explosion, but it never happened. Then it dawned on me, that was the sound of an exploding hand grenade. Immediately a vision of the two hand grenades strapped to the suspenders Dutch was wearing came to mind. I rushed back to the first aid tent just in time to witness several medics peering out the back flap of the tent and looking in the direction of the latrine. Their excited remarks confirmed my suspicions. I pushed my way to the open tent flap. The sight was appalling and accurately described by a medic talking to no one in particular when he said, "He was straddling the slit trench when the grenade exploded right us his ass. God what a mess!"

About to vomit from this horribly gory sight, I moved back into the tent to compose myself. A few minutes later Staff Sergeant Shultz returned, entering from the front entrance. He stopped, surveyed the group of medics, slowly removed the web belt and suspenders, and hung them back on the tent pole. The

45-caliber pistol was still it its leather holster, but one of the two fragmentation grenades was missing. He approached, and with no emotion, he simply said, "Lieutenant, the prisoner tried to escape."

I was so speechless I could not respond. Inside, my guts were churning. I was so frustrated I did not know what to do. I was fed up with killing, with brutality, with inhumanity, but there wasn't one damned thing I could do to change the ugly face of war.

I returned to the Medical Officers tent, sat in his comfortable folding camp chair and drank his 'medicinal alcohol' until I was mercifully drunk!

The Thrust of the Attack is Changed
505th Parachute Infantry Regiment—Operations Center
1 February 1945

By midnight, last night, the regiment had advanced only ten miles. This was far short of the objective set at the beginning of the attack. The advance had been steady, but slow. This was definitely an infantry battle, man against man. It was also a battle of man against the weather, the terrible, terrible weather. The deeper we penetrated into Germany, the more determined the enemy defenders became. They were now defending their homeland. We did feel better knowing Americans now occupied a portion of the Siegfried Line between the German villages of Undenbreth and Loshiem. When the allied supreme command established the objectives for this campaign they obviously had not taken into consideration the inclement weather and the determined enemy defense.

From my point of view, Corps Artillery had performed well. Our artillery units had been able to move with the infantry advance in spite of the icy conditions. We had maintained our ability to deliver effective indirect fire when requested by the infantry. I was extremely proud of my Liaison team. We had remained in contact with Corps Artillery at all times, even while moving forward with the infantry. My radio operator/technicians were skilled in their craft and dedicated to our mission. Quoting Sergeant Wiener, "What more could they ask?"

My feeling of accomplishment was short lived when the regimental commander received a call from Corps advising him the attack had been called off in this sector, and our mission changed.

Like a gigantic ship at sea, steaming at full speed, the momentum of the attack by the XVIII Airborne Corps could not be stopped immediately. The momentum carried us deeper into enemy territory until the inertia of the attack dwindled to a halt.

A Change in Missions
592nd FA Bn – Charlie Battery Rest Area
5 February 1945

My team had served about one week with the infantry and I was glad to be back with our unit. The entire liaison team needed time to wash socks, underwear, and fatigues. We needed to take a real bath, relax, and take a break from fighting a war.

This was not to be. By the time we arrived, Captain Baxter had received orders to move the battery. The 592ns FA Bn had been ordered to move north to support the 9th Army advance on Aachen, Germany and once past Aachen, the attack toward Dusseldorf. The American attack was to be the southern end of a pincers movement. The northern pincer was the responsibility of several Canadian units. I was assigned as a forward observer to man a Corps observation post located west of the large metropolitan area of Aachen. My team was to occupy this post at dawn, the morning of 7 February. The mission, to fire on targets of opportunity for a day, or until my allocation of 155mm ammunition was exhausted. This coordinated attack was scheduled to start the morning of 8 February. The 82nd Airborne and the 78th Infantry Divisions were assigned task of advancing through Aachen, Vossenach, and Bergsten, with the town of Schmidt, Germany being the final objective.

XVIII Airborne Corps – Forward Observation Post
West of Urban Aachen, Germany
February 7, 1945

The morning of 7 February broke cold and clear. The location of the observation post was well chosen and offered an excellent view of the city and surrounding terrain. The abundance of my ammunition allotment surprised me. As we took our stations and waited for the dawn I expected to see many targets of opportunity. But daylight revealed a city which had been utterly destroyed by strategic Air Corps bombing. Not many buildings were standing, and those that were shared various degrees of damage. Jerry and I both manned the OP, our field glassed scanning the city for signs of activity. There was none, the city seemed dead. There were no signs that enemy troops occupied the city. No smoke rising from cooking fires, no light reflections from polished metal or glass, no movements by vehicles nor humans, no sounds of motors running, absolutely nothing! The lack of activity was hard to believe. Jerry commented, "Aachen is like looking at a grave yard covered with broken headstones."

Our first call from Corps consisted of several questions, "Are you in place? Are you ready to observe? Do you have a clear view of the target area?" My answer to all these questions was, "Yes, Affirmative," The second call came from the operations officer himself. He was obviously frustrated and abruptly asked, "Lieutenant, what the Hell is going on up there?"

"Nothing Sir, there is nothing in Aachen to justify wasting ammunition."

"Damn it Lieutenant, there must be something to shoot at. The damned German army hasn't just picked up its marbles and moved to Berlin."

"Major, there are two qualified observers on this hill. As far as we can tell, that's exactly what the Germans have done. They've picked up their marbles and gone home."

After a pause, the Major returned to the telephone and informed me, "I just talked to the Corps Intelligence Officer. He said what you tell me is nonsense. If you can't locate suitable targets of opportunity, drop a few rounds into the city, stir the pot, get things moving."

"As you say sir, we'll have some missions for fire direction in a few minutes."

"You do that Lieutenant, we need to know what we're up against in Aachen. Our preliminary intelligence reports indicates the city is crawling with German troops."

The Major's orders didn't make sense to either of us. We knew there was no sizeable enemy presence in Aachen, never-the-less an order is an order, so Jerry and I went to work. As Jerry scanned the target area with his field glasses, he identified possible locations which German troops might occupy. As he relayed this information to me, I marked these locations on my battle map, assigned them concentration numbers, and recorded the map coordinates. Within fifteen minutes we were adjusting artillery fire into Aachen.

We fired five missions that averaged eight 155mm rounds per mission. Forty rounds of 155mm high explosive shells descending upon various locations is a lots of destructive power. While I was observing the effects of my own fire, I noticed other explosions occurring in the target area. These shell bursts were substantially smaller than mine. I commented to Jerry that other artillery observers were identifying targets of opportunity in Aachen that we seemed to be missing. Jerry had been watching these smaller explosions through his field glasses and replied, "Lieutenant, those are 105mm shell bursts. Some light artillery battalions are wasting ammunition too. Their firing is random and they are not making anything move either. What do you want me to report back to Corps Artillery?"

"Don't report anything to Crops Jerry. Let's put a little fun in our otherwise dull day. Look at the Cathedral just to the right of the bend in the river."

"Jesus Lieutenant, you aren't going to demolish a beautiful old Cathedral are you?"

"Not in your life Jerry. I wouldn't demolish it if it was a Synagogue."

"Come on Randy, that's not funny. You know I don't like to be kidded about being Jewish."

"That was a bad joke Jerry, I'll admit it. You can kid me about being a Methodist if it'll make you feel better. Any way, look about 30 mills to the right of the Cathedral and closer to the river. You should see one huge undamaged smokestack."

"Oh yea, I see it now."

"Well, that is our next target. I think several hundred German SS troops are hiding in that smokestack."

"Come on Lieutenant, you know as well as I do, that is not possible."

"If Corps Artillery wants to play games, why can't I? How large do you think that thing is Jerry?"

"Well, lets take a guess. I'd say it is part of a bombed out factory judging from the rubble around the base. My guess it is about 40 feet across the base and about 150 feet tall. It is built of brick. It is a pretty big structure Randy."

"Do you remember the 'target for destruction' mission we fired to destroy the German 'Royal Tiger' tank?"

"Of course I do. That was damned good shooting."

"Keeping that mission in mind Sergeant Wiener, how many rounds do you think it will take us to topple that Kraut built smokestack?"

"I don't know. The 'airplane jocks' bombed the shit out of the area but that smokestack is still standing."

"You are right Sergeant Wiener, that is how the Air Corps works. They do sloppy work. But we are the Field Artillery, the 'King of Battle,' we put our balls where the 'Queen of Battle' (the Infantry) wants them. The Field Artillery gets the job done right. We don't screw around." After determining the coordinates of the smokestack I gave Jerry the message to send to our fire direction center. When the operations officer asked the nature of the target to be destroyed, Jerry immediately replied, "A fortified strong point."

Our senseless play-acting at destroying something of military importance did accomplish something however. It got Corps Artillery off our backs, and relieved our own tensions, but I did feel the tax paying American citizens did not get their moneys worth when we wasted expensive 155mm artillery ammunition. This game, like all games, had to end some way. Jerry laughed when I told him to give fire direction the message, "Cease Fire! End of Mission! Mission Accomplished!" We both laughed as we looked into the target area. We had to admire the competent Kraut design of the rugged and defiant still standing smokestack.

By noon there were almost no artillery rounds exploding in Aachen. Jerry had one of the jeep drivers to fix lunch. Taking everything into consideration it wasn't too bad. Hot instant coffee with powdered creamer and double sugar, and a heated can of 'C Ration' type pork and beans. It was like having a picnic in the snow. The dessert, a 'D Bar,' was not so good. The story of 'D Bars' goes something like this. They contain rich and tasty chocolate, ease hunger pains quickly, provide almost instant energy, and provide enormous amounts of calories to help keep you warm. This sounds like ideal food for soldiers enduring the most severe cold weather in Europe in years. The truth is, the 'D Bar' was designed for use in desert warfare conditions. Chocolate in the 'D Bar' was processed so it would not melt even when exposed to direct rays of the desert sun. In sub-freezing weather, like we were experiencing, this chocolate had the consistency of cured concrete. When I sucked on my 'D Bar' I was extremely careful. I did not want to break a tooth on a ration that was left over from the battle of the North African Desert.

Toward the end of this cold and dull day, I heard the sound of a jeep motor running behind us at the base of the hill. For a better look, I walked a short distance and observed an American officer talking with members of my team at the bottom of the hill. I noticed my guys motioning toward me and the officer started walking up the trail leading to our observation post. Upon arrival, he introduced himself as Captain Brinson, the CO of the infantry unit that controlled this area. He advised me our observation post would be shut-down for the night and invited us to spend the night with 'Fox' Company. He also offered us hot meals for supper and breakfast tomorrow morning, but added emphatically, "After that you will be on your own because things will be very busy at Fox Company tomorrow morning." I, of course, accepted his offer with gratitude.

As we talked, Captain Brinson asked, "How does the target area look?" In response to his question I handed him my field glasses and replied, "Take a look for your self." The Captain seemed pleased as he scanned the entire target area and detected no signs of enemy activity. As we walked to his vehicle at the base of the hill, Captain Brinson explained he must continue the inspection rounds of his units this afternoon, but would leave one of his men to guide us to his Command Post when the observation post was formally closed. He also stated he was looking forward to talking with me while we enjoyed our supper together.

I could not believe the Captain's hospitable offer, and our own good luck. When I reached the crest of the hill, I asked Jerry to call fire direction and verify if our OP was to be closed tonight. Jerry confirmed the infantry officers information and was advised to 'Ring Off' at 1600 hours, unless otherwise advised. He was also instructed, under the threat of death, to 'Ring on' tomorrow morning no later than 0600 hours.

We arrived at the 'Fox Company' command post with no trouble. It was located in a medium sized farm house, nested in the edge of a forest, facing a relatively large cleared field. Briefed outpost guards were expecting us and waved us into a wooded area some fifty yards from the farm house. After hiding the two vehicles under heavy overhanging branches I asked my radio operator to contact Captain Baxter at 'Charley Battery.' I wanted our commanding officer to know we were spending the night with 'Fox Company' in case he needed to contact us. The attempts to contact the 592nd FA Bn were not successful. Not knowing what the sleeping arrangements were, Jerry and I entered the farm house, but left the other men with the jeeps and our personal gear. We were pleasantly surprised as Captain Brinson showed us a space in one room large enough to accommodate two bed rolls. He then introduced Sergeant Wiener to one of his squad leaders and told us the rest of the men would bed down with the heavy weapons platoon. To make certain he knew where his men would be located, Jerry decided to accompany the squad leader to his bunker and stated he would return with our personal gear and our two bed rolls. I nodded agreement, but the most important thing on my mind right now was to let Captain Baxter where we were.

To ease my anxiety, Captain Brinson asked one of his non-coms to get Charlie Battery of the 592nd FA Bn on the telephone and let the operator know Lieutenant Pierson wants to talk with Captain Baxter. When the non-com asked his CO where the 592nd was located, a peeved Captain Brinson replied, "How in the Hell do I know. All I know is it is attached to the XVIII Airborne Corps Artillery. Just keep trying until you get the 592nd switchboard." He then reached into his bed roll and pulled out an almost full bottle of Cognac and confessed, "I always get jumpy just before an attack. All my men know this, they just humor me, I need a drink."

When I nodded my head in agreement, he asked, "Do you have anything to drink out of?" I took the canteen and cup out of my web holster and extended the cup in his direction. He poured me one hell of a stiff drink, and as we sat there silently watching each other sip the fiery liquid, he finally broke the silence and said, "I think I like you Lieutenant, you drink your spirits straight."

Our little drinking session was interrupted when the switchboard operator motioned for me to come and pick up a phone. I asked the Battalion operator to ring 'C' Battery for me, and then heard a familiar voice answer, "Charlie Battery

Command Post." "This is Lieutenant Pierson, is Captain Baxter available?" "I think he is Lieutenant, hold on a minute and I'll check." After a slight pause an authoritative male voice said, "Baxter here. What is up Pierson?" "Captain, I just wanted to let you know Corps closed our OP until 0600 tomorrow. We are spending the night with Captain Brinson of Fox Company. If you need me tonight you can reach me here."

There was another slight pause as my CO left the line. Upon his return, he said, "I have two pieces of news for you. First, Corps just notified us your OP has been closed permanently, you and your crew are to repost back to Charlie Battery in the morning. Make it as early as possible, the Battalion is moving. Second, congratulate Wiener for me, I received a copy of the orders promoting him to 'Buck' Sergeant today. You apparently had him figured correctly, we have gotten good reports from Corps Artillery concerning his performance. Also the infantry officers he works with think he is first class." "Damn, that is good news Captain. We will eat an early breakfast with the infantry and get started home as soon as we get some light. Any details you can give me over the phone?"

"The details will keep. Just get your lazy butts back to the battery early tomorrow morning. I don't want to leave a man behind just to guide you to our new location." "I understand Captain, don't worry, we'll be there."

When Jerry and I decided to 'hit the sack,' this corner of the Fox Company Command Post was very quiet, most infantry personnel were trying to get rested prior to tomorrows attack. We talked, Jerry was excited about his promotion now being official. Captain Brinson had donated a half full bottle of Cognac to 'wet down' his three stripes. As we stretched out in our bed rolls I was happy to be returning to the artillery instead of staying with the infantry during an attack. We were lucky, we had a roof over our heads, our bellies were full of warm chow, the infantry to guard us, and a 'glow on' from Captain Brinson's Cognac. Ever so slowly the gist of our conversation changed. Even though we had been together several weeks, I didn't know much about Jerry. The Cognac made him more talkative and with no effort on my part he shared the details of his childhood, education, family, religion, his concerns of the present, and his plans for the future. What he shared with me was interesting, he was an unusual individual with a unique background. His dialogue made me realize why he hated Nazi Germans so much.

Finally Jerry wound down and it was time to sleep. I thought of my life, the war, and my plans for after the war. Thoughts of my mother and returning home finally took over and filled my dreams.

592nd FA Fn — Charlie Battery
8 February 1945

As promised, we loaded our two jeeps before dawn for the return trip to Charlie Battery. We were first in the 'chow line' for breakfast with the infantry. Fortunately I ran into Captain Brinson who told me he expected the entire 82nd Airborne Division to be pulled from the line early in the attack and be replaced with an infantry division. He expected the Army to give the 82nd Airborne Division time to 'lick its wounds,' draw replacements to bring the division up to authorized strength, and to replace combat damaged equipment. When I asked why he felt that way, he replied, "It is pretty simple, we will make a jump on the German side of the Rhine. The code name for this jump is 'Bridge Across the Rhine.' Airborne troops are required to establish a large 'beach head' on the East side of the Rhine, and secure the 'beach head' until Army Engineers can build a military bridge across the river. This 'Bridge across the Rhine' operation was new to me, but the way Captain Brinson explained the need, it made sense. He added, "Lieutenant maybe our paths will cross again sometime, in the meantime I wish you all the best." I thanked him for his hospitality and good wishes, then shook his hand as we said good bye.

The experience we had gained while serving with the 82nd Airborne Division for about a month led me to believe it is better to be in an attack mode than in a stale defensive holding action. We had experienced tough fighting with these troopers, but the intensity was usually short lived. Offensive action was not normally drawn out over several days like the holding action of the 589th FA Bn at Baraque de Fraiture, Belgium. The fact the Allies considered the Battle of the Bulge campaign was complete surprised me. I did not know the Allies considered the Battle for the Rhineland a new campaign. Captain Brinson did forewarn me however, with his description of operation 'Bridge across the Rhine.' It was now apparent to me the Allied High Command was actively planning a large campaign to cross the Rhine in force, and latter plan another campaign to conquer central Europe.

Before full light, my two jeeps were on the road headed toward the 592nd FA Bn. Sergeant Wiener asserted himself and told my driver to ride in his jeep, he was going to drive for the Lieutenant because we had important things to discuss. Jerry was so excited about his promotion and so grateful for his third stripe, he gushed forth the entire trip. I did not mind his enthusiasm, I had no immediate worries, so I just relaxed and listened.

Charlie Battery had 'closed station' and was in the process of assembling the vehicles into 'march order' when we reported to Captain Baxter. The Captain was in a good mood. He jokingly chastised Jerry, "Sergeant Wiener, if you are not proud enough of your rank to wear the proper insignia, maybe I can have your promotional order rescinded." A nervous Sergeant Wiener gulped, saluted, grinned, and asked to be excused. I excused Jerry, and turned to the Captain, "Don't be too hard on Jerry, he will make a damned good non-com. He has all the right qualifications. Don't forget, I taught him everything he knows."

"Christ, I don't know which is worse, a new NCO or a smart-ass new 'Shave-tail.' You two deserve each other. Now that the social chit-chat is over Lieutenant, are you interested on learning the details of your next assignment?"

"Yes Sir. I am very interested."

Captain Baxter went on to explain the battalion was being moved father North to the northern boundary of the First US Army, which bordered on the southern boundary of the Ninth US Army. He pulled a map from his canvas map-case and showed me the invisible dividing line between the two American Armies. The boundary line ran roughly northeast through the Hurtgen Forest to the Rhine River about midway between Dusseldorf and Cologne. Once at our destination, and the battery in place, my crew and I would still be attached to Charlie battery, but under Corps Artillery control. As soon as we arrived an officer from Corps Artillery would explain my new assignment to me.

Within an hour, my jeeps were serviced. We drew extra gasoline and field rations, checked the radio equipment, had merged into the slowly moving Charlie Battery convoy, and were headed north toward the Hurtgen Forest. To my surprise, Jerry had decided to drive my jeep again. He had a huge grin on his face when he pointed to the Sergeant Chevrons on the sleeves of his field jacket. He never ceased to amaze me. I had no idea how he got the chevrons so quickly, and decided not to ask.

Well before dark, the battery Executive Officer in the lead vehicle of the convoy spotted Captain Baxter's jeep on the side of the road. The Captain's driver intercepted the convoy and led the column into a bivouac area. While the XO was busy getting the rest of the battery settled, we quickly made our own arrangements for the night. Even though we were miles from our destination, and well in the rear of the combat area, my two radiomen were assigned to perimeter guard duty for the night. Jerry told the jeep drivers to park the two jeeps close together, near the Medics tent, and bed down for the night between their vehicles. As was our custom, Jerry went to the medical section and made arrangements for us.

In the field, but not in a combat area, the mess sergeant stretched a large canvas fly from one side of the mess truck to shelter a folding table and chairs for the officers. I decided to join the other battery officers for supper. After we ate. the weather was not conducive to lingering outside. As we adjourned, the Captain asked me to bring a pitcher of coffee and two cups to his command post. By comparison, the CP tent was warm and cheery, and the Captain was in a good mood. He still did not know what role we would play in the new area of combat, but he surmised his battery would be utilized some where west of Cologne, in general support of operation 'Bridge across the Rhine.'

He asked me if I had ever heard of the 28th Infantry Division and the rough time they experienced in the Hurtgen Forest during October and November 1944. I had to plead ignorance because I was in England at that time and had heard only brief details of the battle. Two of his friends in the 28th Infantry Division had told him of the futile situation the division experienced in the Hurtgen Forest. We were relaxed and under no pressure so he decided to share some of the division history with me.

The 28th Infantry Division was a National Guard unit, born and bred in

Pennsylvania. It was staffed mainly by Pennsylvania citizen soldiers and was known as the 'Keystone Division.' The shoulder insignia is a simple red keystone, the same as the State Seal. Established in World War I, the 28th Infantry Division participated in the WWII liberation of Paris, helped eliminate the German concentration in the French Colmar pocket, endured tremendous losses of men in the Hurtgen Forest, and fought valiantly during the Battle of the Bulge. It was a proud Division with a distinguished military history The futile loss of dead and wounded men in the Hurtgen Forest gave birth to a new name for their honorable Red Keystone insignia. It became known as the 'Bloody Bucket.' The courageous fighting men of the 28th Division spilled much blood in what the commanding officer of the 82nd Airborne Division, General James Gavin, called, "The battle that should have never been." Even the German defenders in the Hurtgen referred to the attacking Americans as, "The men from the Bloody Bucket."

592nd FA Bn — Charlie Battery
In Bivouac — Awaiting Orders
10 February 1945

The men in Charlie Battery were being pushed to get themselves and their equipment ready for the next combat assignment. This preparation was important, however no one knew exactly what to prepare for. This fact increased tensions even though we were not exposed to personal danger in this location, we just didn't know what was going on. As for me, I was still waiting to be told what my responsibilities with Corps Artillery would be. My trend of thought was broken when Jerry informed me the Captain wanted to see me in his command post. Captain Baxter was not in a good mood, and it showed in his body language. "Pierson, sit down. I have news for you that doesn't make sense. Day after tomorrow, you are to report for 'glider indoctrination.' Do you know anything about this?" "No Sir. What is glider indoctrination?" "How in the Hell an I supposed to know?"

"Captain Baxter do you have a copy of my orders?" "No. I just got a phone call telling me you are supposed to be at an air base somewhere in Belgium no later than 1600 hours on 12 February " "Captain, I don't know any more about this so-called training than you. Don't sweat it, I'll get the details and get there on time, One last question, can I use my jeep and a driver for this trip?" "Yes, with my blessings. Now get out of here. I have other things to do." "Thanks Captain, I'll see you in a few days."

The weather for the trip was reasonable for this time of year in Europe. Not great weather, but not lousy weather either. To my surprise Captain Baxter assigned a new driver for the trip, Private First Class James A. Smith. I knew PFC Smith fairly well. He was farm raised, a good mechanic, a good driver, and like most southern born boys, he knew how to shoot a rifle. He didn't talk much, but when he did, I listened. Even though the difference in rank between a PFC and an Officer is great, but we felt comfortable with each other. Getting to a main road was not easy. Smithy drove the jeep in four wheel drive while I read the map and gave him instructions. Finally we reached the paved road and Smithy dropped the jeep into two wheel drive and we relaxed during a long smooth ride into Belgium.

We reached our destination, a Belgian Aerodrome, with time to spare. As we pulled into the operations center Smithy exclaimed, "Holly Shit! What's going on here?" It appeared a majority of the transport planes in the American Air Corps had been assembled here. In addition to the Curtis C46 and Douglas C47 transport aircraft, there were hordes of Waco CG-4A transport gliders parked all over the Belgian country side. To me, a person would have to be 'WACO' to ride in one of those things. They looked like flying, plywood coffins, with flimsy fabric covered wings, and equipped with feeble looking landing gear scrounged from a junk yard. As we stood looking at this huge potential air armada, Smithy put the icing on the cake when he asked, "Lieutenant, you aren't going up in one of those things are you?"

Inside the operations center, other officers and men were checking-in as I presented a copy of our orders to a staff sergeant seated behind the only open desk. The emblem on his jacket indicated he was parachute qualified. He glanced at the orders and then at us. With a 'ho-hum' tone of voice he said, "Lieutenant, take a seat, I'll take care of your driver first." As I sat down, I casually said, "That's fine sergeant. Take good care of him because he takes good care of me." The Airborne Staff Sergeant did not even glance up as he looked at his roster and said, "Private Smith, go to building T-401 and give this assignment sheet to the Corporal-in-Charge. If you loose this assignment sheet before you get there you'll spend the rest of your time here sleeping in your jeep and eating 'C' Rations. Any questions Smith?"

PFC Smith replied, "No questions Sergeant, and let me tell you how nice it is to be here staying with you." "Don't be a smart-ass with me Smith, or you'll find out it don't pay to pull my chain." PFC Smith gave the obnoxious trooper a dirty look, started to say something, decided against it, and left the building. Then the staff sergeant took a good look at me. He quickly noticed I was wearing newly shined jump boots. With a strange look on his face he snarled, "Are you jump qualified Lieutenant?" I really wanted to make this Son-of-a-Bitch squirm a little, so with no explanation I truthfully answered, "No."

"Your orders were issued at XVIII Airborne Corps, you are here to receive Glider Indoctrination. You are out of uniform Lieutenant, you are not authorized to wear jump boots." As aggressively as I knew how, I asked, "Sergeant I see four stripes on your arm. How many stripes do you see on mine?"

"Come on Lieutenant, you know I don't see any stripes on you arm. Besides, what has that got to do with wearing jump boots?" "It has a lots to do with ME wearing jump boots. I have been serving with the 82nd Airborne in combat for two months now. I am an officer and I do not need, or want, any advice concerning jump boots from a rear echelon desk jockey."

Now on the defensive, the trooper replied, "That doesn't make you eligible to wear those jump boots Lieutenant." "Sergeant, you tell the Regimental Commander who gave me these boots that you don't think I'm authorized to wear them. Then listen to what he has to say. I know it will tax your intelligence, but just keep your mouth shut about jump boots and tell me who in the Hell I am supposed to report to. Do you think you can handle that?" With no more conversation about jump boots, he handed me my assignment sheet and directed me to a parachute qualified Captain, who escorted me to the transient officers quarters. On the way I told the airborne captain about the 'hard time' the staff sergeant gave me about not being authorized to wear these boots. He laughed and admitted he also wondered where I got off wearing jump boots. He told me most troopers resented other branches of the service wearing the one piece of equipment which made the troopers distinctive. He also told me I really hit the sergeant below the belt when I referred to his as a rear echelon desk jockey. He knew the staff sergeant had made the 'D-Day Jump', had been decorated for valor, had been wounded twice, and was aware the sergeant's last wound precluded him from ever jumping again.

This news made me feel bad. I had pulled rank and 'mouthed-off' to an NCO who had served his country, and was overly proud of being an airborne soldier. However this feeling did not last long. As far as I was concerned, the trooper brought it on himself. While he was still in the rear, riding a desk, I would be with the infantry and probably get my but shot off. Another thing, he did not show the respect a combat officer deserves!

Glider Indoctrination began early in the morning when a briefing officer asked for my previous combat experience and my current assignment. I explained I had been a technician in artillery fire direction, which he 'waived-off' immediately. I continued with my assignments as a forward observer with different regiments of the 82nd Airborne Division. He seemed pleased and asked if I had any questions. "Yes, why have I been chosen for glider indoctrination?" "Because you are a forward observer." "Why do I need this type training?" "Because the 82nd wants you proficient in glider operations." We seemed to be getting nowhere. "Why does the 82nd want me proficient in glider operations?" With a shoulder shrug, he answered, "You may never know, but if the right day comes along, you will answer your own questions."

He then motioned toward a group of officers gathered under the wing of a Waco CG-4A glider and said, "If you have no more questions, move over to that glider. You will train with that group." The group consisted of about twenty lieutenants, some of whom were milling around the Waco, shaking their heads in disbelief. Most of the officers were young, about my age, in their early 20s. None wore division patches, so I had no idea where they came from. Most had crossed cannons (artillery) on their collars, with a sprinkling of armor and signal corps also represented. There was one serious looking technical sergeant standing at parade rest under the tail of the glider

Finally the sergeant counted heads. Satisfied that everyone was present, he announced in a loud and commanding voice, "OK gentlemen, I am Technical Sergeant Lapinski, your instructor for today. If you gentlemen will form under the port wing of the glider, in the shade facing me, we will get this show on the road. You will notice that I, not you, will be facing the sun. My blessed mother taught me early in life that my students should never be facing the sun." After a pause for a ripple of laughter Technical Sergeant Lapinski continued, "I do not know who used their infinite wisdom to choose you for this training, but this wisdom has given you a golden opportunity to be taught by me. Now 'listen-up' and remember what I say. At the end of my class you will be given a test. Those who pass the test might survive, but those who fail will surely die."

I'll admit this prelude to the indoctrination, plus the military bearing of the sergeant, caught my attention. However he better deliver, if he did not, some member of his class would take him down a peg or two. Technical Sergeant Lapinski continued his lecture by informing us we were at an airborne training and staging location. We were chosen to become familiar with "The vertical Insertion of Artillery and Vehicular Equipment into a Combat Area." He continued by describing airborne operations and nomenclature so we could understand phrases such as, "A 'Tug', is a C47 which tows gliders. A 'Carrier' could be a C47, a Waco CG-4A Glider, or a C46. 'Glider Pilots' are all junior Air Corps officers, with minimal flight experience." He also explained, 'Beginning this afternoon all of you will be assigned to a glider pilot who is also in training. Your training will include learning how to load a glider with vehicles, artillery pieces, ammunition, and other supplies, plus the appropriate number of personnel to accompany this material." The lecture continued, "The pilots have limited experience with landings, and have no experience at towing two 'carriers' with their aircraft. Towing multiple 'carriers' with a single 'tug' is a relatively new concept and yet to be fully tested."

At this point several hands went up, "Why haven't the pilots had more experience in making landings?" "Glider landings should be thought of as nothing more than a controlled crash. Gliders are in short supply, consequently the pilots don't get many opportunities to crash them." One student officer yelled,

"That is great news sergeant, got any more good news for us?" "Yes Lieutenant, we will run experiments with tow lines of different lengths and tests of equal length tow lines. We do not know how much load a tug can get off the ground in a dual tow situation. We do know it is easier to keep the gliders separated in the air using different length tow lines. Different length tow lines also offers the advantage of the tug and each carrier leaving the ground in a sequence of tug, carrier, and carrier. Using same length tow lines puts an additional burden on the two glider pilots. They have to keep their gliders away from each other from take off until release. This can be very difficult With a raised hand an officer student asked, "In your opinion sergeant, which is the best method?"

With a straight face Technical Sergeant Lapinski answered, "Until now, no one has asked for my opinion in this matter. In the final analysis it will be the infinite wisdom of the Commanding Genera of the Air Transport Command that counts." Technical Sergeant Lapinski continued, "Under normal combat conditions, parachute infantry will precede you, have the landing area secured, and provide cover for the gliders as they land with support equipment and personnel." He concluded, "Less than 50 percent of the gliders involved in a combat mission will ever fly again."

This last statement prompted a question, "Are you telling us that you expect to loose more than half of the gliders due to crash landings, sergeant?" "No, not exactly lieutenant. We expect to loose some in mid-air collisions, some to enemy aircraft and anti-aircraft fire, some to enemy small arms fire, and of course we will loose some on the ground due to enemy artillery and mortar fire." The next question to the instructor was. "How do you get out of this fucking outfit?"

Without even entering a glider on the ground, I had come to the conclusion I did not wish to participate in the 'Vertical Insertion' of anything, but it appeared I had no choice. At the end of the lecture session, the instructor showed us a glider loaded with a typical combat load: a jeep, several hundred pounds of ammunition, and seats for six men. He then divided us into groups of six, and introduced us to the glider pilot who would train with us My group drew a young, tall, skinny 2nd Lieutenant from Devils Lake, North Dakota, by the name of Carl Wanamaker. Carl was dressed in highly polished, low cut dress shoes, pink pants, a green Eisenhower jacket, a fifty-mission crushed Air Corps had, and a US 45-caliber pistol in a new leather holster hung from his left shoulder. His 'Class A' Air Corps uniform was in sharp contrast to the wrinkled fatigues the ground officers wore. Other than his flashy uniform, the next thing I noticed was his fair complexion, I don't believe he had started shaving yet. I thought he was younger than I, and estimated his age to be nineteen. He was the youngest looking officer I had ever seen.

Lieutenant Wanamaker greeted the class and said, "This afternoon we will be towed by a C47 and circle the field once. I will release from the tug at 1,500 feet altitude and we will glide gracefully to earth. I will then make a smooth, soft and uneventful landing."

When the murmur of the six students died down, Technical Sergeant Lapinski and Lieutenant Wanamaker led us to a Waco which was loaded with a jeep and a large load of ballast which simulated live ammunition. The Lieutenant entered the gilder first, with a grin of confidence he seated himself in the pilots seat and wiggled the tail assembly and wing controls vigorously. When he and the sergeant were satisfied the controls worker properly, Technical Sergeant Lapinski gave the orders: "Enter the Glider." "Occupy your seat." "Fasten your Seat Harness Securely."

Our tug, a C47, was rigged to tow only one Waco for the first flight. The takeoff was relatively smooth except for the sudden jerk when the tow-line became taught and the jarring bumps caused by the rough runway. One noticeable change occurred in in the wings of the glider during flight. The wings were fairly flexible and as the glider left the ground, the wing tips lifted slightly under the heavy load. Also the plywood body and fabric covered wings acted as sounding boards for the rumbles of the glider during takeoffs. During flight I was aware of the creaks and groans of the flexible fabric covered wings. The interior of the Waco was much more noisy than I had anticipated.

Lieutenant Wanamaker proved to be a good pilot on the takeoff and in the air. I prayed to the Almighty that he also knew how to land this thing. Following the release from the tug he made a graceful turn, lined up on the runway and began his descent. I thought he was going to under shoot the landing area, but in fact his approach was too high. To adjust the altitude, he over-corrected and abruptly dropped the glider onto the ground to avoid flying into the tree line at the end of the landing area. The glider slammed into the ground, bounced and became airborne again. By this time the glider had lost momentum and voluntarily returned to the ground. While bumping along the runway, a sudden cross wind caught the glider broad side, causing one wing-tip to drag along the ground. This resulted in a 180 degree spin which caused the glider to came to rest headed in the opposite direction.

Lieutenant Wanamaker unfastened himself from the pilots seat, approached the passengers with a smile of satisfaction on his face, and asked. "How did you guys enjoy the ride?" When he received on response to his question he briskly exited the glider and made a walk-around tour of the glider to survey the damage. As we exited the glider, I noticed a shift in the position of the jeep and discovered one of the tie-downs had broken during the rough landing. When Technical Sergeant Lapinski appeared on the scene, I reported this fact to him. Neither he nor the pilot seemed disturbed over what I considered to be a poor landing.

As the my group of students rode from the tarmac to our quarters, the sergeant told us, "Airframe mechanics will straighten the bent landing gear, repair the damaged wing tips, replace the damaged tie-down, and the Waco will be as good as new for your flight tomorrow.".

Back at the transient officers quarters I removed a bottle of Cognac from my musette bag, took a healthy swig, and thought of today's experience in 'Vertical Insertion." Frankly, I thought it was for the birds. I also thought of a fourth command for the airborne instructor: "Enter the Glider." "Occupy your Seat." "Fasten your Seat Harness Securely." and, "Pray Reverently!"

Subsequent flights with Lieutenant Wanamaker were interesting, but did not produce as many 'White Knuckles' as the first.

Germany—Overlooking the Rhine River
101st Airborne Division—506th Parachute Infantry Regiment
Mid February 1945

Smithy and I had a hard time finding Charlie Battery. The 592nd FA Bn had moved farther north while we were in Belgium. The Battalion was now in-place on the west bank of the Rhine River, between Coblenz and Dusseldorf. Captain

Baxter was glad to see us, but our conversation about 'Vertical Insertion' was cut short. when he told me of my next assignment. I was to man an Observation Post overlooking the Rhine River which supported a special mission assigned to the 506th Parachute Infantry Regiment of the 101st Airborne Division. For some unknown reason I was apprehensive about their assignment. Maybe it was because I had become 'civilized' again, having been removed from combat for several days while is Belgium. Or maybe it was because I would be working with different people. The people and procedures of the 82nd Airborne were comfortable and predictable, but the 101st Airborne Division had a character of its own. The 'Screaming Eagles' of the 101st Airborne Division had set them apart with their dogged defense of Bastogne during the Battle of the Bulge. The 506th Parachute Infantry Regiment had distinguished itself during this defense. However, no matter what the reason, I still felt uneasy about serving with the 506th Parachute Infantry Regiment.

I assigned Smithy the job of getting out combat gear and supplies loaded into the jeep trailer. I informed Jerry he was to remain behind, and my crew was now his responsibility. He of course, did not think I should 'go this one alone' but assured me everything would be handled properly in my absence, The next morning, after a last minute briefing by Captain Baxter, Smithy and I departed the battery area before dawn and were on the way to the command post of the 506th PIR. We were greeted by the Regimental Executive Officer who expressed his concern about an enemy counter attack across the Rhine River. He emphasized, if this happens he would need all the artillery support he could get. When I assured him XVIII Airborne Corps Artillery would give him all the support he required, he acted as though he had heard that song before, and had been disappointed. During our conversation we poured over his local situation map and the Executive Officer asked me about my experience as a forward observer. The question was legitimate, however it irritated me for some reason. I outlined my experience with the 82nd Airborne Division and told him they referred to me as their 'big stick' because they used me when they were in trouble. Their infantry protected me at all times. I continued, "War is much like football, offense and defense is the name of the game. If the offensive line lets the defense get to their quarterback, he can not throw a pass while lying on the ground. In this war, the 82nd Division company commanders and platoon leaders learned very quickly, a forward observer can not deliver timely and accurate artillery support when he is constantly in a hole with his head down. The men and officers of the 82nd understand this principle which gave me the opportunity to provide the 'big stick' when they needed it."

At the end of my analogy I looked squarely into the eyes of the Lieutenant Colonel to whom I had just reported. He returned my stare and finally spoke, "Lieutenant, you seem to be as concerned about us protecting you as we are about getting effective artillery support from you." After he received an affirmative nod from me, he continued, "Maybe we both worry too much Lieutenant."

The regimental XO then picked up a telephone and called the 2nd Battalion Commander and advised his a Corps forward observer was here and would be reporting to him in a few minutes. The regimental XO then indicated the location of the 2nd Battalion Command Post on his map. The regimental XO then handed me his telephone, and the 2nd Battalion Commander, a Major, indicated he was relieved to have an artillery officer to help him. Over the telephone the Battalion Commander briefed me on the static situation in this sector. His three companies were committed to a defense line that was too long, stretching his men along the west bank of the river. Since he had no company in reserve, he had created several strong points at strategic locations in his defensive line. His troops were housed in buildings facing east with only a narrow road and a water retaining wall separating them from the Rhine River. Since only two hundred yards of flowing water separated his men from the enemy, they had limited mobility during daylight hours. However, American troops could move, almost undetected at any time, in the alleys behind the buildings housing his men.

Upon completion of my call to Battalion, the Regimental Executive Officer summoned a runner to guide us to the Battalion Command Post. The runner climbed into the rear seat of my jeep and assured us it would be OK to drive to the Battalion Command Post. The caviler attitude of the runner concerned me because this was my first experience in riding in a vehicle so close to the enemy. As we made our way through the narrow alleys of the village it became obvious the runner knew his business. Smithy faithfully followed the troopers instructions as we wound our way to the 2nd Battalion, and as the trooper advised, parked the jeep and trailer behind a large stone building. The suggestion to leave the parked vehicle headed away from the river, in case a quick withdrawal was necessary, was sound advice.

The infantry platoon leader who had been acting as an artillery observer was happy to be relieved. He admitted he did not feel comfortable with his ability to call for the right type of artillery support at the proper time. After the Lieutenant left, Captain Rick Sommers, the Battalion Executive Officer, started briefing me in detail. As we read the detailed maps of the area I realized why an untrained infantry officer would feel uncomfortable in this situation. To deliver effective artillery fire into this deep valley, with friendly troops so close to the river, requires a special technique called 'high angle fire,' and all artillery weapons can not be used for this purpose.

When through with the preliminary details. Captain Sommers took us to the house which contained the Observation Post. With the Captain's permission, I asked Smithy to establish radio and telephone contact with the fire direction centers of both the 592nd FA Bn and XVIII Airborne Corps Artillery. I explained to Captain Sommers although we were under the control of Corps Artillery, I still wanted the ability to fire my own battalion in case things got too hot. I told him it was a good idea to have a back-up of twelve 155mm howitzers that could handle 'high angle fire' easily. As Smithy and I worked, Captain Sommers watched intently. It didn't bother me, I knew he was trying to evaluate what type of artillerymen we were. I really did not mind the scrutiny because later I would be evaluating him. I think the Captain sensed this fact.

Some of the time things happen for the best. As it turned out, Captain Sommers was one of the best things that happened to me during the war. Rick Sommers was a powerful man with broad shoulders, a slim waist, a bull neck, arms of steel, thighs which almost split the seams of his fatigue pants, and feet large enough to walk on water. As we talked I asked, "Captain, how much do you weigh?" He responded, "I haven't weighed in a long time. I'm probably in the 250 pound range. How much do you weigh Lieutenant?" My answer was similar to his, "I haven't weighed in a long time either, but I probably tip the scales at 170. The way I figure, you outweigh me by about 80 pounds." Within two hours he had taken me on a tour of his strong points, and introduced me to his key Non-Commissioned Officers. From the reactions I observed during this tour, I concluded these troopers would follow Rick anywhere, including, 'To the Gates of Hell.' We had already started to develop confidence in each other.

Back at the observation post, Rick explained he had to return to his command post to develop plans for tonight's activities. He again expressed his concern with close-in artillery support for his men while on the enemy side of the Rhine. I assured him I could provide supporting fire for his men while in enemy territory. He shook his head and said he still didn't understand the principle of 'high angle fire.' When I compared a howitzer with an infantry mortar, he seemed to understand, and exclaimed, "Well I'll be damned! No wonder we couldn't hit targets in the valley with artillery fire. No one ever explained that technique to me. Lieutenant that may be the reason the Krauts aren't giving us much trouble in this location. We catch Hell every now and then from mortar and direct fire from tanks, but the Kraut artillery doesn't bother us much."

Captain Sommers returned to the observation post shortly after dark and reviewed the night's plans with me. The plans seemed ambitious, however Rick was confident his men could handle their assignments. Each company was to send an intelligence patrol across the Rhine, under the cover of darkness, to determine German strength in the area. These patrols were also expected to return with German prisoners of war, for interrogation purposes. For the life of me, I could not imagine how the troopers could get across the Rhine, let-alone, how they could bring prisoners back to the American side. My responsibilities concerned me, because this was my first time supporting the infantry in this type of endeavor. Sensing my concern, Rick told me, "Lieutenant, if this mission is successful we will not need artillery support at all. However, if my guys run into trouble, we'll need interdiction fire at several locations." The Captain then placed his map-case on the table and placed a clear plastic overlay, marked with crayon, over the map. He pointed to six designated locations and indicated these were places he might require interdiction fire. I studied these potential targets very carefully. If I were to place effective fire on these targets, it would obviously require high angle fire. While I was evaluation these artillery requirements, Rick noticed me shake my head and asked, "What is wrong buddy?"

"Captain, I'd be more confident if I could fire one of these missions and check the results before your men cross the river." "No cam do sport. Preliminary firing would alert the Krauts that something different is going down tonight and they would be waiting. I'd rather depend on quick and quiet action and have the element of surprise in our favor. You know, get it over before they know we are on their side of the river." "OK Captain, it is your show, but I will check with Corps to find out if one of their artillery battalions has surveyed this target area." "What do you mean, surveyed this target area?" "Captain, if an artillery unit stays in one location long enough, we normally run target area surveys. Artillery survey teams locate prominent terrain features which are easy to identify on a map, such as: crossroads, bridges, hill tops, or large buildings. Through the survey data developed, we tie these points to the location of the 'base piece' in each firing battery. Targets which have been surveyed, or targets near surveyed locations are easy to hit. If we are lucky and I find a battalion which has surveyed this section of the target area, interdicting your targets tonight will be relatively simple."

"Well start looking Lieutenant. Where in the Hell were you when I needed you back in France." "To answer your question big guy, I was a T/4 having a damned good time drinking beer and dancing with beautiful girls in Indianapolis, Indiana."

"There is no way I can help you with your job Lieutenant, it looks like you have the artillery part of our show covered. I'd better get to the companies and make certain their inflatable boats, ropes, swimmers, and other gear, are ready for the river crossing. I'll be back about fifteen minutes before the show starts at 2315 hours. I'm going to use this location as the forward command post to coordinate all three river crossings. It will be a little crowded in here with the extra people, but we'll watch the show from hers."

About 2245 hours I heard shuffling feet and muffled voices on the ground floor below. I sent Smithy down stairs to take a look. He came back with the news that a reinforced squad, about sixteen men, had moved into the building. The squad leader, a sergeant, told Smithy they were to wait, and remain quiet, until Captain Sommers returned. Smithy informed me the squad was armed to the teeth with automatic weapons. He told me the squad leader told him this squad was to act as a reserve in case one of the squads crossing the river got into trouble. About the time the reserve squad appeared, three telephone linemen appeared and connected their EE8A field telephones to the lines which connected each company command post to the battalion observation post. Each man made the required test call to his company to make certain all was in order. Then each man made himself comfortable, leaned against the wall, and promptly went to sleep. I could not believe they could be so unconcerned about tonight's activities because I was starting to get hyperactive. My adrenaline was beginning to flow and the old 'fight or flight' feeling was starting to engulf me. The fact that two of the Corps Artillery battalions had developed target area surveys eased my concern somewhat. I had been able to reserve thirty rounds of ammunition for the operation tonight. This gave me five rounds per target which, with surveyed data, should be sufficient. Of course if things got really hot, I knew I could declare an emergency and get permission to expend more ammunition.

Captain Rick Sommers returned about fifteen minutes prior to the beginning of the river crossing, stopped down stairs and chatted with members of his reserve squad, and brought the squad leader upstairs with him. When Rick saw the three sleeping telephone operators, he kicked each one in the foot and curtly asked, "Do you have communications with all three company command posts?" Sleepily, each operator answered, "Yes Sir." "Well get them on the line and keep your line open until we get our men back on this side of the river." The XO then added sternly, "And for Christ's sake, stay awake and pay attention!" This time, the Captain got three rather weak 'yes sirs' as the operators cranked their telephones to establish communications to the command posts of 'Dog,' 'Easy,' and 'Fox' Companies. Captain Sommers then turned to me, looked at this watch, and asked, "Lieutenant, do you have the 'King of Battle' ready to roar?"

I assured him the artillery was ready and we started discussing details. I advised him I had acquired five rounds of 105mm ammunition per target, a total of thirty rounds for interdiction purposes. The potential targets for interdiction he identified had been tied into existing survey data, and firing commands had been developed for each target. Corps Fire Direction had designated his six targets as concentrations "Able' through 'Fox,' and for his convenience, I had marked these concentrations on his operation map. He was pleasantly surprised to learn we would be in direct contact with fire direction during his entire operation. He was almost dumbfounded when I told him if a need presented itself, some one could advise fire direction to fire any concentration from 'Able' through 'Fox' and the mission would be fired. No additional information would be necessary. As tense as he was, I could tell by the look in his eyes, the 'big guy' liked the way I had set up artillery support for his operation tonight.

Captain Sommers looked at his watch again, waited momentarily, and abruptly announced, "On your toes folks. It is show time!" He motioned for the reserve squad leader to come over and join our conversation. The sergeant was in his early twenties and a ruggedly handsome individual. The XO told the sergeant to deploy his squad at the agreed upon positions, and emphasized the mission of the reserve squad was to provide covering fire in the event a patrol experienced difficulty while crossing the river in either direction, Captain Sommers added, "If the initial west to east crossing is executed in a quiet and orderly manner I expect little, or no, problems. However, I feel the return crossing, with German prisoners, can present problems which will require covering fire."

Being privileged to this conversation made me realize that most of my job was completed. Never having witnessed such an operation prompted me to ask the Captain for permission to leave the command post and accompany the reserve squad in order to gain experience. Captain Sommers was not happy with this request. I explained Smithy would remain in the CP during my absence and was fully qualified to coordinate prearranged artillery fire if necessary. I also assured him I would 'hot-foot-it' back to the CP the moment shooting started across the river. Still, not to happy, the XO agreed to let me accompany the sergeant in charge of the reserve squad and advised me to, "Get the Hell inside a building the second you hear small arms fire." This seemed like sage advice, so I readily agreed to seek cover immediately when things started to 'heat up.' The trooper sergeant looked at his XO, then looked at me, nodded his head toward the door as if to say, "You asked for it stupid, now lets get at it."

The Deity responsible for weather conditions gave us a perfect night for this type mission. The night was cloudy and dark and there was no moonlight. However, the Germans had learned how to make their own moonlight by shining their powerful antiaircraft search lights at the cloudy sky. This technique caused light to be reflected from the low hanging clouds back to earth that illuminated the target area with a soft indirect light. I had experienced artificial moon light on various occasions and it provided ample light to spot targets, especially for observers whose eyes had become accustomed to peering into total darkness. This fact was not in our favor, but a wind from the east was. The direction of this wind complicated the west to east river crossing, but helped the more complicated return to the American held west bank. In addition to this help an easterly wind tended to deaden the sounds of the river crossing in both directions.

The reserve squad leader went about his job of placing his weapons and men in a very professional manner. When satisfied, the sergeant returned to the doorway of the building where he had asked me to wait. In hushed whispers he said the crossing tonight would be different than originally planned. Due to the brisk wind and swift river currents, three small inflatable boats would be used instead of one large, hard to handle boat. The changed plans called for one trooper to swim the ice cold river while pulling a light line tied to his waist. Upon reaching the enemy side, the trooper was to give three sharp tugs on this line, signaling he was ready to pull a sturdy rope attached to the lime, across the river. Once the sturdy rope was across the river, he would tie his end to a substantial object and return to the friendly shore by pulling himself 'hand-over-hand' along the now taught rope. When this portion of the mission was complete, the three inflatable boats would be placed in the water. The six men in each inflatable would then pull themselves along the taught rope, instead of paddling, to the enemy side of the rover, and hide the boats for use on their return trip. The trooper patrols would then proceed with their mission to collect intelligence information and take prisoners.

From our vantage point, the reserve squad sergeant and I could follow the progress of the swimmer. I did not know the man, but I knew he had to be a powerful swimmer to complete his task. First, he was hampered by the light line that was being fed to him by troopers on our side of the river. He had to overcome the drag caused by this line in the cold water. Of course, this drag became worse the farther he swam. Second, the swimmer had to anticipate his sideways movement, caused by swift river currents and floating ice, to reach his pre-designated spot on the enemy shore. Third, and most trying for the swimming trooper, was the frigid water. This water was COLD!

No one appreciated the problems of the swimmer more than I. Swimming had been a large part of my life as a youngster, often swimming in the ocean at Cocoa Beach and in the Indian River between Cocoa and Merritt Island. I had also earned my Red Cross Lifesaving Certificate in the University of Florida swimming pool. As these thoughts went through my mind, the reserve squad leader and I watched the swimmer make the trip going both ways undetected. I actually climbed the sea wall and helped the exhausted trooper onto shore. Help came and we carried him into a building, stripped off his wet clothes, patted him dry, wrapped him in a woolen GI blanket and literally poured hot coffee into his almost frozen body. He was a tough trooper! In a few minutes he was laughing and joking, "That's the last time I'll volunteer for anything, except sex."

By the time I returned to the dark street I could barely see the first inflatable silently starting its trip across the river. For some unknown reason the six men were having trouble propelling the boat along the still taught rope. Fortunately the men overcame their problems and arrived undetected on the enemy shore. The second inflatable reached the enemy side of the river without incident. The reserve squat leader whispered to me, "Lieutenant, so far, so good. We've got two squads across the river safely. Let's hope the third squad makes it too."

These word seemed to jinx the third squad. As the last patrol reached midstream, something went horribly wrong. One trooper tried to stand erect, the inflatable tilted and took on water. In a flash all six men were in the water, three hanging onto the taught rope for dear life, while the overturned inflatable boat and the other three men were drifting swiftly down stream. We heard sounds of men flailing around in the frigid water, desperately trying to shed their heavy combat gear and stay afloat. Of course this noise alerted German sentries, and we heard hobnailed boots running along the cobblestone waterfront. We easily heart their guttural shouted commands. The reserve squad leader told me in no uncertain terms, "All Hell is going to break loose in a couple of minutes Lieutenant. Hurry back to the Command Post, the Captain wants you there." Without a question, I left for the CP in a dead run.

Captain Sommers was talking to the reserve squad leader, via radio. when I entered the room. The XO had been advised I was on the way back to the CP and was seeking information about his men and the mission. The reserve squad leader was reporting small arms fire moving down the river. Although he could not see what was happening, he thought the sight of the inflatable and the three men drifting down stream was drawing enemy fire. The sergeant reported the three men who held onto the rope when the inflatable overturned had made it back to shore and were out of danger. His men, though tense, had held their fire and had not revealed their positions. He reported the first two squads were still in German held territory on the east side of the river.

Captain Sommers ordered his sergeant to keep his men in place, to hold their fire, and report anything unusual they could hear or observe. Captain Sommers then advised his reserve squad leader, "I will have Dog Company dispatch men down stream to try and rescue the three drifting troopers." A concerned XO signed off with his sergeant, put his transmitter down, and with a stern look on his face, asked, "Well Lieutenant, did you learn anything?" The question surprised me. I did not wish to appear 'flip' under these circumstances, so I replied, "Captain, I learned that Murphy's law is correct. If mistakes can happen, they will happen."

The operation was completed at about 0230 hours. The final results amazed me. We lost one inflatable, German infantry continued to shoot at the boat until it finally sank some one-half-mile down stream. The troopers from Dog Company rescued all three men who were drifting in the river. During the entire fracas only one trooper was slightly wounded. The two patrols, which successfully crossed the river, returned with more current intelligence information concerning enemy strength, and three German prisoners. These two groups suffered no casualties at all.

One of the German prisoners was an older man, a corporal in his mid-forties. He was sick of being shot at and tried to negotiate a trip to the United States as a prisoner-of-war in exchange for vital information concerning enemy troop , supply dump, and staging area locations. I was present during his preliminary interrogation. This German Corporal was so pissed-off at Hitler and the Nazi Party, I would like to believe he actually got a trip to the states. With the information we obtained from the German Corporal, Captain Sommers and I decided to use our allotted thirty rounds of 105mm ammunition to see if we could slightly cripple the local Kraut war effort. We identified six 'targets of opportunity.' I relayed the new target coordinates to Corps Artillery and requested five rounds of 'fuse quick,' and 'fire for effect' on each target. Of course we could not see the targets in the darkness but, we were able to observe the flash as each 105mm round burst behind the enemy front lines. As Rick and I talked, we wondered if the tax payers back home were getting their moneys worth from these missions. Successful hits on four of the concentrations could not be confirmed, but two hits caused huge secondary explosions, such as exploding ammunition, or exploding fuel. I believe we destroyed an enemy fuel depot and an ammunition storage area. I also strongly believe the tax payers of America got their moneys worth that night.

The operation over, I dozed in the command post for about two hours. At 0530 hours Smithy awakened me and offered me a canteen cup of hot coffee. The smell of the coffee was refreshing, I burned my lips on the hot metal rim of the cup as usual, otherwise the coffee hit the spot. A I relaxed on the floor of the CP, I savored the peace and quiet, and thanked my Heavenly Father for helping me survive another night. After this first action with the 506th Parachute Infantry Regiment of the 101st Airborne Division, I felt better about serving with the 'Screaming Eagles.' All-in-all I felt satisfied, I had no need for anyone to tell me I had handled my responsibilities well.

During the next few days we mainly loafed and performed routine duties during the day light hours, but the nights were always busy. The regiment completed one more successful foray across the river, which netted four more

German prisoners, and the loss of one trooper to sniper fire. I was engaged in a daylight artillery duel with a German forward observer who tried to destroy my observation post. The superiority of the American artillery worked in my favor. I was able to kill him and destroy his observation post before he killed me. This episode made a lasting impression on me because it was extremely personal. I could see him, and he could see me. Smithy stuck by me through the entire artillery duel. He was my trusted friend. I thanked the Lord for our survival.

The only time, during my four campaigns in Europe, I received an order to "Fix Bayonets" occurred the fourth night Smithy and I served with the 'Screaming Eagles.' I had not experienced 'hand-to-hand' combat since December 1944 while the 589th FA Bn was defending 'Parker's Crossroads' at Baraque de Fraiture, Belgium. This situation developed when the Germans tried to counter attack across the Rhine in what was estimated to be in company strength. To describe my feelings at the time as 'uncomfortable' would be a gross understatement, the adrenaline flowed freely and my emotions were high. I was prepared to sell my life dearly and take as many Krauts with me as possible. Fortunately for me, this sacrifice was not necessary. The infantry defenders and their supporting artillery performed magnificently and stopped the attack in midstream. Dawn reveled blood stained ice and snow across the river, but not one enemy soldier reached the American held side.

The next day with the 506th Regiment started out poorly. My stomach was upset, I had diarrhea, and a terrible headache. A medic, and Captain Sommers, told me this was the result of too much stress, too much alcohol, and too much adrenaline in too short a time. I took their word for it but noticed they did not appear to feel as badly as I. 'A little bird' told me I would never get accustomed to people trying to kill me. I took things very personally, but the Captain seemed to be able to remain impersonal about the 'whole dirty, rotten, mess.'

Good news finally came, Smithy and I were relieved from duty when we were replaced by another Forward Observation team. We were ordered to return to Battery C, 592nd FA Bn, and to report to the Commanding Officer, Captain Baxter.

I was ready to be replaced, but had mixed emotions when I told Rick

Sommers good-bye. The 506th was a great outfit, and Rick Sommers was an excellent officer to work with. But all the continuous destruction, chaos, and killing was warping my mind in the wrong direction. Combat was getting to me, and I needed a change!

Charlie Battery—592nd FA Bn
Late February, 1945

It was good to be 'home,' Jerry was happy to see me, he had been hearing tales of action on the Rhine. He too had been busy. Jerry had handled one assignment as an observer himself, and described his experience in detail. We enjoyed talking with each other for a long time before I decided to report to Captain Baxter. My meeting with the Captain was cordial. We swapped notes and I finally told him I need a break from serving with the infantry. He looked at me and admitted, "We all need a break. Maybe it's time for the God of war to smile on us. In the meantime, we must keep on plugging. What is bothering you the most Randy?" "I keep thinking about operation 'Air Bridge Across the Rhine' and the fact I am scheduled to make a glider landing during this operation. I don't like that idea worth a Damn." The Captain laughed as he made a joke, "Maybe something else will happen and you won't have to cross that bridge."

On 7 March 1945, 'something else did happen.' Combat Command B of the 9th Armored Division discovered the Ludendorf Bridge across the Rhine river at Remagen, Germany was still intact. Combat Command B officers quickly 'seized the moment,' crossed the bridge, and established Allied control of the bridge. Orders were issued to all combat troops in the area to cross the bridge, fan out, and establish a bridge-head for the advancing Allied troops. Realizing the seriousness of this Allied intrusion into their homeland, the German High Command tried desperately to destroy the Ludendorf Bridge with Artillery and Air Power. The Germans failed in these attempts, however the Ludendorf Bridge collapsed several days later due to the heavy Allied traffic crossing the war damaged bridge. By the time the bridge collapsed, the US Corps of Engineering had constructed a military bridge across the Rhine and Allied men and equipment maintained a constant flow into enemy territory.

Thus ended the Battle for the Rhineland, and started the Battle for Central Germany. This sequence of events also cancelled the need for operation 'Air Bridge across the Rhine.' It also stopped me from thinking about a glider drop across the Rhine!

20

A Promotional Furlough to London

Charlie Battery—592 FA Bn
The Battle for Central Germany
March 1945

Jerry and I had just been relieved from an observation job with the 82nd Airborne Division, it was good to be on the offensive again. As usual I stopped at the command post to check in with Captain Baxter while Jerry and the men headed to our bunker. The first words Captain Baxter uttered when I entered the CP was, "Pierson, you lucky son-of-a-bitch, you are going to London." Not fully understanding him, I countered, "You must be kidding."

"No Lieutenant, this is no joke. You and a Lieutenant Miller from Corps Artillery have been awarded a ten day promotional furlough to London. The order is already cut, you have to be at Corps Artillery Headquarters at 0800 hours tomorrow. Corps has arranged transportation by vehicle to Paris, where you will report to Army Special Services. They will arrange transportation to London and back for the two of you."

"Well, I'll be damned. I haven't seen Miller since we received 'battlefield commissions' in Stavelot last January. I've talked to him several times when he was on duty. He is as assistant S-3 and helped me a couple of times when I needed special ordnance, like an eight inch howitzer."

"It's always good to have friends in high places. Incidentally, if you want to tell Jerry, I'll have him drive your jeep to Corps tomorrow, I'll ask the XO to release him for the day. I know you 'Gold-Dust-Twins' confide in each other. Maybe this time together will be good for both of you." "Thanks Captain, I'll check with you tomorrow before we leave. Anything I can get you while I'm in the big city?" "Nothing in particular, just relax, have a good time, and drink a gin and tonic for me."

At our bunker, Sergeant Wiener and the crew were busy bathing, shaving and changing into clean socks, underwear and fatigues. I cornered Jerry and told him I had made arrangements for him to drive me to Corps Artillery Headquarters tomorrow morning. Jerry replied, "I'll do anything to get away from this 'chicken-shit' battery. Are you going somewhere?" "We'll talk about it tomorrow. Have my jeep serviced and pick me up at the command post at 0600 hours."

During the jeep ride to Corps Jerry kept talking about his experience as a firing battery section chief. He appreciated the howitzer cross training, but he left no doubt, he was looking forward to getting closer to the action and becoming a forward observer sergeant again. No matter how I tried, I could not convince Jerry I might be gone three or four weeks on a ten day furlough to London. He laughed at the idea that I did not wish to return to sere with the infantry. I did not have the heart to tell him I was going to try my damnedest to get back in fire direction when I returned from London.

This is the way we parted, Jerry looking forward to 'killing those bastards,' and me hoping to remove myself from combat as far as possible.

The Trip to Paris
March 1945

Second Lieutenant Delbert Miller had a grin on his face when I first saw him. Dell looked great in his freshly pressed Class A uniform. By contrast, I was still dressed in fatigues. Of the officers present, the dress was mixed, but the majority wore Class A uniforms. The briefing officer advised the fatigue dressed individuals that fatigues must be changed to Class A uniforms before we reached Paris. I did not know how I could comply with these instructions, but decided I would think of a solution later.

To my dismay, I learned we were to spend an uncomfortable two days in the rear of a 2 1/2 ton GMC truck during the trip to the 'City of Lights.' Despite the loud grumbling, no one refused to make the trip. The rear of the trucks were canvass covered, the weather chilly, but not cold during the trip. Most of the officers slept, but Dell and I had lots of catching-up and planning to do. The trip gave us an opportunity to talk about mutual friends and exchange war stories. During our over-night stop in Belgium I was able to borrow and iron. I was not proficient at ironing, consequently my Class A uniform gave up its duffel bag creases reluctantly. Dell advised me, "Your uniform will look OK after it hangs all night." I didn't agree with him, but his words were comforting.

After the ironing session, Dell and I met some of the other 'mustang officers' and were surprised at the quantity of 'war trophies' these ex-GIs had gathered to sell to rear echelon troops in Paris in order to have spending money in London. Even though Miller kept assuring me he had enough surplus cigarettes in his duffle bag to get spending money for both of us, I was still concerned with having a good time. During the last day of travel, the 'legal eagles' in the crowd arrived at a consensus opinion that the entire group of officers should spend four days in Paris, on their own, before reporting to Army Special Services to obtain transportation to London. If we were questioned about our four day delay in reporting, the universal reason would be vehicle failure. For those four days each man would be on his own. We all agreed and reasoned if we reported in four days late as a group there wasn't much the Army would do if we all told the same story, that a break-down of one truck caused the delay.

Both Dell and I felt uneasy about these plans, but finally adopted the attitude, "What the Hell?" I had two first cousins stationed in Paris I had not seen for years. Mrs. Lucile Nix Adams, the Director of a large American Red Cross recreation center, and her brother, Captain Edward J. Nix, Commanding Officer of the Paris office of the US Army Criminal Investigation Division (CID). We decided obtaining quarters for these four days was our first priority. The first thing I did was get the ARC telephone number and call my 'Cousin Lucy.' Lucile was easy to find, and astonished when she received my call. She was delighted to hear from her younger cousin and promised to pick us up in about twenty minutes at the cafe where we waited. Dell and I were into our second glass of wine, and enjoying the passing females when Lucy arrived. The sight of an attractive blond and leggy ARC female, driving a jeep created a stir in the cafe as Mrs. Adams pulled to the curb, and flashed a shapely pair of nylon covered legs as she dismounted from the vehicle.

I have no idea what effect our close and lingering embrace had on the now assembled crowd. I do remember a strong murmur of approval from the male French patrons of the Cafe, Then I remembered Dell. He was standing there awkwardly, but intently taking in the scene. Lucile nodded toward Miller, and asked with her eyes, "Who is this officer?" She was asking me to introduce my friend.

Over a glass of wine, I explained our situation, the unauthorized delay-in-route, our need for temporary housing while in Paris, and our lack of cash. Lucy laughed and said, "I think I can help, you two really need a friend. To address your unauthorized presence in Paris I suggest you contact your cousin Edward." The thought of getting illicit help from her brother, Captain Edward J. Nix, an Army Intelligence Officer, and the Commanding Officer of the Criminal Investigation Division in Paris did not appeal to me. When I expressed my reluctance, Lucy made a joke, "Why not go see Edward for advice? After all he is in the 'Criminal Business' and should have some cleaver ideas." During this pleasant conversation, Lucy looked at her watch and announced, "We had better get this show on the road." Following her advice, Dell and I threw our belongings into the rear of her jeep. Out of common courtesy I let Dell sit up front with the 'ARC Lady' while I rode in the rear with our luggage.

During the trip I had no idea where we were going, but I felt relaxed while watching the interesting French people and enjoying what was reported to be the most beautiful and the most wicked city in Europe. Dell, on the other hand, hardly took his eyes off of cousin Lucy, whose skirt had worked itself well above her knees, and generously displayed her shapely legs, as they continuously moved, pumping the clutch, the brake, and the gas pedals of her ARC provided jeep.

After a fascinating ride, Lucile parked her jeep in front of a magnificent old building and asked us to wait while she made inquiries inside. Within minutes she returned and advised us our housing accommodations had been arranged.

She explained, "Since you have no orders authorizing your 'stop over' in Paris, I decided against obtaining quarters for you in the transient officer facility. Instead I made arrangements for you to stay in this old French hotel which the ARC uses frequently to house non-military personnel. To help with your shortage of cash, I have asked the manager to forward your entire bill to me for payment. This includes meals and bar service, which you must charge to your room. I highly recommend the food and wine they serve here."

The lobby, bar, and the restaurant were 'old world' elegant. Neither Miller nor I had ever frequented such an ornate hotel. When Lucile accompanied us to our room, Dell and I were totally surprised to find ourselves in a three room suite. My cousin sensing our feeling of awe, quipped, "There is nothing too good for our boys in the service," and guided us out of the sitting room and on to our private balcony. This ancient structure was located on the Place de la Concorde and the view from our third story balcony was extraordinary. We could plainly see the Tower de Eiffel, possibly the most famous structure in the world, as it majestically pointed toward a gorgeous sky. Lucile pointed out other points of interest, Le Madeleline, the beautiful church located nearby on the Rue Royal. Among other events, this church was the location of the Parisian Easter Fashion Parade prior to WWII. But to me, the most impressive location Lucile pointed out was the stately French National Monument, the Arc de Triomphe, located on the broad Champs-Elysees, which connected the monument to the Place de Concorde.

Together, the three of us took in the sights of Paris, and had a view of the city not many Second Lieutenants had been privileged to enjoy.

Back in the room, Dell and I were disappointed when Mrs. Adams declined our invitation to have lunch with us. She told me, "I have a date that I can not break." Hastily, she called her brother Edward, and announced she had a nice surprise for him, and handed me the phone.

My initial conversation with 'Bunny,' the family nickname for Edward, was strained. He immediately reminded me that we were in the Army, and in the Army he was Captain Nix and I should refrain from using his nickname when I talked with him. As my tale unfolded Edward became more relaxed and admitted he understood why a group of young combat officers would want to spend a few days in Paris in route to London. His advice to us was very straightforward. If we did not do something stupid and attract the attention of the military police, they did not bother combat officers who were in Paris on Rest and Recreation (R & R) leave. Captain Nix then asked for our name, rank, and serial numbers and told me if either of us were asked, by the military police, to produce our orders, we should tell the MP our orders are SECRET and can not be displayed. If this does not appease the MP, you must insist he call Captain Nix, the Commanding Officer of the CID Headquarters in Paris. He added, "If things get to this point, you will need my help."

I thanked cousin Edward for the advice and assured him neither Miller nor I would get into serious trouble. I also told him I would like to visit with him before we leave Paris. Edward suggested I call him early tomorrow so we could arrange a get together with Lucile. Lucy reacted favorably to this information. As she was leaving Lucile suggested we lunch together tomorrow. I looked at Dell, who responded, "Don't worry about me, I can make my own arrangements for tomorrow." Lucille nodded and said to me, "Randy expect an ARC driver to pick you in the hotel lobby at 1130 hours tomorrow."

My priorities for the afternoon were very simple, take a lingering bath, get my uniform cleaned and pressed, get my boots shined, and take a nap before our evening meal, and our first night in Paris. After my call, room service appeared promptly to remove my uniform and boots. They assured me both would be ready no later than 1800 hours.

Dinner in the hotel dining room with Miller that night could only be described as tasty and elegant. For the first time in my life I was served gourmet French Cuisine in a world-class restaurant. Due to the war-time shortages we had almost no choice of entrees, but the meal consisted of five courses: soup, salad, fish, entree, and dessert. Beverages consisted of three wines: *an aperitif, beaucoup de vin ordinaire,* and we enjoyed a rich *vin rouge* after dinner with our cigarettes. This was not just a fine meal, it was a wonderful dining experience for me.

The food, the wine, and the ambience, caused us to become philosophic as we discussed the stark contrasts between the Parisian and US Army lifestyles. These differences, which were numerous and extreme, involved the loss of personal privacy through the integration into a totally regimented group of men, lack of choices in food, clothing, education, and personal activities. But the greatest difference of all involved having awesome responsibilities thrust upon you whether you wanted them or not. Sometimes these responsibilities included decisions involving life or death. However, the evolution from 'civilian to warrior' involved a huge plethora of changes. These changes must be experienced to totally understand them.

In less than three days, we were experiencing these traumatic changes in reverse. The change to a care-free and extremely luxurious life in Paris was almost too much for us to fathom. But we were very willing to try. We were happy with our current accommodations filled with luxuries, fine food, and services we had never before experienced. Only two days ago I was living in a rough hewn, cold, and combat damaged, log bunker, eating warned-up 'C' rations out of cans, and wearing under garments and socks which had not been changed in several days. Arriving in Paris straight from a 'kill or be killed' environment was incomprehensible and is difficult for me to explain. Dell described this change as "From Mess Kits to Magnificence" but I believe my simple version, "From Hell to Heaven," was more accurate. Both versions were not bad considering they came from two combat weary Second Lieutenants.

Finally, Miller and I discussed what we would like to do this evening. Dell quickly informed me he was more interested in meeting French females than viewing the architectural wonders of Paris. He planned to visit the *Pigalle* section of Paris, which had been giver the name 'Pig Alley' by the American troops, and asked if I wanted to join him. As we sipped our after-dinner wine, I asked the waiter how we could get to *Pigalle*. *The Garcon de Cafe* smiled, and with a knowing twinkle in his eyes, informed us that taxi service was available, but this service was very expensive and not dependable. He suggested we learn how to use the Metro, the under ground rail system of Paris. As it turned out, understanding, and using the Paris Metro was simple. In the process, we also discovered a high percentage of the French Metro riders spoke English and were eager to help us, and, this rail system was free to American service personnel wearing a uniform.

Upon emerging from the Metro at *Gare St-Lazare,* we found this section of Paris quite different from the area surrounding our hotel. Our walking tour of *Pigalle* produced many interesting sights and several social contacts with French 'women of the night.' I loved the female 'form divine.', but my Army Anti-VD training discouraged us from consorting with prostitutes, so I decided to frequent two well known Paris night clubs, the *Follies-Bergere,* which required an advance reservation, and the *Moulin Rouge,* which was more-or-less, first come, first served. Dell and I decided to part ways and I headed toward the *Moulin Rouge,* in anticipation of witnessing the 'CAN CAN,' a 'naughty' French dance performed by extremely well conditioned female dancers.

At the *Moulin Rouge* I was seated with several American officers, total strangers of course, who were already well into their cups and eager for the floor show to begin. A pleasant *Garcon* paused at the table to take my order. When I ordered Absinthe he questioned me. Noting my tender age, he asked, "Are you familiar with this liquor?" To answer his question I replied, "I am not familiar with this liquor, but I have heard of it and I thought I would try it. You know, when in Rome, do as the Romans do." Politely, and patiently, the *Garcon* explained, "Absinthe is a liquor, perhaps you would enjoy cognac or wine more than a liquor under the circumstances." When I asked, "Why?" he said, "To enjoy Absinthe, one must acquire a taste for it. Also, you must understand how to drink it, and know the effects of over indulging in the use of Absinthe." This prompted my next question, "Just what effect does overindulgence in this liquor have on a person?"

The answer to my question was straight forward, "In the long run, over indulgence with this liquor can cause a man to loose his mind permanently. In the short run, the loss is temporary." As he dramatically waved his arms around the room, he announced, "You young Americans drink Absinthe like you drink beer. The night is young and you can already see the crazy ones in the crowd."

With this explanation I lost my desire to try this famous French beverage. and asked the *Garcon* another question, "What drink do you suggest?" Without pausing, he replied, "The Queen of Wines, Champagne, of course!"

The evening turned out to be, as one British officer put it, "A smashing success!" I missed Miller, but I enjoyed the rousing midnight floor show and the company of the engaging young French females who frequented the crowd. I also enjoyed being pleasantly inebriated by the champagne, even though I had no idea of its relative quality or cost.

As I left the *Moulin Rouge* I was fortunate enough to catch a ride with two British officers who, for reasons unknown to me, rated an American jeep for transportation. These newly made friends decided to show me a portion of Paris I had not yet seen. Their route provided a breath-taking view of the *Arc de Triomphe* at night. This huge monument was dramatically lit by strategically flood and spot lights, which high lighted its artistically sculptured features. This striking effects of this lighting upon the rugged face of the monument made a lasting impression on me. In fact, all the ancient architecture in Paris, undamaged by war, was in stark contrast to the mass destruction of cities I had seen in Germany.

As we circled the Arc in our jeep, I asked my newly made British friends to pull to the curb on the *Champs-Elysses*. While stopped, my request to dismount the jeep started a friendly argument. The Brits thought they should take me all the way to my hotel, but I insisted I wanted to walk the remainder of the way. My point-of-view ultimately prevailed, and the Brits waved goodbye as they pulled from the curb and merged into the late night traffic. It took several trips around the Arc, on foot, to absorb and understand its timeless beauty. However, a quick look at my watch broke the Arc's cultural spell and reminded me I had quite a walk ahead of me to reach the hotel. Oh well, the night was young and so was I, so I started walking briskly down the tree lined *Champs.* By now the cool night air, plus the effects of walking, was beginning to moderate the effects of the French Champagne, and the thought of meeting Cousin Lucy for lunch tomorrow quickened my pace.

Deep in thought, and enjoying the walk, the four approaching American Sergeants scarcely drew my attention. As they came closer I could see they were large men, and judging from their unsteady gait they had been consuming vast amounts of the liquid joys of Paris. As we passed, like two ships in the night, they stopped abruptly and looked at me, displaying a great amount of curiosity in what they saw. To my surprise, one of the men spoke to me in a loud and commanding voice, "Hold up Lieutenant, we would like to have a word with you." Of course I had no idea what they had in mind, but I stopped, turned, and asked, "What can I do for you?"

The four enlisted men turned out to be senior non-commissioned officers from the 82nd Airborne Division. The spokesman for the group was a Master Sergeant. As they approached, the Master Sergeant asked, "Lieutenant, what insignia are you wearing on your left shoulder?" I quickly told the group, "The 106th Infantry Division." The Master Sergeant asked. "Is that the division which was severely mauled and surrendered two Infantry Regiments during the Battle of the Bulge?" "Yes Sergeant, that was the 106th Infantry Division." "Well Sir, meaning no disrespect, we noticed you are not authorized to wear certain parts of your uniform." I thought, "Shit, here I am on leave in Paris, trying to relax and forget the war. Why do I have to get into an argument with four drunken paratroopers, about my authority to wear their precious jump boots? Damn it, this is Paris, France and its the middle of the night."

"Sergeant, are you referring to the jump boots I am wearing?" "Yes Sir." "For your information Sergeant, I am on leave from XVIII Airborne Corps Artillery, and these boots are authorized." "Are you parachute qualified Lieutenant? You are not wearing a qualification badge." "Sergeant, I am not parachute qualified, but you will have to take my word for this, I am authorized to wear these boots, whether you like it or not."

This response generated an animated discussion among these four burly sergeants, who finally decided the word of a lowly 2nd Lieutenant was not good enough for them. Finally the Master Sergeant announced their decision, "Lieutenant, again meaning no disrespect, but you are not qualified to wear those boots and you will have to remove them." "And Sergeant, if I refuse?" "We will forcefully remove them for you, Sir!".

I did not like this turn of events. Technically, the sergeant was correct about non-qualified soldiers wearing jump boots. But I had no plans to meekly surrender my foot wear and walk bare-footed back to the hotel. My problem was simple, but the solution was complex. I could not fight my way through these four belligerent non-coms who now had me surrounded. They could overpower me in less than a minute. I knew I could not outrun them. They were in excellent physical condition and could probably catch a terrified wild deer in full flight. There was only one viable solution left for me, I would have to outsmart them!

"First of all sergeant, I am not accustomed to speaking with enlisted personnel when they are not at attention. If you wish to discuss this matter farther, you must assume the position of attention." To my surprise, all four non-coms snapped to attention. I continued, "For more than two months, I have been in continuous combat with various elements of the 82nd and 101st Airborne Divisions acting as an Artillery forward observer for various Infantry Regiments. You will notice the uniform I am wearing. It is not an officers uniform, it is government issue. Three months ago I received a 'Battlefield Commission' and have been in steady combat since then. I do not own an officers uniform, and I do not wear an Airborne insignia because XVIII Airborne Corps has never issued me one. I'm certain you know, we do not wear unit insignia while in combat. I also am not wearing my Bronze Star nor Purple Heart ribbons. If you look close enough you will recognize the one ribbon on my chest is the Good Conduct ribbon. This medal is awarded only to enlisted men, not to officers."

This lengthy lecture brought looks of surprise to the sergeant's faces, who had sobered-up slightly by now. On a roll, and having attracted their attention, I continued my story. "I was serving with the 505th Parachute Infantry Regiment when these boots were given to me." At this point the Master Sergeant, obviously the ranking non-com in the group, interrupted me, "Lieutenant, you say you served with the 505th Regiment? Tell me the name of someone you know in that regiment," This question deserved serious thought, and I answered it carefully, "I know the Regimental Commander, but I don't think you do. However, you may recognize the name of Staff Sergeant 'Dutch' Schultz, he is a medic." "OK Lieutenant, I know Dutch, we go back a long way, and I know he is one damned fine medic. What I don't know is this, what in the Hell does Dutch have to do with you wearing jump boots?"

"Sergeant, its a long story, but it really is pretty simple. I brought a badly wounded friend of mine, a young platoon sergeant, back to the aid station to be treated. While Dutch was cleaning him up and trying to stop his horrible bleeding, I held this young trooper in my arms to comfort him. When the morphine started to ease the excruciating pain, my friend Bobby relaxed and started to talk. This brave young trooper had already lost most of his blood, and was still loosing it faster than Dutch could transfuse him. Bobby looked up at me, with a peaceful look on his face, and asked me if he was going to die. When I looked away and saw Dutch nod his head in the affirmative, I suddenly realized that all three of us knew Bobby would not make it to the hospital alive. I did not have the guts to tell Bobby the truth, so I lied and assured Bobby he was going to be OK." After this assurance, Bobby called to Dutch, "Dutch I feel weaker and weaker, but I don't hurt any more. Thanks for what you've done for me, I appreciate it, but I want you to do one more thing. Please take off my jump boots and give them to the Lieutenant. He risked his life to save mine and I want him to have my jump boots, he earned them." As Dutch started to remove his boots, Bobby turned to me and said, "No matter what happens to me, and no matter where I go, I won't need these boots any more. Lieutenant Pierson, I would be proud to have you wear my boots in combat for me."

Neither Dutch nor I knew what to say, but as Dutch continued to remove the bloody boots, I said to Bobby, "It will be an honor to wear your boots in combat and I promise I will wear them until I die." I then raised myself to my full 6'-2", looked the Master Sergeant in the eye and continued, "Those were the last words spoken by Staff Sergeant Robert Gilmore, and my promise to him, as he died lying in my lap." "I made a death-bed promise to this fatally wounded trooper, and Dutch Schultz was a witness. I am a man of honor," and paused for emphasis, "you will have to kill me to get Bobby's jump boots!" My adversaries were obviously touched by this story, and the Master Sergeant finally asked, "Is that a true story? Is that really how you got those boots?" Without blinking an eye, I lied to the Master Sergeant, "On my mother's bible. No one is going to take these jump boots away from me."

This false story, and my answer, prompted a hushed, almost reverent, discussion between these four rugged warriors who had stopped me. I did not know what to expect and could only wait and hope, but I knew I had given this story my best shot. I had, of course, changed many of the details, but thought these little white-lies were better than blood-shed. To paraphrase the statement, 'Thinking on Your Feet,' I thought of this situation as, 'Thinking in My Boots.'

After a rather lengthy get-together, the Master Sergeant, an imposing American fighting man, showed me a different face. In the subdued light I could see an almost tender look on his tear-stained face as he asked, "Lieutenant, where are you headed?"

"Sergeant, I'm on the way to my hotel on the *Place de la Concorde*." "Sir, we have made up our minds. There are a lots of troopers in Paris tonight who, like us, would not understand why you are wearing jump boots. With your permission, we will escort you to your billet, and I assure you, No Body will try to remove your boots tonight." With parade ground precision these now sober, premier American fighting men, formed a perimeter around me as we started marching smartly along the *Champs-Elysses,* singing 'The Artillery Song' on our way to the *Place de la Concorde.*

The Second Day in Paris, France
March 1945

The American Red Cross jeep pulled to the curb in front of the hotel at 1120 hours, about ten minutes early. The driver was a female ARC employee, very 'perky looking,' and much younger than my cousin Lucy. She entered the hotel lobby and asked the desk clerk to announce that Lieutenant Pierson's transportation had arrived. With a grandiose bow, the desk clerk motioned toward me as I was starting to rise from a throne sized, antique leather arm chair. We exchanged pleasantries and she explained her name was Elizabeth Ann, but quickly added, "Everyone calls me Betty." Betty informed me Mrs. Adams had instructed her to deliver me to a special restaurant at noon, and had warned her not to be late. Since we had a little spare time, Betty suggested we ride along the Seine River to give me a close-up view of some of the more famous sights of Paris. During this pleasant trip, I learned some of the history, and myths of Paris from an attractive, and well educated, ARC representative.

As we drove along the River Seine, on what Betty said was the 'Right Bank' as opposed to the other side, which she referred to as the 'Left Bank'. The Right Bank contained the glory, fortunes, and noble life of Paris society, whereas the Left Bank contained the French traditions of art, education, life, and love. She explained the differences in terms of French wine. A fine vintage, delicately flavored, and expensive *Vin Bordeau* was the wine of choice for residents of the Right Bank. Whereas, rich, full bodied, and relatively inexpensive *Vin Burgandy* was the wine of choice for residents of the Left Bank. This comparison intrigued me because I was not familiar with the characteristics of French wine and this explanation whetted my desire to learn more about the wines of France.

As we slowly rode along the Right Bank, we passed the *Arc de Triomphe du Carrousel,* the small Arc, and the internationally famous museum, the *Louvre,* came into view. Betty told me the most famous works of art had been removed years ago, to protect them from the ravages of war, and/or removal by the occupying German army. These *Objects de Art* were now slowly finding their way back to the museum for public viewing again. Immediately the River Seine widened enough to surround an island which contained several buildings. The two most famous being the *Palais de Justice*, the Palace of Law Courts, and the imposing Cathedral of *Notre-Dame.* Past *Notre-Dame*, we turned and crossed the Seine River on the *Pont de Sully* bridge to reach the Left Bank section of Paris. We then meandered through a tangled maze of small, rough, medieval lanes which served an older residential section of Paris. Along the way, Betty directed my attention to locations where students of *Sorbonne,* the University of Paris lived, loved, and played. Finally, we broke out of the small streets of this section and onto a much more modern road which gave us a wonderful view of *Sorbonne* itself and it's beautiful surroundings. Betty pulled to the curb to give me more time to view the university, it's immediate surroundings, and the unhurried activities of the students themselves. Here, Betty explained the French word *'flaner'* Apparently there was no one-on-one, French to English, translation for this word. That is because this word explains a feeling, or an attitude, which is more old-world than American. *Flaner* means, 'to hang around.' and/or 'to stroll, or walk, from one place to another with no purpose in mind other than looking and enjoying.' Betty continued, "There is no better place in the world to be a *'Flaneur'* than on the Left Bank in Paris.

Apparently Betty sensed I was interested in her travelogue and asked, "Would you like to hear an interesting myth about the French people and Paris?" In ignorance, I nodded yes, and she told me this story. "In 451 AD, Attila-the-Hun, the so called 'Scourge of God,' marched across Gaul with barbarian hordes. During this march they torched the German city of Cologne and left it in ashes. During the process of devastating Cologne, they reportedly ravished 11,000 virgins." Having attracted my attention, Betty continued her story, "Leaving Cologne behind, Attila and his men moved in a wave of destruction and headed for Paris. When the news of this barbarian advance reached Paris, the Roman defenders withdrew to Orleans, leaving the citizens of Paris to defend themselves. A true French heroine rose to this threat and mustered the defenses of the city. She was a fiery French peasant, a young French maiden named Genevieve. Genevieve convinced the frightened citizens to stand together against the hordes of Attila and defend the honor of the French Republic. At the eleventh hour, Attila and his hordes changed their line of march, by-passing Paris, and made their way to attack the city of Orleans. Although history does not record the specific reason which altered these events, a lingering myth credits this change in plans to the fact that Attila somehow found out there was not 11,000 virgins living in Paris to ravage and decided to try his luck in Orleans.

I liked the way Betty told stories. She was gregarious by nature, and extremely animated as she talked. To me, the icing on the cake was the fact that in addition to her intelligence and great personality, she was extremely appealing to the eye. She obviously enjoyed what she was doing as she did her part for the lonely boys away from home. She explained that Mrs. Adams had made arrangements for my lunch at a *Brasserie.* This term literally meant Brewery in English. The *Brasserie*, which overlooked the enormous *Luxembourg Gardens,* had been a popular dining place for generations. Being ever-helpful, Betty suggested I try their hearty onion soup, the piping hot hard-crusted bread, and of course, their specialty, a full-bodied beer from the Province of Alsace. However she made no recommendations for the entree.

A military sedan was parked in front of the *Brasserie* when we arrived, and Betty observed, "Mrs. Adams is already here." As we stopped, I asked Betty if she would join us for lunch. I was disappointed when she said, "Mrs. Adams did not invite her, and besides, I have other pressing business to attend to." I entered the ancient building as Betty was making a U-Turn in her jeep, apparently headed back to the Right Bank of the River Seine.

The *Maitre d'hotel* promptly welcomed me to the establishment and asked if I had a reservation. I told him no, I was a guest of Mrs. Lucile Adams, of the American Red Cross. With much pomp and ceremony, he led me to a beautifully hand-carved wooden table located next to a large window which provided a panoramic view of the magnificent *Luxembourg Gardens*. Cousin Lucy was seated at the table facing the interior of the restaurant and was talking seriously with a large, athletic looking, blond gentleman, who was dressed in a tailored business suit. This gentleman was seated facing away from me as I approached the table which was prepared with three place-settings.

I caught her eye as the head waiter and I neared the table, and received a smile of recognition in return. Lucile then said something to her gentleman friend, whom I assumed was her current interest. Without turning, the civilian asked, in a rather loud voice, "Is that the infamous international criminal, Lieutenant Randolph C. Pierson?" Without waiting for an answer to his question, the civilian continued, "If it is, it is my duty to inform you this building is surrounded by heavily armed troops, and by the authority invested in me by the President of the Unites States, I place you under arrest."

Not knowing what to do, the *maitre d'hotel* and I froze in place. Slowly the broad shoulders and blond head of the civilian turned to confront me. I fully expected the man to be an FBI agent, or an officer from the French Interpol. To my pleasant surprise, the expensively dressed civilian turned out to be Lucile's brother, my First Cousin, Captain Edward J. Nix, Commander of the Paris Detachment of the Criminal Investigation Division, (CID) US Army Intelligence Service. I held out both hands to be cuffed, but instead, Captain Nix shook my hand and said, "Good to see you Randy, congratulations on your promotion." Then he asked, "Can I buy you a beer?"

The tension, now broken, we drank our beer, ate a delicious meal, and talked up a storm, trying to bridge the years since we had last seen each other back in

Jesup, Georgia. For all three of us, it was a happy reunion.

Lucile dropped her bomb as we were enjoying our cigarettes and *Cafe au lait* after lunch. She said she would be leaving for the states in a few days. While there she intended to use the rest of her accumulated ARC leave and then resign from the American Red Cross. Edward was as surprised as I and asked what she planned to do for the rest of her life. Lucy said it was time to finalize her separation from her husband 'Red,' and hoped for a non-contested divorce. When free, she planned to accept a position with Army Special Services as the Resort Director of a 'Rest and Relaxation Resort' the Army planned to establish in the Bavarian Alps. This resort would accommodate US troops stationed in Europe, after the war, while serving in the Army of Occupation.

Captain Nix nodded his head in agreement, as if he understood her plans and approved of them. However, I was caught totally off guard. After being exposed to the Belgian Count Etienne d'Oultremont's view of post-war Europe during his New Years Eve celebration in his ancestral home, the Chateau Xhos, this was the first news I had heard of Allies plans to occupy Germany after the war. Lucile's knowledge of the plans for an American Army of Occupation amazed me, but Edward seemed to understand completely. This conversation made me start thinking. From my point-of-view, there were many dreadful days of heavy fighting ahead for me. If I survived the war, I fully expected to end the war fighting the enemy face-to-face and house-to-house in the city of Berlin. My view of the war was based upon my personal experience and proved how myopic a soldier's view can be when he is faced with survival in combat. These long-term views made me feel naive, and reinforced my feelings of how we combat soldiers were poorly informed.

This experience reminded me of the techniques used by farmers to produce mushrooms. A close friend of mine from Pennsylvania was from a mushroom producing family. One day during a conversation at the Port of Embarkation, I asked him, "Bill, being from Florida, I know a little bit about raising citrus. How does your family produce mushrooms?" "Randy, growing mushrooms is pretty basic, it involves three things:: location, food, and light. We farm in abandoned coal mine shafts, feed the plants with organic fertilizer, and keep them in subdued light. In Pennsylvania language, we say, feed them shit and keep them in the dark!"

I was beginning to think of the US Army as one giant soldier farm. Like the Pennsylvania farmers, the army fed us shit and kept us in the dark.

The trip to London, England
March 1945

The trip to London was interesting. All officers on leave checked in on time with Army Special Services for transportation to London. From the looks of several of the guys, I wondered what they had done during our brief visit to Paris. They looked like they had tried to get caught-up on wine, women, and fun in three days. The main things they had been missing since November when we left England, more than four months ago. The lady at Army Special Services told us our transportation was divided into three segments: Train from Paris to *Etretat*, a French village on the English Channel, ferry from *Etretat* to a British village on the English Channel, and a train ride from there to London. She advised us we would be met at the train station in London by a bus service operated by Army Special Services. We would not be billeted together, but would be spread among several First Class hotels in the center of London. The assignments of hotels would be strictly random, however, if two officers agreed to exchange hotel assignments for some reason, the changes could be negotiated once we arrived at our destination. She added, the most uncertain portions of the journey were the Channel crossings. This time of year, the Channel can get too rough for the small ferry boats to negotiate, and there was still a small danger posed by German submarines. This was interesting information to receive, but it did not dim the enthusiasm of the majority of the crowd. To me however, the thought of a watery death in the English Channel did not appeal to me. Not after what I had already survived. Never-the-less, the train ride to *Etretat* was full of fun and laughter. We were enjoying the trip!

Upon arrival at *Etretat,* we detrained and were met by a Frenchman in civilian clothes. He herded us into the small train station and announced in broken English, that the ferry scheduled to take us across the channel was still in its British port, unable to make today's trip because of the bad weather. He had made arrangements for us to be accommodated at the one local Inn until the weather cleared. Fortunately for us, he said, the Inn was nearby. Since he was unable to provide a motor carriage to transport us, we must gather-up our personal possessions. He would then walk us to the Inn. This turn of events was not taken lightly by a group of newly commissioned American officers. With much muttering and grumbling, we shouldered our loads, and marched down a cobble stone road to the local watering hole.

The Innkeeper was a typical country type Frenchman. Overly polite, happy to be in the company of American fighting men, and willing to help in our hour of need. He explained his Inn had only five rooms and a small kitchen, but he and his wife were accustomed to handling crowds under these circumstances and they would try to be good hosts. I liked this happy Frenchman and his charming wife. Dell Miller and I, along with two other officers, were assigned to a bedroom which normally accommodated two persons. It was a tight fit, not like the regal arrangements we had enjoyed in Paris The really bad news came when we asked about the bath facilities. The Innkeeper explained there was one bathroom upstairs at the end of the hall which served the guest rooms. In case of emergencies, which he anticipated, there was a public restroom adjoining the dining room and bar downstairs. He added, of course all bedrooms contained slop jars which could be used in the room. By now we were all beginning to get the picture. We were in the country, not the city, and we would have to make do with what was available. On officer, obviously a country lad, asked, "How do you get to the out house?" We all laughed and the Innkeeper grinned as he said, "We do not have your so-called out houses. You are now in France. This is a highly civilized country." His answer was to true to be funny.

For three days, boredom reigned. The weather was so lousy we could not leave the building to enjoy the natural beauty surrounding the village, nor experience the friendliness of its seafaring residents. Miller and I broke the monotony by reminiscing about the Tennessee Winter maneuvers, our life style while stationed at Camp Atterbury, and our experience while at the Port of Embarkation. We compared notes about his assignment at the XVIII Airborne

Corps fire direction center as compared to my assignment as a forward observer with various airborne infantry units. We both agreed that I had been given the 'shitty-end-of-the-stick.' We swapped 'war stories' with the other officers as we consumed what seemed to be an endless supply of locally made wine.

Every one complained about our inactivity. But we unanimously agreed upon one thing. Life at *Etretat* beat the Hell out of being in combat in Germany!

The trip across the English Channel
Three Days Later—March 1945

Dell was up and looking out of the window when I got up. The other two officers sharing the bed room were still asleep. Dell said, over his shoulder, "Randy, the weather cleared last night, maybe we will make it across the Channel today." Almost simultaneously I heard a knocking on our door. Dell opened the door and was met by our smiling Innkeeper, who announced, "We have been contacted by radio, the ferry will arrive in *Etretat* in about two hours. This will give you time to pack your belongings and eat a hearty breakfast before you walk to the pier. It will take the crew about an hour to unload the ferry, then you can board the ferry for its return trip to England."

The conversation between Dell and the Innkeeper failed to awaken the other two 'warriors' in the room. It was a difficult task for Dell to awaken them. These two 'America Fighting Men' had obviously over consumed the delicious locally produced wine last night, but with dogged persistence, Dell finally attracted their attention. Only then they reluctantly reacted to this change of events. Of course all bathing facilities were overwhelmed by this sudden need of twenty people to shave, clean up, and to relieve themselves of 'mother nature's calls.' The Good Lord was with 'us sinners' and everything finally fell into place. The country breakfast was delicious, the weather was beautiful, and all twenty eager American officers had assembled at the foot of the pier to watch the final unloading of the ferry. I was surprised at the size of the ferry. It was a rather small vessel which was manned by a British crew. The ferry was a general purpose vessel, designed to carry both passengers and cargo. On this trip from England the ferry carried almost no passengers, but was loaded with medium sized wooden crates and what appeared to be mail pouches.

When we arrived at the pier, similar wooden crates were being on loaded to be transported to England. I had no idea what these crates contained and no one volunteered this information. Waiting with us were five Frenchmen dressed in business clothes who questioned us about the purpose of our trip to England. Once on board, we found the enclosed passenger area was large enough to accommodate at least fifty passengers and was equipped with restroom facilities that could be used once the ferry reached the open sea of the English Cannel. We soon found out this facility was crude but necessary. Once in the Channel, this small boat moved rapidly up and down as well as rolling from side to side in the turbulent water of the English Channel. Many of the passengers spent more time in the restroom facilities, due to *mal de mer*, than they spent in the relative comfort of the enclosed passenger area.

Other than the discomfort caused by sea sickness, the event which impressed me most was seeing the majestic White Cliffs of Dover shining in the bright morning sun.

Life in London and the Brave British People
March / April 1945

Once in England, Murphy's Law took effect, "If something can go wrong, it will!" No American representatives met us at the English Port. Fortunately for us a sympathetic Port Master arranged transportation to take us from the dock area to the train station. You can imagine the confusion in the train terminal when twenty American officers show up unannounced, with no tickets, expecting a train ride to London. The Station Master, a rather subdued individual, quickly understood our predicament and started making phone calls. Within an hour, he had reserved first class accommodations for us on the next train to London, He also advised us an Army Special Service, or an American Red Cross, representative would meet us when the train arrived in London. This was good news, but with our luck, none of us believed this would happen.

During the wait in the train station lobby the group decided to elect a group spokesman, since no one was officially in charge. We decided to use a technique that all Army Officers of the same rank use. The officer who received his commission first is technically the ranking officer in the group. We then started comparing each 'date-of-rank.' Since we were all 2nd Lieutenants who had been recently commissioned while in combat, this placed the 'dates-of-rank' in a pretty tight group. As it turned out, Dell Miller's 'date-of-rank' was 24 January 1945. This 'date-of-rank' established him as the 'ranking officer' in the group, but this fact surfaced another problem. My 'date-of-rank' was also 24 January 1945, the same as Dell's. The tie breaker then became the two officer's serial number. Dell's serial number was 0-2005352, whereas mine was one digit larger, 0-2005353. Consequently Dell out ranked me by one serial number and became the permanent spokesman for the group. Fate handled this choice wisely. I did not want the distinction of being spokesmen for the group. Dell was the oldest officer in the group and the other guys respected his judgment.

Most of the officers were surprised at the size of the London train station with its multiple tracks and several trains taking on, and detraining passengers at the same time. I could not stop trying to compare it with New York City's Grand Central Station. All though I had never been in Grand Central Station. I had read about it and listened to the radio show 'Grand Central Station' which vividly described this famous New York City train terminal. When the train finally reached its berthing place and stopped, a trainman walked through the coach, announced it was now time to detrain, opened the outer door, placed a steel foot step at the foot of the exit, and motioned for us to leave the train. Our group started to scatter immediately as each individual tried to merge with the multitudes of people struggling with personal gear, headed either to a specific train platform or to an exit gate. We were quickly dissolving as a group. This is when Miller took charge! He jumped onto a cargo wagon and as he waived both arms he yelled, "At Ease! At Ease! Now Hear This! Now Hear This!" This announcement slowed the pedestrian traffic and somewhat hushed to noise. As people turned to look and listen, Lieutenant Miller executed his newly given authority by pointing to the train terminal and loudly commanding, "My officers will proceed to Gate Number 4 as quickly as possible. You will reform the group there, inside the terminal, with your personal gear. You will remain there as a group, Lieutenant Pierson is in charge until I return. Now Move Out!"

With a roar of approval from the mixed audience, Dell jumped from the cargo wagon, grabbed me by the arm, and we headed toward Gate 4. Once inside the terminal and near Gate 4, Dell told me he had to locate the person who was to meet us. If no one was there, he would try to contact someone connected with Army Special Services to help us. He explained he had no idea of how long this would take, but emphasized the importance of keeping the group intact during this waiting period. This seemed logical to me and as soon as Dell left I started assembling the group as they entered the terminal through Gate 4. We quickly found nearby seats and staked our claim. To the groups delight, traffic moved constantly through Gate 4. We had chosen a watching place to the British Empire. Women and men, civilians and uniforms, British, Americans, Canadians, Australians and Scots. Soldiers, sailors, and airmen. You name it and we watched it with interest, as the parade passed our reviewing stand. Of course the young females attracted our attention the most. We were favorably impressed by the general attitude of the passing people. The ladies smiled, men in civilian attire tipped their hats, and service personnel gave us a casual salute. Occasionally someone would stop and talk.

During a lull in the parade, a smiling Lieutenant Miller appeared. He was accompanied by a smart looking female dressed in a uniform that I did not recognize. As they approached our reviewing location, we all decided to stand. Dell introduced her as 'Gracie' and she would escort us to the Algonquin Hotel. When some of the guys tried to introduce himself, Gracie told them we must board our buss immediately and we would get to know each other at the hotel.. She quickly led us to a somewhat private exit to the terminal. For the first time in my life, I boarded a brilliant red double deck British bus.

Life in London, England
March 1945

At the Algonquin Hotel Gracie assembled us in a large room which was normally used for business meetings. She explained she was a Sergeant in the Royal Air Force trained to target enemy aircraft with ground based radar. Her specialty was no longer needed because the Luftwaffe was now unable to bomb London. She was on loan to the American government, to assist in the administration of all U. S. troops on leave in London. She said there were several hundred U. S. officers and enlisted men currently on leave here. She and her assistants interviewed each U. S. serviceman before he was released to his billet in order to determine his special needs or wants while on leave. Since we were the first group of 'Battle Field Commissioned Officers,' who might have unique needs, she wanted to interview each of us herself. She had asked our group leader, Lieutenant Miller, to assist her. She advised us her office was located in the Algonquin Hotel, and for simplicity of communicating with the group had made arrangements for Lieutenant Miller to be billeted here.

When it became my turn to be interviewed, Gracie asked, "You are Lieutenant Randolph C. Pierson? You are a personal friend of Lieutenant Miller?" To both questions I answered, "Yes." "Lieutenant, would you please tell me what assistance I can give you while you are in London?" "Gracie I do need help, but first don't call me by my rank, that is not necessary, just call me Randy." This request drew a knowing smile from Gracie as she responded, "Yes, I'll bet you are! But I cannot help you with you sexual needs." I was just trying to be more informal, but I had forgotten I was in England and the slang word 'randy' meant 'starved for sex.' Miller was laughing so hard he almost fell out of his chair. I quickly tried to explain, but Gracie said she knew what I meant and guided the interview back on track. "Gracie, after getting to my billet I need to get an officer uniform, hat, and low cut shoes so I can get out of this GI uniform I am wearing." Dell chimed in with a definite 'Amen.' "My next problem is, I don't have much money. How do I get enough money to pay for the uniform and live in London for ten days? Rob the Bank of England?"

There was a definite lull in the conversation as the three of us considered my two most pressing problems. Gracie finally broke the silence, "Lieutenant Pierson I have you assigned to a small family type billet, the King George House. It is located within walking distance of the Algonquin. The proprietor's name is Cedric, he is very friendly and will give you royal treatment. Let me have a lorry take you and your belongings there. If you will accept my invitation to dinner tonight, please meet Lieutenant Miller and me here at 1900 hours tonight. I believe your problems can be solved, and if what Lieutenant Miller tells me about the amount of cigarettes he has is true, you two might be more wealthy than you realize." These arrangements sounded great to me, so I told her I would see them at 1900. Miller seemed pleased. As I said, "See you tonight buddy," the next officer stepped up to be interviewed.

When Gracie dispatched the lorry, it contained three officers and their baggage. The lorry driver, a British Corporal, told me I would be the last one of the three to arrive at my billet. The round-a-bout trip to the King George House was pleasant and gave me the opportunity to look at this famous city and ask the driver questions. He explained the Thames River runs mainly East and West, but makes a turn at London and runs North and South. This fact divides the city into two sections, referred to as the East End and West End. The East end was mostly commercial, dominated by the shipping and fishing industries. It was also home of the lower class English citizens called Cockneys. The West End of London was dominated by the Government, churches, museums, parks, banks, retail establishments, hotels, and of course, the Royal Family. He said the King George House is located in the West End, near Piccadilly Circus, in the SOHO section of London. The driver said, "Since you are an officer, I don't know how you want to spend your time, but Piccadilly Circus offers many choices. You might want to check it out." When I told him I had not given this much thought, but I had limited money to spend, he assed, "Well Lieutenant I suggest you get over to the East End and mix with the Cockneys. They are poor people, fiercely proud, but they know how to have fun."

At the King George House we were met by Cedric, who told the driver where to put my belongings. I tried to tip the driver and Cedric, but both declined a gratuity. As he left, the lorry driver reminded me, "Lieutenant, hope you have a nice time in London. Don't forget what I told you about the East End and the Cockneys." I noticed Cedric smiled when he heard the lorry drivers advice.

Cedric accompanied me to my room. The atmosphere pleased me, the Victorian furniture, a large double bed, and an unexpected private 'water closet.' To me, private bathroom facilities had become a luxury. Cedric updated me on the services available to his customers, and the fact that most room service would be billed to the room and Gracie would take care of the payment arrangements. He invited me to have afternoon 'tea and crumpets' with him at 1600 hours and he would help me organize my activities. This was a nice personal gesture on his part and I gladly accepted his invitation. I spent my interim time bathing, shaving, and relaxing. I found out afternoon 'tea and crumpets' was more formal than a ten minute coffee break, it was a deep rooted English ritual. The tea must be 'potted and poured' according to established procedures. The tea may be modified with lemon, sugar, and sometimes milk. The crumpets were small bits of finger foods to be nibbled while enjoying the tea and conversation. This pastime was even followed by British army units while engaged in combat. I never understood the reason for this type of activity while engaged in violent combat. Of course this was not the only thing about the Brits I did not understand, but these differences were what made them interesting.

Our conversation slowly became more personal as I discussed my needs to get an American officers uniform. Cedric said he had a friend, a master tailor, who could easily fit me with a uniform. The problem, he did not have access to the 'pink and green' gabardine material, nor the brass buttons, necessary for an American officers uniform. Perhaps I could obtain these materials from a U. S. Quartermaster Depot. This offer prompted a discussion of my other problem, "Cedric I do not have much money to spend. Do you know how much his services would cost?" "Lieutenant, I can not quote a price, but you can rest assured the cost will be lower than if you go to some famous place of business to purchase a uniform. Remember, the uniform will be tailored to your body and will fit properly, it will not come off of a clothes rack."

"Cedric, do you think your friend would take a payment in cigarettes?" "Lieutenant, the barter system is very common here in London, and is quite legal. Are your cigarettes American, and in the original packages?" "Oh yes, they are American, legal, and still in cartons." "You speak of cartons, how many packs are in a Carton?" "Cedric, these cigarettes come ten packs to the carton, all sealed for freshness." "Lieutenant, may I ask how many cartons have you brought with you?" "Of course you may Cedric, I have no idea how much they are worth, and

I'm not accustomed to paying for things with cigarettes. My friend and I have about fifteen cartons with us. What do you think they would be worth for barter purposes?" "The legitimate value of a pack of American cigarettes is between 5 and 6 dollars a pack. On the black market, possibly more. You and your friend can easily purchase seven to nine hundred dollars of services with your cigarettes. That amount of money gives you considerable buying power right now in London." "This is very interesting information Cedric, I am having dinner with Gracie and my friend at the Algonquin tonight. Will it be OK for me to discuss our conversation with her?" "Of course it will be alright! You will find Gracie is very knowledgeable and experienced in handling these types of problems."

I arrived at the Algonquin a little before 1900, Miller was seated at a table in the lounge socializing with a group of men dressed in civilian clothing. Gracie had not yet arrived. Miller spotted me as I wandered into the lounge, and motioned for me to join the group. Their table was full, but one of the civilians located an empty chair and brought it to the table so I could be seated. Another gentleman asked me what I wanted to drink. This flurry of unexpected activity confused me momentarily, but Miller answered the question,, "He wants a scotch and soda." I was quickly informed the civilians were American businessmen, and everything was 'on them,' because nothing was too good for the 'boys in the service.' We were deep in conversation when Gracie arrived. One gallant Americans offered her his chair, but she politely declined, "I have a reservation for the two Lieutenants waiting in the dinning room, perhaps you will invite them to dinner again." I thought that was nice of Gracie to set us up for a free dinner in the future. We were seated at a table located in a corner of the world famous dining room. Gracie said she preferred this table when she had to discuss business because it was quiet and semi-private. She had preordered our dinners, so we were immediately served. In my mind I started comparing this food with fashionable French food we had enjoyed in Paris. The comparison was difficult. The English and French styles and tastes were miles apart. It seemed to me the French cuisine was lighthearted and pleasing to the eye, whereas our meal tonight was robust and filling. Regardless of the differences, I enjoyed my first English meal in this world class dining room.

Dell and I were surprised when the waiter brought us a pot of coffee to go with our after dinner cigarettes. When Dell asked, to no one in particular, "This tastes like good ole back home coffee. Where did they get this? I thought coffee was scarce." Gracie promptly responded, "Yes, coffee is scarce, it is worth its weight in gold in London. For your information, this came from my private stock. I gave the head chef enough to make this pot. I hope you enjoy the treat." Dell asked, "I know it is none of my business Gracie, but where do you get this stuff?" "Well, to be truthful, I am a friend of an American Master Sergeant who runs a large consolidated mess. His crew prepares about 5,000 meals three times each day. When you handle this much food each day, there is bound to be some leakage. You know, I scratch his back, and he scratches mine, so I get a small amount of that leakage. You two should meet him and tell him Gracie sent you. You will be well fed, and at the same time save money."

As sergeants, both Dell and I hade done some 'wheeling and dealing.' I still felt Sergeants ran the Army, not the Generals, but Gracie made me feel like a rank armature. With admiration I exclaimed, "Gracie, you are amazing!" This more-or-less knee jerk reaction to being served American coffee resulted in Gracie becoming known as 'Amazing Grace.'

Now into the nitty gritty of our meeting, I outlined my conversation with Cedric, and offered his solutions to Gracie for comments. She explained, "I will purchase the pink and green gabardine material, plus the required brass for the uniforms, this will require cash. Of course you must be measured by the tailor first. Lieutenant Miller should accompany you and get measured at the same time. The tailor must give Lieutenant Miller a list of everything he needs and Dell must give the list to me. We will then convert some of his cigarettes to cash which I will use to pay for the goods. Both of you l need an officers gold braid cap, a pair of low cut shoes, and each of you should purchase at least two khaki shirts with epaulets. You can give me your sizes now."

After recording our statistics, Gracie asked, "Do you understand what you must do to get your uniforms?" We both indicated, "Yes" with a nod of our heads. "Lieutenant Miller, will you let me handle the cigarette sale for you?" To which Dell nodded, "Yes." Do either of you have questions concerning what must done?" At this point I said, "Yes Gracie, when should we get started?" She smiled as she answered this question, "Randy, the first thing in the morning. Have Cedric call his friend, the tailor, to meet with you and Dell. I will drop Dell off at the King George House tomorrow morning at 0900 hours. Are we all set?" I could not resist my observation of the change in Gracie's demeanor. "Gracie, I notice we are now Dell and Randy. What made you drop the English formality?" She laughed, "I have learned so much about you two guys, it is almost like you are brothers. Dell, the traveling salesman, and you still the college kid, it is refreshing. I decided to drop the rank, let's forget Sergeant and Lieutenant, just let me be a member of the family, your temporary sister." I had never met a female like her, it was refreshing to me too. That is why she became 'Amazing Grace' to me.

We finished our business with chit chat and small talk. When I decided to leave Gracie asked me how I planned to spend the evening. I told her I wanted to reconnoiter Piccadilly Circus. Gracie nodded agreement, but added, "Frequent only public establishments on main streets, stay out of alleys and 'private clubs.' Do not flash money, avoid street women, and if you get lost, call Cedric, tell him where you are, and he will come get you. And above all things, if you get into trouble, remember that Bobbies are your friend." This was sound advice. I decided to live by it as long as I was in London.

My first night in this strange, huge city, was rather tame, learning to pay for mugs of warm beer with a cigarette, playing darts, and ultimately learning that Americans were not admired by all Brits. In the last pub of the evening, an older Englishman, dressed in civilian clothes, who had obviously had too much to drink, approached me at the bar and belligerently announced, in a loud voice that everyone to hear, "I do not like Americans for four reasons: One, they are over paid, Two, they were over dressed, Three, they are over sexed, and Four, they are over here!" This announcement did not sit well with me. I took an immediate dislike to this man. I knew he wanted to fight, but he did not intimidate me. I knew I could 'polish off' this drunk in about two minutes and not even work up a sweat. But I didn't come to England to fight, I came to England to get away from fighting. But this Limey came on too strong for me to ignore. "You in the civilian clothes! You say you don't like Americans?" "Yea, that's what I said soldier boy. You want to make something out of it?" "I might! Do you dislike me in particular, or all Americans in general?" "You Yanks are all the same, so I guess that includes you soldier boy." "Well, since you don't know me, and you want to make it personal, I'll tell you something about me. First, I am not over paid. You will notice I have no money, I am paying for my beer with my cigarette ration. Second, I am not over dressed. I have seen Cockneys better dressed than I am. Third, I may be over sexed, but remember, God made me that way. And fourth, I sure as Hell I am over here. You know why, ass hole? To put my life on the line to save your lousy Limey ass. If it weren't for Yanks like me, you would be speaking German and eating sauerkraut instead of enjoying mutton.. Do you understand what I just said, stupid, or do I have to repeat these facts to your ugly face again? Now either get off of my back, or lets go outside and settle this thing!"

By this time most of the bar patrons had moved in close anticipating a fight, but I didn't care how many friends he had, I wasn't going to take this kind of shit off of a drunken Limey. As the crowd fell silent, I tensed up and waited for the Limey's first swing. From experience I knew this type of bar brawler, they try to take you out with a quick 'sucker punch.' I was ready, this was not going to happen to me, but the 'sucker punch' never came. Suddenly, several bar patrons grabbed the drunk, dragged him out of the pub and threw him into the street. When they returned, the bar tender called the police and asked them to come get the drunk and hold him in the lock-up over night. This was a valuable lesson to me, I was so naive I thought everyone liked Americans. Then it dawned on me, which is better, to be liked, or to be respected? The fact is, since my altercation with this local drunk I thought some of the pub patrons did not really like me, but I was certain of one thing, they all respected this Yank! For the rest of the evening in this Pub, I never had to pay for another beer.

This was flattering, but the difference between being liked and respected was too deep for this junior artillery officer. The night was young and so was I. My desire to experience the sights and sounds of Piccadilly Circus prevailed. While enjoying this experience I became totally lost and had no idea of how to get back to the King George House. Fortunately an understanding bar tender offered to help. He called the American Military Police, who dispatched a burly Sergeant, in a jeep, to transport me to the King George House. At the King George House, Cedric was fast asleep when the MP Sergeant delivered me to the front desk. I did not know the night clerk and, of course, he did not know me. The three of us had a sincere discussion of who I was, and was I really a registered guest of the King George House. I finally gathered my wits and presented my room key as evidence. Once we reached an agreement on who I was, and where I was supposed to be, the large MP Sergeant said, "Lieutenant, if you get lost again, or get into trouble, call us direct. We'll help you. Have a good time while you are here on leave in London, but please don't drink too much or get into fights with civilians. Getting involved with civilian authority makes it harder for us to take care of our own."

While lying in bed, just before I went to sleep, I realized how lucky I had been tonight, and suddenly remembered that I had to be bright eyed and bushy tailed when I met with Dell, Gracie and the tailor at 0900 in the morning. Having had a long day, now followed with total relaxation, sleep came easily for this young warrior.

Breakfast at 0800 with Cedric was a pleasant occasion. During our conversation, Cedric questioned, "Lieutenant, the desk clerk reported to me that you were accompanied home last night by the Military Police. Did you get into serious trouble? Is there anything I need to know? Do you need my help?" "Cedric, I appreciate your concern, I just got lost and the MPs brought me here. I guess I was a little groggy from too many free beers. In a pub I almost got into a fight with an abrasive Limey who didn't like Americans, but the majority of the patrons were on my side They handles him very nicely and he spent the rest of the night in the lock-up. All's well that ends well." At this point in our conversation, the tailor arrived with his patterns, pins, shears, and a tape measure. He and Cedric greeted each other as good friends do. Then it was Cedric's time to introduce me, a recently commissioned American officers who needs a uniform.

The three of us adjourned to a small room Cedric asked to use as a fitting room. As the tailor was laying out his equipment, Dell and Gracie arrived with the materials and brass. Immediately Gracie, the tailor, and Cedric entered into a 'conference' which did not include Dell or me. Gracie was definitely in charge, with Cedric and the tailor nodding their heads in the affirmative. Once the 'conference was over, Gracie advised us all charges had been agreed upon, the steps necessary to produce our uniforms as quickly as possible were in place, and all bills were to be submitted to her for payment. Only one question remained, what type jackets did we want? She said there were two types, the regulation 'Long Jacket,' or the abbreviated 'Eisenhower Jacket.' Dell chose the regulation length jacket but I preferred the 'Eisenhower.'

For the remainder of out time in London, Lieutenant Miller and I went our own ways. This just happened, it was not planned. Our paths sometimes crossed at the consolidated mess where Gracie's friend gave us special treatment. At other times, he and I were thrown together during a sight-seeing tour which had been arranged by the American Red Cross, or by Gracie's group, but I never saw Dell at night. This was probably for the best. For three long years we had been part of an integrated group. But now, we were able to be on our own and free to follow our own fancies. I personally had some memorable experiences.

One night after pub hopping, enjoying pub entertainment, and consuming several tankards of ale, I decided to walk to the King George House. I was in a part of the city that was not familiar to me, but I felt I could find my way home. As I left the bright interior lights of the pub, I was surprised to find this part of London was in a black-out condition. Even after my eyes became adjusted to the total darkness, I bumped into things and stumbled on the uneven sidewalks. There was a chill in the air, which combined with the warm air currents coming off of the Thames river, produced a damp fog. As I struggled through the foggy darkness I lost my sense of direction and started to have doubts about finding my way 'home.' I decided to keep walking until I bumped into someone who could help me. The farther I walked, the more I became aware of my need to void my bladder. Fortunately for me, I finally blundered into what appeared to be a military guard shack. A 'voice in the dark,' asked, "Can I help you Sir?" I gratefully answered to my unseen benefactor, "I am Lieutenant Pierson and

I am lost. But first, I must urinate, and do it quickly." The 'voice in the dark' answered, "I understand Sir. There are no facilities open in this area at this time of the night. If you will walk through the gate and down the walk, on your left you will find an alcove in the building. Just walk over next to the building and relieve yourself." Without even thanking the 'voice in the dark,' I hurried down the walkway, unzipping my pants on the run. While leaning against the building relieving myself I thought, "P & G, What a Relief!"

My mission now accomplished, I returned to the guard shack in a more leisurely pace and stopped. This time I could see a British enlisted man standing at attention outside the guard shack. As I approached I thanked him for helping me in a time of emergency, and out of curiosity asked, "For the record, what is that building?" With great dignity, he answered, "Sir! You have just pissed on the British Admiralty!"

In retrospect, I have related this true story many times. to highly informed and distinguished historians. To them, this incident illustrates a dramatic change in history. When a very junior American officer 'pissed on the British Admiralty', this became a symbolic act that states, "America, not Britannia, now rules the waves.' This act is indeed, my contribution to the World War II Americana!

† †

On several occasions I visited the Algonquin Hotel early in the evening. I frequented the bar hoping to meet an American business man. This was a nice way to start an evening. All the men I met impressed me, they were executives who represented large U S corporations. They had unrestricted expense accounts, and were very generous to young officers in uniform like me. They gladly purchased us drinks while listening to our 'war stories.' This was profitable time spent for us guys who had little or no money, but I was more interested in listening to them than telling 'war stories' for free drinks. The information about the war I had received from my cousins in Paris was confirmed by these men. They all seemed to have a common cause. They wanted to resume trade with England and the continent, they thought the Allies had already won the war, and of all things, they were all recruiting young men soon to return home from the European conflict.

My first experience in being recruited came from a gentleman in the manufacturing industry. His interest in me intensified when he learned I had earned a battlefield commission. To him, this was a strong indication of leadership ability. As a 21 year old male, with raging hormones, he asked if I was interested in women's breasts. I answered, "Affirmative," with a grin on my face but wondered where this would lead. He relieved my anxiety by explaining he was employed by a company that formerly manufactured the "Lovable" brand of female brassieres. He continued, "The Lovable operation had been suspended for several years and the plant is now manufacturing parachutes, and other equipment, for the armed forces. this change in their business was caused by two factors. First, the three essential materials for making brassieres, nylon, latex, and silk, were no longer available for making civilian clothing, and second, the 'cost plus 10 percent contracts' with the U S Government were more profitable, and less risky, than manufacturing and marketing civilian clothing."

In the restaurant he told me his current assignment was to develop a corporate conversion plan to manufacture and market the Lovable line when the war ends. During a rather enjoyable dinner, the recruitment process continued. He learned I had completed one year of college and had excelled in mechanical drawing and analytical geometry, both in high school and later in college. This fact attracted his attention and he explained that designing brassiere cups, for various sizes and purposes, was really an engineering problem, and 'iced the cake' by adding, that this kind of design required quite a bit of 'hands-on' contact with female models. Of course by this time I was ready to go AWOL from the army, and sign-up to work for free. This was a fruitful learning experience for me and I enjoyed listening to this business man. As I thanked him for a pleasant evening, he gave me his business card and asked me to call him the minute I hit the states.

Now, all these years after receiving this fascinating job offer, I still wonder what my post-war life would have been had I played this role.

The day Dell Miller and I had been waiting for finally arrived. Gracie informed us our uniforms were ready to be picked up and drove us to the small tailor shop where our new uniforms were waiting. Gracie and the tailor watched as Dell and I changed our outer garments. The transition was graphic! I now looked like a commissioned officer in the American army. The pressed pink pants and green jacket, the gold braid hat, the 'spit polished' low cut shoes, and the polished brass insignia made me look and feel like a commissioned officer. I was proud and pleased, and so were Gracie and the tailor.

Of all of the American business men I met at the Algonquin Hotel the one who impressed me most was an executive in the publishing business. His name was William 'Bill' Fawcett, the president of Fawcett Publishing Company. We met when I seated myself next to him at the bar. He looked me over very casually and asked, "Lieutenant, may I offer you a drink?" "Yes sir, but the drinks are pretty expensive here." This made him chuckle when he said, "Lieutenant, don't sweat the cost, I believe my company can afford it. What do you normally drink?" Without thinking, my response was. "A short beer." Mr. Fawcett looked at the bartender and said, "We can do better than that, bring this young man a scotch and soda. That is what I am drinking." He then turned to me, and asked, "Is a scotch and soda OK with you Lieutenant?' "Yes sir, scotch is an expensive drink, but I am learning to like it". "That is good Lieutenant, enjoying scotch does not come instantly, it is an acquired taste." About that time, a dining room employee came into the bar, interrupted our conversation, and told Mr. Fawcett his table was ready.

As he stood up from the bar stool, Mr. Fawcett asked me to join him for dinner. I immediately declined the invitation, stating I usually ate my evening meal at the consolidated mess because the food there was well prepared, and much less expensive. Mr. Fawcett shook his head in disbelief and told me, "I am inviting you to be my guest. To put it bluntly, the meal won't cost you a 'ha-penny.' Why am I doing this? First, I do not like to dine alone, and second, you are an interesting young man and I would like to talk with you more extensively." "Well Sir, under those circumstances, I will be delighted to be your guest for dinner.". As we left the bar, Mr. Fawcett motioned for me to bring my drink and follow him. At the same time he told the bar tender to put the drinks on his dinner check. Judging from the personalized service we received in the dining room, it was easy to surmise that Mr. Fawcett was well known at the Algonquin Hotel.

During the early part of the dinner Mr. Fawcett mainly asked questions. He indicated he wanted to be on a less formal basis than 'Mr. and Lieutenant.' He wanted to know why I kept calling him 'Mister.' I told him I had been taught to address men older than I with 'Mister.' He understood this, but insisted he had rather be called Bill. When I told him my name was Randolph Pierson, he asked "What do your friends call you?" When I told him 'Randy' he really laughed and exclaimed, "I'll bet you have a problem with that knick-name over here!" I told him when my unit was staging in England, I dated a few English girls, and got into trouble when I told them, "I am Randy." Of course I finally learned to say, "My name is Randolph, but my friends call me Randy." For the rest of the evening we became Bill and Randy.

Bill was an interesting gentleman, he grew-up in a family dominated business. He had seen their basic publishing business change several times. The technology to print and store book text and covers was constantly changing. Also changing was the subject matter being read. It was a challenge to convert to ever changing technology, to publish to meet changing readership demands, and to stay profitable in an increasingly competitive market place. The problems he was facing seemed unsolvable to me, but not to him. When we discussed my problems, it was evident that money was not one of his. He was astound at the low pay scale of an unmarried Second Lieutenant because he had secretaries who made more money than I did. To him, my concern over the cost of everything was interesting. He was amazed when I told him I drew only twenty dollars a month in army pay and sent the rest home to my dependent mother. Another thing that interested him was the fact that I paid for my new uniform with American cigarettes, and also paid for my beer in the local pubs with cigarettes. He laughed when I told him the bar here in the Algonquin would not accept cigarettes in payment for bar services. This remark led to his analysis of the tobacco industry. He told me the tobacco industry management was smart. Under the umbrella of being 'Patriotic' they gave millions and millions of free cigarettes to service personnel. This was no gamble, they knew they were creating a gigantic post-war demand for their products, while creating a favorable impression of their companies. To a corporate manager, this was a brilliant idea, the combining of public relations with advanced marketing techniques.

We discussed the status of the war, and realized our points of view were quite different. He was concerned with creating post-war economic advantages for his company whereas I was concerned about getting killed while fighting Germans in the streets of Berlin. I understood him, and he understood me. At our friendly parting that evening, Bill pulled a business card from his jacket pocket, on the back he wrote: "Randy, if you need a job after the war – call me." Signed, 'Bill'

I believe I still have this 'Job Offer' in my WWII Foot Locker.

The most prevailing memories of life in London surfaces when I recall my experience with the Cockneys. But before I tell my true story, let me give you my lasting impression of the Cockney character. Generally speaking, they received little, or no, formal education, yet they were intelligent, self taught, and extremely street wise. They loved the 'Mum' Queen of England, but were loyal to their own elected 'Pearly King.' They were child like in some respects, they could be serious, but enjoyed life and had fun. But what impressed me the most was, they universally understood why American troops were in England, and respected Americans for helping them resist the Nazi war machine which had been pounding them for years. And last but not least, they were hard to converse with. They spoke English, but it was their own version. So you can fully understand this Cockney characteristic, I have included a short table.

ENGLISH TO COCKNEY TRANSLATION TABLE

English	Cockney
† Beer	Pig's Ear
† Boy	Pride and Joy
† Breasts	East and West
† Darts	Horse and Carts
† Face	Boat-Race
† Head	Loaf of Bread
† House	Mickey Mouse
† Money	Bees and Honey
† Stairs	Peaches and Pears
† Suit	Whistle and Flute

Both Cedric and Gracie had ideas about a trip to the East End of London. Cedric was more concerned with the details of getting me over there and getting me back without getting me lost, but Gracie was more concerned about my personal safety while I was there. Fortunately for me, they both had good instincts and offered good advice. As it turned out, I paid attention to what they suggested, and had no trouble at all. In fact, I quickly became familiar with surface and underground transportation routes, schedules, and fares. As far as my personal safety, I was never concerned about this aspect of going to the Ease End. However, I did follow Gracie's advice and never carried more than three shillings and two packs of cigarettes for spending money.

My first trip to the East End was more exploratory than for fun. The first commercial contact I had was with an elderly Cockney man who approached me on the street. He was obviously impressed with my uniform and approached me in a respectful manner. After his initial pleasantries, which I did not really understand, he tried to sell me a souvenir. I looked at what he was holding in his hand. The 'souvenir' seemed to be an empty jar with a screw-on metal top. I commented that this did not seem to be a souvenir to me. His answer was very positive, "Gov, it's valuable! It's a antique jar full of genuine London air. It'll bring you a fancy price back home." His approach fascinated me, the smile on his wrinkled face, the look of expectation in his eyes, and his stained and missing teeth, evoked my sympathy. Not knowing what to do, I pulled a lone 'Lucky Strike' from an opened pack and extended it to the old man, He quickly took the one cigarette, handed me the empty bottle, and bowed as he backed away from me.. If I understood him correctly, his last words sounded like. "Thank ya Governor. God bless ya Yank."

After learning more about building locations and East End customs, my next visits produced nothing but pleasure.

This pub seemed 'happy' to me. I could hear music, people laughing, and not one sound of loud arguments in progress. I decided to enter and 'test the water.' I am glad I did. This was the beginning of a wonderful evening. The building which housed the pub must have been hundreds of years old, but the interior was spotless and filled with males and females. Most were patrons, but some were employees. They mingled so freely, it was hard for me to determine which was which. One thing that pleased me was they all seemed to be either friends or family. As had become my custom, I seated myself on an empty bar stool and negotiated the price of beer. I told the bar tender I had no money, but had an open pack of Lucky Strike cigarettes. The bar tender stuck up two fingers, and I nodded acceptance. He drew a beer and placed it on the bar in front of me. Before I handed him a 'Lucky' he wiped his hands dry so he would not dampen the cigarette. He then smiled and held up one finger, indicating I still had one more beer to go. These actions caught the attention of several other patrons, who suddenly became my newly found 'friends.'

I was soon challenged to a game of 'Horse and Carts.' I had excellent coordination, but try as I did, I could not win at darts. These Cockneys were pros and I was a rank amateur. While awaiting my turn to 'toss' my darts, a man approached me from the rear. When the 'chit chat' suddenly stopped, I turned to see the individual who caused the 'chit chat' to stop. Now facing me stood a man dressed in a full length jacket, matching pants, and a soft cap jauntily perched upon his head. This seemed to be unusual attire for a pub, but what made his costume so elegant was the arrangement of hundreds of mother-of-pearl buttons sewn on his costume in intricate designs. As he stuck out his hand in a gesture of friendship, one bar patron whispered to me, "This is our Pearly King." To my amazement, the Pearly King asked me to join him at his table.

His table occupied the place of honor in the pub. It was situated in a semiprivate alcove which was slightly raised above the level of the main floor. This feature required anyone approaching the Pearly King to look up. Whether this arrangement was intended or not, I did not know, but it did have a profound psychological effect on anyone approaching him. As we took our places at his table, a bar maid immediately placed two beers and finger food on the table. She was thanked by the Pearly King with a big smile and an affectionate pat on her fanny. From the look on her face, I knew she enjoyed pleasing him. The Pearly King was easy for me to talk to, he was an educated man who spoke to me in English, but when our conversation was interrupted by one of his Cockney clan, he spoke to them in their Cockney dialect. After several such interruptions he noticed the quizzical expression on my face and started to explain why each interruption was necessary. These explanations led me to believe he was the sole 'judge and jury' of his small kingdom. He seemed to have a practical solution to each and every problem presented to him. During one of our personal conversations, I made this observation and said, "I don't think I am smart enough to be a Pearly King," His answer surprised me when he said, "I don't think I am smart enough to be an officer in the American army." Half as a joke, and half seriously I suggested, "Let's trade places for a while." He laughed, stood at the table, and started removing his elaborate Pearly King jacket. Following his lead, I stood up and removed my American officer's jacket. We then traded jackets in front of a surprised and attentive audience. He was much shorter than I, but our shoulders were almost equal in width. To my amazement, these differently made jackets looked as though they were tailored for each of us..

With a dramatic wave of his arms, the Pearly King motioned to me to take his seat as he was moving towards mine. This action by their 'King' slowly started to impact his subjects, but soon they realized they had a new 'Monarch' and the U S Army had a new officer. For the next few hours, all clan problems were presented to me in their Cockney dialectic and interpreted to me by the 'King.' I then gave my suggested solution to the 'King,' who relayed my message back to the troubled Cockney. I, of course, had no idea what the 'King' told his subject, but the process seemed to be successful to me. Towards the end of a pleasant evening, the 'King' and I exchanged jackets again, this time to a thundering applause from his subjects.

I will never know, but I believe the applause indicated his subjects were happy to have their 'King' return. As for my performance as their acting 'King,' I doubt the thundering applause was for me!

As a result of my new friendship with the Pearly King, I was invited to attend a Cockney version of an American institution, a Burlesque Show. Having attended American burlesque performances in Boston, at the famous 'Howard Theatre,' while at the port-of-embarkation, and still having fond memories of the pitch-men's corny jokes, the 'bumps and grinds' of the strippers, and the yells of the audience to 'take it off,' 'take it off,' prompted me to accept his invitation.

The English theatre was much like the 'Howard' in design. Maybe I should say the 'Howard' was much like the English theatre in design, because the English theatre pre-dated the 'Howard' by many, many years. Both had a raised center stage behind a sunken orchestra pit. The center stage was flanked by elevated clusters of box seats which gave special patrons an uninterrupted view of the entire stage. The general patrons were seated in the center of the theatre in a normal seating arrangement. Our seats for the evening were in the front box, stage left. The box of the Pearly King and Queen.

The performance was delightful. I could not resist my tendency to compare this performance with those I had seen in Boston at the 'Howard.' The Cockney presentation centered around a 'scroungy looking' older man who told suggestive jokes as he ogled his 'second banana,' a young, innocent looking, sexily dressed female, who was in 'full bloom.' The main difference between American Burlesque and the Cockney performance was the strippers. The Cockneys did not include stripping in their stage show. After the performance, the entire Cockney cast returned to center stage and bowed to an applauding audience. The cast then turned toward the 'King's' box seat and bowed. The 'King,' the 'Queen,' and I, stood and acknowledged the performer's special bow.

After the stage performance ended, this young American officer truly felt like Royalty. This memorable occasion is still fresh in my mind.

† †

For a change, I decided to forgo my 'Pub Hopping' and went to an Officer's Club that 'Amazing Grace' highly recommended. The crowd was mixed, Brits, Aussies, Americans, with a pleasing mixture of males and females. I avoided the all male tables and was invited to sit at a table occupied by congenial females. The atmosphere was relaxed, Glen Miller records were playing, and I enjoyed dancing with the attractive English nurses. At the table, between dances, the conversation covered many diverse subjects, and we shared common concerns about the war. I was enjoying a pleasant evening and was thankful to 'Amazing Grace' for recommending this club, when the mood changed. This change in mood was caused by the entrance of a Scot Infantry Captain. He was resplendent in his dress uniform of high laced shoes, long knee length stockings, a traditional tartan Kilt, a white blouse, his military Regimental Sash, and a jaunty looking cap. He was a handsome man, with a weight lifter's physique, and strikingly dressed. His entrance indicated he had 'it,' and also indicated he intended to flaunt 'it.' His entry created quite a stir at our table. Between the nurses, his entrance surfaced the age old question, "What does a Scots man wear under his kilt?"

This 'age old question' quickly spread to other tables, and a trio of stout Lads decided to assist the females in the crowd and quickly declared, "We will determine the answer to 'the age old question' tonight, for now and for ever." Encouraged by comments from the more aggressive females in the crowd, these stout 'Lads' then approached the Scot Officer and asked him 'the age old question.' His answer was not surprising to me when he said, "Lads, ye shall never know!" The answer from the stout Lads was just as firm, "Oh yes we will!"

The ensuing struggle was egged on by yells of encouragement from the appreciative audience. The determined effort of the stout Lads lasted several minutes. Their alcohol impaired effort was vigorous, but uncoordinated, consequently they failed to lift the kilt of the agile Scot. A senior officer finally decided, enough is enough, and ended the struggle before anyone got hurt. The dejected Lads returned to their tables in defeat, and the Scot Captain strolled to the bar. After downing a straight, double whiskey, the victorious Scot Officer turned to the crowd and announced, "I would like to complement my adversaries, they fought a good fight, but they will never learn the answer to the age old question, "What does a Scots man wears under his kilt?" But to the good people here tonight, I will show you what THIS SCOT wears under HIS KILT!"

With a flair for the dramatic, he turned his back to the audience, bowed and lifted his Kilt. The women screamed in delight, and the men groaned, as the Scot displayed his muscular rear end to the audience. Underneath his Kilt, he wore—nothing at all!

21

Return to Combat

Charlie Battery—592 FA Bn
The Battle for Central Germany
April 1945

Dell Miller and I were not happy when we left London on our way back to Germany, the battle for Central Germany was still raging. We had gone different ways in London and, in our own ways, had become divorced from the war in Europe. Now our personal lives were merging because we were in the same boat. After becoming civilized for almost a month, our animal-like instincts for survival were beginning to surface. Dell knew his job at Corps in Fire Direction was much less dangerous than mine, as a Forward Observer with the Infantry, and promised he would try to get me transferred to Corps Headquarters. When we parted ways at Battalion Headquarters, 592nd Field Artillery, the last thing Dell told me was, "Randy, I'm going to try and get you away from the front lines, that's a promise!" "Dell, I'll take all the help I can get, but buddy, I won't count on it."

At Battalion Headquarters I checked in with the Sergeant Major. The head Sergeant looked up, laughed, and said, "Good to have you back Lieutenant Pierson. You've been gone so long we thought you had gone 'Over the Hill.' I've got some news for you, you have been replaced in Charlie Battery by another officer. Your old Battalion, the 589th, is being reactivated at Rennes, France and they want you back. I believe Captain Baxter at Charlie Battery has all the details. Do you want me to have a jeep take you and your gear to Charlie Battery?" "That would be nice Sergeant Major, and thanks for the good news." The First Sergeant was the first person I encountered at Charlie Battery. He, too, seemed glad to see me. The first thing he asked me was, "Did they tell you at Battalion your old unit is reforming and calling back all of their men they can locate?" "Yes they did First Sergeant." "How was your leave Lieutenant?" "It was super, I was gone a long time. Nothing personal, but I considered not coming back at all." The First Sergeant laughed and admitted he understood, paused and then suggested, "I guess you had better check in with the Captain." As usual, Captain Baxter was 'stressed-out,' the XVIII Airborne Corps was on the attack and moving deeper and deeper into Germany. The hard core SS Troops were making a desperate attempt to defend their fatherland, but many of their conscripted, and untrained, older men were surrendering by the hundreds. At this point in the war, even Field Artillery units were taking prisoners. Being responsible for guarding, feeding, sheltering, and providing basic medical attention to POWs was not normally the responsibility of a Field Artillery Battery Commander.

As Captain Baxter and I were discussing my departure and return to the 589th FA Bn, the Battery Clerk interrupted us and told Captain Baxter that an officer from XVIII Airborne Corps wanted to talk to Lieutenant Pierson. I excused myself and went to answer the telephone. I was not surprised when I heard a voice say, "Randy, this is Dell. Have you been told we are returning to the 589th at Rennes?" "Yes I have Dell, but I don't know the details, you know, when we leave, and how do we get there." "That's why I called Randy, let me fill you in. Orders are being cut today at Corps Headquarters right now for you and me. We leave day after tomorrow, XVIII Corps is furnishing the transportation. I'll pick you up at your Battalion Headquarters at 0900. Be ready, it is a long trip." "Dell I don't know how my Battery Commander will react to this information. We had just started discussing my transfer when you called." "Randy, I can't tell you how to deal with your commanding officer, but the reality is, he doesn't have a vote, Major Goldstein wants his men back and Corps has agreed to release them, this is a done deal. I think he will accept this fact. Anyway Randy, I'll see you day after tomorrow, no later the 0900."

"Before you hang up Dell, I have another question. Are orders being cut on the former 589th enlisted men? We have several men here in the 592nd." "Yep they will be transferred at a later date. I don't think it would be appropriate to discuss this with them right now. Let the process take it's natural course. Incidentally Randy, I hope you don't mind a little side trip on the way to Rennes. Our route goes pretty near the Chateau Xhos. Would you like to have a short visit with the Collenge family?" "Dell that sounds great! Think you can swing a slight delay enroute?" "What do you mean, do I think I can arrange a a slight delay enroute? Have you already forgotten the three day delay we spent in Paris. Buddy I know the rules, I'm on a roll, I'm the convoy commander." "The convoy commander? How many vehicles are making the trip?" "Well there aren't many, it's a two vehicle convoy." "Two vehicles for two 2nd Lieutenants? What do we have to do, drive ourselves?" "No, because there will be four 2nd Lieutenants, not just two. When the motor pool sergeant tried to assign a 3/4 Ton Weapons Carrier for the trip I told him 'no dice,' so he assigned us two jeeps, two drivers, and one trailer for the trip. That is three people in each jeep, with the personnel effects of six people, plus the supplies necessary for the trip in the trailer. I mentioned to the Motor Pool Sergeant the drivers should be able to bring back fresh vegetables, Cognac, and good wine on their return trip. I know he got the drift. I'm certain the two drivers will be well instructed, have plenty of trading materials, and be able to return with 'goodies' not available through normal quartermaster supply channels. If the Motor Pool Sergeant is as smart as I think he is, he will get a case of Napoleon Brandy for the Motor Pool Officer. Hell, that alone should get him another stripe!" "Dell, you still think like a sergeant. Corps hasn't taught you anything about being an officer yet. You still do business like an enlisted man. Dell, I guess I'd better cut the 'chit chat' and get back with Captain Baxter." "OK Randy, see you day after tomorrow about 0900."

Captain Baxter seemed somewhat detached when we resumed our conversation about my pending transfer. He accepted Miller's outline of what would happen without a comment. When I asked him about Sergeant Wiener, he told me Jerry was assigned to observation post duty with his new leader, a 2nd Lieutenant named

Weinberg who is fresh out of The Artillery School at Fort Sill. When I asked how they were getting along, Captain Baxter commented, "They seem to like each other. Weinberg is a good listener, Wiener is a good teacher, and they both like to kill Nazis." "Captain, I would like to see Jerry before I leave. Is he in the battery or up with the infantry?" "Lieutenant, to tell the truth, I don't know. I'm sure the First Sergeant can help you get in touch with him. While we are on the subject, you will be here for two nights, do you have a place to stay? I ask this question because I may have to move the battery forward on short notice before you leave." Thanks for the thought Captain, but I believe I had better get my personal effects together, tell some of the men goodbye, then get back to Battalion. That is where the Corps furnished transportation will pick me up." "Lieutenant, I will tell you goodbye right now, I'm so busy I don't know which end is up. It has been a pleasure to work with you. You have good 'people instincts' and are maturing into a fine officer. Please take my good wishes with you where-ever you go." Without waiting for an answer, he returned to his more pressing matters.

The off duty guys in the Observation Section were surprised to see me. I had been gone for almost a month. We visited for quite some time in their bunker while I answered questions about life in Paris and London. They also wanted to know why Lieutenant Weinberg had replaced me. I told them the whole story about the reorganization of my old Battalion back in France, and the fact that I had been ordered to return to the 589th FA Bn. They accepted my transfer as routine and told me Lieutenant Weinberg was a good officer. When I asked about Sergeant Wiener, I was disappointed to find out he was up with the infantry, and constantly on the move. When I said I wanted to talk with Jerry before I leave, one of the radio men replied, "Lieutenant Pierson, I can arrange that very quickly. I have to make test calls to the Observation Post every day. I'll move a jeep over here to the bunker and set up a call from the jeep radio. Why don't you hang around a few minutes and you can talk to Jerry directly during the test call?" "That sounds like a winner to me 'Sparks.' You go on and set up the call."

That detail underway, I turned to the guys in the crowd, "While we are waiting for 'Sparks' to set up a test call, I need some one to get a jeep and driver to take me and my gear back to Battalion this afternoon. Anyone want to volunteer?" Immediately all the GIs in the bunker volunteered. I left it up to the senior non-com present to handle this 'detail' for me. .

The 'test call' was a 'happy-sad' experience for Jerry and me. I hoped that not too many other people heard our final goodbyes. I was happy Jerry and his new Forward Observer had bonded, and he was glad I was going to be reunited with some old time friends. But the sad part for both of us was the fact that we two had bonded like a strong magnet and hard steel, the type bond formed when opposites attract. I knew I would miss my association with Jerry, and hoped he would also have fond memories of me.

Battalion Headquarters – 592nd FA Bn
The Battle for Central Germany
Late April – 1945

Battalion Headquarters was buzzing when I reported in to the Sergeant Major. The situation in the XVIII Airborne Corps sector was extremely fluid. German resistance was crumbling, the Corps ground units were advancing rapidly, and at higher headquarters, the Allies were discussing who should have the honor of capturing the German capital city, Berlin. Geopolitical decisions for control of post-war Germany were being conducted at the highest level, Roosevelt, Churchill, and Stalin. Even we junior officers knew the final actions in the war depended on how these three powerful world leaders would 'Split the Pot.' At a tactical level, units like the 592nd FA Bn had to continue the struggle for control of the terrain immediately in front of them, and were not too interested in the political controversy of 'who would control what' after the war.

When I asked the Sergeant Major where I should drop my personal belongings, he said, "Lieutenant Pierson, If I were you, I would stay away from Battalion Headquarters until your transportation arrives. Right now, things here at Battalion are a mess. The Battalion Commander is trying to develop new locations for the three Firing Batteries, then he must concentrate on where to locate Service and Headquarters Batteries. Probably the last unit in the Battalion to leave this area will be the Medics. You and the Medical Officer seem to get along OK, would you like to call and get you a temporary spot with the medics?" "Sergeant Major, if you can arrange those accommodations for me, I promise to be your friend for life."

After a brief telephone call the Sergeant Major turned to me, smiled, and said the Medical Officer remembered me and invited me to be his guest. The Sergeant Major also said the Medical Officer mentioned something about grapefruit juice and medicinal alcohol. In response I told the Sergeant Major, " Thanks, I thought the Medical Officer would remember me." When I left the Battalion Command Post tent I found my gear already on board a vehicle and a driver waiting to take me to the Battalion Aid Station.

The next two days with the medics were pleasant even though we remained busy. The Medical Officer obviously enjoyed having another officer around and we both liked to converse with each other. When 'off duty' we discussed many different subjects while savoring our cigarettes with 'medicinal alcohol and canned grapefruit juice.' We joked about the Doctor's 'off duty' time because in reality, he was on duty 24/7. Appointments could not scheduled for an ingrown toenail, or a serious gun shot wound. As a Doctor he handled every case, huge or small, on a demand basis. Even though we enjoyed our 'social drinking' we remained unimpaired while consuming the medicinal alcohol.

To me, Medical Corpsmen were the unsung heroes of the armed forces. They were considered noncombatants by the Geneva Convention, but the prominent Red Cross painted on their helmets was often used as the aiming point by German snipers. Many of these young men were 'conscientious objectors' who's religious beliefs would not allow them to kill another human being. While up front with the Infantry, I witnessed several combat medics killed while exposing themselves to assist a fallen soldier they did not even know. This brave act of human kindness, surrounded by the inhumane act of war, made me think of a Biblical saying, "Greater love hath no man than to lay down his life for another." In one instance I saw a very young combat medic taking enemy fire while assisting a fallen soldier, that I suspect was a friend, pick up the fallen soldier's rifle and return the enemy fire. This aggressive act, committed by a sworn non-combatant, was a catalyst to a group of nearby riflemen who rushed to the assistance of the now wounded medic and dragged both men to safety. I would like to say that both men survived their intended slaughter, but I do not know. I was a combatant, trying to slaughter the enemy and too busy to find out. This is the ugly face of war!

Living and working with these corpsmen was a pleasure, almost an honor. Their devotion to saving lives, instead of taking lives, of giving instead of taking, was in direct contrast to the attitude drummed into us warriors, take the objective and survive, kill or be killed, caused me to ask the Medical Officer, "How can the attitudes of men engaged in warfare be so different?" When we were alone and relaxed, and I would ask him a question of this nature, he would lift his glass and say, "I don't know Randy, all I know is my job is to help the sick and wounded, your job is to kill and survive in order to kill kill again. We've been trained to do each job, and we try our damnedest to do it. I don't think we will ever know why God created people with the ability to be either good or evil."

Battalion Headquarters—592nd FA Bn
Return to the 589th FA Bn
Late April 1945

This was the day, I was going 'home' to my old unit, to be reunited with old friends, and to learn the fate of others. The dawn broke bright and clear, the temperature was perfect, and I was hungry. Eating at the Aid Station, with the medics, was always different. They drew their own rations, prepared their own meals, and when conditions permitted, ate together at a table. This meal arrangement was much different than standing in a Firing Battery chow line, in the cold or wet, waiting to be feed with one hundred other hungry souls, or the meals fixed by a Forward Observation crew, with only limited cooking facilities.

At about 0730 hours I thanked the entire medical detachment for their hospitality, received their good wishes in return, and went to the Battalion Command Post to await the arrival of Lieutenant Delbert Miller and my transportation to Rennes, France. At Battalion, as the Sergeant Major had told me, "Things were in a mess." No one paid any attention to me, which suited me fine. Finally the Battalion Executive Officer noticed me talking with the Sergeant Major. He strolled over, shook my hand, and asked, "Pierson, why are you here?" When I explained I had been ordered back to my old Battalion which was now being reorganized, he acted surprised, wished me well, and returned to his more pressing duties.

I was visiting with the Sergeant Major when we heard the unmistakable sound of jeep motors as they approached the CP tent. We walked out of the tent together just in time to see Dell maneuver his two jeep convoy into a position under the overhang of a huge evergreen tree. Dell dismounted his jeep, like General Patton, and walked the short distance to the CP tent in a brisk military manner. As Dell approached, I explained to the Sergeant Major that Lieutenant Miller had been appointed the convoy commander for the trip back to France. When he reached us, Dell and I shook hands and I introduced him to the Sergeant Major. The Sergeant Major came to attention, saluted Dell, and with a sly smile said, "Nice to meet you Lieutenant Miller. That was an excellent maneuver you and your convoy just made." This remark caught Dell off guard until he realized his leg was being pulled.. Then Dell responded soberly, "Thank you Sergeant Major, I am glad you recognize talent when you see it." We all laughed. It felt good to laugh again..

As usual, Dell was on time. We wished the Sergeant Major good luck, bid him goodbye, and walked to the jeeps. Dell introduced me to the two 2nd Lieutenants going with us to the 105th Division, but I did not recognize either one. Before Dell gave the order to 'Start Engines,' he showed me his proposed route to Rennes with locations marked to spend the night and draw rations. The trip was well planned. Miller was a detail man. I was glad I was not the 'Convoy Commander.' We boarded our jeeps, Dell gave a circular motion of his right arm, the visual order to "Start Engines,' and we were off to a much nicer place than war torn Germany. During the initial slow and bumpy portion of our journey Dell and I talked constantly, trying to get 'caught up,' and exchanging ideas about our future in the reorganized 589th Field Artillery Battalion.

Finally we reached a paved road. Once on a main highway the jeep gained speed and our conversation dwindled. The ride became smooth, the weather was pleasant, as we drove away from the combat area I became more relaxed and fell fast asleep.

The jumping and bumping of the jeep suddenly awakened me. I don't know how long I had been asleep, but I did knew I was tired and completely relaxed because we were out of the war zone by now. The thing that puzzled me was the fact that we were riding an a two rut road, bounded by wire fences and surrounded by fields covered with lush green grass. I yelled at Miller, "Dell, where in the Hell are we?" He laughed and responded, "Randy you should recognize this driveway." I looked around in surprise and finally recognized where we were. We were in Belgium and this was the long and winding driveway to the Chateau Xhos. Suddenly I was fully awake.

We slowly drove past the familiar read entrance to the 400 year old Chateau and to the Belgian block paved courtyard of the Collenge family's home. This one story house, which was constructed during the building of the Chateau, was built of stone with a slate roof. Underneath the building was a spacious 'root cellar' which Madame Collenge used for long term storage of meats, vegetables, and wines year round. It was always well stocked. As the jeeps pulled to a stop, I saw 'Petite Marie' come out of the house. She recognized the American jeeps, she had seen them many times while we were at the Chateau in December, but she hesitated at the open door. After watching Dell and me dismount the jeep, the expression on her face changed to glee as she ran toward me yelling, "Randy, Randy!" With a huge leap, this small child wrapped her legs around my waist, hugged my neck with both arms, and whispered in French, "Randy you are safe! You have returned!" I kissed her on the cheek and said in English, "Yes little Marie, I am safe and I have returned to see you." Petite Marie pulled herself out of my arms, jumped to the ground, and started yelling in French, "Ma Ma, Randy is here, Randy is here," as she ran back into the house. A few moments later, Petite Marie reappeared with her mother, Madame Marie Collenge in tow. Madame Collenge walked toward us, stopped and surveyed us carefully, approached us, and said in broken English, "Randy, you and Mr. Miller have changed. I no longer see your Sergeant Stripes. Are you now Officers?" She then motioned to the gold bars on our collar points. I answered in a combination of broken French and English, "Yes Madame, we are both officers. We are on out way to Rennes and would like to visit with you, your husband Louis, and the children if that is possible." "That is entirely possible with the exception of our son Eugene, who is still in England, and Ruth, who is away at boarding school. I will ring the dinner bell, Louis and Victor are working in the field, they will come when I ring the dinner bell."

Louis, and his young son Victor, appeared riding on a large, throbbing, two cylinder farm tractor shortly after Madame Collenge rang the loud, outdoor dinner bell. Madame Marie talked quickly with Louis while Petite Marie jabbered excitedly with Victor. They were all happy and laughing. I wished I could understand everything they were saying, but I could not. Victor hugged his sister, as Louis, the WWI Belgian Infantryman snapped to attention and gave Dell and me a snappy hand salute. While smiling, both Miller and I returned his salute. It was a joyous reunion for all of us. Inside the spacious kitchen and eating area of the Collenge home, we chatted using a collage of French, German, English, and body language. It is amazing how much love, respect, and friendship, can be passed even though we did not speak, or fully understand each other's primary language. When Petite Marie climbed up onto my lap and started searching my jacket for candy or chewing gum, Miller got the message. He left the room, went outside to our trailer, extracted some goodies we had brought for the Collenge family, and returned with his pockets bulging. He then gave Petite Marie and Victor the candy and chewing gum. He gave Louis three five packs of fresh cigars, and last but not least, he presented a large bag of sugar to Madame Collenge. All the gifts were obviously appreciated, but I believe Madame Collenge valued the sugar the most. At the time, this much sugar, to a lady accustomed to preparing delicious Belgian pastries, was truly a luxury.

As a gesture of friendship, Louis left the room, went into their root cellar, and returned with three bottles of his fine Cognac. He presented each of us with a going away bottle, and masterfully opened the third. Madame Collenge poured the Cognac into brandy glasses and served us with cheese and fresh crackers. Dell, Louis, and I lit the cigars. The children watched as we adults talked, ate, smoked, and drank cognac until we became a little tipsy. While enjoying the comforts and friendship of the Collenge home and hospitality, Dell looked at his watch and suddenly announced, "Randy, it's time to leave. We still have a long way to go."

With saddened hearts, we bid this wonderful family goodbye. While riding down the bumpy driveway, I watched the stately Chateau Xhos slowly disappear, knowing I would never see the Collenge family, or the Chateau again.

East of Beignon, France
589th Field Artillery Battalion
22 April 1945

When our two jeep convoy reached Rennes, we found things rather confusing. We were able to deliver the two other officers, and their gear, to a rear echelon transient facility. I changed jeeps and rode up front in the jeep still pulling the trailer. After much looking and asking, a Military Police Officer advised us to continue toward the coast of France and we should find the 589th in position just east of the small village of Beignon. With Miller in the lead, I followed. We were fortunate to find the 589th located in an area secured by the 66th Infantry Division, and surprised to find out we were now back in a combat zone. The Operations Officer of the 66th Division gave us explicit instructions on how to find the Command Post of the 589th FA Bn and advised us a Major Goldstein was the Battalion Commander. The 66th Division Operations Officer was slightly surprised when we told him we knew Major Goldstein, he was the officer who promoted us from Sergeants to Second Lieutenants.

Northern France Campaign
Command Post 589th Field Artillery Battalion
22 April 1945

Dell and I parked our jeeps with several other vehicles bearing 589th FA Bn markings. The 'parking lot' was in the open and located near the front door of a small French dwelling. There was no guard in front of the house nor evidence of physical activity in the area. This caused Miller and I to exchange questioning glances as we approached the Command Post. We entered the open door and were greeted by a strange Battalion Sergeant Major, who rose from this desk, and asked, "What can I do for you gentlemen?"

For some unknown reason I took the lead and asked, "What happened to

Sergeant Major Hill?" The Sergeant Major responded with a question, "Did you gentlemen know Sergeant Hill?" To answer the question, we both nodded our heads and I asked, "You asked if we 'did' know Sergeant Hill. What does that mean?" "Lieutenant, I am sorry I have to give you the news, but Master Sergeant Hill was captured last December, and died while he was a prisoner of war." Dell and I looked at each other and all I could say was, "Shit! He was a good man."

"Gentlemen all I can say is I didn't know Master Sergeant Hill, but he left some large boots for me to fill. What can I do for you?" "Sergeant Major, we have orders from XVIII Airborne Corps to report to Major Goldstein for assignment." "Is the Major expecting you?" "That is a good question Sergeant Major, we really don't know." "May I give him your names?" "Certainly, our names are Pierson and Miller." "Thank you gentlemen, I will see if the Major can meet with you now."

As we waited for the Sergeant Major to return, we talked about the demise of Master Sergeant Hill, and were interrupted when a smiling Major Goldstein entered the room. He welcomed us back to the 589th warmly and asked us to follow him back to his office. The Sergeant Major had remained inside the Major's office and placed two chairs in front of Major Goldstein's desk. The Sergeant Major remained in the office, standing directly to our rear. Major Goldstein engaged us in personal conversation for a few minutes then said, "I am glad to have you back in the Battalion. I am proud of what you have done as officers. I guess you would like to know what your assignments will be."

Dell and I were both eager to hear what the Major had to say. The Major started his briefing. "First Randy, your fellow Floridian, Barney Alford, is already here, he is assigned to Battery C." "Excuse me Major, I'm glad Barney made it back, but why did you assign him to Battery C instead of Battery A, his old Battery?" "That is a good question Randy, and deserves an answer. As a new officer, I feel it is better to assign him to a battery where he does not have non-coms he formerly worked for, and with. His new rank and responsibilities can be better served with new subordinates and superiors. This principle also applies to Miller, but he older, the Fire Direction personnel has changed, and has served as an assistant S-3 at the Corps level, consequently Dell you will become the Battalion Assistant S-3 reporting to Captain Huxel, our new Battalion S-3. Any questions concerning your assignment Dell?" "No Sir, I know the job and I know I can work with Captain Huxel. Thanks for this assignment Major."

"Now lets discuss your assignment Randy. You may question my decision Randy, because I am assigning you as Executive Officer of Battery A. Your commander is Ted Kendal. Any questions or comments Randy?" "Yes Sir! I guess I assumed I would be going back to the Fire Direction Center. I know Dell is better qualified for that job than I am. I also know you don't need two Assistant S-3s, but assigning me as the number two officer in a firing battery seems strange." "Let me share some thoughts with you Randy. First, Ted is the best firing battery commander in the Battalion. Second, he feels you have a high learning curve. It should be easy to bring your talents up to speed, and third, we are in a very stable area. Realistically, I don't have anyone else more qualified for the job than you. After all, you have almost four months of combat experience in a firing battery. Miller has none. Now you know some of the reasons for your assignment." "Well Sir, I am glad to be back and I promise to give this assignment my best shot." "Randy I know you will, you always have. Now I want to drop the other shoe. Ted is on leave in London, and you will be in charge until he returns. You will have one other officer present in the battery with you until Ted returns. First Lieutenant Romenko actually out-ranks you. He is a nice person and is a qualified Forward Observer, you two have that common bond, but Romenko is actually a professional linguist His parents migrated from Russia to America. Romenko is well educated and speaks four languages fluently; Russian. English, French, and German. He claims he can 'get by' in Italian also. If Romenko does not accept the fact that you are in charge, ask him to call me. I will explain the situation to him. You have a good Master Sergeant who is your 'Chief of Firing Battery,' lean on him hard and trust his judgment until Lieutenant Kendal returns."

The Major then turned to his Sergeant Major and said, "Arrange transportation to Battery A for Lieutenant Pierson, I want him there before dark, and be sure to tell the Battery A First Sergeant to have Lieutenant Pierson fed and a place to stay. As for Lieutenant Miller, ask Captain Huxel to come to the CP and pick up his new assistant."

The Sergeant Major told his Commanding Officer, "Sir, consider it done."

Command Post — Firing Battery A
589th Field Artillery Battalion
Near Dusk — 22 April 1945

In the parking lot in front of the Battalion Command Post, Dell and I removed our gear from the XVIII Airborne Corps trailer. I placed my gear on the rear seat of Major Goldstein's jeep, and was telling Dell good-luck and good-bye when Captain Huxel came wheeling parking lot, driving his own jeep. Dell and I stopped our conversation and Dell started loading his gear into the back sear of Captain Huxel's jeep. It was good to see the Captain again. I had not seen him since I received my commission, and he was as glad to see me as I was to see him. He looked me over carefully, and finally said, "Welcome home Lieutenant, it is good to have you back." We shook hands and he told me, "Randy you better get your butt over to Battery A, they are in pretty rough shape."

As Major Goldstein's driver and I rode down the paved road in the Major's jeep marked '589th FA Bn — Hq Btry 1,' I thought of Captain Huxel's warning about Battery A and wondered what lay ahead for me, its new Executive Officer. My driver knew exactly how to get to Battery A. He pulled off the paved road into an open field which was completely surrounded by ancient and tall hedge rows. The Command Post and Fire Direction Center were housed in two large tents, whose rear entrances snuggled against a hedge row offering limited camouflage and protection. One howitzer was in place in the open field, which had on hiding place and offered no protection for the howitzer nor its Canoneers. The driver parked his jeep close to, and facing the entrance to the CP tent Immediately, a Corporal opened the tent fly, peered out, stepped into the open, read the markings on the jeep, and without looking, he saluted, fully expecting the Battalion Commander to dismount the clearly marked Battalion Commanders vehicle.

The Corporal was apparently confused when a Second Lieutenant approached him and looked quizzically at his friend, the jeep driver. The jeep driver dismounted, walked casually to his friend, where they had a short conversation. As I stood outside the CP tent the Major's driver unloaded my gear and placed it inside the tent, while telling me the 'Charge of Quarters' Corporal had gone to get the First Sergeant. To my surprise, the First Sergeant suddenly appeared with Lieutenant Romenko in tow. I did not know the First Sergeant, but I realized I had met Lieutenant Romenko on the firing range at Camp Atterbury while Captain Huxel was conducting classes for Forward Observers. When I introduced myself I received no sign of recognition from either man. When I told them Major Goldstein had assigned me to Battery A, there was a moment of silence after I informed them I was the new Executive Officer. Then I added, I was also advised by the Major that I was in charge of the Battery until Lieutenant Kendal returned. The First Sergeant looked at Lieutenant Romenko and then at the Major's driver. The driver returned the First Sergeants look with a nod of his head, indicating my statements were correct..

Breaking an awkward silence, Lieutenant Romenko asked me a question, "Lieutenant Pierson have we met?" "Yes we have, it was on the firing range at Camp Atterbury during a class taught by Captain Huxel." "That was where I got my training to become a Forward Observer. I was a Second Lieutenant then." "Yes, I remember you, I was the only enlisted man in the class. I was a Technician Fourth Class in the Fire Direction Center." "I remember you now, Captain Huxel spent more time with you than he did with any of the student officers." "That is true, I suppose I was more dense than the officers." "No, he spent that extra time with you for a special reason. That was obvious. When did you get your commission?" "During the Battle of the Bulge. Major Goldstein promoted three Sergeants to Second Lieutenants. I was one of them. Will it bother you to report to an officer junior to you in rank? If it does I was advised to ask you to call Major Goldstein."

Abruptly the serious look on Lieutenant Romenko's face changed to a smile and he said, "Hell No, it doesn't bother me one damned bit! In fact, you are the answer to my prayers. I am not experienced enough to have the responsibility of commanding this Battery. I gladly pass the torch to you. What shall I call you?" "Lets keep it simple, just call me Randy and I'll call you Romey. Is that OK for starts?" "It's a done deal."

The sun was beginning to set, and I knew I had many things to do. First, I asked the First Sergeant to have the 'Chief of Firing Battery' to report to the CP, next I released the Major's driver with instructions to tell Major Goldstein there was no problem with the chain-of-command in Battery A, but I needed time with the 'Chief of Firing Battery' to iron out some tactical matters, and would check in with Captain Huxel later after I had addressed the Captain's concerns. The jeep driver responded with a, "WILCO (Will Comply), and good luck Lieutenant Pierson."

Romey and I were eating a specially prepared supper the Mess Sergeant had fixed for us when the Sergeant First Class, 'Chief of Firing Battery' reported to us in the CP tent. He introduced him self and I advised him I was the new Executive Officer and he would be working for me. He accepted this information with no comment, but did accept a cup of coffee and the invitation, almost a command, to get a chair and be seated with me while he briefed me on the status of the Firing Battery. He was a straight laced soldier, and I could tell by his body language he was not comfortable with this request. I was certain he thought Lieutenant Romenko was the Battery Commander, after all the bar on . his collar was silver while mine was gold. Romey sensed the same thing and told the Sergeant First Class that Major Goldstein had appointed Lieutenant Pierson Executive Officer, and he was in-charge until lieutenant Kendal returned.

Somewhat relieved the Chief of Firing Battery began to assess the problems faced in this location, and his understanding of our mission here. He said, "Lieutenant Pierson, I don't know your qualifications, but I am sure Major Goldstein has a high opinion of you, or he wouldn't have sent you here." "You are right Sergeant, I have known the Major for almost all of my military life, he knows more about me and the current 589th mission than you or I. For the record, I have about four months combat experience as a firing battery officer. That is all you need to know about me for the present. Feel free to give me your opinion of what is right and what is wrong here in Battery A." Lieutenant Romenko reinforced my statement, "Sergeant you won't hurt my feelings by telling the truth. Lieutenant Pierson needs as much information as you can give him. This is necessary for the good of the mission and personnel in Battery A."

OK Lieutenant Pierson, here goes. Officers from the 66th Infantry Division picked out this battery location. In this hedge-row farm land, we can neither deliver massed artillery fire if requested, nor defend ourselves and our equipment if attacked by foot soldiers. I know we are ordered to contain members of the German Navy in the Laurent Pocket, but I don't have a clue as to how we are supposed to do it. This is a frustration situation for me, and my men in the battery. And Lieutenant, the men in the other firing batteries are just as frustrated as we are." "Thanks for being upfront with me Sergeant. Now I share Captain Huxel's concerns. It may take time to work through the problems but you have my assurance we will." "That is good to know Lieutenant, is there anything you want me to do tonight?" "Lieutenant Romenko and I have some details to work out first. If I need you, where can I get in touch with you?" "I'm staying with section number two, the base piece, you can see it, it's about one hundred yards across this large field. You can call me there. If you need me, I'll come running."

As the tall Sergeant First Class started to stride toward the battery's base piece I said, "First Sergeant get some more coffee, three note books, and three pencils, we have lots of work ahead of us tonight. First we will identify all local security and personnel protection problems, then we will identify what has to be changed to integrate this battery into the Battalion Fire Direction Center. I will keep the master list of tasks to be performed. Then I will assign each problem to be carried out by you. Lieutenant Romenko, you and the First Sergeant, will work with the 'Chief of Firing Battery' on local problems. Lieutenant Romenko and I will work on the ability to cover our assigned sector with accurate artillery fire. Just for the records First Sergeant, what do you and the men call the 'Chief of Firing Battery?'" "Lieutenant Pierson, we all just call him Chief."

Remey and I watched the First Sergeant place his note pad into a jacket pocket, firmly secured his web belt, checked his 45 caliber pistol, returned it to its leather holster, grabbed a flashlight, and briefly said, "Gentlemen things will be a lot more secure in the battery come day light." As he left the tent, he added, "You can count on it." Lieutenant Remenko got the message, went to the telephone and called his Forward Observer Sergeant and told him to get his crew together and come to the CP, they must establish an Observation Post. After a short conversation, the Lieutenant said firmly, "Tonight!"

When the Command Post tent cleared, I asked the Charge of Quarters to get me a line to Captain Huxel. It was reassuring when I discussed my findings with him and I gained more confidence when we discussed our plans to correct the deficiencies I had found. He offered his support to my efforts, made some suggestions, and told me he would discuss the situation with Major Goldstein in the morning. Captain Huxel told me that local security was a problem for the entire Battalion, there were too many civilians wandering around our positions who could be German Navy men dressed in civilian clothes. He confirmed my opinion that our present battery position was not suitable for massed indirect fire, not direct fire, because of the interfering hedge rows. I felt much better when the Captain told me he would try to get to Battery A tomorrow and we could make a joint evaluation of what needed to be done. I was a much more confident Executive Officer when I placed the telephone handset in it's cradle.

When I was finally alone with the Charge of Quarters, I realized I had been thinking, talking, and planning frantically for several hours and realized I needed to get some exercise and fresh air. To break the silence, I stood, stretched, and asked the CQ, "What do your friends call you Corporal?" "Sir, my first name is Bradford, they all call me Brad." "That is a distinguished sounding name Corporal." "Thank you Sir. It is a family name and I am proud of it." "You should be. Brad I am going out and look around the battery area. Have you laid out my bedroll?" "Oh yes Sir! It is in the four man officers tent adjoining this tent. You will be sharing that tent with Lieutenant Romenko until Lieutenant Kendal returns." "Thank you Brad, when you are relieved, tell the new CQ I want to be awakened no later then 0600. Tomorrow will be a busy day."

Command Post – Firing Battery A
589th Field Artillery Battalion
Before Dawn – 23 April 1945

At 0600, when the CQ opened the tent flap, I was already sitting up, but was not fully awake. Lieutenant Romenko was still deep in the arms of amorphous and snoring loudly. I thanked the CQ for checking on me and asked him to arouse Lieutenant Romenko. Romey did not arouse easily, but did respond to my loud statement, "Romenko, get your ass out of bed!" Hot coffee was waiting for us in the CP tent where the CQ asked, "Lieutenant Pierson should I get your breakfast from the mess truck and bring it here?" "Corporal, that's a good idea. Please bring two plates for us." When the Charge of Quarters Corporal left the tent I asked Romenko how much his Forward Observation party accomplished last night?"

He shook his head, laughed, and told me this story. "This is a strange war down here. The German Navy has had a dominant presence in this area for years. The local populous has learned to accepts them as being, shall we say, good neighbors. My vehicle left the battery area under normal black-out conditions. Of course all the local farm houses were well lit and the first village we entered was filled with villagers shopping and being entertained in well lighted bistros. Everything seemed normal, not a trace of war restrictions remained. We felt silly playing war games, it was like we were on maneuvers in Tennessee again, Several members of my crew spoke to local residents as we slowly passes by, obviously indicating they sneak into town at night for their own pleasure. I am not condemning my men, they quickly adapt to the existing environment.

As we got nearer to Lorient and back into the farm areas, we left the main road and started to make our way to a large hill which overlooked the German installations. My map indicated this to be an excellent area to observe what was going on in this German garrison. My instincts were correct. As we approached the crest of the hill, our 'Cat Eye' black-out lights dimly picked up a uniformed man standing in the middle of the farm road we were on. As we slowly approached this man he held his position with an outstretched hand, motioning for us to stop. I stopped the lead vehicle, dismounted,. and approached this armed sentry, who spoke to me in perfect English, "That is far enough Lieutenant. You have come far enough. You must be lost. Turn around and return to your unit." I was flabbergasted and took one more step toward the armed sentry, who raised his weapon and pointed it directly at me. He said again, "Lieutenant you have come far enough!" By now my eyes were starting to adjust to the darkness and there was something strange looking about his uniform, so I told his I was an American officer and knew what I was doing." I then asked him, "To what outfit do you belong?" His answer really surprised me. He told me, "Lieutenant, I know you are an American, but you have blundered into our territory under the cover of darkness. You are not welcome here. To answer your question, I am a member of the *German Kreigmarine*, to you, the German Navy. Now turn around and leave before you start trouble you cannot handle." "Randy, you know what, I took his advice and left quickly. Due to the intervention of the German Navy, we did not establish an Observation Post last night."

Captain Huxel made an unannounced visit to Battery A just in time for lunch. He, Lieutenant Romenko, and I enjoyed the clear spring weather near the Northern Coast of France by eating at the officer's table set near the mess truck. As we ate and enjoyed the balmy spring weather, Captain Huxel started an in-depth explanation of the 'Rules of Combat' which applied in this combat zone. To a soldier like me, fresh out of a 'kill or be killed' combat zone, the campaign here in France seemed like a Boy Scout camp-out. The American Corps Commander of all allied troops in the area had a private telephone line connected to the German Admiral who commanded all Nazi personnel in the French area designated the Lorient Pocket. These high ranking officers were in friendly contact daily. Both agreed there would be no aggressive action taken by either side without prior notification to the other Apparently, both Commanders were willing to maintain the status quo until it was apparent which side was going to win the war.

After lunch, Captain Huxel and I toured the battery and surrounding areas. The Captain was pleased with the small improvements in local security and encouraged me to continue this work. As far as positioning the three firing batteries to enable them to mass fire on a given target, he agreed with me that some of the howitzers would have to be moved. He drew several sketches to support his opinion on how to move certain howitzers when he made his recommendations to Major Goldstein. He added that he thought the Major would agree with our on-site changes because they made sense. When the Captain finally left to return to the Battalion command post he said he would be back in touch with me tomorrow.

I liked, and respected, Captain Huxel. He knew what he was doing and always kept his promises.

The rest of the day was spent getting acquainted with my top non-coms.

589th Field Artillery Battalion — Firing Battery A
North France Campaign
24 April thru 7 May 1945

During the next week we worked daily to improve our howitzer positions and train the unqualified replacements that had been used to bring the battery up to authorized strength. When I arrived in the battery, I was unaware that almost sixty percent of these 'fillers' were not trained artillerymen. Consequently on the job training became a high priority item.

It was difficult for me to comprehend the true feelings of the new men in the battery, and is almost impossible for me to describe it now. I had never been forced to confront such a complex problem in my life. I knew it was my duty to understand and motivate this diverse group of young men and knew I would need help. The circumstances did not grant me unlimited time. To attain success in this endeavor the men of the battery must bond together and become a close knit unit. As a start I knew I must gain the respect and trust of my senior non-commissioned officers. Then I must delegate and work through them. We started with the four howitzer sections. From there we moved to the communications section, the forward observation section, then on to my administrative assistants and even the cooks. I had learned over the years that there is a positive correlation between good food and contented soldiers.

One morning, after several 16 hour days, when I was talking with the Mess Sergeant about his menus and the rations he drew from the Quartermaster Depot, he told me he had almost no choice, and had to take what they issued him. I suggested a more subtle approach. I had learned a good lessen on how to negotiate with most rear echelon type soldiers when I was in Paris. They coveted any kind of German combat equipment. This included pistols, flags, bayonets, insignia. or apparel. These items were quite easy to obtain by soldiers in the field, so I asked the Mess Sergeant to make friends with the Quartermaster Master Sergeant to determine what he and his men wanted. The Mess Sergeant reluctantly gathered some German material and took it on his next trip to the supply depot. While I was at the mess truck, I met the 1st Cook. He was a stocky young man and while we talked I found out he was from the delta country of Louisiana, a commercial fisherman prior to entering the service. He suggested we rent a boat and go fishing in a nearby salt water river. When he told me he thought the troops would enjoy a meal of fresh fried fish, hushpuppies and grits, I agreed, but reminded him it would take a lot of fish to feed one hundred hungry men.

Things were progressing satisfactorily in the Battery so I decided to take some time off and go fishing with the 1st Cook. Little did I know how that trip would turn out!

† †

Dawn broke crisp and clear. After a private breakfast the 1st Cook had prepared for us, we took my jeep and some gear the 1st Cook had accumulated for the trip and drove to a private dock on the river. We loaded our fishing gear into a small commercial fishing boat the 1st Cook had rented for one pack of Camel cigarettes. As we were about to leave the dock, a grizzled looking Frenchman walked out on the dock to greet us. In a combination of French and English he suggested we drift with the outgoing tide, remain there until the tide changed, then drift back to the dock on the incoming tide. He said this would save gasoline, and be less work. We nodded affirmative, and rowed slowly away from the dock and into the river.

The current was slow and gentle with almost no ripple on the surface of the water. As the 1st Cook was separating our fishing gear, he pointed out small areas of the water being disturbed by schools of fish. Although I could not actually see the fish, their telltale ripples indicated where they were feeding. I was about to ask the 1st Cook where our fishing poles were when he explained, "Lieutenant open that top crate in the bow, we might as well start fishing. I think we will have to gather about 150 fish to put on a good fish fry for the battery." I didn't understand what the word 'gather' meant until I opened the first German crate. To my surprise, the 1st Cook had brought about 200 German Concussion Grenades to fish with. I was familiar with this type grenade, as opposed to the American Fragmentation Grenades. I had used both types in combat, but I was puzzled as to how we would use them while gathering fresh fish.

In response to my quizzical look, the 1st Cook asked, "Lieutenant are you familiar with these grenades?" Yes Cookie, I've seen them before." "Then you know the Black Capped ones have a delay fuse and the Red Capped ones have an instantaneous fuse." "Yes I remember. The Krauts used the red capped grenades attached to trip wires when they 'booby trapped' buildings, doors, and things like that. Where did you learn these things Cookie?" "Oh, you'd be surprised Lieutenant. The army taught me how to cook, but life in the bayou country taught me many things. How did you find out about these German grenades Lieutenant? "I learned my lesson the hard way. Early in combat, a friend of mine entered a building ahead of me and stumbled on a trip wire. He was killed about twenty feet from me. That's when I started learning how to kill people."

"I understand Lieutenant. Let me explain how we gathered fish in the back waters of Louisiana with dynamite. This technique works better if two people coordinate their efforts. This technique is not difficult, but it does take practice. The idea is to create an explosive force surrounding a school of fish. Under water this force will either kill, or stun them, causing them to rise to the surface of the water. Then we will gather them with our long handled dip nets as they surface." "Doesn't seem too complicated to me Cookie." "It's not complicated to experienced fishermen, but we will have difficulty in coordination getting the grenades in the right positions and having them explode simultaneously." "Keep on talking Cookie, this is your ball game, tell me what to do."

The 1st Cook then placed two cases of grenades in the stern and kept two cases in the bow of the boat. He explained we should remain quiet and with the oar, he would keep the boat in the center of the river with the bow pointed forward. That would give him the best vantage point to locate the feeding fish. He cautioned, we will work both sides of the narrow river, which meant we will be throwing grenades on both sides of the boat. He would not speak when he located a school of fish, but would point in the direction of the school. It would be my responsibility to have two grenades ready to throw. This meant, two grenades with the black caps unscrewed, ready to pull the fuse igniting wire, so I could throw my grenades into the same area were he threw his. He suggested I duck and wait on the explosion, because if a grenade explodes in shallow water, it will kick water and mud all over us.

Our game of gathering fish went smoothly as we drifted toward the English Channel. We threw grenades, gathered fish, boated them with our dip nets, and watched as the fish holding bin of the boat began to fill. As the tide turned and we began drifting back toward the dock it became apparent we would gather enough fish for the Battery fish fry. The operation had become rather routine by the time we opened the second crates of grenades. I was enjoying the trip and my mind was wandering when Cookie waived frantically to catch my attention. He had spotted a very large school of fish on our starboard bow, and already had his grenades ready to throw. Without looking I reached into my grenade crate, grabbed two grenades, unscrewed the pulling caps and held the grenades ready to throw. Cookie threw his and turned toward me in anticipation of seeing me throw mine. As I pulled the ignition wires from the grenades, Cookie screamed, "No! No, Lieutenant! Don't throw, drop them in the water!" By instinct I obeyed his command, and immediately dropped both grenades into the water beside the drifting boat. Things happened so fast, it is difficult to describe the sequence of events. First, Cookie's two grenades exploded near the school of fish. Second, one of my grenades exploded very close to the boat, but the other grenade did not explode at all. Confused, I looked at the terrified 1st Cook and asked, "What's wrong?" A very shaken Cookie did not speak, but merely pointed at the two grenade caps still in my hand. One was BLACK the other one RED! It took a few minutes for this sight to sink in. There had been one instantaneous fused grenade in the box. I had activated this grenade in my hand. It should have killed us both! For reasons unknown to me, it did not explode.

When I finally realized I had almost killed both of us, my stomach cramped, my body oozed cold sweat, nausea set in, I felt faint, my eyes fluttered, an I almost passed out. As I realized a German mistake in making this grenade had saved my life, I slumped over the boat rail and empted my guts into the river.

✝ ✝

After my 'near death experience' I decided to stay in the Battery and devote more time in becoming a permanent Firing Battery Executive Officer than a temporary Battery Commander. After all, Lieutenant Kendal would be returning shortly to resume his job as Battery Commander and I would like to learn more about the specific duties of a Firing Battery XO before he returned Of course, this type information is readily available in Army Field Manuals, formal class room studies at the Artillery School at Fort Sill, Oklahoma, Army Officers Candidate Schools, or Army ROTC programs offered at many major U. S. Universities. Unfortunately for officers like me, who had received direct commissions in combat, these sources of information were not available. I would have to learn from my senior non-coms, or be self taught.

Units in the army are organized similar to large civilian corporations in that both have 'Line and Staff Officers.' In some instances this separation of duties is not clear cut, and some army officers end up with 'overlapping responsibilities.' However, a Firing Battery XO is mainly a 'Line Officer,' with command responsibilities. He is in charge of the four howitzers and the four howitzer crews who man them 24 hours each day all 7 days each week, and acts as the unit commander when the commander is not present. In military, and civilian terms his duty is, '24/7.'

During this transition period, I depended upon the Chief of Firing Battery to help me learn my XO duties. At the same time, I delegated most of the Battery Commander duties to the First Sergeant, who performed them well. While working with the howitzer crews I noticed a definite change in the men's attitude. When I questioned the 'Chief' about this change he said, "Lieutenant Pierson, the men were told of your suggestions on how to draw better food from the Quartermaster Depot. They helped the Mess Sergeant round up some 'war trophies' for his first meeting with the Quartermaster Master Sergeant, when the Mess Sergeant returned from his first trip, you know what happened Lieutenant? He brought back 'frozen red meat' instead of 'canned pork and beans.' Now the men are regularly gathering 'war trophies' for the Mess Sergeant. This led to another 'ration drawing technique' Lieutenant. One of our new men speaks fluent French. He has made friends with civilians in the village and is now accompanying the Mess Sergeant on trips to farms where they trade canned American rations for fresh food. The French farmers are harvesting huge amounts of fresh food and prefer to be paid with canned food, which can be stored, instead of money. Currency buys almost nothing come winter. According to news we are receiving about the war, lots of guys in the Battery are predicting we will be home for the fourth of July."

"Yes Sergeant, the tides of war seem to be turning in our favor. That is good news." "Lieutenant, I don't know if you are aware of this fact or not, but most of the men in the Battery have been buying bottles of Calvados so they can celebrate the end of the war." "No Sergeant, I was not aware of this fact. What are the implications?" "Lieutenant, what do you know about Calvados?" "Apparently not much." "Well let me educate you. Calvados is an alcoholic beverage made here in Northern France. It is kin to Cognac. Cognac is made from grape juice, whereas Calvados is made from apple cider. If you drink enough of either beverage, you will get stinking drunk! A difference is that Cognac ages well in wooden barrels and becomes more smooth with age. Calvados does not age well and is normally bottled and consumed soon after it is distilled. This gives Calvados a rough taste, and you get a terrible 'hangover'. Americans drink aged Cognac by its other name, Brandy. I'm certain you have tasted smooth Napoleon Brandy." "Yes Sergeant, I'll admit I have 'tipped' a few Napoleon Brandy snifters and consumed some fine Cognac also. In fact, I consider them both a superior beverage than most American Bourbons. But what is your point?" "I guess the point I am trying to make is this, the moment the men in this Battery hear the Germans have surrendered and the war in Europe is over, a tremendous amount of pent-up emotion will be released. The release of these emotions, magnified by the amount of Calvados these guys will drink, in a short period of time, could produce a disaster. I hate to think of what can happen." "Thanks for the warning Sergeant, I will try to be ready for 'one big party' in the event I am still here when the war ends."

The Technical Sergeant 'Chief' was a great help in teaching me the details of firing battery operations. Some of the information I had learned in ROTC training at the University of Florida and some I had learned in combat while serving with Battery C, 592nd FA Battalion in Germany. But many of the details given me by the 'Chief' were new to me. Items such as choosing a proper location for a firing battery included three major items: One, a location in defilade, hidden to the enemy, capable of delivering in-direct fire on enemy positions. Two, a location with easy ingress and egress, easy to defend in case of an enemy attack. Three, open fields of fire, when direct fire is required to defend your position against attacks by enemy infantry and/or armored forces.

An XO must know how to 'Lay the Battery.' This expression outside of artillery circles caused mixed response because the word 'Lay' has sexual connotations in civilian life. Many people would ask , "How does one man 'Lay' 120 other men?" My answer to a naive question of this nature was, "It isn't too hard once you get accustomed to it." or, "Its a tough job, but it goes with the territory." Actually this job must be performed every time a howitzer is moved. This task is normally performed by the enlisted man who is the Chief of Firing Battery. It involves a surveying procedure, using a survey device called an 'Aiming Circle'. This process results in all four howitzer tubes being parallel and pointed in the right direction. This alignment, plus accurate survey data, allows the American field artillery to mass many howitzers and guns on a single target.

NOTE

After WWII, a famous German Field Marshall wrote,

"We would have won the war if we had had

the American Field Artillery

and General George Patton on our side."

This was a great tribute to General Patton and to my Branch of the service!

Possibly the most important responsibility of a firing battery XO is to monitor the maintenance of his four howitzers and maintain the 'Gun Book' of each individual weapon. This 'paper work' is performed by the sergeant in charge of each howitzer section, but monitored carefully by the XO. To understand the importance of maintaining this information, you must understand the weapon itself and the ammunition it fires. First, ammunition comes in three types: Fixed, Semi-Fixed, and Separate. To the uninitiated, think of a rifle round, it is constructed all in one piece and nothing can be adjusted. In other words, what you see is what you get. Every characteristic of this round is 'Fixed'. This type of ammunition is utilized in most weapons smaller then 105mm.

Because of the size and weight, 'Separate Rounds' are delivered to the weapon in three pieces: the Powder Bags, the Projectile, and the Fuse which detonates the projectile. This type of ammunition is normally used by weapons larger than 105mm. Some projectiles weighing several hundred pounds, with powder bags seven feet long.

In my opinion, the Semi-Fixed 105mm ammunition used by my four Howitzers had been developed to the point that made this weapon the most versatile artillery piece on any battlefield during the 1940s. This ammunition had many changeable features: First, these Semi-Fixed rounds were light, well packaged two to a wooden crate, and easily handled by one man. Second, each round contained 7 powder bags, which gave Fire Direction a choice of power they needed for a specific mission, i.e. 'a charge 7' to fire 12 miles, or 'a charge 1' to fire a few hundred yards. The ability to use smaller charges than a full 'charge 7' on each mission materially reduced the wear and tear on the howitzer tubes, a very important innovation. Third, the different types of fuses available, i.e. 'Regular Fuse', to be set by the Cannoneers to detonate upon contact with the target, or with a few seconds delay after striking the target. A 'Mechanical Time Fuse' to be set by the Cannoneers to explode in a fixed number of seconds after firing. This type fuse was ultimately replaced by an electronic operated 'Radar Type' fuse, developed at the University of Florida, which detonated the projectile when it came within 10 yards of the target. This fuse was initially developed to be used by Anti-Aircraft weapons against flying aircraft. After this type fuse proved eminently successful in this role, its importance for use by the field artillery was recognized. When this fuse became available to the field artillery late in WWII, we called it the 'Posit Fuse'. Fourth, the many types of specialized ammunition available to the 105mm howitzer also added to its versatility, the. 'White Phosphorus' projectiles, which start intense fires and produce extensive wounds on exposed troops, the 'Harmless White Cloud' projectiles which produce screening clouds of smoke, or colored smoke used for marking targets, the 'High Explosive Anti Tank' (HEAT) projectile which was far superior to the standard high explosive projectile when used against enemy tanks or to penetrate enemy fortifications. Also miscellaneous projectiles such as: the 'Shell Propaganda' which was used to drop 'Surrender Leaflets' on German troops, and the 'Searchlight Shell' used to illuminate the battlefield at night.

One advantage given the 105mm artillerymen was the wooden crates that contained the Semi-Fixed ammunition. This wood was used to construct bunker walls, floors and ceilings. It was also used for shelving, chairs, tables and wash stands. I can personally vouch for the fact that this Semi-Fixed ammunition crate wood added to the quality-of-life for thousands of U S Artillerymen!

To understand the importance of keeping a 'Gun Book' current at each howitzer, the XO had to understand the amount and type of ammunition being fired on each mission. As explained before, the number of powder bags used with each round fired, had to be translated into a 'Service Round'. The wear and tear on a 105mm howitzer tube, or barrel, is measured in Service Rounds fired. Each 105mm howitzer tube, or barrel, has a 'Breach', a 'Breach Block', a 'Seating Area', and a 'Barrel' with twisting 'Lands and Grooves' inside the barrel. Each projectile is aerodynamically designed with a pointed nose and a slightly tapered bow-tail. Around the larger portion of the bow-tail is a soft brass ring called the 'Rotating Band'. To fire the weapon, a crew member must open the sliding 'Breach Block', firmly insert the entire round into the breach, which 'seats the projectile' properly, and engages the soft brass 'Rotating Band' into the hard steel 'Lands' of the barrel. The crew member then slides the 'Breach Block' into the closed position, and locks it. He then holds up his right arm to signify the round is ready to fire. While this process is being performed the Gunner, sitting on the left hand side of the howitzer is busy elevating and traversing the howitzer tube in accordance with the firing commands sent from the Battalion Fire Direction Center. When the four Gunners signal his howitzer is ready to fire, this information is reported to the Fire Direction Center. After all howitzers involved in this specific fire mission have reported they are ready to fire, Fire Direction gives all Firing Batteries involved the command to "FIRE." Fire Direction then tells the Forward Observer, "ON THE WAY." The Forward Observer, now warned, observes the target area carefully and, in a specific language, tells the Fire Direction Center where the rounds exploded in relationship to the target. This entire process is repeated until the Forward Observer is satisfied the exploding shells are accomplishing the desired results. When this occurs, he gives Fire Direction the command to "FIRE FOR EFFECT." After the Fire For Effect is completed, the Forward Observer sends Fire Direction his opinion of what the barrage accomplished, such as, "MISSION ACCOMPLISHED", or "ENEMY PANZER DESTROYED."

Firing commands sent to the Firing Battery are computed in the Fire Direction Center from a forward observer sightings while he is with the infantry. These three way commands between the Forward Observer, the Battalion Fire Direction Center, and the Firing Battery are transmitted by telephone lines, or radio, depending on the situation.

Of course, if the fire mission is requested by one of the Battalion Air Observers, the communications are always transmitted by radio. Most Field Artillery Battalions are equipped with two light Liaison planes, L-4s, and two or more pilots

By now you are probably wondering what all of this has to do with 'Gun Books'. Maybe not much, or maybe quite a bit, depending on your point of view. The point I am trying to make is, these are just a few of the overwhelming details a new XO must learn. I was a twenty-one year old 2nd Lieutenant with no classroom, or formal training. I had to 'walk the walk and talk the talk' in a short period of time, while trying to accomplish our mission, protect my men, and last but not least, try to stay alive myself.

When a 105mm tube is new and fresh out of Ordinance, the useful life expectancy is approximately 15,000 Service Rounds. Reading the Gun Book of each howitzer was quite interesting, it was a history of the weapon as it matured. Each history started with the test firing of the howitzer at it's original Ordnance Depot. As the howitzer moved from unit to unit, the Gun Book was a roadmap of where the howitzer had been located and the number of rounds it had fired, either in training, or in combat. My four howitzers had reached the Northern France battle ground by entirely different routes and had been serviced in various Ordnance Depots in the United States and in Europe.

Two of our weapons had seen action in the deserts of North Africa, one had hurled shells at the Nazis in Sicily, and one hit the beach at Normandy several days after the D Day Invasion. All of these howitzers were in good condition when I arrived, and I pledged to myself to see that they stayed that way.

† †

As time passed, I began to notice subtle changes within the Battery. The character of the Battery was improving. Nothing specific, or tangible, it was more like a change in the men's attitude. We were eating better, the veterans were working hard with the replacements to attain combat efficiency, and when off duty the men were playing more team sports together, and 'goofing off' less. The new replacements and the old vets were becoming 'buddies' and enjoying each other. My confidence was increasing as I gained the confidence and respect of the senior non-coms. I was learning to 'walk the walk and talk the talk' as I evolved into a more competent XO.

We were getting news of the war in Germany every day. The successful American and Russian advances on Berlin were lifting our spirits. It had become obvious to us the Allies would win the war in Europe. 'Scuttle Butt' had created local betting pools as to the date the war would end in Europe.

Then the first shoe dropped. 'Scuttle Butt' was rampant. The most prevailing rumor was, "The Allies had successfully negotiated an Unconditional Surrender of all German military forces in Europe.

The Northern France Campaign
The Lorient Pocket—April 1945

After three hard campaigns in Germany,
a wonderful reunion
with my surviving old friends
of the Survey Crew from Headquarters Battery, 589th FA Bn

L–R: Kneeling, Sammy Feinberg, Wilmer Ruona, Johnny Kaufman;
Seated, Randy Pierson and Staff Sergeant Andy Andrasofski

22

The End of WWII in Europe

The End of War in Europe
589th Field Artillery Battalion – Lorient Pocket
Northern France Campaign – 8 May 1945

The 589th FA Bn had been ordered to cease reorganization in late April and reinforce the 870th FA Bn in an area of France known, by the military, as the 'Lorient Pocket.' This English Channel enclave contained two gigantic, almost impenetrable, German submarine pens. This enclave housed several operating German submarines, plus several thousand able bodied officers and men of the German *Kreigmarine.* Earlier in the North France campaign, Supreme Headquarters Allied Expeditionary Force (SHAEF) had decided to by-pass these heavily fortified and strongly defended German installations instead of trying to capture them. The theory, these German forces could be easily contained. This theory proved correct because these enemy troops could be re-supplied only by under water vessels. After the Allies broke through the German forces defending Saint-Lo and encircled the French towns of Lorient and Saint-Nazaire, this German Navy garrison was not a threat to the Allies, nor aided the Nazi war machine.

During late April and early May 1945, after the death of Hitler, high ranking German officers began negotiations with the Allies for the surrender of all German fighting forces. Negotiations were tough between these opposing military men.

Germany wanted a surrender with numerous conditions concerning what nation would perform what functions in the post war fatherland. They had specific questions concerning future Russian influence in Germany. The German Admiral commanding the defense of the Lorient Pocket had excellent communications with Berlin and was aware of the details of the surrender negotiations. The Allied Supreme Headquarters, now in Paris, intercepted a message, from the German Lorient Commander, stating he did not think Germany should agree to an unconditional surrender. He said his forces were capable of breaking through the weak American lines encircling him, and marching to Berlin. Once there, his command would assist in the defense of that city. As a result of having this information, the 589th Field Artillery Battalion, along with other experienced combat units, were quickly deployed to this area to make certain the estimated 15,000 man Germans garrison occupying the Lorient Pocket remained contained.

By this time I was no longer a Forward Observer with XVIII Airborne Corps, I was now the Executive Officer of Battery A, of the 589th FA Bn. The combat move to the Lorient Pocket was a new experience for me. I had been a firing battery officer in the XVIII Airborne Corps Artillery, but not an XO. Fortunately for me, my new Battery Commander, First Lieutenant Theodore 'Ted' Kiendl, was a former XO. In civilian life Ted was an 'Ivy League' college graduate, a lettered college athlete, and from a family of influential investment bankers. In the military, Ted was a natural leader, a well liked, and a respected Battery Commander. With his help and training, I was able to mature as a Firing Battery Executive Officer. I owe Ted!

On 8 May 1945, German officials signed an unconditional surrender to the Allies. This day became known as 'V E Day.' The war in Europe was over!
BUT NOT FOR ME !

The End of the War in Europe for Me
Battery A, 589th FA Bn — Lorient Pocket
8 May 1945

When word of the German's surrender reached Battery A, all Hell broke loose! The war was over and it is imposable to describe the dramatic release of pent-up emotions I experienced, and witnessed, that historic day. The reactions ranged from private prayers, with teary eyes, for being allowed to live, to an attempted murder, when a distraught GI drove his truck through a tent, trying to kill his fellow soldiers who where inside the tent, drinking and playing poker. Every GI and officer seemed to have opened his own bottle of Calvados, or Cognac, he had saved for this day. I'm certain each man in Battery A set a new record, on 8 May 1945, for the amount of alcohol he had ever consumed in a single sitting. Some people laughed, some cried, and some just withdrew within themselves and remained silent. This normally well organized and disciplined unit had suddenly become a group of dysfunctional men.

About an hour after the first message advising us the war was over, *the second shoe dropped*, we received a second message, marked urgent, ordering us to maintain a full combat alert. The Admiral commanding the German forces in the Lorient Pocket had refused to accept the word of our Corps Commander that a surrender had been negotiated and hostilities had ceased. The next 24 hours were the toughest I had to endure as a battery officer during WWII. My problems were awesome and the progress in solving them was excruciatingly slow. I would have been lucky to get one howitzer firing that night, instead of the normal four. However, by noon of the next day I had a full battery of 'hung-over sad sacks', who manned all four howitzers. Since we received no missions to fire that day, we will never know if our fire would have been accurate, or not, immediately after the V E Day celebration.

Several days after V E Day, our Corps Commander, who had direct telephone communications with the German Admiral, finally convince the Admiral to negotiate local surrender terms. These negotiations went smoothly, and the German enlisted men started stacking thousands of small arms, and ammunition, in a large field between the two forces, a location agreed upon by the two local commanders. By mutual agreement, all German *Kreigmarine* Officers were allowed to retain their hand guns until they officially became POWs. Once the stacking of arms was complete, another process began. The now docile prisoners began loading into what seemed to be an endless column of American 2 1/2 ton GMC trucks which transported them to a rail head for their train trip to an American Prisoner of War facility for internment.

My friend, 2nd Lieutenant Barney Alford, called form Battery C and asked me if I would like to take a break. I had no idea what he had in mind but I said "Yes" anyway. When Barney arrived at Battery A, he was driving his own jeep. He pulled up to the Command Post and blew the horn, but left the motor running. I stuck my head out of the tent flap and asked, "Barney, what's up?" He spit a wad of tobacco juice onto the ground and answered my question, "I've had it up to here," motioning to his nose, "I've got to get out of my frigging, screwed-up, battery for a while. Maybe we can go some place and talk." This sounded good to me, I had not talked with Barney since our commissioning ceremony in Belgium last January. I turned to the Duty Sergeant and advised him, "Lieutenant Alford and I have to take a short trip. If you need me, you can call Battery C and they can reach me on his jeep radio. But one more thing, Sergeant, I really don't want any calls. Get the message?" In the jeep I asked, "Barney where are we going?" His answer made sense, "Anywhere we can get away from the 'chicken shit' that's going on. How about riding over and watching the Germans leave?" "Sounds good to me ole buddy, you lead the way."

Barney parked on a grassy hill overlooking the intense activity below. We discussed events which had happened since our escape from 'Parker's Crossroads' last December, our current assignments, and shared our plans for returning to the University of Florida to continue our education using the newly passed 'G I Bill of Rights.' We sipped from Barney's bottle of Napoleon Brandy until the trauma of war disappeared as we watched a beautiful orange evening sun slowly start to descend behind a distant tree line. Barney started the jeep motor and said, "Randy, I guess I'd better get you back to Battery A." As I nodded my head in agreement the jeep started to roll down the hill. Barney suddenly stopped the jeep and asked me this simple question.

"RANDY, WHAT WOULD THE WORLD BE LIKE IF WE HAD FAILED?"

EPILOG

More than sixty years ago my friend, Lieutenant Barney Alford, asked me a question, "Randy I wonder what the world would be like if we had lost?" More than sixty years later, we know what the world is like because we did not lose. You can draw your own conclusions about the volatile world of today. Our country is faced with wars of a different nature. Military, Economic, Social, Religious, and Terrorists Warfare, waged by unknown people who, for unknown reasons, wish to destroy our country and our lifestyles. The reasons vary from Hate, Jealousy, Power, or Revenge, you name it.

Three generations have passed since I fought for personal freedom in Europe and in Korea. I can no longer fight, but I know from experience, if the wars in which we are now engaged are not won, things in our country would be much different. The following photos, taken in Germany at the end of WWII, are of dead German and Polish civilians and soldiers, who were either Jews, or political prisoners, who were starved and worked to death in Nazi concentration camps, governed by a deranged Dictator.

We Americans should be thankful that the only major conflict fought to date on American soil was the 'War between the States.' This conflict, as in all wars, there were both military and civilian casualties. Wounds and death reach into the civilian population as well the armed forces. The following two photos are graphic reminders of this truism.

If our country does not prevail in current, or future conflicts, the photo opposite could be of your family, friends, or total strangers. The photo next page, could be a photo of you. The United States of America is the hope of the world.

Dear God, Please Bless America—the Land that I Love!

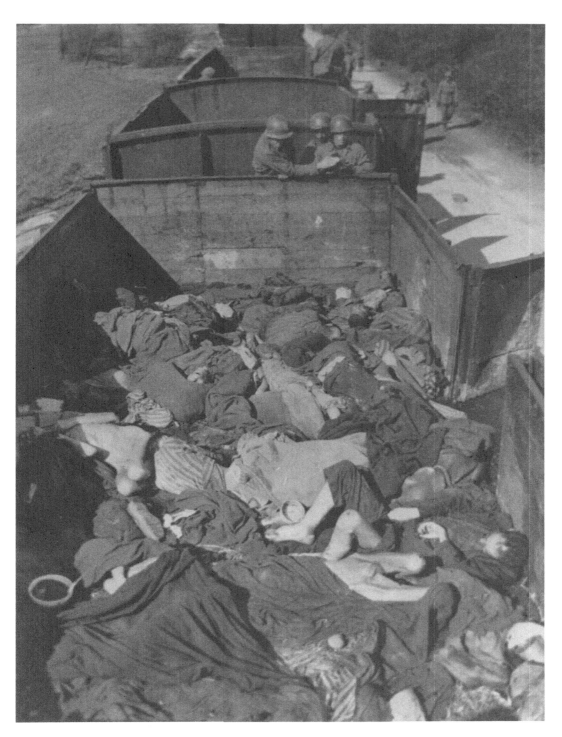

A photo of someone's family and friends!

A photo of You?

You cannot lose to, or compromise with, Evil.